THE SOUND BLASTER LIVE!™ BOOK
A Complete Guide to the World's Most Popular Sound Card

The SOUND BLASTER LIVE!™ BOOK

A COMPLETE GUIDE TO THE WORLD'S *MOST POPULAR* SOUND CARD

Lars Ahlzen and Clarence Song

NO STARCH PRESS

San Francisco

THE SOUND BLASTER LIVE!™ BOOK. Copyright ©2003 by Lars Ahlzen and Clarence Song.

All rights reserved. No part of this work may be reproduced or transmitted in any form or by any means, electronic or mechanical, including photocopying, recording, or by any information storage or retrieval system, without the prior written permission of the copyright owner and the publisher.

Printed in the United States of America on recycled paper

1 2 3 4 5 6 7 8 9 10 – 06 05 04 03

No Starch Press and the No Starch Press logo are registered trademarks of No Starch Press, Inc. All Creative's and its affiliated companies' logos are registered trademarks or trademarks of Creative Technology, Ltd. and its affiliated companies. "Dolby," "Pro Logic," "Surround EX," and the double-D symbol are trademarks of Dolby Laboratories. Other product and company names mentioned herein may be the trademarks of their respective owners. Rather than use a trademark symbol with every occurrence of a trademarked name, we are using the names only in an editorial fashion and to the benefit of the trademark owner, with no intention of infringement of the trademark.

Publisher: William Pollock
Editorial Director: Karol Jurado
Cover and Interior Design: Octopod Studios
Composition: Octopod Studios
Copyeditor: Judy Ziajka
Proofreader: Stephanie Provines
Indexer: Broccoli Information Management

Distributed to the book trade in the United States by Publishers Group West, 1700 Fourth Street, Berkeley, CA 94710; phone: 800-788-3123; fax: 510-658-1834.

Distributed to the book trade in Canada by Jacqueline Gross & Associates, Inc., One Atlantic Avenue, Suite 105, Toronto, Ontario M6K 3E7 Canada; phone: 416-531-6737; fax 416-531-4259.

For information on translations or book distributors outside the United States, please see our distributors list in the back of this book or contact No Starch Press, Inc. directly:

No Starch Press, Inc.
555 De Haro Street, Suite 250, San Francisco, CA 94107
phone: 415-863-9900; fax: 415-863-9950; info@nostarch.com; http://www.nostarch.com

The information in this book is distributed on an "As Is" basis, without warranty. While every precaution has been taken in the preparation of this work, neither the authors nor No Starch Press, Inc. shall have any liability to any person or entity with respect to any loss or damage caused or alleged to be caused directly or indirectly by the information contained in it.

Library of Congress Cataloging-in-Publication Data

Ahlzen, Lars.
  The Sound Blaster Live! Book : a complete guide to the world's most popular sound card / Lars Ahlzen and Clarence Song.
        p. cm.
  Includes index.
  ISBN 1-886411-73-5 (pbk.)
  1..Expansion boards (Microcomputers 2. Computer sound processing. 3. Sound cards. 4. Computer music. I. Song, Clarence. II. Title.
  TK7395.E96 A34 2003
  004.5'3--dc21   2002001658

ACKNOWLEDGMENTS

This book would not be possible without Bill's trust and confidence in offering us, first-time authors, the opportunity of a lifetime to write a book about something we enjoy. Our gratitude also goes out to Karol and everyone at No Starch Press, whose hard work has resulted in what you now hold in your hands.

I wish to thank my family and friends for their patience and support during this busy phase of my life. I would also like to thank Anders Claesson, whose camera is responsible for many photos in the book, and everyone who has supported and contributed to my websites and my music. Last, but certainly not least, without Clarence's great knowledge and attention to detail, this book would have been nowhere near what it has become.
—*Lars Ahlzen*

Thanks to my family, for their understanding and sacrifice when I could not be there. To Guoliang, for the constant encouragement and for graciously offering his help. To Cheng Kiang and Ee Siang, for getting me involved with the sound card. To Melvin, Mingwei, and Raymond, for your invaluable contributions. To Desmond and Jimmy, for making some of the photos in the book possible. And I am not forgetting my partner-in-crime, Lars—thank you for always being there!
—*Clarence Song*

The authors would also like to thank the representatives of these companies for their prompt assistance and for allowing us to feature their products:

Michelle Fradette from Altec Lansing; Anne Khoo, Leslie Lee, Timothy Leong, and Linn Loh from Creative Technology for their support; Manal Ma and Kristen Stonecipher from CyberLink; Kristin Thomson from Digital Theater Systems; Kaleo Willess and Roger Dressler from Dolby Labs; Chris Douglass and Rob Read from Edirol; Hubert Winkler, author of Hubi's LoopBack Device; Chris Cutter from InterVideo; Joshua Ryan Hall from Klipsch; Jamie O'Connell from MIDI-OX; Paul DiComo from Polk Audio; Paul Quinn from Quinnware; Paul McKnight from Really Effective Software; Alan Cheung from StudioAX; Gina Gaffney from Twelve Tone Systems; Roel de Wit from Utopia Sound Division; and David Harold from VideoLogic Systems.

And, thanks to you for picking up a copy of this book!

BRIEF CONTENTS

PART 1: FEATURES & BASICS

Chapter 1
The Evolution of Sound on the PC
3

Chapter 2
An Audio Primer
23

Chapter 3
The Sound Blaster Live! Hardware
39

PART 2: CONNECTING PERIPHERALS

Chapter 4
Accessories Galore!
69

Chapter 5
Connecting Devices
103

Chapter 6
Speakers
137

PART 3: FUN STUFF

Chapter 7
The Mixer
199

Chapter 8
EAX
221

Chapter 9
Drivers and Other Tweaks
235

Chapter 10
Playing Games
273

Chapter 11
Watching Movies
303

PART 4: CREATING AUDIO

Chapter 12
Creating a Music Library
335

Chapter 13
Recording Audio
357

PART 5: COMPOSING MUSIC

Chapter 14
MIDI Explained
373

Chapter 15
Connecting MIDI Instruments
397

Chapter 16
Introduction to SoundFonts
413

Chapter 17
Sequencer Basics
455

Chapter 18
The EMU10K1 Digital Audio Processor
517

APPENDICES

Appendix A
The MIDI Specification
525

Appendix B
The General MIDI Sound Set
535

Appendix C
The GS Sound Set
539

Appendix D
The MT-32 Sound Set
541

Appendix E
The Sound Blaster Live!
MIDI Implementation
545

Index
551

CONTENTS IN DETAIL

PART 1: FEATURES & BASICS

1
THE EVOLUTION OF SOUND ON THE PC

Music Cards	4
Sound in the Real World	5
The Sound Blaster	6
Wave Audio	7
Music Synthesis	8
The Sound Blaster	11
A Timeline of the Sound Blaster Family	11
Advancements in the Sound Blaster Live!	17
The Past and Present	19
Sound Blaster Compatibility	19
The Future	20
The Motherboard Threat	20
The Future of PC Audio	21

2
AN AUDIO PRIMER

How We Hear Sound	24
It's All about Vibrations	24
Sound as Waves	25
Positioning Sound	28
Storing Sound	30
Sound in the Digital Domain	31
Analog vs Digital	31
Digital Audio	33
Sampling	33
A/D and D/A Conversion	36
Working with Digital Audio	38

3
THE SOUND BLASTER LIVE! HARDWARE

Sound Cards Can Look Good, Too!	41
Internal Connectors	41
TAD	*41*
AUX_IN	*42*
I²S_IN	*42*
Playing Audio CDs	*43*
Obtaining Audio from Optical Drives	*44*
Choosing the Connection Method	*50*
Internal Pin Connectors	51
PC_SPK	*51*
VOL_CTRL	*51*
MB_PRO	*52*
JP3	*52*
The Extension Connector	52
AUD_EXT	*53*
SPDIF_EXT	*55*
Backplate Audio Jacks	56
Line Out 1 (Front)	*56*
Line Out 2 (Rear)	*56*
Line In	*58*
Microphone In	*58*
The Mini-jack Digital Output	58
Mini-jack Digital Out on the Second-Generation Live!	*59*
Mini-jack Digital Out on the Third-Generation Live!	*59*
Obtaining A Digital Output	*60*
Summary of Backplate Audio Connectors	*61*
Backplate Joystick/MIDI Connector	62
Summary of Connectors	63
OEM Models	65

PART 2: HOOKING UP

4

ACCESSORIES GALORE!

Digital I/O Cards	70
The Digital I/O Card	*70*
Optical Digital I/O Card	*73*
Digital Output Module	*77*
The Live!Drive	78
Origin of the Live!Drive	*78*
Analog Connectors	*79*
Digital Connectors	*82*
Other Connectors	*83*
Extension Connectors	*86*
Live!Drive Models	*89*
Obtaining Optical Connectors	*91*
Compatibility	*92*
Installing the Live!Drive	*92*
How the Live!Drive Works	*96*
S/PDIF Bypass	96
Uses S/PDIF Bypass	*98*
Compatible Connectors	*99*
Enabling S/PDIF Bypass	*100*
Digital I/O Card or the Live!Drive?	101
Physical Constraints	*101*
Features Required	*101*
Cost	*101*

5

CONNECTING DEVICES

Analog	104
Analog Signals	*104*
Analog Connectors	*105*
Connecting in Analog	*109*
Analog Connectors on the Live!	*114*
Digital	115
Digital Signals	*115*
Digital Connectors	*116*
Connecting in Digital	*120*
Making the Connection	*121*
Digital Connectors on the Live!	*122*
Consumer Devices	*123*
Connecting More Devices	*136*

6
SPEAKERS

Speakers: The Key to What You Hear	138
The Surround Era	*139*
Stereo Systems	140
Why Stereo Systems?	*141*
Multimedia Speakers	141
2.0: Two Speakers	*141*
2.1: Two Speakers and a Subwoofer	*142*
4.1: Four Speakers and a Subwoofer	*142*
5.1: Four Speakers, a Subwoofer, and a Center Speaker	*144*
Home Theater Systems	147
The Old Guard: Dolby Pro Logic Receivers	*148*
The Bridge: 5.1-Ready Receivers	*149*
The Ultimate: Dolby Digital and DTS Receivers	*150*
Subwoofers: Providing the Rumble	152
Headphones	153
Making the Decision	153
Number of Speakers	*153*
Sound Quality	*154*
Power and Amplification Ratings	*156*
Magnetic Shielding	*158*
Space Constraints	*158*
Convenient Features	*159*
Budget	*161*
Research and Listen	*161*
Speaker Support on the Live!	163
Speaker Connectors	*163*
Connecting Speakers	168
2 Speakers Mode	*170*
4 Speakers Mode	*172*
5.1 Speakers Mode	*176*
Headphones Mode	*180*
Live!Surround Mode	*180*
Other Speaker Technologies on the Live!	*182*
Speaker Placement	185
Front Speakers	*186*
The Center Speaker	*188*
Surround Speakers	*190*
Subwoofers	*194*

PART 3: FUN STUFF

7
THE MIXER

Mixing Audio	200
How the Live! Routes, Mixes, and Resamples Audio	200
Audio Sources	*200*
Using Mixers	205
The Windows Mixer (Volume Control)	*205*
The Surround Mixer	*207*
Keeping the Live! Hiss Free	215
Set High Enough Levels	*215*
Mute Unused Sources	*215*
The Digital I/O Advantage	*216*
Recording Audio	216
Choosing the Correct Sound Source	*216*
When to Use What-U-Hear	*217*
Recording Audio CDs in Optical Drives	*218*
Adding EAX Effects to Audio Recordings	*218*
Voice Chat and Videoconferencing	*218*
Volume Controls in Software	219

8
EAX

Environmental Audio?	222
Now, It's Just EAX!	222
An Open Standard	223
Behind the Scenes	223
Using EAX	224
Other Uses for EAX Effects	*224*
Environment Controls in the Surround Mixer	225
The EAX Control Panel	228
EAX Control Panel Basics	*228*
Adding EAX Effects to Sound Sources	*229*
EAX Presets	230
Adding and Removing Effects	*230*
Customizing Effect Types	*230*
Editing Effects Parameters	*232*
Tweaking the Reverb	*233*
Have Fun!	*234*

9
DRIVERS AND OTHER TWEAKS

What Drivers Do	235
Bad Drivers	237
Windows Drivers	238
The Windows Evolution	238
VXD and WDM Drivers	241
Windows Drivers for the Live!	244
Determining the Driver Version	250
Verifying Driver Installation	251
What Drivers Are Available Today?	253
Completely Stable Drivers: A Misnomer?	254
Alternative Windows Drivers for the Adventurous	255
The APSLive!	255
The kX Project	256
Linux Drivers	257
Creative's Open-Source Drivers for Linux	258
ALSA	259
DOS Drivers and Sound Blaster 16 Emulation	259
Why SB16 Emulation?	260
SB16 Emulation in Windows 95/98/ME	260
SB16 Emulation in DOS	262
SB16 Emulation in Windows NT/2000/XP	262
Hardware Tweaks: How to Build an External Volume Control	262
A Few Words of Warning	263
The Idea	263
Locating the VOL_CTRL Pins	263
Building the Volume Control	264
Testing It	265
Software Tweaks: Windows Multimedia and Sound Settings	265
Sounds	265
Audio: Sound Playback and Recording	266
Audio: MIDI Music Playback	268
Advanced Audio Properties: Hardware Acceleration	270
Advanced Audio Properties: Settings That Don't Work	271

10

PLAYING GAMES

Looking to Hollywood	274
Music in Games	275
From Beeps to Music	275
General MIDI	277
Custom Instrument Sounds	278
Recorded Audio	279
The Interactive Music Future	280
Sound Effects in Games	281
Before the Sound Blaster	281
The Sound Blaster–Compatible Era	282
DirectSound and Sound Mixing	283
3D Positioning	285
DirectSound3D and A3D	287
OpenAL	289
3D Streams	289
EAX	290
EAX 1.0	290
EAX 2.0	291
EAX 3.0	293
I3DL2	294
EAGLE	294
Dolby Digital API	295
3D Sound on the Live!	296
Speaker Configuration	297
2 Speakers Mode	297
4 Speakers Mode	297
5.1 Speakers Mode	298
Headphones Mode	298
Live!Surround Mode	298
Playing Games with the Live!	299
Games with 3D Positioning	299
Games with EAX Support	301
Games without EAX Support	302

11
WATCHING MOVIES

From the Cinema to the Living Room	303
Matrix Surround	*304*
Discrete Multichannel Surround	*307*
Encoding in Digital Formats	*309*
What about THX?	*310*
Summary of Common Surround Formats	*311*
Surround Setups	311
Not Everything Is 5.1!	*313*
Dolby Surround Soundtracks Encoded in Dolby Digital	*313*
Playing 5.1 Soundtracks on Fewer Speakers	*314*
Home Theater on the PC	314
Surround Sound on the Live!	316
Playing Matrix Surround Soundtracks	*316*
Playing Digital Surround Soundtracks	*320*
Choices, Choices!	*328*

PART 4: CREATING AUDIO

12
CREATING A MUSIC LIBRARY

Audio Compression	336
Frequency Masking	*337*
Temporal Masking	*337*
Hearing Range	*337*
Sensitivity	*337*
Stereo Encoding	*337*
Codecs	338
The MP3 Phenomenon	340
The MP3 Standard	340
Sample Rate	*341*
Bit Rate	*341*
Joint Stereo	*343*
Audio Software: PlayCenter and Winamp	344
Ripping CDs	346
Other Ways to Get Audio	347
Recording with PlayCenter	*349*

Tweaking the Audio	350
Equalization	*350*
Plug-Ins	*351*
Time Scaling	*351*
Organizing Your Music	352
Organizing with PlayCenter	*352*
Winamp's Playlist	*353*
More Tips	353
Drag and Drop!	*353*
Archiving Your Music	*354*

13
RECORDING AUDIO

Recording Sources and Equipment	358
Analog Inputs on the Live! Card	358
Line In	*359*
Microphone	*359*
On-Board Inputs	*359*
Live!Drive Inputs	*359*
Digital Inputs	*359*
Mixer Settings for Recording	360
Selecting the Right Source for Recording	*361*
Adjusting the Recording Level	*361*
Recording with EAX Effects	*363*
Audio Editing Basics	363
Recording Audio	*365*
Memory Requirements	*365*
Normalizing	*366*
Cutting, Trimming, and Other Editing	*366*
Adding Effects	*367*
After Recording	370

PART 5: COMPOSING MUSIC

14
MIDI EXPLAINED

Overview of MIDI	374
MIDI Hardware	375
A Little About Sequencers	376
Hexadecimal Numbers	376
A Simple Example	376
The Structure of a MIDI Message	378
MIDI Message Types	380
General MIDI and Other Standards	383
Standard MIDI Files	384
The Problems with General MIDI	385
GS and XG	385
General MIDI 2 (GM2)	386
Synthesizer Basics	387
A Brief History of Synthesizers	387
Other Electronic Instruments and Studio Equipment	387
Sound Cards	389
Synthesizer Jargon	390
Polyphony	390
Multitimbrality	390
MIDI Capabilities of the Live!	391
The Live! Synthesizers	391
The SB Live! MIDI Synth	392
Why A and B?	392
The Software Synthesizer	392
FM Synthesizer Emulation	393
MIDI Ports for External MIDI Instruments	393
Summary of the MIDI Devices of the SB Live!	394

15

CONNECTING MIDI INSTRUMENTS

The MIDI Interface on the Live!	398
The Original Live! with a Digital I/O Card	*398*
Live!Drive and Live!Drive II	*398*
Live!Drive IR	*398*
Other Live! Models	*399*
Sample Setups	399
Example 1: MIDI Keyboard to Synthesizer Module	*399*
Example 2: MIDI Keyboard and Sequencer	*400*
MIDI Thru	*400*
Using a MIDI Keyboard for Input	401
Choosing the Right MIDI Keyboard	*401*
Example: The Author's Choice	*404*
Software Synthesizers	405
Types of Software Synthesizers	*405*
The Pros and Cons of Software Synthesizers	*407*
A MIDI Loopback Device	409
Hubi's MIDI LoopBack Device	*409*
MIDI Yoke	*410*
Using the Loopback Device	*410*

16

INTRODUCTION TO SOUNDFONTS

What Is a SoundFont?	413
Where to Find SoundFonts	414
The Standard SoundFonts	*414*
SoundFont Archives on the Web	*415*
Commercial SoundFonts	*416*
The SoundFont Control Panel	416
Replacing the Synth Bank	*417*
Loading Additional SoundFonts	*418*
About the Bank Stack	*418*
Variation Banks	418
Replacing One or More Presets	*420*
SoundFont Cache and Other Options	*421*
Creating Your Own SoundFonts: Introduction to Vienna SoundFont-Studio	422
Getting and Installing the Software	*423*
The Program Parts	*423*
Playing Sounds	424
Using a MIDI Keyboard	*424*

Using the Mouse	424
Using the Computer Keyboard	424
Using the Controller Toolbars	425
The SoundFont Structure	425
Samples	426
Instruments	427
Presets	427
Getting Your Own Sample Material	427
The Sample Section	428
Importing .wav Files	428
Creating New Samples	428
Looping	429
Creating Instruments	430
Getting Creative with Zones: Multisamples, Splits, and Layers	431
Velocity Range and Velocity Splits	432
Exclusive Classes	433
Looping – On the Instrument Level	434
Generators	434
Pitch	435
Effects, Filter and Pan	436
Volume Envelope	436
Modulation Envelope	438
Low-Frequency Oscillators (LFOs)	439
The Global Zone	440
Creating Presets	440
Creating a New Melodic Preset	441
Editing Preset Zones	442
Editing Generators at the Preset Level	442
Adding a Global Preset Zone	442
The Percussive Section	443
The Advantage of the Sample-Instrument-Preset Structure	443
A Full Example	443
Before We Start	443
Step 1: Loading the Samples into Vienna	444
Step 2: Looping the Samples	444
Step 3: Creating the Instrument	446
Step 4: Adjusting Key Ranges	447
Step 5: Adding a Global Zone	448
Step 6: Creating a Preset	449
Step 7: Creating Another Preset	450
Listening to the Result	450
SoundFont Management	450
Copying Samples, Presets, and Instruments from Other SoundFonts	451
Converting Other Formats into SoundFonts	451

Other Features of Vienna ... 452
   Information and Statistics ... 452
   Print ... 452
   Full-Screen Editing ... 452
   Tools ... 453
   Preferences ... 453

17
SEQUENCER BASICS

Finding the Right Sequencer ... 456
   Bundled Software ... 456
   Choosing Your Own ... 456
Installing and Configuring Your Sequencer ... 457
   Selecting the MIDI Ports ... 458
The Building Blocks of a Modern Sequencer ... 459
   The Track or Arrange View ... 459
   Piano Roll and Other Edit Views ... 460
Basic Sequencer Use: Recording Tracks ... 462
   Tempo ... 463
   The Metronome ... 463
   Quantization ... 463
   Recording in Real Time ... 466
   Non-Real-Time Recording ... 466
   Using the Editor Views ... 466
   Step Recording ... 466
   Using SoundFonts ... 467
SoundFont Support in Cakewalk ... 468
   Configuring Instruments ... 468
   Creating Your Own Instrument Definition ... 469
   Loading SoundFonts within Cakewalk ... 470
   Using SoundFont Banks on MIDI Tracks ... 472
SoundFont Support in Cubase ... 472
   Configuring Cubase for SoundFont Support ... 473
Using SoundFonts in Any MIDI Sequencer ... 475
   Using the Bank Field ... 475
   Changing Banks Manually ... 476
Using MIDI Controllers ... 477
   Entering MIDI Controllers ... 478

Controllers on the SB Live! MIDI Synth ... 478
   CC0: Bank Select ... 479
   CC1: Modulation ... 480
   CC6 and CC38: Data Entry ... 480
   CC7: Volume ... 481
   CC10: Pan ... 481
   CC11: Expression ... 482
   CC64: Sustain Pedal ... 483
   CC91: Reverb Depth ... 483
   CC93: Chorus Level ... 484
   CC98 and CC99: NRPN ... 484
   CC100 and CC101: RPN ... 484
   CC120: All Sounds Off ... 484
   CC121: Reset All Controllers ... 484
   CC123: All Notes Off ... 484
Common Controller Problems ... 485
Controlling Effects ... 486
Selecting and Configuring Effects ... 487
   Using the Default Effects with MIDI ... 487
   Customizing Effects ... 489
   Using Other Effect Types ... 492
   A Note on Recording Effects ... 493
The Available Effects ... 494
   Reverb ... 494
   Chorus ... 495
   Flanger ... 495
   Echo (Two Tap) ... 495
   Distortion ... 496
   Auto Wah ... 496
   Ring Modulator ... 497
   Pitch Shifter ... 497
   Vocal Morpher ... 498
   Frequency Shifter ... 498
Saving Environment Presets ... 498
Introduction to RPN and NRPN ... 498
   RPN ... 498
   NRPN ... 499
   How RPN and NRPN Messages Are Sent ... 499
   Sequencers with RPN and NRPN Support ... 500
RPNs on the SB Live! MIDI Synth ... 500
   Changing the Pitch Bend Range ... 500
   Changing the Global Coarse Tuning ... 502
   Changing the Global Fine-Tuning ... 503

NRPN: The Key to Real-Time SoundFont Control 504
    How to Use NRPN Messages 505
    Example: Filter Cutoff 506
Audio Sequencers 508
    Configuring Audio Settings 508
    Optimizing Software 509
    Optimizing Hardware 510
    Using Audio Tracks 510
Automation 512
    Mixermaps and StudioWare 512
    CAL 513
Sequencing Tips and Tricks 514
    Don't Give Up! 514
    Experiment! 515
    Get to Know Your Sequencer! 515
    Try Some Cool MIDI Effects! 515

18
THE EMU10K1 DIGITAL AUDIO PROCESSOR

A Backgrounder 517
The EMU10K1 Chip 518
    Many Functions on One Chip 519
    Sample Rate Conversion 519
    The 48-kHz Sample Rate Conundrum 519
The FX8010 Effects Processor 522
The Wavetable Synthesizer 523
    SoundFont Support 523
PCI Bus Communication 524

A
THE MIDI SPECIFICATION

MIDI Messages 525
Voice Messages 526
    About MSB and LSB 527
    Running Status 528
    Control Change Numbers 528
    Examples of Voice Messages 530
System Messages 531
    System Exclusive (SysEx) Messages 532

B
THE GENERAL MIDI SOUND SET
535

C
THE GS SOUND SET
539

D
THE MT-32 SOUND SET
541

E
THE SOUND BLASTER LIVE! MIDI IMPLEMENTATION

The MIDI Implementation Chart	545
MIDI Implementation Chart: SBLive! MIDI Synthesizer	*545*
MIDI Implementation Chart: Creative Software Synthesizer	*547*
RPNs on the SBLive! MIDI Synth	548
NRPNs on the SB Live! MIDI Synth	548
Resonance Coefficients Table	*550*

INDEX
551

PART ONE
FEATURES AND BASICS

1

THE EVOLUTION OF SOUND ON THE PC

Beep. That's all PCs could do before sound cards existed. The engineers and designers at IBM, where the PC was born, added a very simple tone generator that produced simple electrical waveforms that were channeled to a tiny speaker mounted on the PC casing. The *beeper*, as the PC speaker is affectionately called, is used to provide audio beep codes for diagnostic purposes and allow the PC to alert users to certain conditions.

At that time, the PC was deemed a serious business machine, to be used for office applications such as word processing. After all, IBM stands for International Business Machines. Fortunately, processors that provide computing power in PCs were designed to be multipurpose and to process information for a wide variety of tasks. Naturally, the PC's potential as an entertainment machine helped it gain popularity in homes, and people quietly snuck games into their PCs at work. (Many games of that time had the all-important "boss key" feature. Or: When the boss walks in, a quick tap on the boss key, like the F5 key, and the game changes the screen to a mockup of some office application like a spreadsheet, and you'll seem to be hard at work!) Interactive entertainment such as games became a part of computing, and audio played a huge role in the effectiveness of such applications—definitely more so than spreadsheets. Even then, audio can also add value to business applications. For instance, a slide presentation can have far greater impact with the mere addition of audio and video clips.

The beeper became woefully inadequate; something was needed to bring music and sound in PCs to the quality level of musical recordings and movie soundtracks.

Music Cards

Many enterprising companies came to the rescue by taking sound and music synthesizer chips found in electronic musical instruments and placing them on circuit boards that could be inserted into the expansion slot on a PC's motherboard. (We have to thank the designers of the PC for including such expansion capabilities!) These expansion cards were the precursor to the sound cards of today, and were termed *music cards* because of their capabilities derived from technology used in electronic musical instruments.

You can read more about music cards and game music in Chapter 10, "Playing Games."

Music cards, like the popular AdLib card with its FM synthesizer, provided music generation capabilities that were characteristic of the technology available in the late 1980s and early 1990s. They offered a basic set of features for PCs to adequately produce music for games and other software:

- Simple methods were used to simulate instrument sounds. This was crucial because processors and electronics were not very advanced like today, and if they had been, they would be too costly for a mass-market product like the PC. It was also not possible to play back real recorded instruments and sound because of the large storage space required, and also because memory chips were slow, expensive, and had limited capacity. This resulted in the use of electronically simulated audio derived from simple mathematical algorithms. The music resulting from such technology was often characterized as electronic sounding, tinny, and metallic—sounds really bad to most of us today, but at that time heavenly compared to the beeper.

- Because music often relies on layering and harmony of different instruments and sounds, these electronic music generation techniques also provided the ability to play several instrument sounds simultaneously to create a coherent piece of music. This "polyphonic" ability is a huge improvement from the monophonic PC speaker that could play only a single tone at a time. The AdLib synthesizer can play 11 basic FM instrument sounds at one time.

- With this music generation hardware, small and manageable music files were possible. Small music files allowed games and other applications to communicate and send instructions to the card to produce music, without clogging up the tiny amount of communication bandwidth available between the PC and other components.

With the popularity of music cards, many game developers saw the potential and added support for cards like the AdLib to further immerse players in their games. Many PC gamers and enthusiasts snapped up these cards from the stores to hear the exciting stereo and polyphonic soundtracks that give the PC the musical capabilities of video game systems from Nintendo and Sega. Music cards paved the way for sound cards in the PC and played a huge role in the success of the Sound Blaster.

Read more about the evolution of game music in Chapter 10, "Playing Games."

Music cards also gave musicians a much better environment to write music by making it possible to compose and sequence music by looking at notes on the computer monitor, and freely change and shuffle them around. This form of music composition eventually evolved to the point today where computers can be used as full-fledged desktop music production tools that rival professional studio equipment costing tens of thousands of dollars. In fact, many music sequencing and digital audio editing workstations in studios today use high-end professional sound cards installed in the same Macs and PCs we find in our homes!

Find out more about how to use the Live! for music composition in Chapters 14 to 17.

Sound in the Real World

Despite technological limitations of early music cards, they adequately generated polyphonic music that sounded cohesive as a tune, though electronic-sounding; it still served its purpose for the games and electronic music applications of that time. However, the "real world" was still missing from these music cards, because they could not generate or playback sounds that occur around us. For instance, the complex waveforms of shattering glass could not be generated with a simple music card.

It would be ideal if computers could also do what audio tapes and vinyl records can: by using recording equipment to capture the vibrations of the air that make up sound, storing that on media like tape, and reversing the process to translate the recorded sound stored on the media for playback on speakers. Because computers work with information in digital format with only two absolute values of 0 and 1, it was not straightforward to represent the minor graduations, as well as the widely differing components of analog audio. Several fundamental issues had to be addressed:

- How to represent analog audio waveforms in digital 0s and 1s.
- How to reliably capture and convert analog waveforms to a digital format.
- How to store digital audio in various data storage media, including analog tapes, optical discs, and many other formats.
- How to convert digital data back to analog waveforms that can be heard.
- How to store and output audio that covers the entire hearing range of humans.
- How to build such digital audio devices cheaply, so they can be included in consumer products like CD players and sound cards.

The solution is now generally known as *digital audio*, and the predominant method of implementing this is through the use of digital-to-analog converters (DACs) and analog-to-digital converters (ADCs) that convert between digital and analog methods of representing sound. The sound provided by an audio source, such as a microphone, is captured in analog form and converted to digital 0s and 1s by the ADC. The reverse conversion is performed by the DAC, so that the original captured audio can be retrieved and played back. Just like the addition of sound to silent movies sparked off an artistic transformation in Hollywood, the invention of DACs and ADCs gave electronic equipment the ability to realistically capture and reproduce sound that occurs in the real world, ushering a brand-new aural dimension for audio equipment and sound cards.

The next chapter will delve more into the DAC and ADC process.

The DAC and ADC are the most basic and essential components of any sound card, and remain so today, as they act as the bridge between the analog world of vibrations of air creating sound, and the digital world of 0s and 1s. They are used to play back MP3s, music, and sound effects recorded in games, and to allow recording from various audio sources like microphones and CDs.

The Sound Blaster

When introduced in 1989, the first Sound Blaster broke new ground by integrating the popular FM synthesizer found on the AdLib music card with the ability to record and play back digital audio—all at an affordable price. The significant improvement in audio over the PC speaker enticed enthusiasts and gamers. Soon, the sound card became an essential component in PCs, and Creative would make millions of Sound Blasters and become the sound card powerhouse that it is today.

Figure 1.1: The very first Sound Blaster

Wave Audio

The first Sound Blaster could manage only mono FM synthesis and 8-bit mono digital audio, resulting in sound that is close in quality to an AM radio. The Sound Blaster Pro added stereo to the FM synthesizer and Wave audio capability, making sound from the Sound Blaster produce stereophonic sound that can be differentiated by our two ears, like the predominantly stereo sound systems available. Games could play back sound effects with this capability; sounds like gunshots and the evil laughter of a boss character in a game could be effectively conveyed by playing back true-to-life recordings of such sounds. Many sound card owners also shared audio recorded in digital form, exchanging floppy diskettes or transferring Wave files over modems.

The Sound Blaster 16 finally brought sound cards to the much-desired CD-quality audio benchmark with its 16-bit, 44.1-kHz ADC and DAC. With the increase in the number of bits used to store digital audio, recorded sounds became much smoother and more realistic compared to the electronic-sounding nature of 8-bit audio. The Sound Blaster Live! has the maximum sampling rate improved from 44.1 kHz to 48 kHz, increasing the number of times that "snapshots" of the audio are taken and stored, thereby increasing the detail of the resulting digital audio recording. 48 kHz is also commonly used in consumer digital audio technologies like DVD.

Today, sound cards like the Live! can reproduce clear and crisp audio that covers the full range of sound that can be heard by humans. The quality of DACs used are much better than older Sound Blasters, because of better sound card design, advancements in electronics, and improved manufacturing processes. This ended the age-old complaint of Sound Blasters making "computer bleeps," hisses and noises in the speakers, and lets the Live! work admirably with high-end speakers and sound systems.

The patented *8-point interpolation* of the EMU10K1, the audio chip used in all Live! cards, helps smooth out lower-quality Wave audio files that are less than the preferred 16-bit 44.1 or 48 kHz format, making them sound clearer than other sound cards. Many programs like audio streamed over the Internet, and sound effects of the majority of games today still use Wave audio that is around 16-bit 22 kHz, which is half the quality of audio CDs.

Unlike earlier Sound Blasters that could play only a single Wave file at a time, the Live! can mix and play back many Wave audio channels simultaneously, thanks to hardware Wave mixing built into the EMU10K1. There can be many audio applications playing Wave audio, and the Live! will output all of them at the same time. Contrast this to sound cards of the past, where the first application that manages to grab hold of the sound card gets exclusive use of the DACs, and subsequent applications that need to play Wave audio will be rejected. Although this capability seems useless at first, it has its benefits. For instance, you wouldn't want to miss out on an alarm from your scheduler or the alert sound from an instant messenger just because MP3s are playing in the background.

Audio Sample

CD Folder: Chapter 1 – The Evolution of Sound on the PC
File: Sample Size Comparison.wav

Listen to the sound quality of the same piece of music, first recorded from a sound card in 8-bit mode, and compare it with the 16-bit version that follows. You'll notice that the 8-bit version is less able to store a detailed representation of the original audio, especially in the higher frequencies, because less space is used to store the digital audio information. We have included the orginal files as **Sample Size Comparison - 8-bit.wav** and **Sample Size Comparison - 16-bit.wav,** so that you can hear how much better the 8-bit file sounds on the Live! compared to the older sound card we recorded from.

Music Synthesis

The early Sound Blaster cards, including the Sound Blaster AWE cards, all had the electronic-sounding FM synthesizer based on the Yamaha OPL2, and later the OPL3 FM synthesizer chips. This form of music generation was essential in the early days when PC hardware was not as advanced and affordable as today, where streaming a large prerecorded piece of music from an audio file to the Wave output is common.

Wave Audio for Music?

Of course, playing back prerecorded music through the DAC would enable the sound card to reproduce audio as it was recorded, just like a consumer CD player using its built-in DACs to play back Wave audio data read from the compact disc. This method called "streaming audio" negates the need for a music synthesizer on the sound card. However, storage space was scarce in the early days, especially before the CD-ROM emerged as a viable storage medium. Even then, the constant transfer of data from the CD-ROM to the sound card required a significant amount of CPU power, which was little compared to the multi-gigahertz processors available today.

In games, it was unwise to spend a large percentage of this power just to play back a music track in the background when a less costly option was available, especially because CPU power can be put to better use to perform other operations that can enhance game play, for example, to produce dazzling on-screen graphics and effects, and to perform artificial intelligence computation for more realistic computer-controlled opponents. Despite the lack of realism, the music synthesizer was essential to sound cards in those days, as it offloads much of the chore of generating music away from the CPU.

> Composers writing music for synthesizers use the musical instrument digital interface (MIDI) format, where only the instructions on which notes to play, which instruments to use, and how long to play them are stored. No actual audio recordings and instrument sounds are stored in MIDI files, making them small, manageable, and easy on PC resources.

Realistic Instruments with Wavetable Synthesis

Naturally, people wanted the realism of music produced by sound cards improved, but at the time, only costly high-end electronic music equipment had the hardware necessary to generate music that sounded very close to real-life musical instruments. It was not until the Sound Blaster AWE cards released in 1996 that Creative provided a more realistic form of music generation called *wavetable synthesis*, right on the sound card. The wavetable synthesizer in the AWE cards utilized E-MU's expertise in wavetable technology to produce the cost-effective EMU8000 synthesizer chip.

Audio Sample

CD Folder: Chapter 1 – The Evolution of Sound on the PC
Files: FM synthesis.wav and **Wavetable synthesis.wav**

Listen to the instruments generated by the Sound Blaster 16's FM synthesizer and compare it to the wavetable synthesizer of the Live! Although the same MIDI file was used to record both audio samples, they sound significantly different because MIDI stores information only on the notes to be played back. Therefore the realism of the music depends on the technology employed in the music synthesizer hardware on the sound card. This is also true with the professional synthesizers used in studios, because they also rely on the MIDI standard.

Instead of mathematically generating instruments with techniques like FM synthesis, wavetable synthesis stores actual recordings of Wave audio of instrument sounds, which can then be manipulated by the wavetable synthesizer to produce music. This feature is carried on in the EMU10K1 chip found on all Live! cards, with even better wavetable sound quality and effects.

> Unlike the EMU10K1 on the Live! which handles both Wave audio and wavetable music synthesis, the EMU8000 chip on the AWE series handled only music synthesis, and similar to the Sound Blaster 16, used a separate set of ADCs and DACs for Wave audio.

Affordable Music Composition

The Sound Blaster is popularly known as a multimedia and gaming sound card, especially the Live!, with its vaunted EAX technology for games. However, do not be surprised when someone tells you that the Live! is a very capable music-making tool, as well. Since the Sound Blaster AWE cards, many musicians have turned to the Sound Blaster as an affordable means of composing music—some of which has even been used in commercial recordings.

In addition to the wavetable synthesizer in the Sound Blaster AWE32, Creative threw another advancement into the mix that made the Sound Blaster ideal for musicians: SoundFont technology. Like typographic fonts used for screen display and printing with operating systems and word processors, SoundFonts are files that contain custom instrument sounds. They can be loaded on any Sound Blaster that has SoundFont support, and subsequently are used in MIDI compositions as regular instrument sounds.

Find out more about SoundFonts in Chapter 16.

Such capabilities were already available to professional musicians and studios, but these devices, called *samplers*, cost thousands of dollars. With this *sampling* feature available on Sound Blaster AWE and Sound Blaster 32 cards using the EMU8000 synthesizer chip, and on the EMU10K1 chip found on the Live! cards, the Sound Blaster becomes an affordable sampler, which costs a few hundred dollars compared to the thousands of dollars for professional samplers. They can also render these compositions as Wave audio to be compressed to MP3 or even mastered to CD audio discs.

> Most of the Sound Blaster cards that use chips from E-MU can support SoundFonts, like the EMU8000 and EMU8008 used on many Sound Blaster cards, the EMU10K1 on the Live! and even the EMU8710 chip used in a previous E-MU product that puts a sound card inside a small PC card to be used in notebooks.

The faster peripheral component interconnect (PCI) connection between the Live! and the PC allow SoundFonts to be loaded into the main system memory. By using the main system memory, users can easily add more RAM to their PCs to load many SoundFonts at the same time and load SoundFonts that are large and contain many instrument sounds. Instead of being limited to the meager half-megabyte of SoundFont RAM built into most Sound Blaster AWE cards, the Live! can use up to 32 MB of your PC's memory to load SoundFonts.

The Live! also adds features such as higher-quality effects processing, SoundFont and wavetable synthesis, and 8-point interpolation to keep the instrument sounds smooth and realistic when manipulated by the wavetable synthesizer. The *polyphony*, which determines the number of instrument sounds that can be generated simultaneously by the music synthesizer, has been increased from 32 in the earlier EMU8000 Sound Blasters to 64 in the Live! to allow more complex instrument sounds and SoundFonts to be layered in a composition.

The Sound Card as an Audio Hub

With sound cards, faster video cards, and the emergence of the CD-ROM as an economical storage medium, *multimedia* quickly became a buzzword for PCs. These computers could play smooth video and high-quality audio and allow interactivity in games, educational software, and even business presentations. With the development of hardware such as CD-ROM drives, MPEG and DVD decoders, telephony cards, and other devices that need to output sound to the speakers, the sound card had to evolve from a simple Wave audio and music synthesizer combination to an audio hub supporting many of these capabilities:

- Provide connectors to accept sound from all these different hardware peripherals.
- Mix all the different sound sources together and send them to speakers connected to the sound card.
- Allow individual volume, mute, and balance controls for each sound source.
- Allow the user to balance the volume of each source and control the overall volume.
- Facilitate Wave recording from any of these sources.

The *mixer* is the nucleus for consolidating the myriad of sound sources together on the sound card. Earlier sound cards used analog mixers that were prone to hiss and noise, because the sound card had to be connected to the motherboard inside the PC, which is an electrically noisy environment. Newer sound cards like the Live! make use of a digital mixer and tightly integrated electronics that reduce the possibility of noise affecting the sound that is sent to the speaker outputs behind the sound card.

Read more about the Live! card's mixer in Chapter 7.

Chapter 4, "Accessories," will cover the extension connector found on every Live! card. The extension connector gives Live! owners the flexibility to add more inputs and outputs on the Live! by connecting it to digital I/O devices like Creative's Live!Drive and other third-party digital I/O cards. You can connect CD players, MiniDisc recorders, microphones, VCRs, satellite and cable receivers, DVD players, and other analog or digital audio equipment to the Live! to record and play back sound, making the Live! the center of a PC-based home entertainment system.

Chapter 5, "Connecting Devices," will illustrate how to connect audio and audio-visual equipment to the Live! and an attached digital I/O device.

The Sound Blaster

Creative has come a long way since the first Sound Blaster was launched more than a decade ago. In the early days, the company faced strong competition from other companies who relentlessly made "Sound Blaster-compatible" sound cards, threatening to seize the crown from Creative. However, Creative was able to stave off much of the competition and remain at the top of the PC sound card market for over a decade. The company is constantly innovating and adding features to sound cards to improve sound quality and realism, with the ultimate aim of providing effective and affordable audio solutions for PCs to attain Hollywood-quality audio.

A Timeline of the Sound Blaster Family

So many models of Sound Blaster cards have been released that many Creative staff, not to mention the general public, can barely keep track of them! The following is an overview of some of the more significant developments in the evolution of the Sound Blaster, leading up to the Sound Blaster Live!, affirmed by many users and publications as a revolution in PC audio.

Before the Sound Blaster, Creative made a card called Game Blaster. It used a simple 12-voice music synthesizer dubbed the Creative Music System (C/MS), and was aimed at gamers who wanted better and yet affordable music for their games. It had some support from a few developers but did not gain widespread acceptance compared to the huge support for the AdLib card and its FM synthesizer. It also did not have Wave playback capability, which, thankfully, the Sound Blaster had.

1989 Sound Blaster

The first sound card was launched with 8-bit mono Wave audio and FM synthesis. The first version, simply called the Sound Blaster 1.0, also had Creative Music System (C/MS) stereo music synthesizer chips to retain compatibility with Creative's Game Blaster music card released in 1987. However, this feature was removed in subsequent 1.5 and 2.0 versions to save cost, since the AdLib-compatible FM synthesis on the sound card sounded better (even though it was mono compared to C/MS's stereo) and had excellent support in software and games. Future Sound Blasters do not have C/MS.

1991 Sound Blaster Pro

With the great success of the Sound Blaster, Creative took the next logical step by adding stereo for both parts of the sound card—the 8-bit Wave audio and FM synthesis.

This year also marked the beginning of the multimedia revolution, with CD-ROMs and multimedia upgrade kits gaining in popularity, especially with home PC users. Creative jumped in the fray by retailing upgrade kits consisting of a Sound Blaster and a CD-ROM drive.

1992 Sound Blaster 16, Sound Blaster 16 ASP, and Wave Blaster

Creative brings the Sound Blaster to CD-quality level, with support for 16-bit, 44.1-kHz digital audio recording and playback. The music generation portion of the sound card continued to use FM synthesis.

The first version of the card was the more advanced *Sound Blaster 16 ASP* (Advanced Signal Processor; later renamed the CSP, for Creative Signal Processor), which had a simple processor that could apply algorithms to Wave audio. It was initially used for QSound 3D positioning and acceleration of voice recognition, but developer support for the ASP was not strong. In addition, including the chip in all sound cards was costly, so this feature is not found most Sound Blaster 16 and future generations of Sound Blaster cards.

Around this time, the Plug-n-Play standard was adopted by the market to allow PC peripherals to be easily configured without requiring users to fiddle with switches on the hardware, like having to move little plastic jumper caps on the Sound Blaster's circuit board. Creative introduced new versions of the Sound Blaster cards and tagged on a "PnP" behind their names to signify Plug-n-Play compatibility, like the *Sound Blaster 16 PnP.*

Multimedia became a hot buzzword and was the must-have for enthusiasts and gamers. Before CD-ROM drives were able to work with the standard hard drive connections found on all motherboards, early CD-ROM drives had their own connection standards. PCs did not come with connectors for these various CD-ROM standards, and it was up to the sound card to provide a controller so that the CD-ROM drive could communicate and send data to the PC. To allow the Sound Blaster to be affordably used with CD-ROM drives in multimedia upgrade kits and new PCs, CD-ROM controllers were added to the Sound Blaster cards for the most popular CD-ROM drives from Mitsumi, Panasonic, and Sony. A *Sound Blaster 16 MultiCD* was also sold that supported all three CD-ROM interfaces, and a *Sound Blaster 16 SCSI-2* supported CD-ROM drives with SCSI connectors.

As wavetable synthesis became more affordable, Creative added a 26-pin wavetable connector at the top of some Sound Blaster 16 cards so that daughterboards like Creative's Wave Blaster, Roland's excellent SCD-10 and SCD-15, and Yamaha's DB50XG could be attached to the sound card. These wavetable upgrade cards provided more realistic music from MIDI files and games. The Wave Blaster had 4 MB of instrument samples and used wavetable technology based on the professional synthesizers made by E-MU, a manufacturer of electronic musical equipment used in music and movie studios around the world. This partnership would lead to Creative's subsequent acquisition of E-MU and the use of its expertise in the development of audio chips for future Sound Blasters, including the EMU8000 and the EMU10K1 used in the Live!

Budget versions with fewer features — for instance, no wavetable connector — these were sold under the "Value" name, like the widely used *Sound Blaster 16 Value.* This strategy allowed the Sound Blaster 16 to penetrate the OEM and budget segments of the market, providing an affordable sound card for PC manufacturers to bundle with their PCs. Many older PCs still use the Sound Blaster 16.

1994 Sound Blaster AWE32, Vibra Pro, and Vibra 16

With rising consumer awareness of the increase in quality provided by wavetable synthesis, and the popularity of wavetable sound cards like the affordable Gravis Ultrasound, Creative introduced the *Sound Blaster Advanced WavEffects* (AWE) sound cards based on the EMU8000 synthesizer chip. These cards had 1 MB of instrument samples stored in ROM and 512 KB of RAM for uploading custom SoundFonts. There are two empty memory slots on the sound card, allowing it to use up to a maximum of 28 MB of SoundFont memory by adding 30-pin SIMM memory modules also used in PCs at that time. Vienna SoundFont Studio was released several months later to give musicians the ability to create their own instrument samples for the AWE32.

Instead of moving to a brand-new sound card design, Creative retained Sound Blaster 16 compatibility in the AWE32, including the old FM synthesis chips. This allowed software and games to slowly transition to this new wavetable capability, which developers quickly warmed up to, supporting the EMU8000 in their software.

The 32-note polyphony of the wavetable synthesizer in the EMU8000 allowed it to play back 32 instrument sounds at the same time. Consumers often mistook the AWE32 for a 32-bit sound card because of the number 32. Unlike the 16 in Sound Blaster 16 referring to the bits supported by the Wave audio's DAC, the AWE cards referred to the polyphony of the EMU8000 wavetable music synthesizer and not the Wave audio portion of the sound card. (In those days, bits were attributed to performance, just like the number of megahertz is a big selling point today and is significant in marketing and public perception of the power of PC hardware.)

Creative also introduced the *Vibra Pro* and *Vibra 16* chips based on the Sound Blaster Pro and Sound Blaster 16, respectively. Unlike the Sound Blaster cards, which required many chips to make (for instance, one for ADC/DAC and another for the FM synthesizer), the Vibra integrated all the essential features of a Sound Blaster into a single chip. This drove down manufacturing costs and allowed the chip to be used on motherboards as a built-in audio solution, negating the need for a sound card. Some affordable Sound Blaster cards were also made with this chipset.

1995 Wave Blaster II

An upgrade to the Wave Blaster was introduced. The *Wave Blaster II* used the EMU8000 chip with 2-MB ROM of instrument sounds. This gave owners of Sound Blaster 16 cards with the wavetable connector the ability to upgrade to wavetable synthesis similar in quality to the one found in the AWE cards.

1996 Sound Blaster AWE64 and Sound Blaster AWE64 Gold

Despite the name and marketing efforts, the AWE64 was still a minor upgrade from the AWE32 and is definitely not a 64-bit sound card. (It is still capable of only 16-bit Wave audio.) The 32-note polyphonic EMU8000 chip remained in the AWE64. The quoted 64-note polyphony comes from a Sondius WaveGuide software synthesizer that relied on the CPU instead of the EMU8000 to produce the extra 32 notes of polyphony, and only for selected instruments.

SoundFont worked only with the hardware synthesizer chip and not the software synthesizer, so in effect, the AWE64 has the same features as an AWE32. On the AWE64, the SIMM memory slots were removed and replaced with a proprietary memory slot that required users to purchase a Creative memory upgrade module to add more SoundFont RAM.

The *Sound Blaster AWE64 Gold* was marketed as a high-end audio solution and came with RCA instead of mini-jack outputs, an S/PDIF output bracket for digital connectivity, and brass-colored connectors.

SoundFont 2.0 was introduced, and added several features to the popular SoundFont standard that is still in use today in the Live!

1997 Sound Blaster AWE64 Value, Sound Blaster AWE64D (OEM), EMU8008, and Vibra 16x

The EMU8008 and Vibra 16x audio chips were introduced as upgrades to their older counterparts, providing new features like 3D stereo enhancement and full-duplex Wave audio. Internet use exploded and videoconferencing, Internet telephony, and "voice over IP" were hot applications of this global communications network. *Full-duplex support* in the sound card was needed to let users speak into a microphone and hear the other party simultaneously, and also to use different playback and recording sampling rates at the same time.

To provide this feature cheaply, Creative updated the Windows drivers of older Sound Blaster cards to simulate full duplex by quickly switching between recording and playback modes, while future Sound Blasters would have full duplex as a standard feature, implemented in the sound card's hardware.

Permutations of the EMU8000-based cards like the *Sound Blaster 32* and *Sound Blaster 64* were introduced without the 512 KB of SoundFont RAM. This made sense because most applications do not use the SoundFont RAM (except for the minority that compose music with SoundFonts).

Other cards like the Sound Blaster AWE64 Value and Sound Blaster AWE64D (OEM) were also introduced to target budget customers and the OEM markets, respectively.

The year also saw Creative acquire Ensoniq for its PCI sound card and Sound Blaster emulation technology, which permitted sound cards using the PCI connector on the motherboard to work like all the older Sound Blaster cards that use the much slower industry standard architecture (ISA) connection. Like E-MU, Ensoniq has its roots in professional synthesizers and electronic musical equipment. This acquisition led to the introduction of a new range of PCI-based Sound Blasters in the following year, aptly called the *Sound Blaster PCI* platform.

At the end of the year, Creative showcased the EMU10K1 at Comdex Fall and outlined the strategy for more advanced effects and audio processing for a new line of Sound Blaster cards that would be introduced less than a year later as the Sound Blaster Live!

By this time, motherboards had support for CD-ROM drives and the on-board CD-ROM controllers on sound cards were not necessary. Subsequent PCI-based Sound Blasters including the Sound Blaster PCI and Live! would have the controllers removed. The wavetable connectors were also removed in these sound cards.

1998 Sound Blasters based on Ensoniq AudioPCI, Sound Blaster Live!, and Sound Blaster Live! Value

At the beginning of the year, Creative adapted and sold Audio PCI sound cards brought over from newly acquired subsidiary Ensoniq under the Sound Blaster brand name, resulting in products like the *Sound Blaster PCI 64*. This was widely seen as an interim measure to quickly get the Sound Blaster to the PCI platform, as many other low-cost PCI sound cards appeared on the market with features better than those of the dated EMU8000 sound cards.

In September, Creative officially launched the Sound Blaster Live! and the EMU10K1 as the next-generation platform for Sound Blaster cards. The marketing tagline, "So Real It Has to Be Live!," highlighted the ability to add reverberation and effects to any audio played back by the sound card. This feature was known as Environmental Audio.

Creative also heavily promoted Environmental Audio eXtensions (EAX) to game developers as a quick and easy way to add Environmental Audio to games. EAX, together with the support for surround sound with four-channel speakers and DirectSound3D positioning, would make the Sound Blaster Live! one of the most popular gaming sound cards for the next three years.

The audio quality of the wavetable synthesizer was improved over the EMU8000 cards, and the faster PCI connection allowed the removal of costly memory chips that had to be included in EMU8000 cards for SoundFont support. Now, SoundFonts are stored in the memory of the PC and obtained directly by the wavetable synthesizer in the EMU10K1 when needed.

A full version of the product known simply as the Sound Blaster Live! was marketed alongside the Sound Blaster Live! Value, which was an affordable version with fewer connectivity options, but otherwise retained all the features and sound quality of the full Live! product. A much more affordable US$99 compared to the full product's US$299, helped the Live! penetrate the market and garner a wide installed base. The new features and huge leap in audio quality offered by the Live! gave many PC users an incentive to upgrade their sound cards.

1999 Sound Blaster AudioPCI 128, Sound Blaster Live! Platinum, Sound Blaster Live! Player, Sound Blaster Live! MP3+, and Sound Blaster Live! X-Gamer

February saw the number of Sound Blaster Live! cards hit the one million mark, while in November, Creative announced that the total number of Sound Blaster cards reached 100 million units—just in time for the tenth anniversary of the Sound Blaster. The lower-end sound cards based on the Ensoniq AudioPCI design continued to be sold in retail and OEM markets to be included in new PCs, while the Live! does its rounds in the retail channel as well as bundled with some new high-end multimedia PCs from popular PC manufacturers.

Live!Ware 2 and 3 were released to the public. These software upgrades added new functionality to the Live! They included better 3D positioning algorithms, new utility applications such as the Surround Mixer, and more features for users to customize the effects of the Live!

EAX quickly became a standard supported by many game developers, and Microsoft licensed EAX for inclusion in DirectX used by Windows games and multimedia applications.

EAX 2.0 was added to support occlusion and obstructions, allowing games to simulate muffling of sound when blocked by objects in the gaming environment. EAX 3.0 was also announced at the same time to counter the popularity of competitor Aureal's A3D 2.0 3D audio rendering technology. Unfortunately, EAX 3.0 was never released.

In September, the Sound Blaster Live! cards were upgraded with a digital output that supported digital speakers from Creative's speaker subsidiary, Cambridge SoundWorks. The Sound Blaster Live! product line was diversified to reflect the different software bundles available. The X-Gamer bundle included the same second-generation Live! card with EAX game titles, while the MP3+ cashed in on the popularity of MP3s with applications and tools for digital music. The new Platinum product had a wide-ranging software bundle, but most importantly, the new Live!Drive was bundled to add more analog and digital inputs and outputs for greater connectivity.

2000 Sound Blaster Live! 5.1 series

Environmental Audio Graphical Librarian Editor (EAGLE), a graphical 3D audio modeling software to easily add EAX and 3D audio, was introduced to the game development community.

Creative built on the success of the Live! with the Sound Blaster Live! 5.1 series of cards. The product diversification and naming convention remained similar to those of the second-generation products introduced in 1999, including the X-Gamer, MP3+, and Platinum. The Live! 5.1 added another analog center/woofer output to the existing front and rear outputs, allowing the sound card to be connected to 5.1 speaker systems and home theater receivers.

The new Live!Drive included in the 5.1 Platinum product was a new model called the *Live!Drive IR* that had IR remote control capability.

Dolby Digital decoding became a standard feature and made the Live! 5.1 an affordable solution for watching DVDs on the PC with the full impact of 5.1 surround sound.

Advancements in the Sound Blaster Live!

The Live! was an advancement from the older Sound Blaster cards, but among the new features that were introduced, two of them stand out. These features proved to be very popular and became essential in sound cards today.

Effects Processing

Echoes and reverberations occur all around us. Shouting in a hollow tunnel will produce eerily long, repeating echoes. A choir performing in a concert hall will not sound majestic or grand when you move it to your bedroom, as the reflection of sound waves provided by the architecture of the concert hall is gone. Reverberation and echoes are key to realism, and are often employed in movie soundtracks, to add ambience to vocals, as well as augment musical instruments in audio recordings. Effects processing allow electronic devices to simulate these repeating echoes. Other interesting things can also be done to audio, like the imaginative use of pitch-shifting effects (known technically as a "vocoder" effect) to make Cher's vocals in her hit single, "Believe," out of the ordinary.

Effects processing requires significant processing power, and it was only after the mid-1990s that it moved out of professional recording studio equipment and into consumer sound cards like the Sound Blaster AWE series. Earlier sound cards had limited ability to add reverb and other effects to music generated by a wavetable synthesizer, but the Live! is the first mass-market sound card to provide effects processing not only on wavetable synthesis, but also all other sounds including Wave audio and audio from external audio devices connected to the Live! It definitely sounds much better than the primitive echo controls on cheap karaoke systems. In fact, many musicians attest to the quality of the effects processing in the Live!

The EMU10K1's built-in effects processor handles this feature, providing the flexibility to place sounds in any environment and allow pitch shifting, muffling, and other interesting effects to be applied to Wave audio and music. Creative markets the effects processing of the Live! as Environmental Audio and Environmental Audio eXtensions (EAX), and they were successful in garnering support from game developers, as well as recognition from consumers. With effects processing, sound cards can now simulate different realistic environments — especially useful for first-person games like Unreal!

> Visit your local gaming store, and you'll probably find a lot of game packaging with the EAX logo imprinted alongside other logos like the ubiquitous Windows logo.

Chapter 8, "EAX," will tell you more about EAX on the Live! and show you how to use the driver utilities to change or create your own environments.

3D Audio

Sound can emanate from any direction, but audio systems and sound cards have largely been limited to the two-speaker stereo format for decades. The use of surround sound in movies and home theater helps to underscore the benefits of surround sound. When playing first-person games where you explore an environment, it would be advantageous for the game's sound effects to clue you in about the direction of every event occurring in the game world. When 3D positioning is used, players can hear sounds from all directions — even from behind. This gives gamers a strategic advantage, since telling the direction of an opponent would be less of a chore, unlike plain stereo-sound cues that place all the sound in front of the player even when it is supposed to come from behind.

> The Live! uses virtual 3D surround when it is placed in two-speaker mode and games with 3D audio are played.

Before the Live! was introduced, some sound cards tried to provide virtual 3D surround algorithms that made use of two speakers to simulate sound behind the listener, but that was not particularly realistic for many because of the need to stay in the same sweet spot from the speakers for the virtual algorithms to be effective.

A few sound cards supported more than the usual two-speaker stereo configuration, including Creative's own Sound Blaster PCI 64, but it was the Live! that popularized the use of 3D audio and four-speaker setups for PCs, which Creative calls a "four-point surround" configuration. Together with affordable multichannel speakers from subsidiary Cambridge SoundWorks, Creative successfully converted many PC enthusiasts and gamers to multi-speaker configurations. It wasn't difficult to convince gamers and developers alike, because the benefits of 3D audio are readily apparent! Today, 3D audio support in every sound card is a must, especially for serious gamers.

The Past and Present

Creative's history is synonymous with the evolution of sound cards on the PC. Several factors contributed to this, including tactics used on the technical and legal fronts to keep the competition at bay. Factors that helped make Creative a success today were the foresight by the founders that a sound card is a great device for the PC and the vision to put sound cards in every PC. Also, as you have seen in the timeline and the many other Creative products, the company has a willingness to try new things and innovate, while most of the early competition merely copied and made cheaper "Sound Blaster–compatible" sound cards.

Sound Blaster Compatibility

One of the things that helped Creative and the Sound Blaster maintain dominance for such a long time is definitely Sound Blaster compatibility, which stemmed from the hardware and software architecture of early PCs. You may have seen in promotional material, news articles, and reviews that proclaim the Sound Blaster as the "de facto standard" for sound cards, especially before 1996 when DOS games were predominant. This meant that a Sound Blaster–compatible sound card supports all the features of, and works in a way similar to, an original Sound Blaster card. This was important for DOS games because of the proliferation of Sound Blaster cards and the abundance of software (mainly games) that support the Sound Blaster. Developers could write code to support and use the features of the Sound Blaster; they did not have worry about supporting many different sound cards that did not conform to an established standard.

Windows changed things. With a driver layer and hardware abstraction, Windows acts as an arbitrator, requiring all instructions and requests sent to the hardware (for example, requests to print information to the screen or play back audio on a sound card) to be sent to Windows first. It then communicates these instructions sent from the applications to the hardware using the drivers provided by the hardware manufacturer. Windows drivers are required for any hardware peripheral that wants to operate with Windows and its software.

With this abstraction provided by Windows, Sound Blaster compatibility is moot. Sound card manufacturers can use their own designs and need not implement Sound Blaster compatibility. As long as a sound card has functioning Windows drivers, Windows applications can use the sound card.

Previous cards up to the Sound Blaster AWE series still had Sound Blaster compatibility, as many games were still using DOS and relied on the Sound Blaster as an audio platform. It was not until the Sound Blaster PCI cards, including the Live!, that Creative moved away from Sound Blaster compatibility in hardware. Instead, Creative opted to include software emulation so that some (but not all) older DOS games can still work in Windows 95 and 98. Today, we seldom hear the term *Sound Blaster compatible*. Rightly so, the focus has shifted to audio features like surround sound, effects, and 3D audio support in games.

The Future

With an illustrious history in the PC audio market, Creative is not immune to changes in the marketplace. Competition is still strong, especially when more affordable sound cards providing similar features than the Live! are available at lower prices. Audio is becoming an essential part of computing. Today, every notebook and many personal digital assistants (PDAs) come with built-in audio. In desktop PCs, sound chips on many motherboards threaten to encroach on the sound card business.

The Motherboard Threat

In the past few years, the sound card has become ubiquitous in the PC, prompting Intel and motherboard manufacturers to cater for sound chips right on the motherboard. This motivation is mirrored in the integration of video chips on motherboards as an affordable replacement for graphic cards, because every PC needs a display output. The motherboard is a vital component for every PC to function, and it acts as an arbitrator and hub between all the various components used to make up a PC, like the CPU, graphic cards, hard drives, USB ports, and all other peripherals.

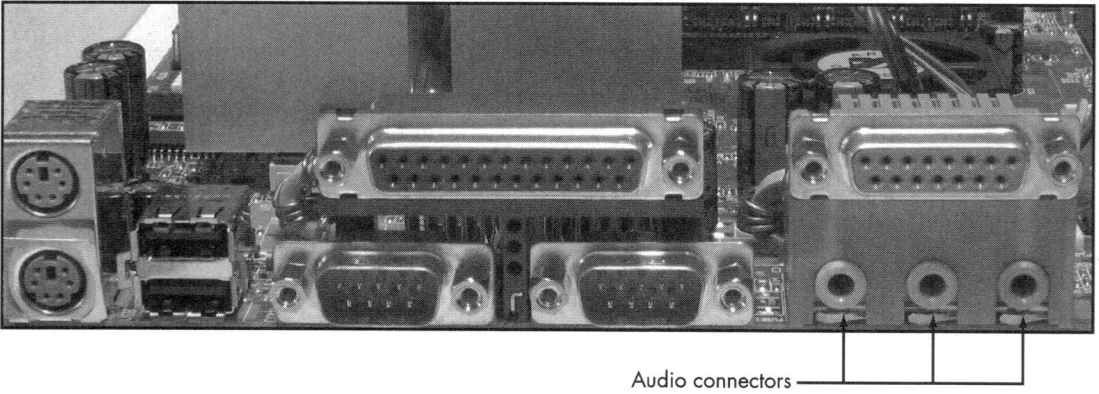

Figure 1.2: Audio connectors on a motherboard

Some motherboards today come with non-Creative sound chips, which are adequate for normal use, especially in office PCs where bells and whistles like multispeaker support and effects processing are unnecessary and may even affect productivity. When the initiative to embed sound on the motherboard was announced by Intel in the late 1990s, many predicted the death of Creative's sound card business. The company has proven critics wrong and that sound cards still have room to grow with new high end features that promise to enhance audio. In the coming years, we'll be watching how Creative innovates to provide better audio products for games and entertainment on the PC, and continues developing products with features that surpass those in the increasingly sophisticated audio chips used on motherboards.

The Future of PC Audio

PC audio will remain an important and essential part of computing, with applications for games, the Internet, audio, videoconferencing, voice mail, movies, MP3s, and many other purposes. The Sound Blaster Live! played an important role in the evolution of PC audio, especially in improving gaming audio, and promoting multi-channel speaker systems for PCs. Newer sound cards are poised to continue this advancement, as more powerful audio technologies emerge. One day, the audio from your PC may sound so true to life that you'd think it was something real! That's exciting to look forward to.

2

AN AUDIO PRIMER

Sound is an interesting phenomenon caused by the mere movement of air. They come in many forms—from the subtle whiff of a breeze, the jarring sound of thunder, to the rhythmic blending of musical instruments in music. Many of us do not pay attention to it like we do with our visual senses. Most would notice that a movie has great scenery, balanced lighting, and good-looking actors, and that a game has dazzling 3D graphics and special effects. However, many would not notice or comment that a movie or game has an effective and enveloping soundtrack, or notice that the audio quality was subpar. And still, sound has the power to move us in unimaginable ways. How is it that the mere movement of air can do so much and provide such a wide range of sounds for our ears to feast on?

This chapter delves into the more technical aspects of audio, but avoids going into details that only engineers would understand. We hope this chapter will give you an idea of how analog sound occurs in our world and how digital audio has changed and improved the way we can record, use, and manipulate sound.

How We Hear Sound

Part of the reason why audio affects us in profound ways is that our ears are linked closely to our brains, giving music and sound the power to affect us greatly. Even though to many of us, this may seem abstract and difficult to comprehend at times, we can still enjoy and appreciate the music and great audio quality produced by our sound cards and audio systems.

It's All About Vibrations

Sound is nothing but vibrations of the air. Every time an object moves and pushes against the air, it creates compressions and rarefactions, or differences in air pressure, which we perceive as sound. Unlike most matter in our physical world, air can be easily compressed and moved about, allowing it to act as a medium to transmit sound from one place to another. Compressions and rarefactions create *sound waves,* which are propagated in all directions from the object. The different way in which each object vibrates the air results in a seemingly unlimited palette of sounds that inhabit our world, from animal noises to earth-shaking explosions.

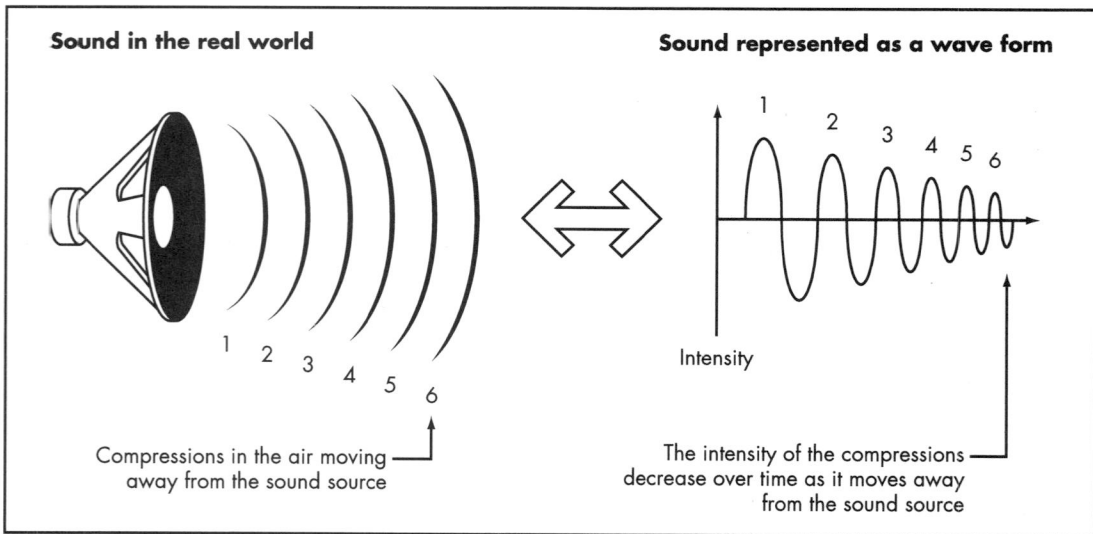

Figure 2.1: Sound waves

> The speed with which sound waves are propagated in the air is relatively low compared to light waves. This is why you can hear echoes when you speak in a relatively small empty room, but you never see a delay when you move in front of a mirror. While depending a little bit on conditions such as temperature and air pressure, the speed of sound (in air) is approximately 340 meters per second (1,110 feet per second).

For instance, when you speak, your vocal cords excite the air around you and cause neighboring air particles to vibrate in a similar manner. This process continues until the air hits something, like the eardrums of a person nearby. In the ear, the sound and vibrations are further transmitted via a few small bones (the hammer, anvil, and stirrup) to the elements in the ear that are sensitive. These elements pick up the minute vibrations of the air and transmit nerve impulses to your brain, creating different thoughts and sensations.

Sound as Waves

Compressions and rarefactions of the air can be captured rapidly at equal intervals of time and represented on equipment such as an oscilloscope. The graph on the oscilloscope would show a continuously evolving plot or line that moves up and down in tandem with the increase and decrease of air pressure. These are known as sound waves. A common measure of sound waves is *frequency*. Many sounds are repetitive in nature, like a sustained note on a flute, the repetitive chugging of an engine, or even when you open your mouth and say "aaaaa" for the doctor. The sound waves produced are relatively consistent and occur at equal intervals of time, resulting in a reasonably steady frequency in the waveform.

Frequency

Frequency measures the number of vibrations per second of the sound and is represented in hertz (often abbreviated as Hz). If, for example, something (let's say a speaker cone) is vibrating back and forth 85 times a second, we say that it produces an 85-Hz tone. Different elements in the ear are sensitive to different frequencies. Altogether, the human ear can hear sound with frequencies in the range of about 20 Hz to 20,000 Hz (or 20 kHz). The lower frequencies, called *bass*, are deep and rumbling like those of an earthquake, while the higher frequencies, known as *treble*, can be very sharp and ear-piercing, like a cymbal or glass breaking. There are more elements in the ear that are sensitive to mid-range frequencies between 200 and 2,000 Hz. Therefore a 500-Hz tone will sound louder than a 50-Hz tone with the same intensity.

Frequencies below the hearing range of 20 Hz are known as subsonic, and those above 20 kHz are known as ultrasonic. Dogs can hear frequencies up to 67 kHz, which is much higher than humans can hear. Imagine the myriad of high-pitched sounds that they have to contend with every day. Dog whistles don't seem to make any sound but work miraculously!

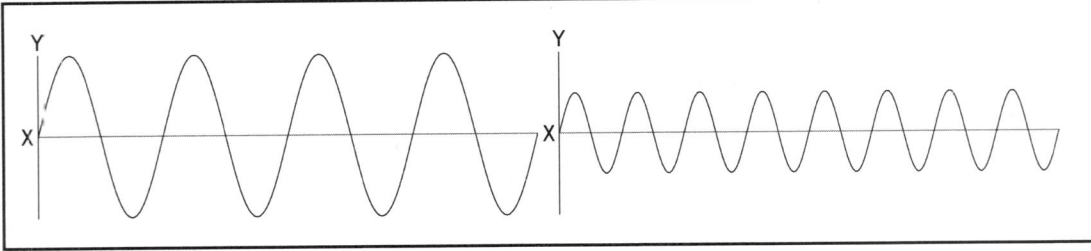

Figure 2.2: Two pure tones as they are usually represented on paper, on an oscilloscope, or a computer screen. The amplitude is pictured on the vertical (y) axis, and the time on the horizontal (x) axis. The right waveform has twice the frequency (twice as many compressions and rarefactions per second) as the left one, but only half the amplitude.

Depending on the way the sounds vibrate the air, the waveforms reaching the brain can be very irregular, resulting in a muddled combination of very different frequencies. This will be interpreted as noise, like the sound of tires screeching. A waveform may also be made up of smooth and constant waves, like the sound of a sustained piano note; we interpret these sounds as music because the waveform repeats itself in a way so that we can easily make out common musical characteristics like volume and pitch of different notes.

Audio Sample
CD Folder: Chapter 2 – An Audio Primer
Files: screech.wav and piano.wav
Using a sound editor like SoundForge or CreativeWaveStudio that is included in most Live! driver CDs, open screech.wav and compare it to piano.wav. You should be able to see that the waveforms of the piano sound has smooth and recurring peaks and troughs, while in contrast, the screech is very randomized.

When we deal with instrument sounds that may consist of many frequencies with different intensities, we talk about the pitch of the sound rather than its frequency. Pitches are often expressed as note values (such as "A in the fourth octave"), rather than according to their frequencies.

Sound Intensity, Amplitude, and Decibels

Measuring absolute values for the amplitude or intensity of a sound (which would be measured with formulas like N/m^2 and W/m^2, respectively) is sometimes, but not very often, useful, but the physics are beyond the scope of this book.

Comparing Ratio of Intensities

We are often interested in comparing the *ratio* of the *intensities* of a sound to another sound, the latter known as a *reference sound*. For this purpose, we use a unit known as *decibel* (dB). The decibel scale is what is known as a *logarithmic scale*. We won't bore you with the mathematics behind it, but will instead describe what such as scale means in practice. (For the technically inclined, there is a mathematical definition of the decibel at the end of this section.)

If the first sound has twice the intensity of the reference sound, their ratio is always (approximately) 3 dB, regardless of the first sound's actual absolute intensity. If the first sound has four times the intensity of the second sound, their ratio, expressed in decibel, will be 3 + 3 = 6 dB, eight times (doubling three times) will be 3 + 3 + 3, which gives 9 dB, and so on. (Every time we multiply or divide the ratio, we add or subtract on the decibel scale.) If instead, the sound intensity is lower than the sound you compare it to, you'll end up with a negative number. For example, half the intensity gives −3 dB. This method is mainly used to compare two sound intensities. For example, if we compare two fans, we may say that the second one is three decibels quieter than the first one.

Comparing Amplitudes

Furthermore, the decibel can also be used for comparing *amplitudes* of signals. In this case, an amplitude ratio of 2 is instead (approximately) 6 dB. Comparing signal levels is common in electronic music, recording equipment, and many consumer audio systems and home theater receivers.

Instead of using a simple scale of 0 to 10, some of these devices have the maximum amplitude defined as 0 dB, which is the level that other signals are compared against. Therefore, we usually end up with negative decibel values for volumes that are lower than the maximum of 0 dB. For example, a signal at −6 dB is about half the maximum amplitude. Because decibel is a logarithmic scale, an amplitude of zero (silence) can't be expressed in dB and is usually written as minus infinity (-∞ dB).

This measurement is used when dealing with amplitudes, such as on a mixer or in a sound-editing program. If you look at the scale in an audio editor, it's usually marked with -6, -12 dB, at 1/2 and 1/4 of the maximum amplitude. The computer uses this form of representation because there are no actual sound intensities, only signal levels.

Absolute Measurements

The dB unit is also used for absolute measurements of sound, by comparing sound pressure levels and setting the reference sound intensity to the lowest sound intensity that the human ear can perceive at the frequency where the ear is most sensitive. As a consequence, sound perception at 0 dB and below doesn't mean absolute silence—just that the sound intensity is weaker than humans can hear. As an example, normal speech is usually about 55 to 65 dB. This "absolute" scale is also used to measure sound levels that we hear, like the sound level at a rock concert or how much noise a fan makes at a distance of one meter.

> For those of you who are not mathematically challenged, the following formula defines the decibel unit. Given the intensities, I and J, of two audio signals, the ratio of their intensities, Ri, expressed in dB, is:
>
> Ri = 10 log10 (I/J)
>
> When used to compare amplitudes, the ratio Ra between the amplitudes K and L, in decibel, is:
>
> Ra = 20 log10 (K/L)
>
> Thus, comparing a signal with an absolute amplitude of 184 to another signal with an amplitude of 457 (never mind the amplitude units; we're interested only in their ratio), their ratio is:
>
> 20 log10 (184/457) = -7.90 dB
>
> Or, put another way, the amplitude of the first signal is 7.90 dB below that of the second signal.

Positioning Sound

It's no secret that human beings have two ears and that our eyes all point to the front, although many of us wish we had eyes behind our heads to see what people are doing behind our backs! Likewise, the main advantage of having two ears is that it adds another dimension to our hearing and makes finding the source of a sound much easier than if we had only one ear. There are many reasons for this, and the two significant ones are:

- **Loudness**. If a sound comes from your left, your left ear will hear a louder sound than your right ear.
- **Time difference**. Almost as important for the sense of direction of a sound is the time difference between the moment the sound reaches one ear and then arrives slightly later in the other ear. Because the ears are spaced apart, a sound that comes from the left or right will reach one ear a fraction of a second before it reaches the other. The brain can sense this time difference to determine the source of the sound even more accurately, and you'll instinctively be able to tell where sound came from.

These two reasons, together with the fact that human beings move their heads a little bit all the time (which the balance sensors in our ears are very good at keeping track of), make it easy to determine the direction of a sound.

Stereo

We have two ears, so why not take advantage of the benefits in sound reproduction? A common application of the human ability to listen with both ears is to use two channels. This is commonly known as *stereophonic sound*, giving rise to the term *stereo* being used for many decades to refer to any audio system that produces stereophonic sound (although we now use the word *stereo* interchangeably to mean stereophonic sound, as well). The left speaker plays one channel of the sound, and the right speaker plays the other channel. By changing the balance to vary the intensity of sound in each speaker, the sound can be made to appear to come from anywhere between the two speakers. If the sound is played back equally loud in both speakers, the sound will appear to be centered between the two speakers (provided the listener is seated equidistant from each speaker). A stereo recording adds variety and breadth to the resulting audio compared to mono sound.

Figure 2.3: A stereo setup creates a sound stage in front of the listener

Multichannel Audio

When stereo is not enough, additional channels can be used to provide more accurate positioning and/or positioning in more dimensions. Stereo gave us the possibility to position sounds in one dimension, namely anywhere on a line between the two speakers in front of the listener. By adding two rear channels, we can position the sound anywhere in the rectangle of the four speakers, achieving two-dimensional sound positioning.

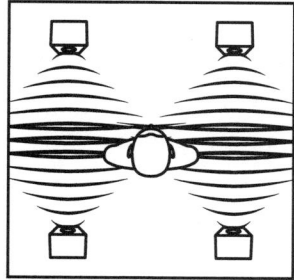 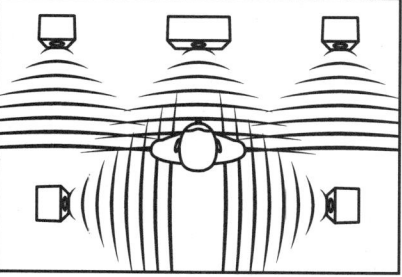

Figure 2.4: Four-speaker and 5.1 surround sound fields

An Audio Primer **29**

Other configurations have been popular for movies. Dolby* Surround and Dolby Pro Logic surround add a center channel (which is the average of the left and right channels) and a surround channel (which is usually placed behind the listener) to improve the directionality of sound. These extra channels are encoded in the two stereo channels of a movie, which makes the technology cheap to implement and compatible with existing stereo equipment, but somewhat limited in functionality.

More recently, Dolby Digital, which uses five totally independent channels, plus an extra channel with bass information, has become popular. For the ultimate playback of such audio tracks, a five-speaker setup is necessary. This arrangement is known as *5.1*, and it is a must for DVD and film buffs.

The Live!, which is designed particularly with gamers in mind, has support for four independent audio channels for total freedom of positioning between four speakers. Although this configuration is usually referred to as 3D sound, keep in mind that we have very little ability to position the altitude of the sound source, so effectively we're limited to sound positioning in two dimensions (which is enough in most cases because often the ability to tell which direction a sound came from is far more important than being able to tell how high or low a sound is; adding a third dimension would make speaker placement close to impossible, as you would need to have the same multispeaker configuration duplicated above and below ear level). In addition to this, the 5.1 series of Live! cards offers extra analog outputs for the center and bass (subwoofer) channels, for playback of DVD movies, and for games that support 3D audio positioning.

> Although subtle, the Live! does use algorithms to virtually simulate a sound above and below ear level for games that support 3D sound. Chapter 10, "Games," will cover more on 3D audio in games.

You can read more about multichannel audio configurations in Chapter 6, "Speakers." Chapter 11, "Watching Movies," will touch on surround sound technologies in movies and how you can play them back with the Live!

Storing Sound

Before digital technology became common, many ways to store sound signals were invented. Most of these methods aim to record and reproduce analog audio waves as accurately as possible. Some record the vibrations on bumps on a plastic surface and use a sensitive needle over the bumps to translate the vibrations back to sound, while others translate the vibrations to equivalent electrical signals or align magnetic particles on tape, to be converted back when playback is needed. One of the first approaches was to create a score in a material and vary its thinness or thickness depending on the strength of the sound signal at a particular point in time. When a small needle (later referred to as the *pickup*) is forced through the score, it vibrates and, when connected to additional elements, produces sound. This is essentially how a record player works.

Another way of storing analog sound is using magnetic particles on a plastic tape. To record sound, the tape is passed over a magnetic head that aligns the small magnetic particles with varying magnetic polarity between north and south. During playback, another type of magnetic head picks up the different alignments of magnetic particles on the tape and produces a corresponding electric signal. This is the way tape recorders work.

Although there are many ways to reduce imperfections on a sound source (which can be anything from dust on a record to badly aligned particles on a magnetic tape), a certain amount of noise is always introduced in analog recordings. As a consequence (and contrary to digital recordings), every time sound stored on analog media is copied, the quality is reduced. Many types of analog media, such as tape, also degrade over time.

Sound in the Digital Domain

Digital technology brings several advantages to the audio world, particularly the ability to represent data discretely in 0s and 1s. It eliminates the quality degradation of analog recording because 0s and 1s are easier to recognize and pick up by equipment.

Analog vs. Digital

One major benefit of digital over analog is that small fluctuations or interference in media carrying digital signals will not cause much harm, because the signal can still be uniquely identified as a 0 or a 1. Let's use an example to illustrate this:

Imagine that we are transmitting analog audio through electrical signals and have a simple scale ranging from a low intensity of 0 to a high intensity of 10. Analog signals would occupy any number between 0 and 10. Using only whole numbers would be too limited because tiny increases or decreases in analog audio cannot be represented precisely, just like the tiny variations in temperature or even the Richter scale require decimal places to measure accurately.

So on our hypothetical scale, we would possibly have values like 0.000145, 4.95637, or 9.9991 to represent different electrical intensities. Values that are very near to one another, like 9.985 and 9.986, may still need to be differentiated so that these small fluctuations in the analog waveform can still be accurately recreated when converting electrical signals back to analog. Any unwelcome interference would skew the value of the electrical signals, even the decimal places, resulting in a modified representation of the original analog sound.

> In addition to the technique used to store and recover analog audio, the conversion circuitry used during the translation process between analog audio and electrical, magnetic, or other signal formats also has to be of high quality so that the conversion is accurate. This is also true in the digital world of DACs and ADCs used in digital audio equipment and sound cards.

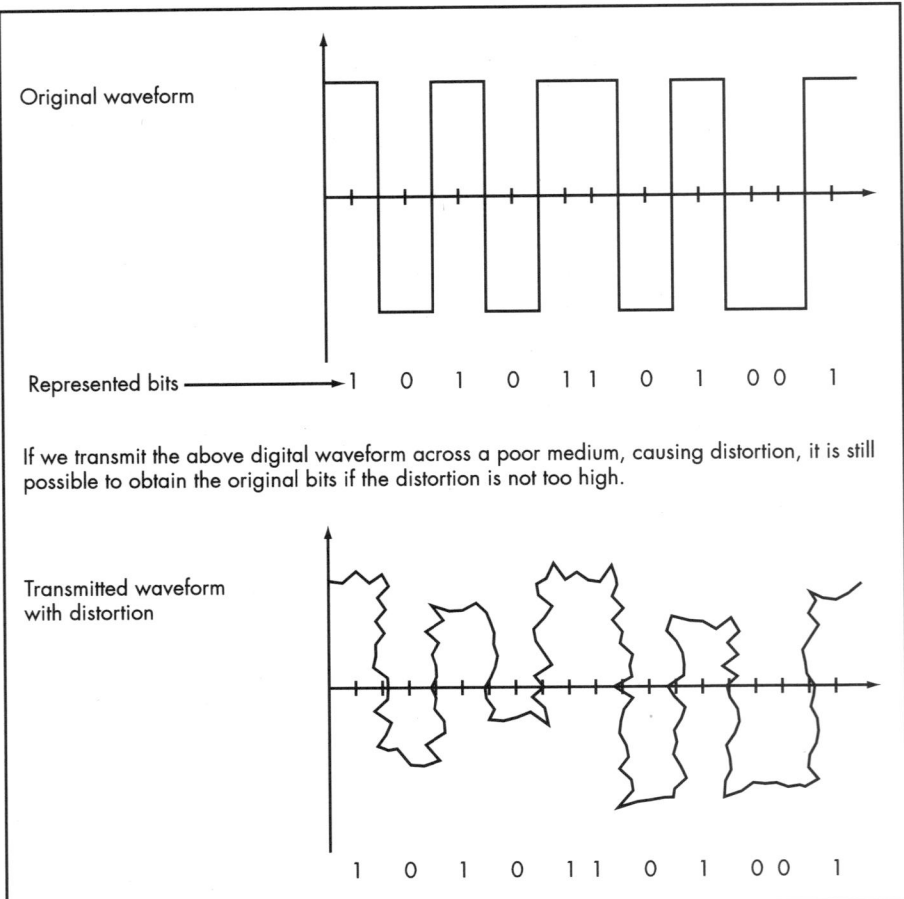

Figure 2.5: Distortion in digital audio

Contrast that to the digital way of representing information, where analog signals representing digital 0s and 1s have a huge difference, making them easy to differentiate. How is this so? If we look back at the previous example, we could use the two extremes of our hypothetical scale to represent a digital 0 and 1. An electrical intensity of 0 (i.e., no electrical signal) could be used to represent a digital 0, and the maximum intensity of 10 can signify a digital 1. When interference occurs, the circuitry converting electrical signals to digital 0s and 1s can accommodate a wider margin of error. For instance, electrical intensities from 0 to 5 indicate a digital 0, and any intensity above 5 implies a digital 1. If a digital 0 is sent over an electrical wire with an intensity of 0, and an unwanted surge causes the value to be changed to 4.5, the electrical signal will still be recognized as a digital 0 at the receiving end.

Likewise for other forms of digital transmission media, for instance, the use of the presence and absence of light in optical cables, or the extreme north and south poles of magnetization to represent discrete digital 0s and 1s, digital data can be easily recovered due to the larger margin for error, and results in a format that is much less susceptible to noise, distortion, and loss of data.

Digital Audio

As you will see, we can never represent an analog audio signal perfectly in digital form. We can, however, make very good compromises using sampling, analog-to-digital (A/D), and digital-to-analog (D/A) conversion techniques.

Sampling

As analog sound evolves continuously, you will probably see that its waveform is made up of smooth, rounded curves with varying intensities and frequencies. If you took snapshots of the analog waveform at regular intervals and converted them to absolute values in 0s and 1s, you would have a digital representation of the waveform.

Doing this requires a way to convert from analog to digital. For instance, if we record sound with a microphone, the electrical signal level generated by the microphone at any point in time would be proportional to the relative air pressure (sound) around it. An electronic circuit transforms this signal to a digital number according to the signal strength. This process is usually referred to as *taking a sample of*, or *sampling*, a signal.

Together, large groups of samples taken at frequent intervals of time make up a pool of digital measurements that can be used to reproduce an analog waveform in its entirety. The digital measurements can then be written to Wave files and other digital audio formats and stored on media such as a hard disk, CD, or DVD. Stored digital audio data can also be duplicated accurately with the exact 0s and 1s found in the original digital recording.

Sampling Rate

If an analog waveform is sampled often enough, we can get a very good representation of the sound signal. To get reasonable sound quality, we must perform sampling tens of thousands of times every second. The number of samples taken every second is called the *sample* (or *sampling*) *rate*, and it is measured in hertz (Hz), which simply means "samples per second." The CD audio format uses a sample rate of 44,100 Hz (often abbreviated as 44.1 kHz), while most DVDs and the Live!'s Wave capability support sampling rates of up to 48 kHz.

> The hertz (Hz) measure can be used to represent the number of times something is done each second. In the case of frequency, it is a measurement of the number of air compressions and rarefactions per second. For sampling rate, it is the number of "snapshots" of a waveform that are taken per second. Even though they use the same hertz (Hz) measure, frequency and sampling rate are two very different things.

Although infinitely high sampling rates seem to be beneficial, a theory known as Nyquist's Theorem states that a sampling rate of at least double the maximum of the analog waveform's frequency is sufficient to represent the waveform. Going by this theorem, our 20-kHz hearing limit can be adequately reproduced with digital audio by sampling at 40 kHz and above; therefore, most consumer digital audio formats and equipment are able to provide crisp and clear sound at 44.1 kHz or 48 kHz. Most high-end digital audio equipment exceed 48 kHz, and many devices

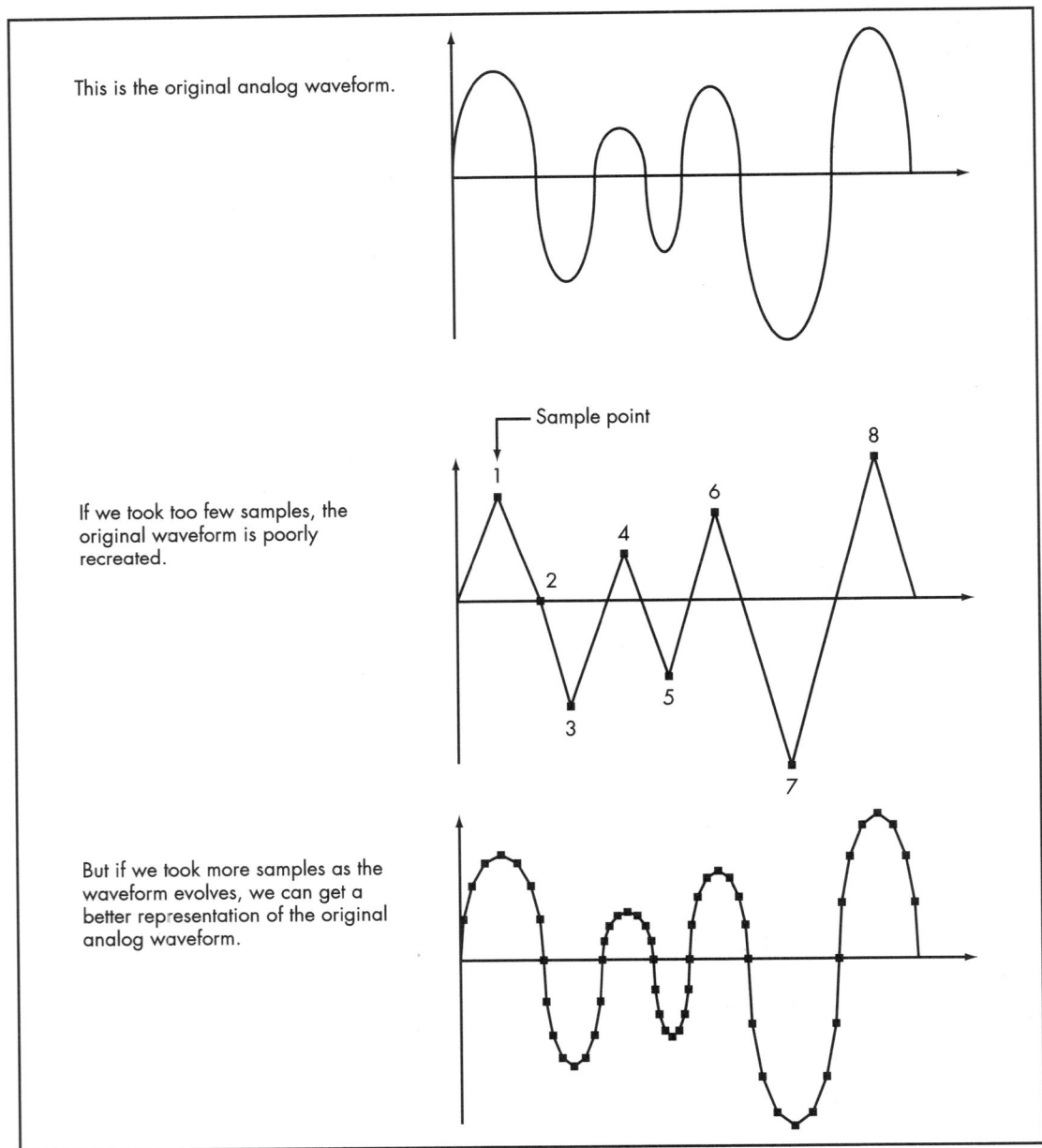

Figure 2.6: High vs. low sample rates

use 96 kHz or higher sampling rates to provide a wider margin for error and allow the audio to be edited with less deterioration. This is especially true of digital recording and mixing equipment used in sound studios, as well as professional sound cards.

Low sample rates reduce the sound information that is captured every second and therefore does not accurately record the sound that we hear, especially in the high frequency ranges. The results are like watching a jerky video file on a PC that uses fewer frames per second than the usual 24 to 30 frames per second used in broadcast TV, DVDs, and VCRs to create smooth moving images. Although it is desirable to use CD-quality sampling rates for the best sound quality, lower rates like 22 kHz and below are still used in applications like video-conferencing where reducing network bandwidth, processing time, and storage space are more important than sound quality. Some games also use sound effects recorded in 22 kHz, while some use CD-quality sound effects at 44.1 kHz, providing greater fidelity and realism for gamers.

Audio Sample

CD Folder: Chapter 2 – An Audio Primer
File: Sample Rate Comparison.wav
Similar to small sample sizes, reduced sample rates result in lower audio quality. The low sample rate that plays first is recorded from an older sound card at 22 kHz, while the later half sounds more dynamic because it is played back at the 44.1 kHz sample rate also used in the CD audio standard. Sample rates and sample sizes work hand-in-hand to deliver high-quality audio. The original files used to produce this recording are **Sample Rate – Low.wav** and **Sample Rate – High.wav**. Notice that the Live! produces a much clearer output of the low sample rate Wave file because of the 8-point interpolation performed by the EMU10K1.

Sample Size

Because computers cannot store an infinite number of values, we must allocate a certain amount of storage space to represent every sample captured from a sound wave. Computers are capable of representing data only as 0s and 1s, so one bit of data can either be a 0 or 1—which is not very helpful for storing the different states of a waveform. The *binary system* in computers uses a group of bits to represent values. If we put two bits together, we can use the bit sequence *00* to represent the number 0, the sequence *01* to represent the number 1, the sequence *10* for number 2, and the sequence *11* for 3. Thus, two bits can represent four distinct "analog" numbers, from 0 to 3. If we increase this to three bits, we can store eight numbers. Hence, adding more bits allows a wider range of numbers to be represented.

> The general formula to obtain the number of integers that can be stored in binary is to take 2 and raise it to the power of the number of bits allocated. Thus, 2^3 yields 8, and 2^4 yields 16.

Depending on the quality we need, the capabilities of the hardware, and memory constraints, we may use 8, 12, 16, or even 24 bits of data for every sample of audio. The higher the number of bits per sample, the greater the range of possible values (which gives a finer resolution), and the more memory the sound will occupy. For example, if you are asked to represent numbers from 1 to 2, but can use only whole numbers, you will have only the digits 1 and 2 for the representation. But if you can also use a single decimal point, you can represent the range from 1 to 2 in finer detail, as 1.1, 1.2, 1.3, and so on.

Adding more bits, like the EMU10K1's ability to process audio in 32 bits, is like giving processors more decimal points to work with, resulting in more precise calculations. Similarly, if you were doing your financial statements and the calculator works with only whole numbers and does not support decimal points, you would quickly lose precision in your calculations.

Because sampled analog waves don't always map exactly to an available digital number (represented by a series of 0s or 1s), they have to be rounded up or down to the nearest available value. The difference between the real signal and the result (the error) decreases as the sample resolution increases. If the difference is huge and the digitally reproduced waveforms deviate from the original analog waveforms by a large margin, the playback will not sound exactly like the original, and noise may be introduced, as well. Sixteen bits are generally considered to give noise-free, clean playback. That is why 16 bits are used as the resolution for sample data on CDs.

Smaller sample sizes (and hence lower resolutions) were often used in computer applications where memory requirements were a big problem. For instance, games on older ISA sound cards used 8-bit sound because it was smaller and required less overhead to play back. Memory is less of an issue today, and so 16-bit is now the dominant sample size used in consumer digital audio, while high-end professional digital equipment and sound cards have moved up to 24-bit sample sizes for more accuracy.

> The Live! can work with digital audio and Wave files of a maximum sample size of 16 bits and a sample rate of 48 kHz.

A/D and D/A Conversion

The process of converting continuously evolving analog signals to digital samples is called analog-to-digital conversion, or A/D conversion. The electrical component that performs this operation is called an A/D converter, or ADC. Each sound card has at least one ADC that performs conversion in stereo (two channels) simultaneously. The Live! has several ADCs that convert audio from analog devices to digital for further processing and mixing in the EMU10K1.

To play back digital sound, we need a circuit that does the opposite of an A/D converter; namely, take a list of digital numbers and produce an analog sound signal. Such a circuit is called a digital-to-analog converter (D/A converter, or DAC, in short). The resulting analog signal from the D/A converter gets amplified by

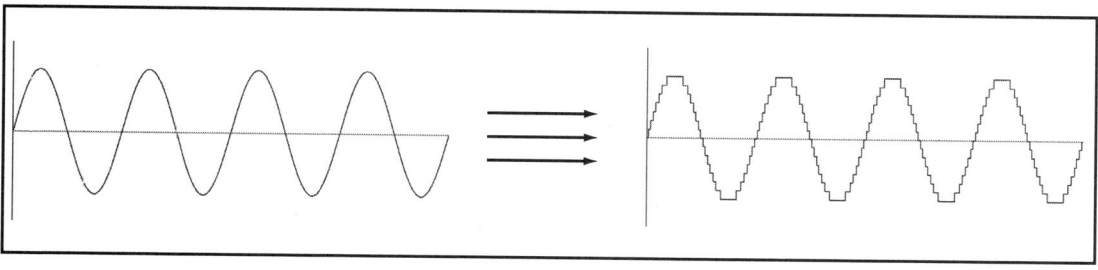

Figure 2.7: The process of converting an analog audio signal into a series of digital numbers, known as A/D conversion. At regular intervals, the value of the analog signal (on the left) is sampled, rounded to the nearest number, and stored in computer memory. Pictured, the digital signal would appear as in the right picture. Note, though, that in practice, much higher sample rates and resolutions are used; therefore the waveform after A/D conversion will be similarly smooth and rounded like the original waveform on the left. That is when we perceive that the sound is indistinguishable from the original.

an amplifier unit either built in to your speaker system or housed in a separate unit, and sent to a connected speaker. The speaker cone moves in and out with this signal, producing vibrations in the air similar to those of the original sound. This process is usually performed in parallel for two digital signals because most sound systems are in two-channel stereo. For multi-channel surround configurations, the sound system has to perform the same D/A and amplification process for more channels simultaneously. However, the reproduced sound may not be 100 percent similar to the original sound because of factors such as the loss of information when converting to digital, the quality of the storage media, the design of the amplifiers and speakers, and the quality of the cables used, among other factors. The DAC is one critical component in digital audio equipment. There is a huge cost difference between CD players and high-end dedicated DAC units because some DACs perform and sound better than others. Given the same digital audio signal, different DACs provide a different recreation of the analog sound. Most produce bright and sharp sound that is great for pop, techno, and other forms of modern music, while some are described as "warm" for their analog-like and smooth-sounding character. The ability to tell these differences apart isn't a gift only for audio enthusiasts. Just listen closely, and you'll soon be able to spot the characteristics that make digital audio equipment and their DACs sound different.

The Live! can sample as well as play back digital Wave audio at sample rates up to 48 kHz. Sample sizes accepted are 8 or 16 bits. It can also record in mono or stereo. Stereo recording records two mono tracks, one each for the left and right speakers, and therefore doubles the file size.

> Digital audio is stored on the computer in files called Wave files because they store numbers that can be passed through a DAC to obtain the sound waves. Even then, how the individual bits are arranged and stored in the file can be different, and this leads to different digital audio file formats.

Working with Digital Audio

Once converted to digital, sound can be more easily managed, transmitted, and archived without much interference compared to analog audio. A few changed bits will not severely affect the quality of the resulting sound. Moreover, most digital storage and transmission media have error-correction facilities to aid recovery of damaged or missing data—for example, to fix data that is lost to scratches on a CD.

Digital audio can be stored permanently on optical discs such as CDs and DVDs or transmitted over the air on radio waves, through cables that carry electrical signals, on magnetic hard drives and digital tapes, and even sent to any place in the world via satellite transmission and underwater submarine cables carrying Internet traffic. The discrete nature of digital audio makes it much easier to send such data without serious degradation. Previously agreed specifications for storing and transmitting digital information over these different media types help different companies make compatible products that are able to create as well as correctly decode digital audio.

In the PC, digital audio fits nicely into the digital nature of computers and provides an easy way to distribute audio and audio-visual material in software, applications, and Web sites. You can use the sound card's ADCs to quickly record sound in digital form and store them in hard drives and removable media like inexpensive recordable CDs. With the Internet, you can also share them with anyone around the world without worrying about loss in quality, which is readily evident in the file-sharing phenomenon. With a proper audio setup and a sound card, the person playing the recorded audio would hear it with a similar quality as you would on your own PC. The digital audio possibilities provided by sound cards are endless.

3

THE SOUND BLASTER LIVE! HARDWARE

Like many other devices in the PC, the Live! is made of chips and other electronic components mounted on a printed circuit board (PCB). At the bottom of the circuit board is a row of pins that makes up the PCI connector. It is inserted into the (typically) white slots found on motherboards to allow the sound card to communicate and send data to the rest of the PC. To the left edge of the circuit board are connectors that are exposed through the backplate behind the PC, allowing speakers and other audio devices to be connected to the sound card after it is installed in the PC case. This chapter describes the layout and connections available on the Live! and highlights the differences among the common models that were retailed.

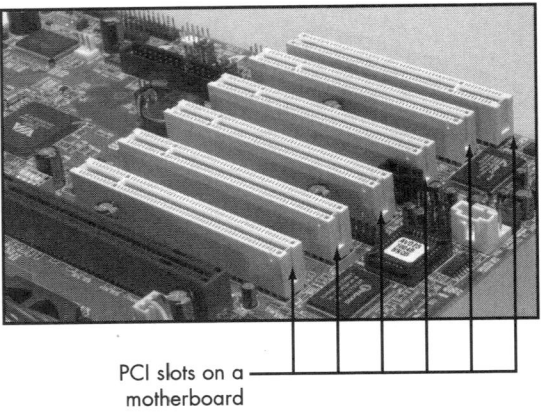
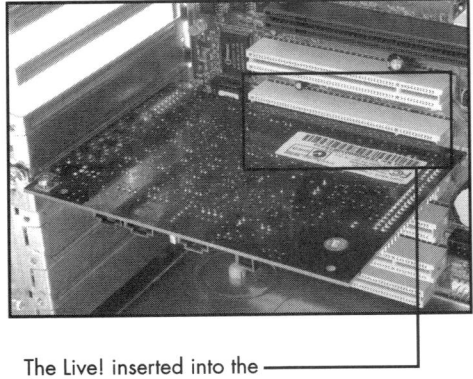

PCI slots on a motherboard

The Live! inserted into the motherboard's PCI slots

Figure 3.1: PCI connectors on a motherboard

The EMU10K1

Take a look at the Live! card. Among the numerous electronic components, you'll definitely notice a large, square chip with "EMU10K1" printed among other letters and numbers that make up the part number of the chip. That's the EMU10K1 digital signal processor (DSP) chip that powers the Live! Just like the CPU does the processing work in the PC, the EMU10K1 is the workhorse of the Live! and performs vital tasks like playing and recording of digital audio, generating of MIDI music, effects processing, 3D audio positioning, controlling the sound that is sent to each speaker, and mixing of the different sound sources piped into the sound card.

Chapter 18, "The EMU10K1," covers the technical aspects of the EMU10K1.

Figure 3.2: Different versions of the EMU10K1 chips used on the first-, second-, and third-generation Live! cards

Older sound cards, such as the earlier Sound Blaster cards using the old ISA connection standard, were built with many different chips etched onto the PCB: for instance, a wavetable chip for MIDI music, a DAC to provide digital audio and Wave playback, or a mixer chip to combine various sound sources together into a single speaker output. In this configuration, sound data has to travel along the PCB many times in analog format, making such designs more susceptible to electromagnetic interference from other components in the PC, resulting in hiss, digital noise, and beeps from the speaker outputs. Using many components also makes sound cards complicated and costly to build.

Newer PCI sound cards like the Live! have all-in-one DSP chips that integrate many of these components into a single silicon chip. Interference is reduced because much of the data that used to travel between separate components on the PCB now stays within the DSP. It is only during the final stage of processing that the digital audio data is converted back to analog audio and output to the jacks behind the card, lowering the chances of signal degradation. These sound cards use a smaller PCB and require fewer parts and resources to manufacture, and we consumers ultimately benefit from this advancement, as it provides very affordable and noise-free sound cards.

Sound Cards Can Look Good, Too!

The green PCB has always been synonymous with PC motherboards and add-in cards. However, in recent years, manufacturers have tried to differentiate their products by using different-colored PCBs. Many years back, the popular Gravis UltraSound sound card came on a distinctive red PCB. Popular motherboard and video card manufacturers have used brown, black and even red PCBs. We have even seen blue sound cards out there!

The Live! was Creative's first product to use a dark brown PCB—a departure from the green PCBs that all other Sound Blasters were manufactured with. The brass-colored connectors on the early Live! cards was a nice match for the brown PCB and gave the Live! an expensive and unique look. There are rare special edition Live! cards with gold-plated backplates and oscillators (in addition to the gold-plated mini-jacks) that only a handful of people own, while the rest of us who bought the retail versions have backplates and oscillators that are silver in color.

> Oscillators are the metal components soldered on Live! cards. They keep the clock timing in EMU10K1 synchronized. Some Live! cards use oscillators from Hosin, while later ones do not have prominent metallic oscillators on them.

Internal Connectors

Aligned on the top edge of the card are industry-standard Molex connectors that connect to many add-in cards and optical drives housed in the PC casing. One of them is a two-pin connector, while the rest are four-pin Molex 70553 connectors. Depending on the model of your Live! card, some of these connectors may be missing.

TAD

This connector hooks up to an internal data or voice modem and allows the dialing and connection sound from the modem to be channeled to speakers connected to the Live! The microphone output from the sound card is also trans-

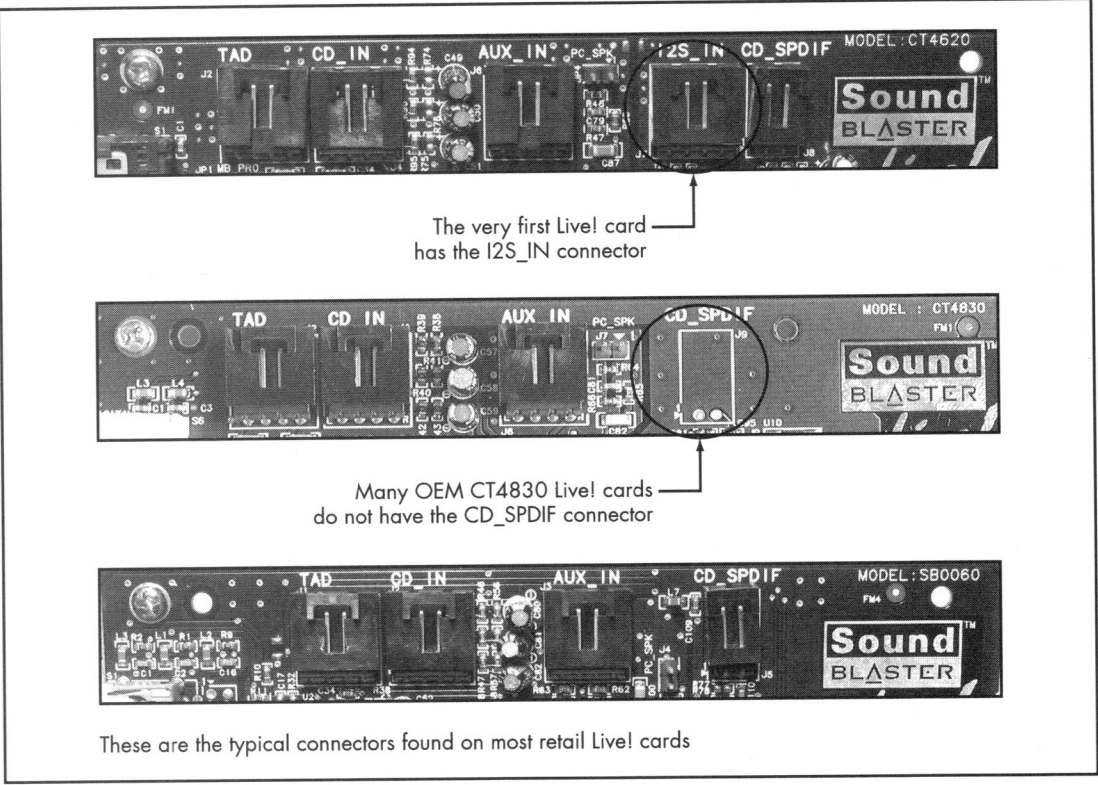

Figure 3.3: Internal connectors on various Live! cards

ferred to the modem card for certain uses, such as a speakerphone. Unless an internal modem or telecommunications card with a similar TAD output is installed in the PC, this connection is not needed in most cases.

AUX_IN

The auxiliary input also takes a stereo signal from internal add-on peripherals such as MPEG/DVD decoders, TV/FM tuner cards, and video capture cards that support this form of output. The pin assignments are similar to those for the CD_IN connector, so this connector can be used as a second CD_IN. This is especially useful if you have many optical drives and both CD_IN and CD_SPDIF are already used.

I²S_IN

Inter-IC sound (I²S) is a digital transmission protocol that improves on the S/PDIF format widely used for digital audio in consumer products. It uses more data wires to further minimize audio artifacts that may occur inside an electrically noisy PC casing due to reasons such as inferior cables and faulty digital audio equipment, as well as allow more control information to be sent between devices in addition to digital audio.

Some add-on cards have an I²S output, and most notably, it is found on the DVD decoder card bundled with Creative's PC-DVD DVD-ROM upgrade kit. Because PCs above 400 MHz can play DVDs without the need for hardware assistance from a DVD decoder card, most PCs with DVD-ROM drives do not come with such cards, leaving this I²S connector unused. Because of this, you will find this connector only on the very first generation of Live! cards released in 1998 when 200- to 300-MHz PCs were common. Subsequent generations of the Live! do not have this I²S connector.

> The S/PDIF (Sony/Philips Digital Interface Format) was standardized to allow digital audio to be transmitted and recognized across different digital audio equipment made by different manufacturers. This format is now supported in many consumer audio devices and was first popularized in CD players. Data is transmitted in 1s and 0s either electrically through a cable or over an optical fiber cable, which uses light.

Playing Audio CDs

The most frequent audio connection made between sound cards and other devices inside the PC is to CD-ROM or DVD-ROM drives, CD-RW and DVD writers, or other optical drives that can play audio CDs. This connection allows the sound from audio CDs played on such drives to be heard on the speakers connected to the sound card. The Live! can accept such audio from the optical drive either in analog or digital form.

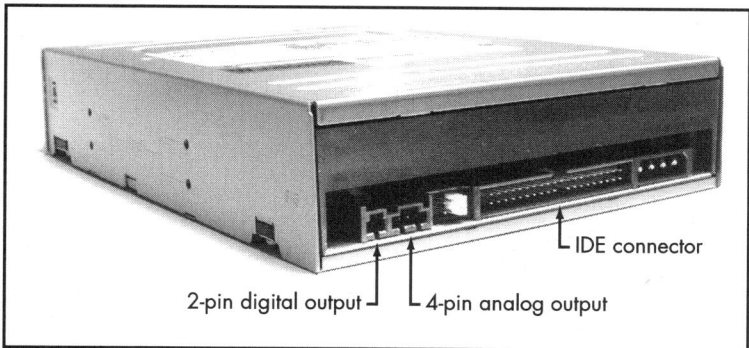

Figure 3.4: The CD analog and CD digital output on most optical drives

Audio connections between sound cards and optical drives are used only when audio or music CDs are played. Most of them also have the ubiquitous "Compact Disc" logo printed on the disc or on the inserts in the packaging. Sound on other types of CDs, like games and application CD-ROMs, as well as data CDs that contain audio files like MP3s and video files with sound, are all regarded as computer data and can be sent only through the data connection to the PC for processing and playback through the sound card's Wave audio output. If you look behind the optical drive, you will probably see a flat IDE data cable that provides the data connection between the optical drive and the motherboard of the PC.

> IDE stands for Intelligent Drive Electronics or Integrated Drive Electronics, where the controller that handles the transmission of data to and from the PC is built into the drive itself. It is the predominant method used in storage devices like hard drives and optical drives found in most PCs. Physically, the standard uses 40 wires to transmit data so flat cables with wires arranged side-by-side in parallel are used to keep the cable size manageable inside a PC case.

TIP *Like the CD audio and CD digital outputs behind the optical drive, the headphone mini-jack output provided at the front panel of these drives works only when audio CDs are played back. It does not output sound that is produced or played back on the sound card.*

Obtaining Audio from Optical Drives

At the top of the sound card are two connectors labeled CD_IN and CD_SPDIF that accept audio output by optical drives in analog or digital formats, respectively. There are three ways to connect an optical drive to the sound card so that audio CDs can be heard on the speakers.

CD_IN Analog Connection

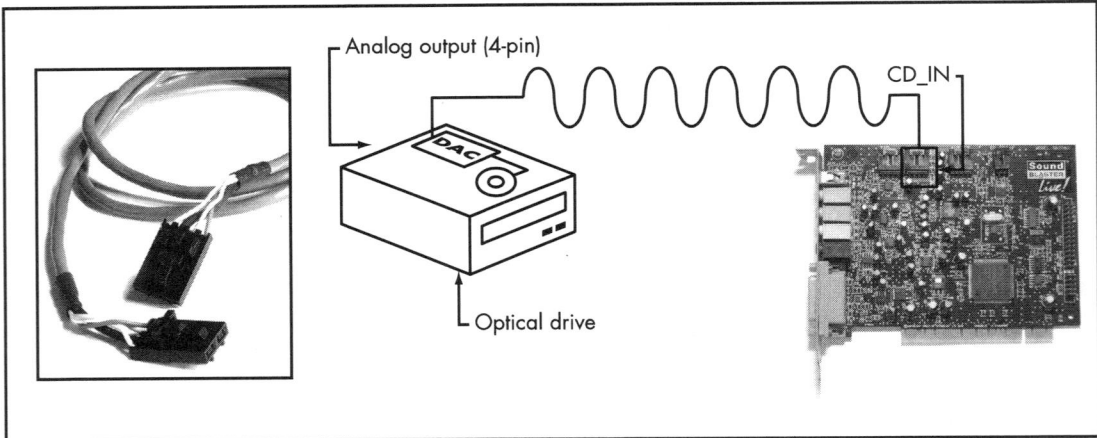

Figure 3.5: The CD_IN analog connection

Nearly all sound cards have the CD_IN analog CD input that connects to the 4-pin analog stereo output found at the back of virtually all optical drives. Such cables have an identical plug at each end and are usually provided along with the optical drive. This type of connection has been around for a long time, so if you are upgrading from an older sound card, the audio cable may already be present and can be reused.

Like consumer CD players, all optical drives with an analog CD audio output have DACs built in to them to convert digital audio read from the CDs to analog. The analog audio is then directed to the 4-pin analog output behind the drive, as well as the stereo mini-jack headphone output to the left of the drive's front panel.

CD_SPDIF Digital Connection

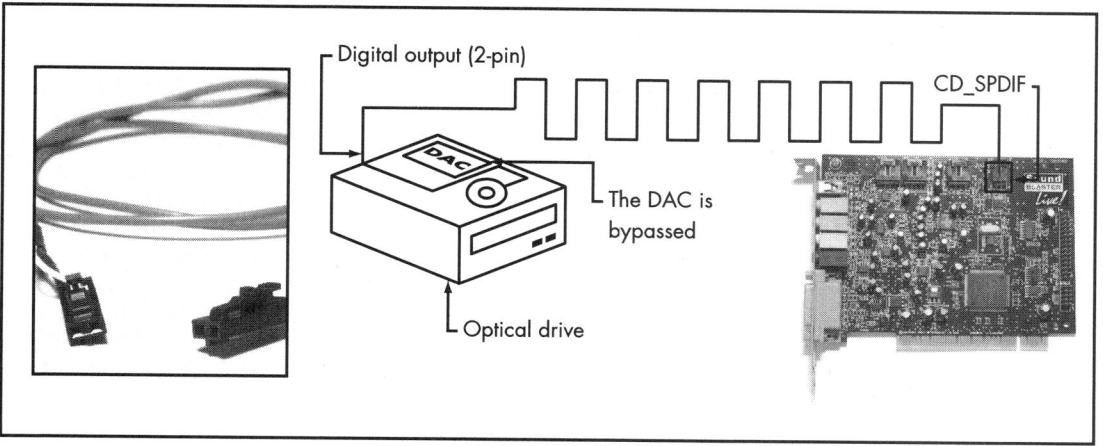

Figure 3.6: The CD_SPDIF digital connection

The CD_SPDIF connector is similar to the other internal connectors lined at the top of the sound card, but has only two pins. The Live! is the sound card that popularized this form of input, allowing the DACs in the optical drive to be bypassed. Digital audio read from the CD in the optical drive travels to the sound card in digital form largely unaffected by electrical noise inside the PC case, resulting in cleaner audio.

TIP *You can regard the CD_SPDIF connection as a digital version of the CD_IN connection, which therefore works only when audio CDs are played in the optical drive.*

Because this connector is not a standard feature in sound cards, most retail versions of the Live! include the 2-pin CD digital cable required for the connection. However, not all optical drives have the 2-pin digital audio output. For such drives, the standard 4-pin analog output should still be provided for connecting to the analog CD_IN connector on the sound card.

> Some optical drives, especially very early CD-ROM drives, may not provide proper audio through the 2-pin digital output. Some don't work, while others produce audible pops and clicking noises, especially when changing tracks. This should not occur with recently manufactured drives.

Data Connection

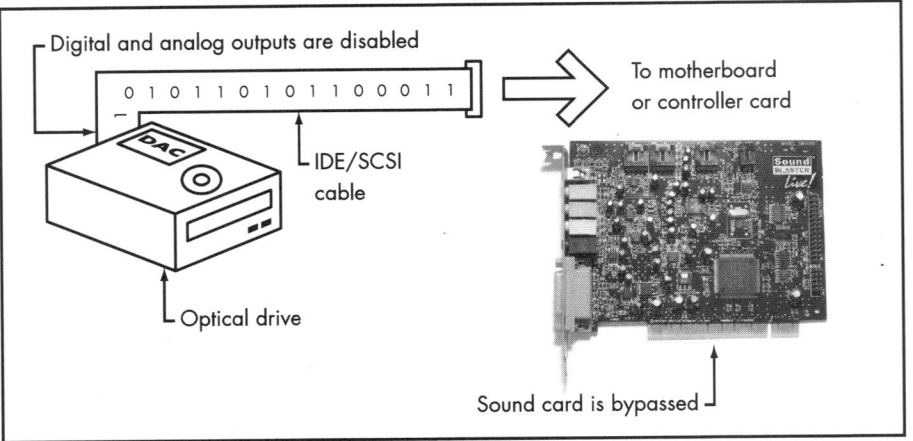

Figure 3.7: Data connection

A data connection uses the digital audio extraction (DAE) capability of optical drives to read CD audio as Wave data. This data is sent digitally to the PC through the IDE cable connected between the motherboard and the optical drive, and the OS will redirect the audio to the Wave output DACs of the sound card for playback. Because this method uses an existing IDE data connection, no cables need to be connected between the optical drive and the sound card's CD_IN or CD_SPDIF connectors.

> IDE may be the most common form of connection found on optical drives, but other standards, like Small Computer System Interface (SCSI) used in a small minority of PCs, do exist. Some PCs also have external optical drives that use a universal serial bus (USB) or FireWire connection. For external drives, they are not mounted inside the PC casing and cannot reach the CD_IN and CD_SPDIF connectors, so the data connection method described here is the only way to play back audio CDs via the sound card.

TIP *DAE is the best method to obtain a direct digital copy of audio CDs. The sound data read by the optical drive is saved to standard Wave files and passed to a MP3 encoder for compression. Many "CD ripping" applications use this method to "rip" audio from CDs.*

Digital CD playback is available in Windows Me, Windows 2000, and Windows XP. However, this approach does not work correctly on a small number of optical drives, especially older CD-ROM drives where the DAE feature is faulty and produces occasional clicks and crackling sounds. Most recently manufactured drives do not have problems with DAE, and many have high-speed DAE that extracts audio from entire 74-minute CDs in 5 to 10 minutes.

To enable this feature, look for the name of the optical drive in Control Panel • System • Device Manager. In Windows Me, Device Manager appears as a tab labeled Device Manager. In Windows 2000 and Windows XP, it is a button in the Hardware tab.

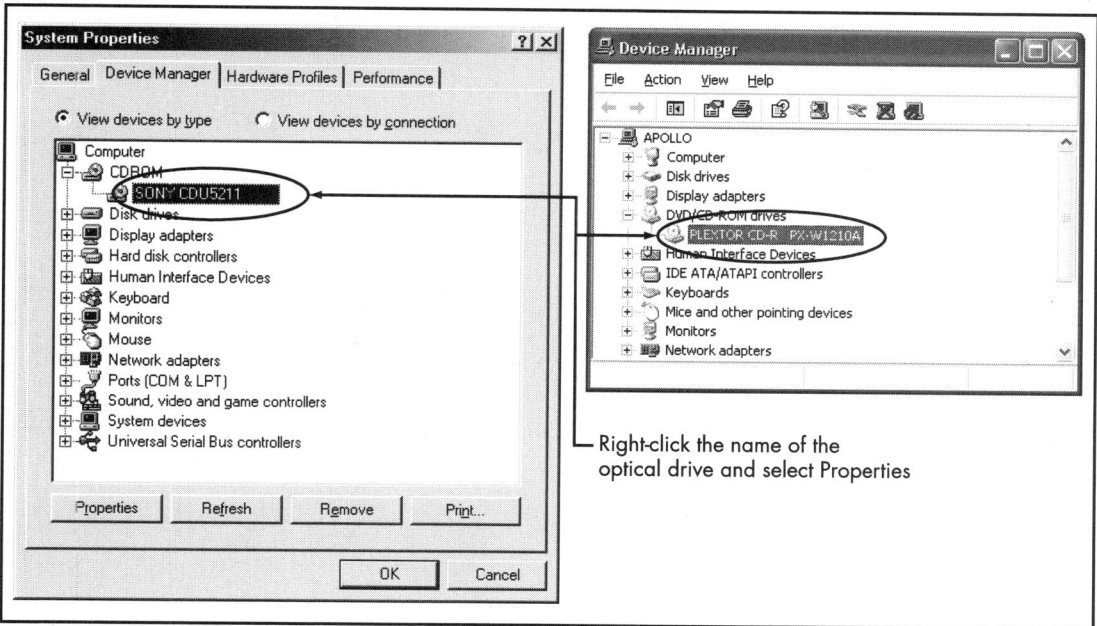

Figure 3.8: Device Manager

Right-click the name of the CD-ROM drive and click Properties to display the settings screen for the optical drive. Click the Properties tab, and you will see the window in Figure 3.9.

The Digital CD Playback setting at the bottom has a checkbox labeled "Enable digital CD audio for this CD-ROM device." Checking it will enable DAE and negate the use of the CD_IN or CD_SPDIF connection.

Alternatively, Windows Media Player version 7 also has an Options window that can control the DAE feature. To do this, load the Options screen, click the CD Audio tab, and enable the "Digital playback" checkbox.

TIP *The Copy Settings section shown in Figure 3.10 changes the method used when Media Player converts audio CDs to compressed audio files in the hard drive. The Digital copying checkbox should ideally be checked, as well.*

Windows Media Player version 8 (introduced with Windows XP) also allows you to enable DAE, but the way it is done is slightly changed. After going to the Options screen, click the Devices tab and choose the drive you wish to turn on DAE. Cick the Properties button, and you'll see a Properties screen of that optical drive. Under the Playback section, selecting the Digital option button will enable DAE when audio CDs are played.

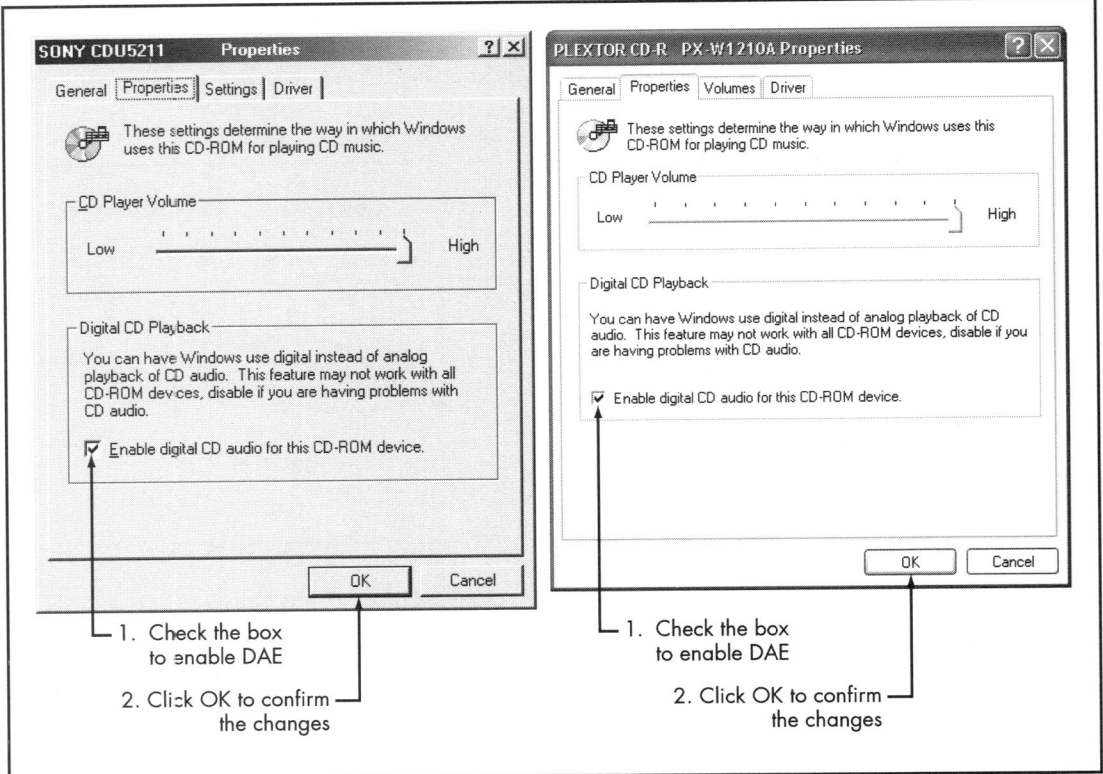

Figure 3.9: Drive Properties

TIP *The Copy section shown in Figure 3.11 changes the method used when Media Player converts audio CDs to compressed audio files in the hard drive. It should ideally be set at Digital, as well.*

Depending on the OS, you may need to reboot your system before the changes take effect. After Digital CD Playback is enabled, the CD Audio slider in the mixer will control the volume of the CD audio played back using DAE. Drives connected to the CD_IN connector cannot be heard or controlled by the sound card's mixer.

> A few jukebox and multimedia playback software applications may play audio CDs using DAE, even though the drive is not configured to use DAE in Windows.

TIP *A quick way to check whether DAE is enabled is to plug a pair of headphones into the mini-jack headphone output on the front panel of the optical drive and play an audio CD. If there is sound from the headphones, the drive is not using DAE.*

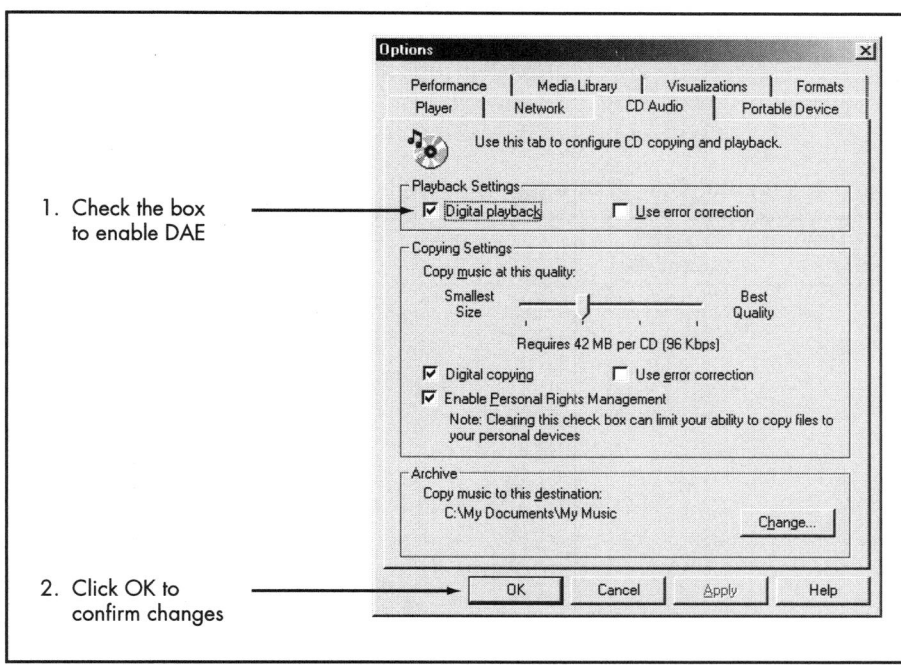

Figure 3.10: Turning on DAE in Windows Media Player 7 in Windows Me

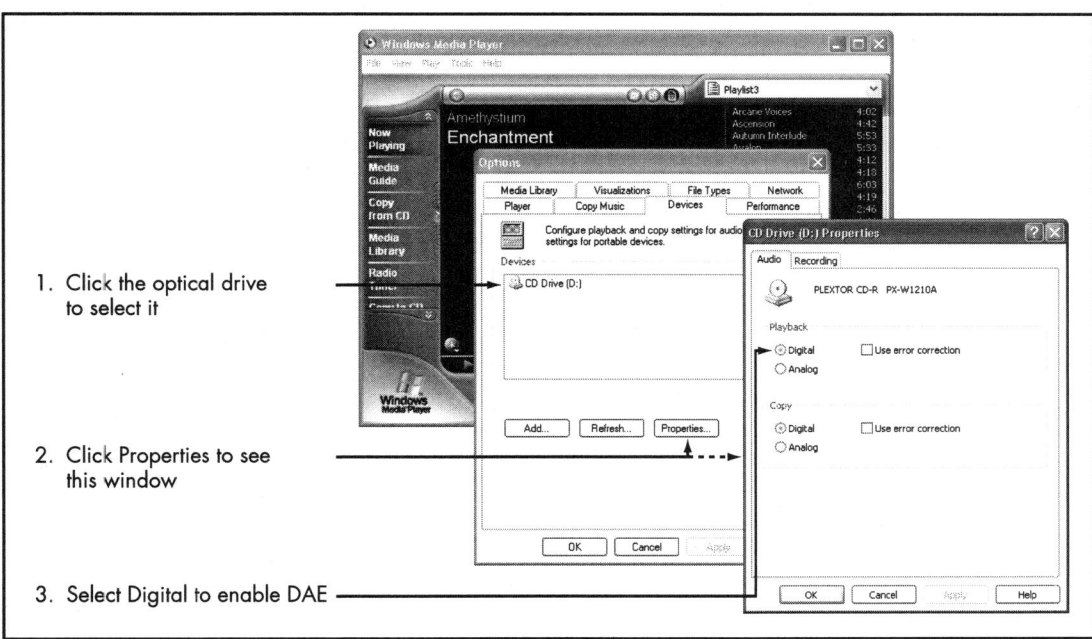

Figure 3.11: Turning on DAE in Windows Media Player 8 in Windows XP

The Sound Blaster Live! Hardware **49**

Choosing the Connection Method

There are benefits when digital connections are used, and the different connection methods consume different levels of CPU power. This table summarizes the pros and cons of the different methods:

Table 3.1: Pros and Cons of Different Connection Methods

Connection Method	Physical Connection	Sound Quality	CPU Hit	Notes
CD_IN Analog Connection	4-pin audio cable from optical drive to CD_IN on the sound card.	Analog transmission. Susceptible to noise in the PC case.	Minor. Audio travels directly from the optical drive to the sound card, requiring little CPU processing.	CD_IN cannot be used when the data connection method is turned on.
CD_SPDIF Digital Connection	2-pin audio cable from optical drive to CD_SPDIF on the sound card.	Audio is transmitted digitally. Less distortion and noise. The DACs on the Live! performing the D/A conversion are usually better than most DACs in optical drives.	Minor. Similar to the CD_IN analog connection method, audio travels directly to the sound card, requiring little CPU processing.	
Data connection (DAE)	Relies on the existing data connection between the optical drive and the PC. No audio cable is required to be connected between the sound card and the drive.	Audio is transmitted as digital data. Similar to CD_SPDIF digital connection, there is little opportunity for distortion.	More CPU processing and bandwidth required. The OS has to constantly read digital audio data from the optical drive and pass it on to the sound card for D/A conversion.	Takes over the CD Audio slider in the mixer, disabling the CD_IN connector.

With the low CPU hit and clarity of digital audio transmissions, the CD_SPDIF digital connection offers the best of both worlds. Therefore, this connection method should always be considered first, unless the optical drive does not have such a connection or has problems with its digital output.

Alternatively, use either CD_IN or DAE to play audio CDs. In a minority of PCs, there may be noise or hiss present in the CD_IN connector, especially when the volume is turned up high, but on most PCs, the hiss is minor and does not become a nuisance. If you prefer not to use analog connections, DAE is also a good choice because it sends audio digitally. However, to many users, the quality difference is not great and any choice is just as acceptable.

TIP *For the adventurous, connect to both CD_IN and CD_SPDIF on the sound card and mute and un-mute the sound sources in the mixer to perform a comparison between the different methods of connection.*

DAE may slow down the PC, especially if it has a slow CPU with speeds under 300 MHz, or has many applications running at the same time. In such circumstances, the CD_SPDIF or CD_IN would be better options because they use little CPU when audio CDs are played.

For typical setups, only one connection method is necessary. No problems will occur if both the CD_IN and CD_SPDIF are connected to the same drive, but be sure to mute either the CD Audio or CD Digital mixer sliders, or the audio will be duplicated and heard twice with the mixer, and with a few CD-ROM drives may sometimes result in a weird slurring effect due to the small time delay between the analog and digital outputs from the optical drive.

TIP *The AUX_IN connector is similar to the CD_IN connector and can be used when you have many optical drives.*

See Chapter 7, "The Mixer," for more information on the mixer sliders for CD audio playback.

Internal Pin Connectors

There are more pins located at various positions on the card (depending on the model). These pins are not Molex connectors enclosed in plastic, but are just bare metal pins protruding from the sound card's PCB.

PC_SPK

The PC_SPK is a two-pin connector located to the right of the AUX_IN connector. It allows audio from the PC speaker output on the motherboard to be routed to the Live!, instead of using the tiny PC speaker in the casing. We do not recommend this setup, however; the PC speaker is seldom used in today's PCs because more often than not, they come with sound cards. However, the PC speaker is still a useful tool for diagnosing any errors that may occur when the PC starts and performs the power-on self-test (POST) procedure. Sound cards (including the Live!) are not initialized until after the POST is successful and the operating system and drivers are loaded; therefore, you will not be able to hear any error code beeps from the PC speaker if you redirect the audio to the sound card. Still, if you wish to make this connection, you will have to purchase a compatible two-pin cable from your local computer hardware store, because Creative does not provide these cables with the sound card.

VOL_CTRL

The VOL_CTRL connector can be found on some models. This allows PC manufacturers to control the volume of the Live! with external hardware: for example, a volume control knob mounted on the front of the casing. Chapter 9, "Drivers and

Other Tweaks," contains instructions on how you can build a simple external volume control using this connector.

MB_PRO

The early Live! models include this connector for internal modems, but this connector is rarely used and was removed in the second- and third-generation Live! cards.

JP3

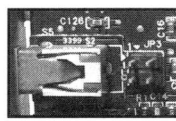

One some Live! cards with the yellow mini-jack digital output, like the CT4760, there is a set of four pins located just to the right of the connector and labeled JP3. These provide the same digital output signals as the mini-jack digital output connector, but in normal circumstances, these pins need not be used. These pins are removed from many Live cards, too.

The Extension Connector

At the right edge of the sound card, you will find two vertical columns of pins that give access to input and output signals available in the EMU10K1. Creative was smart to include such a connector on every Live! card so that its capabilities can be enhanced with add-on digital I/O devices such as digital I/O cards and the Live!Drive. With the extension connector, these devices can tap into the audio and electrical signals used by the EMU10K1 and provide extra connectors for more audio equipment to be connected to the Live! The extra audio input and output jacks can be placed in another backpanel expansion card behind the casing, a drive bay device like the Live!Drive installed in front of the casing, or even a breakout box that can be placed anywhere outside the PC casing.

The presence of these extension connectors, together with the huge sales of Live! cards also provided a lucrative opportunity for other computer peripheral makers to design add-on boards and other custom digital I/O solutions to cater to different needs of Live! users. We will take a look at some of these products in Chapter 4, "Accessories Galore!"

Two different types of extension connectors were produced in the Live!'s history. However, in any one Live! model, only one of them is present. The first type is the AUD_EXT connector, which exists on a majority of the Live! cards. The second is the scaled-down SPDIF_EXT connector, found on budget cards.

In Chapter 4, you will find out more about the popular accessories available. Most of them use the extension connector on the Live! to transfer audio to and from the EMU10K1. Let's take a look at these two connectors and find out how they differ.

AUD_EXT

At the right edge of the card is the AUD_EXT connector consisting of a set of 40 pins arranged in two vertical columns of 20 pins each. A few pins are grouped together to provide a particular input or output connection to and from the EMU10K1. Audio signals are always transmitted digitally, and other signals like the MIDI input and output are also provided, enabling digital I/O devices to include these connections for greater convenience. The following diagram shows the pin assignments.

> Warning! The AUD_EXT connector and cables may look similar to the common motherboard IDE connectors that hook up to hard drives and CD-ROM drives, but do not connect a hard drive to the AUD_EXT, or the hardware may be damaged.

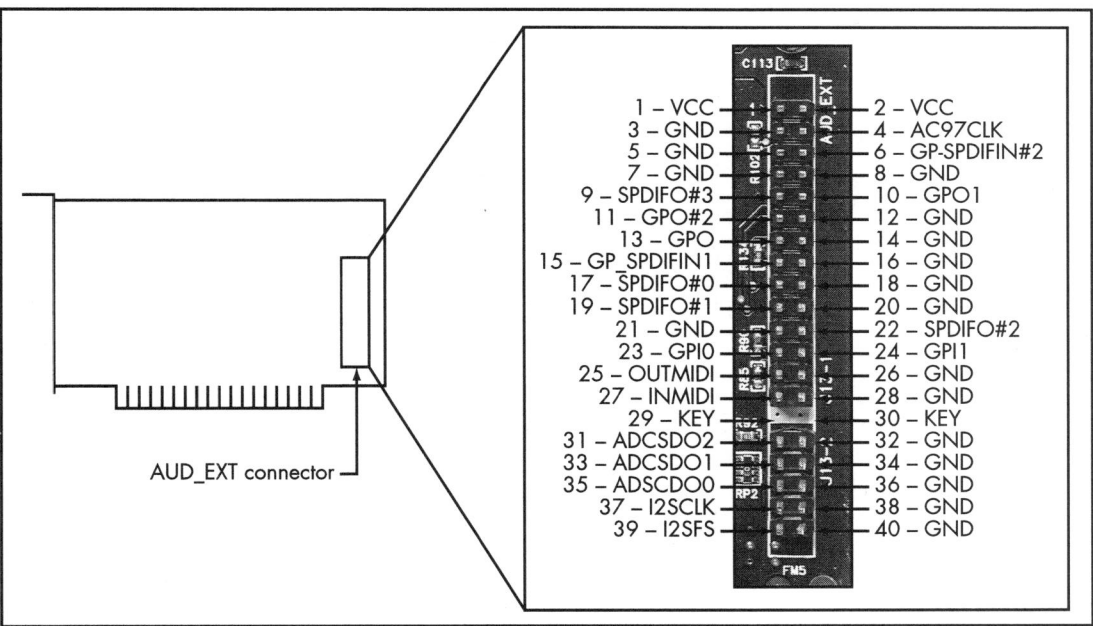

Figure 3.12: The AUD_EXT connector

Table 3.2: Pinouts of the AUD_EXT Connector

Type	Pin Number	Name	Description
Digital Audio Inputs	6	GP_SPDIFIN#2	Two S/PDIF input signals allowing digital I/O devices to provide up to two extra audio inputs.
	15	GP_SPDIFIN1	

The Sound Blaster Live! Hardware   53

Table 3.2: Pinouts of the AUD_EXT Connector (continued)

Type	Pin Number	Name	Description
	31, 33, 35	ADCSDO2, ADCSDO1, ADCSDO0	These pins provide the signals for the I²S digital input.
	37	I2SCLK	I²S serial bit clock. A clock-timing signal to keep digital I/O devices using I²S digital input synchronized for audio transmission.
	39	I2SFS	A frame sync signal for the I²S digital input.
Digital Audio Outputs	9 17 19 22	SPDIFO#3 SPDIFO#0 SPDIFO#1 SPDIFO#2	Four S/PDIF digital outputs providing support for up to eight speaker channels. Two of these pins are used for up to 4-channel output on Live! cards, and three pins are used with the Live! 5.1 cards for 5.1 output. All these pins are provided on the Digital DIN connector available on some digital I/O devices.
MIDI Inputs and Outputs	25	OUTMIDI	Allows MIDI output to be sent to a digital I/O device.
	27	INMIDI	Obtains MIDI data from MIDI devices connected to digital I/O devices with MIDI connections.
Other Pins	1, 2	VCC	Provides five volts of power supply to power digital I/O cards.
	4	AC97CLK	This is a 24.5 MHz clock output to keep external digital I/O devices in sync with the Live! card.
	10, 11, 13	GPO1, GPO2, GPO0	Three general-purpose output and two general-purpose input pins for control signals to be sent and received. These are used for features on digital I/O devices like the remote control in the Live!Drive IR.

23, 24	GPI0, GPI1	
3, 5, 7, 8, 12, 14, 16, 18, 20, 21, 26, 28, 32, 34, 36, 38, 40	GND	Provides electrical grounding.
29, 30	KEY	Two key pins that aren't actually pins on the card, but are missing from the card. They also help to ensure that the flat cable is connected in the correct orientation.

A flat cable with 40 wires is used to pass these signals to and from the Live!

This connector was found on the digital I/O card introduced with the very first version of the retail Sound Blaster Live! product in 1998. Creative kept the AUD_EXT connectors available in nearly all Live! cards, with the exception of some budget versions released earlier in 1998 and 1999. Peripherals that use this connector include the Live!Drive and nearly all third-party digital I/O products.

Find out more about digital I/O devices in Chapter 4, "Accessories Galore!"

SPDIF_EXT

Some of the budget first-generation Live! cards, especially the popular Sound Blaster Live! Value product, came with another extension connector, labeled "SPDIF_EXT." It has only 12 pins, carrying a fraction of the signals available in the AUD_EXT connector.

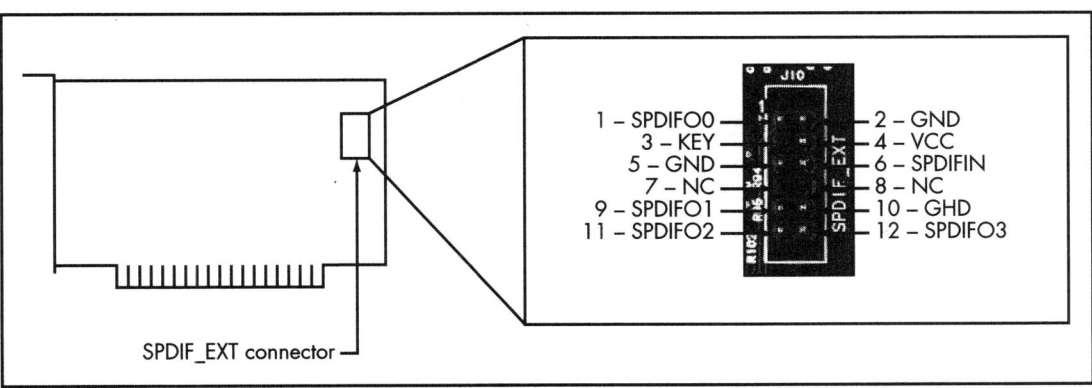

Figure 3.13: The SPDIF_EXT extension connector

Because the first-generation Live! Value product was intended to be a budget product, Creative decided to reduce its digital I/O capabilities probably for product placement reasons, even though the same EMU10K1 chip was used in these cards and could in fact support all of the signals present in the AUD_EXT connector. Digital I/O devices that use the SPDIF_EXT have less functionality, providing one instead of two S/PDIF digital inputs, and the four S/PDIF digital outputs for the digital outputs on digital I/O devices and digital multimedia speakers. Users who wanted to tap the full digital I/O capabilities of the EMU10K1 had to purchase the more expensive full Live! product with the bundled digital I/O card.

During the second generation in the Live!'s evolution, in 1999, Creative developed the Live!Drive to provide extra inputs and outputs placed conveniently at the front of the PC case. The Live!Drive is bundled with the top-of-the-line Sound Blaster Live! Platinum product and the third-generation Platinum 5.1. The Live!Drive uses the full capabilities of the AUD_EXT connector and does not support the SPDIF_EXT connector.

The full AUD_EXT connector was restored in budget versions of the second- and, subsequently, third-generation products to give owners the option to upgrade their Live! cards by purchasing Live!Drives or other digital I/O cards.

Backplate Audio Jacks

After installing the Live! in the motherboard's PCI slot, the jacks on the backplate will be exposed behind the casing. These jacks provide permanent connection to external peripherals such as speakers, microphones, amplifiers, music keyboards, and joysticks.

Line Out 1 (Front)

The line out 1 carries line-level analog audio signals of the front left and front right speaker channels to powered speakers and amplifiers. Any audio that is produced and mixed digitally in the EMU10K1 is converted to analog with DACs and output through these jacks. Headphones can also be used with this line output.

> Many older sound cards have a speaker-level output that amplifies line-level signals so that it is powerful enough to drive multimedia speakers that do not use any form of power source such as the mains, power adaptors, or batteries. The line out signal on the Live! is too low to drive these speakers adequately, so be sure to get powered speakers.

Line Out 2 (Rear)

The line out 2 carries audio for the rear left and rear right speakers and is normally used to produce positional and surround effects with multichannel speaker systems with rear speakers. These outputs produce sound only when the Live! is set to 4 Speakers, Live!Surround, or 5.1 Speakers (for Live! 5.1 cards) mode. Unlike line out 1, this line output is not designed for headphones.

See Chapter 6, "Speakers," for more information on how you can connect the Live! to different speaker systems.

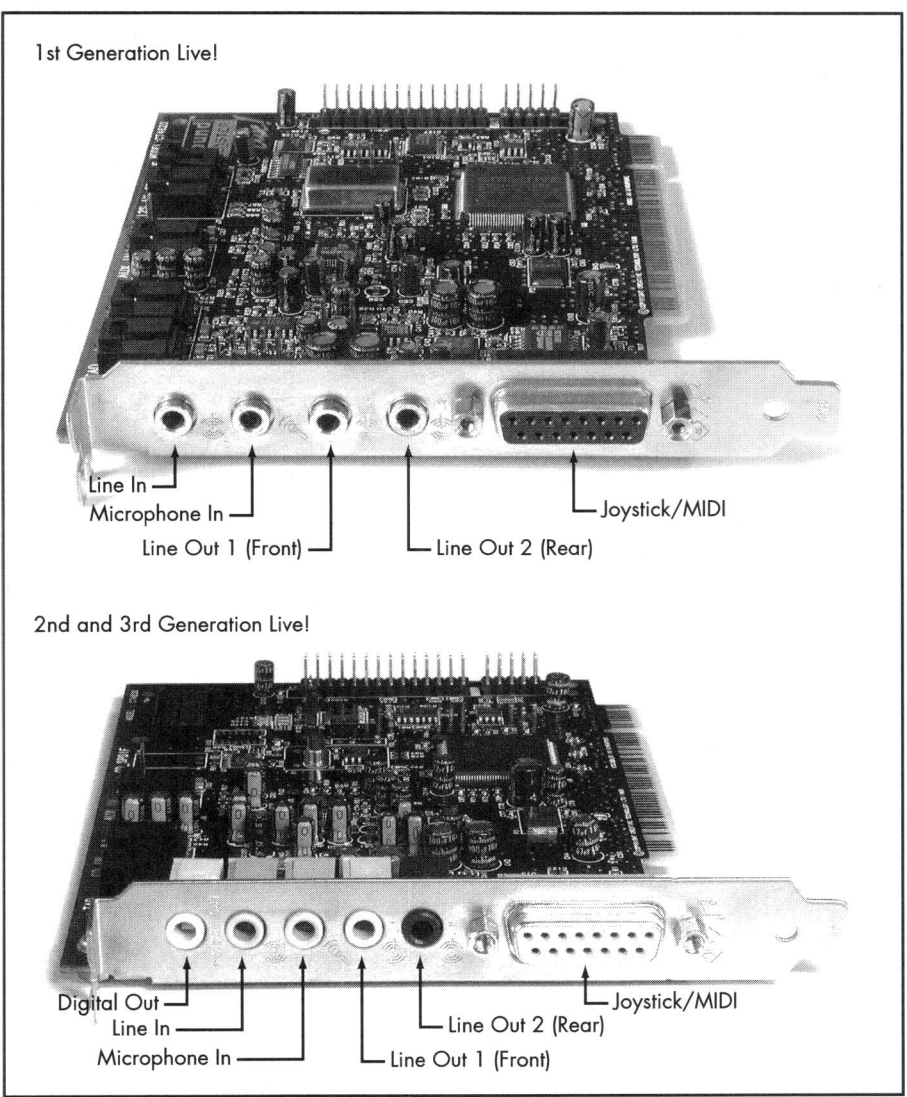

Figure 3.14: Compare the backplate of the first-generation Live! card with the backplate of the second- and third-generation Live! cards. With the addition of the digital output jack, the connectors are closer together.

Line In

The line-in jack accepts audio from devices that output line-level signals, such as CD players, tape decks, and almost any other consumer audio equipment that has an output, usually marked "line out." You can play back and record audio from devices connected to the line input.

Microphone In

The signal from a microphone is weaker than a line-level signal; therefore, an amplifier known as a mic preamp is needed to boost it to audible levels so that it can be heard. The Live! has a built-in preamp, and the volume can be boosted by 20 dB in the mixer. Only microphones can be connected to this input, and not other types of audio equipment. Do not connect line-level signals to this jack because the preamp will boost the audio way above line levels, and the audio equipment and Live! card may be damaged!

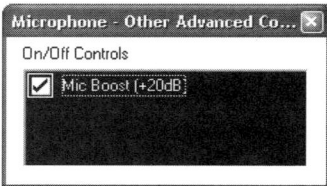

Figure 3.15: Clicking the red plus symbol above the Microphone In slider will open this window and allow the 20 dB mic boost to be turned on or off

The Mini-jack Digital Output

The digital I/O card bundled with the first Live! product came with a proprietary Digital DIN output that worked only with certain digital multimedia speaker models, notably those from Creative and its subsidiary Cambridge SoundWorks, that have the same Digital DIN input. No other sound card used the Digital DIN format, making it a proprietary Creative-only format. However, this did not stop speaker systems such as the Cambridge SoundWorks FPS2000 Digital and Desktop Theater DTT2500 Digital from gaining popularity. Users welcomed the ability to preserve audio quality by transmitting audio digitally from the sound card to the speaker before it is converted to analog audio.

Figure 3.16: The Digital DIN connector

Creative hit upon a dilemma. The Digital DIN output was available only on the digital I/O card that came with the non-Value version of the Live!, which cost

US$299. Bundling any additional hardware with the US$99 budget models would mean that the company had to either increase prices and risk losing buyers in the budget market, or incur a higher production cost for every Live! card manufactured. The backplate of a Live! was nearly full with four mini-jacks and the huge joystick/MIDI port, so it was impossible to add a Digital DIN output to the backplate. Users of first-generation Value cards had to purchase an optical digital I/O card to obtain the Digital DIN output.

Nevertheless, the company wanted to give budget users the option to use digital speakers, and at the same time sell more digital multimedia Cambridge SoundWorks speakers, which usually cost more than their analog counterparts, so a compromise was born. The mini-jack digital output was added to the second-generation products released in 1999 and was enhanced in the third-generation products in 2000 to cater to the new 5.1 support. A Digital DIN–to–mini-jack converter was manufactured to allow these cards to connect to the digital speakers.

> Because of the addition of a fifth mini-jack on the second- and third-generation Live! cards, the backplate is a little cramped. If you have two cables that have large plugs and connect them to adjacent mini-jack connectors on the Live!, they may push against one another. If they push against one another very lightly, you can still use them, but if they push very hard, you may need to change cables or risk damaging the mini-jack connectors on the sound card.

Mini-jack Digital Out on the Second-Generation Live!

Mini-jack digital output was introduced in the second-generation Live! cards primarily to connect to Creative's Inspire and Cambridge SoundWorks line of digital speakers and the digital output module. (You can find out more about the digital output module in Chapter 4, "Accessories Galore!") It carries two stereo S/PDIF signals, one for the front speakers and one for the rear speakers, providing a total of four channels of digital audio.

Mini-jack Digital Out on the Third-Generation Live!

Located at the same position as the second-generation Live! cards, mini-jack digital output on the third-generation Live! carries the same two S/PDIF signals, but it includes support for the card's Dolby digital decoding and 5.1 speaker output, which required another analog output to provide the center and woofer signals. A switch was added to allow the mini-jack to operate in either digital or analog mode.

Find out more about using the mini-jack digital outputs in Chapter 6, "Speakers," and Chapter 11, "Watching Movies."

To output the center and woofer signals in digital form using the same mini-jack digital output, a third S/PDIF signal is added to carry the center and woofer channels. In digital S/PDIF mode, all six channels of a full 5.1 surround system are transmitted from this mini-jack to support compatible 5.1 digital speakers, such as the Cambridge SoundWorks DTT3500 and the Creative Inspire 5700.

The third-generation digital mini-jack output can also be switched to analog mode. This enables it to be used as a third line output, similar to line outputs 1 and 2, which carry the front and rear channels. The third line output carries the center and woofer channels. Taken together with the other two analog line outputs, the Live! provides a total of six channels for analog 5.1 multimedia speaker systems and many 5.1 home theater receivers.

> The digital S/PDIF format carries two audio channels over one wire inside a cable, whereas a single wire can carry only one audio channel if transmitted by analog means.

Obtaining a Digital Output

The voltage of the digital output on various models of the Live! differ, affecting their compatibility with the standard S/PDIF coaxial digital inputs used by the consumer electronics industry. Only the more recent models like the CT4830 second-generation Live! card made for the OEM market, and all third-generation Live! cards (including the SB0060 sold in retail) are compatible.

In addition to being able to Connect to Digital DIN speakers, the mini-jack digital outputs on these Live! cards can be used as coaxial outputs to send digital audio to amplifiers and recorders with digital inputs (for playback and recording purposes) without the need for an additional digital I/O device.

However, coaxial outputs on most equipment use RCA connectors, while the digital output on the Live! is a mini-jack, so a mini-jack–to–RCA cable is used to convert between the two different types of plugs. The cable has a stereo mini-jack that is connected to the digital output of the Live!, and at the other end are two RCA plugs. The front left and front right channels will be sent to the white (or sometimes black) RCA plug, while the rear channels will be output from the red RCA plug. A less commonly available mini-jack–to–RCA cable with only one RCA plug can also be used to obtain just the front channels of the Live!

TIP *Use cables of a reasonable quality for this connection, because the S/PDIF standard requires the thicker and more shielded 75-ohm coaxial cables instead of standard analog audio cables. Audio dropouts may occur if poor-quality mini-jack-to-RCA cables are used.*

> This connection method can also be used to output Dolby Digital or DTS surround sound signals from DVDs played back on a DVD-ROM drive and a software DVD player in S/PDIF mode. The digital signals of the front channel will be used to output the surround soundtracks, and this signal can be connected to a consumer home theater receiver's coaxial inputs for surround sound decoding. For more information on this feature, see Chapter 11, "Watching Movies."

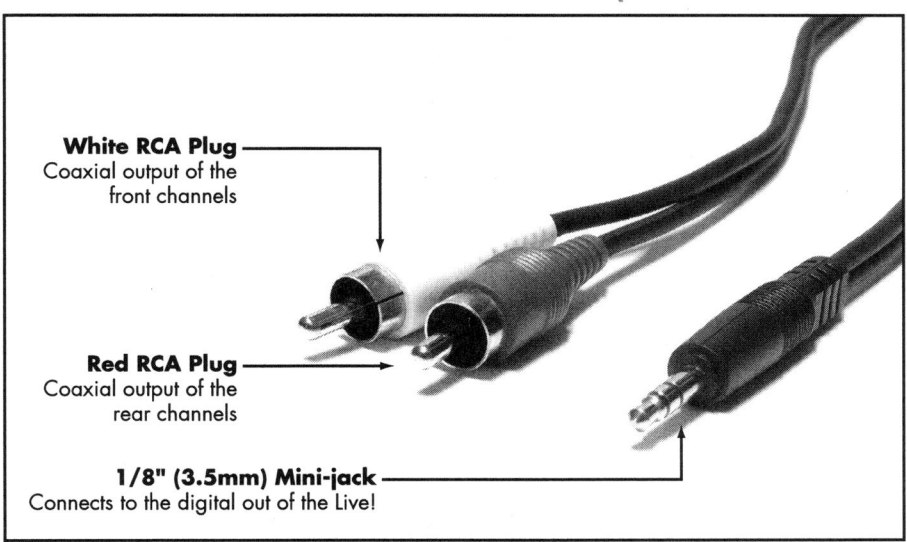

Figure 3.17: Digital signals carried by a stereo mini-jack to RCA cable connected to the mini-jack digital output of the Live!

Voltage Differences

The voltage of the S/PDIF signal from the mini-jack digital output of many retail (non-OEM) second-generation Live! cards, especially the widely sold CT4760, use transistor-transistor logic (TTL) voltage levels which go up to 5 volts. Consumer coaxial inputs and outputs work at only 0.5 to 1 volt, which makes TTL levels a huge increase! Therefore, if your Live! card uses TTL levels, it is not advisable to use the above method to connect to digital audio equipment with coaxial inputs and outputs, as it may cause them to be damaged. Only Cambridge SoundWorks digital speakers and digital I/O products from Creative are guaranteed to work correctly, but many have reported that some other digital audio equipment may also work fine. If you are not sure, always check with Creative technical support to find out the specifications of the digital output of the particular Live! card you have before making any connections.

Summary of Backplate Audio Connectors

The following table summarizes the backplate connectors and audio formats that the Live! supports.

Table 3.3: Mini-jack Connectors on the Live!'s Backplate

Connector	Color	Audio Format	Number of Channels	Audio Channels
Line Out 1 (Front)	Green	Analog	2	Stereo: front left and front right
Line Out 2 (Rear)	Black	Analog	2	Stereo: rear left and rear right
Line In	Blue	Analog	2	Stereo: left and right
Microphone In	Pink	Analog	1	Mono
Mini-jack Digital Output (Second-Generation Live!)	Yellow	Digital	4	S/PDIF Channel 1: front left and front right S/PDIF Channel 2: rear left and rear right
Mini-jack Digital Output (Third-Generation Live!)	Orange/Yellow	Digital mode	6	S/PDIF Channel 1: front left and front right S/PDIF Channel 2: rear left and rear right S/PDIF Channel 3: center and woofer
		Analog mode	2	Stereo: center and woofer

Backplate Joystick/MIDI Connector

The DB-25 joystick connector was a mainstay in the very early PCs, providing a standardized way to connect joysticks and console-like gamepads to the PC. Today, the USB peripherals are more popular, but the antiquated joystick port can still be found on many sound cards and built in to some motherboards.

Not all the wires in the joystick port are used; hence, in the very first Sound Blaster, Creative incorporated the MIDI input and output signals into some of the unused wires to provide easy access to the MIDI functionality with an optional adapter cable, which was good news for a small group of users who composed music with the sound card and needes MIDI ports.

Other sound card manufacturers have adopted this standard, and joystick-to-MIDI cables can be found in many computer accessory stores. One end of the cable connects to the joystick port on the sound card, and the other end provides two MIDI plugs (for input and output), as well as a joystick connector, so that MIDI hardware and a joystick can be used simultaneously.

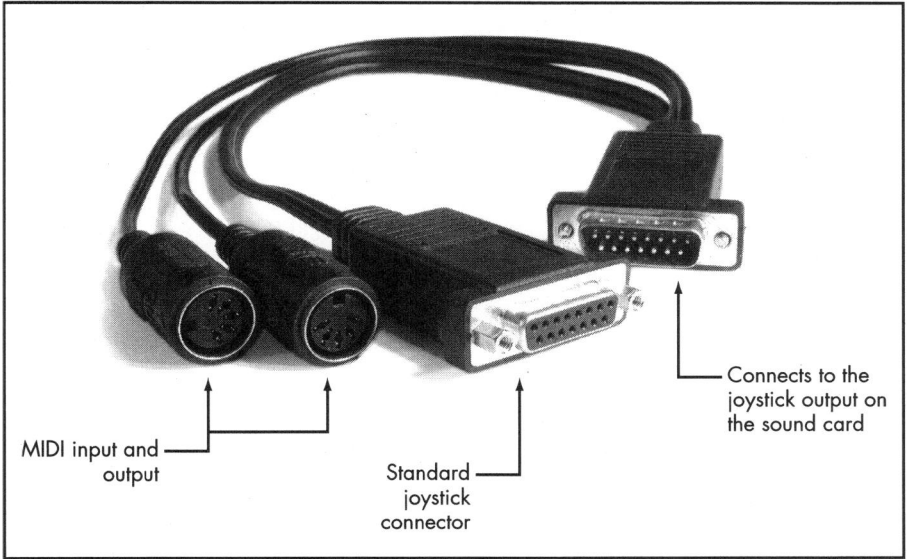

Figure 3.18: A joystick-to-MIDI cable

Summary of Connectors

As Creative upgraded and added new hardware features to the Live! during its three-year evolution, many variations were produced. There are versions that cater to specific markets, such as OEM versions for PC manufacturers like Dell, a special Live! card with special connectors needed for the customized case used by Creative's personal computer line, the BlasterPC, and models that target popular applications in markets like Japan, where MiniDisc recording and digital video editing require optical digital outputs and FireWire connections.

> Creative has used the "CT" prefix for Sound Blaster cards since the very first one released in 1989. The first- and second-generation Live! cards also have model numbers beginning with "CT," but with the third-generation Live! cards, Creative moved away from that and new Sound Blaster cards after 2000 now have model numbers beginning with "SB."

The following table summarizes the differences among the most popular models that are sold in majority of retail products worldwide.

Table 3.4: Connectors on Retail Live! Cards

Product Name	First Generation		Second Generation	Third Generation
	Sound Blaster Live!	Sound Blaster Live! Value	Sound Blaster Live! (Platinum, MP3+, X-Gamer, Player)	Sound Blaster Live! 5.1 (Platinum, MP3+, X-Gamer, Player, Digital Entertainment)
Model Number	CT4620	CT4670	CT4760	SB0060
TAD	✓	✓	✓	✓
CD_IN	✓	✓	✓	✓
AUX_IN	✓	✓	✓	✓
I2S_IN	✓			
CD_SPDIF	✓	✓	✓	✓
PC_SPK	✓	✓	✓	✓
Extension Connector	AUD_EXT	SPDIF_EXT	AUD_EXT	AUD_EXT
Mini-jack Digital Out			4 channels	6 channels (switchable to analog Line Output 3)
Line Out 1: Front	✓	✓	✓	✓
Line Out 2: Rear	✓	✓	✓	✓
Line In	✓	✓	✓	✓
Microphone In	✓	✓	✓	✓
Joystick/MIDI Connector	✓	✓	✓	✓

> **Where is the model number?**
> You can usually find the model number printed in white at the top-right corner of the card, just above the Sound Blaster Live! logo. In some countries, a white FCC label on the back also indicates the model number, bar code, and serial number of the card.

> The Live! Player is sometimes known as the Live! Player 1024, and the Live! Value is known as the Live! 1024 in some areas.

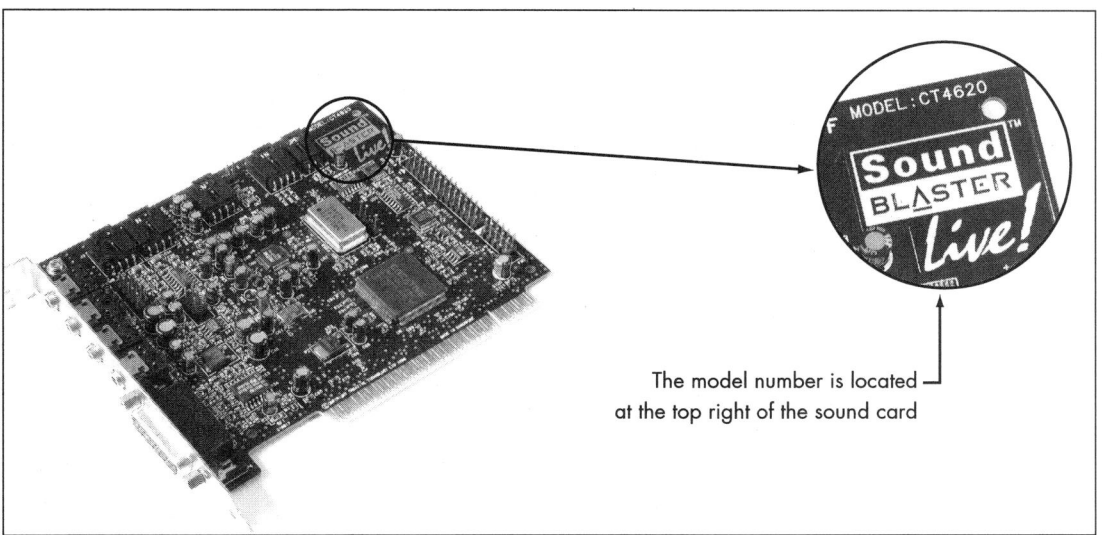

Figure 3.19: The model of the Live! card is usually located above the logo

OEM Models

The Live! is also available in original equipment manufacturer (OEM) versions that are manufactured by Creative, but instead of being put into boxes with freebies such as microphones, audio cables, games, and audio software, OEM cards are sold in bulk, mainly to PC manufacturers who bundle sound cards with their machines. However, many retailers also sell these cards separately without the bundled software and accessories, and sometimes even without the driver CD. (Beware! Creative does not provide the complete application suite for download over the Internet. The driver CD-ROMs have to be purchased directly from Creative.)

The OEM version of the first-generation cards was the same CT4670 model included in the retail Sound Blaster Live! Value product. This model was sold in the OEM market without the software bundle and accessories.

The second-generation Live! cards with the new mini-jack digital output also had OEM models that were made of less costly parts. Some features, such as the two-pin Molex connector for the CD digital (CD_SPDIF) input, were removed on many units. The mini-jacks on the backplate were also color coded, instead of having the brass-colored analog mini-jacks used on all retail products based on the CT4760 card. These models still had the mini-jack digital output and the full AUD_EXT extension connector.

The most common second-generation OEM model is the CT4830. Other variations, such as the CT4831 and CT4832, also exist. Because they lacked a name, many dealers and users started calling these cards Sound Blaster Live! 1024 and Sound Blaster Live! Value and referring to these cards as new versions of the first-generation CT4670 Value card. Dell used the CT4780 in its PCs, which was a slightly modified CT4760.

Creative manufactures many Live! versions, but all of them are, in general, functionally equivalent. The same EMU10K1 DSP is used on all cards; therefore, all the audio processing features, such as the mixer, MIDI playback, and EAX, are present. The same drivers and utilities are used, and EAX games all sound alike. The general audio quality is also similar, but it is difficult to pinpoint exactly which cards are superior, because Creative tends to change DAC brands on different production runs, resulting in slight audio quality differences that are generally unnoticeable to most users.

The most discernable differences among the different models are the upgraded or removed connections in each model and new generation. Features are enabled (or disabled) by the presence (or absence) of these connections, thus determining their value and placement either as premium or budget products. Before you purchase a digital I/O device, hook up an optical drive or connect to speaker systems, and check that the required connectors are present on your card.

**PART TWO
HOOKING UP**

4

ACCESSORIES GALORE!

Most consumer sound cards provide all audio inputs and outputs on the backplates, and that's what users lived with for many years. However, with the increasing sophistication of technology and use of PCs for entertainment, music, and gaming, many users discovered that they can use their computers for even more when armed with a sound card, like more advanced applications such as music composition, audio recording, and digital audio interfacing and recording—tasks that used to belong only in professional studios costing thousands of dollars.

Creative smartly included the extension connectors on the Live!, making it possible for other peripherals to tap into and enhance the potential of the Live! This chapter covers some of the accessories available for the Live!, and the various types of connections that they provide.

Find out more about the extension connector in Chapter 3, "The Sound Blaster Live! Hardware."

The cramped backplates of most sound cards make it impossible to squeeze in more connectors without removing the essential ones such as the line outputs and the microphone input users expect to find on every sound card. An early and still popular solution is to include a digital I/O card that connects to the sound card with an internal cable. This card is placed in an expansion slot behind the casing with the connectors exposed, just like a sound card; however, it does not make use of the connector on the motherboard.

The back of an expansion card is narrow, though and can only contain smaller-sized connectors, limiting them to scaled-down versions of popular consumer and professional connection standards used today. Many users also prefer to have the connectors easily accessible in front of their casings, and Creative's answer is the internal 5 1/4-inch drive bay device called the Live!Drive.

> Due to the way the EMU10K1 was designed, the Live! can output digital audio at only 48 kHz, and not at any other sampling rates. This affects all the digital outputs of digital I/O devices connected to the Live! The section titled "The 48-kHz Sample Rate Conundrum" in Chapter 18, "The EMU10K1 Digital Audio Processor," will explain Creative's design choice in greater detail.

Digital I/O Cards

Digital I/O cards have been very popular with Live! users, especially those who need digital inputs and outputs from the Live! for various digital audio applications, such as to record MP3 tracks to MiniDisc recorders or play and record audio from audio equipment with digital inputs and outputs.

The Digital I/O Card

The very first Live! product came with a digital I/O card that provides various digital inputs, outputs, and MIDI connectors to extend the I/O capability of the Live! card. Creative did not retail this card as a separate upgrade for other Live! cards, and this card was also not bundled with later Live! products released after 1998.

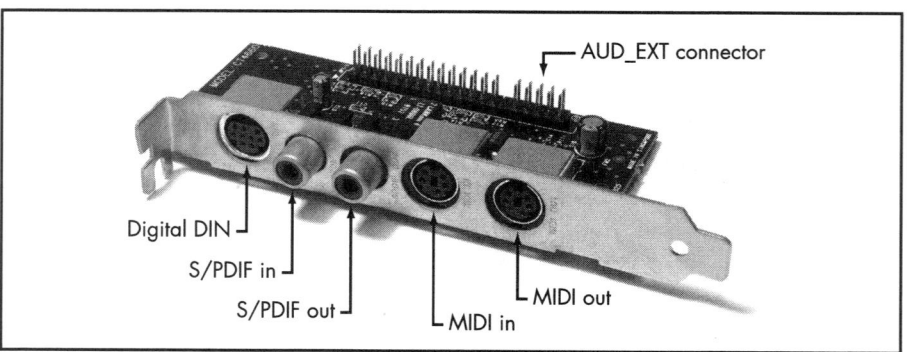

Figure 4.1: The CT4660 Digital I/O card bundled with the CT4670 Live! card

This card interfaces with the AUD_EXT connector on the CT4620 Live! card that came with it, and it also works with newer Live! cards that have the AUD_EXT connector. It can also be cascaded to a Live!Drive. (You will find out more about cascading digital I/O cards to the Live!Drive later in this chapter.)

The following table summarizes the connectors available on the CT4660 digital I/O card.

Table 4.1: Connectors on the CT4660 Digital I/O Card

Connector	Type	Audio Format	Number of Channels	Channels
Digital DIN	Mini-DIN (9-pole)	Digital	4 (with non-5.1 cards) 6 (with 5.1 cards only)	S/PDIF 1: front left and front right S/PDIF 2: rear left and rear right S/PDIF 3: center and woofer (with 5.1 cards only)
S/PDIF In	Coaxial/RCA	Digital	2	S/PDIF: left and right
S/PDIF Out	Coaxial/RCA	Digital	2	S/PDIF: front left and front right
MIDI In	Mini-DIN (5-pole)	N/A	N/A	N/A
MIDI Out	Mini-DIN (5-pole)	N/A	N/A	N/A

> **Poles**
> Although both the Digital DIN and the MIDI connectors use Mini-DIN plugs, they differ in the number of poles (or pins). If you have both of these connectors or plugs, take a look at the different number and arrangement of the pins.

The functionality of the I/O card depends on what it is connected to: the AUD_EXT connector on the Live! card itself or cascaded to the DIGITAL I/O CARD connector on the Live!Drive. The S/PDIF In on the I/O card will be disabled when it is connected to the Live!Drive, because the same S/PDIF In is already available and assigned to the Live!Drive. The following table summarizes the differences in function when the I/O card is connected to the Live! card or the Live!Drive.

Figure 4.2: The Digital I/O card connected to the CT4620 Live! card

Table 4.2: Functionality of the CT4660 Digital I/O Card

Connector	Connected to the **AUD_EXT** connector on the Live! card	Connected to the **DIGITAL I/O CARD** connector on the Live!Drive	Uses
Digital DIN	✓	✓	Connects to speakers with a Digital DIN input.
S/PDIF In	✓		Allows playback and recording of audio from digital audio equipment with S/PDIF coaxial outputs.
S/PDIF Out	✓	✓	Outputs the front channels of the sound card to audio equipment with S/PDIF coaxial inputs, such as digital audio recorders, digital speakers, and A/V receivers.
MIDI In	✓	✓	Accepts MIDI data from MIDI instruments, such as a music keyboard.
MIDI Out	✓	✓	Connects to a MIDI device, such as a synthesizer or sound module for MIDI playback.

Optical Digital I/O Card

By allowing users to record digital audio at a quality that is seldom discernible from that of CDs and with minimal degradation even when played back and rerecorded many times, the portable MiniDisc (MD) format gained popularity, like other digital audio formats, such as digital audio tape (DAT). Ever since MDs were introduced, most consumers have used digital cables to record their favorite tracks from music CDs to MDs. With the popularity of MP3s, many also wanted to record MP3s from sound cards to MD, but sometimes ended up with poorer quality because most consumer sound cards often had only analog line outputs that can be affected by noise in the PC and may also pick up some amount of hiss.

A digital output from the sound card solved this problem. However, due to the electrical nature of sound cards and electronic equipment in general, many manufacturers provide only the S/PDIF coaxial output, because it uses electrical signals to transmit digital audio, and was convenient to implement compared to the optical output found on most consumer MD equipment. Creative also took this route with the earlier Sound Blaster AWE64 Gold and the Digital I/O Card bundled with the first Live! product. Fortunately, Creative also makes the Optical Digital I/O Card for users who need optical inputs and outputs.

Versions Available

An early optical digital I/O card was developed and quickly discontinued by Creative due to lack of demand. Subsequently, a new version known as the "Optical Digital I/O Card II" was released. This is the card covered here. Many refer to it as the "optical I/O card" as it is the only I/O card with optical digital input and output connectors currently available from Creative.

Hardware

In addition to the Optical Digital I/O Card itself, a Digital Input/Output (DIO) module is also included. It has a digital mini-jack plug that goes into the white Digital In/Out jack on the I/O card and is placed outside the PC case.

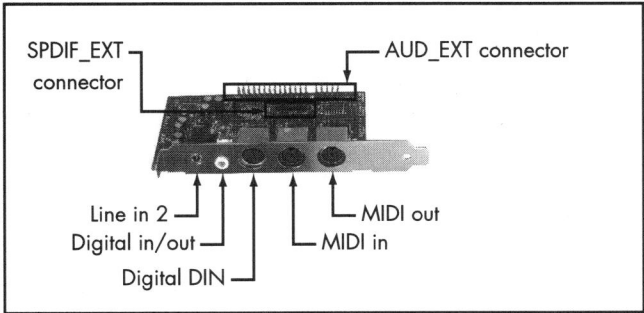

Figure 4.3: The CT4770 Optical Digital I/O card

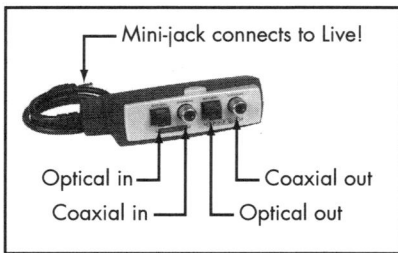

Figure 4.4: The CT4800 DIO module

Connectors

The I/O card's backplate has connectors that offer a second analog line input, a Digital DIN speaker output, and MIDI connectors. It is the DIO module connected to the card's digital in/out mini-jack on the backplate that provides the coaxial and optical inputs and outputs. Here is a list of the connectors on both the I/O card and the DIO module.

Table 4.3: Connectors on the CT4770 Optical Digital I/O Card

Hardware Item	Connector	Type	Audio Format	Number of Channels	Channels
CT4770 Optical I/O Card	Line In 2	Stereo mini-jack	Analog	2	Stereo: left and right
	Digital In/Out*	Mini-jack	Digital	N/A	S/PDIF In (for Coaxial In and Optical In on the DIO module) S/PDIF Out (for Coaxial Out and Optical Out on the DIO module)
	Digital DIN	Mini-DIN (9-pole)	Digital	4 (with non-5.1 cards) 6 (with 5.1 cards only)	S/PDIF Channel 1: front left and front right S/PDIF Channel 2: rear left and rear right S/PDIF Channel 3: center and woofer (with 5.1 cards only)
	MIDI In	Mini-DIN (5-pole)	N/A	N/A	N/A
	MIDI Out	Mini-DIN (5-pole)	N/A	N/A	N/A

*The Digital In/Out connector is a proprietary design and is used only to interface with the included DIO module. It does not connect to other digital audio equipment or speaker systems.

Table 4.3: Connectors on the CT4770 Optical Digital I/O Card

Hardware Item	Connector	Type	Audio Format	Number of Channels	Channels
CT4800 DIO (Digital Input/Output) Module	Optical In	Optical/TOSLink	Digital	2	S/PDIF: left and right
	Coaxial In	Coaxial/RCA	Digital	2	S/PDIF: left and right
	Optical Out	Optical/TOSLink	Digital	2	S/PDIF: front left and front right
	Coaxial Out	Coaxial/RCA	Digital	2	S/PDIF: front left and front right

Compatibility

Early versions of the first-generation CT4620 Live! card will disable the Line In 2 connector because some signals from the EMU10K1 were not fully tapped. You can contact Creative technical support, who will be able to help you determine if your card will work correctly. Apart from the CT4620, the Optical Digital I/O Card works with all other Live! cards.

> CT4620 owners: Because the CT4620 has an I2S_IN connector that is also shared by Line In 2 input on the Optical Digital I/O Card, a red + button will appear above the I²S icon in the mixer. Clicking this button will allow you to switch between the internal I²S connector on the sound card and the analog Line In 2 on the I/O card.

The I/O card supports the AUD_EXT connector found on most Live! cards. It is the only digital I/O device from Creative to also support the SPDIF_EXT connector on the CT4670 Live! Value. The I/O card comes with flat cables for both types of connectors. The I/O card can also be connected to a Live!Drive for extra digital outputs, but the audio and MIDI inputs will be disabled.

Due to the different extension connectors and the option to hook the I/O card directly to the Live! or cascade it to the Live!Drive, the functionality of the card depends on the means of connection. The following table summarizes the connectors that are enabled or disabled with the different forms of connection.

Table 4.4: Functionality of the Optical Digital I/O Card

Hardware Item	Connector	Connected to the AUD_EXT connector on the Live! card	Connected to the SPDIF_EXT connector on the CT4670 Live! Value card	Connected to the DIGITAL I/O CARD connector on the Live!Drive	Uses
I/O Card	Line In 2	✓ (may not work on early versions of the CT4620 Live! card)			With an appropriate cable, you can connect to any equipment with line-level analog outputs, such as CD players, MiniDisc players, and VCRs.
	Digital DIN	✓	✓	✓	Connects to speakers with Digital DIN input.
	MIDI In	✓		✓	Accepts MIDI data from MIDI instruments such as music keyboards.
	MIDI Out	✓		✓	Connects to a MIDI device, such as a synthesizer or sound module, for MIDI playback.
DIO (Digital Input/Output) Module	Optical In*	✓	✓		Allows playback and recording of audio from digital audio equipment with optical outputs.
	Coaxial In*	✓	✓		Allows playback and recording of audio from digital audio equipment with coaxial outputs.
	Optical Out	✓	✓	✓	Outputs the front channels to audio equipment with an optical input, such as digital audio recorders, digital speakers, and A/V receivers.
	Coaxial Out	✓	✓	✓	Outputs the front channels to audio equipment with a coaxial input.

* Optical In and Coaxial In cannot be used simultaneously because they are connected to the same S/PDIF input signal on the extension connector.

Using the MIDI Inputs and Outputs

Standard MIDI devices use a DIN connector, but because of the size limitations of expansion cards, DIN connectors cannot fit on the backplate of an I/O card, so pin-equivalent Mini-DIN connectors with a smaller diameter are used instead. Unfortunately, the required Mini-DIN–to–DIN adapter cables are not bundled with the Optical Digital I/O Card and have to be purchased separately from Creative.

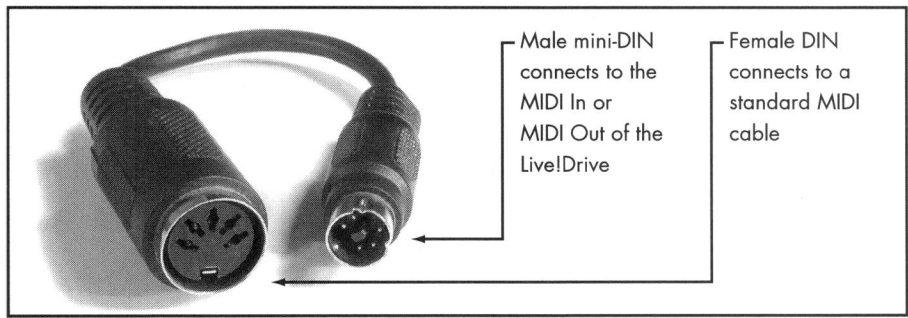

Figure 4.5: A Mini-DIN–to–DIN adapter cable

TIP *Be sure to have the position of the plug correct before inserting it into the Mini-DIN connector. The pins are fragile and may break off very easily.*

> The Live!Drive IR has similar Mini-DIN MIDI input and output connectors, and Creative does include the adapter cables. If you own a Live! Platinum 5.1, the adapter cables provided for the Live!Drive IR can also be used to obtain MIDI connectivity from the Optical Digital I/O Card.

Alternatively, you can use the joystick/MIDI connector on the backplate of the Live! to tap the same MIDI input and output signals. Joystick-to-MIDI adapter cables are also more common because sound cards have used this method to provide MIDI inputs and outputs for the past decade.

Digital Output Module

A digital output module was sold in Europe for a short while but was later discontinued. The Digital Output Module looks similar to the DIO module included with the Optical Digital I/O Card, but the connectors on them are different. The Digital Output Module offers only two coaxial/RCA outputs and two optical/TOSLink outputs and does not have any inputs.

A mini-jack plug from the module hooks up to the mini-jack digital output on the second-generation CT4760 Live! The second-generation CT483x OEM cards do not work because the mini-jack digital output cannot provide enough power for the module. (See the "Voltage Differences" on page 61 of Chapter 3, "The Sound Blaster Live! Hardware" for more information.) If you already use the mini-jack digital output on the Live! as a permanent connection to a Digital DIN speaker system, this may not be the most convenient solution.

Because of a redesign of the mini-jack digital output on the third-generation 5.1 Live! cards, the module will not work as well.

If you have this module, remember to turn on the Digital Output Only option in the mixer so that the mini-jack digital output on the Live! card is

Accessories Galore! **77**

enabled and the S/PDIF signals are sent to the module. (See Chapter 7, "The Mixer," for more information.)

> The Optical Digital I/O Card and the Live!Drive support a feature known as S/PDIF bypass to allow the digital inputs to be channeled directly to the digital outputs of the sound card. It will be explained later in this chapter.

The Live!Drive

The Live!Drive is possibly the most popular accessory for the Live! cards, providing users with convenient access to headphones and analog and digital inputs and outputs, right from the front of the PC case. Gone are the days of having to get all dusty and dirty crawling behind the PC casing just to search for the correct jack to plug in a pair of headphones!

Origin of the Live!Drive

When the first-generation Live! was introduced, E-MU decided to make its own sound card with the EMU10K1. Because E-MU has its roots in music synthesis, making digital musical instruments and tools for musicians, the card was christened the Audio Production Studio (APS) and marketed as a digital audio and music production tool. It had better hardware and audio quality, and the minijacks were upgraded to the larger 1/4-inch stereo jacks that are common on digital musical instruments. It also came with a different set of drivers and utilities geared toward digital audio production and MIDI composition.

The APS had an add-on device known as the E-Drive that provided extra analog and digital S/PDIF inputs and outputs supported by the APS card. It is sized like other 5 1/4" devices, like CD-ROM drives, and can easily fit inside an available drive bay in the PC case, with all the connectors exposed in the front panel. This is extremely convenient because many users have their PCs in a fixed position or tucked away in a corner, making it difficult to move the casing or reach to the back of the PC to attach and remove cables.

In the second-generation Live!, Creative adapted the E-Drive for the Sound Blaster Live! product line by replacing the professional connectors with convenient, consumer-oriented features such as headphone outputs, microphone inputs, and extra analog and digital audio inputs and outputs for connecting to consumer digital audio equipment. The result was aptly named the Live!Drive.

Two models of the Live!Drive were introduced together with the second-generation Live! products. The first is known simply as the Live!Drive (and is sometimes referred to as the Live!Drive I). The Live!Drive II is like a Live!Drive, but includes an extra analog input, as well as optical inputs and outputs.

The third-generation Live!Drive IR replaced both previous Live!Drives. It has the same features as the Live!Drive II, but adds an IR receiver above the MIDI connectors to receive remote control signals from the included infrared remote control unit.

The following pages describe the types of connectors and jacks available with each version of the Live!Drive and the devices that can be hooked up to the various inputs and outputs.

Analog Connectors

The Live!Drive connects to the Live! using a flat cable that transmits audio and control signals in digital form. This provides less opportunity for electromagnetic interference and noise to seep into the audio signals that are carried over the cable. Because audio is exchanged digitally through the flat cable, every Live!Drive has its own set of DACs and ADCs so that analog connectors, like the second line input and headphone outputs, can be provided as well.

When connecting to analog audio equipment, the Live!Drive usually provides relatively cleaner analog inputs and outputs, and should therefore be the first choice over the Mic In and Line In on the backplate of the sound card. However, on some rare occasions, the particular position and mix of electrical and hardware components inside the PC casing may cause more noise in the Live!Drive's analog connectors than the sound card. To do a test, simply turn up the volume and compare the inputs on the sound card and the Live!Drive. Listen for any noticeable hiss, distortion, or computer "bleeps" in the connected speakers. This should help you decide which to use for playback, and especially, recording from analog sources, because it is always key to use the input that provides the cleanest audio.

Here is an overview of the connectors on the Live!Drives and what they can be used for:

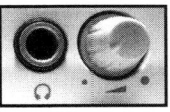

Headphone Out

You can connect stereo headphones to the 1/4-inch Headphone Out jack. Creative sometimes include a mini-jack–to–1/4-inch-stereo-jack adapter so that portable headphones and ear buds with smaller 1/8-inch stereo mini-jack plugs can be used. These adapters are also widely available in consumer electronics stores.

A convenient volume control knob is provided to the right of the headphone jack. If the volume of the headphone output is too soft, even when the volume knob is turned to the maximum, increase the volume of the audio source and the master volume control in the mixer.

Automatic Speaker Muting

Automatic speaker muting is a very convenient feature available only on the Live!Drive. When a 1/4-inch plug is inserted into the headphone jack, the speakers will automatically be muted. This feature is great for nighttime music listening and gaming. However, this behavior can also be disabled and both speakers and headphones will have sound.

To disable this feature, go to AudioHQ and load Device Controls. Click the Live! Drive tab, and this window will appear:

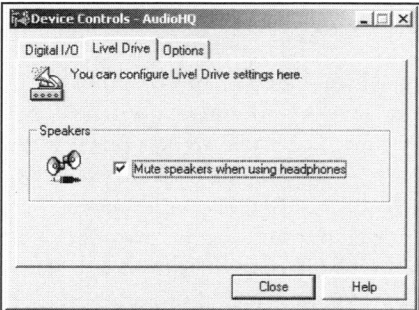

Check the "Mute speakers when using headphones" box to automatically mute the analog and digital outputs at the back of the Live! card. On the other hand, if you have a pair of headphones permanently connected to the Live!Drive and would like to hear sound from the speakers, do not check the box.

When a pair of headphones is connected to the Live!Drive and the speakers are muted, the mixer will not indicate this. The mixer sliders continue to be used to adjust the volume that goes to all audio outputs of the sound card as well as the Live!Drive, while the volume knob acts as a regulator to decrease the volume level that is output from the mixer to the Live!Drive and the connected headphones

Mic In 2/Line In 2

Mic In 2/Line In 2 is a switchable microphone and line input and appears in the mixer as a single slider labeled "Line-In2/Microphone2." The connector is named Line In 2 and Mic In 2 because the first line and microphone inputs already exist on the Live! card's backplate. The knob to the right of the jack lets you switch between microphone and line input modes, and when in microphone mode, control the volume of the microphone input.

If the knob is turned counterclockwise to minimum, past the click sound, the jack goes into line-in mode, allowing it to accept a stereo line-level input. A cable that has RCA plugs at one end and a stereo 1/4-inch jack at the other can be used

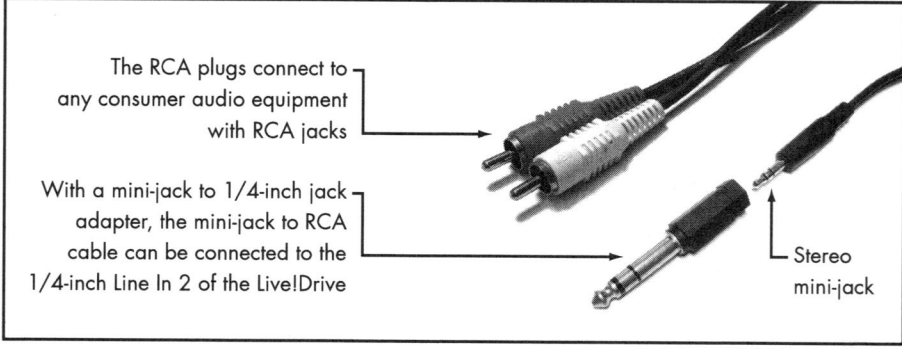

Figure 4.6: Stereo mini-jack–to–RCA cable with mini-jack–to–1/4-inch jack adapter

to send audio from consumer audio equipment to the Live!Drive. Alternatively, a stereo mini-jack–to–RCA cable can also be paired with a mini-jack to 1/4-inch jack adapter to obtain the same connectivity.

> **Mini-jacks on portable audio equipment**
> Mini-jacks are usually found on portable CD and MiniDisc players because manufacturers opt for the space savings provided by combining the stereo (left and right) signals into a single mini-jack, instead of using two RCA jacks or a larger 1/4-inch stereo jack.

To engage the microphone mode, turn the knob clockwise, past the click. When the knob is turned further clockwise, the amount of amplification (known technically as *gain*) applied on sound picked up by the microphone is increased. Adjust this such that a comfortable volume is obtained from the microphone, but not so much that there is excessive hiss or feedback from the speakers. In microphone mode, the Live!Drive outputs the microphone audio in monaural format.

Many affordable microphones have mini-jacks; they are known as *condenser microphones*, such as the Telex microphone bundled with the Live! Platinum. Microphones used for vocal performances are called *dynamic microphones* and usually come with 1/4-inch jacks. The Live!Drive supports condenser microphones. Some models of the Live!Drive also support dynamic microphones, like the CT4860 model. If the manual for your Live!Drive says that there is a two-pin jumper named C85 on the PCB of the Live!Drive, you can place the included jumper cap over the two pins of the C85 jumper to set the Live!Drive to accept dynamic microphones.

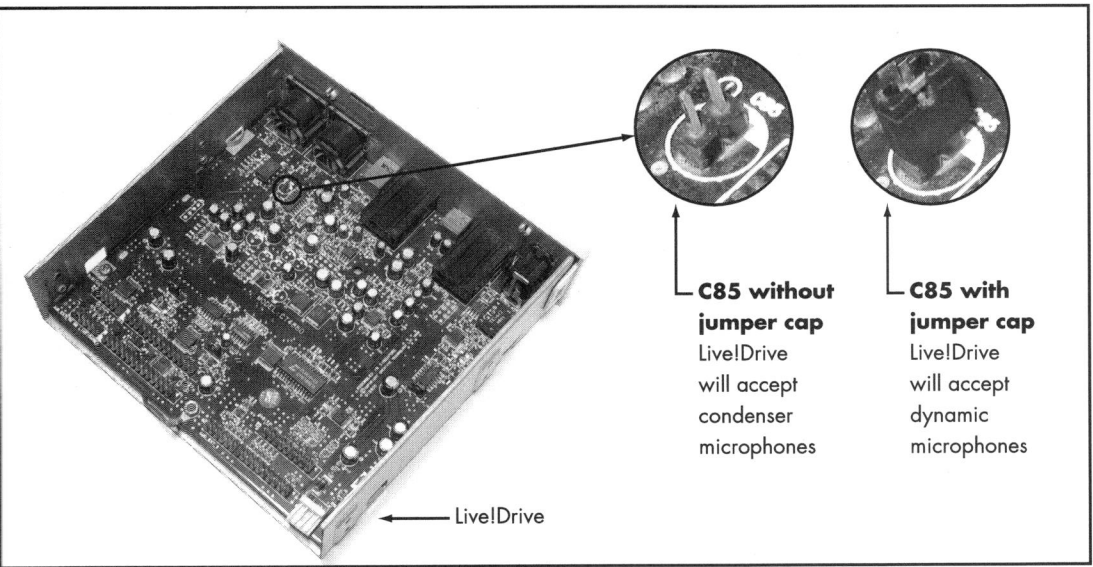

Figure 4.7: The C85 jumper

Aux In 2

The Aux In 2 input has two RCA jacks, providing a stereo analog line input that connects to audio equipment such as VCRs, CD players, and tape decks. As with all the other audio inputs available on the Live! and Live!Drive, you can record and listen to audio from these inputs.

Either Aux In 2 or the S/PDIF In (or Optical In) can be enabled at any one time, because they share the same slider in the mixer. To enable Aux In 2, go to the Surround Mixer and locate the mixer slider labeled "SPDIF-In/Auxiliary2." Above the icon for the slider is a red plus symbol, which will open up a window. If the checkbox is checked, the Aux In 2 will be turned on. Clear the checkbox to use the S/PDIF In.

Digital Connectors

The digital inputs and outputs located on the left side of the Live!Drive provide a direct audio path from the EMU10K1 to digital audio equipment, allowing noise and interference to be minimized. If an audio player or recorder has digital as well as analog inputs or outputs, connecting them digitally to these digital inputs and outputs on the Live!Drive will likely result in better audio quality.

S/PDIF In

> In consumer audio equipment, the word *coaxial* is commonly used to indicate connections that accept S/PDIF data in electrical form, and *optical* refers to connections that accept S/PDIF data in the form of light pulses. Creative labeled these outputs as S/PDIF on the Live!Drive, while most consumer digital audio devices use the term *coaxial*. In any case, they are both the same type of signals and can be connected to one another without difficulty.

The S/PDIF In input accepts a standard S/PDIF signal from coaxial cables with RCA plugs. You can listen to and record audio from digital equipment such as MiniDisc and DAT decks that have similar coaxial digital outputs.

> S/PDIF is a digital audio format—a means of transmitting digital audio across compatible equipment. You can also look at it as a standardized arrangement of 1s and 0s used in digital data that all compatible equipment can recognize and successfully convert to analog audio. The standard also specifies the hardware and electrical specifications involved in S/PDIF connections. The more common method is to send them electrically across wires, while another costlier method is to transmit S/PDIF as light across optical fiber cables.

Aux In 2 has to be disabled in the mixer to allow S/PDIF In to work because both inputs share the same mixer slider. Also, the S/PDIF In and Optical In are connected to this same digital input signal, so only one can be connected to the Live!Drive at one time.

S/PDIF Out

The S/PDIF Out connector outputs the front channels of the Live! in digital S/PDIF format. You can use this to record and play back audio from digital audio equipment such as MiniDisc recorders or pipe the audio of the Live! to another sound card with an S/PDIF input. Instead of connecting to speakers with analog cables, which may cause some signal degradation, you can connect digitally to speakers and A/V amplifiers with coaxial inputs.

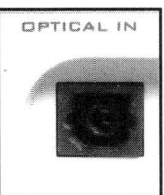

Optical In

The Optical In connector accepts standard TOSLink cables that transmit audio in digital form through light pulses. Like the S/PDIF input, this allows you to obtain sound from compatible digital audio equipment for playback or recording with the Live!

Aux In 2 must be disabled in the mixer to allow Optical In to work. Both cannot be enabled at the same time. Also, you can use only the S/PDIF In or the Optical In at any one time.

Toshiba Link (TOSLink) is a digital interconnection standard that allows transmission of S/PDIF data by sending light over optical fibre cables, and also standardizes the physical jacks and connectors used. The plug itself is squarish and has grooves around it to allow it to fit into an optical jack with a nice click.

Optical Out

The Live!Drive takes digital audio from the front channels of the EMU10K1 and converts it to light pulses sent to the Optical Out. Optical cables are connected to the Optical Out and to digital audio equipment with optical inputs. As with the Optical In jack, TOSLink plugs and connectors are used.

This output is ideal for recording MP3s to MiniDisc format, because most MD recorders provide optical inputs. However, many portable MiniDisc recorders do not use the square TOSLink connectors, but rather smaller mini-jack–sized connectors to allow the same jack to double as an optical and an analog input. With such connectors, an optical cable with a TOSLink plug for the Live!Drive and a mini-jack optical plug at the other end is needed. Creative bundles such a

Accessories Galore! **83**

TOSLink–to–mini-jack optical cable in some Live! Platinum and Live! Platinum 5.1 shipments that come with the Live!Drive II and Live!Drive IR, respectively.

Other Connectors

The right of the Live!Drive houses some non-audio connectors, including the MIDI inputs and outputs that musicians will be most interested in. In addition, the Live!Drive IR bundled with the Live! 5.1 cards also has an IR receiver for remote control.

MIDI In

The MIDI In input connects to MIDI keyboards and other musical instruments for input of music data into music sequencing and audio programs. The Keyboard application in AudioHQ can also be configured to accept notes from the MIDI input of the Live!

Figure 4.8: The TOSLink and mini-jack plugs

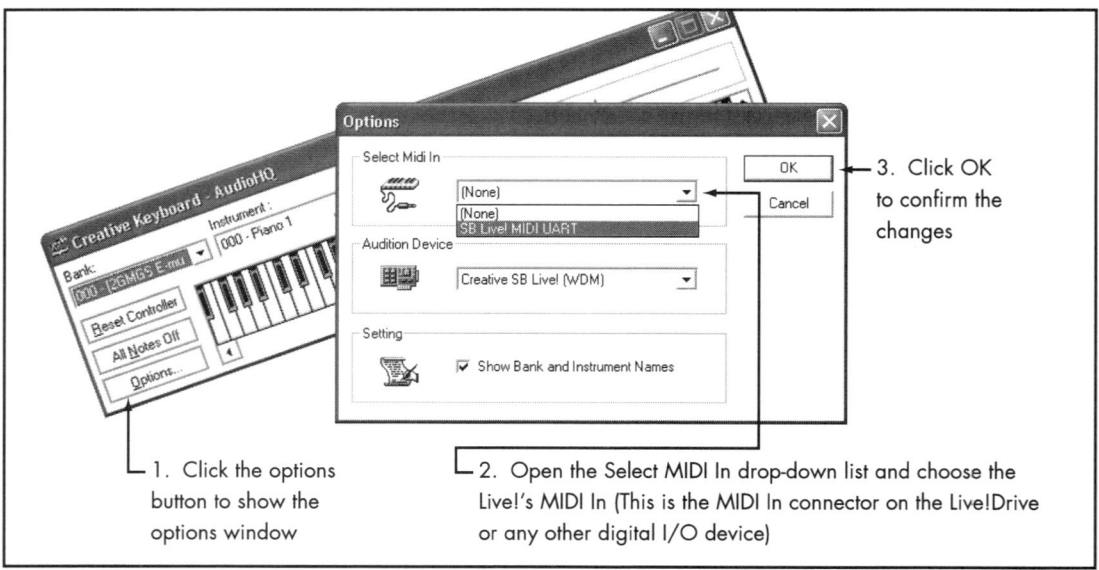

Figure 4.9: Choosing a MIDI input in Creative Keyboard

The MIDI In connectors are full-sized DIN connectors on the Live!Drive and Live!Drive II. However, with the added IR receiver on the Live!Drive IR, the DIN connectors are shrinked to the smaller pin-equivalent Mini-DIN version, so Mini-DIN–to–DIN adapter cables are needed to allow standard DIN MIDI cables to be connected to the Live!Drive IR. These Mini-DIN connectors and adapter cables are the same as those used by Creative's other digital I/O cards described earlier in this chapter.

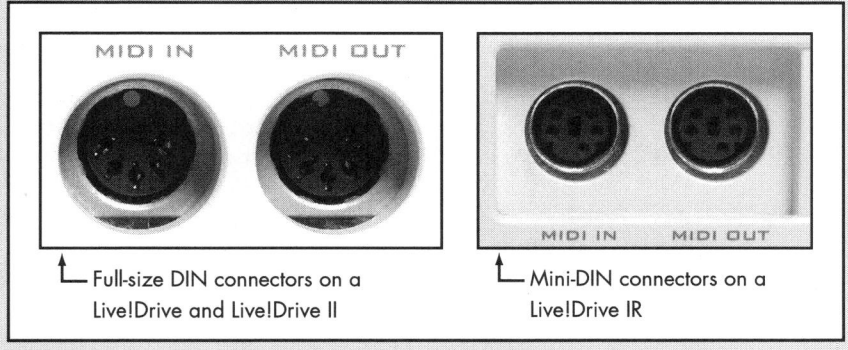

Figure 4.10: DIN and Mini-DIN MIDI In/Out jacks

MIDI Out
The MIDI Out can be used to connect to sound modules, music synthesizers, or any device that recognizes MIDI data. This is mainly used to reproduce music from any game that uses MIDI for music, a sequencer with MIDI support, or a media player that plays MIDI files. The drivers default to the internal EMU10K1 synthesizer for this purpose and should be suitable for most users, but if you want to route MIDI data to external equipment, change it from the EMU10K1 synthesizer to the Live!'s MIDI output in Windows Control Panel and connect the MIDI hardware to the MIDI Out on the Live!Drive.

The section "Audio: MIDI Music Playback" on page 206 of Chapter 9, "Drivers and Other Tweaks," describes how you can change the MIDI device used for input and playback.

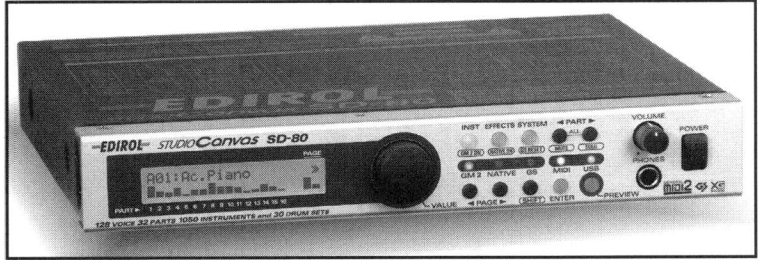

Figure 4.11: A MIDI sound module

> You might realize that your PS/2 keyboard and mouse also use Mini-DIN connectors. Look closer! Although the plug looks similar on the outside, the number of pins (also known as poles) and the way they are laid out is different from that used by the 9-pole Digital DIN plug.

IR Receiver

Behind the black rectangular piece of plastic above the MIDI connectors on the Live!Drive IR is an infrared (IR) receiver similar to those found on most A/V equipment that comes with a remote control. (If your TV doesn't, we won't recommend that you buy it!) This receiver works together with the remote control included with the Platinum 5.1 package. The remote control unit is also provided when the Live!Drive IR upgrade is purchased separately for non–Platinum 5.1 Live! cards. The sensitivity of the IR receiver can be changed in the included RemoteCenter software if commands from the remote control are often not registered. A clear line of sight is required for the remote control to operate reliably, so be sure to place the PC casing in a position that is in close proximity to where you would normally point the remote control.

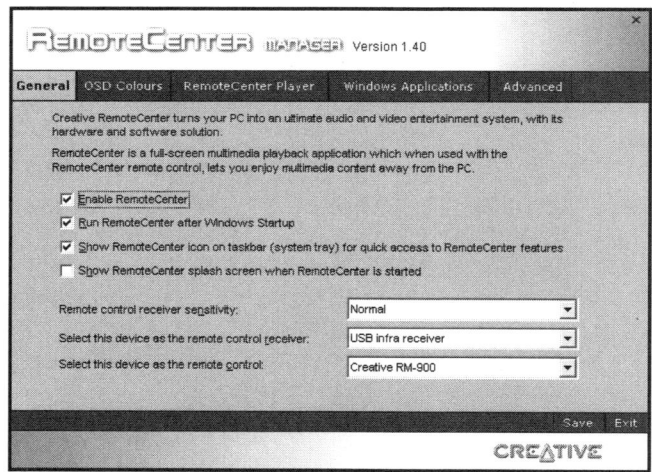

Figure 4.12: RemoteCenter for the Live!Drive IR

Extension Connectors

Four extension connectors are available on all Live!Drives. Their main purpose is to allow some of the signals from the Live! card's AUD_EXT connector to be passed to other add-on peripherals such as digital I/O cards and Digital DIN backplates. This feature allows far more audio connectivity than normal sound cards can provide with just the connectors on their backplates.

Figure 4.13: The IR receiver located above the MIDI In and MIDI Out on a Live!Drive IR

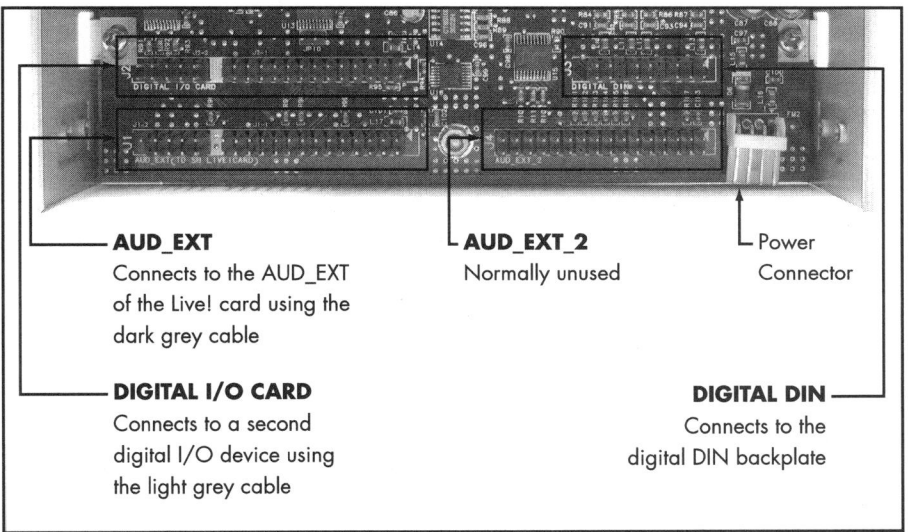

Figure 4.14: The extension connectors on the Live!Drive

AUD_EXT

The AUD_EXT connector interfaces with the similarly labeled AUD_EXT connector on the Live! It allows the Live!Drive to obtain input and output signals from the sound card.

DIGITAL I/O CARD

Using the DIGITAL I/O CARD connector, a digital I/O card can be cascaded to and used together with the Live!Drive. This connector is similar in configuration to the AUD_EXT connector found on the Live!, allowing it to connect to a second digital I/O device that works with the AUD_EXT connector.

Accessories Galore! **87**

TIP *You can even cascade a second Live!Drive to the primary Live!Drive.*

Live!Drive Inputs Have Priority

Similarly labeled inputs on a cascaded digital I/O card, such as the Line In 2 input found on Creative's optical digital I/O card, will be disabled if they are also found on the Live!Drive. This happens when the I/O card is connected to the Live! through a Live!Drive acting as an intermediary device, compared to a direct connection from the digital I/O card to the Live!, where there will be no conflicts or duplicated inputs. The inputs on the Live!Drive are always given priority, and this behavior cannot be changed.

On the other hand, all *outputs*, including the MIDI outputs, will still be available on the connectors of cascaded digital I/O cards, as well as on those of the Live!Drive. Therefore cascading another digital I/O device to the Live!Drive provides extra analog and digital audio outputs, as well as extra MIDI outputs. The tables presented earlier in this chapter for the Digital I/O Card and the Optical Digital I/O Card will give you an idea of the connectors that are enabled, or disabled due to duplication, when the I/O cards are connected to the DIGITAL I/O CARD connector on the Live!Drive instead of the AUD_EXT connector on the Live!

DIGITAL DIN

The DIGITAL DIN connector is used to connect to a Digital DIN backplate included in some shipments of the Live! Platinum and Live! Platinum 5.1 products. This backplate provides an alternative way to connect to Creative or Cambridge SoundWorks speakers with Digital DIN inputs, instead of using the mini-jack digital output found on second- and third-generation Live! cards. Both the Digital DIN and mini-jack digital output are functionally equivalent, and they provide four channels of audio with first- and second-generation Live! cards and six channels with Live! 5.1 cards.

Figure 4.15: Digital DIN backplate connected to the Live!Drive

AUD_EXT_2

The AUD_EXT_2 connector is provided for future upgrade options, possibly for additional digital I/O devices. At the time of this writing, no products are known to use this connector.

> Some versions of the Live!Drive have extension connectors that are named differently. However, the location and function of the connectors remain the same in all models.

Live!Drive Models

Three Live!Drive models are commonly sold with the second- and third-generation Sound Blaster Live! products. Some countries, like Japan, have specialized Live! cards and Live!Drives to cater to the needs of the consumers there, but a large majority of Live!Drives are one of the three listed below. The major difference between these models is the optical digital connectors and the auxiliary analog input.

Table 4.5: Connectors on the Live!Drives

	Second Generation Live!Drive	Second Generation Live!Drive II	Third Generation Live!Drive IR
Model Number	CT4860	CT4861	SB0010
Headphone Out	✓	✓	✓
Mic In 2/Line In 2	✓	✓	✓
S/PDIF In	✓	✓	✓
S/PDIF Out	✓	✓	✓
Optical In		✓	✓
Optical Out		✓	✓
Aux In 2		✓	✓
IR Receiver			✓
MIDI In	✓ DIN	✓ DIN	✓ Mini-DIN
MIDI Out	✓ DIN	✓ DIN	✓ Mini-DIN

Live!Drive

The Live!Drive is the most basic model available and is bundled with the second-generation Platinum product in the Americas and Asia. In Europe, the Live!Drive II is bundled with the Platinum instead of the Live!Drive.

The lack of optical digital outputs caused some consternation among users in the Americas and Asia who own MiniDisc recorders and prefer to record from the sound card in digital format. Most consumer MiniDisc portable recorders and decks (except those in the midrange to high end) come with only optical inputs and do not use the coaxial outputs commonly found on sound cards.

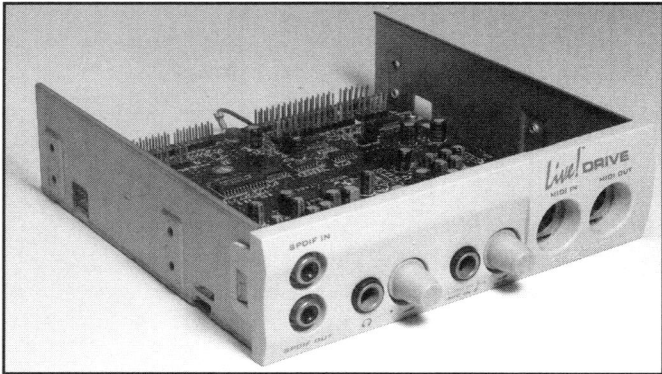

Figure 4.16: The Live!Drive

Live!Drive II

The Live!Drive II has all the connectors found on the Live!Drive but adds more analog and digital connectors. The Live!Drive II includes the Aux In 2 analog line input that connects to standard RCA cables and connectors used by most consumer audio equipment. Optical digital TOSLink inputs and outputs are also included for connecting to consumer digital audio equipment such as MiniDisc and DAT decks, as well as receivers with digital inputs.

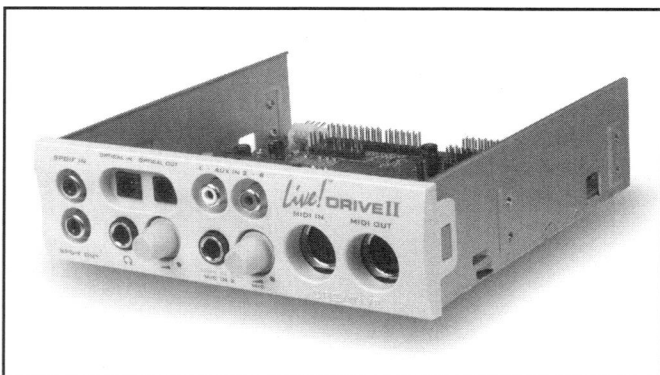

Figure 4.17: The Live!Drive II

Live!Drive IR

The Live!Drive IR was introduced in 2000 during the launch of the third-generation 5.1 Live! cards and is sold as an upgrade option for all Live! cards with the AUD_EXT connector. Creative took all of the features of the previous Live!Drive II and added an IR remote control receiver just above the MIDI input and output.

This IR feature was previously seen in the exclusive Japanese version of the Live!Drive for the second-generation Live! Platinum product, which is available only in Japan.

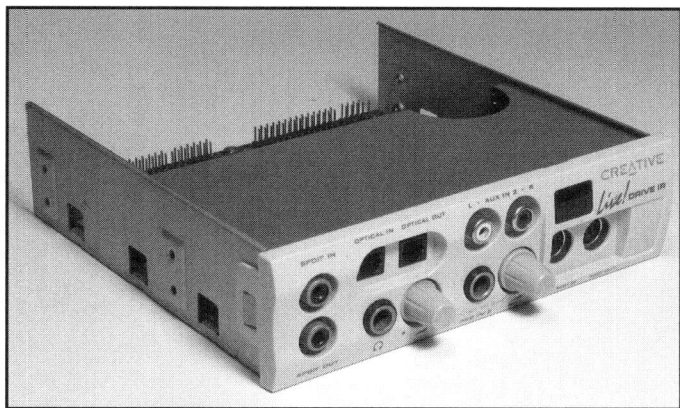

Figure 4.18: The Live!Drive IR

> The Japanese sometimes have better Live!Drive products than the rest of the world. There is also a Japanese model that has an IEEE-1394 FireWire port to tap into the large market of DV (digital video) camera users there.

To make way for the IR receiver located above the MIDI connectors, Creative had to change the standard full-sized DIN connectors to the smaller Mini-DIN connectors, thus requiring users to use a Mini-DIN–to–DIN adapter cable so that normal DIN MIDI cables can still connect to the Live!Drive. Fortunately, the adapters are provided with most Live!Drive IRs; they are not commonly found in stores. You can also purchase them directly from Creative or at the company's online store.

Obtaining Optical Connectors

Because of demand from users who want optical inputs and outputs on their Live!Drive, Creative has, for a short while, offered a trade-in program to allow customers to swap their Live!Drive for a Live!Drive II. In the third-generation products, Creative decided to avoid this issue entirely and make the Live!Drive IR standard on all Platinum 5.1 products sold worldwide. All Live!Drive IRs bundled with the third-generation Live! Platinum 5.1 come with the Optical In, Optical Out, and Aux In 2 connectors, as well as the new remote control feature.

Compatibility

The Live!Drive connects to the AUD_EXT connector on a second- or third-generation Live! It will not work with Live! cards that have the SPDIF_EXT extension connector, such as the first-generation Live! Value (model CT4670).

Like the Optical Digital I/O Card, the Live!Drive works only partially with some batches of the very first Live! card (model CT4620), because some signals from the EMU10K1 were not fully tapped and prevent connectors like the Mic In 2/Line In 2 from functioning correctly. This problem was corrected in later shipments. If you have a CT4620, check with a Creative customer service representative. They will be able to help you determine if your CT4620 fully supports the Live!Drive.

With the above exception, all other second- and third-generation Live! cards with the AUD_EXT connector will work with any of the three common Live!Drives. An easy way to determine whether your Live! will work with the Live!Drive is to check if it has a mini-jack digital output, because the digital output became a permanent feature of the Live! when the second-generation was introduced.

> A second-generation Live!Drive (Live!Drive and Live!Drive II) will work with a third-generation Live! card such as the SB0060. The third-generation Live!Drive IR will also work with second-generation Live! cards.

Table 4.6: Live!Drive Compatibility

	First Generation		**Second Generation**	**Third Generation**
Model Number	CT4620	CT4670 (Live! Value)	CT4760 CT483x	SB0060
Compatibility (all Live!Drive models)	✓ Partial compatibility especially for early batches, which may disable the Mic In 2/Line In 2	✓ No AUD_EXT extension header	✓ Full compatibility	✓ Full compatibility

Installing the Live!Drive

Like most 5 1/4-inch PC peripherals, such as CD-ROM drives, the Live!Drive fits nicely into one of the drive bays. Creative provides two flat cables in the box for installation. One is darker and has a black circle on the underside near one end of the cable, while the other cable is in a lighter shade of gray.

The two flat cables provided with each Live!Drive look similar to the IDE cables that connect hard drives to the motherboard. In spite of this, do not use IDE cables to connect the Live! to the Live!Drive or you risk shorting out both devices!

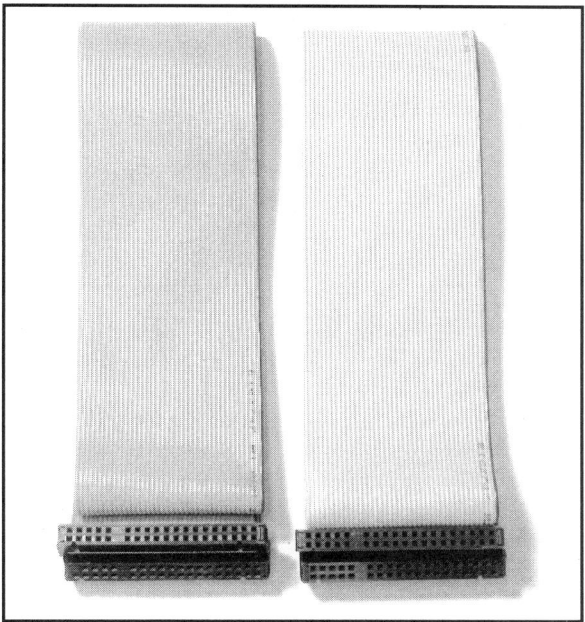

Figure 4.19: The flat cables provided with a Live!Drive

Connecting to the Live!

The dark gray flat cable is used to provide the data connection between the AUD_EXT connectors found on both the sound card and the Live!Drive. Make sure that the end of the cable with the black circle on the underside is connected to the AUD_EXT connector on the Live! and not the one on the Live!Drive. The cable provided by Creative is usually of adequate length for most PC cases. However, if you own a large full-tower casing, be sure to check the length before installing the Live!Drive, in case it ends up too far away from the Live!

TIP *When the Live!Drive is in full use, many cables will dangle from it, so you may want to install it in a drive bay that is below drives that open and close (like CD-ROM drives) and removable floppy, cartridge, or hard drives.*

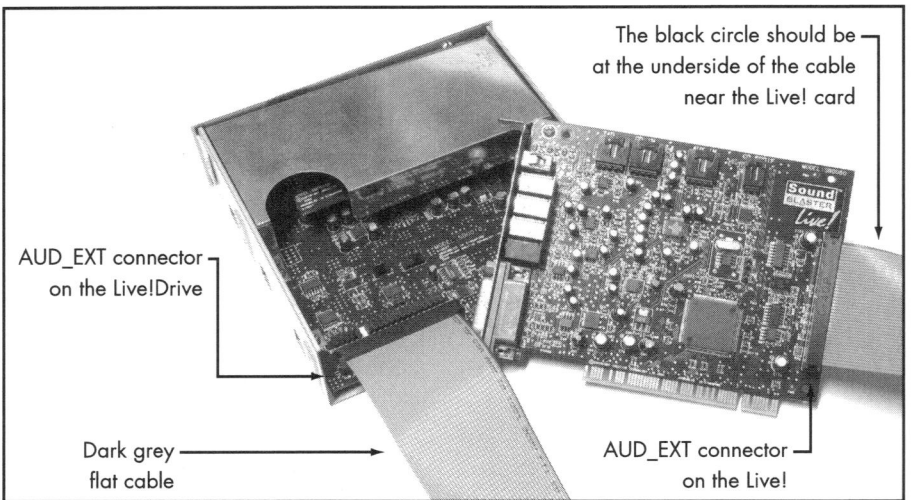

Figure 4.20: The Live!Drive connected to a Live! card

Cascading a Digital I/O Card

The light gray flat cable is also included in the package, in case you have an additional digital I/O card that you want to continue to use with the Live! To cascade an I/O card from the Live!Drive, connect one end of the cable to the DIGITAL I/O CARD connector on the Live!Drive and the other end to the connector on the I/O card.

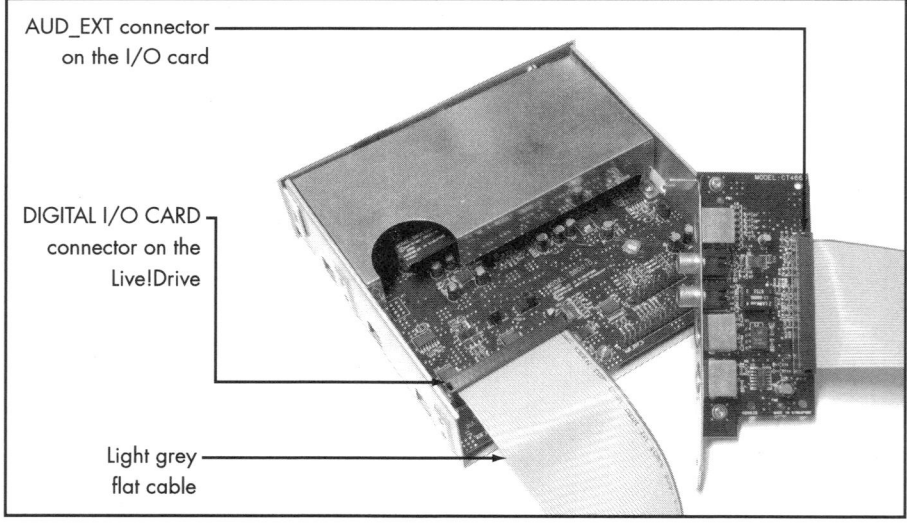

Figure 4.21: The Live!Drive with a cascaded digital I/O card

> If you do not have a digital I/O card, keep the light gray cable for future upgrades because manufacturers expect digital I/O cards to be connected directly to the Live! and installed in slots that will probably be located near the Live! card, so very short cables are usually provided. These cables are just long enough to reach a nearby Live! card and not the Live!Drive, which may be located far away from the motherboard, especially with tall PC cases.

Powering the Live!Drive

The Live!Drive also includes DACs and ADCs because all of the audio input and output by the AUD_EXT connector are in digital form. All of these functions on the Live!Drive require power; therefore, you will also see a power splitter in the package to allow you to tap the power from the power supply unit in the casing. Make sure it is correctly connected according to the manual before it is powered up.

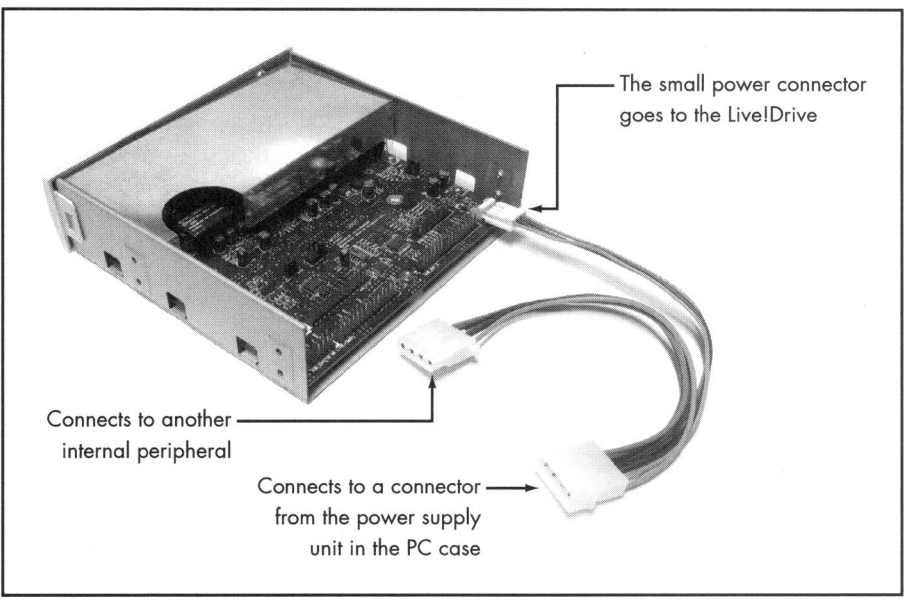

Figure 4.22: The Live!Drive with the power splitter connected

No Drivers Needed

Like digital I/O cards, the Live!Drive does not require any driver installation, and if you purchased it separately from the Live! card, do not be alarmed if there is no CD included in the package. It is pretty much a plug-and-play solution. The drivers have built-in support for these accessories and will automatically enable or disable the respective applets and mixer settings when these devices are detected. All you need to do is to make sure that your PC has the latest drivers.

How the Live!Drive Works

Here is the diagram of the Live! card's AUD_EXT connector from the previous chapter with the inputs and outputs on the Live!Drive added to give you an idea of how audio is sent and received from the Live!

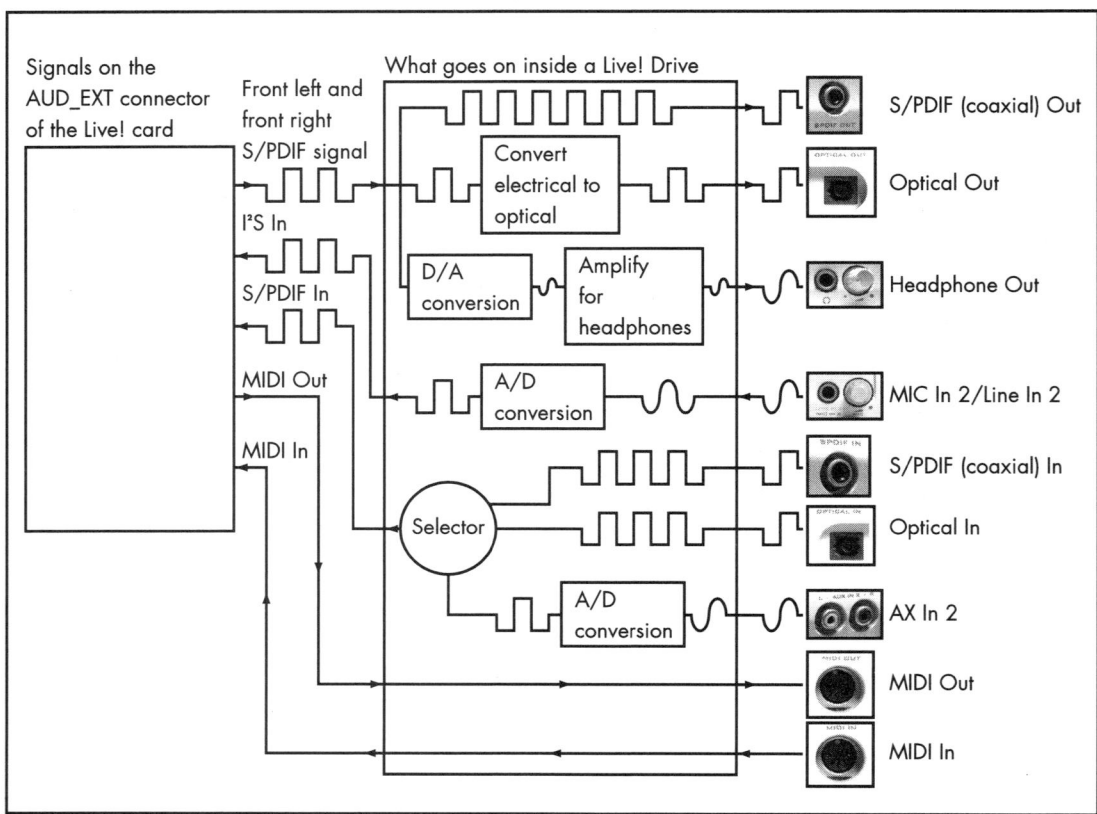

Figure 4.23: Live!Drive diagram

S/PDIF Bypass

This feature is available on the Optical Digital I/O Card and the Live!Drives. It allows you to pass a digital signal from the digital input to the digital output without having it enter the Live!'s mixing circuits. S/PDIF bypass works not only with PCM audio, but also Dolby Digital and DTS signals from a DVD decoder card installed in the PC or in a consumer DVD player.

Table 4.7: Connectors on the Live!Drives

Signal from EMU10K1/ AUD_EXT	Connector	Type	Volume (for Analog Connectors)	Audio Format	Number of Channels	Channels
Front Output	Headphones	1/4-inch stereo jack	Controllable with knob	Analog	2	Stereo: front left and front right
	S/PDIF Out	Coaxial/RCA		Digital	2	S/PDIF: front left and front right
	Optical Out	Optical/TOSlink		Digital	2	S/PDIF: front left and front right
I²S Input	Mic In 2*	1/4-inch mono jack	Controllable with knob	Analog	1	Mono
	Line In 2*	1/4-inch stereo jack	Fixed (line level)	Analog	2	Stereo: left and right
S/PDIF In	S/PDIF In**	Coaxial/RCA		Digital	2	S/PDIF: left and right
	Optical In**	Optical/TOSlink		Digital	2	S/PDIF: left and right
	Aux In 2**	2 RCA jacks	Fixed (line level)	Analog	2	Stereo: left and right
MIDI In	MIDI In	DIN (or 5-pole Mini-DIN on the Live!Drive IR)	N/A	N/A	N/A	N/A
MIDI Out	MIDI Out	DIN (or 5-pole Mini-DIN on the Live!Drive IR)	N/A	N/A	N/A	N/A

* Only one can be used at any time. The position of the knob determines which input mode is used.

** Only one can be used at any time. Also, you need to use the mixer to set either analog (Aux In 2) or digital (S/PDIF/coaxial or optical) mode. When Aux In 2 is enabled (analog mode), both S/PDIF In and Optical In will not work. When Aux In 2 is disabled (digital mode), connect either to the S/PDIF In or the Optical In, and the Live!Drive will choose the correct input to use automatically. There is no need to use the driver software to switch between S/PDIF In and Optical In— the Live!Drive will detect which is connected and use the signal from that physical input jack.

Accessories Galore! **97**

> Some digital I/O cards, like the CT4660 digital I/O card and other third-party I/O cards may have S/PDIF input and output jacks, but they may not necessarily support S/PDIF bypass.

Using S/PDIF Bypass

You will need this feature only for specific setups and purposes, and most users would not even need this feature at all. This feature will come in handy if you have many digital audio equipment or a complex setup. The following is just one of the many situations where this feature will be useful:

Consider a setup with a DVD player's digital output connected to a digital input on the digital I/O device (either coaxial or optical), and a surround AV receiver (or a 5.1 multimedia speaker system) that supports Dolby Digital or DTS decoding connected to a digital output from the Live! The user regularly listens to audio CDs played on the DVD player and has music piped into the Live! and mixed with the other audio sources from the Live! This mixed audio from the Live! is then sent digitally to the AV receiver so that it can be heard.

The problem arises when DVD movies with surround soundtracks are played, like those encoded in Dolby Digital or DTS. Because the Live! is not able to decode Dolby Digital or DTS signals from its digital inputs, no sound would be heard when such DVDs are played back. Fortunately, the AV receiver supports surround decoding, so the digital output from the DVD player should be connected directly to the AV receiver to get surround sound. However, manually disconnecting the DVD player from the sound card and connecting it to the AV receiver every time a DVD needs to be played would be too troublesome.

The S/PDIF bypass feature enables the digital signal from the DVD player (going into the digital I/O device) to be sent directly to the digital outputs of the digital I/O device. The digital signal does not enter the Live! at all, so it can be viewed as a direct connection from the device connected to the digital input, to the device connected to the digital output. After finishing with a DVD, S/PDIF bypass is disabled and audio CDs played on the DVD player can once again be heard through the sound card and the connected AV receiver.

Other devices can also be used in such a configuration. For instance, when a CD player is connected to the input, and the output is connected to a MiniDisc recorder, the CD can be recorded to the MiniDisc directly by turning on S/PDIF bypass. This allows the audio from the CD player to go directly to the MiniDisc recorder, without mixing in the other sound sources that may be playing back on the Live! at that time, eliminating recording of unwanted audio in the MiniDisc.

With S/PDIF bypass, the digital audio signal can pass through the digital connectors on the Optical Digital I/O Card or the Live!Drive without being processed by the Live! S/PDIF bypass is a convenient feature to eliminate the need to reconnect cables and should not be turned on if you do not need it.

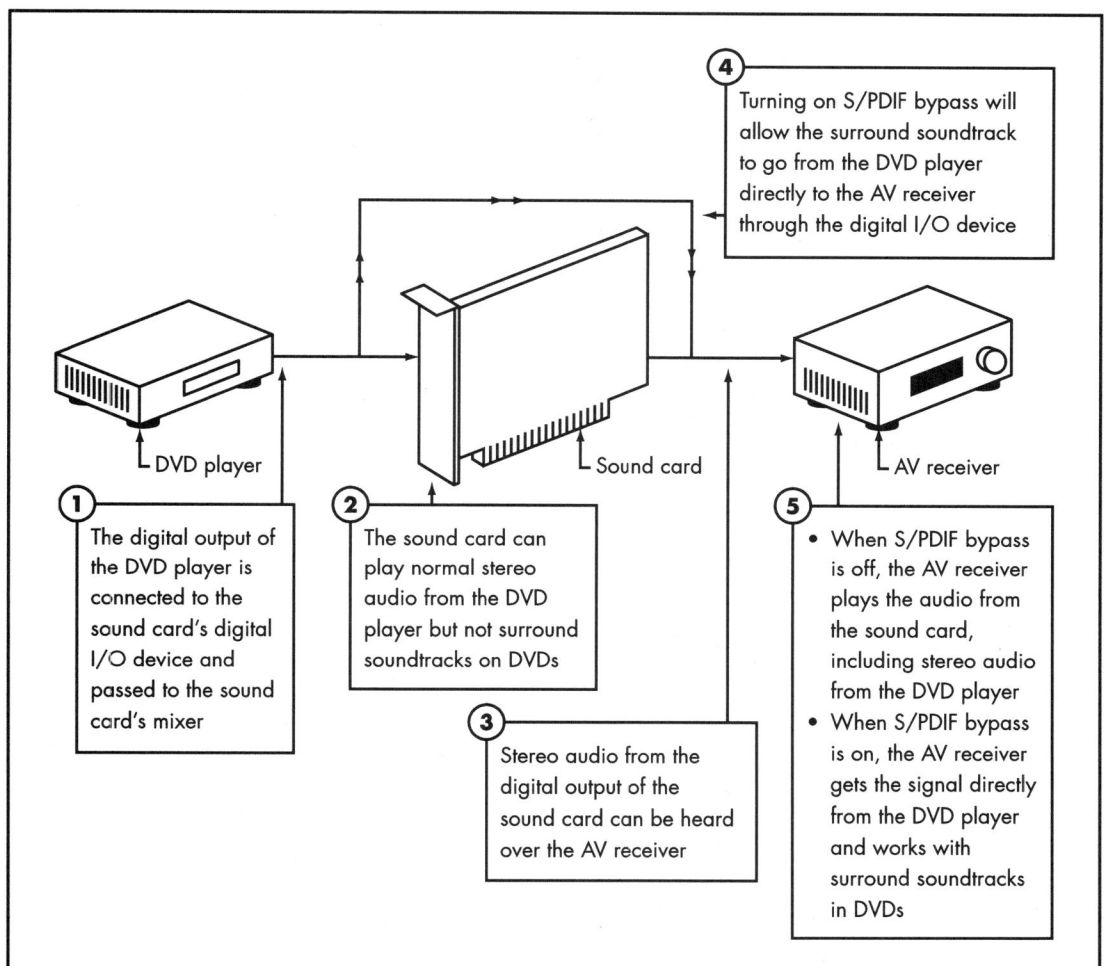

Figure 4.24: The S/PDIF bypass feature

Compatible Connectors

S/PDIF bypass works with both coaxial and optical connections, but apart from bypassing between connectors of the same type (either coaxial or optical), it is also possible to use the S/PDIF bypass feature to convert between coaxial and optical.

> Both coaxial and optical signals carry audio data in the same S/PDIF format. It is only the physical transmission medium that is different. Coaxial uses electrical signals, while optical uses light pulses. With some added circuitry in these devices, coaxial can be converted to optical (and vice versa).

This table summarizes the coaxial and optical connectors available in these devices and which ones can be used for S/PDIF bypass:

Table 4.8: Coaxial and Optical Connectors Available for S/PDIF Bypass

Digital Connector	Optical Digital I/O Card	Live!Drive	Live!Drive II	Live!Drive IR
Coaxial In	✓	✓	✓	✓
Optical In	✓	N/A	✓	✓
Coaxial Out	✓	✓	✓	✓
Optical Out	✓	N/A	✓	✓

Enabling S/PDIF Bypass

S/PDIF bypass can be enabled in the drivers. If you have an appropriate digital I/O device like the Optical Digital Card or one of the Live!Drives, there will be extra options available in AudioHQ's Device Controls applet. Click the Digital I/O tab and you will see this screen:

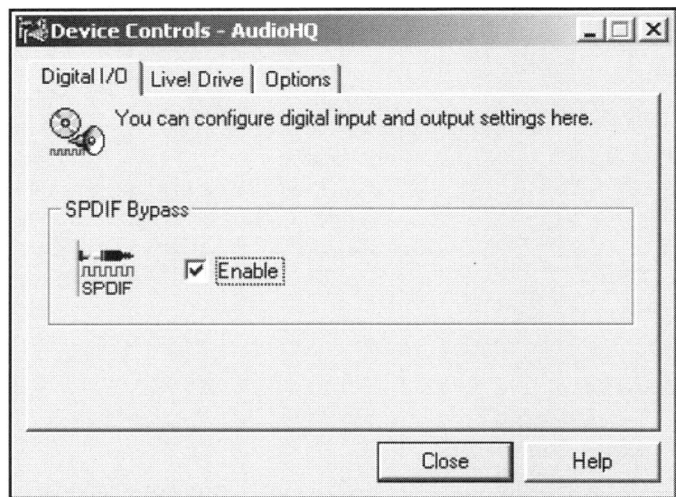

Figure 4.25: Select the Enable checkbox to turn on S/PDIF bypass

Once enabled, all the coaxial and optical digital outputs of the digital I/O device that are supposed to carry the front left and front right channels will be used to carry the bypassed signal instead. However, the other digital and analog audio outputs on the Live!'s backplate and the analog outputs on digital I/O devices will continue to function. The front channel (left and right) signals of the Digital DIN output and the mini-jack digital output are not affected when S/PDIF bypass is enabled.

> S/PDIF bypass will not be affected by the 48-kHz rate that the EMU10K1 operates with. The input S/PDIF signal will be channeled to the output S/PDIF jack directly without any resampling. This allows it to bypass non-PCM audio like Dolby Digital and DTS formats.

Digital I/O Card or the Live!Drive?

You should generally consider three things when choosing a digital I/O device for the Live!: physical constraints, features required, and cost. Then, with these factors in mind, hop down to your nearest store. Some digital I/O devices are not readily available in many stores as they are not high-volume items. If you are unable to find the digital I/O device that you want, the Internet is a good place to shop for it. Creative also sells the Live!Drive products at the Sound Blaster Web site, at http://www.soundblaster.com.

Physical Constraints

Because digital I/O cards take up a slot's space in the casing that would otherwise be put to good use for connecting peripherals that actually use the ISA, PCI, or AGP expansion slot on the motherboard, a drive bay solution like the Live!Drive may be preferable.

However, if the PC casing is small, or no 5 1/4-inch drive bays are available, a digital I/O card would be an appropriate purchase. Be sure to look behind the plastic cover to make sure that the bay really is empty, because some system manufacturers put an internal hard drive there.

Features Required

Make a list of the analog and digital equipment that you would like to connect to the Live! Note the connectors and jacks they have so that you will be able to match them to the connectors available on the digital I/O device. Also take into account any future expansion, if you anticipate that you will need to use more inputs to the Live! in the future. This will help you decide which product is most suitable.

Cost

The Live!Drive products are much more expensive than digital I/O cards, but they do provide more functionality and the convenience of easy access from the front of the PC casing. If you intend to permanently leave the cables connected, an affordable digital I/O card with jacks exposed behind the PC case would suffice. Weigh your options carefully and decide for yourself whether the cost of such an add-on is justified.

5

CONNECTING DEVICES

Although technologically less complex than a state-of-the art 3D video accelerator, a sound card is more complicated in terms of the setup and the number of cables and connections you'll have to make to get it up and running. You may have electronic gadgets like portable CD players, VCRs, MiniDisc recorders, and even an old tape deck that you want to integrate with the Live!

This chapter focuses on how to get audio in and out of the Live! so that you will be able to hear the sound from other devices with the sound card's speakers. Sound card mixers can combine and output the sound from several audio sources simultaneously, which allows you to do things like play a game with a favorite CD playing music in the background. EAX allows you to add effects and enhance the Live! card's audio, and you can also transfer all of your treasured tape albums and keep a copy of them digitally in an audio file. Does it sound like there's much to do to obtain this type of functionally from the Live!? The good news is that you'll have to do this setup only once to get everything all hooked up. And it isn't difficult, so let's get started!

Analog

In the audio primer, you read that audio transmitted through analog means is easily susceptible to interference. However, the industry has been using analog connections for decades simply because analog is what we hear! Even if an analog signal is converted to digital for purposes of distribution, as with CDs and MP3 files, or for transmission over digital cables, it ultimately has to be converted back to analog format so we can hear it.

Analog Signals

Analog audio signals are transmitted across wires at varying levels of power for different purposes. The speaker cables that connect to an amplifier carry high levels of power to drive the speaker cones. The signals sent over an audio cable connected to the Phono Out jack of a record player are of low level because they are obtained from a tiny stylus vibrating on the little grooves on a vinyl record. The following paragraphs discuss some of the more common types of analog signals that you will likely encounter in consumer audio.

Line-Level Signals

The line-level signal is a low-level electrical signal standard that exists industry-wide. This standard ensures that analog audio transmitted between standard audio equipment is within specified levels. If the level is outside this range, it may be too soft to hear or so loud that distortion and crackling sounds will sometimes occur. This may damage amplifiers and speakers because they assume line-level signals and are designed to accept and amplify only signals within that range. Conversely, signals that are too low will result in under-amplification, and the volume of the sound source will be barely audible. Many amplifiers also have protection circuitry or fuses to automatically stop the unit from operating when such mishaps occur.

You can assume that most consumer audio equipment outputs line-level audio, except where there is a volume control for the output, as on portable disc or tape players, which will likely indicate that the output is amplified for headphones and can produce output that is above line-level.

Low-Level Analog Signals

Low-level analog signals operate at lower voltages than line-level signals and therefore require an additional amplification stage. A preamp is commonly used to boost the power of such sound to line levels. Microphones, phono outputs from record players, and electric guitars all produce extremely low levels from their outputs and require some form of preamplification.

> There are DIY instructions available on the Internet that show you where to find or how to build a converter to convert a phono input that is originally meant only for record players, to a line-level input.

On microphones, a mic preamp is usually used. You will be able to hear only a very soft sound or even no sound at all if you connect a microphone directly to a line input. Likewise, guitar pickups require preamplification because the strings produce only tiny vibrations that are barely audible when connected directly to line-level inputs. Amplifiers that have phono inputs connect to record players and provide amplification and equalization to the audio before it is amplified on the speakers.

> Do not connect line-level audio to phono inputs on amplifiers, guitar amps, and mic preamps because of the preamplification that these devices apply to the audio signal.

Amplified Signals

Analog signals are used for speakers and headphones, too, but they are different. Line-level signals are too low in power to cause the magnetic speaker drivers to vibrate and produce sound that we can hear. Therefore, the audio needs to be increased in power while at the same time preserving the basic characteristic shape of the signal so that it sounds the same—only louder and powerful enough to move the speaker drivers. Amplifiers are used for this purpose. They can be hidden inside the body of most TVs and multimedia speaker systems. Hi-fi systems usually come with a separate amplifier unit. Usually, volume control knobs are added to allow the amplification level to be regulated.

Although portable devices do not have dedicated amplifier units like hi-fi systems do; they still need to integrate a headphone amplifier to boost the audio signals for the headphone outputs. Larger headphones require more energy to move the speaker drivers in them and therefore require more amplification. Hooking up a headphone-amplified output to a line input is possible, if the volume is turned down low enough to approximate the volume of line-level audio outputs.

Besides headphone outputs, most of the amplified outputs on hi-fi systems are the speaker outputs behind the amplifier. Bare wires and banana plugs are commonly used. This is not a strict standard, however, and some manufacturers, like many multimedia speaker manufacturers including Creative and Cambridge SoundWorks, do make use of connectors such as RCA jacks to hook up speakers, so do take note of the type of signal carried, as well as the type of connectors used. Never connect an amplified speaker output to a line-level input because amplified signals are very strong and will fry your equipment!

Analog Connectors

There are different analog connectors for different purposes. Unfortunately, there is no simple distinction that enables us to easily tell the particular purpose or audio equipment that a specific type of connector is used for. Here, we will attempt to highlight the common connectors used for analog audio.

Most connectors are either male or female—sounds weird, but it's the dirty truth! Plugs are usually male because they connect into female jacks or sockets. Transmission of analog audio requires one wire for each channel. Therefore two wires are needed to send a stereo signal. These are usually bundled neatly into a single cable; however, some cables have two plugs for each of the left and right channels, while others also combine the left and right channels into a single plug.

RCA (Phono) Jacks

The Radio Corporation of America introduced RCA cables in the 1970s as a consumer audio interconnection standard. They are sometimes called *phono cables*. There is one plug for each channel of analog audio. Therefore, stereo systems require two plugs at each end of the cable. The white plug is for the left channel, and the red plug is for the right channel. Some cables use black plugs instead of white for the left channel, but they work the same way. The RCA jacks on consumer audio equipment are also color coded in this way to make setup easy: match the colors, and you'll never go wrong.

eStereo RCA-to-RCA cable with two RCA plugs on both ends. One end connects to the outputs, while the other goes to the inputs on another piece of equipment.

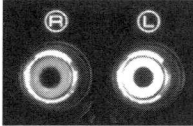

Figure 5.1: The left and right female RCA jacks on typical consumer audio equipment

Things may be a little more complicated sometimes because RCA jacks and cables are not limited to connecting analog line-level audio. After all, they are just plugs connected to the end of wires! RCA connectors are also used for other types of signals, such as video and digital audio. These higher-bandwidth signals require that the cables be built from better quality wires to allow more electric data to pass through at any one time—a requirement similar to mandating a larger water pipe to allow more water to flow through.

Typical audio cables are designed to accommodate the bandwidth required for analog audio. However, there is also a large market for high-grade cables that

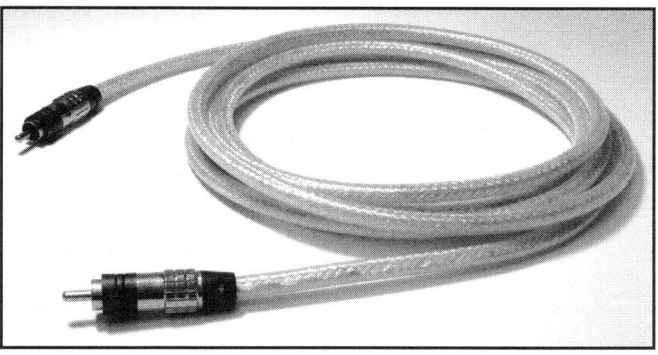

Figure 5.2: A higher-quality single RCA-to-RCA cable with a thicker cable

transmit signals with less interference and resistance, resulting in better audio quality on equipment that is properly set up. For multimedia audio systems, a cable with gold-plated plugs would suffice, but then again, you'll probably feel better with cables of reasonable quality, so the decision ultimately depends on your budget and the quality of the audio equipment you are connecting.

Apart from the common copper wires used to make RCA cables, coaxial cables are preferred for video and digital audio signals because of their ability to carry more information across, at a higher bandwidth, and with more resistance to noise due to the design of the cable. Coaxial cables with RCA plugs are common for the more costly digital audio cables.

RCA cables are designed to shield the audio signal from noise. Inside the cable, a wire in the center carries the audio signal, and an insulation material that does not conduct electricity encloses the wire. An outer layer of wire or metal, such as twisted copper or aluminum foil, is wrapped around the insulation material to help absorb the electrical noise from the environment. This provides acceptable shielding in normal circumstances, although stronger electromagnetic interference may still seep through. If you want better insulation, you can find converters to allow you to outfit BNC coaxial cables (like those that connect to your TV antenna or cable tuner) with RCA plugs so that they can be used like normal RCA cables.

Connecting an RCA cable is easy. On an RCA plug, the metallic outer shield conductor that encircles the center pin is separated in half, so gently nudging the plug into an RCA jack should keep it in place. However, do be careful of the labeling on audio equipment. It is easy to accidentally connect the left and right channels in reverse or accidentally connect a video or coaxial digital RCA jack because of the use of similar connectors. In addition to the markings on the outputs, color coding is often used as an aid to help differentiate the various RCA outputs on a device. Typical composite video outputs have yellow RCA jacks, while coaxial digital outputs are normally black. Be sure to look closely!

1/4-inch (6.3mm) Jacks

The 1/4-inch jacks are widely used on equipment such as headphones, microphones, and musical instruments like electric guitars and keyboards. An interesting thing about these plugs is that they fit into the jacks with a very smooth and satisfying click!

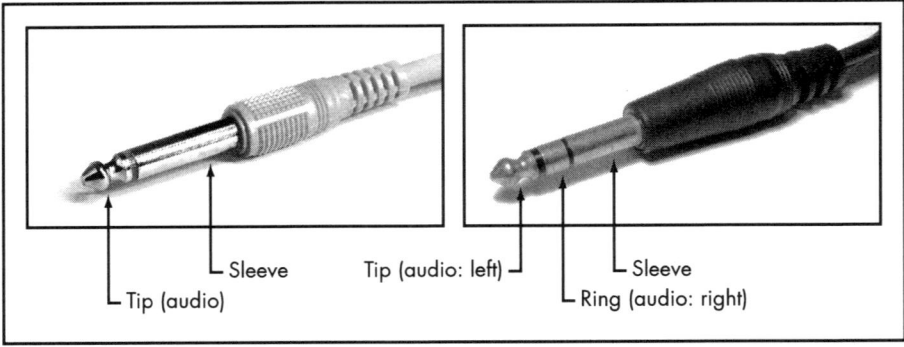

Figure 5.3: Mono and stereo 1/4-inch jacks

There are two common varieties of 1/4-inch jacks. The first is a stereo plug with three segments, separated by rings that are often black in color. These are also known as *TRS plugs*, after the names of each segment on the plug: tip, ring, and sleeve. The tip and ring carry the left and right audio signals, respectively, and the sleeve is used to shield the audio signals from interference (also known technically as *grounding*). A mono version of the 1/4-inch jack has two segments, omitting the ring segment and leaving the tip for the audio signal and the sleeve to provide grounding. Different types of wires are also used for 1/4-inch cables. Cables used for connecting musical instruments such as guitars are thicker because of added material, insulation, and improved shielding. This additional thickness helps to reduce noise and improve resistance to wear and tear from rough use. Electric guitar and microphone cables do tend to get stepped on very often!

Microphones are the most common equipment used with mono 1/4-inch jacks, although they sometimes use stereo 1/4-inch jacks in a TRS configuration, with one of the segments used to power the microphone. (You'll find out more about microphones later in this chapter.) Some musical instruments such as MIDI synthesizers also have separate mono 1/4-inch jacks for the left and right channels, instead of using a single stereo 1/4-inch jack.

For stereo 1/4-inch jacks, there are stereo microphones and those large headphones that are commonly used with hi-fi audio systems. You can tell whether a plug is mono or stereo by counting the number of segments, but it is a little difficult to tell whether a 1/4-inch input on a piece of audio equipment is mono or stereo, so you'll have to check the manuals or verify the specifications with the manufacturer.

1/8-inch (3.5mm) Mini-jacks

Mini-jacks are very useful in the portable audio market. Imagine lugging around a portable CD player with a large 1/4-inch jack that invites dust and a pair of tiny in-ear earphones with a heavy and unwieldy 1/4-inch plug at the end that may be larger than the earphones themselves! Ridiculous, isn't it?

Mini-jack plugs mirror the functionality of the 1/4-inch connectors, with the same three-segment tip, ring, sleeve (TRS) configuration for stereo plugs. There is also a two-segment version used for carrying a single mono channel. The 1/8-

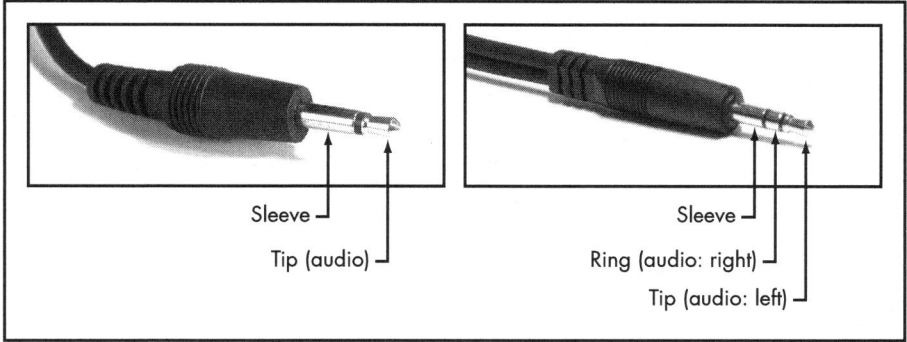

Figure 5.4: Mono and stereo 1/8-inch mini-jacks

inch mini-jacks are generally perceived as more for the consumer. A rusted and dirty plug can affect the quality of the signal that the cable transmits, although sometimes only minimally.

Mini-jacks are commonly used on sound cards because of the small and cramped backplates. Instead of two RCA jacks or a larger 1/4-inch jack, a sound card maker can squeeze more connectors behind a sound card by using mini-jacks. Conversely, the Live!Drive covered extensively in Chapter 4, "Accessories Galore!" uses 1/4-inch connectors instead of mini-jacks.

> There are mini-jacks that carry three signals and are typically used for audio-visual equipment that needs one signal for video and the other two for the left and right audio channels.

Connecting in Analog

Wow! Lots of connectors and analog signals, eh? Not to worry, because setting up analog equipment is very simple. Just take note of these three points:

TIP *Before you proceed to hook up an audio system, make sure your PC and audio equipment are all turned off. When connecting new equipment to the sound card, it is advisable to mute the particular channel in the mixer before you make the physical connection and then slowly turn up the volume to a comfortable level. An accidental microphone feedback or static that is too loud may damage your equipment and the Live! card, not to mention your ears!*

1. The Plug

Note the type of connectors found on both devices. You will need to match the plugs on both ends of the cable with the jacks. Many types of cables are available with different plugs, so it is possible to connect two different jacks with the correct cable. Moreover, adapters can also be purchased to convert between different types of plugs.

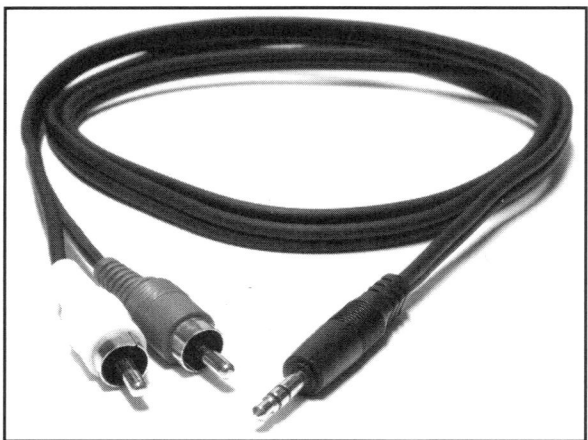

Figure 5.5: A stereo mini-jack–to–RCA cable

Figure 5.6: A stereo mini-jack–to–mini-jack cable

Remember that each RCA plug can carry only one audio signal, while 1/4-inch jacks and 1/8-inch mini-jacks can come in mono or stereo configurations. So, a cable that has a stereo 1/4-inch or mini-jack would most probably come with a similar jack, or two RCA plugs, at the other end. If the 1/4-inch or mini-jack is mono, there would be one RCA plug at the other end of the cable. You can find mono 1/4-inch–to–RCA or mono mini-jack–to–RCA cables, although they are less common than their stereo counterparts.

The stereo mini-jack–to–RCA cable is commonly used to connect sound cards to audio systems with RCA inputs. Stereo mini-jack–to–mini-jack cables are commonly used to connect the line output of a sound card to multimedia speakers and to get the audio from portable devices (such as MP3 and CD players) into the Live!'s line inputs.

Creative used to include stereo mini-jack–to–RCA cables with many Sound Blaster cards but has opted not to with the Live! cards because of the popularity of mini-jack connectors in multimedia speakers.

TIP *It is possible to turn down the volume on the headphone output of a portable player and connect it to a line input on the Live!, but the quality may suffer because of the extra amplification and volume control electronics that the audio signal has to go through to drive headphones. However, it's worth a try if that is the only output available on your audio equipment.*

Adapters are also available to change the type of plugs on audio cables. A 1/4-inch jack–to–1/8-inch mini-jack adapter allows mini-jack devices to work with 1/4-inch jacks like those on the Live!Drive. An inverted version of this adapter is also available to convert the larger 1/4-inch jacks to mini-jacks, mainly to allow microphones and headphones to work with portable audio devices that sport only the smaller mini-jacks. Female-to-female RCA adapters (also sometimes known as female barrel connectors) allow two RCA cables to be connected together to extend the cable's length.

In addition, RCA, 1/4-inch jack, and mini-jack splitter adapters are available that allow you to obtain two outputs if the device has only one. Using such an adapter may affect audio quality because the signal now has to be fed to two input

Figure 5.7: A mini-jack–to–1/4-inch jack adapter

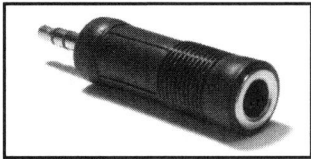

Figure 5.8: A 1/4-inch to mini-jack adapter

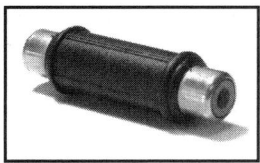 

Figure 5.9: Single- and double-barrel female-to-female RCA adapters

Connecting Devices **111**

devices at the same time, so do an A-B comparison to see if you can detect any serious quality degradation or a huge drop in volume.

Figure 5.10: RCA and mini-jack splitter adapters

TIP *Splitter adapters can be used for output signals but not inputs.*

Manufacturers have adopted different plugs for different purposes; therefore, it is not possible to say exactly what each one is used for. For example, you can't conclude that a mini-jack is always used for headphones and is used only for signals amplified for headphone use. Amplifiers and speaker manufacturers (including Creative) have even used RCA plugs on the amplified speaker outputs, so anything is possible!

The most important thing is that you note the other two factors that we will mention below and get the correct cable with the correct plugs. Your local electronics store should have the right cables and adapters in stock. If you have some electronics skills, you can buy the wires and plugs and assemble your own cables. This ability will be especially useful if you need a certain cable length or a special wire and plug configuration isn't readily available in stores.

2. The Wire

The wires that make up the cables are designed and produced for many purposes and vary according to the signal characteristics of the types of information they are intended to transmit. Cables that are of a higher quality and lower resistance, made of better materials, and generally thicker, are tailored to transport higher-bandwidth digital audio and video, while thinner and lower-quality ones can be used for lower-bandwidth signals like analog audio.

You may be able to interchange types of wires, and usually you may not even notice the difference, especially when substituting a higher-quality cable for low-bandwidth applications, like using a coaxial cable meant for digital audio to transmit analog signals. However, it is still advisable to get the correct cables, because the connection will be optimized, and you will be getting the best out of your audio system. Spending a fortune on expensive wires for a pair of budget multimedia speakers is foolhardy if you can't make out the difference in audio because of the quality of the equipment. Likewise, using a low-grade analog audio cable to carry digital audio is imprudent.

Table 5.1: Analog Connectors Provided by the Live! and Digital I/O Devices

	Connector	Type	Channels	Signal Type	Sound Blaster Live! (first- and second-generation)	Sound Blaster Live! 5.1 (third-generation)	Optical Digital I/O Card	Live!Drive	Live!Drive II and Live!Drive IR
Inputs	Line In	Mini-jack	2 (stereo)	Line-level	✓	✓			
	Mic In	Mini-jack	1 (mono)	Low-level	✓	✓			
	Line In 2	Mini-jack	2 (stereo)	Line-level					
	Line In 2/ Mic In 2	1/4-inch jack	2 (stereo) when in Line In 2 mode	Line-level (when in Line In 2 mode)			✓		
			1 (mono) when in Mic In 2 mode	Low-level (when in Mic In 2 mode)				✓	✓
	Aux In	RCA jacks (left and right)	2 (stereo)	Line-level				✓	✓
Outputs	Line Out 1 (Front)	Mini-jack	2 (stereo)	Line-level	✓	✓			
	Line Out 2 (Rear)	Mini-jack	2 (stereo)	Line-level	✓	✓			
	Line Out 3 (Center and Woofer)	Mini-jack	2 (stereo)	Line-level		✓*			
	Headphone Out	1/4-inch jack	2 (stereo)	Amplified				✓	✓

* Only when the Live! 5.1 is set to 5.1 speaker mode and the mini-jack digital output is switched to analog mode to output the center and woofer channels.

3. Audio Levels

We have mentioned three general types of analog audio signals: line-level, low-level, and amplified. These are used regardless of the type of connectors, although certain connectors are more commonly used for particular types of signals. It is important to match the audio levels supported by the input and output equipment before hooking them up. Wrong audio levels are a big killer of speakers and audio equipment!

Analog Connectors on the Live!

Analog connections are available primarily on the Live!, but some digital I/O products like the Live!Drive also provide analog inputs and outputs for connecting to more analog equipment. Table 5.1 summarizes the connectors available on the Live! and the digital I/O devices from Creative.

As with other audio equipment, connecting sound sources to the Live! is easy as long as you take note of the three things mentioned previously. The Live! card's backplate uses mini-jacks, so you should have stereo mini-jack–to–mini-jack cables on hand if you want to connect portable players and other equipment with mini-jacks to the Line In, or record to a portable tape recorder from the Line Out. Mini-jack–to–RCA cables are great if you have audio components with RCA outputs that you want to play through the Live! card's Line In. This cable also comes in handy for some of the speaker setups that will be discussed in Chapter 6, "Speakers."

> Both the front and rear line outputs on the Live! output the same sound when you set the sound card to four or 5.1-speaker mode. The only exceptions are when you are playing a game that uses 3D positioning, have CMSS turned on, or when you have used the mixer to move the sound sources around, thereby changing the left-to-right and front-to-rear balance of that particular sound source.

A 1/4-inch–to–1/8-inch adapter will be convenient if you need to connect a headphone or microphone with 1/4-inch plugs to the Live! card's mini-jack Line Out. The common 1/8-inch–to–1/4-inch adapter is also useful for the Live!Drive's Headphone Out and Line In 2/Mic In 2 jacks, as they both use 1/4-inch jacks instead of the smaller mini-jack.

Like other sound cards, the Live! supports the two most common audio interconnects used for consumer audio: line-level and microphone inputs. These will be sufficient for most users. The Live! does not have inputs for other analog audio equipment that uses different signal types, such as phono inputs for record players. To connect a record player, you will need to use an amplifier that has phono input jacks and connect the line-level outputs of the amplifier (commonly RCA jacks) to the Live!

Generally, if you want to connect nonstandard low-level analog equipment to the Live!, the signals will need some form of preprocessing with an amplifier or preamp unit outside the sound card. After preprocessing, the device will output line-level audio that can be sent to the Live!'s line inputs.

If digital outputs are available on the preprocessing device, connect them to the digital input on a digital I/O device installed with the Live! This eliminates opportunities for noise to seep into the audio. The Live! card's line inputs cannot be compared to the inputs available on good-quality external audio equipment, partly because of the noisy PC environment with which the card has to contend.

Digital

Now let's take a look at the digital format, the connectors available, and how to connect digital devices to the Live!

Digital Signals

As discussed in the audio primer, digital signals are converted from analog signals and use rather discrete waveforms to represent the 1s and 0s; therefore, a slight distortion of the digital signal will not affect the audio in significant ways. Digital is a huge benefit for PC audio, because the PC is an electrically noisy environment, and analog signals are very susceptible to electromagnetic interference. Nevertheless, digital audio can also be garbled and appear as pops or loud screeches in the resulting audio.

On the other hand, noise may vary from PC to PC because of the different combinations of hardware components and motherboards used. If you have many computers, you may notice that, with the same Live! card, some computers produce more hiss and noise than others. The good news is that in most cases, the Live! is surprisingly noise free for a peripheral that has to live in a noisy PC casing.

Still, it is difficult to know exactly when some unwanted noise or computer bleeps will slip into the audio signal, so you should use digital connections over analog for the Live! if your audio device supports digital. If you have a Live!Drive or the Optical Digital I/O Card, the Line In 2 or RCA line input and analog outputs may also provide better results than those found on the backplate of the Live! card, because the Live!Drive is located further away from the motherboard and does not plug in to the motherboard (which is a common source of computer noise).

Digital Formats

For the uninitiated, digital signals can sometimes be extremely baffling. Why can a digital signal carry so many channels and yet use a cable with only one wire carrying the signal (such as an RCA cable with one plug on each end)?

In digital format, the signals are in discrete pulses of 1s and 0s are not constant waveforms like analog signals. Therefore, with only one wire for audio data transmission, it is possible to make a rule, for example, that tells the equipment to send eight bits of data of the left channel, followed by eight bits of the right channel, and then again eight bits of the left channel, and so on. The digital equipment at the receiving end would recognize this protocol and be able to decode the digital audio data correctly into the respective audio channels. The S/PDIF standard specifies such a protocol to be used by all consumer audio equipment when transferring digital audio.

Unlike analog audio, more than one audio channel can be transmitted over a single wire with S/PDIF. S/PDIF is commonly used in consumer digital audio applications to transmit uncompressed stereo (two-channel) PCM audio, but it can also transmit non-PCM and multichannel audio formats like Dolby Digital and DTS over a single-wire connection.

> S/PDIF also transmits other miscellaneous information known as *subcode*. This subcode can include the time information that allows a CD player to display the correct time of the track that is currently playing and copyright information that indicates whether the digital audio data being transmitted is copyrighted.

> Although Dolby Digital, DTS, and MP3 are all digital audio compression formats, the MP3 format does not specify how MP3 audio can be transmitted and received over digital cables. Therefore, it has to be uncompressed to Wave audio and output as S/PDIF. The MP3 player software performs the decompression and playback, and the sound card sequences the decoded audio into uncompressed Wave/PCM format to be sent to the digital output jacks via S/PDIF.

Digital Connectors

S/PDIF tells us how bits can be timed and sent digitally. The specification also encompasses two physical methods to transmit the data between digital audio equipment. One popular transmission method uses electrical signals by quickly varying the voltage of the electrical signals to represent the 1s and 0s in digital audio data. Another method uses optics, by rapidly turning light on and off to represent the 1s and 0s in the digital data.

Coaxial: RCA

Coaxial cables use the same RCA plugs found on analog RCA cables, but the wires used are similar to the ones used for connecting television to antennae systems. The cables are commonly labeled "75 ohm," and they are usually thicker and provide better signal integrity and shielding compared to the standard analog cables. Low-quality RCA cables increase the probability that digital 0s may be read as 1s instead, or vice versa, resulting in incorrect data picked up by a digital input.

> Coaxial cables used for TV connections do not use RCA plugs, but slightly different ones called BNC. You can purchase BNC-to-RCA adapters so that you can use the cable as a coaxial RCA cable. Coaxial cables with RCA plugs meant for digital audio are also readily available.

Coaxial connectors are commonly found on home and deck-sized digital audio recorders for digital compact cassette (DCC), digital audio tape (DAT), and MiniDisc (MD) devices. Many AV receivers and DVD players also use coaxial connectors, including those for Dolby Digital and DTS signals.

> DCC was introduced by Philips in the early 1990s to compete with Sony's MiniDisc format. However, it did not gain wide acceptance, and the technology was discontinued.

Coaxial: Mini-jack
Manufacturers of portable DCC and DAT recorders found RCA jacks cumbersome, so they adapted the design of mini-jacks for coaxial digital audio transmission. Except for portable digital tape recorders, coaxial mini-jacks are not commonly used by consumer audio equipment. Manufacturers have opted for optical transmission instead.

> The mini-jack digital output on the backplate of a second- or third-generation Live! also uses a mini-jack to transmit S/PDIF signals. However, the assignment of the TRS signals on a mini-jack from this output is proprietary to Creative products and therefore cannot be considered part of the industry standard.

Digital I/O devices for the Live! do not provide coaxial mini-jack connectors, instead providing the more commonly used RCA coaxial connectors. You can, of course, purchase cables that will convert a coaxial mini-jack signal to RCA and connect such equipment to the Live! and the optical I/O devices. The quality of the wires used and other considerations are similar to those for coaxial RCA cables, because the digital signal is essentially the same, and only the plugs differ.

Optical: TOSLink
Optical connectors and plugs provide digital equipment with an interconnection model for transmitting S/PDIF data using quick pulses of light. The TOSLink connectors are unique in the audio world because they are square in shape, and the wires and plugs do not use metal as conductors. Instead, a red light-emitting diode (LED) is used in an optical output to produce the light pulses to the connected optical cable.

Optical cables are marvels of technology. They are typically made of plastic fibers that are around 1mm in diameter. The fibers allows the cable to work as though there are tiny little mirrors spanning the entire length of the cable, reflecting light from one end to the other. When connected correctly into an optical output socket, the red light is sent over the other end and picked up by the optical receptor behind the optical input jack.

Some more expensive cables also use other materials like glass fibers, aiming to increase the conductivity of light. The connectors may also be metal instead of plastic to dampen vibration that may cause some light pulses to be lost.

TIP *If you have an optical fiber cable, try pointing one end at a bright light, and you'll see the light appear at the other end!*

Although an optical output has a LED behind it, while an optical input has a receptor, both input and output use the same TOSLink jacks, allowing either end of the cable to be used.

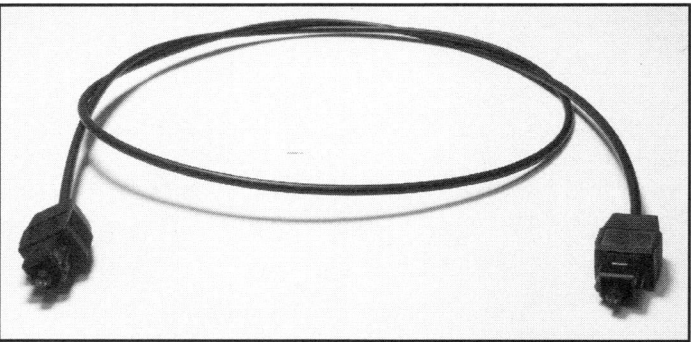

Figure 5.11: Optical TOSLink cable

TIP *Optical jacks usually have small, square caps that cover them to prevent dust from entering. Be sure to cover optical jacks when they are not in use because dust and dirt can accumulate, and soon the light emitted from an optical output will be too weak for the receiving equipment to pick up.*

Because they are not electrical in nature, optical cables are immune to the electromagnetic interference that plagues poorly shielded electrical cables, thereby eliminating the need to make shielding and grounding an important part of the cable design. On the other hand, compared to optical cables, electrical cables made of copper and other metals are cheaper to manufacture and are consequently more affordable.

Still, optical connections can become problematic when the equipment or the optical cable is faulty, or the cable exceeds the ten-meter limit such that not all light reaches the receiving equipment at the other end. Problems may also occur if a cable is not fully inserted into the TOSLink connector. Light attenuates and loses its strength more significantly than electrical signals over the same length of wire, so it is advisable to keep the length of the optical cable to a minimum.

Optical: Mini-jack

Sony was one of the companies that helped popularize the optical mini-jack connector by including it in almost all of its portable CD and MiniDisc products. Due to the ever-increasing need to shrink the size of these portable devices, they usually have a combined mini-jack output that carries both a stereo line-level analog output and an optical digital output.

Optical mini-jack–to–mini-jack cables are available to allow a portable CD player with an optical mini-jack output to send digital audio to a portable MD recorder with a similar optical mini-jack input. However, most optical I/O devices available for the Live! use the larger TOSLink connectors, so TOSLink–to–optical mini-jack cables are used instead. This cable can also be used to connect a portable CD player to the digital I/O device's TOSLink optical inputs.

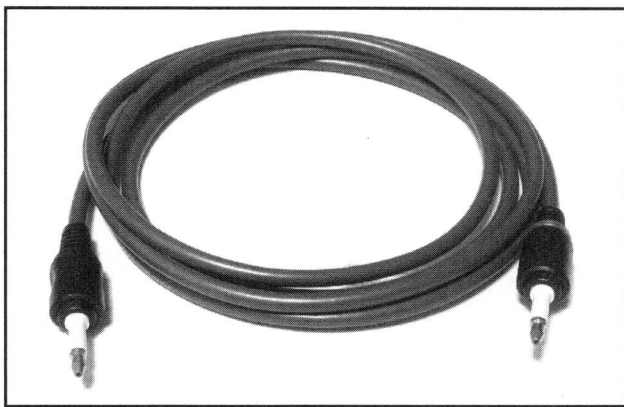

Figure 5.12: An optical mini-jack–to–mini-jack cable

TIP *The Live!Drive II and Live!Drive IR come with a TOSLink optical input and output, so a TOSLink–to–optical mini-jack cable will come in handy when connecting equipment with optical mini-jack inputs and outputs.*

Creative's Proprietary Digital Outputs

Creative introduced two additional digital outputs with the Sound Blaster Live! family, primarily to allow connection to the company's own digital multimedia speaker systems that sport the Digital DIN connector. The Digital DIN output available on Creative's digital I/O cards can carry up to four S/PDIF signals for eight channels of audio.

The second- and third-generation Live! cards also have an equivalent mini-jack digital output that delivers two S/PDIF signals on the second-generation Live! and three S/PDIF signals on the third-generation Live! In the first-generation Live!, Digital DIN speakers could only be used when a digital I/O card with Digital DIN output was installed. With the mini-jack digital output on the second- and third-generation Live!, a mini-jack-to-Digital DIN adapter cable will allow the sound card to be connected to four- or 5.1-channel speakers with Digital DIN inputs without requiring a digital I/O card with the Digital DIN output.

Find out more about how you can use the mini-jack digital outputs on some Live! cards as a coaxial output in Chapter 3, "The Sound Blaster Live! Hardware."

These connectors are primarily used to send the speaker outputs of the Live! digitally rather than through analog line-level outputs, bypassing the DACs on the sound card and circumventing any noise that may potentially affect the analog outputs or the cables that are connected to the sound card.

The use of the Digital DIN and mini-jack digital output to connect to speakers are discussed more fully in Chapter 6, "Speakers."

Because these connectors and cables are proprietary, Creative bundles them with its products that use them. The Digital DIN–to–Digital DIN cable and the mini-jack–to–Digital DIN adapter cable are included with every speaker that has a Digital DIN input. If you need extra cables, they can be purchased directly from Creative and its online store. If you have the technical know-how or a friend experienced in electronics, you can consult the schematics and pinout diagrams of these connectors that are readily available on the Internet. These can help you tap the signals from the Live! and construct custom-made cables to connect to your digital audio equipment.

Connecting in Digital

Unlike analog, where the signal format may differ (like amplified or line level), digital data from the Live! uses the S/PDIF format no matter what physical medium is used to transmit the data. It can either use coaxial or optical cables, and the plugs may vary, as we have described above. The uncompressed PCM digital audio that is used by the Live! also supports different sample sizes and sampling rates.

Digital Input and Output Specifications of the Live!

The S/PDIF digital inputs of the Live! card (and any connected digital I/O device) support 32-kHz, 44.1-kHz, and 48-kHz sample rates. The sample size must be fixed at 16 bits. These specifications also apply to the S/PDIF In (coaxial and optical) found on digital I/O devices and the internal CD_SPDIF connectors. Most digital audio equipment output audio at 16-bit 44.1 kHz or 48 kHz, so they will work with the Live!

Because of the way that the EMU10K1 is designed, digital audio sent to the Live! will be converted and processed with the internal 48-kHz sample rate used by the EMU10K1. Consequently, all digital outputs of the Live! will output a S/PDIF signal at 16-bit 48 kHz. Therefore, digital outputs from the Live! will not produce an exact 1:1 version of the signal from any digital input.

Find out more about the 48-kHz issue of the EMU10K1 in Chapter 18, "The EMU10K1 Digital Audio Processor."

TIP *If you have a Live!Drive or the Optical Digital I/O Card, you can set it to S/PDIF bypass mode so that an exact copy of the digital input will be passed to the digital output without the output having to enter the Live! and be processed by the EMU10K1. This procedure is explained in Chapter 4, "Accessories Galore!"*

> The Live! can play back digital audio at other unusual sampling rates, such as 8 kHz and 32 kHz, but through the S/PDIF inputs, only 44.1 kHz and 48 kHz are supported because these are the most common sampling rates carried with S/PDIF.

> The Live! can also be put into S/PDIF passthrough mode, allowing a software DVD player to take over the S/PDIF output of the Live! and send non-PCM formats, such as Dolby Digital and DTS compressed audio through the output. In this mode, the S/PDIF outputs (either coaxial or optical) from a digital I/O device connected to the Live! can be sent to an AV receiver, surround sound decoder, or multimedia speaker system that supports Dolby Digital or DTS decoding for surround sound playback.

Making the Connection

Compared to analog, it is much easier to physically make a digital connection. Just note these two points:

1. Both devices must use the same physical medium: either coaxial or optical.
2. The cable must have the correct plugs for the connector on the input device and the output device: likely RCA for coaxial and TOSLink or mini-jack for optical connections.

> Do not try to connect speakers or headphones to a digital output, even if the connectors are similar (for instance, mini-jacks or RCA connectors). There will be digital noise and bleeps, and equipment may be damaged if the volume is too high.

Converting Between Coaxial and Optical

Some digital I/O cards and the first Live!Drive model provide only coaxial inputs and outputs. This has left many users frustrated, especially the growing number of users with MiniDisc recorders that have only optical inputs. Good news, though: there are products that can convert between coaxial and optical formats. If you have a budget MD recorder, you won't have to purchase a more expensive Mini-Disc deck just to get the coaxial inputs and outputs.

If you have a Live!Drive II or Live!Drive IR, you can also turn on the S/PDIF bypass feature (explained in Chapter 4) and use the coaxial and optical inputs and outputs to perform coaxial-to-optical or optical-to-coaxial conversion. There are also many schematics and instructions on the Internet for DIY coaxial-to-optical converters. Perform a search with your favorite search engine, and you should be able to find quite a few. With a little electronics savvy and the readily available parts, you can create your very own coaxial-to-optical converter!

Digital Connectors on the Live!

Besides the mini-jack digital output available on second- and third-generation Live! cards, digital I/O devices like the Optical Digital I/O Card or the Live!Drive have to be paired with the Live! for the coaxial and optical digital connectors. The following table lists the common connectors found on the Live! cards and the accompanying digital I/O devices produced by Creative.

Table 5.2: Digital Connectors on the Live! Cards and Digital I/O Devices

	Digital Connector	Sound Blaster Live! (first-generation)	Sound Blaster Live! (second-generation)	Sound Blaster Live! (third-generation)	Digital I/O Card (CT4660)	Optical Digital I/O Card with DIO Module	Live!Drive	Live!Drive II and Live!Drive IR
Inputs	Coaxial In				✓	✓ *	✓	✓
	Optical In					✓ *		✓
Outputs	Coaxial Out				✓	✓ *	✓	✓
	Optical Out					✓ *		✓
Proprietary Digital Outputs	Digital DIN				✓	✓	✓ With Digital DIN backplate attached	✓ With Digital DIN backplate attached
	Mini-jack Digital Output		✓	✓				

* These connectors are found on the DIO module attached to the Optical Digital I/O Card.

You can see that the only digital output available on the Live! cards is the proprietary mini-jack digital output meant for speakers with Creative's proprietary Digital DIN input. To obtain the full range of digital inputs and outputs in coaxial and optical form, a digital I/O device is necessary. There are also third-party digital I/O cards that provide different combinations of connectors to cater to diverse needs.

Find out more about digital I/O devices and the Live!Drive in Chapter 4, "Accessories Galore!"

Table 5.3: Format of Digital Connectors on Live! Cards and Digital I/O Devices

	Connector	Type	S/PDIF Signals	Audio Channels	Audio Channel Assignment
Inputs	Coaxial In	RCA	1	2 (stereo)	Left and right
	Optical In	TOSLink	1	2 (stereo)	Left and right
Outputs	Coaxial Out	RCA	1	2 (stereo)	Front left and front right
	Optical Out	TOSLink	1	2 (stereo)	Front left and front right
Proprietary Digital Outputs	Digital DIN	9-pole Mini-DIN	2 on first- and second-generation Live! 3 on third-generation Live! 5.1*	4 on first- and second-generation Live! 6 on third-generation Live! 5.1*	Front left and front right, rear left and rear right. (Additional center and woofer channels for the Live! 5.1.)
	Mini-jack Digital Output	4-pole Coaxial Mini-jack	2 on first- and second-generation 3 on third-generation Live! 5.1	4 on first- and second-generation 6 on third-generation Live! 5.1	Front left and front right, rear left and rear right. (Additional center and woofer channels for the Live! 5.1.)

* The Digital DIN connector physically supports up to four S/PDIF signals, for a total of eight audio channels; however, Creative uses only two of those channels to transport audio on the first- and second-generation Live! cards, and three of those channels for the third-generation Live! 5.1 cards.

You'll notice that the optical and coaxial outputs are all taken from the front left and front right channels of the Live!, which is what you'd want to record from. Only the proprietary Digital DIN and Mini-jack Digital Output have additional channels because they are used primarily to connect to digital speakers with Digital DIN inputs.

Consumer Devices

There are so many consumer devices that use myriad connection standards that we cannot cover everything here. Nevertheless, this section attempts to give you an idea of how a majority of such devices are configured, so that you can easily hook them up to the Live! If your equipment is different from what is discussed here, fall back to the basics presented earlier in this chapter, and you should do great!

Hooking up audio equipment, especially with analog connections, is a little like playing with Lego blocks because, in some cases, you will need to combine cables and adapters. It's quite fun! Once you master the basic techniques and issues involved, no connector or cable will baffle you ever again. So let's begin.

CD Players

The most common home CD players come in standard-sized decks that stack nicely in a separate component hi-fi system. Because CDs store audio digitally, CD players contain DACs to convert the audio to analog form, and it is then output to RCA line-level outputs. Nearly all CD players come with RCA outputs, and many of them have a 1/4-inch headphone jack for private listening. You can use a stereo RCA–to–mini-jack cable to connect the player to the Live! If you are using the RCA inputs on the Live!Drive II or Live!Drive IR, the RCA-to-RCA cable normally bundled with CD players connected to the Aux In 2 would suffice.

If you want to connect the RCA outputs to the Live!'s Line In, you can purchase an RCA–to–mini-jack cable.

Digital Outputs

Some CD players also come with coaxial and optical outputs. Data is read from the CD, formatted as S/PDIF data, and sent directly to the digital output. The device that receives the S/PDIF signal, either with a coaxial or optical input, will need to have a DAC to decode the digital audio signal. Some audiophiles purchase separate DACs and pair them with CD players with high-quality laser pickups to get the best possible sound.

Similarly, the benefit of connecting devices such as a CD-ROM drive to the Live! digitally and connecting the Live! digitally to speakers and amplifiers cannot be ignored because the Live! card itself must contend with much electrical noise in the PC casing. Analog connections can easily be affected by noise.

Portable CD Players

Portable CD players are miniaturized, battery-efficient versions of deck CD players. Generally speaking, the analog sound quality of portable CD players is slightly lower than that of their deck-sized counterparts because of the trade-offs that manufacturers have to make to reduce the size. They usually sport mini-jack headphone outputs. Some models also include analog mini-jack line outputs. You can use a stereo mini-jack–to–mini-jack cable to connect the mini-jack Line In on the Live! or the Line In 2 on the Optical Digital I/O Card. If you want to connect to the RCA connectors on a Live!Drive II or Live!Drive IR, a mini-jack–to–RCA cable is required. Alternatively, the 1/4-inch Line In 2 on Live!Drives can also be used.

Some portable players also have a TOSLink or mini-jack optical output. Optical I/O devices for the Live! come with TOSLink inputs, so make sure you have an optical cable with the correct plugs.

Listen!

Listen closely: The DACs on good CD players may give a different tonal quality to the audio. You may even prefer using an analog connection to take advantage of the DAC on the CD player if the audio somehow sounds better. Other CD players sound better when you connect them digitally to the Live! Always let your ears decide!

Table 5.4: Connections for CD Players

Output Format	Jacks on a CD Player	Sound Blaster Live!	Digital I/O Card (CT4660)	Optical Digital I/O Card with DIO Module	Live!Drive	Live!Drive II and Live!Drive IR
Analog	Line Out (stereo RCA jacks)	Line In (stereo mini-jack)		Line In 2 (stereo mini-jack)	Line In 2 (stereo 1/4-inch jack)	Line In 2 (stereo 1/4-inch jack) Aux In 2 (stereo RCA jacks)
	Line Out (stereo mini-jack)	Line In (stereo mini-jack)		Line In 2 (stereo mini-jack)	Line In 2 (stereo 1/4-inch jack)	Line In 2 (stereo 1/4-inch jack) Aux In 2 (stereo RCA jacks)
Digital	Coaxial Out (stereo RCA jacks)		S/PDIF In (RCA)	S/PDIF In (RCA)	S/PDIF In (RCA)	S/PDIF In (RCA)
	Optical Out (TOSLink)			Optical In (TOSLink)		Optical In (TOSLink)
	Optical Out (TOSLink)			Optical In (TOSLink)		Optical In (TOSLink)

Tape Players

In our increasingly digital world, tape players are generally considered obsolete. However, with billions of cassette tapes sold in the past decades, many still own them. Wouldn't it be great to transfer them to digital form with the Live! and maybe keep them in MP3 or CD audio format to enhance their longevity?

Tape players are analog beasts through and through. Expect to find line-level RCA input and output jacks on a tape deck. A stereo mini-jack–to–RCA cable will come in handy if you want to record from the Line Out of the Live! to a tape deck, or if you want to play back or record the tape deck's sound with the Live!

Portable tape players seldom come with line outputs, but it is still possible to use the amplified headphone output if the volume is turned low enough. Set the volume to its minimum level and slowly increase it both on the player and the mixer until it is at a level that is high enough, but does not cause the sound to crackle through the speakers.

Many portable tape recorders come with only a mic input, so it is not possible to feed the line-level output from the Live! to such recorders to record audio from the sound card. The sound will be distorted due to the extra amplification performed on low-level analog signals from microphones.

Table 5.5: Connections for Tape Players

Purpose	Jacks on a Tape Player/Recorder	Sound Blaster Live!	Optical Digital I/O Card with DIO Module	Live!Drive	Live!Drive II and Live!Drive IR
Playback	Line Out (stereo RCA jacks)	Line In (stereo mini-jack)	Line In 2 (stereo mini-jack)	Line In 2 (stereo 1/4-inch jack)	Line In 2 (stereo 1/4-inch jack) Aux In 2 (stereo RCA jacks)
	Headphone Out (stereo mini-jack)*	Line In (stereo mini-jack)	Line In 2 (stereo mini-jack)	Line In 2 (stereo 1/4-inch jack)	Line In 2 (stereo 1/4-inch jack) Aux In 2 (stereo RCA jacks)
Recording	Line In (stereo RCA jacks)	Line Out 1: Front or Line Out 2: Rear (stereo mini-jacks)			
	Line In (stereo mini-jack)**	Line Out 1: Front or Line Out 2: Rear (stereo mini-jacks)			

* Use this as a last resort only if your portable tape player does not have line outputs.

** Found on only a rare few portable tape recorders.

TV Sets and VCRs

Most TV sets and VCRs are either mono or stereo; they have one RCA jack for the input and output if they are mono, and two RCA jacks if they are stereo. To connect a mono output from a TV or VCR to the Live!, you will need a mono RCA–to–stereo mini-jack cable, which can be difficult to find.

Mono RCA–to–stereo RCA cables are more commonly available if you want to connect to the RCA inputs on the Live!Drive II or Live!Drive IR. Also, known as a Y-cable, it has a RCA plug at one end and splits into two RCA plugs at the other end. This allows a single RCA output to be available on two RCA plugs, allowing equipment with stereo RCA inputs (like the Aux In 2 on the Live!Drive II and Live!Drive IR, or any standard consumer hi-fi amplifier or receiver) to play mono audio sources on both speakers.

But that still leaves us with a problem of how we can connect to the mini-jack inputs on the Live! or the 1/4-inch jacks on a Live!Drive. You can make a custom cable for this purpose, or you can create a special cable by connecting a mono RCA–to–stereo RCA cable with a double female barrel connector and a stereo RCA–to–stereo mini-jack cable. You can add the mini-jack–to–1/4-inch jack adapter if you are using the 1/4-inch Line In 2 jacks on the Live!Drive.

Connecting TVs and VCRs with stereo outputs is easier. The usual RCA cables or stereo mini-jack–to–RCA cables are readily available in stores.

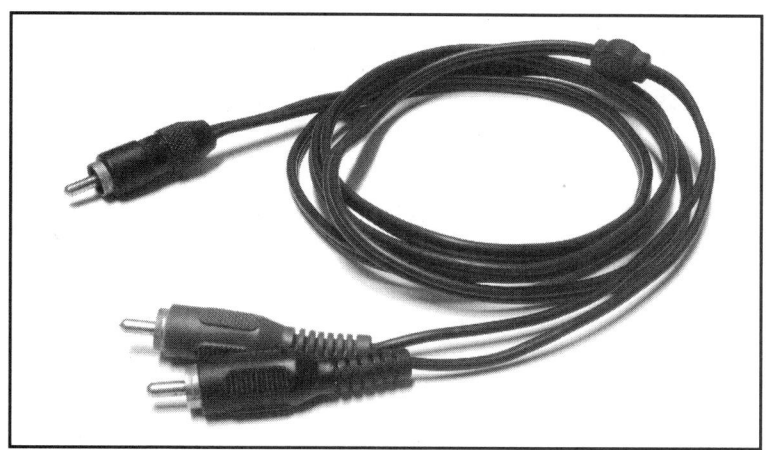

Figure 5.13: A mono RCA–to–stereo RCA cable

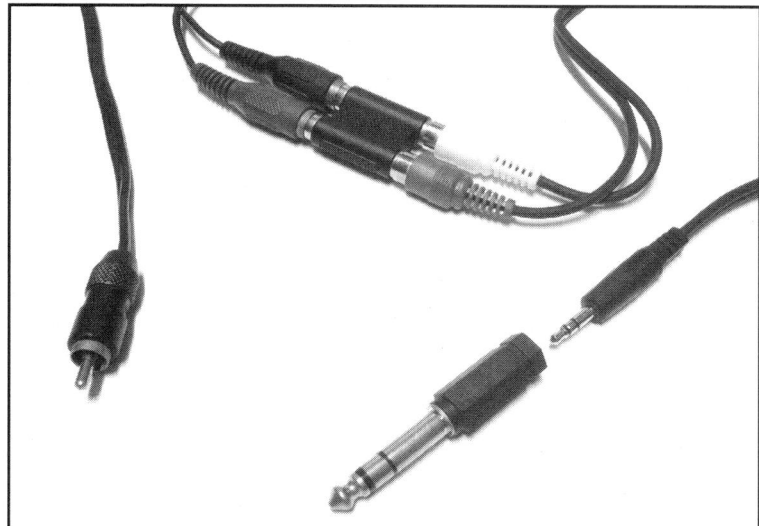

Figure 5.14: A mono RCA–to–stereo RCA cable is connected to a double female barrel connector, allowing a stereo RCA–to–stereo mini-jack cable to be connected. The mini-jack at the end of the cable can be connected to the Live!'s Line In, so that a mono output can be heard on both speakers. If you own a Live!Drive, a mini-jack–to–1/4-inch jack adapter can be snapped on to the mini-jack to allow it to be connected to the 1/4-inch Line In 2.

Table 5.6: Connections for TVs and VCRs

Purpose	Jacks on a TV/VCR	Sound Blaster Live!	Optical Digital I/O Card with DIO Module	Live!Drive	Live!Drive II and Live!Drive IR
Mono Output	Line Out (mono RCA jack)	Line In (stereo mini-jack)	Line In 2 (stereo mini-jack)	Line In 2 (stereo 1/4-inch jack)	Line In 2 (stereo 1/4-inch jack) Aux In 2 (stereo RCA jacks)
Mono Input	Line In (mono RCA jack)	Line Out 1: Front or Line Out 2: Rear (stereo mini-jacks)			
Stereo Output	Line Out (stereo RCA jacks)	Line In (stereo mini-jack)	Line In 2 (stereo mini-jack)	Line In 2 (stereo 1/4-inch jack)	Line In 2 (stereo 1/4-inch jack) Aux In 2 (stereo RCA jacks)
Stereo Input	Line In (stereo RCA jacks)	Line Out 1: Front or Line Out 2: Rear (stereo mini-jacks)			

TIP *You can connect the Live! card's output to a TV's audio inputs, but we do not recommend that because most TV speakers sound really bad. Instead, the audio outputs of TVs and VCRs should go to the sound card to be played back on the connected speakers. With a multichannel speaker system, you can even use CMSS to get surround sound from normal stereo sound sources.*

Satellite and Cable Receivers

Some older satellite and cable services use primarily analog audio, but digital is increasingly being adopted because of its high-quality video and multichannel audio capability. A majority of the receivers have RCA outputs so they are compatible with most TVs and AV receivers. Some older cable services provide only mono outputs, so you'll need to use the same methods described earlier in the TV and VCR sections to connect them. Digital satellite and cable services also provide coaxial and/or optical outputs on their receivers.

Remember that the Live! is able to input and play back only uncompressed PCM audio through the digital inputs, and not Dolby Digital audio that some networks use. A Dolby Digital signal needs to be connected directly to an AV receiver that has a Dolby Digital decoder built in. If you have the Live! card's digital outputs connected to an AV receiver and there are no more digital inputs left, you can enable the S/PDIF bypass for the Optical Digital I/O Card and the Live!Drive. (See Chapter 4, "Accessories Galore!" for information on S/PDIF bypass.)

Table 5.7: Connections for Satellite and Cable Receivers

Purpose	Jacks on a Satellite or Cable Receiver	Sound Blaster Live!	Digital I/O Card (CT4660)	Optical Digital I/O Card with DIO Module	Live!Drive	Live!Drive II and Live!Drive IR
Analog Playback	Line Out (stereo RCA jacks)	Line In (stereo mini-jack)		Line In 2 (stereo mini-jack)	Line In 2 (stereo 1/4-inch jack)	Line In 2 (stereo 1/4-inch jack) Aux In 2 (stereo RCA jacks)
	Line Out (mono RCA jacks)	Line In (stereo mini-jack)		Line In 2 (stereo mini-jack)	Line In 2 (stereo 1/4-inch jack)	Line In 2 (stereo 1/4-inch jack) Aux In 2 (stereo RCA jacks)
Digital Playback*	Coaxial Out (stereo RCA jacks)		S/PDIF In (RCA)	S/PDIF In (RCA)	S/PDIF In (RCA)	S/PDIF In (RCA)
	Optical Out (TOSLink)			Optical In (TOSLink)		Optical In (TOSLink)

* Make sure the digital outputs are S/PDIF and not Dolby Digital. The Live! cannot accept a Dolby Digital signal.

MiniDisc, DAT, and Other Digital Recorders

Note the issues mentioned earlier in the section "Digital Input Specifications." Because the Live! can output digital audio only at a 16-bit 48 kHz, you need to ensure that your digital recorder can accept digital audio at this sample rate. When recording from a MiniDisc, DAT, or other digital recorder, make sure the recorder outputs S/PDIF with a 16-bit sample size and uses a sample rate of 32 kHz, 44.1 kHz or 48 kHz. Most MD recorders have optical connectors, and a smaller number, notably high-end deck models, also have coaxial jacks. RCA coaxial connectors are the norm for DAT decks, and portable DAT recorders use the less common mini-jack coaxial connectors.

> Do not be alarmed because the Live! outputs at 16 bits and some MiniDisc recorders, such as those from Sharp, are advertised to have "24-bit recording." This only means that the recorder performs MiniDisc's ATRAC compression at 24 bits; the data will be converted to 16 bits when the audio is written to the MD and when the recorded MD is played back. The quality of MD depends on the ATRAC implementation in the MD recorder, and increasing the sample size headroom while performing compression is one way to yield better accuracy and audio quality but MD devices still interface in 16-bit sample sizes.

> Most portable MiniDisc players are meant to be used on the go; therefore, they have only mini-jack headphone outputs. Digital and line outputs are usually not provided.

Almost all of these digital recorders have analog inputs and outputs to let them work with analog sound sources, which are still widely used today. The deck-sized home versions normally sport RCA jacks, whereas portable devices use mini-jacks. Most portable MD recorders have mini-jack line inputs that also work as a mini-jack optical input but do not have any analog line-level or digital outputs; they have only headphone outputs.

However, some manufacturers have realized this shortcoming, and some recent models do include an internal software switch that disables the headphone preamp to change the headphone output to a line output. You can connect a headphone output to a line input on the Live! but, as always, be careful not to set the volume too high, or damage may result.

> At the time of writing, there is only one portable MD recorder from Sony that does not support analog recording. Most provide microphone and line inputs. MDs are popular because they are easy to use, and tracks can be erased, reordered, and rerecorded over and over again.

Table 5.8: Connections for Digital Recorders

Purpose	Jacks on Digital Recorders	Sound Blaster Live!	Digital I/O Card (CT4660)	Optical Digital I/O Card with DIO Module	Live!Drive	Live!Drive II and Live!Drive IR
Analog Playback	Line Out (stereo RCA jacks)	Line In (stereo mini-jack)		Line In 2 (stereo mini-jack)	Line In 2 (stereo 1/4-inch jack)	Line In 2 (stereo 1/4-inch jack) Aux In 2 (stereo RCA jacks)
	Line Out (stereo RCA jack)	Line In (stereo mini-jack)		Line In 2 (stereo mini-jack)	Line In 2 (stereo 1/4-inch jack)	Line In 2 (stereo 1/4-inch jack) Aux In 2 (stereo RCA jacks)
Analog Recording	Line In (stereo RCA jacks)	Line Out 1: Front or Line Out 2: Rear (stereo mini-jacks)				

Table 5.8: Connections for Digital Recorders (continued)

Purpose	Jacks on Digital Recorders	Sound Blaster Live!	Digital I/O Card (CT4660)	Optical Digital I/O Card with DIO Module	Live!Drive	Live!Drive II and Live!Drive IR
	Line In (stereo mini-jack)	Line Out 1: Front or Line Out 2: Rear (stereo mini-jacks)				
Digital Playback*	Coaxial Out (stereo RCA jacks)	S/PDIF In (RCA)	S/PDIF In (RCA)	S/PDIF In (RCA)	S/PDIF In (RCA)	
	Coaxial Out (mini-jack)*	S/PDIF In (RCA)	S/PDIF In (RCA)	S/PDIF In (RCA)	S/PDIF In (RCA)	
	Optical Out (TOSLink)			Optical In (TOSLink)		Optical In (TOSLink)
	Optical Out (mini-jack)			Optical In (TOSLink)		Optical In (TOSLink)
Digital Recording	Coaxial In (stereo RCA jacks)	S/PDIF Out (RCA)	S/PDIF Out (RCA)	S/PDIF Out (RCA)	S/PDIF Out (RCA)	
	Coaxial In (mini-jack)*	S/PDIF Out (RCA)	S/PDIF Out (RCA)	S/PDIF Out (RCA)	S/PDIF Out (RCA)	
	Optical In (TOSLink)			Optical Out (TOSLink)		Optical Out (TOSLink)
	Optical In (mini-jack)			Optical Out (TOSLink)		Optical Out (TOSLink)

* This connector is rare except on some portable DAT and DCC recorders.

DVD Players

Like other digital audio devices, DVDs store data digitally, but for compatibility, they do provide analog outputs in the form of line-level RCA jacks. These will connect to stereo TVs and hi-fi sets. However, to take full advantage of DVD players and the superior surround sound of DVD movies, you should purchase a speaker or AV system that is capable of decoding Dolby Digital and the increasingly popular DTS surround sound formats that the DVD player provides through its coaxial or optical outputs. Turn to Chapter 11, "Watching Movies," for coverage of this topic in greater detail.

Table 5.9: Connections for DVD Players

Purpose	Jacks on a DVD Player	Sound Blaster Live!	Digital I/O Card (CT4660)	Optical Digital I/O Card with DIO Module	Live!Drive	Live!Drive II and Live!Drive IR
Analog Playback (stereo)	Line Out (stereo RCA jacks)	Line In (stereo mini-jack)		Line In 2 (stereo mini-jack)	Line In 2 (stereo 1/4-inch jack)	Line In 2 (stereo 1/4-inch jack) Aux In 2 (stereo RCA jacks)
Digital Surround-Sound Playback*	Coaxial Out (stereo RCA jacks)		S/PDIF In (RCA)	S/PDIF In (RCA)	S/PDIF In (RCA)	S/PDIF In (RCA)
	Optical Out (TOSLink)*			Optical In (TOSLink)		Optical In (TOSLink)

* The Live! does not support compressed surround sound formats like Dolby Digital or DTS on its S/PDIF (coaxial or optical) inputs. There will be no sound if these signals are fed into the Live! However, CDs or other stereo PCM audio tracks recorded on DVD (some concert and music DVDs) played on DVD players can still be heard when output to the Live!

MP3 Players

Most MP3 players are portable devices; hence, most have only amplified headphone outputs. A few models do have line outputs, so this should be used if it is available. Digital I/O is rarely found on MP3 players because they rely on parallel or USB connections to the PC to transfer MP3 audio directly to the on-board memory. A few players, such as Creative's Nomad Jukebox, can record audio through provided mini-jack line inputs, and some other players can also do voice recording with a built-in microphone.

You may want to have a cable with a mini-jack–to–mini-jack cable permanently connected to the Live! card's line inputs so that when you are at your PC, you can quickly hook up your MP3 player through the Live! for playback. A few players also come with a dock or cradle that has line outputs that can be permanently connected to the Live! or an audio system. You can listen to the MP3 player by placing it in the dock.

As with most portable players, if your MP3 player has only headphone outputs, you can still connect it to the Live!, but make sure the volume is turned down low initially while you increase the volume gradually to obtain a distortion-free volume level through the line inputs of the Live!

Table 5.10: Connections for MP3 Players

Purpose	Jacks on a MP3 Player	Sound Blaster Live!	Optical Digital I/O Card with DIO Module	Live!Drive	Live!Drive II and Live!Drive IR
Analog Playback	Line Out (stereo RCA jacks)	Line In (stereo mini-jack)	Line In 2 (stereo mini-jack)	Line In 2 (stereo 1/4-inch jack)	Line In 2 (stereo 1/4-inch jack) Aux In 2 (stereo RCA jacks)
	Line Out (stereo mini-jack)	Line In (stereo mini-jack)	Line In 2 (stereo mini-jack)	Line In 2 (stereo 1/4-inch jack)	Line In 2 (stereo 1/4-inch jack) Aux In 2 (stereo RCA jacks)

Headphones

Headphones are great for private music listening and multiplayer gaming during the wee hours of the night. They come in all shapes and sizes, but as we all know, the jacks on them are standard, allowing them to be used for different brands of audio equipment.

Headphones are available for mini-jacks and 1/4-inch jacks. The smaller in-ear type of earphones usually use the mini-jacks. Many large headphones use 1/4-inch jacks, but an increasing trend is to provide a mini-jack and bundle a mini-jack–to–1/4-inch jack adapter to allow the buyer to use it on all possible headphone outputs available on audio equipment on the market. Although they are less common, 1/4-inch–to–mini-jack adapters can also be used to convert 1/4-inch jacks to mini-jacks.

The specification of the Live! state that the front line output supports a 32-ohm load, which basically means that the Line Out 1 (Front) connector is designed to support the higher power required by headphones, but not the Line Out 2 (rear) connector. The Live!Drive has a 1/4-inch headphone output that can automatically mute the speakers when used. A volume control knob on the Live!Drive allows quick volume control.

Certain high-end headphones require tremendous power to drive them and will sound very soft and weak even when the volume of the sound source and the master volume control is set to maximum in the Live!'s mixer. For such headphones, you should use a headphone amplifier that is specifically designed to provide greater amplification.

Table 5.11: Connections for Headphones

Headphone Plugs	Sound Blaster Live!*	Live!Drive, Live!Drive II, and Live!Drive IR
Stereo 1/4-inch Jack	Line Out 1: Front (stereo mini-jack)	Headphone Out (stereo 1/4-inch jack)
Stereo Mini-jack	Line Out 1: Front (stereo mini-jack)	Headphone Out (stereo 1/4-inch jack)

* Do not use Line Out 2 (rear) to connect to headphones, as this output is not designed for the loads and power that headphones require.

Microphones

The world of microphones is particularly confusing due to the different techniques used to make them and the different power requirements. Microphones are also known technically as *transducers*, because they convert a signal from one medium to another—in this case, from sound waves, such as the vibrations in the air caused by your voice to equivalent electrical signals that can be transmitted across wires. In fact, if you think about it, this is what speakers do, too, but in reverse.

How do vocalists sound so good on their recordings? Clever use of microphones is a critical part of the process, because a well-chosen vocal microphone can make a singer's voice sound warmer and have more presence. There are all sorts of microphones, with different tonal characteristics and different *directions* of pickup. Some can pick up sound in all directions (omnidirectional microphones), while others are less sensitive to sound from the rear and sides (directional) and are great for applications where the majority of the sound that needs to be captured comes from a particular direction, as in videoconferencing, where all you want is voice and not other noise in the surrounding environment.

Different microphones are also constructed differently. There are generally two types of microphones: *condenser* (also sometimes called *electret*) and *dynamic* microphones. Dynamic microphones are sometimes preferred because they can color sound to make it more pleasant, making these microphones great for recording acoustic musical instruments. Condenser microphones usually capture sound more accurately and in a wider frequency range than dynamic microphones; they are available in a variety of qualities and prices, ranging from a few dollars to thousands of dollars. Most small multimedia microphones, like the Telex microphone included with some Live! products, are usually low-cost condenser microphones with a limited frequency range.

The important thing to know is that microphones have a very weak power output that is much lower than line level. Usually, a preamp is needed to boost these levels to make sound audible. The Live!'s microphone input has a preamp built in, and if you find that the level from the microphone is too low, you can set the mixer to give it a 20-dB boost. This is especially useful for professional microphones, which sometimes put out a signal that is much weaker than that of typical microphones. However, note that boosting the microphone inputs will also boost the noise that is induced or picked up by the microphone. If all else fails and the volume is still too low, you may need a dedicated mic preamp to make full use of the microphone. In any case, with an expensive professional microphone, you will almost always find it necessary to pair the microphone with a good mic preamp for the best results.

Condenser microphones require a power source to operate. On the Live! and Live!Drive, this is usually supplied through the microphone cable itself. This approach works well with common multimedia microphones and headsets used for Internet telephony.

> **TIP** *Headsets are considered two devices in one — a combination of a headphone and microphone — becausee they need an audio output from the sound card and send audio from the microphone to the sound card. The volume of the output and microphone recording slider has to be set individually for optimum performance.*

Because of the way they work, dynamic microphones do not require power, but the outputs are usually lower than for condenser microphones, so more amplification is required. An advantage to this is that the microphone can capture a wider range of volumes. A loud sound may cause distortion in a condenser microphone, while a dynamic microphone may be able to handle the same sound without problems.

A dynamic microphone connected to a Live! may be too soft even when you turn it to maximum volume in the mixer and scream into the microphone; in this case, you should connect the microphone to an external preamp, which will amplify the recorded sound before passing it to the Live!

> On some Live!Drive models, such as the first Live!Drive, you can add a jumper to enable dynamic microphone support in the Mic In 2/Line In 2 connector. See Chapter 4, "Accessories Galore!" for more information and pictures on the jumper.

If you want to record high-quality audio such as vocals or musical instruments to be mixed into your own music compositions or other audio projects, a mic preamp is definitely a must. The line-level outputs of the preamp will connect to the line inputs available on the Live! or an attached digital I/O device. An even better approach is to locate the microphones and recording gear, such as amplifiers and mic preamps, away from the noisy PC environment and pass the audio from the microphone to the Live! via the digital inputs.

> All the microphone inputs on the Live! and Live!Drive are mono, and both the left and right speakers output the same sound obtained from the microphone.

Microphones that need power, such as most multimedia and videoconferencing microphones for the PC, also make use of the tip, ring, sleeve configuration. The tip carries the microphone audio signal, the ring provides the power from the Live!, and the sleeve is for grounding. Microphones that have mono plugs would probably be dynamic microphones because they do not need the power line.

Table 5.12: Connections for Microphones

Microphone Plugs	Sound Blaster Live!	Live!Drive, Live!Drive II, and Live!Drive IR
1/4-inch Jack	Mic In (mono mini-jack)	Mic In 2 (mono 1/4-inch jack)
Mini-jack	Mic In (mono mini-jack)	Mic In 2 (mono 1/4-inch jack)

> The Live! does not support stereo microphones. All the mic inputs on the Live! and Live!Drive are mono.

Connecting More Devices

If the Live! with an attached digital I/O device is still unable to provide all the connections and inputs that you need for your audio equipment, there are several alternatives. You can purchase an audio or AV switch that allows you to connect a few devices to the switch, and you can select which device the switch will output to the Live! If you have an old hi-fi or amplifier lying around with several inputs, you can use it as a switch, as well.

Alternatively, if you prefer all your sound sources to be mixed together, as they are on the Live!'s mixer, instead of being able to listen to only one sound source at a time, you can purchase a hardware mixer, commonly available in stores that sell electronic musical instruments.

6

SPEAKERS

Selecting the best sound card is the first step to great PC audio, but do not overlook the importance of speakers; they can make or break your resulting audio experience. Audiophiles spend years, and lots of money, in pursuit of the ultimate audio experience, and they know very well that the choice and correct combination of speakers, amplifiers, and audio playback equipment can make or break the pristine sound quality provided by any sound source.

TIP *Don't expect the Live! to sound alive if the speakers are not up to scratch!*

In the early days when sound cards were just beginning their journey toward becoming an essential peripheral in the PC, cheap multimedia speakers were all the rage. They had limited frequency ranges and an utter lack of bass that would make any serious multimedia enthusiast cringe. Fortunately, the multimedia speakers of today come in multichannel configurations and sport bass-pumping subwoofers that can literally rock the house. Thanks to the increasing quality of sound cards in recent years and the availability of digital I/O for pristine audio transmission, the PC has become a home entertainment machine—but, of course, only with the right speakers!

Speakers: The Key to What You Hear

Speakers come in all shapes and sizes. There are full-range speakers—the big rectangular boxes that have two or more speaker drivers. They can be a few feet in height, or they can be the floor-standing variety that can be taller than you. The smaller bookshelf and satellite speakers are great space savers, and when paired with a subwoofer, can become a capable home theater system.

Take a look inside a speaker and you'll see that it includes one or more speaker drivers. The drivers use the sound energy provided by an amplifier to vibrate air particles and create sound. Each driver is tasked to reproduce audio in a certain frequency band, and the drivers work together to collectively reproduce a broader frequency range than each driver would be capable of reproducing on its own. This is similar in concept to work allocation in the physical world. If a particular amount of work is assigned to more people, each individual will have a lighter load, and can therefore concentrate on and perform better at that task than if one person handles the entire job.

The human ear can usually detect sounds from 20 Hz to 20 kHz (although this range narrows as people age), but due to design and physical limitations, most speakers do not cover this frequency range entirely. For example, a speaker may go down to only 50 Hz and hit 18 kHz at the high end. Therefore, purchasing the right speakers and matching them to the correct subwoofers is necessary to ensure a smooth response across the entire frequency range.

Different types of speaker drivers are used to reproduce sound in different frequency bands. A subwoofer provides the deep vibrations that are felt as much as heard. The woofer handles the bass, while midrange drivers reproduce sounds such as vocals. Tweeters are responsible for treble, which is at the higher end of our hearing range.

There is a correlation between the size of the driver and the audio frequencies it can reproduce. Consider this example: A bee can move its tiny wings very rapidly, and this allows it to push enough air to keep aloft. This results in the high-pitched buzz that we hear. On the other hand, an eagle requires much more energy to move its wings, and it does so at a slower pace than a bee because it can push more air. The resulting sound from an eagle is a lower-pitched and slower flapping sound.

Subwoofer drivers are huge because of the amount of air they need to displace to produce the deep vibrations required. On the other extreme, tweeters are small because they need to move in and out 20,000 times a second. By making them small, less energy is required to move the driver, making it easier for them to move 20,000 times a second (20,000 Hz or 20 kHz) than if large drivers were used. Woofers move fewer times a second because they reproduce bass in tens or hundreds of cycles a second. For example, the lower end of our hearing is 20 Hz, which is only 20 times a second. This causes less excitement of air particles, so to make bass effective at such slow movement rates, woofers need to move in and out farther than do tweeters, to displace more air. (This movement of speaker drivers is also known as *excursion*.) Because of the number of cycles a driver is required to move, you won't be able to notice a tweeter vibrating because it is too fast for the eye, but you can definitely see a woofer vibrating.

> A single speaker driver will not be able to reproduce the entire frequency range because of the high power output required to produce vibrations in the air. Therefore, at least two drivers are required to reproduce an adequate frequency range. This is unlike headphone drivers, which use one small driver for the entire frequency range because they need to output at only low volumes in our ears to be heard.

Advancements in technology have made satellite speakers possible. These small, inconspicuous speakers are housed in tiny cubes and produce crisp, clear sound. With the aid of a subwoofer to reproduce the lower bass frequencies, satellite speaker systems have become very popular for PC audio. They can fit in many small homes and tight corners because of the small footprint, and the subwoofer can be tucked away from sight. Satellite speakers are also available for home theater systems, and home theater retailers also stock a wide range of satellite speakers, including in-wall designs that fit inside a wall to allow a home theater system to blend with a home's décor.

The Surround Era

Stereo has served us well for music and is a huge step up from the monaural sound used in the early days. Since then, the popularity of home video and the proliferation of Dolby Surround has brought the cinema into the home, and the term *home theater* was born. With the five-speaker setup of a home theater, we hear not only sounds directed from the front by the left and right speakers, but also screen-specific audio and dialogue from a center speaker, and surround sound effects and ambience with surround speakers to the sides or behind us. Many surveys and listening tests have shown that the number of speakers and the use of surround sound increases the emotional impact and overall perceived quality of a movie.

Sound card makers brought the multichannel concept to the PC by introducing 4- and 5.1-channel support on their sound cards. This technology has taken the market by storm. Today, many hard-core gamers and PC enthusiasts insist on multichannel sound systems for their PCs. The multimedia speaker industry also took notice of this change from stereo to multichannel speakers, and many 4.1 and 5.1 speakers now vie for a place beside your PC.

> The dot method of representing channel configuration, for instance, 5.1, traditionally applies to surround formats, but some have also been using them to describe speaker configuration, especially for multimedia speakers. In speaker systems, the *.1* suggests the presence of a separate woofer unit, while *.0* indicates that there is none. The number before the decimal point indicates the number of speakers in the main channels. These are typically 2 for stereo systems, 4 for four-point speakers, and 5 for a full surround speaker configuration including a center speaker.

Stereo Systems

Stereo audio systems have been with us for a long time. They come in all shapes and sizes, but the common characteristic among them is that they have two speakers to reproduce stereo audio found on everything from radio broadcasts to cassette tapes and compact discs.

> The only pervasive applications of mono sound are television broadcasts and mono VCRs. Many broadcasters in some countries still provide only mono sound for their programs. Even then, as you learned in the previous chapter, with the right cable you can connect mono sound sources to stereo systems and the Live!

Minicomponent Systems

Minicomponent systems with an integrated tape deck, radio tuner, and CD player are very popular among consumers because of their large feature set and affordable prices. They are very consumer oriented and boast radical designs, with flashy graphic equalizers and colorful fluorescent displays. The greatest benefit of minicomponent systems is the high level of integration among the different functions. This makes it easy to make recordings and dubs: for example, to dub a CD to tape. Users can easily control all the functions from a single remote control.

In the past, many minicomponent systems had very bad sound and an overemphasis on bass and treble—things that might easily wow an uninformed consumer. However, more and more models today, especially those from high-end audio manufacturers, offer very respectable performance and great value and would be ideal companions for sound cards.

Hi-Fi Systems

For the more discerning, a separate hi-fi system with different decks (for instance, a CD player deck and an amplifier deck) performing different functions has appeal. Each deck can be from a different manufacturer, so such a setup is perfect for enthusiasts and audiophiles, who tend to prefer to mix and match different brands of equipment and cables for the best possible sound. The integrated amplifier unit has the important task of consolidating and allowing users to switch among the various input and output of audio and AV equipment. Analog RCA cables are commonly used to connect playback equipment to the amplifier. Hi-fi systems are primarily used for music playback, and when properly assembled, they can sound very good.

Why Stereo Systems?

If you primarily listen to music on the PC, a stereo system makes an ideal speaker system for the Live! However, most stereo systems are just that—stereo—so you can't take advantage of the Live!'s multichannel and 3D positioning capabilities. Then again, if you use the sound card for simple audio tasks such as playing MP3s and streaming audio, you can't go wrong with such a setup. If you are interested in exploring the possibility of having more speakers, read on!

Multimedia Speakers

Multimedia speakers were made when music cards and sound cards rose in popularity. Simplicity in design was key because manufacturers wanted to push prices down. Unlike the speakers for consumer audio and hi-fi systems, multimedia speakers are much simpler in design. The required amplification circuitry is usually hidden in one of the speaker cabinets, reducing the space requirements on a computer desk. Fancy equalizer displays, built-in CD players, and dozens of knobs and buttons are seldom seen.

2.0: Two Speakers

In the early days of the sound card, tiny multimedia speakers were sufficient for most needs because sound cards did not have the audio quality of consumer CD players, and many were affected by computer noise. The 8-bit limit on Wave playback caused these sound cards to sound less dynamic and clear compared to a good hi-fi system, so very simple speakers usually sufficed.

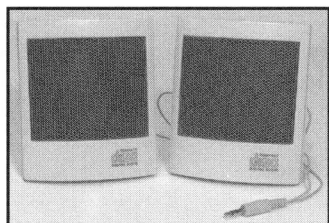

Figure 6.1: Unpowered multimedia speakers

These multimedia speakers are either unpowered, requiring connection to amplified headphone outputs of the sound card (which most sound cards today do not have), or they require power from batteries or a DC adapter. They have limited bass output because of the lack of a woofer unit. To be immersed in the

CD-quality audio that the Live! is capable or producing, you shouldn't use such speakers unless you have a serious space constraint or you use the Live! in an office or with headphones and don't need speakers very often.

2.1: Two Speakers and a Subwoofer

Fortunately, with the increasing audio quality of sound cards like the Live!, speaker options are much more appealing. The multimedia speaker has evolved into a powerful beast, boasting subwoofers and clear, crisp sound at an affordable price — so affordable that many people use multimedia speakers as their primary audio system.

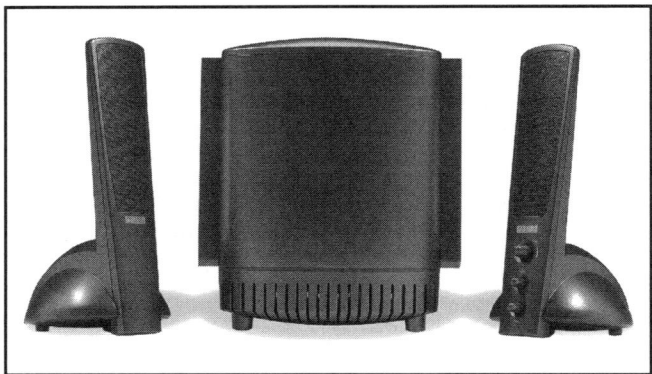

Figure 6.2: The Altec Lansing ATP3 2.1 multimedia speaker system

A majority of multimedia speakers come in a 2.1 design that includes small satellite speakers for the left and right channels for easy placement on a computer desk. The subwoofer unit typically incorporates the woofer speaker driver for bass reproduction, the amplification unit, and the connectors to the sound card. The volume control is usually found on a wired remote, along with some balance control, and, at times, a headphone jack.

A 2.1 speaker system is perfect if you primarily play music, surf the Internet on your PC, and use office or productivity applications. You also will not need anything more than stereo support from the Live! if you do not play games or watch DVDs often.

4.1: Four Speakers and a Subwoofer

But, of course, the hard-core PC audio enthusiast and gamer would not settle for just two speakers! Before multichannel multimedia speakers were widely available, owners of four-channel sound cards had to pair two sets of stereo speaker systems together to play back the four channels of audio from the sound card. This made common tasks extremely troublesome, such as simultaneous adjustment of the volumes of all four speakers, ensuring that the volume from each speaker is similar, and turning the speaker on and off.

When the Live! was introduced, Cambridge SoundWorks (Creative's speaker subsidiary) adapted its popular PC Works speaker design to produce the first four-channel multimedia speaker system: the Cambridge SoundWorks FourPointSurround FPS1000. These 4.1 speakers were very inexpensive, not costing much more then their 2.1 counterparts.

The quality difference in 4.1 multimedia speakers can be wide ranging, depending on the speaker design and the ability of the manufacturer to maximize the performance of the design and at the same time make the product cost effective.

Figure 6.3: Cambridge SoundWorks FourPointSurround FPS1000

> Many four-channel multimedia speakers will automatically duplicate the sound on the front speakers to the rear speakers, if only the front line input is used.

The cheaper models sometimes lack low bass because of their smaller and less powerful subwoofer and amplification units. Sometimes, the satellites that produce the higher treble sounds may lack sparkle or sound metallic. Midrange frequencies as in vocals may sound thin if the satellites are poorly designed.

As the price increases, the specifications and power handling of 4.1 speakers generally improve. The bass is deeper and more robust, and the treble is clear, crisp, and warm sounding. Manufacturers like Klipsch and VideoLogic produce very good sounding multimedia speakers for consumers who expect nothing less than the best. Klipsch even had its speakers THX certified for quality and sound.

> DVDs can also be played on 4.1 speakers by using a software DVD player and selecting the four-speaker mode to allow the surround channels of a Dolby Digital track to be sent to the rear speakers. Find out more about this in Chapter 11, "Watching Movies."

Figure 6.4: Speakers like the Klipsch ProMedia 4.1 are for PC audio enthusiasts who want nothing less than the best

Because of the wide range of speakers available, you should listen to speakers before buying to determine what level of performance and quality is satisfactory for you.

5.1: Four Speakers, a Subwoofer, and a Center Speaker

There are two main types of 5.1 multimedia speakers available for 5.1 sound cards. The more affordable ones, which do not come with surround decoding, are perfect for sound cards that have built-in Dolby Digital decoding for DVD playback, like the Live! 5.1. The costlier 5.1 speakers have Dolby Digital or DTS decoding capability built in to the hardware and function like miniature home theater systems.

In 2000, sound card manufacturers noticed the popularity of DVD movies on the PC and decided to improve the four-channel design by adding another stereo output for the center and subwoofer channels. This enables the sound card to support the 5.1 configuration of a typical Dolby Digital and DTS home theater system. In the same year, Creative updated the Live! products to support six-channel outputs and Dolby Digital 5.1 decoding.

When used with an appropriate software DVD player and a DVD-ROM drive, the Live! can take the six channels of compressed audio from a Dolby Digital 5.1 soundtrack and decode them to six separate analog signals. These signals are then sent to an analog 5.1 speaker system with the Live! card's analog outputs. This is a great money saver for consumers because people can now use their CPUs, a DVD-ROM drive, an affordable analog 5.1 speaker system, and the Live! 5.1 card to play DVDs on the PC in full Dolby Digital surround sound that otherwise requires more expensive decoder hardware such as a Dolby Digital AV receiver.

Analog 5.1 speakers are built like their 4.1 counterparts, the only difference being the addition of a center and subwoofer input and a physical center speaker. Like 4.1 speakers, they depend on the sound card provide the six channels of audio and do not perform any Dolby Digital decoding.

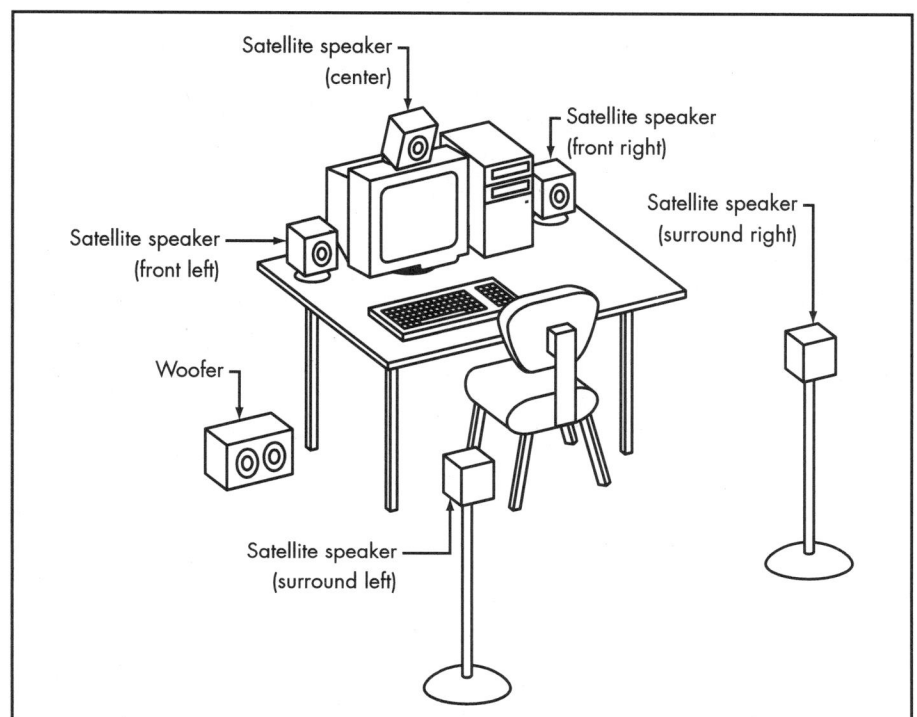

Figure 6.5: A 5.1 PC audio setup

Figure 6.6: The VideoLogic ZXR-500 has six-channel (5.1) analog inputs that connect to 5.1 sound cards like the Live! 5.1

Figure 6.7: The three mini-jack 5.1 inputs on an analog 5.1 multimedia speaker system

The 5.1 multimedia speaker systems with built-in decoders were introduced when earlier sound cards could not decode Dolby Digital by themselves and required external decoders. These speaker systems are made for users to connect to a sound card or DVD/MPEG-2 decoder card that can output a compressed Dolby Digital signal.

When playing back DVDs entirely on the PC became possible, these 5.1 multimedia speakers with decoders became more popular as affordable home theater systems for dormitory rooms and other small spaces, rather than for PCs. Manufacturers responded with new consumer features like DTS decoding, consumer DVD player connectivity, and infrared remote control capability, while maintaining the features that allow these speakers to be connected to sound cards.

> As with stereo multimedia speakers, manufacturers of 4.1 and analog 5.1 speakers try to keep the amplification unit inside the subwoofer to preserve the space-saving qualities of multimedia speakers and keep costs down.

Figure 6.8: The Cambridge SoundWorks DTT3500 has inputs for sound cards, as well as an amplifier unit to decode surround sound from consumer digital audio equipment like DVD players

USB speakers

USB speakers make use of the USB connection and cannot be connected to the Live! or the audio outputs of other audio equipment. They appear to the operating system as sound card devices, and the computer sends digital audio signals to the speakers via the USB cable. The signals are converted to analog by a sound card–like DAC circuitry in the speaker unit and amplified for the speaker drivers. Because the Live! cannot use such speakers, you should purchase USB speakers only if you do not want to install a sound card or do not have access to the inside of the CPU casing: for example, if your PC at work is locked for security reasons.

Home Theater Systems

A home theater is the perfect means of bringing the cinema experience to the comfort of your own home, and the use of multichannel surround sound helps place viewers in the heat of the action. These systems normally come with five to seven main channels, and many also have a subwoofer unit to accentuate the deep rumbles and bass effects from high-quality audio sources such as laser discs (LDs) and DVDs.

If you are one of the lucky people who own a Live! 5.1 and have a home theater system near your PC, connecting the Live! to it is a definite plus because these systems are generally more powerful than multimedia speakers. Playing MP3s, and watching movie trailers and other media files would be a truly room-shaking experience. This is also a great option for users who want to play PC games on big-screen TVs with multichannel sound!

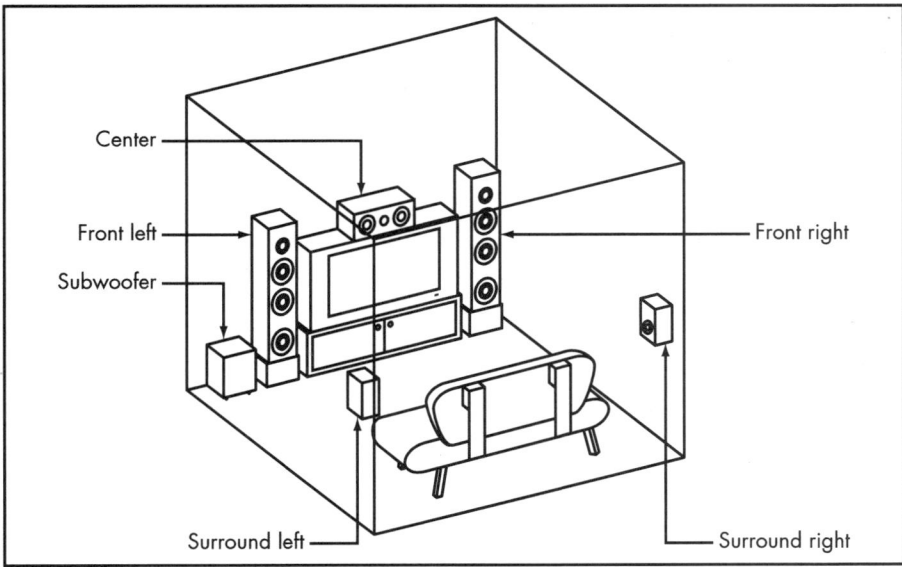

Figure 6.9: A 5.1 home theater system

> The AV receiver is the nerve center of a home theater system. It acts as a hub to accept multiple audio and video inputs from audiovisual (or audio-only) equipment and also allows the selection of the connected equipment to be heard on the speakers and played on the video device (direct-view TV, rear-projection TV, or front-projection screen) connected to the AV receiver. Integrated surround decoders allow them to recognize encoded surround soundtracks and play them back after amplifying audio sources to levels that are powerful enough to drive the speakers.

AV hardware comes in many different brands with different features and reproduction quality. AV receivers also differ in their decoding abilities. This directly affects the connection method and speaker mode that the Live! should be set to, so let's take a look at this aspect now.

You'll learn more about Dolby technologies and home theater sound in Chapter 11, "Watching Movies." For now, we'll concentrate on how to correctly connect the Live! to home theaters.

The Old Guard: Dolby Pro Logic Receivers

Dolby Pro Logic receivers decode the older Dolby Surround soundtracks, which are delivered over normal stereo audio sources. When the Live! is connected to a Pro Logic receiver, these prerecorded soundtracks can be converted into surround. The Pro Logic decoding can also be turned off on these receivers, so they can be used as stereo systems when surround sound is not needed.

Dolby Surround is an encoding method that mixes four channels into two channels for storage on media such as LDs and stereo TV broadcasts. Dolby Pro Logic is a decoding method that does the opposite: it extracts the four channels from the two stereo channels.

What about software such as games, for which the multichannel sound is not prerecorded but generated using 3D positioning APIs like DirectSound3D? Fear not; the Live! has a Live!Surround speaker mode that converts them into a Pro Logic–compatible signal output through the front channels of the Live! This allows receivers with Pro Logic decoders to be used as a speaker system for surround sound from the Live!

Unfortunately, there is a caveat. Because the surround channel of Pro Logic receivers is mono, sounds in that channel will be output on both surround speakers, so the positioning of sounds behind the listener will not be as accurate as surround channels that are stereo. (In discrete surround systems, such as a 4.1 multimedia speaker or Dolby Digital DVD playback, positioned sounds can appear to come from the rear left or rear right surround speakers independently because of the separate surround left and surround right channels.)

The Bridge: 5.1-Ready Receivers

In the mid-1990s, a new update to the aging Dolby Surround standard was announced as Dolby AC-3 (now known as Dolby Digital). It was a huge leap up from the limited two-channel delivery method used with Dolby Surround. The Dolby Digital format supports six individual speakers by carrying the audio for each of the six channels separately in digital form, but at that time, the home theater market was still dominated by Dolby Pro Logic equipment. Manufacturers wanted to continue selling Dolby Pro Logic products while waiting for the market to warm up to Dolby Digital and let the standard become more affordable before adopting it for low- to midrange consumer products.

To ensure that consumers could upgrade to Dolby Digital in the future, six analog inputs (for each of the speaker channels in a 5.1 setup) were added to the design of existing Pro Logic AV receivers. These receivers still supported only Pro Logic decoding (and not Dolby Digital decoding), but manufacturers tagged them as "Dolby Digital-ready" or "5.1-ready" to reflect their capability to take in six separate analog channels and feed them to each speaker individually—something older Dolby Pro Logic receivers could not do.

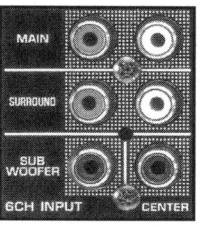

Figure 6.10: Six RCA inputs behind 5.1-ready AV receivers

The six inputs on a 5.1-ready decoder can be connected to any audio or AV equipment that can output six channels of audio corresponding to the front left, front right, center, rear left, rear right, and LFE/subwoofer channels in a typical 5.1 surround configuration. These include the following types of equipment:

- DVD players that have built-in Dolby Digital and/or DTS decoders, so they can convert the 5.1 sound in DVDs to six analog outputs that are connected to a 5.1-ready receiver.
- Dedicated surround decoders that support Dolby Digital and/or DTS decoding. These decoders take the compressed 5.1 signal (usually from a DVD player, LD player, or digital satellite box) and decode it into six analog outputs.
- 5.1 sound cards, like the Live! 5.1, which works in a similar way as DVD players with decoders and stand-alone surround decoders. The six channels are output via the three mini-jack line outputs on the card's backplate, for a total of six analog outputs.

> Many affordable DVD players save cost by not including Dolby Digital or DTS decoding features. These models can only output surround sound in its undecoded, compressed form, leaving the decoding task to external equipment like the AV receiver. If you have a Dolby Digital– and/or DTS-capable receiver or speakers, you won't need to spend extra money on a player with built-in surround decoding because you'll be using the one on your receiver or speaker system (unless the particular DVD player has excellent video quality or other features that you are looking for).

The Live! 5.1 cards support five-speaker output in DirectSound3D-supported games by taking the 3D positional sounds and spreading them across five speakers. The Live! 5.1 cards' Dolby Digital decoding feature built in to the drivers allows discrete six-channel analog outputs for surround sound.

> Dolby Digital can output up to six channels of audio, with five channels being full range and one channel that is limited in bandwidth because it carries only low bass information. Therefore, the bass channel is termed the *.1 channel*, and the entire Dolby Digital setup is known as *5.1*.

Do these 5.1-ready receivers seem to be similar to 5.1 multimedia speaker systems? You are right! Just like 5.1-ready receivers, 5.1 multimedia speaker systems also have six discrete analog inputs that accept audio from sources that have already decoded the sound into separate speakers. The only difference is the physical connectors used.

But what if your Live! is not a 5.1 model? The four-channel output from the first- and second-generation cards can still be connected to 5.1-ready receivers. You will need to leave out the center and woofer connections because the four-channel Live! cards do not provide them. Therefore, only the front left, front right, rear left, and rear right speakers will have sound. If your speaker system is configured to route bass from these speakers to the subwoofer, the subwoofer will also output bass. (Multimedia speakers and many AV receivers do this automatically.)

The Ultimate: Dolby Digital and DTS Receivers

We've come to the Holy Grail of home theater systems: discrete multichannel audio that eliminates all the problems of Dolby Surround in one fell swoop. Surround-encoded DVDs, not to mention the blockbuster sales of DVD players, are making such home theater systems a must. Everybody wants DVD!

Dolby Digital and DTS are two prominent surround sound encoding schemes found in DVDs today. They use different encoding algorithms, but are similar in speaker configuration. Both support discrete 5.1- and 6.1-channel surround sound, which are already widely used in soundtracks for cinema playback. Using digital cables, these AV receivers accept the compressed Dolby Digital or DTS signals from equipment like DVD players and satellite receivers, and decode them into six analog channels to be sent to each of the six speakers.

> Dolby and DTS updated their technologies to support extra surround channels for 6.1 and 7.1 speaker configurations. They have named the new systems Dolby Digital EX and DTS-ES, respectively. Some DVDs are encoded in such formats, and at the time of this writing, manufacturers have incorporated this advancement into high-end and midrange models. As costs fall, these enhancements may also be made available in budget home theater systems and multimedia speakers. Read more about this advancement in Chapter 11, "Watching Movies."

These digital inputs for Dolby Digital and DTS can also be connected to the Live! to receive Dolby Digital– and DTS-encoded signals when playing DVDs or AC-3 files with software DVD players that support the S/PDIF passthrough feature (described in Chapter 11, "Watching Movies"). Unfortunately, all other forms of audio output by the Live!, such as music playback and sound effects from games, cannot be in Dolby Digital or DTS format, so a digital connection to these receivers or decoders will yield only a standard stereo output. In such cases, turn on Live!Surround, and switch on Pro Logic decoding so that at least you get a surround effect when games use the 3D positioning of the Live!

> Surround-encoded signals take quite a bit of processing power to create; therefore, they are more commonly found on DVDs in their encoded form. Unfortunately, the EMU10K1 cannot encode and compress multiple audio channels into Dolby Digital or DTS signals in real time so that they can be sent to a digital surround–capable receiver or decoder.

> You can also find other audio equipment, like minicomponent systems, that come with a built-in DVD players and Dolby Digital decoding. However, they may not have six-channel discrete inputs for connecting to the Live! You would have to use Live!Surround mode to connect to such systems.

The only way to get four speakers (for first- and second-generation Live! cards) or 5.1 channels (for third-generation Live! 5.1 cards) of audio from games and other sounds on the PC is to use discrete connections with the line outputs on the Live!'s backplate, as described earlier in the section, "The Bridge: 5.1-Ready Receivers." Most Dolby Digital and DTS receivers have six-channel analog inputs, just like 5.1-ready receivers, so this connection method will work very well.

Subwoofers: Providing the Rumble

We have mentioned subwoofers many times, and you probably know that their job is to enhance the bass and make action movies sound great, especially when T-Rex is out looking for lunch. Subwoofers are used in many sound systems, from home theaters to multimedia speakers. However, their roles vary in different speaker systems. Let's find out why.

> It is possible to play back a 5.1 sound source on a 5.0 home theater system that does not have a subwoofer—hence, the .0 instead of the .1. In such setups, the AV receiver is configured to direct all bass to the full-range front left and front right speakers. (Satellites cannot be used for this configuration because they do not have woofers; a subwoofer is mandatory if the front speakers cannot reproduce bass.)

Ideally, the speakers used for every channel should be able to reproduce the entire frequency range, from 20 Hz to 20 kHz. This would cover the frequency range that most audio systems and media formats can carry. In reality, this range is hard to attain because very large speaker drivers are needed to provide lower-frequency vibrations in the air for bass. It is cost prohibitive and impractical to have huge speakers with multiple drivers for the center speaker, to be placed atop a television set, or large speakers to be hung on the wall for the surround channels. The woofers on full-range speakers are usually smaller than those on a subwoofer. The amplifier driving full-range speakers also has to both provide power for bass and amplify the other frequencies in the hearing range. This approach is less efficient than that of a dedicated subwoofer speaker, where the amplification power and speaker driver are dedicated entirely to reproducing bass.

> The .1 LFE channel in Dolby Digital requires one-tenth the bandwidth of a full-range channel because it takes care of only the bottom one-tenth of the frequency range that people can typically hear (and feel).

> In multimedia speakers, the use of the term *subwoofer* is actually a little misleading because many of these systems do not go down as low as home theater subwoofers with 10-inch drivers can. Usually, they do not output low-bass sound at loud enough volumes, and many can only hit 50 or 60 Hz, not the 20 or 30 Hz that larger and more powerful home theater subwoofers can. We use the terms *woofer* and *subwoofer* interchangeably, because many still refer to them as subwoofers.

Subwoofers have large speaker drivers because they need to move large amounts of air to produce deep vibrations. The cabinets are also specially designed with materials and shapes that maximize the bass output of the particular subwoofer speaker driver used. Extra amplification power is required for such large drivers; therefore, many subwoofers incorporate their own amplification circuitry. Such subwoofers are known as *active* (or *powered*) *subwoofers*, and they are the most common type of subwoofers found in home theater systems. A different type of subwoofer, known as a *passive subwoofer*, works like other speakers and require an external amplifier unit to drive it.

Headphones

Listening on a pair of headphones is a markedly different experience from listening to speakers because the effect and potential interference of sound traveling through air to reach your ears is minimized. Headphones are also less affected by outside noise because sound can travel straight to the ears without obstruction. When speakers are used, sound quality can be foiled by many more factors: for example, bad speaker positioning, poor room acoustics, or the positioning of your head away from the speakers.

On speakers, many drivers are used to reproduce each frequency band effectively so that the entire frequency range is covered. Most headphones use only one driver to reproduce the entire frequency range, and as a result many headphones (except the very best) have some inconsistencies in their frequency response in the hearing range of 20 Hz to 20 kHz. Like speakers, some frequency bands may be emphasized more than others, and many typically cannot go as low as 20 Hz. Most people can notice the huge difference in sound quality among different brands and models of headphones, especially in the amount of bass and treble. It is crucial to select the right pair that reproduces the kind of sound that you like.

TIP *Test headphones with music that is familiar to you.*

Making the Decision

The Live! supports a wide range of speaker configurations, so knowing the features you want can facilitate your buying decision. Here, we will touch on some of the issues and factors that may affect your choice.

Number of Speakers

With the flexible speaker configuration available on the Live!, you have various speaker options at your disposal. Here are some tips to help you decide on one configuration that can meet your needs and budget.

Is Stereo Sufficient?

Are you the occasional PC user who uses the computer mainly for office applications, Web surfing, and emailing? Do you play stereo sound sources like MP3 files and CD audio most of the time? If your answer is yes, a stereo speaker system will be sufficient. You can connect the Live! to a nearby stereo hi-fi system or purchase a 2.0 or 2.1 multimedia speaker system.

Going Multichannel

On the other hand, if you frequently play games and watch DVD movies, going multichannel will definitely increase the impact. Multichannel sound is also beneficial for games because it helps players pinpoint the direction an enemy is approaching from, and the Live! card's EAX processing adds ambience to the game's sound effects and immerses you more deeply in the gaming environment. Surround sound has been standard on movies for more than ten years because filmmakers know that an audience's involvement with a movie increases when the soundtrack is effective, and it is fortunate that today's technology enables such soundtracks to be reproduced in the home audio systems and PCs.

Is a Center Speaker Necessary?

With the Live! 5.1, the addition of a center speaker output allows on-screen dialogue and gaming sound effects in the middle of the screen to originate from the center of the front soundstage, usually right above the display. When listeners are seated away from the screen, on-screen sound will still appear to originate from the screen. However, unlike with home theater systems, where the listeners are many feet away from the screen, most PC users sit very near and central to the left and right speakers, or place the speakers close together, so the effect of a center speaker may be less pronounced. In such cases, a 4.1 setup (which omits the center speaker) can also be very feasible and cost effective.

Which Live! Card?

On the PC, 4.1 and 5.1 multimedia speakers are affordable and effective means of obtaining surround sound. However, your choice of multimedia speakers also depends on the sound card you own. A four-channel one like the first- or second-generation Live! can work with all audio systems and speakers except multimedia speakers or AV receivers with 5.1 analog inputs. With the newer 5.1-channel cards like the third-generation Live! 5.1, nearly all speaker types (including equipment with inputs for each of the six channels in a 5.1 setup) can be used.

Sound Quality

But, of course, sound quality is definitely high on the list of considerations. The sound quality of a speaker system depends on many factors. The most important are the speaker drivers, the solidity of the speaker cabinet, and how the drivers and speakers are set up to work together.

Bass and Subwoofers

The bass capabilities of sound systems also vary widely. Without a subwoofer, you may lose much of the low bass information that really gives games and movies that extra kick. Good bass is also essential for realistic music reproduction. Some subwoofers for home theater systems are even able to go really deep down—even to 10 Hz, to produce vibrations and rumbles that we cannot hear but can feel.

At the other extreme, the satellites of multimedia speakers sometimes compromise the reproduction of higher bass frequencies, which can be easily localized. In such speaker systems, the satellite speakers cannot go low enough to cover directional high bass frequencies, so the matching woofer unit has to take over part of the task of reproducing high bass frequencies. Because of this, some people can easily locate the position of a multimedia speaker's woofer when it is not placed close to listening position, near the left and right speakers.

This is less of an issue with larger home theater and speaker systems because the full-range left and right speakers have woofers that adequately cover the high bass frequencies, as well as nearly all of the frequencies that are directional. In such a setup, the subwoofers can be configured to handle the truly low bass frequencies below 50 Hz and need not waste energy reproducing the higher bass frequencies.

Timbre Matching

In multichannel surround systems, timbre matching is an important factor that easily affects the realism of the sound system. *Timbre* is an aspect of sound that makes one sound distinguishable from other sounds, even when the sounds are at the same pitch and volume. A trumpet and saxophone playing the same note at the same volume will sound different because of the different tonal characteristics. Similarly, different speakers produce a slightly different sound, even when they are connected to the same amplifier and play from the same audio source, because of myriad factors, such as the different materials used for the enclosures and different speaker drivers.

Imagine using different speaker models for the left and right speakers. The results would sound weird, won't they? Likewise, it is crucial to match the timbre of the speakers used in a surround setup. This is especially important for speakers in the same plane: the front left, front right, and center speakers need to have similar characteristics so that sounds moving between them have a smooth and convincing transition, and the sound characteristics don't seem to suddenly change. The surrounds need to sound the same when sound moves from one to the other. Of course, it is best to purchase an entire set of home theater speakers from the same manufacturer and product range so that all channels are timbre matched.

This is seldom an issue with multimedia speakers because the satellite speakers provided are usually the same. Games that use 3D positioning also move sounds not only among the front speakers, but to the rear left and rear right speakers, as well; therefore, it will also be beneficial if the front and rear speakers are well matched.

Digital vs. Analog

As we covered in Chapter 2, "An Audio Primer," there are two main things that need to be performed for us to hear digital audio processed by digital audio equipment like sound cards:

1. Perform D/A conversion to obtain the analog signals.
2. Amplify the analog signals to levels that are strong enough to move the speaker drivers.

In the Live!, the D/A process is done in the sound card, while the amplification duties are handled by the speaker system connected to the sound card. The only exception to this is when speakers that accept digital inputs are connected to digital outputs on the Live! or an attached digital I/O device. In such setups, both D/A and amplification are performed by the speaker system.

Unless you have a bad combination of hardware components in your PC or a faulty power supply or motherboard, the Live!'s analog line outputs should be relatively quiet and noise free, so analog and digital connections do not differ very much for most people. The sound quality of the speakers is more important.

Power and Amplification Ratings

Amplifiers with high-power outputs can handle loud movie soundtracks and music efficiently and with minimal distortion. When the audio tracks get very complex, with many sounds playing at different frequencies and requiring different output power, a lower-quality amplification system will attempt to amplify the audio, but the result will sound messy. The characteristics of each of the individual sounds will be lost or will not be as clearly defined as with a more powerful amplifier that can amplify these sounds with less difficulty.

Besides handling loud sounds and complex audio passages, the ability to reproduce subtle nuances in recordings is also important. For example, the light, breathy sounds of a flute player as air enters the instrument, or the plucking and fret sounds of a guitar, or a singer's breathing are all subtle, but the ability to hear them adds to the realism of a recording. Such details are easily lost with less capable amplifiers and speakers.

If you have a big room to fill, there is more air to move, so a powerful amplifier would definitely be advantageous. On the other hand, if you have a small room, or if you do not usually listen at very high volumes, a lower-powered speaker system may suffice.

Technical Specifications

Sound quality is subjective and is difficult to measure in exact terms. Because of this, many consumers base their buying decisions on specifications provided by manufacturers because it is much easier to compare figures on paper than to go through the process of listening to every sound system available. But the latter is exactly what you should do to guarantee that you get the sound system that sounds best to your ears.

Design and the quality of components used also play a huge role in sound quality, and these factors cannot be easily evaluated just by looking at technical specifications. Moreover, manufacturers measure the specifications of their components differently and sometimes do so to put their products in the best light possible. Use technical specifications to get a general idea of the capabilities of a sound system, but do not base your buying decisions solely on them. Listening tests will reveal more.

The PMPO Game

Beware of the power ratings game that some consumer electronics manufacturers have been playing for years, especially in countries where there is weak legislation or consumer protection laws to prevent manufacturers from misrepresenting their products. Some manufacturers tout the peak music power output (PMPO) rating because it yields higher numbers, and the way it is measured is not standardized. A minicomponent system that screams "5000W PMPO" on a shiny label is certainly attractive, but alas, it is completely misleading.

> Power is measured in watts (W).

So, what exactly is PMPO? It is basically the maximum power output that the amplifier can produce without distortion. In many cases, if the amplifiers run at such a high power output for even one second, the speakers will blow up! A more realistic way of measuring the power output capabilities of an amplifier is the root mean square (RMS) rating, which measures the power that can be produced consistently over long periods of time. This figure may be around ten times smaller than the PMPO rating. Fortunately, many manufacturers of multimedia speakers and home theater systems use RMS in their product literature.

Center Speaker Power

Since the advent of Dolby Digital, each of the five channels in a 5.1 setup (excluding the .1 LFE channel used by the subwoofer) carries the full range of frequencies and has the potential to carry sound from 20 Hz to 20 kHz. Many recent AV receivers, usually in the middle and high ranges, allocate equal amplification power to every speaker so that sounds in all channels are reproduced with equal intensity. This is extremely beneficial for movies that have powerful sound effects directed to all five main speakers, as well as for games on the Live!, where sounds can potentially range from 20 Hz to 20 kHz for every speaker channel.

To cut costs, some 5.1 multimedia speaker systems come with a center satellite speaker that has higher amplification power than the front and surround speakers. Some lower-end home theater equipment also reduces the power of the other speakers, allocating the largest share of the amplification power to the center and subwoofer speakers. This is usually acceptable if you do not watch movies at a very high volume. In surround movies, most of the action and sound effects originate on the screen, so it is natural for such audio to come from the center speaker, while the left and right front speakers play back the music and the occasional sound effects that match the action occurring at the left or right of the screen and can therefore be of lower power.

Of course, the ideal situation would be for the sound system to have equal power for all channels, but many other factors that are mentioned in the following paragraphs are also important. Do not be unduly worried if the speaker system you are purchasing has a very high power output only for the center speaker, as the other speakers would also be adequately amplified. Perform a listening test on a movie that has an active sound mix and directionality on the front and surround channels to determine the true capability of the setup.

Efficiency

Efficiency is an often overlooked characteristic of amplifiers and speaker systems. Because speakers and amplifiers are all made differently, some are more efficient than others. For example, assume that two speaker drivers have similar timbre and sound quality, but one of them is less energy efficient than the other. The less efficient speaker would require more power to drive it to produce the same level of power and quality as the other speaker. A more efficient speaker rated with a higher sensitivity will be able to produce the same results with much less amplifier power, thus making efficient use of the amplification energy from the amplifier. Therefore, you will see that some sound systems list sky-high amplifier power outputs in their specifications, but they don't sound as loud as a lower-powered sound system because their speakers are less efficient in making use of the power provided by the amplifier to move the speaker drivers.

> There are also other factors and characteristics working together that can affect the quality and power output of a speaker and amplifier combination. Even then, efficiency plays a huge role and practically eliminates the usefulness of many of the brief specifications that manufacturers provide.

Ultimately, you will need to listen to a speaker system using a wide range of audio sources, preferably with the speakers in the location where they are going to be permanently located, to get an accurate idea of the performance of the system in your particular listening environment.

Magnetic Shielding

Speaker drivers contain powerful magnets that can affect television screens and monitors, causing permanent distortion and visual artifacts such as flickering and odd color patches. Magnetic shielding is accomplished by adding components in the speaker cabinet to cancel the magnetic field produced by the speaker driver. Magnetic shielding is especially important in speakers made for home theater and multimedia because of the presence of CRT screens. It is definitely a must on center speakers because they are placed on top of the monitor. Most multimedia speakers are magnetically shielded, although this may not be the case for low-priced models. Most home theater speakers are magnetically shielded, as well. However, do remember to check the specifications or ask the dealer to make certain before you fork out your money!

TIP *LCD monitors are not affected by the magnetism of speaker drivers.*

Space Constraints

Whether you are one of the lucky folks who has a dedicated home theater room with plush carpeting and cinema seats, or has a moderate-sized living room or just a small bedroom, there are speaker systems to fit your setting.

Placing stereo speakers are easy, because they are usually placed on the left and right side of the screen, while the woofer unit is placed under the desk. In many cases, a multimedia speaker system will usually suffice. However, multichannel setups are a little more challenging. The most problematic aspect is definitely the placement of the surround speakers.

Before you decide to adopt surround, make sure there is space beside or behind you for these speakers. They usually need to be directed at or above ear level, so they are normally placed on floor-standing speaker stands, screwed into walls, or placed on furnishings behind the listening position. This is common for home theater surround speakers, and manufacturers do offer different mounting accessories to accommodate different setups.

However, manufacturers of 4.1 and 5.1 multimedia speakers are more constrained by the requirements of the market—they need to offer speakers that provide good performance and at the same time are very affordable. Therefore, mounting choices are somewhat limited. The satellite speakers of most multimedia speaker systems are not designed for wall mounting, nor are brackets often available as optional accessories. Similarly, not all come with speaker stands, and many manufacturers go the cost-saving route by providing no mounting options at all, so these speakers can only be placed on tables or other furniture. When purchasing speakers with surrounds, make sure your room can support such a setup, and check with the dealer to see whether the model you are interested in has the appropriate mounts or speaker stands.

Convenient Features

Even though multimedia speakers offer the bare minimum, there are still some nice features that can help make daily operation a much breezier affair.

Volume Controls

Where will you be placing your speakers? If it is far away from the PC, like a stereo system or an AV receiver, an infrared remote control would be nice. If you intend

Figure 6.11: The wired volume control unit provided with some Creative Inspire speakers

Speakers **159**

to buy multimedia speakers, find out where the volume controls are. If they are found only on the subwoofer, you might want to reconsider that speaker. Most well-designed multimedia speakers have volume controls on one of the satellite speakers, or even better, on a wired volume control unit that can be placed in a convenient location, such as near the keyboard.

Audio Inputs

Many people own other audio and video equipment, such as CD players and VCRs, that would definitely benefit from good speakers. If you want to connect these devices to the speaker system so they can be used while the PC is turned off, look for speaker systems that have more than one audio input, because one will already be permanently connected to the sound card. Stereo and home theater systems usually have more than one audio input and allow you to switch among them to determine which source is heard on the speakers.

Unlike stereo and home theater systems, multimedia speakers usually have only one input for the sound card. To connect other devices, use the inputs available on the Live!, such as the Line In found on the card's backplate, to channel the sound from these devices to the speakers connected to the sound card. You may want to consider adding a Live!Drive or one of the digital I/O cards if the inputs on the Live! do not suffice, or if digital audio inputs are needed. A caveat, though: You will need to keep the PC turned on for these devices to be heard on the speakers connected to the sound card, so this may not be a good idea if you do not leave the PC turned on while, for example, listening to music from a portable CD player.

An affordable way to get switching capability for multimedia speakers with one audio input is to purchase a switch from your local electronics store. The switch should have a few RCA cables to connect to the audio outputs of these devices, and a single RCA output will connect to the speaker system. Buttons or knobs on the switch will allow you to choose which audio output to send to the speakers.

Some multimedia speakers do have more than one audio input. Some speakers work in a fashion similar to switched hi-fi systems, where only one of the connected audio inputs can be selected at any one time. Other multimedia speakers mix the sounds from all of the audio inputs so they can be heard on the speakers simultaneously.

Apart from the number of inputs, you should also note the audio connectors provided, so that they can be matched with those found on the Live! or an attached digital I/O device. If the connectors are different, make sure converter cables are readily available. This is especially important for digital connections, which differ from analog connections, where the signals themselves are similar (line-level audio) and only the plugs vary. Optical connections use light, and coaxial connections use electrical signals, so converting between them requires a converter device, which usually costs more than cables.

Headphone Outputs

If you frequently listen to headphones, it will be useful if the speakers have headphone outputs so that you need not remove the cable connected to the line output of the Live! just to plug in headphones. Most AV receivers and hi-fi systems have a 1/4-inch headphone output. Some multimedia speakers have headphone outputs that are located on one of the satellite speakers. The speakers should automatically mute when the headphone jack is inserted. (Of course, with a Live!Drive, this feature on speakers becomes less important because the Live!Drive has a volume-controllable headphone output that automatically mutes the speakers when used.)

Budget

There are, of course, really expensive, high-end products that promise the best audio from your sound card, but ultimately it is your budget that determines the choices of speakers that are available to you and the balance between performance and price that you can accept. But the old mantra, "expensive does not equal good," applies here, as well. There are many budget systems that sound like systems that cost twice the price, and others that look classy (and are expensive) but that do not produce sound to match.

All the Parts Make Up the Whole

If you are looking at a home theater or stereo system, do not spend the majority of your budget on speakers, leaving the balance for a low-powered and compromised amplifier or receiver. A good amplifier can make a speaker sound sweet, and good speakers can make good use of the energy that is pumped out by an amplifier and produce the sound that you prefer.

Even though this book is about sound, we encourage you to spread your budget among all the different computer components, especially on good video hardware. A good-quality, large monitor of at least 17 inches coupled with a powerful video card will definitely increase your enjoyment of games and movies, just like good sound will. For home theater and hi-fi systems, the sky (and your budget) is the limit. The range of available video equipment is far and wide—from low-flicker 100-Hz direct-view television sets to wide-screen plasma displays and DLP or LCD projectors.

Research and Listen

You can begin by searching the Internet and consulting audio and AV magazines. Compare the prices and find out the pros and cons of each speaker system, but keep in mind that opinions about the audio characteristics of a speaker can be highly subjective. Make sure the amplifiers and speakers match in power handling and timbre. But this is just the first step.

Auditioning is the next and most important step because everyone has preferences and opinions about how they want things to sound. Some prefer powerful, rumbling bass, while others equate good sound quality with good vocal reproduction. Nevertheless, there are a few basic guidelines that can help you make the most of your time at the dealer.

To test 5.1 sound systems, use movies that are known to have good soundtracks and make decent use of each of the speakers in a 5.1 setup. This will help you gauge the power handling and surround capabilities across all channels. Listen for clear and natural-sounding dialogue from the center that isn't too tinny or sharp. Scenes set in the jungle, a club, or the rain can help you test the envelopment provided by the surrounds. Here are some popular DVDs that many people recommend when auditioning a surround system:

- The subtle environmental noises in *Cast Away* make good use of the surrounds to create ambience. (An interesting fact about this movie is that there is absolutely no music used during the scenes on the island, which attests to the ability of a good soundtrack to keep viewers in the moment.)
- The scene in *Dragonheart* where the dragon is circling above and around the viewer is a good test for timbre matching of transitioning sounds among all the five speakers in a surround setup.
- The opening beach landing sequence in *Saving Private Ryan* is a fantastic test of surround capability and power handling. Many sounds are happening at one time, and there is also lots of bass in the surround channels.
- Some scenes in *Apollo 13*, *Fight Club*, *The Haunting*, *Titan A.E.*, and *U-571* are known to give subwoofers a real workout.

> Older movies are not designed with discrete digital surround in mind, so even though they come in Dolby Digital on DVDs, they may not sound as dynamic and enveloping as recent films.

Unlike movies, with their random bursts of dialogue and sound effects, music provides more constant sound, which helps when auditioning sound systems and speakers. Avoid using unfamiliar material when auditioning speakers because many dealers will play something that accentuates a speaker's particular strengths. Bring a few of your favorite recordings to the store and use them for testing. You'll be able to make a valid comparison because you know how a particular track sounds on other speaker systems.

Listen for treble that is crisp and clear without sounding too harsh or overly bright. A system that has a very brash and bright sound might be extremely impressive when you first hear it, but listening to such sounds for prolonged periods can be very fatiguing. Vocals should not sound thin but full and lifelike, as if the singer were right in front of you. Acoustic instruments such as a piano and drums played in blues and jazz recordings, or a well-recorded symphony orchestra, can be very telling, especially if you have been to live performances and know how real instruments should sound. A good audio system should be close to that.

Bass should be deep and tight and not so boomy that the low frequencies of, for example, a kick drum or bass guitar sound like a confused smattering of bass instead of being well defined and punchy, allowing you to individually make out each hit.

Also be aware that many people conclude that a system played at a higher volume has better sound. To make a fair comparison, it is vital to test different sound systems at similar levels. A slight increase in volume can easily influence your buying decision. Likewise, something that sounds "detailed" may just have treble that is too high, or something that has good bass may actually be too boomy and unrealistic instead.

We hope that after reading this section, you will not go around shopping for a home theater system based entirely on the manufacturer's specifications, the look of the product, or how much air comes out of the subwoofer's bass ports. You do not need an audiophile's ear to know what is good sound, because you have been listening to real sounds all your life. Close your eyes, listen closely, and trust what your ears tell you!

Speaker Support on the Live!

The Live! is very flexible in terms of speaker support and can be used with nearly every type of sound system—from stereo to 5.1 speaker configurations. The first- and second-generation Live! cards support a maximum of four channels for two front speakers and two rear speakers. The 5.1 cards can output up to six channels, while retaining support for four-channel and two-channel configurations.

In this section, you'll find out what type of cables can be used to connect speakers to the Live! and learn about the different types of input jacks available on multimedia speakers and consumer audio equipment.

> The Live! does not come with speaker cables, like the mini-jack–to–RCA cable provided with many previous Sound Blaster cards. Today, multimedia speakers will include the audio cables necessary to connect to the mini-jack outputs of sound cards.

Speaker Connectors

There are several connectors on the Live! and digital I/O devices that can be used to connect to speakers.

Analog

The Live! uses mini-jack connectors on the backplate to output analog line-level audio to speakers. On first- and second-generation Live! cards, two mini-jacks output the front and rear channels to four speakers. On the third-generation Live! 5.1 cards, the mini-jack digital output also doubles as a third analog mini-jack output for the center and woofer channels.

> The mini-jack digital output on second-generation Live! cards cannot be switched to analog mode to output the center and woofer channels. This capability was introduced in the third-generation Live! 5.1 sound cards.

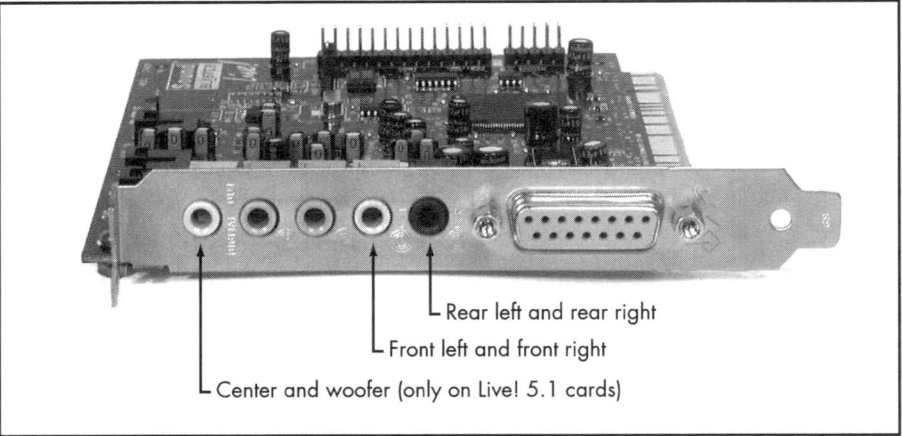

Figure 6.12: The mini-jack analog line outputs of the Live!

Digital

The Live! can also output the front (left and right) channels digitally to AV receivers and other digital audio devices that have digital inputs (with coaxial or optical connectors). To get the optical or coaxial digital outputs from the Live!, you will need to use a digital I/O card or a Live!Drive. A digital connection will allow you to bypass the DAC on the Live! and use the ones on a hi-fi system, AV receiver, or multimedia speaker that has digital inputs. This reduces the opportunities for noise, which may affect the digital-to-analog conversion process when it is performed by the sound card in the electrically noisy innards of a computer casing.

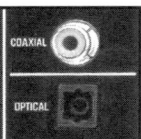

Figure 6.13: Coaxial and optical inputs are usually found on AV receivers. Some digital multimedia speakers will also have either one or both of these inputs.

Connecting for S/PDIF Passthrough

The Live! can be set to a S/PDIF passthrough mode that allows the same digital output of the front channels to be used to carry compressed surround sound formats such as Dolby Digital and DTS instead. These surround formats usually support up to six channels of audio, and all of the channels can be transmitted with a single coaxial or optical digital cable connected to an output on a digital I/O device attached to the Live! On the other hand, when the Live! is not in S/PDIF passthrough mode, uncompressed PCM audio format is used, and each digital output will carry only two channels of audio.

Chapter 11, "Watching Movies," covers the S/PDIF passthrough in further detail.

To connect to AV receivers or 5.1 multimedia speakers that come with Dolby Digital or DTS surround decoders, you will need to connect from the digital outputs of the Live! (provided with a digital I/O device) to the coaxial or optical inputs of the decoding equipment. The connectors themselves look the same as those in the picture above, but they must be configured to auto-detect Dolby Digital and/or DTS and switch to the appropriate decoding modes whenever the DVD playback software uses the Live! for S/PDIF passthrough. Also, the Live! always outputs in PCM format when it is not in S/PDIF passthrough mode, so the decoder must also support stereo PCM sound on the same coaxial or optical input connector and be able to automatically detect and switch between PCM and Dolby Digital/DTS audio formats.

Digital DIN

Creative introduced the proprietary Digital DIN connector to allow more than one wire, each carrying a digital signal, to be bundled together in a single cable. Like other sound cards and audio equipment, the Live! works with uncompressed PCM audio, where one wire in a cable carries one digital signal consisting of two channels of digital audio. Digital DIN uses cable that has several wires to carry up to four digital signals, for a total of eight audio channels. With a single Digital DIN cable, you will be able to connect all the speaker channels that are output by the Live! to a speaker system with a Digital DIN connector.

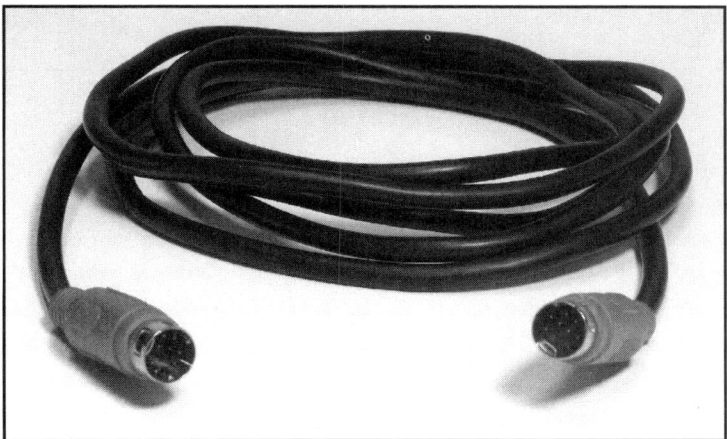

Figure 6.14: A Digital DIN cable

The first- and second-generation four-channel Live! cards use only two digital signals because there are only two front and two rear channels. The third-generation Live! 5.1 uses a third digital signal on the Digital DIN cable to transmit the center and woofer channels.

The fourth digital signal in a Digital DIN cable is not used, but if 7.1 configurations become popular in the marketplace in future, it is technically possible for the Live! to support them.

When the Live! was first introduced, Creative and Cambridge SoundWorks were the only manufacturers that sold digital speakers with Digital DIN connectors, and they continue to support Digital DIN for obvious reasons. A few models, like the Logitech Xtrusio DSR-100 and Polk Audio AMR-150, do support Digital DIN, but most manufacturers and models in the market do not.

Figure 6.15: Polk Audio AMR-150

Most 4.1 or 5.1 digital multimedia speakers not made by Creative or Cambridge SoundWorks will likely use the conventional optical or coaxial S/PDIF connectors instead of Digital DIN. Only a few third-party optical I/O cards provide the rear speakers in the form of optical or coaxial digital outputs, so you may need to fall back to analog connections when connecting to these types of digital speakers.

There are two types of connectors used to output Digital DIN signals. The first is using the mini-jack digital output on the backplate of second- and third-generation Live! cards. Due to the physical differences between a mini-jack and a Mini-DIN plug used by Digital DIN, Creative provides an adapter cable to allow the Digital DIN cable to be connected to the mini-jack digital output of the Live!

Another way to get a Digital DIN output is to use one of Creative's digital I/O cards or the Digital DIN backplate provided with some Live!Drives. These connect directly to the Mini-DIN plug on a Digital DIN cable, and do not need the mini-jack–to–Digital DIN adapter cable pictured above. Chapter 4, "Accessories Galore!" covers these peripherals in detail.

Figure 6.16: A mini-jack–to–Digital DIN adapter

Figure 6.17: A Digital DIN output

> **TIP** *If you are using the mini-jack digital output and find that there is no sound, check that the "Digital output only" option in the Speaker configuration in AudioHQ or the Surround Mixer is checked.*

Here is a summary of connectors that are enabled when the Live! is set to a particular speaker mode.

Table 6.1: Outputs Enabled with the Various Speaker Modes

Output Format	Connector	2 Speakers, Headphone, or Live!Surround	4 Speakers	5.1 Speakers*
Analog Outputs	Line Out 1 (front left and front right)	✓	✓	✓
	Line Out 2 (rear left and rear right)		✓	✓

Speakers **167**

Table 6.1: Outputs Enabled with the Various Speaker Modes (continued)

Output Format	Connector	2 Speakers, Headphone, or Live!Surround	4 Speakers	5.1 Speakers*
	Line Out 3 (center and woofer)*			✓
Digital (S/PDIF Outputs**	Coaxial Out (front left and front right)	✓	✓	✓
	Optical Out (front left and front right)	✓	✓	✓
Digital DIN Outputs***	Mini-jack Digital Out	✓ The front outputs are still enabled, but no 2.1 speakers support this connector	✓ Front left, front right, rear left, and rear right	✓ Front left, front right, rear left, rear right, center, and woofer
	Digital DIN Out	✓ The front outputs are still enabled, but no 2.1 speakers support this connector	✓ Front left, front right, rear left, and rear right	✓ Front left, front right, rear left, rear right, center, and woofer

* Only available on Sound Blaster Live 5.1 cards.

** Digital outputs can be found on the Live!Drive and digital I/O cards connected to the Live! However, not all of these devices feature both coaxial and optical outputs.

*** Digital DIN inputs are found only on Creative and Cambridge SoundWorks digital speakers.

Changing Speaker Modes

The speaker mode on the Live! can be changed with the Surround Mixer to allow the Live! to support the various types of sound systems available on the market (see Figures 6.18 and 6.19).

Connecting Speakers

Most speaker systems come with well-written instructions and the necessary cables and accessories. When setting up your system, follow the diagrams and the color coding of the connectors and speaker wires. Take care not to reverse the polarity of speaker connections, as this may cause the speaker to be out-of-phase, making it sound dispersed and lack bass. Setting up multichannel speakers can get messy, so you may also want to label the wires and audio cables as you go along. Make sure the speaker wires are not near strong electromagnetic emissions from electrical equipment such as power adapters, because this may induce noise and hum in the speaker output.

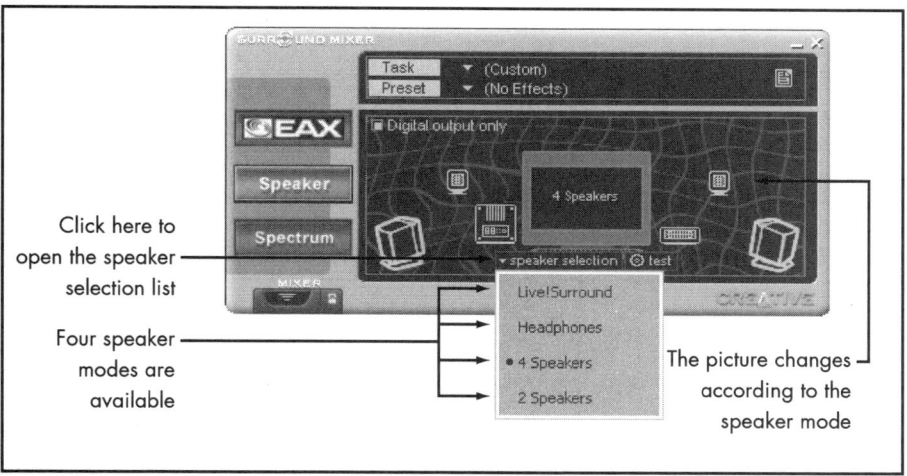

Figure 6.18: Speaker configuration for four-channel first- and second-generation Live! cards

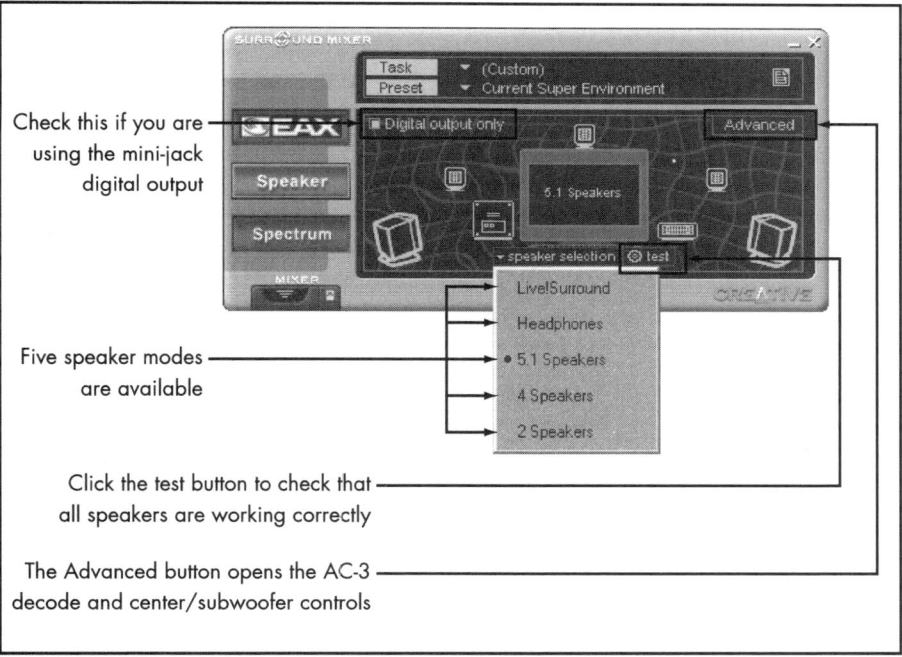

Figure 6.19: Speaker configuration for third-generation Live! 5.1 cards

This section is organized according to the speaker modes available on the Live! It explores the types of connectors commonly used on sound systems that can work with each speaker mode. You'll find out how to physically connect your system to the Live!, including the cables to use.

2 Speakers Mode

Using the front outputs of the Live!, the 2 Speakers mode outputs a standard stereo signal carrying the left and right channels. The digital outputs on the Live! (available on digital I/O devices) will also output the front channels to sound systems that accept digital inputs. Other outputs, such as the Line Out 2 carrying the rear channels, are disabled in this mode.

When DirectSound3D games are played in this mode, the Live! will use a virtual 3D positioning algorithm to simulate a 360-degree sound field using two speakers. (See the section "Virtual Surround" later in this chapter.) Other non–3D-positioned audio will be output as stereo in the front outputs without any virtual audio processing (unless CMSS is used).

Analog: RCA Connectors

RCA jacks are commonly found on stereo systems and are usually labeled with the name of the sound source, corresponding to the sound source to be selected in the amplifier, like "CD," "Tape/MD," "Aux," or "DVD." This is sometimes followed by the word "in" to indicate that it is an input, rather than "out," which is an output. The plugs and jacks are color coded white and red, for the left and right speakers, respectively. (Some RCA cables substitute white plugs with black ones, but the cables still work in the same way.) You will need a stereo mini-jack–to–RCA cable to connect to such equipment. The mini-jack plug connects to Line Out 1 on the Live!'s backplate.

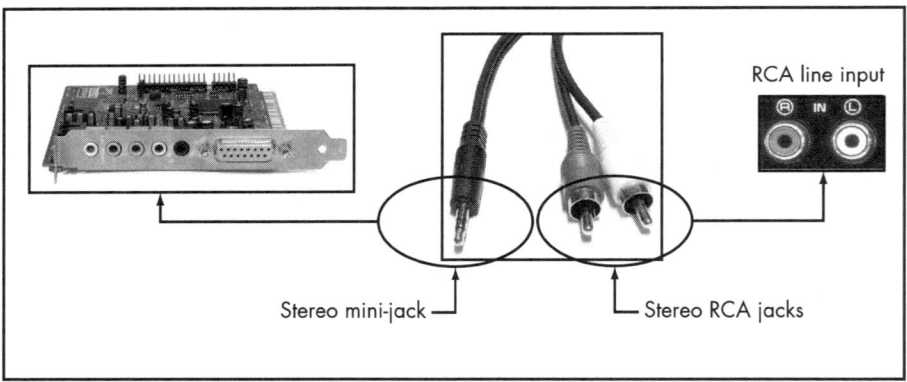

Figure 6.20: Connecting to stereo systems with RCA inputs

Analog: Mini-jack Connectors

Two-channel multimedia speakers have a mini-jack input, usually at the back of the woofer unit. You can use a stereo mini-jack–to–mini-jack cable to connect to the Live!

Some budget multimedia speakers have cables where the wire is fixed inside the speaker unit and extends out to a stereo mini-jack plug at the other end of the cable. You can connect this mini-jack plug directly to Line Out 1 on the Live!

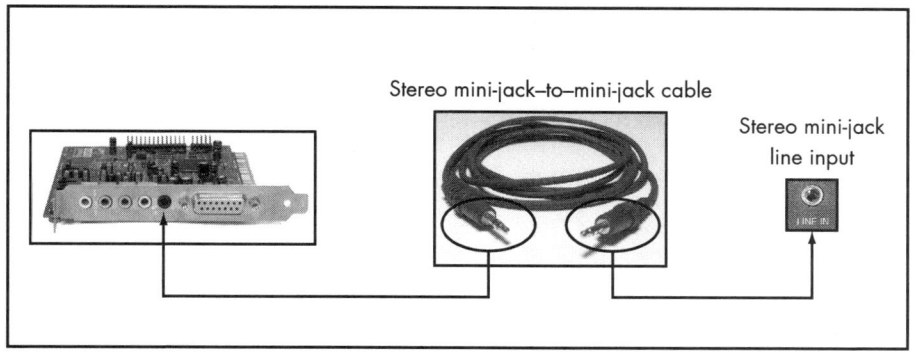

Figure 6.21: Connecting to stereo systems and multimedia speakers with mini-jack inputs

> If you have small unpowered multimedia speakers, you can use the Line Out 1 on the Live! card or the Headphone Out on the Live!Drive for audio output. Do not use the other connectors for unpowered speakers and headphones, because they are not designed for this purpose, and using them in this way may damage the Live! card.

Digital Connectors

Digital speakers normally have an optical TOSLink or a coaxial RCA input. Optical TOSLink outputs are available on the Live!Drive II, Live!Drive IR, and Optical Digital I/O Card. A TOSLink-to-TOSLink optical cable is used to connect from the Live!'s digital I/O device to the digital sound system.

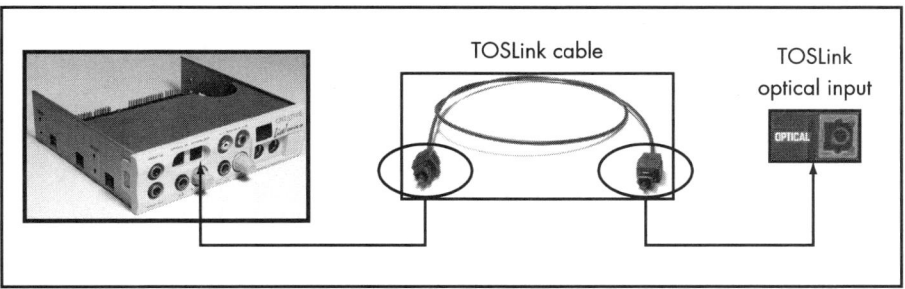

Figure 6.22: Connect the TOSLink output of a digital I/O device like the Live!Drive to the TOSLink input on the digital equipment

Speakers **171**

Optical cables may also use mini-jack optical plugs, but they are not commonly found on digital multimedia speakers. They are more widespread in portable digital players such as CD and MiniDisc players. See Chapter 5, "Connecting Devices," for more information.

Coaxial connections are made in the same way. Using a coaxial cable with RCA plugs, you can connect digitally from the digital I/O device to a digital multimedia speaker system or AV receiver that has coaxial inputs.

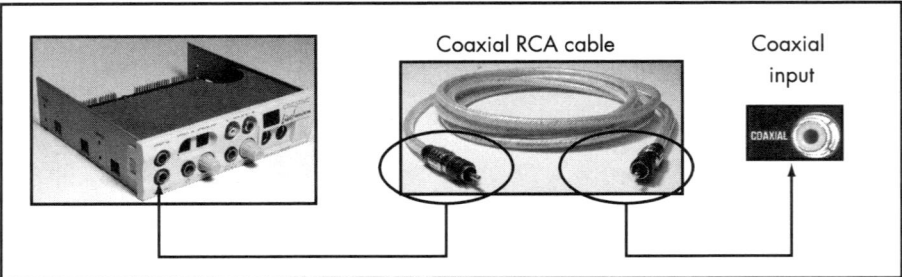

Figure 6.23: Connect the S/PDIF coaxial output of a digital I/O card or the Live!Drive to the coaxial input on the digital equipment

The Optical Out and Coaxial Out can also be switched to S/PDIF passthrough mode when a software DVD player is used. When this mode is engaged, the speakers may output noise, or there may be no sound at all unless your speakers support surround sound decoding for Dolby Digital or DTS.

4 Speakers Mode

4 Speakers mode works with 4.1 multimedia speakers unique in the PC audio world. When playing back audio from normal sound sources, the Live! duplicates the front speakers to the rear with the same volume unless you have specifically positioned an audio source in 3D using the Surround Mixer or turned on CMSS.

Find out more about positioning sound sources in Chapter 7, "The Mixer."

The Live!'s four-speaker output is fully utilized to place and move sounds among the four speakers only when you are using a software DVD player to decode and output a surround soundtrack, or a 3D game that supports DirectSound3D or OpenAL.

Analog: RCA Connectors

You may come across the rare 4.1 multimedia speaker system that sports four RCA inputs (two red, two white) instead of the commonly used mini-jacks. You'll need two mini-jack–to–RCA cable to connect to these speakers to the Line Out 1 and Line Out 2 on the Live!'s backplate.

Alternately, you may wish to connect to a 5.1-ready home theater receiver that has six analog RCA jacks (for a 5.1 input) by leaving out the center and subwoofer RCA inputs. With only four speakers output from the 4 Speakers mode of the Live!, no audio will be heard from the center speaker. A connected subwoofer may still be utilized, if you correctly set your home theater receiver to redirect bass from the main speakers to the subwoofer. For lower-end receivers that do not perform bass redirection for discrete 5.1 inputs, the subwoofer will not be used, and the bass output may be weak if the main speakers do not have woofers.

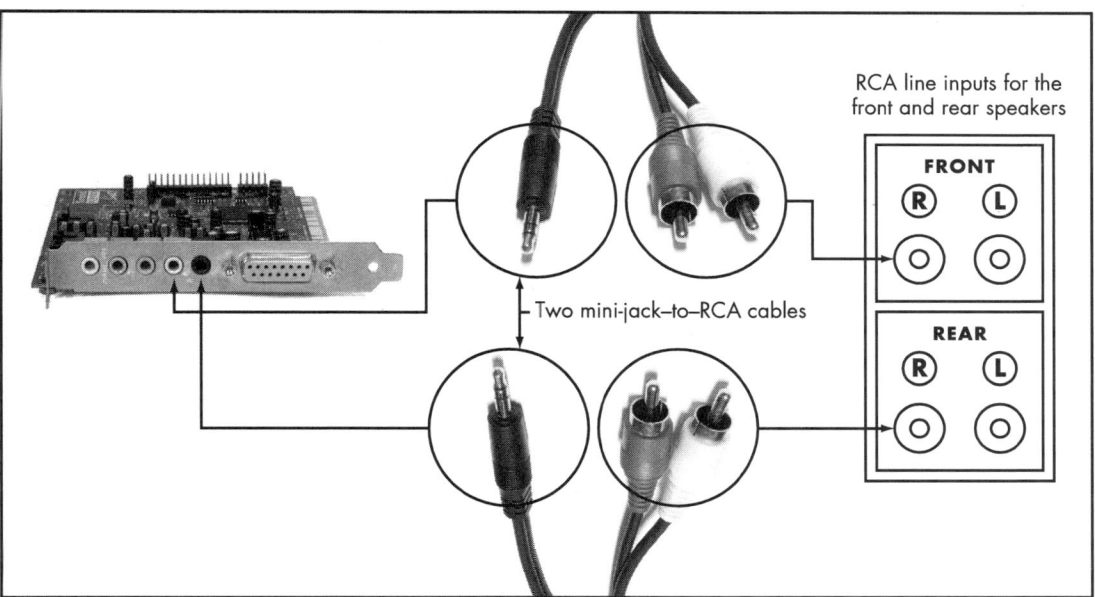

Figure 6.24: Connecting the front and rear mini-jack outputs of the Live! to a multimedia speaker system or AV receiver with front and rear RCA inputs

Analog: Mini-jack Connectors

Take a look at the back of a 4.1 multimedia speaker system; more often than not, you'll find two mini-jack connectors: one for the front speakers and the other for the rear speakers. These correspond to Line Out 1 and Line Out 2 on the Live! Usually a cable with two stereo mini-jacks at each end is included with the speaker system.

Alternatively, if you have two pairs of stereo speakers, you can use them together to reproduce the four channels output by the Live! Using the appropriate cable, connect Line Out 1 on the Live! to the front stereo speakers and connect Line Out 2 to the rear speaker system.

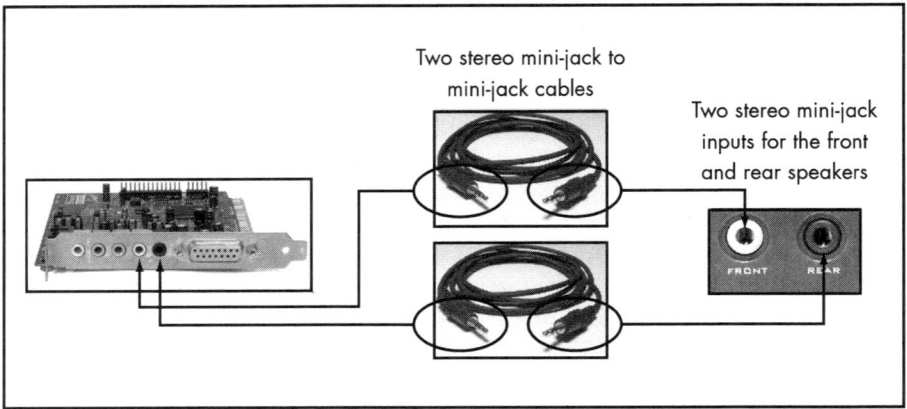

Figure 6.25: Connecting the Live! to the front and rear mini-jack inputs of a four-channel multimedia speaker system

> An important point: If you have read the section "Timbre Matching" earlier in this chapter, you will realize that it is crucial to match the audio characteristics of all the speakers to obtain seamless transition of sounds when they move among the four speakers, so for optimal transitioning of sounds, make sure speakers with similar audio characteristics for both the front and rear are used.

Digital DIN Connectors: Mini-jack Digital Out

Cambridge SoundWorks speakers such as the 4.1-channel FPS2000 are very popular because they use the Digital DIN connector that allows a clean digital signal to be obtained from the Live! The mini-jack digital output found on the backplates of second- and third-generation Live! cards can be used to connect to these speakers.

TIP *"Digital output only" should be checked in the Speaker settings in AudioHQ or Surround Mixer, when the mini-jack digital output is used.*

Two cables are normally included in the speaker package: a mini-jack–to–female Digital DIN adapter cable and a Digital DIN–to–Digital DIN cable. Both cables are bundled with the speakers.

On earlier shipments, especially those prior to the second-generation Live! cards (when the Mini-jack Digital Out connector was introduced), digital Cambridge SoundWorks speakers such as the FPS2000 and the DTT2500 did not come with the mini-jack–to–female Digital DIN adapter cable. You can call Creative to get a hold of this cable.

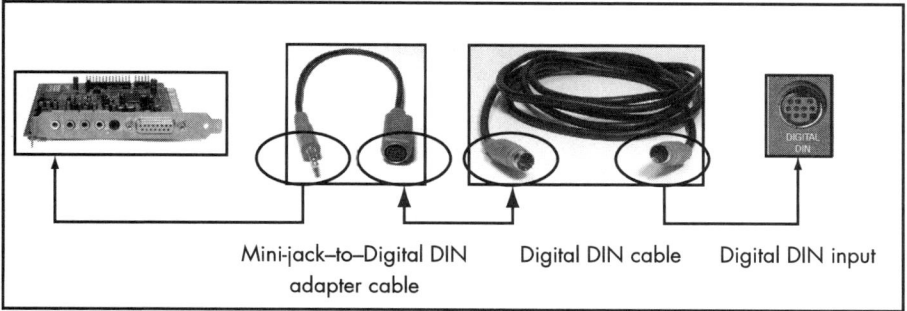

Figure 6.26: *Connecting the Live!'s mini-jack digital output to the Digital DIN input behind a multimedia speaker system*

Newer speakers from Cambridge SoundWorks, like the MegaWorks 210D and MegaWorks 510D, do no have a Digital DIN input, but rather a mini-jack digital input that is compatible with the mini-jack digital output of the second- and third-generation Live! cards. A custom-made digital mini-jack–to–mini-jack cable is included for this purpose.

Digital DIN Connectors: Digital DIN Out

The first Live! product with the CT4660 digital I/O card, the optical digital I/O card, and the Digital DIN backplate all have a Digital DIN output so that you can use the Digital DIN–to–Digital DIN cable without the mini-jack–to–female Digital DIN adapter cable (see Figure 6.27).

Digital DIN Backplate

In some versions of the Platinum, a Digital DIN backplate (Figure 6.28) is included in the package. It is a female Digital DIN connector screwed onto a backplate. The black rectangular connector at the end of the cable connects to the connector on the Live!Drive labeled "DIGITAL DIN."

This backplate requires a free slot behind the casing but does not connect to the PCI slot on the motherboard, which is a little wasteful, especially if you have many PCI cards. If your casing has a nine-pin COM port opening, you can remove the screws, separate the female Digital DIN connector from the backplate, and use the same screws to attach it to the COM port opening. There, you saved a slot's space!

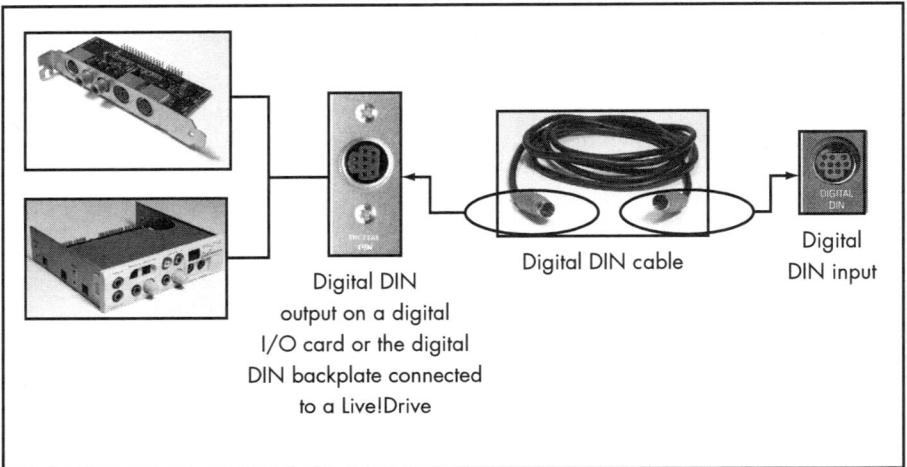

Figure 6.27: Connecting the Digital DIN output on a digital I/O device to the Digital DIN to Digital DIN input behind a multimedia speaker system

Figure 6.28: Digital DIN backplate

5.1 Speakers Mode

The 5.1 Speakers mode is available only if you have a third-generation Live! card. The 5.1 support is primarily used for playing back 5.1 soundtracks in DVDs and 3D audio in games.

When Will There Be Sound from the Center Speaker?

The center speaker is used only when the Live! is decoding Dolby Digital 5.1 soundtracks or when a 3D game is using the hardware to position sounds in 3D. This provides the benefit of a wider front soundstage with a left-center-right configuration compared to only the left-right arrangement with the 2 speakers and 4 speakers modes.

Do not be alarmed if there is no sound from the center speaker when it is used to play back other sounds. If you want the center speaker to be used, turn on CMSS/movie mode to convert stereo audio to 5.1.

Alternatively, if you have a Creative or Cambridge SoundWorks 5.1 speaker system that has built-in Dolby Digital decoding, such as the DTT2500 or DTT3500, you can use the built-in CMSS Music and CMSS Movie modes, as well. (These will not use the CMSS mode on the Live! because the processing occurs in the amplifier unit of the speaker system.)

When Is the Woofer Channel Used?

The woofer channel is provided because the Dolby Digital standard incorporates a LFE channel (also called the .1 channel). This channel outputs audio in several situations:

- When DVDs with .1 surround soundtracks (like 5.1 or 6.1) are played using the sound card decoding method.
- When DVDs with .1 surround soundtracks (like 5.1 or 6.1) are played using the software decoding method, with the DVD playback software set to output in six (5.1) channel mode.
- When DVDs with surround soundtracks of any speaker configuration (even .0) soundtracks using the software decoding method, with the DVD playback software set to output in six (5.1) channel mode, and bass/LFE redirection is turned on in the software.
- When the Bass Redirection option is turned on in Surround Mixer, the sound from all channels will also be copied over to the woofer channel.

For more information about the sound card decoding and software decoding methods used for DVD playback, see Chapter 11, "Watching Movies."

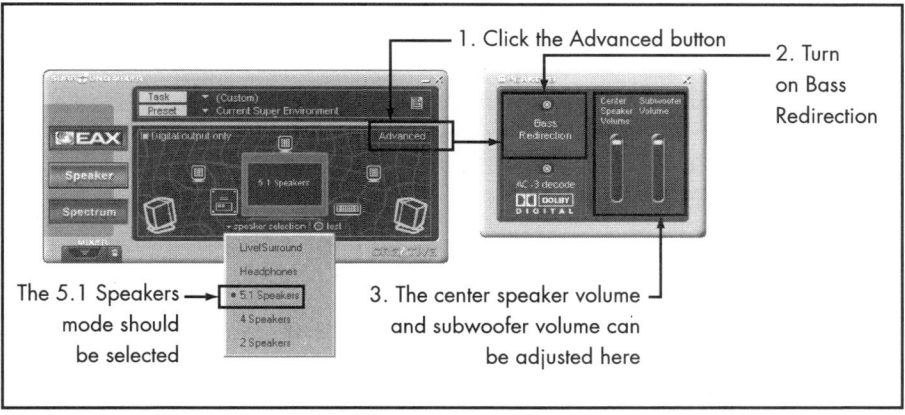

Figure 6.29: Turning on Bass Redirection and adjusting the subwoofer volume in the Surround Mixer. The volume of the center speaker can also be adjusted here.

If the Live! 5.1 does not output sound on the woofer channel, it does not mean that physical subwoofers will not be used. The subwoofers of most home theater systems will still be used when the AV receiver or decoder is set to normal/small speaker mode instead of the large speaker mode. This causes low bass

Speakers **177**

information of the five main speakers to be routed to the subwoofer. However, some AV receivers do not perform this redirection when its 5.1 discrete analog inputs are used, which is the recommended way to connect a Live! 5.1 to such speakers. For these receivers, turning on bass redirection will help.

Multimedia speakers do not have a similar mode, but because most of them use satellite speakers that already require a woofer unit to take on the bass reproduction tasks, most of them are already hardwired to reproduce bass information of the main channels, as well as the woofer output from a 5.1 sound card. However, a few 5.1 multimedia speakers do not do that, and only play back sound on the woofer unit when the sound card provides bass on its woofer output. What's worse is that this isn't very obvious to owners, because manufacturers do not clearly state how their speakers handle bass. Experiment with bass redirection and choose the setting that produces better bass output for your particular speaker system.

Analog: RCA Connectors

You can connect the 5.1 outputs of a Live! 5.1 to a 5.1-ready home theater system or other AV receivers that have discrete six-channel analog inputs. You will normally find six RCA jacks: one for each channel, namely the front left, front right, center, rear left, rear right, and woofer channels.

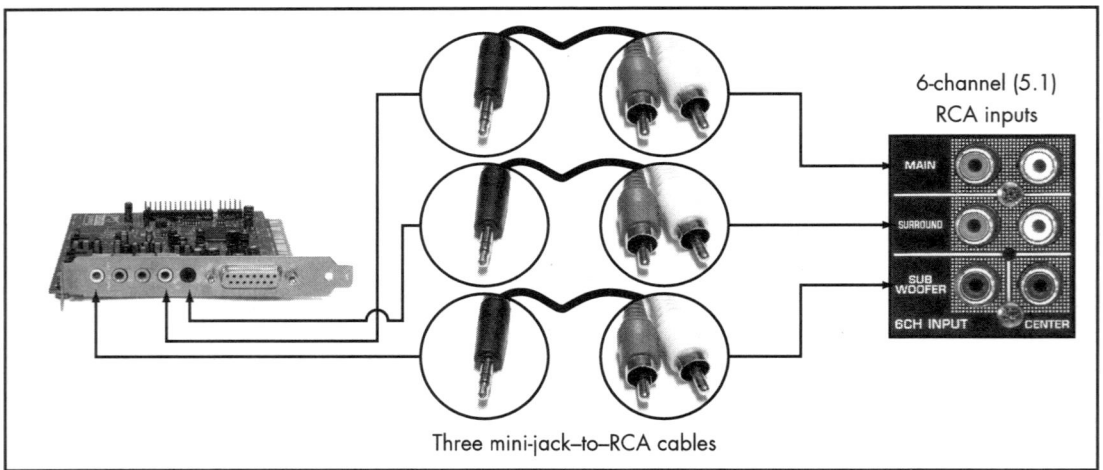

Figure 6.30: Using three mini-jack-to-RCA cables to connect a Live! 5.1 to an AV receiver with six (5.1) RCA inputs

You will need three stereo mini-jack–to–RCA cables to make this connection. Remember to use the test feature on the Surround Mixer to ensure that the speakers are set up correctly. It is very easy to accidentally swap the cables while connecting them.

TIP *To get the Live! 5.1 to output the center and woofer channels from the mini-jack digital output on the backplate, instead of a Digital DIN signal, ensure that the "Digital output only" option is not checked in the Speaker configuration in AudioHQ or Surround Mixer.*

Analog: Mini-jack Connectors

On 5.1 multimedia speakers, you will find three mini-jack connectors. The manufacturer will probably include three stereo mini-jack–to–mini-jack cables to connect the Live! to the speakers. Sometimes the three separate wires are bundled neatly together, with three different-colored mini-jack plugs at each end of the cable.

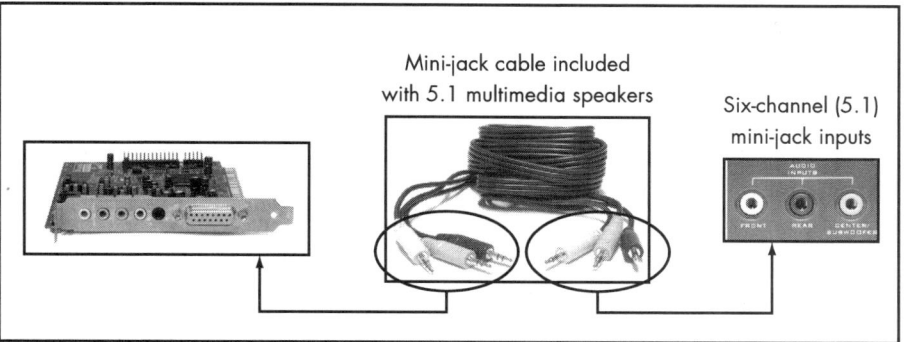

Figure 6.31: Use the color-coded cable included with the 5.1 multimedia speaker to connect the three mini-jacks at each end of the cable to the respective mini-jack outputs on the Live! 5.1 to the mini-jack inputs behind the multimedia speaker

Digital Connectors

No digital connection standard exists for uncompressed six-channel PCM audio that is output by the Live!, so most equipment has only six (5.1) analog inputs. The only exception is with Creative's Digital DIN connector found on a few multimedia speakers, which we will cover now.

Digital DIN Connectors

You can use the same mini-jack digital output and Digital DIN Out connectors described earlier in the "4 Speakers Mode" section to connect to 5.1 Digital DIN speakers. But there is a catch: some 5.1 Digital DIN speakers, such as the Cambridge SoundWorks DTT2500, work only in four-channel mode, even when connected to a 5.1 Live!

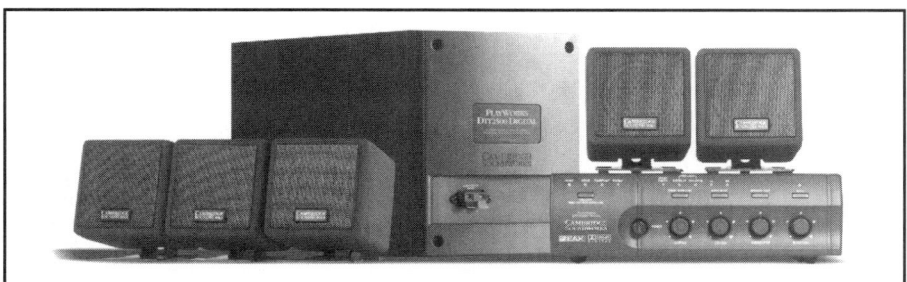

Figure 6.32: The Cambridge SoundWorks DTT2500

Speakers **179**

At the time of this writing only the Cambridge SoundWorks DTT3500, Cambridge SoundWorks MegaWorks 510D, and the Creative Inspire 5700 speaker systems support the 5.1 output from the Live! 5.1. These speakers were released after the new 5.1 cards hit the market and were therefore reworked to support the extra center/woofer signal carried over the Digital DIN connection.

TIP *On Creative and Cambridge SoundWorks 5.1 speakers with amplifier units, like the DTT series, ensure that it is in FourPoint/5.1 mode so that it uses all the channels output by the Live!*

Other 5.1 digital speakers with Digital DIN input, most notably the Cambridge SoundWorks DTT2500, were released before the third-generation Live! 5.1 cards, and do not recognize the extra center and woofer channels present on the Digital DIN cable. For the most accurate 3D positioning and surround playback with these speakers, use the 4 Speakers mode of the Live!

> It is technically possible to program a four-channel Live! card to work in 5.1 mode and enable the Digital DIN output to send the center and woofer channels. However, for market positioning reasons and because of the existence of the Live! 5.1 products, Creative has no plans to provide this as a driver upgrade to owners of existing four-channel Live! cards, although we hope the company will change its plans in the future.

Headphones Mode

The Live! has a special Headphones mode that equalizes the output from the Live! so that most headphones sound much better than when the 2 Speaker mode is used. The quality of the audio from this mode may be inferior to some, and furthermore, Creative does not allow tweaking of the parameters used in Headphones mode, so you either use it or you don't. Use the stereo mode if you prefer, because it does not alter the sound quality from the original audio source.

TIP *Use the Live!'s Line Out 1 or the headphones output on the Live!Drive. They may not provide enough amplification power enough for large headphones, so you may need to feed the line output from the Live! into an amplifier and use that to drive the headphones.*

Dolby Headphone

Dolby Headphone is a virtual surround technology that recreates a realistic 5.1 sound system with just the left and right channels piped to a pair of headphones. Find out more about this in Chapter 11, "Watching Movies."

Live!Surround Mode

Stereo signals carry audio for the left and right speakers and work with almost any audio system. A stereo signal can also have extra center and surround speaker channels hidden in them, by using a technique known as *matrix encoding*. The most popular matrix-encoding format is Dolby Surround. Such surround technologies still use a stereo connection (with two wires) to transmit audio, so the physical connection is similar to stereo. Chapter 11, "Watching Movies," will talk about how you can play back such surround soundtracks with the Live!

Live!Surround is a Creative-developed sound processing technology that takes the multichannel output from the Live! and converts it to a stereo signal that is compatible with Dolby Surround and Pro Logic decoders. (Officially, Creative does not mention compatibility with any particular type of matrix decoding, probably because of licensing issues.) When Live!Surround signals are fed into a multimedia speaker or AV receiver with matrix decoding, you will get four channels of audio: front left, front right, center, and surround. To use Live!Surround, be sure that your audio system can perform matrix decoding, like Circle Surround, DTS Neo 6, Pro Logic, or Pro Logic II.

A Small Drawback

Because of the limitations of masking extra channels in a stereo signal that also has to be heard like a normal stereo signal, there is only one surround channel in Dolby Surround. On a typical 5.1 home theater setup, this surround channel is sent to both surround speakers. As you may realize, 3D sounds in games that are positioned behind you cannot sound like they are coming from a particular position behind you. But with discrete surround channels provided by the 4 Speakers or 5.1 Speakers modes, you can pinpoint whether a sound is close to the rear left or rear right or 180 degrees behind you.

> More discrete channels of audio result in more accurate 3D positioning (though more than 7.1 speakers is considered overkill and would cause speaker placement problems, not to mention budgetary concerns).

Do Not Use Live!Surround for *All* Surround and AV Receivers

The Live! manual vaguely mentions that Live!Surround will allow you to use the card with home theater systems, without mentioning in detail the type of decoding that can be used. This has confused many Live! users.

Live! 5.1

If your Live! card is a 5.1 model and your home theater system has discrete 5.1-channel inputs, connecting the Live! to the home theater system using three mini-jack–to–RCA cables (as described earlier in the section "5.1 Speakers Mode") would allow the Live! to send each of the 5.1 channels directly to the receiver or decoder. Therefore, if discrete inputs are supported by the AV receiver, use it as a first choice. Use Live!Surround and matrix decoding only when the AV receiver does not have discrete 5.1 inputs.

Other Live! Cards

With a four-channel Live! and an AV receiver that supports discrete 5.1 inputs, your preference determines which of the two speaker configurations you use:

- Connect in stereo and use Dolby Pro Logic decoding for a front, center, left, and mono surround channel using the connection methods described in the "2 Speakers Mode" section earlier in this chapter.
- Connect the four channels using two stereo cables from the Live! to the front left, front right, rear left, and rear right on the 5.1 discrete input jacks. (The center and woofer inputs will not be used.) Use the "Analog: RCA Connection" method described in the "4 Speakers Mode" section earlier in this chapter.

With a four-channel Live! and a receiver that does not have discrete 5.1 inputs, always use the Live!Surround mode so that you can get the center and surround channels from the Live! unless you do not like the Live!Surround effect, in which case you can switch the Live! to 2 Speakers mode to send an unaltered stereo signal to the receiver.

If you often play games that use 3D audio, using the second method to obtain the rear left and rear right output from the Live! will result in better 3D positioning. Otherwise, the Live!Surround mode would usually suffice.

Connecting Live!Surround

Use the same methods, cables, and connectors as described earlier for 2 Speakers mode to connect to an AV receiver or multimedia speaker that supports matrix decoding like Pro Logic. You have a choice of either analog connections using RCA jacks and mini-jacks, or digital connections using coaxial or optical cables.

The decoder has to be manually switched to Dolby Pro Logic mode. Your receiver will not be able to auto-detect and switch to Dolby Pro Logic mode even if you use digital connections.

If your sound system has Dolby Digital decoding, the Dolby Digital mode will not be activated even if you connect to the Live! using digital cables (unless you use the S/PDIF passthrough mode while playing DVDs with a software DVD player). The digital cable will continue to output a stereo PCM audio, not a multichannel Dolby Digital compressed signal.

Other Speaker Technologies on the Live!

Creative Multi-Speaker Surround (CMSS)

CMSS works when the Live! is set to any speaker mode, but is most effective in creating a surround channel with physical rear speakers when the 4 or 5.1 Speakers modes are used. It works like other matrix-decoding techniques—taking a stereo signal and creates a surround channel (and a center channel if the 5.1 Speakers mode on a Live! 5.1 is used). Unless you are performing matrix decoding like Pro Logic decoding using an external decoder or AV receiver, CMSS will work fine with any speaker configuration and can provide decoding for Dolby Surround–encoded soundtracks.

Find out how to enable CMSS in the "Sound Card Decoding with CMSS" section in Chapter 11, "Watching Movies."

> The two-channel–to–5.1 conversion feature on more costly Creative and Cambridge SoundWorks multimedia speakers also uses the CMSS name. The CMSS Movie and CMSS Music modes on the speakers sound slightly better than the Live! card's single CMSS mode.

Virtual Surround: Many Channels with Two Speakers

Another feature of the Live! card's speaker support is virtual surround. Using as its basis the way that a human with just two ears can determine whether a sound is coming from the front or back, the virtual surround theory suggests that it is possible to use algorithms to process sound so that the sound from two speakers can give the illusion of many speakers. Interestingly, Creative has not branded this feature with any fancy name, but it is present in the drivers, working in the background when you set the Live! to 2 Speakers or Headphones mode and play a game that uses 3D positioning APIs like DirectSound3D or OpenAL.

Games that support 3D positioning have their sound effects coded with instructions to specify the position of the sound 360 degrees around the listening position. This feature works best on multichannel setups with more than two speakers because it is difficult to simulate surround without speakers actually behind the listener. However, in 2 Speakers and Headphones modes, the Live! does not have rear speakers to work with, so the virtual surround algorithms are used to simulate them. (These algorithms are different from the ones used by Live!Surround to encode and generate positional audio that can be decoded with Dolby Pro Logic.)

Find out more about 3D positioning in Chapter 10, "Playing Games."

> Virtual surround is different from other 3D sound technologies that take a stereo sound source and expand the stereo image to make it sound very wide and dispersed, but without any form of active directional positioning like what the Live! and other 3D positioning techniques do. This form of pseudo–3D surround, commonly known as *stereo expansion,* may change the sound so much that it may not be what the recording engineers and artists originally intended.

These virtual surround systems make use of a sound-processing technique known as the *head-related transfer function* (HRTF). HRTFs are applied to the original sound to produce an altered sound that attempts to take into account the changes a sound would undergo after traveling through the air and reaching a person's ear. This technique is especially useful for simulating a slightly muffled and delayed sound that is coming from behind a person's head, eliminating the need for surround speakers.

> The Live! does not use virtual surround when playing back non-DirectSound3D audio.

One way to research the proper HRTFs is to record the properties of a sound that is being played back from known directions around a model of a human head. Microphones placed inside the ears of the model are used to take measurements of the sound, to be compared to the original sound being played back to determine which characteristics of the sound have changed. With these measurements, HRTFs can be developed to simulate these changes on other sounds.

Virtual surround can be very effective for some people; however, in reality, it just does not sound realistic for most people when compared to real surround speakers firing from behind. Moreover, many implementations require you to place your head in a sweet spot, which is a small area where the virtual surround will be most effective. Once you turn your head around, it will foil the audio image. It's hard to keep your head completely still when you're in the middle of an exciting game! Different head sizes have different distances between the ears, so most virtual surround implementations use an average head size, which probably is one of the reasons why some people find that HRTFs are not effective.

Height Positioning

The Live! also uses HRTFs for DirectSound3D gaming in four-channel and 5.1-channel modes to simulate the up-down movement of a sound to help you pinpoint whether a particular sound is above your head or below it. This is a very subtle effect, and many users seldom realize that this feature exists. This effect is also diminished when the front and rear speakers are not firing toward the listener at the same angle, like when the front and rear speakers are placed at different heights.

> Height positioning was added with the release of Live!Ware 2.

This is a good feature because it enhances realism of sound. It is also expensive to use extra speakers aligned in a vertical column at a fixed spot just to position sound that moves up and down. This is less important than having speakers around a listener to obtain the surround effect, so height positioning is attempted virtually in the Live!

Speaker Placement

Have you already gone through a long selection process and countless hours at the store auditioning to find the perfect pair of speakers? How and where you place the speakers will also play a crucial role in a good audio experience.

Making Speakers Work for You

Many people place speakers in the absolute worst positions, and most of the time it is because of convenience or to fit the speakers into the existing décor or layout.

Some use a minicomponent system for the Live!, where both speakers are located on a shelf to the left or right of the computer desk. The sound always comes from a corner from the seating position—no use for stereo here!

Many people place surround speakers on top of the front left and front right speakers, or elsewhere around the front soundstage. We have seen dealers do it, and to our horror, people do it when they bring the speakers home, too! Sure, it looks really nice, but it makes the front soundstage such a mess that we would rather recommend using the Live! in stereo mode. Admittedly, it is a chore to set up surround speakers, but it is a one-time task. Once it is done, you'll benefit from a much more involving aural experience.

Many people fit speakers into their environment, sometimes compromising their placement and ruining the soundstage that the speakers are capable of reproducing. To rephrase a popular saying: Do not let your environment dictate where you put your speakers. Change your environment to suit yourself and, of course, the speakers!

There are too many room sizes and room and furniture configurations to cover every variation in detail. As a result, the placement tips mentioned here are not meant to be hard and fast rules. In the end, listening closely and experimenting with different setups will help you find the optimal speaker configuration for your listening environment. After all, the speakers are here for your listening pleasure!

Room Acoustics

Speak in an empty house, and you will hear your voice drowned in a damp and cold echo caused by sound reflecting off the walls, floor, and ceiling. After the room is populated with furniture and carpeting, it becomes a whole new audio environment, with the reflecting sounds absorbed by items in the room.

Room acoustics play an important role in audio, and a good listening environment should not cause so many reflections that the sound is excessively colored. The speakers should have a direct line of sight to the listening position. The location of the speakers in a room also plays a big part. Having the left and right speakers equidistant from the walls to the left and right will cause the reflections from each speaker to be equal, and in some rooms this results in a markedly improved soundstage. If you are at liberty to move your PC around, you should experiment with different listening positions to hear how the audio from the speakers is affected by the changes.

Front Speakers

The front speakers should be placed at the same distance to the left and right of the listening position. The speakers should be far apart enough that you can hear a dynamic front soundstage that seems to come from a wide area in front of you. If the speakers are placed too close together, the soundstage will not be as wide, and the sound will be less dispersed—as if it is coming from a narrow area in the center. This is a very common problem because many people place satellite speakers to the sides of a small computer monitor.

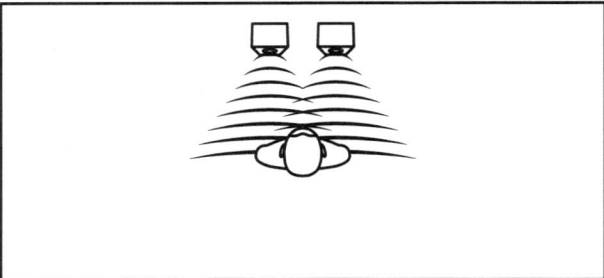

Figure 6.33: Speakers placed too narrowly together

Conversely, if the speakers are too far apart, you will get an effect known as a "hole in the center," where sound seems to come from the sides instead of from the front, and the center will be hollow, as if there is a huge gap without sound. Try placing the speakers far apart enough to form a 45-degree angle from the listening position.

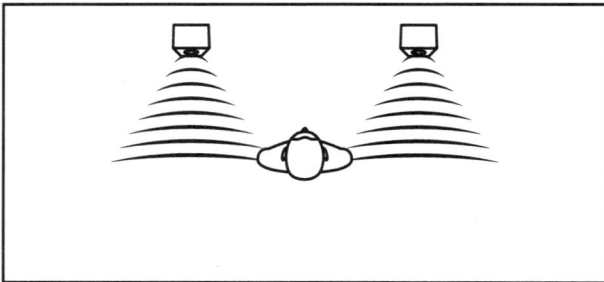

Figure 6.34: A "hole in the center" effect, caused by speakers placed too far apart

Another solution to this problem is to angle the speakers inward, toward the center, so that the soundstage is narrowed. This method is called *toe in*.

> You will notice that sound takes on a subtly different characteristic and timbre when it is nearer to or in a direct line of sight with your ears.

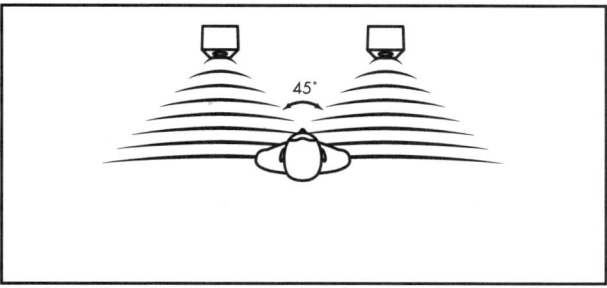

Figure 6.35: Left and right speakers placed at a 45-degree angle from the listening position

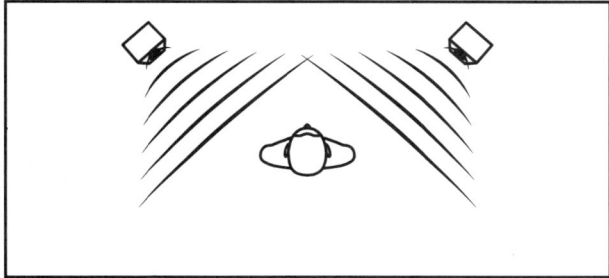

Figure 6.36: Speakers that can only be placed far apart can be angled toward the listener

If your room layout only allows the speakers to be placed far apart, consider a 5.1-channel sound system, where the center speaker can be used to fill the gap in the center.

The height of the speakers is also crucial. Both speakers should be placed so that the sound waves travel to ear level when you are seated at the listening position. Many times, multimedia speakers placed beside the monitor come with stands that are angled so low that the speaker drivers are firing way below ear level. Elevating the speakers may result in an improvement in sound.

> Humans hear high frequencies better than low ones.

Test and modify the position of speakers while in a comfortable listening position. If you sit in a sofa in the listening position, be sure to test the height while sitting down because a change in height can alter the characteristic of a sound, especially in the middle (or midrange) and high frequencies. If the speakers have stands that can pivot up and down, make sure both speakers are set to the same angle so that one speaker is not aimed higher than the other (unless, of course, the speakers are placed on separate pieces of furniture of different heights). Another potential problem may arise with speakers at different heights because when the height of the listening position is slightly changed, the speakers will again be aimed at different angles.

Figure 6.37: The front speakers should be angled such that the sound seems to be coming at ear level

The Center Speaker

A 5.1 home theater or multimedia speaker system adds a center channel that is used primarily to reproduce on-screen sound; thus, the center speaker is usually placed on a monitor or television set. This speaker also has to work together with the left and right speakers to provide a convincing front sound field where sound can move smoothly between the speakers and not seem to hop from one speaker to another. The dialogue should also be intelligible and not be difficult to make out from the listening position.

The center speaker should be at the same distance from the listening position as the front left and front right speakers. If the left and right speakers are farther away from the listening position than the center speaker, the split-second difference can cause the human ear to believe that a sound played on all front speakers is coming primarily from the center. Use a measuring tape or string to measure the distance from the left, right, and center speakers to the listening position and then move the center speaker backward, or the left and right speakers forward, accordingly.

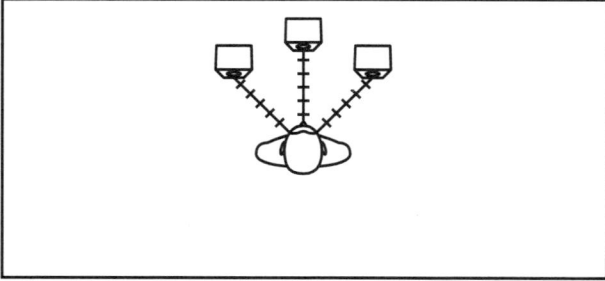

Figure 6.38: The center and front speakers should be at the same distance from the listening position

Another way to compensate for different distances between speakers is available on most AV receivers (and also a few 5.1 multimedia speakers with built-in decoders). They will allow you to set the center and left/right channel delays individually to compensate for the differences in distance to the listening position. Check your manual to see how this can be achieved.

In addition to distance, the height of the center speaker is just as important, because the human ear can easily localize midrange and treble sound. The mid- and high-frequency drivers of the front and center speakers should be aligned at the same level so that sound from any of these speakers will appear to come from the same level. If this is not possible, you can try tilting the speakers.

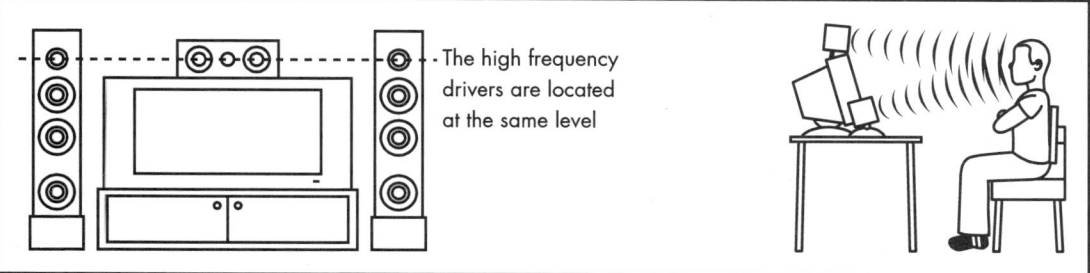

Figure 6.39: The size of the speakers may automatically allow them to be aligned to the center speaker. Otherwise it will have to be tilted downward, like in a 5.1 multimedia speaker system.

If the center speaker is so high above the listening position that sounds appear to go over your head instead of being directed toward you, you should tilt the speaker lower.

Many multimedia speakers come with two stands for the center speaker: one tilted downward, and the other angled upward, like the stands for the other speakers. If there is no space above the monitor for the speaker, you can use the stand that tilts upward and place the speaker close to the front of the monitor.

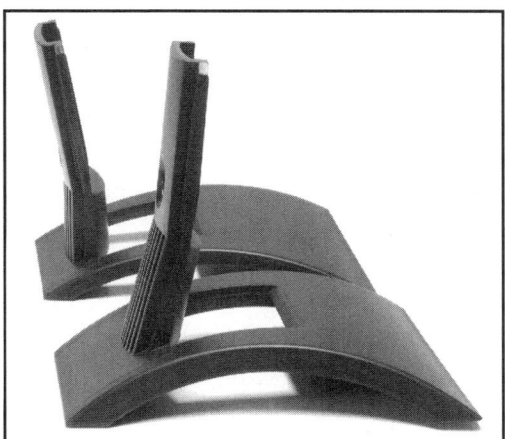

Figure 6.40: Two types of speaker stands provided with the Creative Inspire 5300 5.1 speakers. The stand in the foreground is angled downward and should be used if the center speaker is placed atop a monitor.

Surround Speakers

Surround speakers are found on four-channel multimedia speakers, as well as 5.1 home theaters and multimedia speaker systems. Surround speakers were born out of the necessity to effectively reproduce an enveloping sound field matching the environment represented by images on the monitor or television screen, not only behind, but also around the listener. Another more recent use of surround speakers, with the advent of discrete surround sound formats like Dolby Digital, and 3D positional audio, is to place the sound in an exact location behind or to the sides, or to facilitate a smooth transition when a sound has to gradually move from the front left or front right speakers to the surrounds.

There are many ways to place surround speakers, but there are two methods to position them, depending on the type of audio you normally listen with the Live! The first is to position them by following the traditional recommendations described in most home theater publications, which work best for movies and other surround-encoded material. The other way is to position them for gaming, in arrangements that optimize the 3D positioning algorithms used by the Live! to place sounds in a 360-degree sound field. Choosing between them shouldn't be difficult once you know how often you watch movies versus how often you play games with 3D positioning.

Positioning for Surround Sound

Surround speakers in this purpose are used more often to create an enveloping sound field, than to place sounds in a particular location behind the audience. These speakers can be pointed at walls and ceilings so that sound waves bounce off these surfaces and become diffused, or they can be pointing directly at the listening position for a more directed sound. Some of the positioning tips may help you place the surround speakers in positions that create a wide sound field to the rear. However, always be open to experimentation to determine the positions that are best for you.

> Many AV receivers and 5.1 multimedia speakers with decoders have speaker tests that help you determine if you have connected the speakers correctly. They can also help you adjust and balance the volume from the main speakers. Aim to have all speakers at the same volume level.

The surround speakers can be located further behind the listener than the main speakers, and if you are using a home theater system, the delay settings found on most AV receivers can help compensate for the difference. The left and right surround speakers can be farther apart than the front left and front right speakers, because having them too close together will cause the surround soundstage to be very narrow, and the sound will not feel wide enough to literally surround the listeners.

Ideally, surround speakers should not be placed so that the sound is aimed directly at ear level, because it will diminish the surround effect when listeners can tell where the speakers are. The surround speakers should ideally be two to four feet above ear level and aimed across the room to provide a more open and spacious sound field.

If there are two walls beside the listening position, you can mount the surround speakers on the walls, at least two feet above ear level. If the walls are not of equal distance from the listening position, consider shifting the seat to the center so that the sound from both surrounds reaches the listener at the same time. Alternatively, if your surround speakers have compatible speaker stands, you can place them to the sides of the listening position. The stands should be slightly higher than ear level, as well. Alternatively, the stands should be tilt-adjustable so that you can aim them higher. This is an important feature to look for because some multimedia speakers come with stands that are very short.

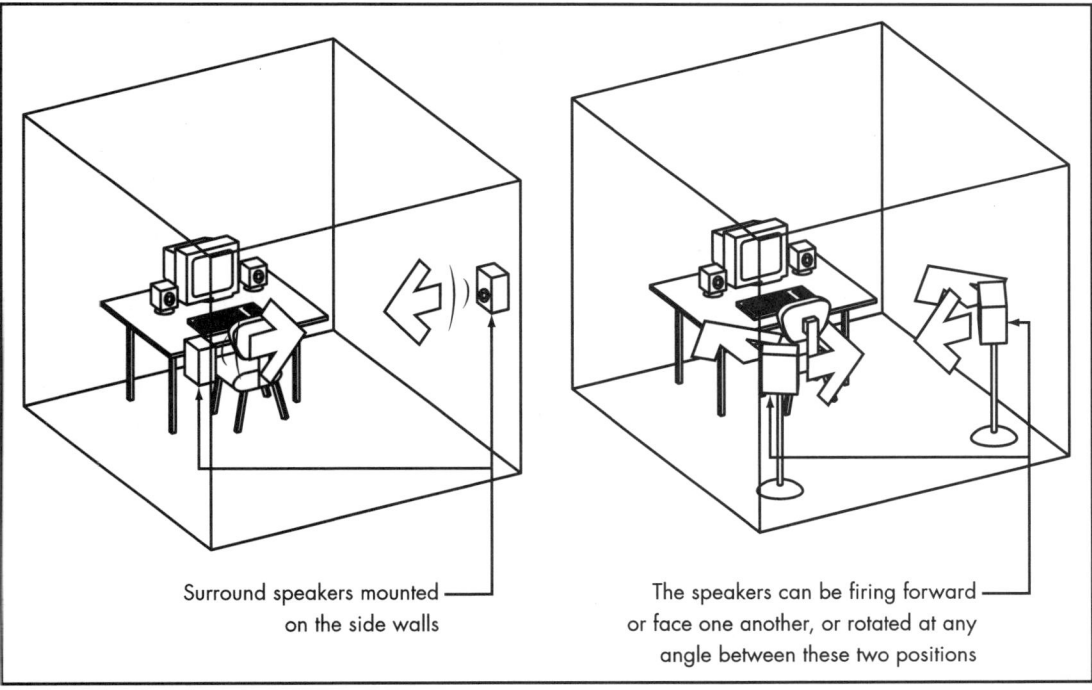

Figure 6.41: The surround speakers can be mounted on walls to the sides of the listening position, or on speaker stands

TIP *Many multimedia speakers do not come with speaker stands or other mounting options, so be sure to decide how you can install the speakers before purchasing them.*

A wall behind the listening position can also be used to mount the surround speakers. You can align the speakers so that they point toward one another, or you can face them toward the opposite end of the room. If your surround speakers have mounting brackets that allow the angle to be changed, you can experiment to pick an angle that provides the best coverage for your particular speaker and room dimensions.

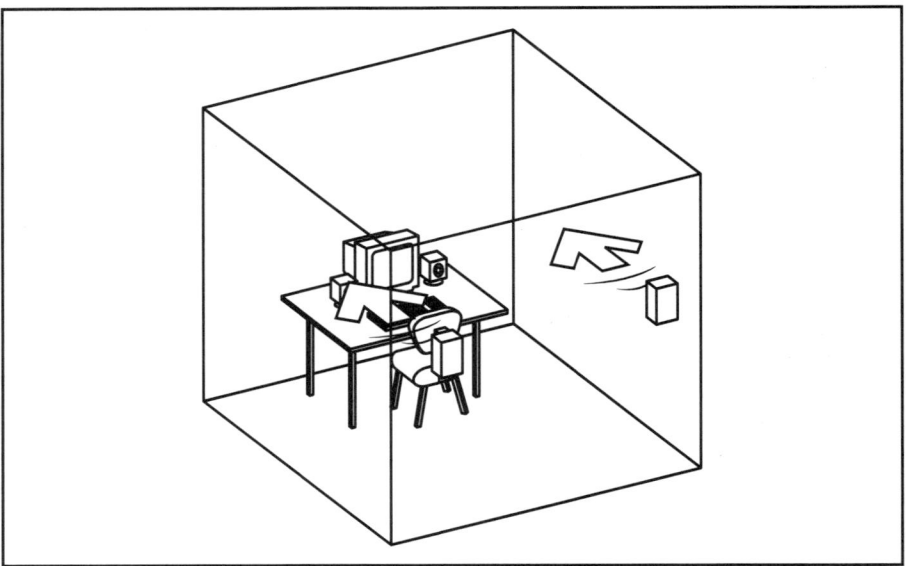

Figure 6.42: The surround speakers can also be mounted on a wall behind the listening position

If you are having difficulty placing the surround speakers anywhere behind or to the sides of the listening position and must have them in front, a last resort would be to try placing them far apart at the edge of, say, a table and point them toward the back (as shown in Figure 6.43). This may cause the sound to appear from behind the listening position if you don't sit too far back that the surrounds sound like they are coming from the front. Experiment with the placement angles of the surround speakers to find the position that gives the surround soundstage that you prefer.

When setting up these speakers, you may need to replace the included speaker cables with longer ones. Please do so! Do not let the length of the speaker cables restrict your placement choices. If you are moving into or redesigning a new home or room, take into account the location of the speakers and where the wires can be hidden. In-wall speakers and flat speaker cables are readily available.

Positioning for Games with 3D Audio
Unlike general surround sound, games using 3D positioning APIs like DirectSound and OpenAL use parameters to precisely define the angle, height, and distance of a particular sound source in the game world. The sound card uses these parameters to reproduce the sounds in the correct position, in relation to the position of the listener, but this is accurate only when the surround speakers are placed correctly. This is important for the surround speakers of 4- and 5.1-channel speaker systems.

The surround speakers should ideally be placed as far behind, and as far apart, as the front left and front right speakers are (see Figure 6.44). The speakers can be pointing forward or toed in, but the sound should always reach the listener such that sounds that come directly from behind (and in front) can be located accurately. You can use games with 3D audio to test the effectiveness of a speaker placement.

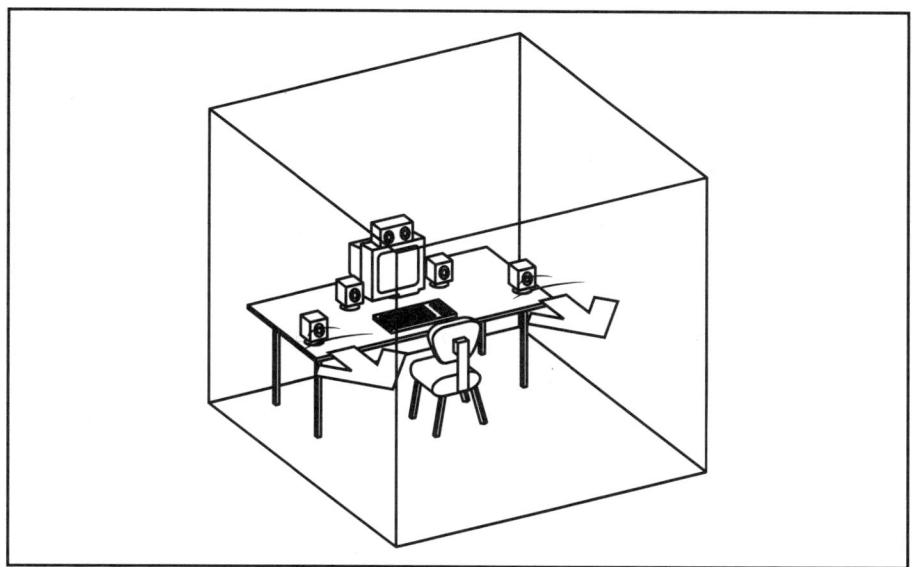

Figure 6.43: If there is no space behind, the surrounds can also be placed in front, pointing to the back

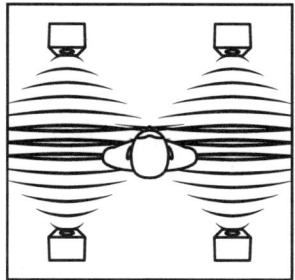 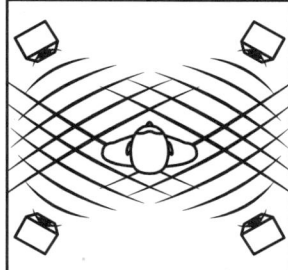

Figure 6.44: The surround speakers for 3D games should be placed in relation to the front speakers. They can be pointed straight forward (as shown at left), or toed in (as shown at right).

The Live! also uses audio processing techniques like crosstalk cancellation to ensure that sounds meant for a particular direction appear and move among the speakers accurately, and the four (or five) equally positioned speakers in the front and rear work together to create a precise 3D soundstage. This is marred when the distance of each of the speakers to the listener is altered, causing sounds from further speakers to arrive later then sounds from nearer speakers.

HRTFs and other techniques are employed to perform height positioning, so the surround speakers should ideally be located at the same height as the front speakers. An alternative is to tilt the speakers such that they hit the listening spot at the same angle as the front speakers. If the surrounds are placed too high up, the height positioning is lost, and the timbre of sounds coming from behind also changes, causing the sound effects to lose some directionality.

This configuration is more stringent than home theater placements, and of course, it would be ideal for the positions of the surround speakers to be a mirror image of the positions of the front speakers. However, not all rooms can accommodate that, so try the alternative speaker placements suggested in the previous section, while trying your best to place the rear speakers to get the same effect as the sound from the front speakers. The distance that the sound travels and the angle at which the sound hits the listening spot should be consistent for both the front and the rear.

Subwoofers

Placing subwoofers requires a fair amount of trial and error because of different room sizes and walls and furnishing, which alter the audio characteristics of bass. Bass is omnidirectional, and the sound waves spread out in all directions instead of moving in a straight line like mid- and high-frequency sound waves do. It is difficult to tell the location of an earthquake or machinery from its low rumble, compared to the location of a bee that is whizzing around. This characteristic of bass gives us the freedom to place the subwoofer in other positions, but it also means that the characteristics of the room can potentially hamper the performance of the subwoofer.

Placing Woofer Units of Multimedia Speakers
The "subwoofers" (actually woofers) of some multimedia speakers output high-bass sound to compensate for satellite speakers that cannot reproduce them effectively. If the woofers of such speakers are placed too far away from the front speakers, you would probably be able to pinpoint the location of the woofer unit, which isn't ideal. Such woofer units need to be placed below and between the front speakers—in the middle of the front soundstage. For example, if you have the front left and front right speakers at the corners of a desk, the woofer unit should be placed in the center, below the desk. The best position is the position where the woofer unit sounds like it is integrated with the front left and front right speakers, and not like a separate speaker by itself.

Placing Subwoofers
Subwoofers (and also front speakers that have woofer drivers) that are placed near the corner of a room, close to a wall and floor, will reflect bass off these hard surfaces and increase the dispersion of bass. However, this placement does not always mean that the bass will be as tight and punchy; some surfaces and subwoofers can sound extremely boomy and muddled. Conversely, placing a subwoofer away from the walls, at the center of a room, may cause the bass to be weak.

Experiment with the different positions and subwoofer volume levels to find the bass that you like. In some cases, a particular spot in the room may have weak bass. If these weak spots are around the listening area, change the subwoofer placement, or if your subwoofer has a switch labeled "Phase," flip it to see if it the bass will be more apparent.

Here's a recommended way to set up a subwoofer: Place the subwoofer *at* the listening position and play something that outputs bass frequently. Then walk around the room to determine the spots in the room that have punchy and powerful bass. These would be ideal places for the subwoofer.

Ultimately, the subwoofer should blend in with the other speakers, especially the front and center speakers, because its main role is to augment the bass capabilities of these speakers. It should not sound like a separate speaker or as if it is coming from a particular direction.

**PART THREE
FUN STUFF**

7

THE MIXER

On a hi-fi system, you normally have a knob or buttons to choose one sound source you want to listen to, such as tape, CD, or tuner. Sound cards, however, work somewhat differently. Anything connected to the sound card can play at any time, be it Wave audio, music from the CD-ROM drive, or sound from any other source. Some games may use CD audio to play background music, while Wave features may be used for sound effects, requiring both audio sources to be heard at the same time. This multitude of possibilites makes switching audio sources impossible in a sound card. To overcome this, all sound cards use a mixer to combine and allow multiple sound sources to be heard together.

Mixing Audio

In a music studio, the *mixer* is the device that all audio outputs and microphones are connected to. There is a vertical slider for each sound source, allowing the volume of each sound source to be adjusted individually. The mixer in the Live! has exactly the same purpose, although you can access it only through a software program, which is usually known as—surprise, surprise—the mixer, or sometimes the Volume Control. Mixers blend two or more sound sources together so that any number of sound sources can be played simultaneously on the speakers without having to switch among them. For example, you can play a MIDI file or audio CD and sing along using a microphone connected to the Live! The Live! will let you adjust the relative volume levels of the various sound sources and mute those sources that are not used, producing a balanced mix of sound sources over the speakers.

How the Live! Routes, Mixes, and Resamples Audio

In contrast to previous sound cards from Creative, all audio routing (what sound is sent to what output), resampling (conversion between audio sources with different sample rates and resolutions), and effects processing on the Live! are done within the EMU10K1 (the card's main audio processor) and therefore kept within the digital domain as long as possible. This ensures that there is minimal loss of sound quality and less noise than is commonly associated with traditional sound card mixers because of their analog mixing circuits and the electrically noisy environment inside a PC case. Analog signals are used only for obtaining audio from external audio equipment (such as when you record from a microphone) and outputting the audio to external sound systems (like connecting the line outputs on the Live! card to speaker systems).

Audio Sources

All Live! cards have a number of sound sources that are mapped to mixer sliders to allow the volume of each source to be individually controlled. The following table lists the audio sources available on Live! cards. Depending on the model or whether a digital I/O device is installed, some of these sources may not be available. For example, the OEM models sometimes omit the CD_SPDIF internal connector, so the CD Digital input will not be operable in the mixer.

Refer to Chapter 3, "The Sound Blaster Live! Hardware," for more information on the Live! hardware and the available connections on the different generations and models.

Table 7-1: Sound Sources Available on the Sound Blaster Live!

Audio Source	Description	Analog	Digital
Wave	This is the most important audio source on a sound card. It plays back all Wave audio from media players, 3D and sound effects from games, Dolby Digital soundtracks decoded internally by the Live! 5.1, and even the sound events in Windows. This sound source is sometimes labeled DirectSound and/or MP3, because game audio and MP3 playback all use the Wave output and can be controlled with this slider.		✓
MIDI	This input includes all sounds played back by the MIDI sequencer of the EMU10K1 (including SoundFonts), as well as the software synthesizer included in the Live! drivers. A few games still use MIDI for music, but the majority now come with prerecorded music that is played back through the Wave output instead. Some Web pages also embed space-efficient MIDI files that can produce music with a quick download.		✓
Line In	This input controls the volume of the equipment connected to the analog mini-jack line input on the card's backplate.	✓	
Microphone	This input corresponds to the Mic In input on the Live! card's backplate. It connects only to microphones and is monophonic, so the sound will be duplicated in the left and right channels.	✓	
CD Audio	This input allows control of the CD_IN connector on the Live! card. As explained in Chapter 3, "The Sound Blaster Live! Hardware," this input is connected to optical drives that can play audio CDs. CD audio inputs are used only when normal audio CDs are played. Any other data discs, such as those for games, movies, and MP3 files, are read digitally and played through the Wave output on the sound card instead of the CD Audio output.	✓	
Auxiliary	This input works just like the CD Audio input, so you can connect another optical drive or an internal peripheral with a similar output. Mute this slider when nothing is connected.	✓	

Table 7-1: Sound Sources Available on the Sound Blaster Live! (continued)

Audio Source	Description	Audio Format Analog	Digital
TAD In	This input corresponds to the TAD connector that connects to some internal telephony and modem cards. You can hear and control the level of audio and dialing sounds from these peripherals.	✓	
CD Digital	This input is a digital connection with optical drives like CD-ROM, DVD-ROM, or CD-RW drives, and is used only when audio CDs are played. If your drive has a two-pin digital output, use this input instead of the CD Audio input. All other digital audio in data discs read by the optical drive will be output through the Wave output instead. Some OEM Live! cards do not have this connector.		✓
I^2S In (PC-DVD)	This seldom used input is found only on first-generation Live! cards, including the CT4620. It does not accept a standard digital input such as CD digital and works with only a limited number of peripherals. It was removed in subsequent generations of the Live!		✓
S/PDIF In/Auxiliary 2*	This input will appear if you have a digital I/O device such as the Live!Drive. The Live!Drive II and Live!Drive IR have a stereo RCA input that will work through this mixer input if it is switched to Aux In mode. (See Chapter 4, "Accessories Galore!" for instructions on how this is done in the mixer.) If the digital I/O device is not a Live!Drive, this input will be labeled "S/PDIF In." You cannot input any nonstandard PCM format, or PCM data that exceeds 16 bits and 48kHz. Dolby Digital and DTS soundtracks from consumer DVD players cannot be input to the Live! in this manner.		✓
Line In 2/Microphone 2*	Found on the Live!Drive, this input provides an extra line input through a 1/4-inch jack. This input is also available on the optical digital I/O card but is labeled "Line In 2" (without "Microphone 2") because unlike the Live!Drive, it does not have a knob that can switch the jack to a microphone input.		✓

* Although Auxiliary 2 and Line In 2/Microphone 2 are analog inputs on the Live!Drive and the optical digital I/O card, these digital I/O devices communicate with the Live! using a digital connection. Remember the flat cable connecting the sound card to the digital I/O device? The Live!Drive has its own set of analog-to-digital and digital-to-analog converters to support the analog connectors on the Live!Drive. Therefore, to the sound card, these inputs are considered digital sources and work as such in the mixer.

Refer to Chapter 3, "The Sound Blaster Live! Hardware," for a description of the internal and backplate connectors on the Live! card.

> Mic and Mic In 2 are mono sound sources. The rest of the sound sources are stereo. However, if you are using more than two speakers and use software like games and DVD players that produce multichannel audio with DirectSound3D (or Dolby Digital soundtracks decoded by the Live! 5.1), these outputs all use the Wave slider in the mixer to control the volume of all channels, including the surrounds and center/woofer channels (found on Live! 5.1 cards only).

Some inputs, such as Line In, Mic In, CD Audio, and S/PDIF In, are *external sound sources*—in other words, the audio signal comes from a device outside the Live! card. There are also *internal sound sources*, such as the MIDI synthesizer and the digital audio playback (Wave) channel. These sound sources are played internally by the sound card and don't rely on input from an external device. The Live! doesn't distinguish between internal and external sources, as long as you have them set up correctly in the mixer.

The following table shows what type of external connector or internal sound source each input in the mixer corresponds to.

Table 7.2: Inputs in the Live! Mixer and Their Corresponding Sound Sources

Audio Source	Symbol in the Mixer	Internal	External (on the Live! card's backplate)	External (on the Live! card)	External (on a digital I/O device)
Wave		✓			
MIDI		✓			
Line In			✓		
Microphone			✓		
CD Audio				✓	
Auxiliary				✓	

Table 7.2: Inputs in the Live! Mixer and Their Corresponding Sound Sources (continued)

Audio Source	Symbol in the Mixer	Internal	External (on the Live! card's backplate)	External (on the Live! card)	External (on a digital I/O device)
TAD In				✓	
CD Digital				✓	
I²S In (PC-DVD)				✓	
S/PDIF In/Auxiliary 2					✓
Line In 2/Microphone 2					✓

S/PDIF Passthrough

The behavior of the mixer is slightly different when S/PDIF passthrough is enabled in the settings of a software DVD player. This feature allows the Live! to output a Dolby Digital or DTS signal to an external decoder through the front digital output on an attached digital I/O device. While S/PDIF passthrough is in effect, the mixer is completely bypassed, and the master volume and other settings usually available for sound sources cannot be used to control the volume of the surround soundtrack from the DVD. However, changes made to the mixer will continue to be registered on the sound card and the changes can be heard once S/PDIF passthrough is turned off by stopping the DVD playback.

> Passthrough takes effect only when a DVD with a surround soundtrack is played, but not when the player is loaded on the desktop but is not playing anything.

S/PDIF passthrough is covered in detail in Chapter 11, "Watching Movies."

Live! 5.1 Cards

This behavior is a little different on a Live! 5.1 when AC-3 Decode is enabled in the mixer. If the software DVD player is also configured to use S/PDIF passthrough, and AC-3 decoding is in effect when playing a Dolby Digital–encoded DVD, the outputs of the sound card are not entirely disabled. Rather, the Dolby Digital soundtrack will be mixed and heard together with the other sound sources of the sound card.

The decoded surround sound is not assigned to any audio slider, but the overall volume of the soundtrack can be controlled with the master volume slider. Unlike non–AC-3 decoding mode (or when S/PDIF passthrough is used with non–Live! 5.1 cards), the master volume control and changes made to the other sliders and settings in the mixer can be immediately heard even when S/PDIF passthrough is turned on together with AC-3 Decode mode.

Using Mixers

To change the mixer settings (such as what sound sources to listen to and the overall volume and tone controls), you can use either the Windows built-in mixer application (usually called the Volume Control) or the Live!'s Surround Mixer. If you have the latter installed, it will most likely be the application of choice, because it is tailor-made for the Live! and makes all the unique features easily accessible. However, if your PC is slow, you may notice that Creative's mixer takes slightly longer to load than the Windows mixer.

> Most sounds cards today, including the Live!, conform to Intel's AC'97 specification. Therefore, you can also use a generic AC'97 mixer program to control sound cards that conform to the AC'97 specifications.

The Windows Mixer (Volume Control)

Windows includes a standard mixer application, or Volume Control (as it is known in most versions of Windows), that works with any supported sound card, including the Live! By default, a small speaker icon will be displayed in the system tray (at the lower right corner of your screen) if a sound card is installed in the PC (except for Windows XP). (The speaker icon can be enabled or disabled in Sounds • Multimedia in the Control Panel.) The Windows Mixer can be quickly brought up by double-clicking the icon. The mixer can also be run from the Start menu, under Accessories • Entertainment.

In the Mixer window, audio sources are displayed in a separate column (also known as a *mixer strip*), with balance, volume, and mute controls for each source. The leftmost column shows the master audio controls, consisting of the overall volume and balance sliders.

By default, the Play Control settings are shown. These are the settings that determine what sound sources you hear in the speakers. At first, only some of the available audio sources may be displayed. If so, from the Options menu, select Properties, and you'll see a list of all available audio sources that can be added to the mixer display.

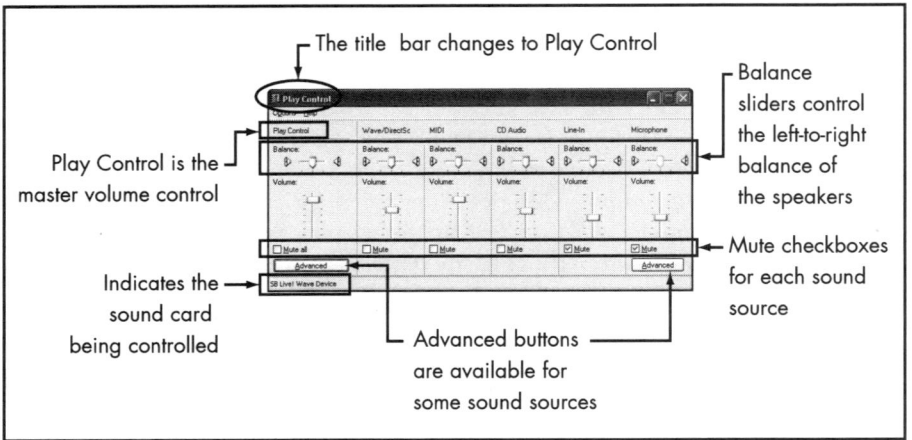

Figure 7.1: Play Control settings in the Windows mixer

From the mixer, you can set the volume of the various audio sources using the vertical volume sliders. Unused audio sources can be muted by checking the Mute checkboxes at the bottom of each column.

TIP *If you feel that you need a higher volume for one output and it is already at maximum, lower the volume of all the other sources and increase the master volume.*

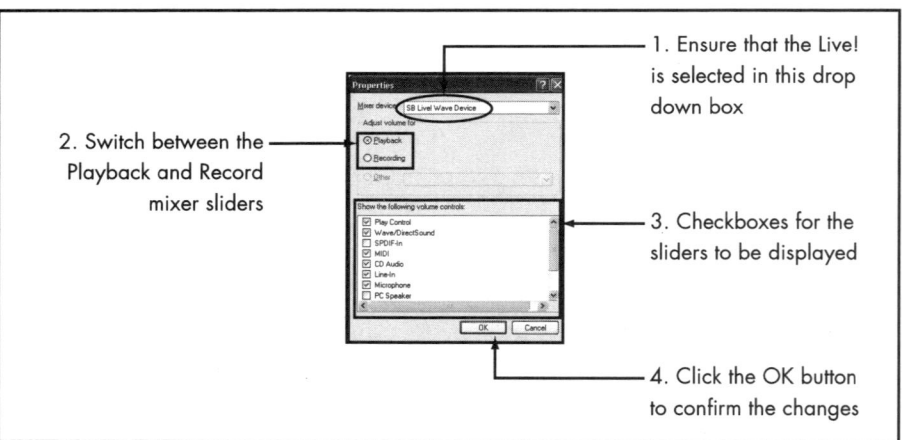

Figure 7.2: Properties of the Windows mixer

Recording settings can be controlled from the Windows mixer as well. To do so, select Properties from the Options menu and then select Recording. Just as with the Play Control settings, you can select what recording sources to display by checking them in the list below.

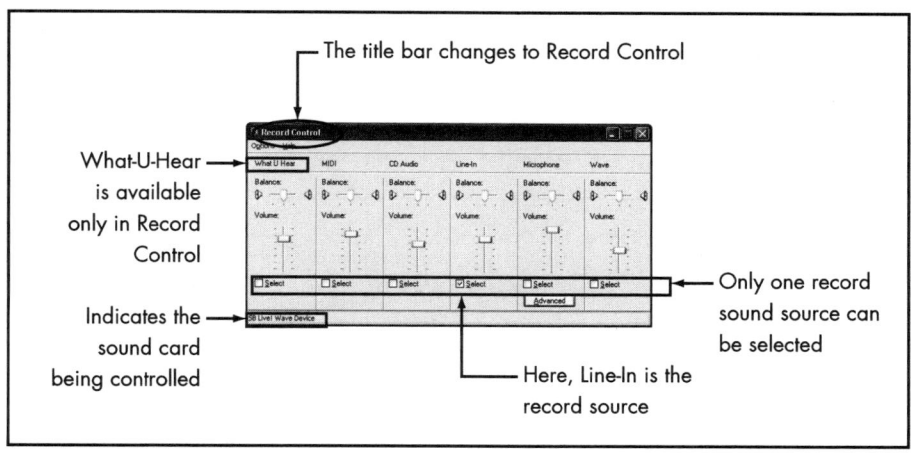

Figure 7.3: Record Control settings in the Windows mixer

The Record Control view looks similar to the Play Control view. Only one input can be selected at a time, so the Mute checkbox is replaced with a Select box. The recording settings are totally independent of the play settings (except when What-U-Hear is selected as the recording source; see "Record Control" later in this chapter), so changing the record volume for the sound sources will not affect the volume levels that are set in the Play Control sliders. This allows the playback volume of the sound source to remain, while a different record volume can be assigned to the same sound source solely for recording purposes. The audio source can even be muted while recording from it so that it is not heard over the speakers.

In the menu, you can also choose Advanced to display additional buttons for some sound sources. These settings correspond to the features described in the "Advanced Controls" section later in this chapter.

The Surround Mixer

The Surround Mixer is designed to control many of the settings available on the Live!, making it more ideal than the Windows Mixer if advanced settings need to be made. It has two windows that can be attached together or detached and used separately. The top window houses the EAX, speaker, and spectrum analyzer features, while the lower window is the traditional mixer application with sliders for sound sources and the mute button.

TIP *You should be able to find the Surround Mixer in Start • Programs • Creative • Sound Blaster Live! (or a similar name) • Surround Mixer after successful installation of the driver CD. It can also be loaded in AudioHQ and the round AudioHQ icon in the notification tray of the taskbar.*

When the mixer is loaded from AudioHQ, only the bottom mixer window will appear. If it is loaded from the Surround Mixer item in the Start menu, the full Surround Mixer with both the top and bottom windows will be displayed.

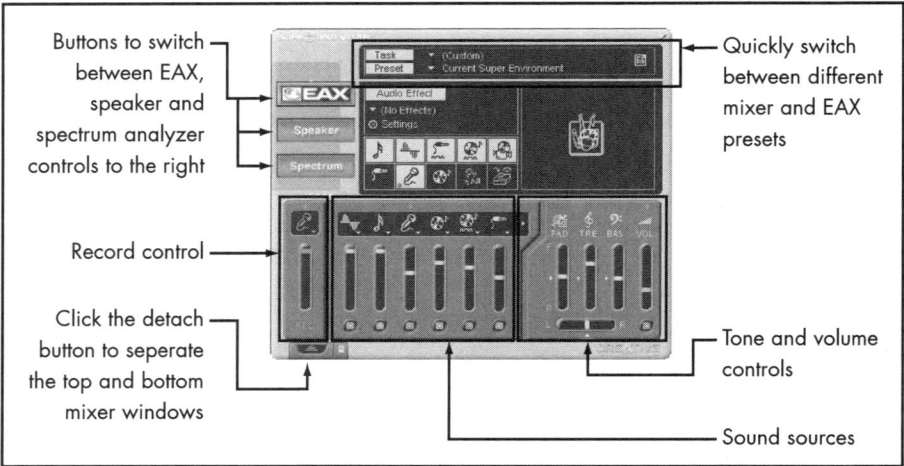

Figure 7.4: The Surround Mixer with the top and bottom windows

Sound Sources

One difference between the Windows Mixer and earlier versions of Creative's mixer applications for the older Sound Blasters is that this mixer has a fixed width and displays only six input sources at once. (Previously, the width of the mixer was expandable to accommodate more sliders that were controllable with the keyboard.) It uses icons to represent each sound source, so you will need to be familiar with what each icon represents to use the mixer effectively. You can also pause the mouse cursor over an icon to pop up a tool tip with the name of the slider.

Unlike Windows applications, where buttons are easily identifiable because of their bevels, Creative has chosen to use icons and change the standard mouse cursor to a hand cursor to indicate that an element in the mixer can be clicked or controlled. As you move over the icons of each sound source, the hand cursor appears, and you can click them to change the particular slider to another sound source. For convenience, try to have six of the most often used sliders in view, and mute and hide the other unused sound sources. You can also right-click any of the sound source icons to quickly toggle all six sliders between the available sources.

Muting

The yellow round buttons below each slider allow you to quickly mute and unmute any of the sound sources. When a sound source is muted, the round button changes to gray, but the slider volumes can still be modified. Muting is a great aid to keep out unwanted noise from the speaker outputs. Find out more about

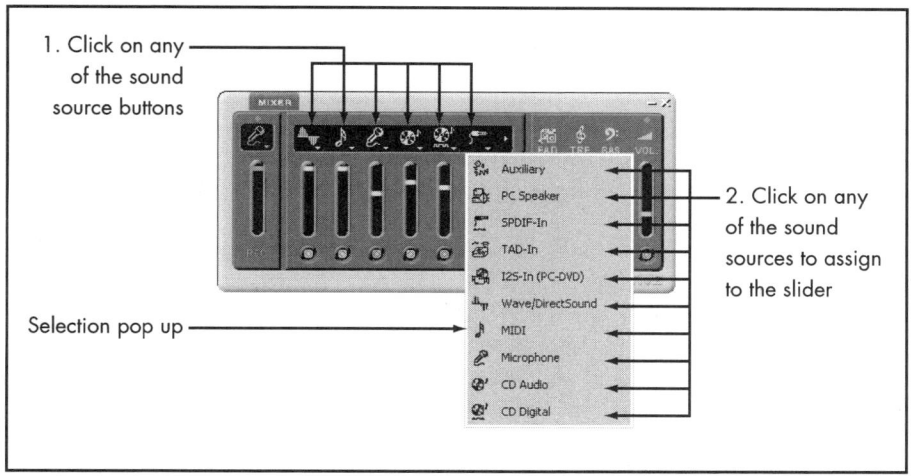

Figure 7.5: Changing the sliders to other sound sources

keeping the Live! noise free in the section "Keeping the Live! Hiss Free" later in this chapter.

Advanced Controls

Above some of the sliders, like the master volume control and the microphone control, you will notice a clickable button in the shape of a small red plus symbol labeled "Other Advanced Controls." This brings up a dialog box that allows you to enable or disable additional settings applicable to that particular sound source.

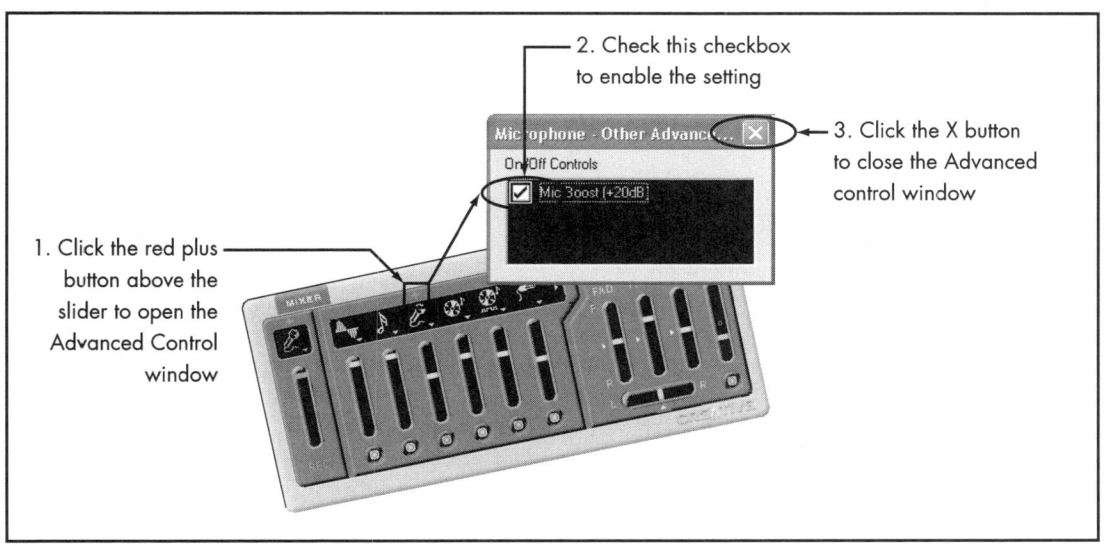

Figure 7.6: Changing Advanced Control settings

The Mixer **209**

The following table summarizes the additional settings that can be adjusted using the surround mixer.

Table 7.3: Additional Mixer Settings in the Surround Mixer

Slider Name	Additional Setting	
Master Volume Control (labeled "Play Control Volume")	Digital Output Only	Enabling this turns on digital output through the yellow mini-jack digital output on the backplate of second- and third-generation Live! cards. The front and/or rear analog line outputs may also be disabled when this is enabled. This setting can also be changed in the speaker applet. Turn this on when you are connecting to speakers that sport a Digital DIN (or for more recent speakers, a compatible multichannel mini-jack digital input).
Microphone	Mic Boost (+20 dB)	The mic input requires a sensitive microphone for a good sound level; however, many consumer and multimedia microphones are not loud enough. This setting in the mixer will increase the sound from the microphone by 20 dB (about 10 times) for a stronger signal.
S/PDIF In/Auxiliary 2	Enable Auxiliary 2	This is available only for the Aux In 2 RCA jacks present on the Live!Drive II and Live!Drive IR. Only one input can be used at a time, and this additional setting allows switching between these two inputs.

> Because the S/PDIF In on the Live! is digital, there is an ADC in the Live!Drive to convert the RCA inputs to digital. Changing this additional setting will enable or disable the ADC, switching between Aux In 2 and S/PDIF In.

Tone and Volume Controls

The right side of the mixer houses five sliders relating to tone (equalization) and volume settings. The first slider on the left is the FAD (fader) setting and is available only when the Live! is in 4 Speakers or 5.1 Speakers mode. Pushing it upward toward the F (front) position lowers the volume of the rear speakers, and pushing it down toward the R (rear) position makes the rear speakers louder than the front. If your multichannel speakers do not have a front-rear balance control, this is a good aid to help you balance the relative volumes of the front and rear speakers, especially when the speakers are at different distances from the listening position. Ultimately, all speakers should mesh seamlessly to produce a coherent 360-degree soundstage. A sound should not suddenly increase or drop off in volume when moving from the front to the rear.

To the right of the front-rear fader are the TRE (treble) and BAS (bass) sliders. These allow you to modify the tonal quality of the sound to compensate for speakers that are weak in these areas. Like applying EAX effects, these settings apply to all sound sources at once, so use them with caution, especially when recording using What-U-Hear (described later in this chapter).

> Some media players have their own treble and bass controls or even a graphic equalizer. Because the TRE and BAS sliders affect all sound that is played back, including sound from media players, any equalization you set in the media players will also be affected by the TRE and BAS sliders and may result in excessive treble or bass.

The horizontal slider controls the balance between the left and right speakers. Typically, the left and right speakers should be placed at equal distances from the central listening position, like mirror images. You do not usually need to change the left-right balance unless the speakers are placed at awkward positions or there is a problem with the speaker such that the apparent volume of the speakers on each side is different. The balance control affects both the front and rear speakers in 4 Speakers or 5.1 Speakers mode.

> Unlike the Windows mixer, the Surround Mixer does not allow modification of the balance of individual sound sources. If you need to do this—for example, if an external device is playing back the left and right channels at different levels—use the balance sliders in the Windows mixer or the EAX positioning window of the upper part of the Surround Mixer to place the sound source in the desired position.

The rightmost blue VOL (Play Control Volume) slider is the master volume control that affects all sounds playing through the sound card. You can consider this slider the arbitrator of volume levels on the speaker outputs of the Live!, with the individual sliders controlling the volume of each sound source and passing the preset volume to the master volume control to determine the final volume output of the sound card.

Near the FAD (Front/Rear Balance), TRE (treble), BAS (bass), and Balance (left/right balance) sliders are a small white triangles indicating the center position. You can click the triangle to move the slider back to the center. Leave the sliders there if you want flat settings. Many audiophiles prefer to leave such settings dead center so the sound is not colored in any way. However, poor speakers or headphones do warrant some adjustment for your listening enjoyment.

The goal of adjusting the relative levels of the sound sources is to ensure that every sound source is balanced and at a reasonable volume. For example, CD audio input is usually louder than other audio, especially MIDI; therefore, you might want to set it to a lower volume than the rest. Once all the individual sound sources are set correctly, you will need to use the master volume control only to adjust the volume or mute the sound card.

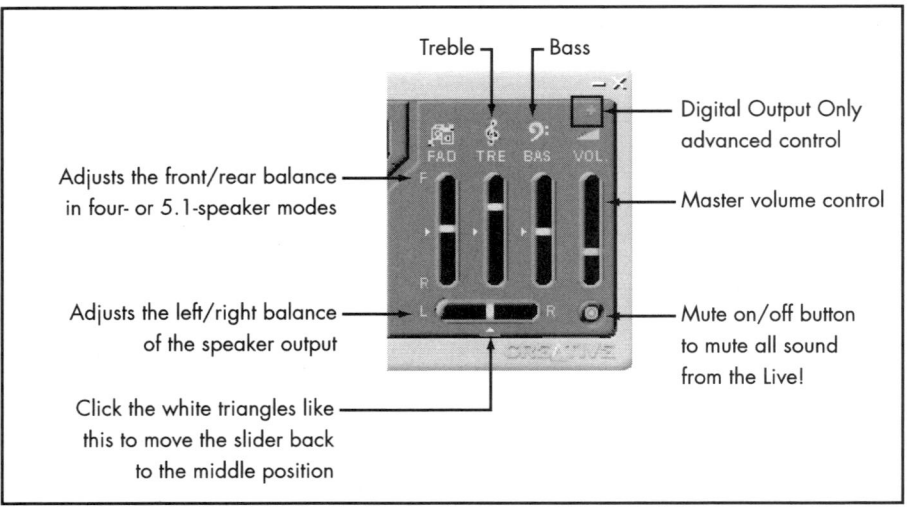

Figure 7.7: The tone and volume controls to the right of the mixer window

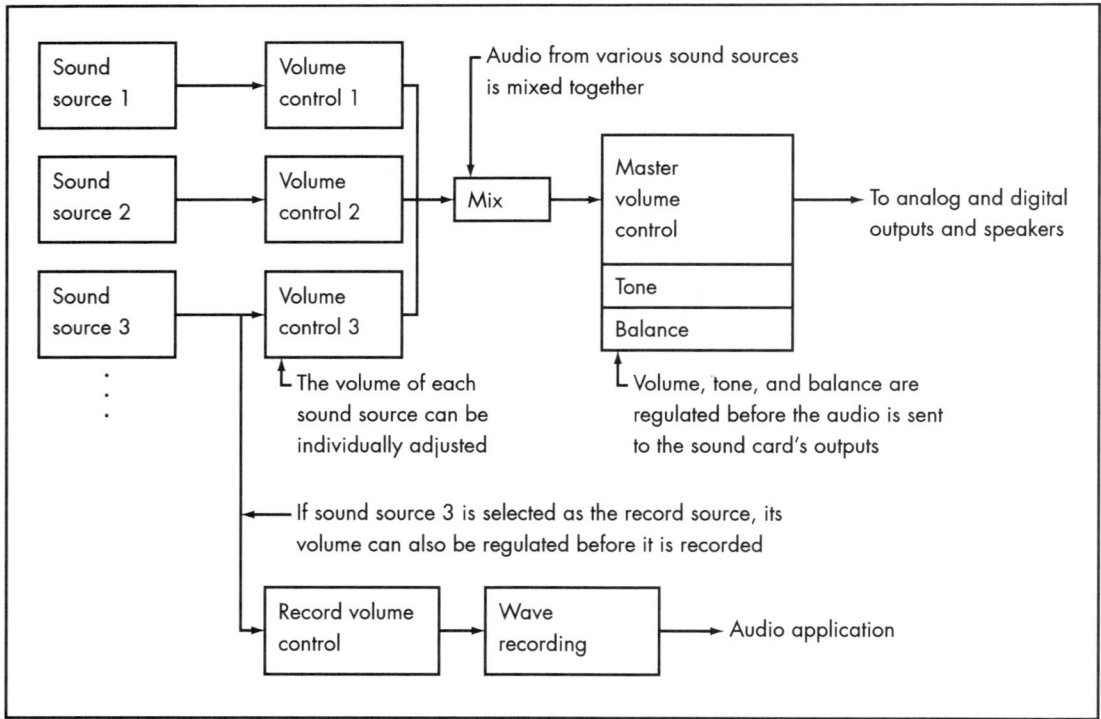

Figure 7.8: The master volume control affects the volumes of the individual sound sources

TIP *You can deliberately set the volume such that the maximum possible volume through the speakers is not loud enough to hurt your ears and unknowingly damage your hearing.*

Record Control

The leftmost slider, in red, allows you to select which source to record from. The volume level at which the sound source gets recorded is determined by the volume level of only the red slider and not its corresponding yellow playback slider. For example, if you record from a microphone, you will usually want to eliminate microphone feedback by muting the playback so that the sound does not play through the speakers. Sound from the microphone will still be recorded when the record source is set to the microphone.

Unlike previous Sound Blaster cards, the Live! is designed to allow only one sound source to be recorded at a time, which can be limiting for more complex recording tasks. A special recording source known as *What-U-Hear* is made available to allow the sound that is being heard to be recorded. This setting works in the same manner as the interaction between individual sound sources and the master volume control, but instead of the sound going to the speakers, the sound goes to the Wave recording input of the Live! In What-U-Hear mode, the volume set by the yellow playback sliders affects the volume that is recorded, and the red What-U-Hear slider controls the overall volume of all sound sources that are being sent to the Wave input for recording.

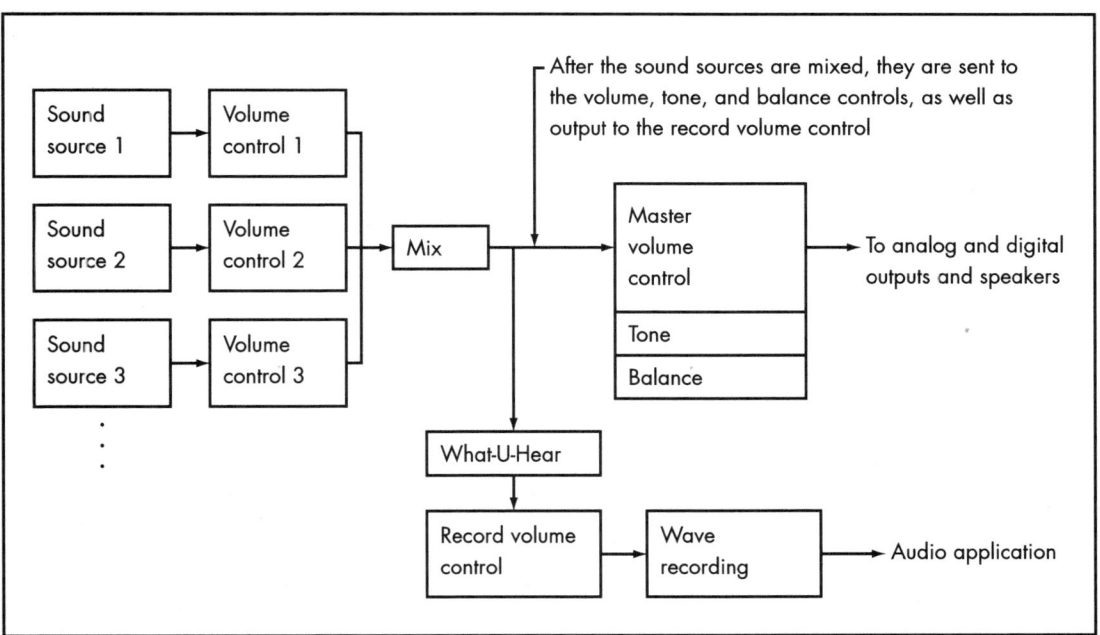

Figure 7.9: Differences between What-U-Hear and individual record sources

The Mixer **213**

Audio Analyzers

Audio software, media players, and visualization plug-ins are able to display dazzling animation and equalizer displays in tandem with the music that is being played back. This is achieved by recording the audio from the same record source specified in the mixer and analyzing the characteristics of the audio signal to generate the graphics on the screen.

There is only one record source available on the Live! to record from, so this source must be selected correctly so that the visualization and equalizers can get the correct audio samples to generate the graphics. The spectrum analyzer in the top part of the Surround Mixer also uses this record source to monitor and produce the spectrum analyzer display. For most uses, you want the spectrum analyzer and other visualization software to work with all sounds from the Live!, so the What-U-Hear record source should be selected in the mixer.

The Analog Caveat

You may notice in the table in the "Audio Sources" section earlier in this chapter that several inputs of the Live! are analog. Because of a design limitation, the Live! can play back audio from only one of these sources at a time. This makes operation of the mixer particularly quirky, which can be a problem for many users.

There are a few things you can do so that sound from analog sources can be played back:

- The sound source should not be muted.
- The sound source should be set to a reasonable volume level with the yellow slider.
- The record source above the red slider must also be set to the same analog input that you want to hear. It can also be set to What-U-Hear.

TIP *If the source still cannot be heard, try muting and unmuting it.*

Because of a hardware limitation of the Live!, when an analog input (not What-U-Hear) is selected as recording source, you will not be able to listen to any other analog sound sources (even if they are active in the mixer).

For example, if the record source is set to Microphone, you will hear the microphone in the speakers (unless it is muted) but no other analog sound sources (such as CD Audio), regardless of whether they are muted.

When What-U-Hear is used, the Live! will automatically switch to play back the analog source that was last unmuted.

This is a limitation of the AC'97 design adopted by the EMU10K1, which also limited the Live! to output digital audio only at a 48 kHz sample rate. Read more about this issue in Chapter 18, "The EMU10K1 Digital Audio Processor."

Keeping the Live! Hiss Free

You can do a great deal to reduce the noise in the output signal of the Live! While the D/A converters of the Live! cards offer a very good signal-to-noise ratio with very little noise, the Live! can still be a major source of noise, hiss, and even distortion when incorrectly configured.

Set High Enough Levels

Always set the sound levels for audio sources as high as possible, but without causing distortion. The louder the sound itself, the less apparent the inherent noise in the resulting sound, especially when additional noise may be introduced in the sound after it is amplified for speaker output. Rather than turning the volume knob all the way up on your amplifier or speaker system (which increases the background noise level), try using a higher master volume level. The volumes for individual sound source should also be set as high as possible (while still keeping the desired relative levels). Be careful, though, because levels that are too high may introduce *clipping*, where the waveforms hit their maximum limits (known as *peaking*), causing distortion. This distortion will be heard as an ugly, crackly noise in the loudest parts of the sound, which is much worse than background noise. Equipment may also be damaged if the distortion is excessive.

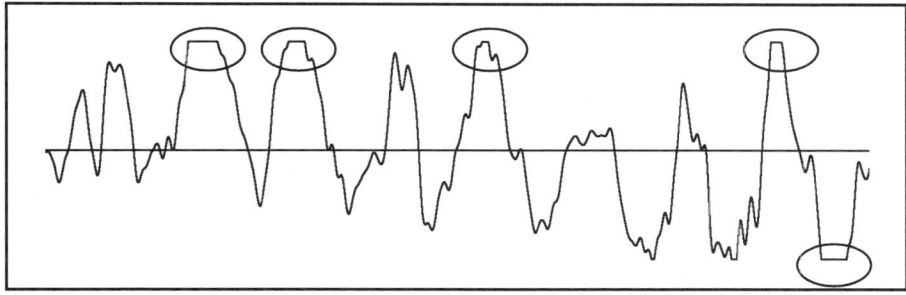

Figure 7.10: The circled parts of the waveform look flat because they are clipped off at the maximum point that can be represented by digital audio

Mute Unused Sources

Last, but not least important, mute all unused audio sources. In the mixer, make sure that all audio sources that you don't have anything connected to are muted. This is especially important for analog audio sources (such as Microphone, Line In, and CD Audio), since these, when not muted, always produce a significant amount of noise. If you are recording to an external device such as a MiniDisc or tape recorder, mute all other sources except the source from which you want to record to cut off unnecessary noise.

> **TIP** *If you are recording to an external audio recorder from the Wave output of the Live!—for instance, by playing MP3 files—also ensure that no other audio or Windows background sound will pop up during the course of recording, since the Wave output of the Live! can play back multiple channels of Wave audio simultaneously.*

Other ways to reduce noise and improve audio quality are to use good cables and a good amplifier/speaker system. Try to keep the length of audio cables down, because longer cables tend to pick up more noise and cause audio signals to weaken as they travel across to the other end. It is also a good idea to keep audio cables separated from speaker cables and power cords, because electromagnetic interference from them can affect audio quality and cause noise and hum.

Some hiss will always be present in amplifier or speaker systems, because they are analog in nature and have to amplify line-level audio to produce a sound level that can be heard comfortably. If you turn up the volume, you'll probably still hear some noise despite the lack of input signal. There's not much you can do about this other than try to keep the output of the Live! as high as possible so you can use a lower volume level on the amplifier.

The Digital I/O Advantage

Digital I/O devices like the Live!Drive send audio to and from the Live! digitally using the connected flat cable. By using digital connections instead of analog, the possibility of interference is significantly reduced. As the Live!Drive is located farther away from the motherboard, there is less interference, noise, and hiss—problems especially noticeable with analog inputs and outputs. The analog inputs on the Live!Drive are usually better in quality than the inputs on the Live!'s backplate. For instance, the Line In 2 jack on the Live!Drive is quieter than the Line In mini-jack on the backplate of the sound card. If you own a digital I/O device, use the analog inputs there first if such inputs are available, and whenever possible, always use digital connections for external digital audio equipment.

Recording Audio

When recording audio, it is often useful to be able to record something other than what's playing back in the speakers. For this reason, the recording mixer settings can be adjusted using the mixer software, but they are separated from the playback and output sliders.

Remember: The Live! will let you record exactly what is playing back, using the What-U-Hear source, thus allowing you to record from any number of audio sources simultaneously.

Choosing the Correct Sound Source

Suppose that you have created a piece of music in a MIDI sequencer using several MIDI and audio tracks. Now you want to add vocals to the song by singing into a microphone. In this case, you would make sure that the MIDI, Wave, and microphone sources are enabled for playback. Set the recording source to Microphone, and you're ready to start recording. To prevent feedback and avoid background noise in the vocals, it's best to use headphones to monitor the resulting audio.

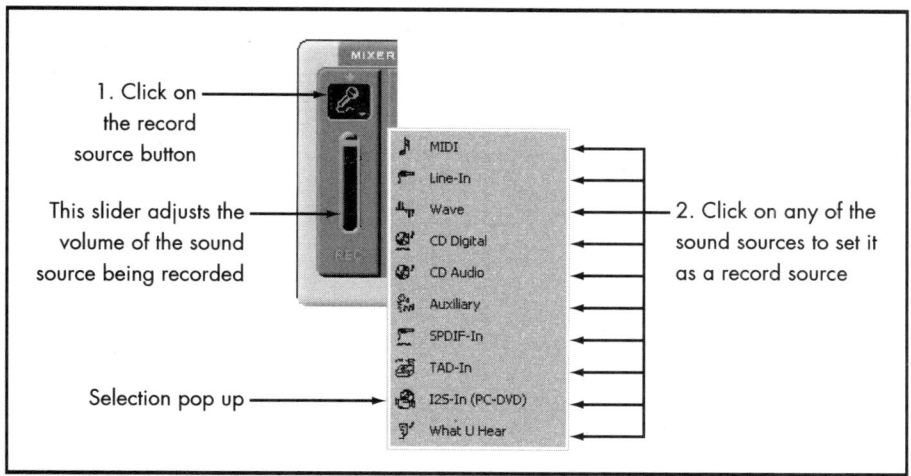

Figure 7.11: The recording controls of the Surround Mixer

When to Use What-U-Hear

When using this feature, it is basically "what you hear is what you record," so it is advisable to mute all unused playback sound sources so that noise and hiss is reduced in the recorded audio file. You should use the What-U-Hear recording source rather than a single source particularly under the following conditions:

- When you need to record from more than one source at a time.
- When you want to include EAX effects as part of your recorded audio.

For instance, continuing the previous example, imagine that you have the MIDI and audio tracks (including the vocals) and now want to create a final mix. The MIDI channels are played back using the MIDI sound source, and the audio tracks are played back using the Wave sound source. In this case, you would mute all sources but MIDI and Wave, set the recording source to What-U-Hear, and start recording.

Or consider this example of the second condition. Suppose you've created a piece of MIDI music with reverb, chorus, and/or other effects and want to record it. Sure, you can set the recording source to MIDI, but this will record the song without the effects. To get the effects, mute all play sources except MIDI, set the recording source to What-U-Hear, and record the MIDI source. Don't forget to unmute the Wave channel when you're finished recording, or you won't be able to hear the recorded material when it is played back.

Recording Audio CDs in Optical Drives

In Chapter 3, "The Sound Blaster Live! Hardware," we mentioned that there are three methods that music from audio CDs played on optical drives can be channeled to the Live! If you have connected the drive to the CD_IN analog connection on the Live! card, you can record directly from the CD Audio recording source. Similarly, with the CD_SPDIF digital connection, the CD Digital recording source is used.

However, when the optical drive is using the digital connection to digitally extract audio from the CD to the Wave output of the Live!, you should record from the Wave output. Of course, recording from a digital or data connection provides the best results, compared to the analog connection.

Despite the methods described here, the best method to obtain audio from CDs is to use software that supports digital audio extraction (DAE) to digitally copy the data on the CD to Wave files, without using any form of audio recording. This method is also faster and produces the best sound quality.

Adding EAX Effects to Audio Recordings

There are times when the What-U-Hear setting may not work for what you want to do. Let's go back to the example of recording vocals to an audio track in Cubasis while playing back other MIDI and audio tracks simultaneously. In many cases, you'll want to use a reverb on the recorded vocals, and what could be better than the high-quality built-in reverbs of the Live! card? However, when you record from the microphone source, the reverb is not recorded. If you try to record using What-U-Hear, the reverb is there, but so are all the other tracks that you don't want to record. Recording the vocals without playing back the other tracks is hardly an option, so obviously you're in trouble.

What is described here is one of the limitations of the Live!'s way of selecting recording sources, a problem also described in Chapter 17, "Sequencer Basics," in the section, "Audio Sequencers." Here is one possible workaround:

1. Record the vocals without effects onto one track.
2. Temporarily mute all play sources except Wave, use the EAX effect of your choice, and select What-U-Hear as the recording source.
3. Rerecord the audio data onto a new track by playing back the recorded vocal track. This will add EAX effects because What-U-Hear is enabled.
4. Delete the original track without the effects (unless you want to keep a copy of the dry audio data).

Voice Chat and Videoconferencing

For videoconferencing applications (and other similar uses such as real-time voice chat in games), the incoming audio is played using the Wave sound source, and the outgoing audio comes from the microphone input (assuming that you're using a microphone or a headset). You normally don't want to hear yourself speaking, so enable only Wave in the mixer for the game audio, and mute the Microphone sound source. Since videoconferencing applications essentially record your voice in real time and send them to the other party, you need to select Microphone as the recording source (if the application doesn't automatically do this for you).

Because the audio in videoconferencing applications is usually compressed to reduce its size when sent across the network, and thereby reduced in quality, it's important that it has good quality from the start when it is recorded. Try keeping the microphone at a fixed distance, not too far away from your mouth. Of course, a telephony headset is the best way to go if you use this type of application frequently. Make sure that the recording level is adjusted to a suitable volume—not too low but still with a bit of a margin for louder volumes, to prevent clipping.

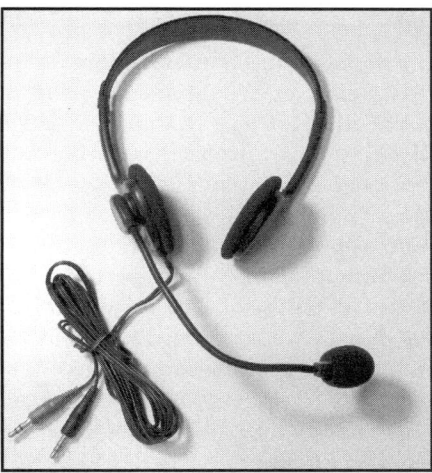

Figure 7.12: A typical headset used for Internet telephony

Volume Controls in Software

Besides controlling the volume of the sound card in mixer applications, many audio and media players also provide volume controls within the software. These sliders may or may not affect the settings in the mixer, depending on how the developer implemented the volume control. These are the common ways these volume controls work:

Table 7.4: Volume Control Methods in Multimedia Software

Volume Control Method	Affects Sliders in the Mixer?	Description
Software	No	Volume controls in most audio software, like Winamp and Windows Media Player, do not modify any of the mixer settings. Changes to the volume control affect only the sound that is played back by the media player.
Individual Sound Source	Yes	Some software, especially CD players, changes the volume of the sound source directly, like the CD Audio slider.
Master Volume Control	Yes	Other sound sources.

It is fortunate that most media players have disciplined when interacting with the mixer. It is disruptive to find the mixer settings altered because these changes also affect the sound output of other software. It would be bad if an MP3 player's volume control modified the Wave slider in the mixer instead of only the audio that it is playing back, because the Wave output of the Live! is also used by many other software applications.

Many voice chat and videoconferencing applications will also change the mixer's record source to the Microphone sound source. If you have a Live!Drive and the microphone is connected to the Mic In 2 ¼-inch jack, you will have to manually load up the mixer and change the record source to Mic In 2/Line In 2.

Some software will also mute and unmute sound sources when you open and close them, or set the volume to previous levels stored when you last exited the software, which can affect the mixer settings that you have carefully tweaked. To prevent such situations, remember to save your preferred mixer settings to a Super Environment preset so that it can be restored at a later date.

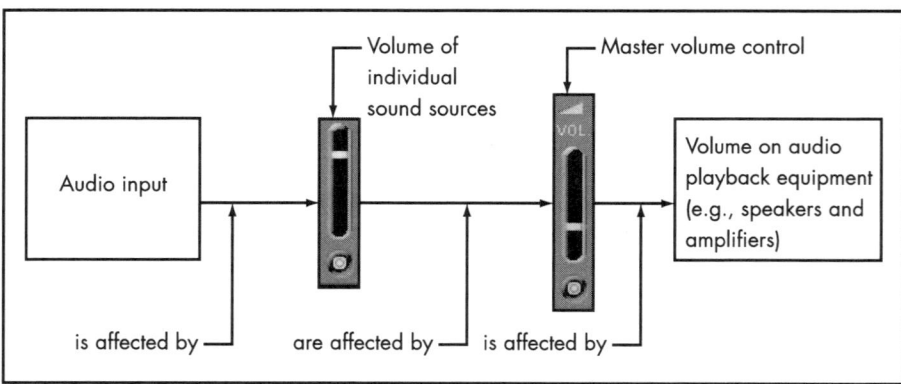

Figure 7.13: The various stages where volume control can be performed

8

EAX

The audio cues created by ambience and reverberation of sound can quickly clue us in on the characteristics and size of the place we are in. Games attempted to bring us into a different world with the use of sound effects, but many of them were limited to simple Wave playback, resulting in sound effects that have no sense of environment to them.

Game developers had to work around this limitation by prerecording sound effects with reverb or adding echo to sound effects by using the CPU to process the wave audio as the game is running. The resulting audio often sounded unrealistic because developers had to limit themselves to simple echo and reverb algorithms to keep the use of CPU power to a minimum.

The Live! changed all of this with *EAX* and *Environmental Audio*, Creative's effects-processing technology developed by E-MU and introduced with the Live! family. They allow effects such as echoes, reverbs, and various types of filtering and 3D positioning of sound to be performed by the sound card in real time. These are all achieved through the programmable effects processor in the EMU10K1 chip found on all Live! cards.

Instead of allowing EAX only in games, Creative has also enabled the effects processing capability of the EMU10K1 to be used with all other sound sources coming from the Live! In this chapter, you will learn how to set the EAX presets with the utilities provided by the drivers, tweak effects levels and parameters, and customize your own environments. The EAX technologies for gaming will be covered in Chapter 10, "Playing Games."

Environmental Audio?

Figure 8.1: The early Environmental Audio logo

When the Live! was first introduced, two different terms were used to market the effects processing capability of the EMU10K1. The first was *Environmental Audio*, which was used to indicate the ability of the Live! to place sounds inside different environments, such as a cave or concert hall. The second was *EAX* (Environmental Audio eXtensions). This was initially used as a marketing name for the software instructions that were packaged in the EAX API, a set of functions to allow game developers to easily implement Environmental Audio for audio in software and games. With the API, software can easily use and switch between the various environmental presets available on the Live!

The EAX API allows developers to control and modify the card's environmental effects without the need to study and reprogram the EMU10K1. For example, `SetEnvironment cave 50` could be implemented as one of the available instructions in the API and then used by game developers to change the Live! to the cave environment preset with a 50 percent volume whenever the gamer walks into a cave.

Now, It's Just EAX!

Then something interesting happened. The EAX API, being the key enabler for enhancing games with effects, made the EAX name ubiquitous in the gaming industry. Gamers have come to relate this term to the environmental effects capability of the Live! products, more so than the Environmental Audio name.

Figure 8.2: The current EAX logo

In the latter half of the Live!'s three-year evolution, Creative decided to do away with the unwieldy Environmental Audio term and focus solely on marketing the EAX brand name. Today, the name Environmental Audio is not used anymore, and EAX now refers to the entire effects capability of the Live!, encompassing the environmental audio–processing capability of the sound cards, as well as the EAX API used by developers. A new EAX logo was introduced with this change, and this move also tied in with the company's plans to introduce EAX capabilities in other audio products like portable audio players.

An Open Standard

Instead of keeping the EAX API proprietary, Creative released the specifications and allowed other sound card manufacturers to support EAX in their products. Seeing the wide support by game developers, other manufacturers quickly introduced EAX-compatible sound cards and drivers to tap into the increased realism in games offered by EAX. This helped Creative gain a foothold for the EAX standard.

EAX-compatible sound cards are able to recognize and respond to the EAX presets defined in the EAX API. However, the hardware, DSP algorithms, and techniques used by each sound card to render an EAX environment—for example, the sound of a hallway—is very much dependent on the manufacturer. Even though the EAX preset and parameters may be the same, the resulting sound may be slightly different between sound cards from each manufacturer. Most developers use Creative sound cards to program EAX in their games, so sound cards like the Live! are deemed to produce EAX environments that are closest to what the sound programmer intended.

> Some sound cards that have EAX support for games do not support EAX for normal audio sources to allow effects to be added to, for example, the Wave, MIDI, or CD audio output.

Behind the Scenes

So how does all of this work? The EMU10K1 chip is at the heart of the Live!'s ability to deliver EAX effects. This chip contains a programmable effects-processing unit known as the FX8010, which is designed specifically to process sound data efficiently so that effects can be added in real time to audio that is playing back on the sound card.

Find out more about the EMU10K1 in Chapter 18, "The EMU10K1 Digital Audio Processor."

When the game switches to a new environment, such as a simulation of ambience and reverberation in a cave, a small program is loaded into the effects processor that takes the original game audio and processes it with the loaded program to add an echo similar to that of a cave. All of this is handled automatically by the EAX programming interface and the Live! drivers, making it easy for game programmers to support the special features of the Live!

Using EAX

There are many ways that EAX can be applied to sound sources, and this depends largely on whether the software supports EAX. In some cases, you will still need to turn on or enable EAX manually, unless the software has automatic detection for EAX-supported sound cards.

1. Games with EAX Support

Some games with EAX support will automatically detect the Live! and begin to send EAX instructions to the sound card without requiring any configuration. Alternately, the developer may choose to ship the game with EAX turned off, while providing a menu item in the game configuration for more adventurous users to turn it on. In any case, games should work without a hitch with the Live!, and you need not use the mixer or EAX applications to enable or disable EAX—it is turned on and handled by the game.

2. Games Without EAX Support

If a game does not support EAX, you can still create or use an existing environment for the game with applications provided in AudioHQ. For example, if most of a game takes part in a dungeon, but the game lacks EAX support, you may select a suitable EAX environment (such as the cave preset) for this game. This does not provide the same high-precision interactive environment simulation as in a game with native EAX support—for instance, the automatic switching of EAX presets according to the level or map of the game—but using a manual EAX preset can still add realism to the game. The Live! drivers come with a set of pre-defined EAX environments for some old games like Diablo and Starcraft, which can be selected in Surround Mixer, Creative Launcher, or the EAX Control Panel in AudioHQ.

See Chapter 10, "Playing Games," for more information on how you can configure games to exploit the 3D sound and gaming capability of the Live!

3. Other Software and Audio Equipment Connected to the Live!

EAX environments can also be added to normal audio sources by changing EAX presets in the Surround Mixer. Any software that is used to play back the audio will not be EAX aware; therefore you will need to use the mixer and EAX applications provided with the drivers to turn on and tweak the EAX effect. The selected EAX preset will be applied to all audio sources that can be heard through the mixer. Later, we will explain how you can tweak existing EAX presets to create custom environments and set the amount of EAX for each sound source.

Other Uses for EAX Effects

The use of EAX is not limited to game effects. In fact, it's very easy to customize effects and use them on any sound source, making the list of possibilities virtually endless. For example, EAX effects can be applied to the microphone input for exciting effects (such as pitch shifting) on karaoke players. Plug in a guitar and use the chorus, wah-wah, distortion, reverb, or any other effects instead of an effects pedal. Use EAX effects (such as reverb and chorus) on your MIDI tracks; you can set the effects levels separately for each MIDI channel.

Environment Controls in the Surround Mixer

The EAX pane in the top window of the Surround Mixer shows icons representing the digital sources in the first row and icons representing the analog sources in the second row. The icons are actually buttons that look similar but behave in very different ways. The right part of the window is a 3D positioning area that shows the top view of a man on a chair, representing your seating position. To move sounds around you, drag the icons of the sound sources around the seating position.

The buttons:

- Allow the display and hiding of icons in the 3D positioning area.
- Toggle between analog sources that can be played back, which affects muting and record source settings in the mixer.

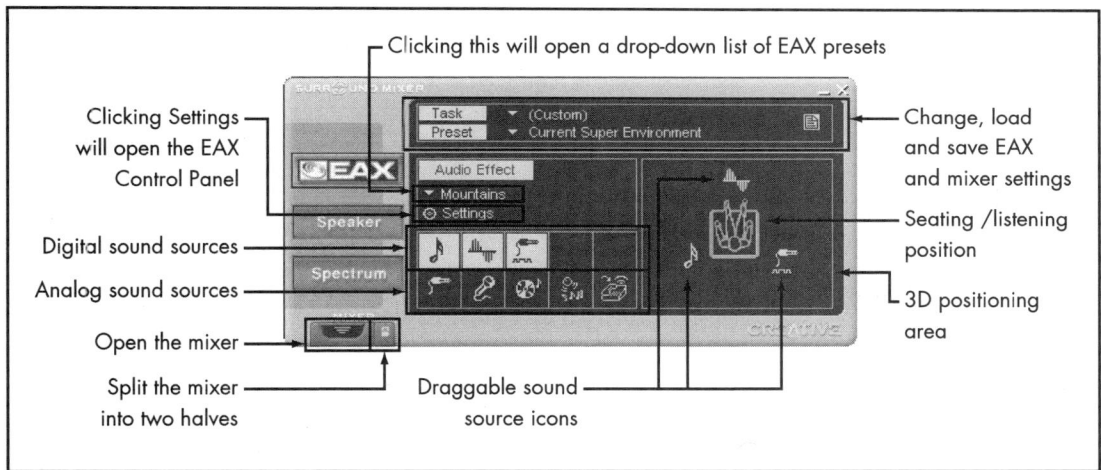

Figure 8.3: The EAX pane of the Surround Mixer

Because the digital sources are not inhibited by a single analog source playback limitation, as explained in the section titled "The Analog Caveat" in Chapter 7, "The Mixer," they can be muted and unmuted in any combination. The icons in the first row are toggle buttons that turn the digital sources on and off, much like checkboxes that can be independently toggled and do not affect each other. When turned on, the icon is highlighted in yellow, and it also appears in the 3D positioning area. You can drag the icon around to balance the volume of the sound source between the front and rear speakers, assuming that you are using at least four speakers. In 2 Speakers or Headphones mode, you can drag the sound source only left and right, like a balance control.

Figure 8.4: In this screenshot, the MIDI and S/PDIF-In digital sound sources are enabled, and they appear in the 3D positioning area. The record source is not What-U-Hear, so only one analog sound source can be enabled at one time. The CD Audio analog sound source is enabled and positioned to the rear left of the listener.

The icons in the second row work differently. In addition, their behavior also depends on whether What-U-Hear is enabled as a recording source. When What-U-Hear is not used, the buttons work like option buttons, and only one analog sound source can be selected at one time. Selecting one will disable the other analog sound sources. The icon of the selected analog sound source will also appear in the 3D positioning area and will change to a yellow highlight. A red dot at the bottom right of the icon also indicates that the record source has been changed to correspond to the sound source. This is necessary to allow the Live! to work within its hardware limitation and allow the analog sound source to be positioned in 3D.

Things are different when What-U-Hear is the record source. Only the CD Audio source can be toggled on and off, while only one of the other analog sound sources can be enabled at any one time. All analog sound sources are combined into a single icon and treated as a single sound source in the 3D positioning area, so enabled analog sound sources will all come from the same position when moved around in the 3D positioning area.

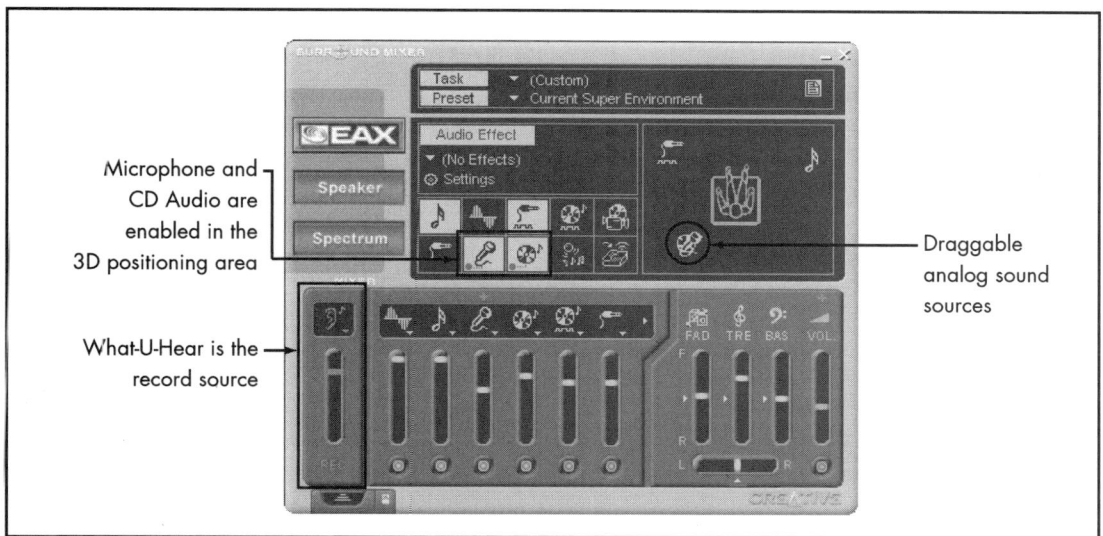

Figure 8.5: In this screenshot, the record source is changed to What-U-Hear, so the Microphone and CD Audio sound sources can be enabled and placed in the 3D positioning area. The icons for Microphone and CD Audio are stacked on one another, and they can only be moved together like a single icon.

Here is a summary of the behavior of the icons in the EAX window of the Surround Mixer:

Sound source type	The selected record source	What happens when a sound source icon is clicked	Affects the playback setting of the sound source in the mixer?
Digital sound sources (Wave, MIDI, CD Digital, I^2S In, S/PDIF In/ Auxiliary 2, Line In 2/ Microphone 2)	Any sound source.	Toggles between enabling and disabling the sound source in the 3D positioning area. The icon will also change to yellow when the sound source is in the 3D positioning area.	The playback setting of the sound source is not affected.
Analog sound sources (Line In, Microphone, CD Audio, Auxiliary, TAD In)	Any sound source except What-U-Hear. Will automatically change to the enabled analog sound source.	Clicking a highlighted icon will remove it from the 3D positioning area. Clicking an un-highlighted icon will enable the sound source in the 3D positioning area and remove all other analog sound sources from the 3D positioning area.	The playback setting of the sound source is not affected.

EAX   **227**

(Table continued)

Sound source type	The selected record source	What happens when a sound source icon is clicked	Affects the playback setting of the sound source in the mixer?
	What-U-Hear	Toggles and switches between the sound source in the 3D positioning area. CD Audio can be enabled or disabled independently from the other analog sound sources. Apart from CD Audio, only one other analog sound source can be enabled at any one time.	When a sound source is enabled, it will also be unmuted in the mixer. When a sound source is disabled, it will be automatically muted.

You can also click the small, downward-pointing arrow under Audio Effect to pop up a list of EAX effects that can be applied to all sounds playing through the mixer. The Settings button will take you to the EAX Control Panel, where you can tweak the EAX preset further.

The EAX Control Panel

The EAX Control Panel is included as part of AudioHQ in all Live!Ware versions. This software gives full control for selecting, loading, saving, and customizing sound environments and effects and is particularly useful for the following:

- Games that lack EAX support. Use the EAX Control Panel to create a custom audio environment to use throughout the game, or use it to tweak an existing one.
- Creation of environments for purposes other than games—for instance, a guitar or vocal effect.
- MIDI music effects. The same effects that are used for game environments are also useful when creating music.

A number of the effect types are especially useful for music; however, here we'll focus primarily on the first and second items in the preceding list. For more information about using EAX effects with MIDI and sequencers, see Chapter 17, "Sequencer Basics."

EAX Control Panel Basics

The EAX Control Panel can be used to do the following:

- Select, load, and save audio environments.
- Tweak, edit, and customize environment presets.
- Create new effects settings.

- Apply the currently selected effects to audio sources.
- Set up how effects are controlled by MIDI (see Chapter 17).

Adding EAX Effects to Sound Sources

The currently selected EAX preset can be applied to the various audio sources of the Live! (such as CD Audio, Microphone, and Line In, as well as the Wave playback sound source and any digital inputs). The controls are on the second tab of the EAX Control Panel (labeled Source).

To control the active effects for a particular audio source, simply select the source from the drop-down list; you can then control the effects level by selecting an effect and adjusting its level with the slider below. EAX presets usually use the Reverb setting, so modifying the value will change the volume of the reverberation against the volume of the Original Sound that does not have effects added to it. Keep in mind that this level is relative to the effect's master level (as set on the Master tab), so make sure that the effect's master level is not zero, or you won't hear any effect no matter what this setting.

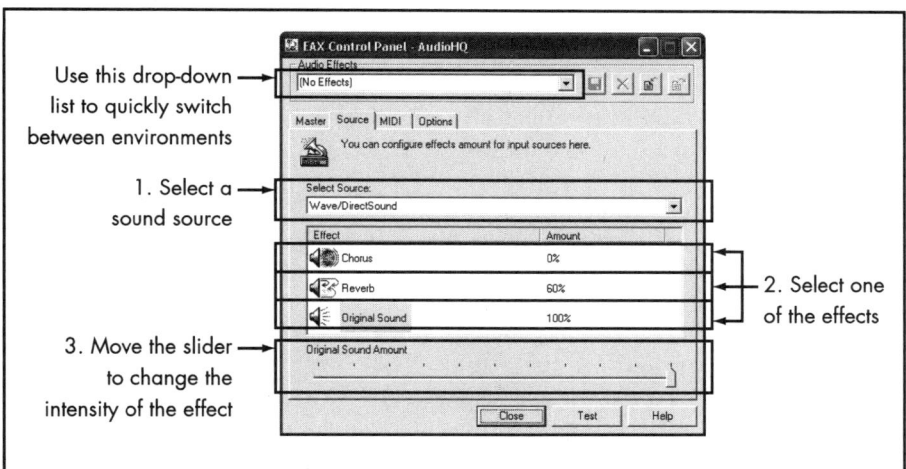

Figure 8.6: The Source tab of the EAX Control Panel allows different EAX settings to be applied to individual sound sources of the Live!

> Digital audio sources can be selected and adjusted individually, while analog audio sources have only one entry, and therefore all EAX settings made here will apply to all analog inputs of the Live! The name of the entry in the drop-down list also changes depending on what is selected in the EAX window of the Surround Mixer.

TIP *EAX presets are enabled on all audio sources by default, so if you want to use an effect on only a particular source or MIDI (which is a very common case), you'll use this tab to disable, rather than enable, effects for the available audio sources by setting the reverb level to 0.*

The MIDI synthesizer is not included in the list of sound sources because MIDI effects are controlled separately for each channel by MIDI messages, eliminating the need for a separate control here. The third tab labeled MIDI in the EAX Control Panel will allow effects to be configured for the Live!'s MIDI synthesizer.

> **Adding EAX Effects to Games**
> Because games use the Wave output of the Live!, setting any EAX preset will also affect the sound from the game, unless you use the Source tab of the EAX Control Panel to set the Wave/DirectSound sound source to a reverb of 0. If the game you are playing already has EAX support, do not set any EAX preset before loading the game as this may interfere with the game, when it tries to switch environments.

EAX Presets

All settings on the EAX Control Panel, including the loaded effects and the effects levels on the individual sound sources, can be saved as *EAX presets* (sometimes referred to simply as *environments*). These EAX presets can then be recalled from various locations, such as the EAX Control Panel or the Creative Launcher.

EAX presets make it easy to quickly select the correct settings for the task you will perform. For example, you can save a preset for karaoke applications that contains a pitch shift and reverb effect on the microphone input, and you can save an effects preset for each game on you system that doesn't have EAX support. Whenever you want to use the karaoke player or play one of these games, simply select the corresponding EAX preset, and the effect will automatically be configured.

Naturally, many presets are included with the Live!Ware package (too many, some may say), but you can easily delete those that you don't find useful.

Adding and Removing Effects

The Live! can use four simultaneous effects for environmental audio, including Reverb and Chorus, and excluding Original Sound. To simulate natural environments, reverb (a dense echo effect) is by far the most important one. For this reason, reverb is always one of the four effects (unless you are using a very old version of the drivers).

To add a new effect, follow these steps:

1. On the first tab of the EAX Control Panel, click the Add button.
2. The dialog box that appears displays any (not yet used) available effects. Select the effect that you want to add and click OK.

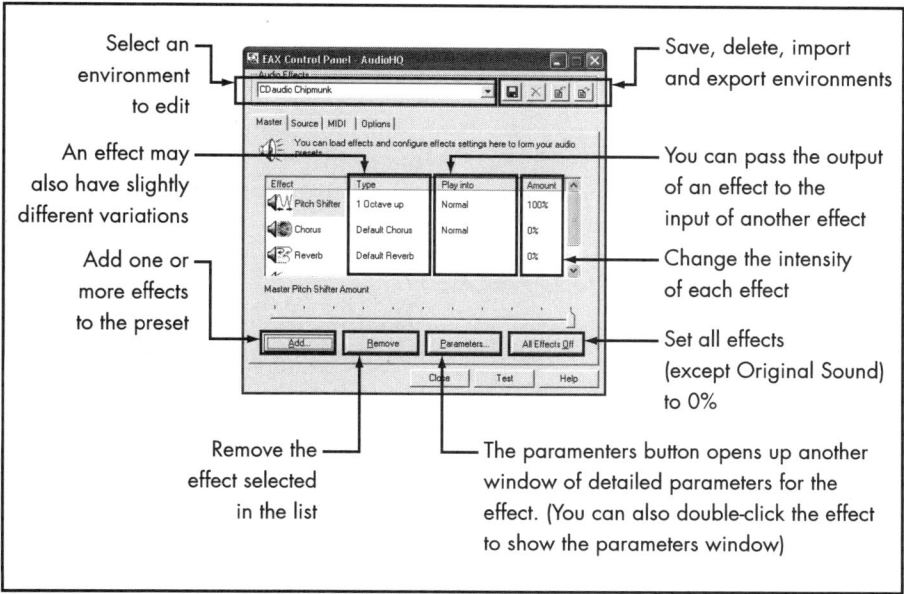

Figure 8.7: Create and edit EAX presets in the Master tab of the EAX Control Panel

3. The selected effect appears in the list of currently used effects. For most effects, there are several types to choose from. To select one, highlight the effect in the list and then select a new effect type from the drop-down list in the Type column.
4. With the effect highlighted, set its master level (amount) with the slider below.
5. On the second tab, make sure that the effect is applied to only those audio sources that you want.
6. If you want to use the effect with a MIDI sequencer, see Chapter 17 for information on how to map the effect to a control change number.

To remove an effect, simply highlight it and click the Remove button.

Customizing Effect Types

The EAX Control Panel lets you edit the available effect types to create your own customized effects. To create your own effect type, follow these steps:

1. Select the effect you want to modify from the list of effects currently in use.
2. Click the Parameters button. This brings up a dialog box with all editable effect parameters for the selected effect.
3. Modify the effect parameters. If the effect is applied to a sound source, you will hear the result in real time as you edit the effect. Otherwise, you can try the effect at any time with the Test button (if you use this feature, make sure that the effect is enabled on the Wave channel).

4. When you are satisfied with the result, you'll most likely want to save it as a new effects type. Name it in the Type field and click the Save icon on the right side of the Type field.

If you don't save the preset, it will be lost when you select another effect type or restart your computer. Also note that only the names of the effect types are saved in an environmental audio preset, not the parameters themselves, which is another good reason for saving the new effect type when you are finished editing it.

Editing Effects Parameters

With most effects, the editable parameters are quite self-explanatory. Reverb is the most important effect for simulating natural sound environments. Unfortunately, for this reason there are so many parameters for the reverb effect that it can be difficult to know how to adjust them to get the desired result.

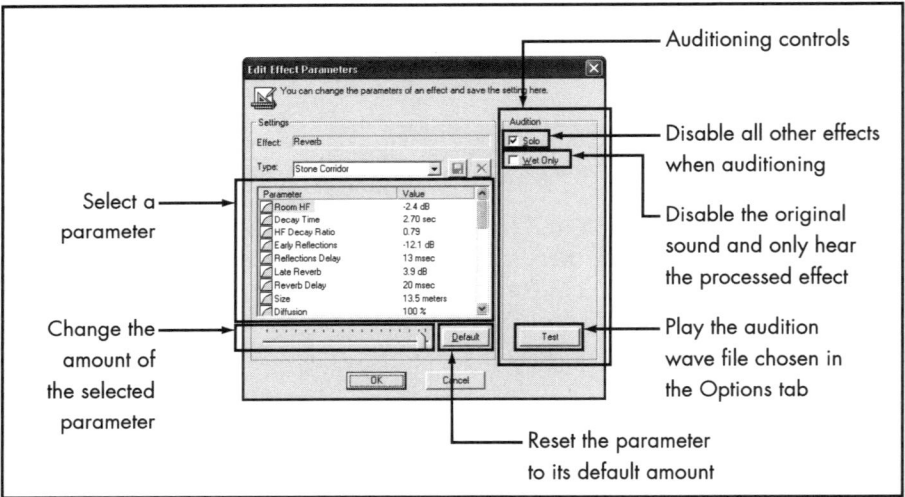

Figure 8.8: The Edit Effect Parameters window

TIP *Chapter 17 provides brief descriptions of the parameters for those effects that are interesting for MIDI music.*

You can take a look at the available parameters for the reverb by selecting this effect on the EAX Control Panel and clicking Parameters. Before exploring some of the most important parameters in detail, note these two general tips for finding the correct settings:

- Look at other effects. If, for instance, you want a longer reverb effect, find a long reverb effect among the available presets and see what parameters are different from those of the shorter reverbs.

- Try out the parameters. There's no better way to find out what a parameter does than to try it. If you mess up the entire effect, you can always go back to the previous settings by selecting the effect type from the Type drop-down list again.

Tweaking the Reverb

The reverb effect is meant to simulate the type of dense echoes that you hear in large rooms, such as a concert hall or a cave. To simulate an arbitrary sound environment, it's important to know a little about how reverb is simulated and how the particular parameters affect the final result.

A sound with reverb consists of three parts: the original sound (the *dry* signal), *early reflections*, and *late reverb*. Early reflections and late reverb make up the effect part and are mixed with the original sound at the proportions specified by the master and individual audio source levels for the original sound and reverb.

The early reflections are the first echoes that strike the listener after the original sound. They are not extremely dense and usually last for only a fraction of a second. The late reverb is the denser, smoother sound that follows the early reflections. The time between the original sound and the early reflections, as well as the decay time of the late reverb, can be adjusted to simulate different room sizes. Every time the sound bounces off a wall, some of the sound energy is absorbed, leading to decay of the reverb. In many environments, high frequencies are absorbed more quickly than low frequencies. This can be simulated as well. In addition, the reverb on the Live! lets you simulate other factors, such as slight detuning of the reverb and different levels of reverb density. The parameters listed here are the most important for customizing the reverb to your liking.

Table 8.1: Important Parameters for Customizing the EAX Reverb

Early Reflections	This parameter controls the level of the early reflections (in decibels below the original sound level) that are heard directly after the sound. The early reflections level will vary with the size and shape of the room, as well as the material of the walls and any sound absorbents. A higher setting will make the reflections more pronounced.
Reflections Delay	This parameter controls the delay (in milliseconds) between the original sound and the first early reflections. In general, the larger the room, the later the general reflections will come, and thus the larger this value should be.
Late Reflections (or Reverberations)	This parameter controls the intensity of the late reflections that occur right after the early reflections. This effect is denser and is intended to simulate sound that continually bounces between walls and objects, as in a cathedral.
Reverb Delay	This parameter controls the delay between the original sound and the beginning of the late reverb. Small values create a smooth reverb, and larger values simulate rooms where the listener is far from the nearest reflecting wall.
HF (High-Frequency Cutoff)	Through this parameter, you can set the highest frequency that the reverb contains. Frequencies above this value will not be reverberated.

Table 8.1: Important Parameters for Customizing the EAX Reverb (continued)

Room HF	This parameter controls the high-frequency damping of the room. Certain materials absorb high frequencies more easily than lower frequencies. More high-frequency damping will create a warmer, smoother reverb.
Echo	Unlike reverberations, echoes are distinct reflections of a sound that occur far enough apart to be individually discernible. Echo parameters allow you to control the level of echo.
Detuning	This parameter helps simulate the change in pitch of the sound in unusual environments, such as under water.
Size	Changing this parameter affects the length of the reflections. A higher value simulates a larger room, and a smaller one reduces the reflections.
Density	This parameter controls density in terms of reflections. Higher density settings make the reflections mesh together faster to produce smooth reverberation much earlier than do lower density settings.

Have Fun!

The effects-processing capability of the Live! is a groundbreaking feature in sound cards and is very fun to play with. Modifying a few parameters may change the sound drastically, but do not hesitate to experiment and try new parameters. This will help you understand the intricate details of the often neglected phenomenon of sound, which occurs constantly in our everyday lives.

9

DRIVERS AND OTHER TWEAKS

The *drivers*—programs that control and give the operating system (OS) access to a particular hardware device—are as vital to the operation of the sound card as the quality and features provided by the hardware. The Live! drivers have gone through many releases, each with incremental improvements to add enhancements to the 3D audio engine used for gaming, new EAX effects, and better utilities for the Live!, and to quietly fix bugs that seeped into earlier drivers.

What Drivers Do

To allow software applications to use the Live! in operating systems like Linux and Windows, several things need to happen:

- The operating system must work with any sound card; therefore, a generic set of specifications and routines known in technical terms as an *application program interface*, or API, is supplied with the OS (for example, DirectSound used by Windows-based games).

- The API is designed to encompass a generic set of features supported by a majority of sound cards in the market and also cater to the features required by application developers.
- An application running in the OS communicates with the API when it needs to use the sound card.
- The API receives audio instructions from the application and interprets and passes the instructions to the sound card in a format that is understood by its drivers.
- The driver is written according to the specifications of the API to support the audio features that the API provides to applications.
- The drivers take the instructions given by the API layer and convert it to a native format that is compatible with the specific hardware—in this case, the Live! card. This native format is transmitted to the EMU10K1 directly to control its operation and reprogram it.
- The desired audio is reproduced by the hardware on the Live! card.

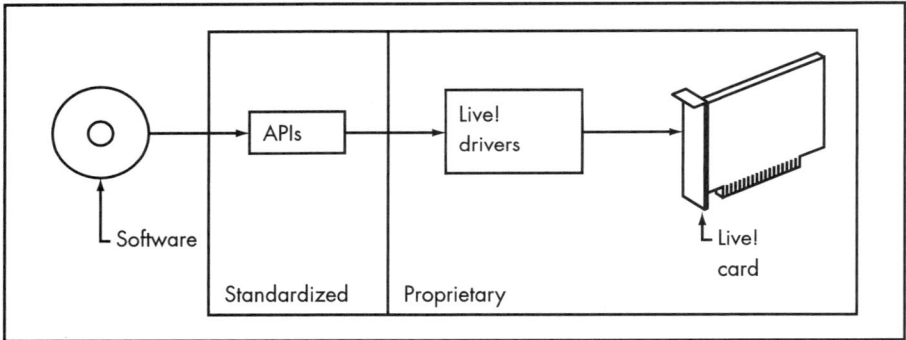

Figure 9.1: The relationship between APIs and drivers

The API provides a standard set of commands and features so that applications requiring the services of a sound card have a uniform way of communicating with it. This benefits the application developers, as they are freed of the laborious task of writing their programs to support the dozens of sound cards in the market.

For instance, before using the sound card, the application requests the services of the sound card by issuing an "open sound card" instruction through the API. The application will also set parameters such as sample rate and sample size to tell the API the format of the Wave audio it will be sending. Once this is done, the application can begin sending audio data and playback instructions to the sound card using functions provided by the API.

In turn, the drivers will have to respond to the instructions from the API by translating the instructions to commands understood only by the sound card. These commands are transmitted across the motherboard to the sound card's hardware components via electrical signals, where the physical hardware such as the sound chips and the EMU10K1 DSP will respond and generate the sound through the speakers.

Bad Drivers

There are many bad drivers on the roads, and poorly written drivers are just as prevalent and unwelcome on PCs. Without stable drivers, the Live! will not function correctly. Some users have experienced the various glitches and bugs that have surfaced with some of the Live! drivers released in the past.

Applications can be monitored and easily terminated by the OS when errors occur, but hardware drivers work at a different level of the operating system and typically have full and direct access to the hardware. The OS cannot easily monitor what drivers do. Therefore, there is a huge responsibility for hardware manufacturers to provide extremely stable and well-tested drivers. However, it is not an easy task to write drivers for hardware used in PCs because the PCs we own can come in so many configurations and combinations of hardware. It is nearly impossible to test every combination of hardware to ensure that the OS and drivers interact correctly and don't cause problems.

Poorly written sound drivers can cause system instability and audio artifacts and easily bring about OS freezes, blue screens, sudden reboots, and many other unwanted and often frustrating symptoms. Unstable drivers also affect the more crash-proof operating systems such as Windows 2000/XP, based on Windows NT, and the generally stable Linux. Crashes became widespread, causing consumers to attribute such malfunctions to a bad OS, not suspecting that the drivers of the hardware have an equal part to play in the overall stability of a PC.

With newer versions of Windows, Microsoft initiated a driver signing program where the company tests the drivers and awards Windows Hardware Quality Labs (WHQL) certification only to drivers that pass a suite of Windows compatibility tests. If you try to install non-WHQL drivers in Windows ME/2000/XP, a warning will be issued, and you will be asked to confirm that you are *very sure* you want to install an uncertified driver.

> Most drivers from hardware manufacturers, especially the latest ones, are not signed because Microsoft takes some time to evaluate and certify drivers. Some hardware manufacturers do not bother to certify their drivers, but fortunately Creative isn't one of them. This leads back to the problem of consumers unknowingly installing unstable drivers in their PCs because "it's the only one available." This is where the System Restore feature in Windows ME and Windows XP can help prevent a potential disaster, in case the PC completely refuses to start after a driver is installed.

The Live! drivers have had their fair share of bugs and teething problems that Creative has gradually fixed over time. Fortunately, the latest drivers work very well for most users.

Windows Drivers

Because most of the world relies on Windows for computing and entertainment, the Live! naturally has the most functionality in Windows. Let's first take a quick look at the evolution of the various Windows operating systems that the Live! runs on, especially because major architectural differences between the various versions of Windows have led to different types of drivers used by the Live!

The Windows Evolution

When the first popular Windows operating system, version 3.1 was introduced, the PC industry was still using disk operating system (DOS) applications. DOS was a primitive, non-multitasking, mostly text-based operating system that provided rudimentary support for program execution, file storage, and other basic system functions. DOS applications generally worked by accessing and modifying memory and hardware directly: for example, if an application wanted to print a word on the monitor, it simply wrote that information to the video card directly. This model allowed software to take control of the PC, including hardware peripherals like the sound card and the entire memory space, thus allowing poorly written software to affect the OS and crash the PC.

The PC world discovered the graphical user interface, the ability to run many programs at once, and font support in Windows in the early 1990s; sales of Windows 3.1 skyrocketed, sealing Microsoft's position in the software market. To retain compatibility with DOS and the thousands of applications that run on it, Windows was designed to run on top of DOS like any other application. As in the "do anything you please" operating environment provided by DOS, badly written Windows applications could crash the OS. A poorly written Windows 3.1 program could easily hijack the resources of the entire system and affect the operation of other applications running in the background.

By the mid-1990s, the world had seen all the flaws and limitations of Windows 3.1 due to its weak foundation based on DOS and needed an upgrade that was more stable and provided more features. Many programs, in particular CPU-intensive graphical software such as games, still had to use DOS because Windows 3.1 was not designed as a multimedia OS and was largely unsuitable for games that required close control of the PC hardware for best performance. This was crucial in those times because CPU speed and system performance were not very high; game developers were trying their best to squeeze the most performance out of the hardware available in typical PCs in the home, and DOS was the way to do it efficiently.

The Windows 9x Operating Systems

Given the growing dissatisfaction with Windows 3.1, Microsoft was not resting on its laurels. The company had been working for several years to come up with another operating system that provided 32-bit computing, more stability, native networking features, and a new graphical interface (with the familiar Start menu and taskbar that is still used today). However, the OS had to retain compatibility with many DOS applications that still existed, particularly multimedia applications such as games.

> Windows 9x operating systems include Windows 95 (including OSR1 and OSR2), Windows 98 (including SE, the second edition), and Windows ME (Millennium Edition).

When Microsoft finally completed this new OS in 1995, after grappling with numerous delays during the course of development, this new version was christened Windows 95 and released worldwide to much fanfare. It was more stable and could run multiple applications simultaneously. But as many users discovered, it was still subject to crashes, although it was more resilient than Windows 3.1. Nevertheless, the numerous new features, better user interface, and stronger foundation it provided was a huge step up from Windows 3.1. Games could have near-direct access to hardware and sound cards using the DirectX API, and developers quickly took to the new Windows OS. The number of DOS programs and games gradually decreased.

Future versions of Windows, such as Windows 98, Windows 98 SE, and Windows ME, added some new features and improved the user interface, but because they were still based on Windows 95, these operating systems inherited the stability issues and fundamental flaws inherent in the way the OS was designed. Even so, consumers purchased these new operating systems for important functionality such as support for large hard drives with FAT32 and USB support for the increasing number of plug-and-play peripherals.

Windows NT: Reliable Windows

Around the time when Windows 3.1 dominated the PC market, Microsoft had already realized the shortcomings of an operating system that had to sit on top of (and be limited to) the primitive DOS operating system and sought to create a fully multitasking and protected operating system to be ultimately used as the foundation of all future Windows operating systems. This OS was dubbed NT, which stands for new technology.

Windows NT was a remarkably stable Windows OS and contained many features found in operating systems like Unix, used in servers and commercial deployments. An important prerequisite for producing a stable operating system is not to allow applications to arbitrarily modify and change properties of the PC directly. Instead, NT verifies that each operation of a program is valid and does not jeopardize the OS or other applications running on the PC at the same time. Think of it as a traffic cop for PC resources. Applications run separately in their own memory spaces, and the moment they perform an illegal operation and corrupt another application or the operating system's memory space, NT generates the familiar "protection fault" error and terminates the program.

Contrast that to the operation of Windows 3.x and Windows 9x, where an error in one program would sometimes cause system instability and affect other programs that may also be running at the time. In many cases, users had no choice but to go through a long reboot process to get a safer and clean operating environment so that the PC would be less likely to crash again.

As they say, there's no such thing as a free lunch, and this form of protection comes at a price: more PC resources are required. This was tough for PCs of the past, when CPUs were not very fast and the capacity of PC memory was only in the 8 to 32 MB range. This effectively kept the NT operating system from dominating the home market due to the hefty system requirements and lack of compatibility with DOS applications due to the operating system's protected nature—not good news for budget home PCs. Hence, Windows 9x-based operating systems were developed to bridge this gap between DOS/Windows 3.1 and NT, and Windows 9x became widely used in consumer PCs.

Realizing this, Microsoft focused on retooling the operating system for the enterprise market. In subsequent years, the NT platform moved from the Windows 3.1 interface to the Windows 95 interface with the familiar Start menu and taskbar. The product line was split into two general versions—workstation and server—where the workstation version of NT had fewer features, and the server version was designed to run as a server in networked environments.

But things couldn't stay still. This multipronged approach of carrying several different underlying operating systems under the Windows brand name was troublesome for both hardware manufacturers and software developers. They had to ensure that their products worked on all variants of Windows, which increased development costs and time. Microsoft planned to ultimately move all Windows OSes to the more stable NT platform and quash all these issues once and for all, but at the time, the protected environment of NT was not optimized for multimedia applications and games that needed close and efficient access to hardware.

Windows 2000: It Plays Games!

In 2000, a radically updated version of the NT platform was released as Windows 2000. It finally provided DirectX, USB support, video and audio acceleration, and other features sorely missing in the earlier Windows NT operating systems but already found in the consumer Windows 98 and Windows ME operating systems.

There were new features to circumvent some of the difficulties caused by the system's protected nature, such as a new way to write drivers for hardware like sound cards, known as the Windows Driver Model (WDM), and support for the latest DirectX version. Windows 2000 was a huge surprise for many consumers, who always thought that the NT platform was not suitable for games. To the contrary, many games and applications ran very well under Windows 2000. In addition, Windows 2000 was much more crash resistant than Windows 9x/ME, and even surpasses Windows NT in speed and stability. Microsoft maintained that Windows 2000 is for the enterprise market, but this did not stop some consumers from purchasing a copy of the OS as a replacement for Windows 9x/ME—and hence the demand for WDM drivers for the Live! when Windows 2000 was released.

Windows XP: Finally, a Stable Consumer OS!

In October 2001, after many years of talking about plans to use the Windows NT as a base for both enterprise and consumer Windows operating systems, Windows XP was finally released to fulfill this vision. It was an updated version of Windows 2000, with all of its stability meshed with the multimedia bells and whistles of Windows ME. With an updated user interface and, most important, stability inherited from Windows 2000, Windows XP is now becoming the OS of choice for home users purchasing a new PC and is also a great upgrade for users of Windows 9x/ME who are incessantly frustrated by stability issues.

VXD and WDM Drivers

The more open nature of Windows 9x/ME gave developers near-direct access to the hardware, especially the video and sound cards, resulting in efficiency gains that were crucial for resource-hungry games. With the slower PCs and hardware peripherals in the mid-1990s, computing resources were scarce; thus, Windows 9x operating systems were viewed by many as a compromise between stability and efficiency.

VXD drivers are used for hardware devices in Windows 9x operating systems to allow them to work in the OS. The Live! comes with VXD drivers that give applications close control of the sound card through the WaveOut and DirectSound/DirectSound3D APIs in Windows. Parameters such as sampling rates can be modified directly, and this can potentially affect other applications that may also need to use the sound card. This problem is solved by permitting only one application to access certain functions of the sound card—for example, the MIDI playback features.

> Before DirectX 5.0 was released in 1997, a year before the Live! was introduced, the 3D audio portion (DirectSound3D) of the DirectX API was limited to software rendering of 3D sound using the CPU, and could not work with sound cards that could efficiently generate 3D audio in hardware.

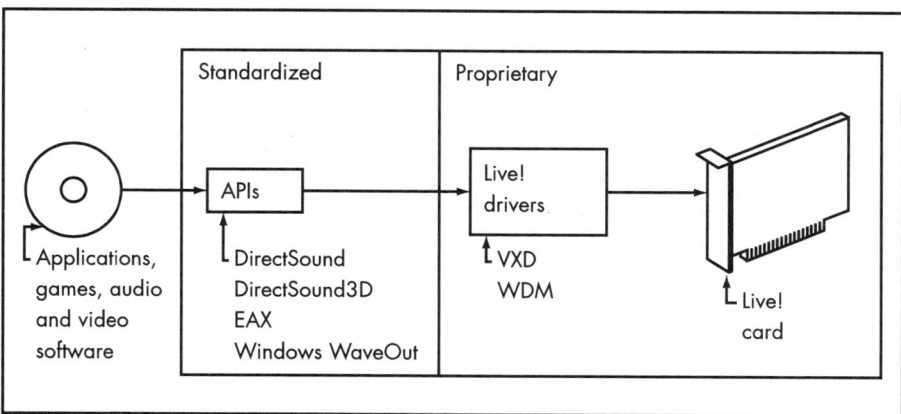

Figure 9.2: APIs and drivers in Windows

> VXDs are also known as *virtual device drivers*. The OS allows these drivers to communicate directly with the hardware on the sound card.

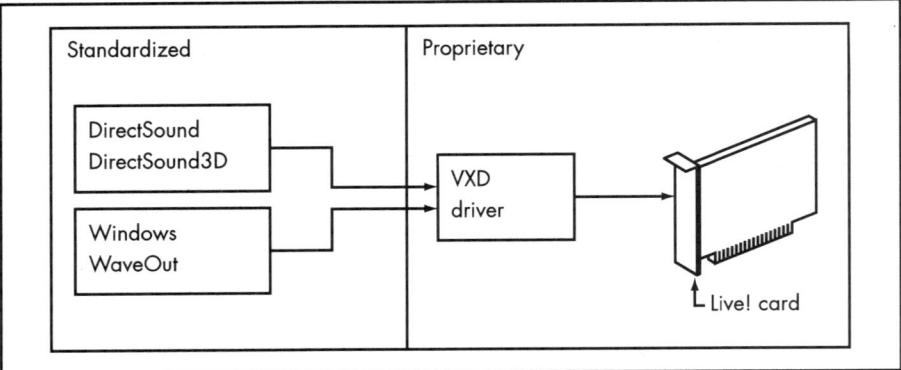

Figure 9.3: Interaction between Windows APIs and the VXD driver

The protected NT-based operating systems cannot provide applications with direct access to the hardware, because this may cause system instability when an application does the wrong thing. This has limited the DirectX and gaming features available in Windows NT. It was not until Windows 2000 that WDM was added to NT-based operating systems to circumvent this problem.

To allow the industry to transition from the older VXD drivers to WDM, later Windows 9*x* operating systems, including Windows 98 SE and Windows ME, do support WDM drivers. However, Creative has opted to use the VXD drivers for all Windows 9*x* operating systems, using WDM only for NT-based operating systems like Windows 2000 and Windows XP.

For sound cards, WDM adds another layer of arbitration and processing between the sound card drivers and the audio APIs and offloads to the OS some of the common tasks traditionally handled by VXD drivers. This WDM audio layer consists of several components that preserve the integrity of the protected operating environment provided by the OS, while allowing the possibility of near-direct access to sound card features through APIs such as DirectSound and DirectSound3D.

> One of the components present in the WDM audio layer is the kernel mixer (KMixer), which obtains audio from these APIs and performs preprocessing and mixing before passing the audio to the WDM driver of the sound card. For instance, it helps mix and convert Wave audio if the sound card does not support the particular format.

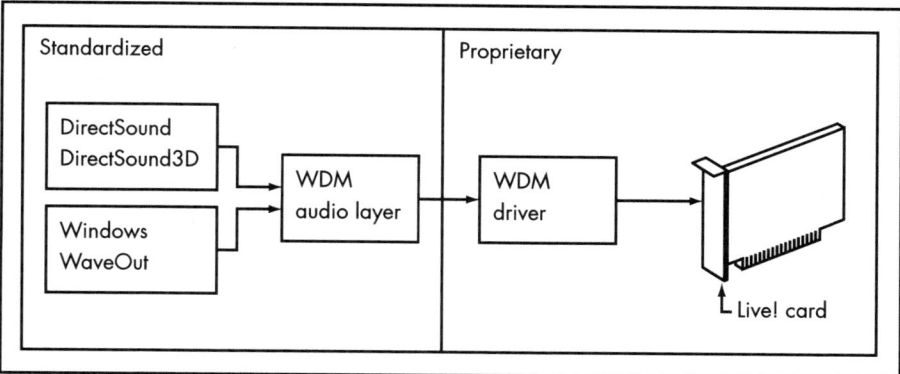

Figure 9.4: Interaction between Windows APIs, the WDM audio layer, and WDM driver

> The *kernel* is the essential portion of an operating system that provides functions critical for a computer to operate, such as memory management, storage management, hardware interfacing, and allocation of system resources. The kernel mixer can be viewed as an arbitrator of sound card resources, just like the OS is the arbitrator of disk space on a hard drive.

Applications that want to use the sound card are written like their Windows 9*x* counterparts to talk to the WaveOut, DirectSound, or DirectSound3D APIs. However, these APIs now need to go through the WDM audio layer to access the sound card, and the drivers are retooled to respond to instructions from the WDM audio layer. With WDM, the drivers and APIs do not talk directly all the time. Sound card manufacturers like Creative write only the part to interface with their particular hardware, leaving the audio-processing tasks common on all sound cards to the WDM audio layer.

The addition of the WDM audio layer provides a few advantages:

- APIs and WDM sound card drivers have a common means of communicating with one another.
- New APIs can be quickly developed to work with KMixer.
- Sound card manufacturers need to support only KMixer and the WDM audio layer and do not have to support every new API that is introduced.

You can see that VXD and WDM drivers are different in their implementation, and Creative had to write these drivers separately, while making sure that they provided similar functionality in any Windows OS and did not cripple the abilities of the EMU10K1.

Looking forward, the entire PC industry will be using WDM drivers for hardware in Windows, because they provide cross-platform compatibility between Windows 9*x*- and NT-based operating systems. The VXD driver model will be phased out, and with Windows XP gaining acceptance in the consumer space, WDM drivers are essential for multimedia hardware like the Live!

Windows Drivers for the Live!

Due to the ubiquity of Windows, the advanced features of the Live! are exploited in Windows and not other operating systems. The drivers usually consist of small, optimized files that can be downloaded quickly, but the applications and utilities take up much space. Therefore, Creative had to come up with creative methods for distributing this software:

- **Live!Ware:** Full package consisting of the driver and sound card applications like MiniDisc Center, PlayCenter, and Vienna SoundFont Studio.
- **Driver-only releases:** These drivers provide basic functionality for the sound card and include only essential software like the Surround Mixer and AudioHQ.
- **Driver patches:** These driver-only releases are used to fix problems and upgrade an existing driver or Live!Ware installation.

TIP *You can open AudioHQ from four places: the Control Panel, the tray notification area on the taskbar, the Creative Launcher, and the Start menu.*

Live!Ware

The reprogrammable design of the EMU10K1 DSP has often been touted because it gives Creative the flexibility to add new capabilities to the Live! with a simple software installation, not requiring a hardware change. These upgrades are integrated into the drivers and distributed to users through the Live!Ware program. New product shipments also have the latest Live!Ware provided on CD-ROM. In addition to enhanced features like an improved 3D positioning engine for gaming, applications and utilities like the Surround Mixer and PlayCenter were also introduced and upgraded throughout the three-year evolution of the Live!

Figure 9.5: The Live!Ware logo

Driver-Only Releases

Today, the drivers provided on the Internet by Creative are all driver-only releases, with only the VXD or WDM drivers for specific Windows OSes, and the standard utilities and applications for controlling the basic features of the sound card.

Unofficial Drivers

Sometimes, newer unofficial drivers are available on the Internet. These drivers are contributed by users who purchased a Live! recently and found these drivers bundled. Creative often releases new driver versions to OEM and PC manufacturers without providing similar driver upgrades on its Web site for other owners who bought the retail versions. This has left some users frustrated, especially if the drivers they have are causing problems.

The pent-up demand for updated drivers has been compounded by the teething problems of the WDM drivers, which continued to have missing features many months after Windows 2000 was released. Users who had the newer WDM drivers created their own driver packages and made them available over the Internet for others to try. Many enthusiasts would also like to install new drivers when they are available, in anticipation of new features and better performance.

Nevertheless, you should not use these drivers unless you are experiencing serious problems getting the Live! to work. Some of these unofficial drivers have not been tested on a wide range of system configurations and may introduce new glitches. Furthermore, the official drivers available today should work very well, so there is no need to use unofficial drivers unless you have no other options.

Driver Patches

Creative occasionally provides driver upgrades and patches on its Web site for users to download. These are usually provided to fix common problems and issues experienced in previous Live!Ware or driver releases. These drivers are tested extensively and work for a large majority of users. Upgrade to these official drivers when you find them, as they may fix known issues and improve performance of the sound card.

TIP *To be sure that you are getting drivers from a legitimate source, download or purchase them directly from Creative or the Sound Blaster Web site at http://www.soundblaster.com.*

Windows 9x Drivers

When the Live! was introduced in September 1998, Windows 95 and 98 were the dominant operating systems, and of course, a VXD driver was supplied. Major changes to the Live! drivers and features occurred with these drivers, because they were the first and only drivers available early on when the Live! was introduced. By the time the later Windows (Windows ME, Windows 2000, and Windows XP) operating systems were launched, many of the changes and upgrades had already been made, so all Creative had to do was develop drivers that work with the OS and make the utilities compatible with the new operating systems. The following table presents some of the major changes and milestones in the drivers released for the Windows 9x operating systems.

TIP *When installing the drivers, the last part of the process will seem to pause with no indication of progress and take an extremely long time to complete. Nevertheless, give it some time as the installation is writing a huge amount of EAX and other configuration information into the Windows registry before the Live! and EAX presets are installed correctly for use.*

Table 9.1: Major Sound Blaster Live! Driver Releases for Windows 9x Operating Systems

Date	Version	Major Features
September 1998	Live!Ware 1	• The first version of the drivers and applications bundled with the first generation of Live! products. • Provided support for eight 3D positioned sounds. A patch came later and raised this to thirty-two 3D positioned sounds. • EAX 1.0 for environmental reverb.
Early 1999	Live!Ware 2	• Enhanced the 3D positioning algorithms and added positioning of the vertical axis, so sounds above and below the listener can be simulated. • EAX 2.0 was introduced, with new occlusion and obstruction effects. • The polyphony of the software synth was increased to 1,024. • New utilities like Surround Mixer and AutoEA were added. • Other applications like the Live! Experience demo were improved.
October 1999	Live!Ware 3	• The third Live!Ware release. • EAX is still at version 2.0. There are many misconceptions that Live!Ware 3.0 contains EAX 3, which is incorrect. • A new EAX demo was added to showcase the 3D positioning, occlusion, and obstruction effects. • The interface of Surround Mixer was slightly changed. • The Live!Task utility was added for computer novices. • Time-scaling was added to PlayCenter.
October 2000	Live!Ware 3 for Windows ME	This is a Windows ME-compatible version of Live!Ware 3 released around the same time that Windows ME was introduced.

Subsequent releases after 1999 were small driver patches and updates that fixed problems with certain software and hardware, especially for some games that use EAX. Unfortunately for the thousands of users who were anticipating "Live!Ware 4" and "EAX 3.0," the Live!Ware program ran out of steam as Creative focused its resources on forthcoming audio products, resulting in a lack of major new features in 2000 and 2001. With successors to the Live! being released, Creative is less likely to improve the features of the Live! much further than what is currently available, even though the hardware may be capable of such features.

> **Windows NT Drivers**
>
> Drivers for Windows NT provide only basic audio functionality because of the protected nature of the OS and the fact that it was not until Windows 2000 (and subsequently Windows XP) that the NT platform had WDM support to allow sound cards to function fully. Games and multimedia do not work well in Windows NT, so users should install Windows 98, Windows ME, Windows 2000, or Windows XP to exploit the full capabilities of the Live! in these applications.

Windows 2000 Drivers

Compared to the Windows 9*x* drivers, Windows 2000 drivers had a rough start because of problems with certain features, most notably S/PDIF passthrough, hibernation, and symmetric multiprocessing (SMP) support. It took Creative some time to bring the WDM drivers to the same level of functionality as the Windows 9*x* VXD drivers. Today, most of the features work well and are largely similar to those on the Windows 9*x* operating systems, so you will not lose functionality when using multimedia application and games.

Because Windows 2000 Professional is the version that most desktop PCs and workstations use, most game developers, and Creative's drivers for the Live!, target this desktop variant of Windows 2000 and not the Windows 2000 server version.

The following table lists the major driver releases for the Live! in Windows 2000.

Table 9.2: Major Sound Blaster Live! Driver Releases for Windows 2000

Date	Major Features
March 2000	The first Windows 2000 drivers were released about a month after the launch of Windows 2000. They provided very basic features, and some utilities sported a look similar to that of Live!Ware 1 for Windows 9*x* and were not as advanced as Live!Ware 3 available for Windows 9*x* users at that time.
July 2000	Live!Ware for Windows 2000 skipped the second generation and was released as Live!Ware 3. This brought the drivers and utilities of the Live! to the same level as the those for the Windows 9*x* operating systems.
September 2001	The long-awaited driver update that finally fixed S/PDIF passthrough and SMP problems was released.

Hibernation

Most PCs can be put to a sleep mode. This turns off the main components of the PC, while still drawing some power to maintain the memory contents and operatingstate of other critical components in the PC. This allows the PC to be turned back on very quickly, but you may notice that the power supply unit of your PC still continues to operate.

Windows ME and 2000 bring another advancement by enabling the CPU to power down completely, while the desktop and applications that are running are retained. This is done by saving the state of Windows on the hard drive. The next time the PC is turned on, the desktop is restored from the hibernation data on the hard drive, and the desktop looks the same as it was before the PC was hibernated.

TIP *Hibernation can be turned on in the power settings in Control Panel.*

Early drivers for the Live! could not work with hibernation because Creative did not take in to account the need to support this feature. The most commonly experienced symptom was that the system could go into hibernation correctly, but when attempting to power it up again, the PC could not be restored and had to be reset. The hibernation data is completely lost, which is no different from a sudden Windows crash or blue screen.

Driver versions after 3110 are reported to work well with the hibernate feature built in to Windows ME/2000, and you should download the latest drivers if you encounter this flaw.

S/PDIF Passthrough

The S/PDIF passthrough feature is used by software DVD players to output a DVD's Dolby Digital or DTS soundtrack to external decoders like home theater receivers. With earlier drivers, no signal is present on the S/PDIF output (optical or coaxial) of a digital I/O device. This has nothing to do with the hardware, as it is caused by both the drivers and Windows 2000's ability to support this feature. To fix this, install the latest drivers, as well as Windows 2000 Service Pack 2 (SP2) or higher.

> **Service Packs**
> From time to time, Microsoft releases a collection of updates and fixes to NT-based Windows operating systems to bring them up-to-date. These are collected into a service pack. Many software and hardware products indicate the minimum service pack release required on their boxes and manuals. The latest service packs can be download from Microsoft at http://www.microsoft.com/windows/ as well as the Windows Update Web site at http://windowsupdate.microsoft.com.

TIP *S/PDIF passthrough works fine in Windows 95/98/ME operating systems.*

Chapter 11 explores the various ways to play movies and DVDs with the Live!, including using S/PDIF passthrough.

Compressed multichannel audio formats like Dolby Digital AC-3 and DTS are not standard PCM signals; therefore, the Windows WaveOut API has to provide a way for applications like DVD players to bypass PCM processing and mixing in the OS and sound card, and send out the soundtrack unaltered as it is read from the DVD. These signals are then delivered to the sound card's digital outputs and a connected surround decoder built in to home theater receivers and some more costly multimedia speakers. Microsoft omitted this non-PCM WaveOut capability in Windows 2000; it was added to the OS in May 2001 when SP2 was released.

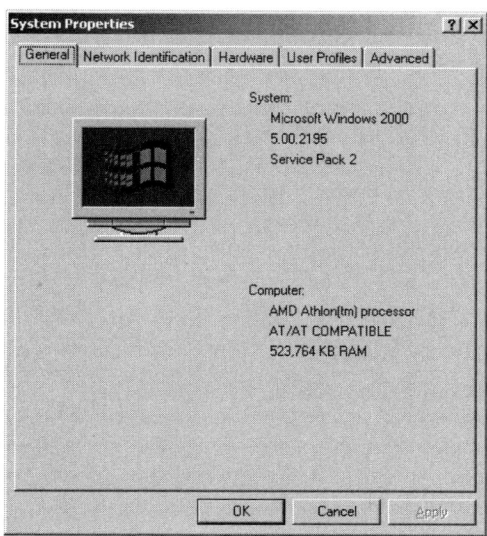

Figure 9.6: To determine the version of Windows 2000, choose Start • Control Panel • System, and this window will open. If a service pack is installed, it will be indicated below the version number.

Even after SP2 allowed S/PDIF passthrough, the Live!'s drivers did not work with the feature until the second half of 2001 when WDM driver versions 3219 and higher were made available on new shipments of the Live! Owners who purchased new Live! cards repackaged the drivers and shared them over the Internet, so the new WDM drivers were available unofficially for a while. The September 2001 driver update officially fixes this issue, and all Windows 2000 users should download the latest driver updates directly from Creative.

> Driver versions are generally given based on the version number of the EMU10K1 driver file. See the section "Determining the Driver Version" later in this chapter to determine the version of the drivers that are installed on your PC.

Symmetric Multiprocessing (SMP) Systems

NT-based operating systems (except versions for consumers like Windows XP Home Edition) support PCs with two or more CPUs running concurrently. These PCs are mainly used in enterprises as servers, but some PC enthusiasts do go the multiprocessor route for an extra speed boost. The WDM drivers for the Live! had problems with such SMP PCs, but this was fixed in drivers released after late 2001. Earlier drivers had problems like pops, stuttering audio, very loud screeching sounds, and distorted EAX effects.

> **TIP** *If you are still experiencing problems with SMP, try decreasing the hardware acceleration as described in the section "Advanced Audio Properties: Hardware Acceleration" later in this chapter.*

Windows XP

Windows XP is based on Windows 2000 and uses similar WDM drivers and utilities. However, incompatibilities may arise due to minor differences between the operating systems, so always install the latest driver updates that Creative states as compatible with Windows XP. Fortunately, by the time Windows XP was released in October 2001, most of the WDM driver issues that plagued Windows 2000 users had been resolved, and the new Windows XP drivers work just as well for a majority of Windows XP users.

Native Windows Drivers

Windows 2000 and Windows XP come with built-in drivers for the Live!, and the OS will use them automatically when a Live! card is detected in your PC. However, these drivers are very basic and do not provide the full set of features like multispeaker support, EAX, and other crucial features of the Live! To ensure that the Live! can be exploited fully, install the drivers provided by Creative.

Determining the Driver Version

Most software developers and hardware manufacturers tag their drivers with version numbers and increase the number when features and bug fixes are added. However, Creative does not do that with the Live! drivers made available to the public for download. Instead, the drivers are usually given a release date, and this is pretty much the only way users can gauge how new the drivers are before downloading and installing them. Make a note of the date of the last driver update you have installed, so that when you come across a new one, you can decide if you want to use it.

> **TIP** *Remember to have a copy of the Windows CD or the Windows installation files in the hard drive when installing the Live! drivers, as Windows may need to install additional components for audio support.*

In spite of this approach, the driver development team at Creative does make use of internal version numbers, so if you're curious to find out which driver is installed on your PC, here's how you can find out. The most important driver file that determines the operation of the Live! always has a file name beginning with

EMU10K1. In NT-based OSes like Windows 2000 and Windows XP, it is the EMU10K1F.sys file and is usually found in the winnt\system32\drivers folder for Windows 2000 or windows\system32\drivers folder for Windows XP. In Windows 9*x* operating systems, look for EMU10K1.vxd in the windows\system folder. The version number will be separated by several periods. The rightmost number after the last period is the usually the one that is changed most often, and many people abbreviate it as the version number.

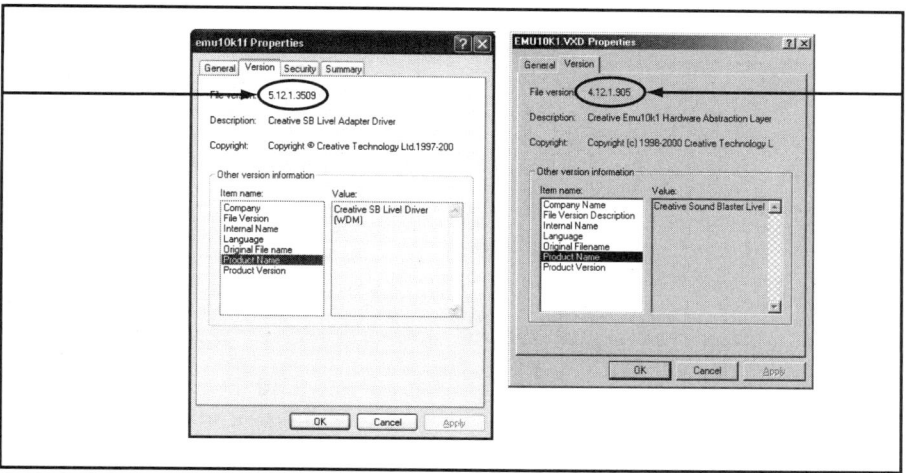

Figure 9.7: Finding the version number

TIP *WDM drivers usually have a .sys file extension, while VXD drivers end with a .vxd extension. You may not be able to see the file names in full if you have hidden system files and file extensions in Windows Explorer. This can be disabled by going to Tools • Folder Options in Windows Explorer.*

TIP *Microsoft's Windows Update service at http://windowsupdate.microsoft.com sometimes has new drivers for the Live! that are certified by Microsoft to comply with Windows. Check this site often and update your copy of Windows, especially with security fixes and the latest hardware drivers.*

Verifying Driver Installation

After installing the drivers, you should see a new program group named Creative on the Start menu. The group will contain all of the new software that was installed in your PC. You should also find a subgroup called Sound Blaster Live! that contains the essential utilities such as the Surround Mixer and AudioHQ.

To ensure that the drivers are installed correctly, make sure there are no errors in the Windows Device Manager. First, you will need to load Device Manager, where Windows lists the categories of hardware and devices installed on your PC, as well as the installed audio and video codecs and drivers.

Table 9.3: How to Load the Device Manager in Windows 9x, Windows 2000, and Windows XP

To load Device Manager in Windows 95/98/ME:	To load Device Manager in Windows 2000:	To load Device Manager in Windows XP:
1. Click the Start button.	1. Click the Start button.	1. Click the Start button.
2. Move the mouse to select Settings.	2. Move the mouse to select Settings.	2. Open the Control Panel.
3. Open the Control Panel.	3. Open the Control Panel.	3. If the Control Panel is in Category view ("Pick a category" is displayed), click Performance and Maintenance, and at the bottom, click System.
4. Click the System icon; a System Properties window opens.	4. Double-click the System icon; a System Properties window opens.	4. If the Control Panel is in Classic view, double-click the System icon.
5. Click the Device Manager tab.	5. Click the Hardware tab.	5. Click the Hardware tab.
	6. Click the Device Manager button.	6. Click the Device Manager button.

After Device Manager is opened, find the Sound, video and game controllers category. Click the plus (+) symbol to the left of the item (or double-click the item), and the list will expand to show the Live! driver. The name changes slightly between different operating systems, but you'll see something like "Creative SB Live!" listed there. If the driver is WDM, you may also see "(WDM)" appended to the device name.

In Windows 2000/XP, you will also see a Creative SB Live! Gameport device for the joystick connector on the Live! card's backplate. In Windows 95/98/ME, the game port is labeled Creative Gameport Joystick and is found under another category of devices labeled Creative Miscellaneous Devices. This category will also contain a Creative MultiMedia Interface device and a Creative SB16 Emulation device. The emulation device allows Sound Blaster–compatible games and programs to work from DOS command prompts in Windows; it was removed from newer Windows 9x drivers (more on SB16 emulation later in the chapter).

TIP *You can disable the game port device if you do not intend to use it.*

Usually, the devices listed will not have problems, but if you see a question mark (instead of a normal icon) beside the Live! driver entry, or any of the other devices related to the Live!, there is a problem. Most likely, there is a resource or hardware conflict. Creative tech support is most qualified to step you through the troubleshooting and installation process unique to your PC and hardware configuration. Nevertheless, the following may help solve some of the more common problems:

- Remove the SB Live! device and reinstall the drivers. In Windows 2000/XP, you can right-click the device and use the Uninstall option.
- Uninstall the drivers and software completely and then reinstall them.

- Upgrade to the latest drivers available from Creative over the Internet.
- Move the Live! card to another PCI slot on the motherboard.

What Drivers Are Available Today?

With the introduction of next-generation Sound Blasters to supercede the Live!, Creative will probably not add new features. Innovations and improvements could expectedly go to the new sound cards, but due to the huge user base for the Live! cards amassed since 1998, new drivers will still be released if any major problems and compatibility issues crop up in the future.

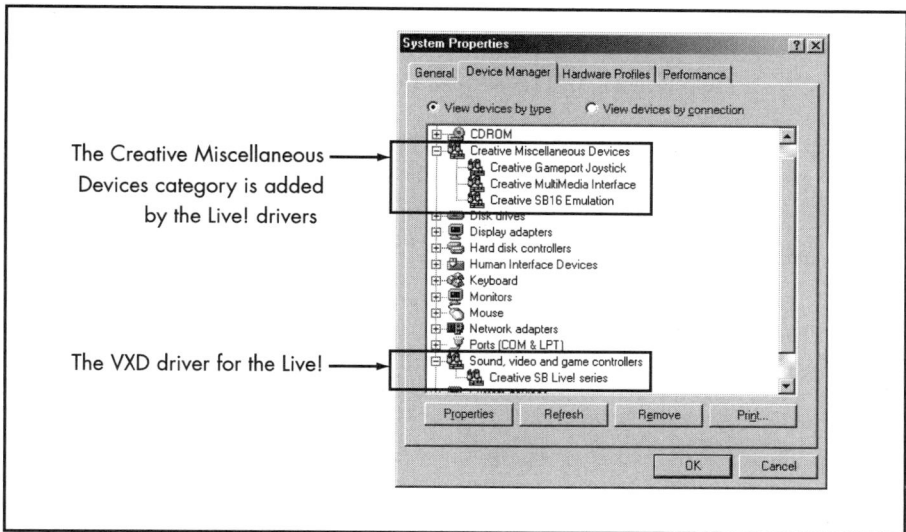

Figure 9.8: The Device Manager window in Windows 95/98/ME

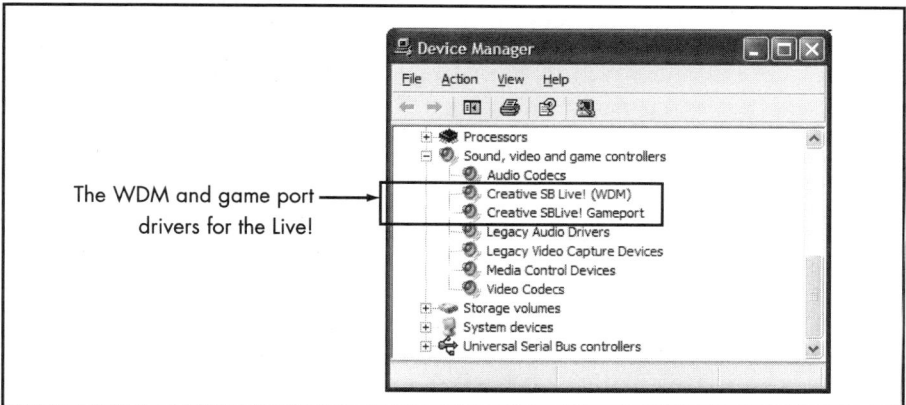

Figure 9.9: The Device Manager window in Windows 2000/XP

Drivers and Other Tweaks   **253**

What about new operating systems? Not to worry. With the ubiquity of the Sound Blaster, Creative will also have to release updated drivers whenever a new Windows OS is released. This has already happened to the Live! with the release of Windows ME, Windows 2000, and Windows XP; Live!Ware supported only the Windows 9x and Windows NT operating systems when it was first introduced.

> Creative dropped the "Live!Ware" name and focused on marketing the more generic "CreativeWare" name for some of its products that feature upgradability. These include the Sound Blaster and Creative's line of portable music players.

In fall 2001, Creative decided not to provide the complete suite of Creative-Ware/Live!Ware drivers and applications for customers to download over the Internet. Past releases of Live!Ware have caused massive slowdowns and disruptions on Creative's Internet servers, and Creative does not allow third parties to mirror these files, so some users were unable to get them until many days later.

Today, the full suite of drivers and applications is available only on CD-ROM and must be purchased directly from Creative. The download versions contain only the bare minimum needed for the Live! to function, including the following:

- Drivers for your Windows version
- Essential utilities like the Surround Mixer
- AudioHQ for configuration of the sound card

Other software like PlayCenter, MiniDisc Center, and Vienna SoundFont Studio are included only in the retail driver CD-ROM.

> Be sure to get the correct CreativeWare/Live!Ware CD when you are purchasing a bulk or OEM version of the Live! (in general, a version that does not come in a retail box). Some new users purchased their Live! cards without the CD and then discovered that Creative does not provide the full suite of software over the Internet.

Completely Stable Drivers: A Misnomer?

It is not easy to write drivers that work on 100 percent of the PCs that exist because many different applications, hardware, and drivers can be put together in a PC. Buggy drivers of other hardware may affect the operation of the Live!, or an application developer may make a mistake and set the sound card to an invalid state and cause it to be unusable by other applications, or perhaps Windows itself has a bug that causes the whole PC to behave unexpectedly—there are just too many ways that things can go wrong.

> Unlike many companies, which openly list the current known issues and problems with their products, Creative seldom discloses or acknowledges existing problems and issues on its Web site, preferring to quietly fix and release new drivers when they are ready. Sometimes these fixes are announced in the obligatory "what's changed" list, but at other times, the fixes are not disclosed. This uncertainty causes some users to experiment with new drivers in the hope of solving issues that they have encountered.

Unlike platforms that have a fairly uniform and standardized hardware design, such as game consoles like the PlayStation 2 and Xbox or even computers like the Apple Macintosh, PCs consist of a myriad hardware and software that are mixed and matched to build the machine. Regrettably, the probability of problems occurring in PCs is high enough that some unfortunate users will experience them. In these cases, a call or email to Creative technical support is in order.

Proper software development and testing procedures by hardware and software developers do play a part in determining the quality of software such as drivers. Also, tight development deadlines and unrealistic schedules are a hard fact in the IT industry. Some companies take the easy route and adopt a "release first, patch later" attitude, because "everybody's doing it"; others have strong commitments to product quality and customer satisfaction and will opt to delay a product or driver release until it is working correctly.

Alternative Windows Drivers for the Adventurous

Although Creative has provided very good support for game audio through the Live!Ware upgrades, not everyone is satisfied with the feature set of these drivers. Particularly, some musicians have felt that important features are missing in the drivers, and that they therefore can't use the full potential of their Live! cards. For example, there is no or little support for multiple cards in one computer, multiple analog outputs (using the rear out), or ASIO. In addition, the effects system for MIDI music is quite limited compared to what is possible with the powerful capabilities of the EMU10K1 DSP.

The APSLive!

The E-MU APS, the Live!'s more professional sibling, clearly targeted at musicians rather than gamers, was introduced around the same time as the first-generation Live! cards. Because both are based on the EMU10K1 processor, these cards are (despite the huge difference in price) virtually identical. As a consequence, a minor modification of the APS drivers will allow it to work with Live! cards. Users abbreviated Live! cards running APS drivers as the "APSLive!"

This is great for musicians, because these drivers include much more flexible effects, support for ASIO (Steinberg's high-performance and low-latency audio driver system), and software clearly made for musicians. Still, for several reasons, we cannot recommend these drivers. Among other things:

- These drivers are based on copyrighted software developed for (and only for) the E-MU APS card. As a consequence, modifying, as well as using, these drivers with a Sound Blaster Live! is clearly illegal.
- For these drivers to be useful, you need the basic APS software. This software is also copyrighted, and using it without owning an APS card would be software piracy. Keep in mind that part of the (significantly) higher price of the APS comes from its more professional software and drivers.
- These drivers do not support the Windows Driver Model (WDM) and can therefore not be used with more recent Microsoft operating systems, such as Windows 2000 and XP.
- Needless to say, Creative does not support the use of these drivers. Don't expect Creative's tech support to help you if you run into trouble.

The kX Project

The kX project is a set of free, independently developed WDM drivers and basic software for EMU10K1- (Live!, APS, PCI512) and Audigy-based cards. The fact that they are WDM drivers means that they are compatible with all modern versions of Windows (Windows 98 SE, ME, 2000, and XP). Because they are not based on any copyrighted software, you need not worry about legal issues when using them.

At the time of this writing, these drivers were recently released to the public, and new features are being added. At the very least, you should expect these drivers to support the following set of features (several of which are missing from Creative's drivers for Windows):

- Playback and recording of analog and digital audio sources
- Digital output support and AC-3 bypass
- ASIO support
- DirectSound support (DirectSound3D and EAX support planned)
- Hardware wavetable synthesizer and SoundFont support
- Support for external MIDI and joystick
- Custom routing (for advanced users)
- DSP manager with support for loading of custom effects programs (including an integrated FX8010 assembler/disassembler that can be used for developing your own effects)
- Support for multiple sound cards in one computer
- A custom, very powerful mixer application

These drivers still lack some important features present in Creative's drivers for Windows and may not (yet) be quite as user friendly. However, despite their young age, they have an impressive set of features—some that could previously be found only in the open-source drivers for Linux. Because of such features as the multiple sound card support and the ASIO implementation, musicians in particular should not overlook these drivers.

For the latest list of features, documentation, and download locations, visit the project's official Web site: http://www.kxproject.com.

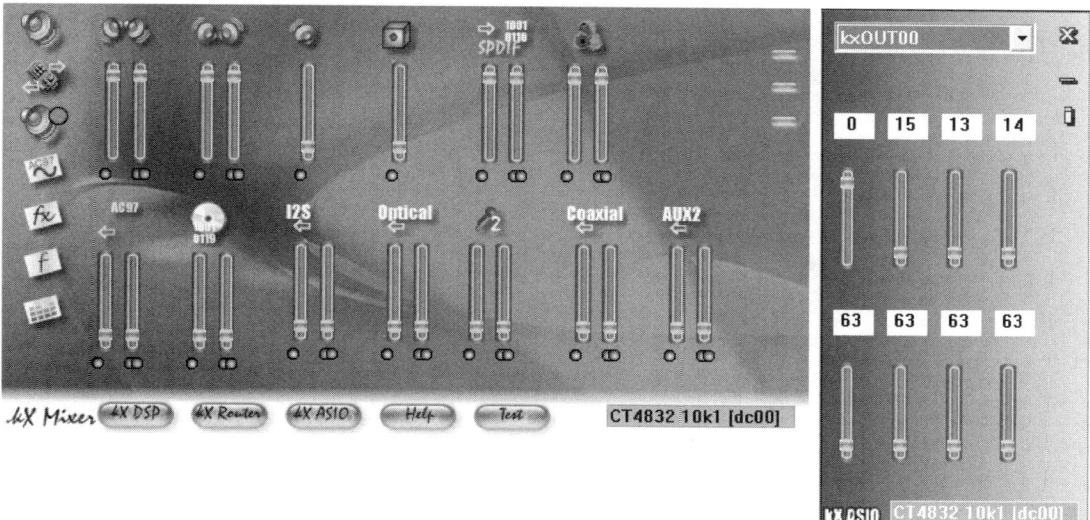

Figure 9.10: The kX mixer with the ASIO configuration panel open (from release 5.10.0.3517). In addition to the standard mixer features, the kX drivers come with a DSP manager you can use to load, connect, and modify effects in virtually any way you like.

Linux Drivers

Because Creative and E-MU (the companies that together developed the Live!) have revealed few technical details about the design of the card (and the EMU10K1 processor), it took quite a long time before there was support for the card under operating systems besides Windows. Eventually, however, Creative released an open-source driver for Linux that gave Live! users basic functionality in Linux. Since then, other alternatives have appeared, as well.

Installation of a sound driver under Linux may include compiling it yourself (although a configuration script and/or makefile is normally included, as well as instructions how to install it). Note, though, that many Linux distributions already come with support for the Live!, probably making it unnecessary to compile it yourself.

Normally, a Sound Blaster Live! driver for Linux is compiled as a module that can be loaded and unloaded as necessary. To check whether such a driver is already loaded, you can switch to the administrator account (root) and type lsmod, which gives you a list of loaded modules. If there's a module named emu10k1 or something similar, you should be all set.

```
root@apollo: /root                                        _ □ X
[root@apollo /root]# lsmod
Module                  Size    Used by
sr_mod                  15520   0  (autoclean)
emu10k1                 48928   0  (autoclean)
soundcore               4432    4  (autoclean) [emu10k1]
autofs                  11136   1  (autoclean)
3c59x                   25312   1  (autoclean)
ipchains                38944   0  (unused)
ide-scsi                8352    0
scsi_mod                94336   2  [sr_mod ide-scsi]
ide-cd                  27104   0
cdrom                   27392   0  [sr_mod ide-cd]
nls_iso8859-1           2880    1  (autoclean)
nls_cp437               4384    1  (autoclean)
vfat                    9168    1  (autoclean)
fat                     32832   0  (autoclean) [vfat]
[root@apollo /root]#
```

Figure 9.11: Typing lsmod *as root on a Linux system gives you a list of loaded modules. In this case, Creative's open-source drivers for Linux are loaded (the emu10k1 module). This module, in turn, is used by soundcore to provide the basic functionality of the sound card.*

Creative's Open-Source Drivers for Linux

As is common in the world of open source, Creative's Sound Blaster Live! drivers for Linux are constantly in development. At the time of this writing, the latest version was 0.17. Some important features are still missing, but as you read this, new features may be available in a later version. It's also worth noting that these drivers support several quite important features that are missing from the Windows drivers. For the latest information, and to download the driver sources, visit the official Web site at http://opensource.creative.com.

Some of the most important features of Creative's open-source drivers (at the time of this writing) are support for:

- Simultaneous hardware-mixed playback of Wave streams
- Full-duplex playback and recording
- Multiple Live! cards in one computer
- External MIDI in/out and joystick
- AC-3 passthrough
- OSS compatibility

> OSS stands for Open Sound System and is used by many Linux applications to play audio through the sound card.

If you have some knowledge of the internals of the EMU10K1 processor and you are not afraid of experimenting, included with the drivers (or available from the project's Web site) are tools that let you customize the sound routing (which, for example, can be used for analog multichannel output), as well as create and load your own (or others') effects programs.

As you can see from the preceding list, support for the wavetable MIDI synth (or SB Live! MIDI Synth, as it is known in Windows) and for SoundFonts is lacking. This may, of course, be added in a later version.

Installation instructions, a more complete list of features, and documentation of the advanced features of the drivers and included software can be found in the driver package available for download from the URL mentioned earlier.

ALSA

Advanced Linux Sound Architecture, or ALSA, is an open-source project meant to provide a modular driver set for most popular sound cards to replace the Linux kernel's built-in sound support. A large number of sound cards, including EMU10K1-based cards such as the Live!, are already supported. Just as in the case of Creative's open-source drivers, these drivers are constantly in development, so be sure to visit http://www.alsa-project.org, the project's official Web site, for the information on the status of the latest drivers.

The ALSA EMU10K1 (Live!) driver supports the basic features like Wave playback and recording, mixer settings, and external and (to some extent) internal MIDI. With add-on modules (normally included in most releases), the driver is also OSS compatible (compatible with the way the kernel sound drivers work)—something that many programs require to function properly.

Information about installation and configuration can be found in the documentation included in the driver package (which can be downloaded from the project's Web site). If the installation (which may require compilation of the driver module) seems too complicated, there may already be binary (precompiled) packages available for your Linux distribution.

DOS Drivers and Sound Blaster 16 Emulation

DOS is a primitive operating system used by early PCs, and it did not have a compulsory model in place where drivers and APIs play a part in sound card support. Therefore, the missing API layer and drivers have to be implemented by either the sound card manufacturer or the application developers. This task often fell to the application developers, who either supported the Sound Blaster with their own routines built in to the software or licensed sound card programming libraries like the popular Miles Sound System used by many DOS game developers.

> DOS emulation drivers are not necessary unless you want to use very old DOS-based applications and games that require Sound Blaster support.

The Live! has a Sound Blaster–compatible mode, which lets it act like an original Sound Blaster card so that older software can still work with it. This feature works only in Windows 9x, because only these operating systems are based partly on the old DOS platform. Many DOS applications that access hardware directly, like games, cannot work in protected operating systems like NT-based Windows 2000 and Windows XP. But even in Windows 9x, there are no guarantees that all games will work successfully with the emulation mode, because many applications were written before Windows 95 was introduced, so there was no way to make them compatible. Nevertheless, most are well behaved and do work in DOS windows in Windows 9x.

Why SB16 Emulation?

When Creative moved its line of sound cards from the ISA to the PCI bus (the type of interconnection between the sound card and the rest of the computer), there was one big problem: compatibility. Although, at that time, newly released games were designed for Windows and DirectX, older DOS-based games were written specifically for Sound Blaster 16 (and compatible) cards and would not work without an ISA Sound Blaster card.

As a solution, Creative released software that made new PCI sound cards look like old ones (sounds great, doesn't it?). This is called *Sound Blaster 16 emulation,* because this feature pretends to be a Sound Blaster 16 card to the software, while translating audio instructions from the software to one that is compatible with the new PCI sound card. It's probably safe to say that 99 percent of the Live! users won't need SB16 emulation. However, the remaining 1 percent (which is still quite a large number, considering how many Live! cards Creative has sold) will find it very important to be able to run their favorite DOS software—hence, the effort....

SB16 Emulation in Windows 95/98/ME

In Windows 95, 98, and ME, the installation programs for Live!Ware or driver packages from Creative will install not only the normal audio drivers for Windows, but also a special driver called Creative SB16 Emulation. You can verify that it is installed by opening System in the Control Panel and selecting the Device Manager tab. This driver should be listed under Creative Miscellaneous Devices.

Double-clicking the SB16 Emulation device will open the SB16 Emulation Properties window. The Settings tab displays the resources in use (such as IRQs, DMA channels, and I/O ports), which is useful because many older programs and games require you to manually specify these during the initial setup.

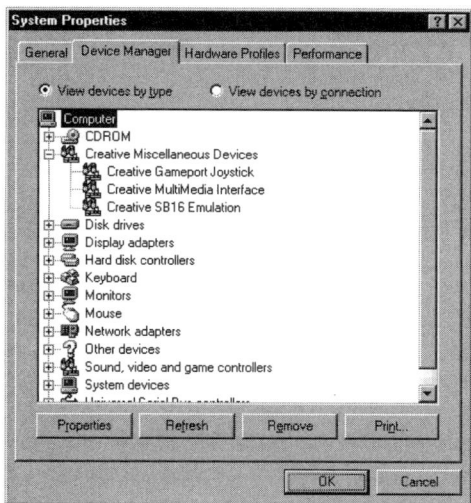

Figure 9.12: The Device Manager in Windows 98 Second Edition after Live!Ware 3 was installed. Note the Creative SB16 Emulation device.

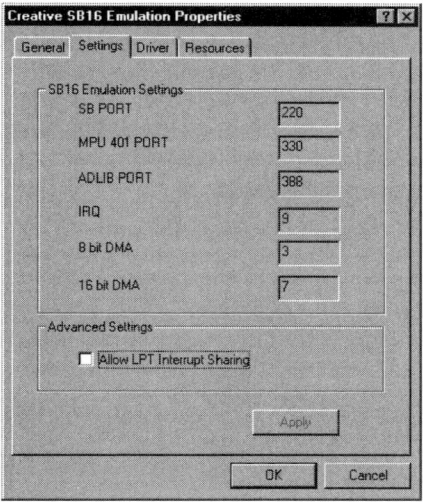

Figure 9.13: View the settings for the SB16 emulation driver by double-clicking it in the Device Manager. You can change them on the Resources tab.

TIP *Because a Sound Blaster 16 (real or emulated) requires quite a lot of resources (at least one additional IRQ, two DMA channels, and several I/O ports), you may want to disable it to make these available to other hardware. To do this, open the Properties for Creative SB16 Emulation, check Disable, and reboot Windows for the changes to take effect.*

Drivers and Other Tweaks **261**

Having this driver installed will let you run DOS software with sound just as if you had a Sound Blaster 16 installed in your computer. While most software works fine, some software may not work with the SB16 emulation driver.

The emulation device requires many system resources and may conflict with existing hardware. Disable the device if you do not need to use DOS programs in command-prompt windows with audio. If you encounter system conflicts, you can try adjusting the BIOS settings if you are familiar with them. First, take down the resources listed in the Settings tab of the SB16 Emulation Properties window. Go to the BIOS settings accessible when your PC boots up. (Check the user or motherboard manual for information on how to display the BIOS screen.) Most BIOSes will allow you to reserve IRQ and DMA resources so that when Windows boots, it will not automatically assign plug-and-play hardware to these resources unless it runs out of them.

SB16 Emulation in DOS

With early versions of Live!Ware and on some installation discs, a set of DOS programs was included that could be used for SB16 emulation in pure DOS mode (which means Windows is not running in the background). On systems with Windows 95 or 98, these drivers would also (by default) use the same settings as the Windows SB16 emulation driver, if available, so that software would work when run inside a Windows Command Prompt, or in pure DOS mode.

Unfortunately, this software is not included with current Live!Ware versions and does not seem to be supported by Creative anymore.

TIP *For hints on where to find the SB16 emulation software for DOS, as well as tips on how to use it, check the various Sound Blaster sites on the Internet.*

SB16 Emulation in Windows NT/2000/XP

There is no support for SB16 emulation in Windows NT, 2000, or XP, as these operating systems were not designed to run old DOS software. If you run one of these operating systems, there are a couple of options you may consider.

Although it may require a substantial amount of work if your computer is already set up, creating a dual-boot setup with the option of booting between Windows 98/ME (or even MS-DOS) and Windows NT/2000/XP at startup would most likely solve the problem, because SB16 emulation is available for the former operating systems.

Another possibility is to create a bootable floppy disk or CD with the SB16 emulation DOS software on it. Then use this disk to boot the computer every time you need to run your DOS-based programs or games.

Hardware Tweaks: How to Build an External Volume Control

This little do-it-yourself hack was published on the author's Web site shortly after the Live! was introduced. The basic idea is to connect external switches to pins on the Sound Blaster Live! that will let you control the master volume of the card (which is also in the software mixer). At the time it was published, I had few ideas what this discovery could be used for. It didn't take long, however, before I started receiving lots of feedback and creative uses (no pun intended) for the volume buttons.

For example, it can be used as a quick volume control when your headphones are connected directly to the line out of the Live! Also, if you use separate amplifiers or speaker systems for the front and rear channels, using this control will be more convenient than adjusting the volume on both amplifiers.

A Few Words of Warning

To build the volume control buttons described here, you need to modify your computer's hardware. Do not attempt to do this if you are not comfortable with computer hardware and electronics. Also keep in mind that modifying, or even opening, your computer may void your warranty. If you still want to consider trying it, read the entire description before you start.

> Disclaimer: The procedure described here has been built and tested by the author, as well as many other Live! users. Nevertheless, as there is risk involved with electronic work like soldering, the author and publisher will not be responsible for any damage it may cause to your Live! card, computer, or other hardware, or for any misprints or errors in this description.

The Idea

The Sound Blaster Live! card has three pins that can be used to control the main volume of the card. Grounding one of the pins (which can be done by pressing a switch) will increase the volume; grounding another pin will decrease it. Finally, grounding both pins will mute/unmute the card. Of course, what actually happens depends on the drivers. As someone has pointed out, by modifying the drivers (which is possible, for example, with the open-source drivers for Linux), you can make these buttons perform virtually any task. However, let's focus on the hardware for now.

Locating the VOL_CTRL Pins

The pins controlling the volume, labeled VOL_CTRL, are located next to the card's clock generator (crystal). The clock generator may look slightly different depending on the Live! model, but it is always located near the EMU10K1 chip. Pin number 1 is marked with an arrow. Notice that there's no pin 2.

NOTE *On some "value" versions (like the CT4830 shown next), the pins may be missing. In that case, you should not attempt this project.*

Figure 9.14: The VOL_CTRL pins. Note that the clock generator (crystal and other circuits) may look different from your version. Look for pins labeled "VOL_CTRL."

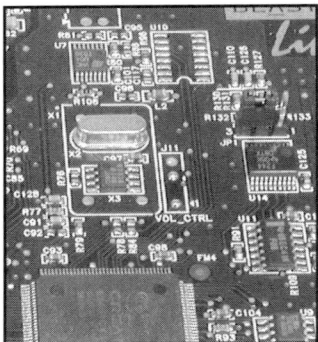

Figure 9.15: The VOL_CTRL pins missing on an OEM Live! Value card

Building the Volume Control

All you need to build the basic volume control buttons are the following:

- Pin connectors that will fit on the VOL_CTRL pins
- Wires
- Two switches (that conduct only when depressed)
- Tools (including soldering iron)

The switches should be built and connected according to the following diagram.

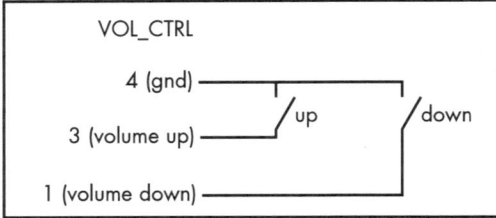

Figure 9.16: Wiring diagram for Live! volume control

As you can see, all you need to do is connect (solder) the wires to the switches and mount them somewhere (either in your computer case or in an external unit). If you have trouble finding pin connectors that will fit the pins on the Live! board, see if you can find an old computer case. Since the Live! uses the same pin spacing as most other computer components, the same type of connectors that are used for case switches and LEDs can be used here.

Testing It

Before you connect and test the project, make sure that the power is turned off (unplug the power cord) and check the circuit once again. Then connect it and turn on your computer. No special drivers or software should be required for this to work, so once the computer boots up, open the mixer and watch the main volume slider go up and down as you press the buttons. Pressing both buttons simultaneously should mute (or unmute, if already muted) the audio. If everything is working, congratulations—you're finished!

Software Tweaks: Windows Multimedia and Sound Settings

Windows includes a few settings in the Control Panel to configure the sound card, including:

- Sound schemes (what sound effects, if any, play at various Windows events, such as when Windows starts or when you close a window)
- Default audio quality used for recording (in programs that don't specifically ask you for it)
- The sound card (if you have more than one installed) used by default for audio playback and recording
- The synthesizer used for MIDI playback

You can find these settings in Sounds (in Windows 95/98), Sounds and Multimedia (in Windows ME/2000), or Sounds and Audio Devices (in Windows XP) in Control Panel. A few of these settings can be adjusted from the Live!Ware utilities, as well, and most are already correctly configured after installation. Nevertheless, what follows are a few tips that may help you tweak your audio setup to your liking.

Sounds

Sound effects can be fun—for a while. Most people, however, seem to be happier the quieter a device (including their computer) is. By default, most Windows installations come installed with sound schemes that adds all sorts of clicks, beeps, and other sound effects. Most Live!Ware installations will also add sounds such as replacing your startup sound with an extremely loud thunder sound with a pseudo-surround effect.

A Wave file is associated with each sound event listed. You can change the Wave file used for a particular event, or completely turn off the sound for that event. After confirming the list of events and sounds you want, you can save the entire list as a Scheme. You can later switch between schemes quickly to use different sets of event sounds.

To change, add, or (more likely) remove sounds, do the following:

1. Switch to the Sounds tab (unless you're using Windows 95/98, in which case there's only one tab).
2. There is a list of pre-defined sound schemes that you can choose from. Simply select the scheme you like to use.
3. If none of the pre-defined schemes suits you, select the sounds to use for particular events from the list below.

If you are sick and tired of sound effects, you can remove them all by selecting the No sounds scheme from the drop-down list.

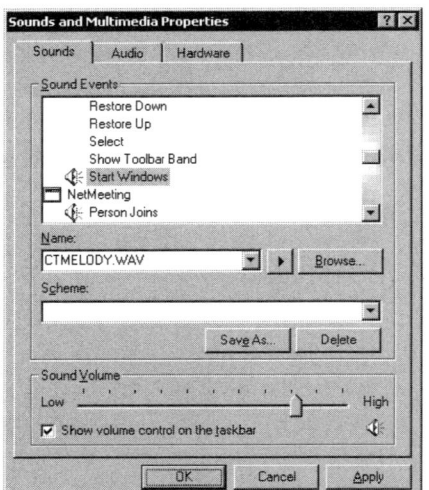 

Figure 9.17: The sound scheme settings in Windows 2000 and Windows XP

TIP *Turning on sounds will use some PC resources, as Windows will often need to load the sound from the hard drive before sending it to the sound card. If your PC has a slower processor or is running many tasks in the background, you may find the performance of the PC a little sluggish with sounds turned on.*

Audio: Sound Playback and Recording

The Audio tab allows you to choose the preferred audio device used for sound playback (digital audio playback), sound recording (of Wave files), and MIDI playback. The device selected for sound playback will be used to play any audio and sound effects of nearly all applications that use sound, such as instant messengers, browsers, and media players. The chosen sound recording device is used by software that records sound from any of the audio inputs of a Live! or an attached digital I/O device. For example, a videoconferencing or Internet telephony application will use the microphone input on the designated sound recording device.

> Windows XP uses the term *default device* instead of *preferred device* in the menus, but the terms mean the same thing.

If the Live! is the only sound card installed, the sound playback and recording drop-down lists will show only the Live! If you have more than one sound card but want to use the Live! for most audio purposes, you should select the Live! in these two boxes so that when applications request the services of a sound card, Windows will direct these requests to the Live! and not any other sound card.

There are two main ways audio applications use audio devices in Windows:

- They always use the preferred audio device set in the Windows Control Panel (as discussed).

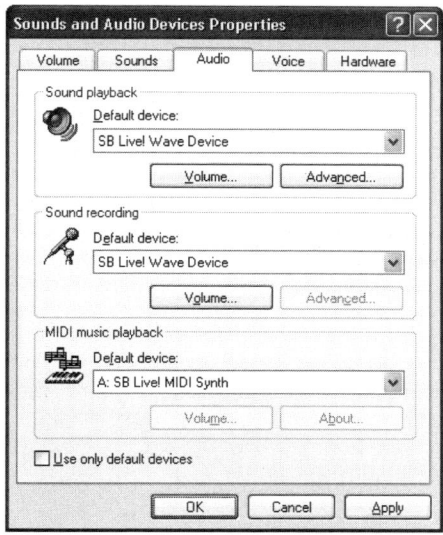

Figure 9.18: The "SB Live!" devices should be selected in the drop-down lists for playback and recording

- They allow users to choose the audio device.

Many applications automatically use the preferred device configured in Windows, while others provide drop-down lists on their own configuration screens so you can select another audio device for playback and/or recording. This is useful for digital audio workstations where there may be more than one sound card, so such flexible configuration options are essential in digital audio and multitracking applications. With this feature, you can choose another audio device if you have more than one sound card in your PC and need to direct audio to specific audio outputs on different sound cards.

In addition to the names of all installed sound cards, the drop-down lists of these applications will also contain a Microsoft Sound Mapper (for the waveOut API) or Primary Sound Driver (for the DirectSound API) device. More often than not, applications that allow selection of other audio devices will still default to the Windows preferred audio devices (either Microsoft Sound Mapper or Primary Sound Driver). Conversely, selecting a specific device in the list will cause that application to use that device all the time, and bypass the preferred devices selected in Windows.

 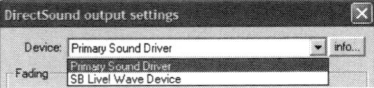

Figure 9.19: The audio device selection in Winamp's waveOut and DirectSound plug-ins

Allowing Windows to choose the audio device has an advantage. When the "Use only preferred devices" (or "Use only default devices in Windows XP") checkbox is cleared, Windows will attempt to use the preferred device. If it is not available, it will try the other devices, assuming that you have other sound devices installed. An error message will be displayed or no sound will be heard if no audio device is available.

On the other hand, when this checkbox is selected, Windows will use only the chosen preferred device. If it is tied up, Windows will not attempt to try any other sound device that may exist, but instead, it will display an error message immediately (or no sound will be played). For most uses, though, either setting will work well.

Audio: MIDI Music Playback

On the Audio tab, you'll also notice a MIDI music playback option that allows you to choose a preferred device. As you may already know (if not, you will after you read Chapter 14), the Live! has not one, but a number of synthesizers that can be used to play back MIDI files. Many applications that play MIDI files, such as Windows Media Player and Winamp, don't specifically allow you to pick a synth to use, but instead they rely on the selected MIDI device in the Control Panel.

> More advanced MIDI applications like MIDI sequencers will bypass the Windows settings and rely on their own internal configurations to determine the MIDI devices used. This allows greater flexibility, because MIDI sequencers are designed to work with more than one MIDI device at the same time.

To change the MIDI devices, do the following:

1. Open the sound controls from the Control Panel (Windows 95/98: select Multimedia; Windows 2000: select Sounds and Multimedia; Windows XP: select Sounds and Audio Devices).

2. Switch to the Audio tab (or MIDI, if you're using Windows 95/98).
3. Select the preferred synthesizer from the list.

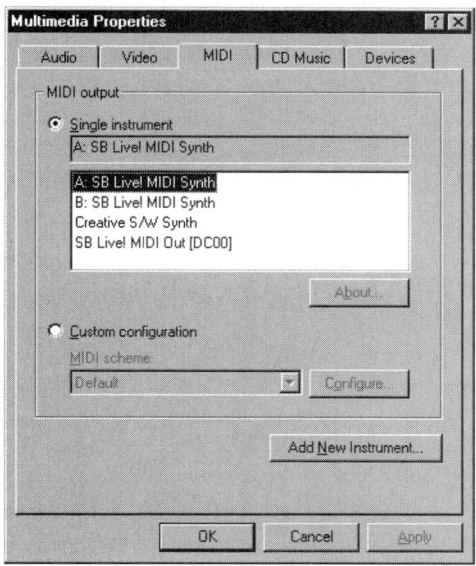

Figure 9.20: Selecting the preferred synthesizer for MIDI playback in Windows 98

You would typically find four of these five devices in the drop-down list:

- A: SB Live! MIDI Synth
- B: SB Live! MIDI Synth
- SB Live! MIDI UART
- SB Live! Soft Synth (also labeled Creative S/W Synth in some driver versions) (only in Windows 95/98/ME)
- Microsoft GS Wavetable SW Synth (built into Windows 2000 and Windows XP)

The different synthesizers are explained in more detail in Chapter 14, but usually the SB Live! MIDI Synth (A or B doesn't matter) will give you the best playback quality. If MIDI playback quality is important, also make sure that a good General MIDI SoundFont is loaded in AudioHQ's SoundFont Control Panel. Many installations come with several different quality levels; more information about where to find them and how to change them can be found in Chapter 16.

The SB Live! Soft Synth, installed with the drivers in Windows 95/98/ME, and the Microsoft GS Wavetable SW Synth, provided by Microsoft in Windows 2000/XP, will also show up in the list. These are software synthesizers that use the CPU to play back MIDI music and should be used only when no other MIDI devices are available, or when you need particular instrument sounds from this device for MIDI music composition.

The Microsoft GS Wavetable SW was licensed and based on a software synthesizer made by Roland, known as the Virtual Sound Canvas. The accompanying CD-ROM for this book includes a demo of the latest version of Virtual Sound Canvas.

TIP *You can switch between these MIDI devices and play back the same MIDI file to find out which sounds best! (Playback has to be stopped and started again for the change to take effect.)*

Advanced Audio Properties: Hardware Acceleration

Hardware acceleration determines how much of the work of processing and producing audio is balanced between the CPU and the sound card. Newer sound cards like the Live! have features built in to the hardware to handle nearly all the audio processing tasks, so it is crucial to configure this setting correctly. You can set four modes: None, Basic, Standard, and Maximum. To shift the work of producing audio to the sound card, hardware acceleration should always be set to Maximum. This ensures that the CPU will not be bogged down by audio processing tasks and that enough power is available for processor-hungry applications, particularly games. When maximum acceleration is enabled, Windows will use all of the capability provided by the sound card and its drivers. EAX will be enabled only when the slider is at Maximum. 3D positioning using APIs like DirectSound3D only works when acceleration is set to Standard or Maximum.

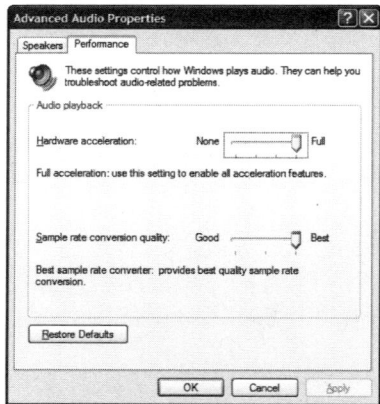

Figure 9.21: Hardware acceleration can be changed in this window. It can be opened by clicking the Advanced button when the Live! is selected as the playback device in the Audio tab.

Fixing Problems on SMP PCs

However, on certain setups like some SMP PCs, the Live! may produce frequent loud noises and screeching sounds. Decreasing the hardware acceleration to Standard or Basic may help alleviate some of these problems. However, dropping the acceleration will cause the CPU to take up more of the audio-processing tasks, and enhanced features like 3D audio with DirectSound3D and EAX will be disabled, as well. It would be a trade-off, especially if your PC has sound-quality problems with the Live! (Also upgrade to the latest drivers as it may fix these issues.)

Advanced Audio Properties: Settings That Don't Work

Below the hardware acceleration slider is another slider labeled Sample Rate Conversion Quality. This does not affect the actual quality of audio produced by the Live!, because it performs sample rate conversion in the hardware and does not rely on Windows to do it. Nevertheless, keep this slider at the default Best position anyway.

Beside the Performance tab is a Speakers tab that lets you choose the speaker type. Ignore this tab, as well, because it does not work for the Live! To change speaker settings, use the Speaker configuration in AudioHQ or the Surround Mixer.

10

PLAYING GAMES

Computer games are remarkable software—collections of 0s and 1s—that can keep us entertained and glued to the screen for hours on end, simply by allowing us to control images on the monitor with a keyboard, mouse, or joystick. As hardware manufacturers roll out cheaper and faster CPU, graphics, memory, and sound chips, games are getting more sophisticated. Take a look at any modern game on the console or PC; games like Half-Life and Quake were not technologically possible even just ten years ago!

In the early days, games were simple: place the player in a repetitive but compelling situation and up the ante by increasing the number and speed of the opposing elements. Remember games like Frogger, Lode Runner, and Tetris? Accompanying these classics were beeps and simple tunes produced on the PC speaker in an attempt to provide a soundtrack and auditory accompaniment synchronized to our actions. As the player progressed to higher levels and the action became more exciting, all developers did was increase the tempo of the same tune, and adrenaline would start pumping. Talk about easy!

From the simple beeps of the PC speaker to the use of orchestras for music accompaniment and 3D positional audio for sound effects, sound for games has come a long way and is slowly closing in on the ultimate benchmark—Hollywood-quality audio. As market leaders who are in a position to define and enhance the operating system and tools that are available to game developers, companies like Creative and Microsoft have an important role to play in producing sound cards and new technologies that enable developers to approximate the sounds of the real world as closely as possible.

In this chapter, we will look at the history of gaming sound, how it has changed in the recent years, and some of the technologies available in sound cards such as the Live! that make it all possible.

Looking to Hollywood

These days, we are fortunate to have sophisticated technologies available that allow sound and music in games to approach the quality and complexity of movie soundtracks. Movie soundtracks set an important benchmark for gaming audio because of the quality of the technology employed and the way that effective music steers audiences toward the particular emotional responses intended by the filmmakers. Sound effects and surround sound are exploited to envelop the viewers and keep them engrossed. Massive explosions in action movies have little impact if the earth-shattering rumbles are not conveyed effectively through sound.

Directors also consider the film composer, who writes the musical score for a movie, one of the actors, with the power to subliminally influence and steer audience reaction with masterfully written music (although sadly, they don't get paid as much as Jim Carrey or Julia Roberts). The music of the soundtrack normally does not appear up front, unlike the rock and techno music used in many games, but instead stays in the background, playing at the right moment and pushing all the right buttons to evoke an appropriate emotional response in the audience. No horror or suspense movie would work as well without effective music.

> Try turning off the sound of a movie or imagining it without music. It will likely be much less engaging and frustrating to watch and understand.

Dolby is one leading film audio technology establishment that is bringing its standard-setting audio technologies such as Dolby Digital to the gaming world. The PlayStation 2 console included Dolby Digital capability and a digital output for AV receivers. In March 2001, Creative took the next step for PC audio by introducing a Dolby Digital API that gives game developers the ability to easily incorporate 5.1 surround sound in their games using the same technology and tools used to create Dolby Digital movie soundtracks.

This is great news for all gamers. With multichannel sound cards and affordable but great-sounding speaker systems, gamers can look forward to an improved sonic experience on the PC. Things are getting exciting!

Music in Games

Music that accompanies games is basically computer generated. Here are a few factors that make it effective:

- Realistic instruments
- Customized instruments, to allow composers to reproduce the same instrument and sound quality on any sound card
- The use of many instruments at the same time, to create the illusion of a band or orchestra
- Standardized technology, to allow developers to support many music synthesizers easily
- Music files that take little processor time to generate, so the game engine can perform more critical tasks such as graphics rendering
- The ability to seamlessly change the music in tandem with the scenario and gamers' actions

Let's take a look at the evolution of music in games and the technologies that drive it.

From Beeps to Music

Before the advent of sound cards, the built-in speaker found on every PC was the only tool for sound reproduction. It is monophonic and could create only simple waveforms, limiting it to beeps that can accommodate only simple melodies without any form of background accompaniment. Music is predominantly polyphonic, requiring a few instruments playing together in harmony to sound complete and be enjoyable.

Fortunately, early music cards like the AdLib and the Roland MT-32 sound module gave game developers an avenue for creating more realistic soundtracks for their games. Introduced in 1987, the AdLib relied on a simple technique known as frequency modulation (FM) synthesis, which uses mathematical algorithms to simulate instrument sounds. At an affordable US$99, the AdLib was considered a huge step up from the PC speaker.

> FM synthesis was so pervasive in games and sound cards that future generations of the Sound Blaster cards, like the Sound Blaster 16, Sound Blaster 32, and Sound Blaster AWE cards, all had FM synthesizers for backward compatibility.

The Roland MT-32 used an advanced form of synthesis that made its output a cross between realistic and electronic sounding, but these results were much better than those from FM synthesis. It was primarily a music-making tool, and at US$400, only dedicated gamers who appreciated the difference between good and bad music would fork out that sum to purchase one without using it for music composition.

Roland does not sell the MT-32 anymore, but you can visit the company at http://www.rolandus.com to find out more about its current products.

However, with strong advocacy by game companies like Sierra On-Line (makers of best-selling adventure games like King's Quest and Space Quest) and the demonstrably huge difference music adds to the gaming experience, the AdLib and MT-32 made significant inroads, and many gamers bought them. The success of the Sound Blaster introduced in 1989 was largely due to the AdLib-compatible feature that enabled it to work with existing games that supported the AdLib card.

> In 2000, in a bid to refocus its efforts on the popular action and strategy gaming market segments, Sierra laid off many of its employees who had been responsible for the well-loved adventure and other classic games that built up the Sierra brand name. We will miss these adventure games and their pioneering use of music synthesis on the PC to push the boundaries of interactive gaming.

MIDI

Before the advent of CD-ROM as a storage medium, games came on floppies. The limited disk space did not allow games to store and play back prerecorded audio as game soundtracks. Moreover, CPUs were not very powerful at that time, so the sound-generating tasks had to be passed on to dedicated synthesizer chips that were specifically designed to generate music by receiving from the game simple parameters that described the music. MIDI was the common means of storing and transmitting these music instructions to synthesizers.

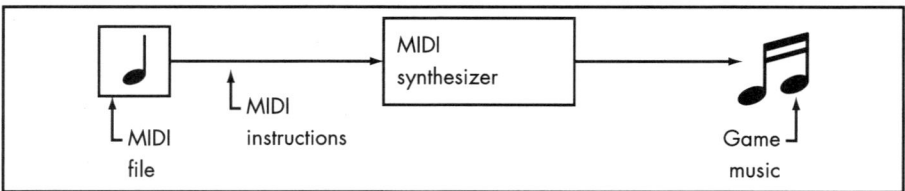

Figure 10.1: The MIDI synthesizer is used to generate music from simple MIDI instructions provided by the game

MIDI instructions describe such tasks as which note to play, how long to play it, and what instrument preset to use. The game that is producing the MIDI output for the music need not be concerned with such tasks as generating the instrument sounds, changing the pitch of the sound, and mixing all the instrument sounds together. The hardware does all the hard work.

MIDI files typically range from a few hundred to a few thousand bytes and are much smaller than recorded audio, where a second of CD-quality music can take up 176,400 bytes. MIDI allows music to be quickly transferred over to the sound card, which was especially important when PCs were not as fast as they are now.

Wavetable Synthesis

Still, many people were not satisfied. The tinny and metallic sounding approximation of instruments created by FM synthesis was unrealistic. Something better had to come. The answer came in a new form of synthesis technique known as *wavetable synthesis*. It had been used for electronic musical instruments for some years, and by miniaturizing these sound-generating engines so that they fit onto a small chip that could be etched on a sound card, it became possible to build such technology into sound cards.

Unlike FM, wavetable synthesis does not depend on mathematical algorithms to simulate instruments. If you look at the waveforms of real instruments, they are far more complex and random in nature, making them impossible to represent using simple equations and formulas. The best solution is to use recorded sounds of real instruments and reproduce them with the correct pitch and duration. The instrument, pitch, and duration parameters come in the form of MIDI instructions provided by the games.

General MIDI

Because most developers could not directly access and modify the instrument sounds stored in ROM on the sound card, a standard set of instruments had to be established so that games could use MIDI to select the correct instrument for each part of the music to be played back. The General MIDI (GM) standard provides a set of 128 common instruments and sound effects, as well as a drum kit. Game developers can write music that conforms to this instrument list. For example, instrument 1 is always a piano on a General MIDI device, whereas a non-GM instrument may place some other sound in that slot.

> ROM stands for read-only memory, and is usually a piece of silicon that stores data. In the case of ROM for wavetable synthesizers, instrument sounds are stored on chips and mass manufactured for inclusion in every wavetable sound card.

FM did not need such a standard; the FM synthesizers used by early sound card manufacturers operated the same way because of the need for AdLib compatibility. Developers could create instruments for the AdLib and be sure that it would work on other AdLib-compatible cards as well. This is not the case for wavetable synthesizers, because each sound card manufacturer may use different wavetable chips and instrument sounds, which are stored in ROM.

GM was initially adequate but became less and less desirable because every manufacturer *did* include the 128 instruments, but they tended to sound different because of the different sound sets used by different manufacturers. A General

MIDI track did not sound like what the composer originally intended if it was played back on a wavetable synthesizer other than the one used by the composer to write the piece of music. This problem plagued all games that used GM soundtracks, leading many developers to move to prerecorded wave audio.

> The Roland Sound Canvas is widely regarded as the standard GM sound set, and many game music composers write and optimize GM music for this sound set.

Custom Instrument Sounds

To make their music more consistent, composers need to ensure that the instrument they use in composing a track is available on every wavetable synthesizer chip. The SoundFont standard introduced by Creative aims to provide this assurance by allowing custom instrument sounds to be used in MIDI compositions. The final music tracks for a game includes the instrument sounds stored in SoundFont fiiles, and the game uploads the instruments to the memory of the synthesizer on the sound card before sending over MIDI instructions for music playback.

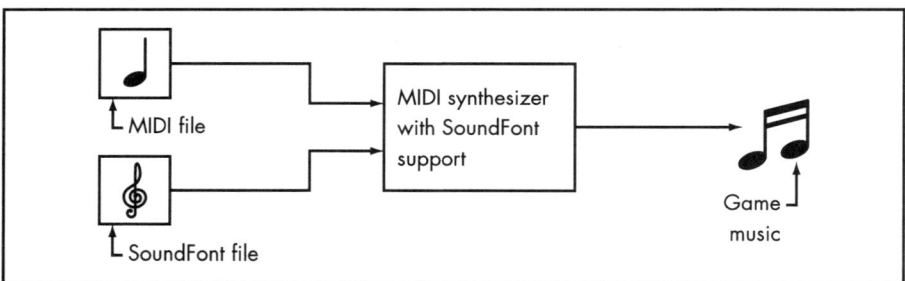

Figure 10.2: MIDI instructions in a MIDI file use custom instruments in SoundFonts to generate music

However, few developers made use of SoundFonts because of the work it requires. Furthermore, SoundFont support is available only on Sound Blaster AWE and Live! cards, while most other sound cards, especially non-Creative sound cards, support General MIDI. This caused most game music composers to settle on GM because it is a common format supported by all sound cards.

> Despite the limited success of SoundFonts with game developers, musicians quickly took to this format because they did not have to worry about distribution and SoundFont compatibility issues, since their music will probably be recorded and distributed as Wave or MP3 files.

Downloadable samples (DLS), conceptualized by the Interactive Audio Special Interest Group (IA-SIG) in the late 1990s, aimed to standardize the use of custom instrument sounds in wavetable synthesizers across manufacturers. The updated DLS2 specifications (based on the SoundFont 2 specifications) are now available in Microsoft's DirectX 8 API. Unfortunately, like SoundFont, DLS met with limited success, partly because recorded audio is already entrenched as the preferred delivery method for game music. Few games today use MIDI for music.

You can visit the MIDI Manufacturers Association at http://www.midi.org to find out more about General MIDI and DLS.

Recorded Audio

In the early 1990s, CD-ROMs gained wide adoption as the preferred storage medium for games. The huge (at that time) storage space of CD-ROM discs allows game developers to store and reproduce any kind of prerecorded sound and music through the Wave playback feature available on any sound card. Recorded audio can be delivered through CD audio tracks on game CDs, or as Wave or compressed audio (like MP3 files) that is read continuously from the CD and piped through the DAC on the sound card. (This technique is known as *streaming*.)

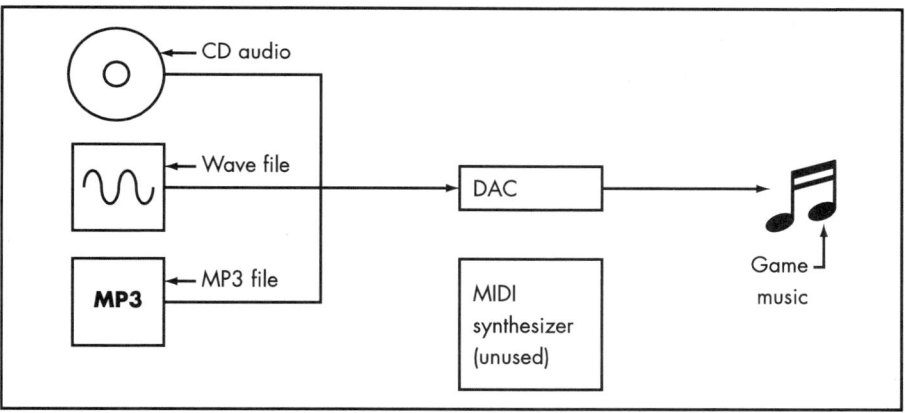

Figure 10.3: Recorded audio is sent to the DAC of the sound card to playback game music

With recorded audio, composers are no longer limited to the idiosyncrasies of different synthesizers. They can use familiar studio recording techniques and finalize the sound of each track and its instruments. They have the freedom to add effects with the advanced signal processing available on studio equipment, including vocals, and to use live session players or a real symphony orchestra to make game music to sound more real and human — achievements that synthesizer technology is not capable of. This approach has overtaken General MIDI as the preferred method for delivering game music. Nearly all of the games today use recorded audio for music.

The Interactive Music Future

Although recorded audio gives the most accurate sound, remember that games, unlike movies, are nonlinear, and events change depending on players' actions. The player may suddenly "die" after losing too much health, and the game will need to quickly segue from the current music track to a gloomy game-over piece. An enemy may suddenly pop up behind the player, and the music needs to change to a battle piece and turn up the adrenaline by a few notches.

With prerecorded audio, it is tricky to transition between different tracks because the structure, form, length, and progression of the music is already finalized. Transitioning is especially distracting on games that use CD audio music. When the music needs to change, the current track abruptly stops, and the playback jumps to the next track. With Wave and MP3 streaming used by most games today, fade-ins and fade-outs help facilitate a smooth transition between different pieces of music, making the experience much more seamless.

Although this process is adequate for many games, the continuous looping of the same piece of prerecorded music throughout an entire game level gets annoying over time. The use of interactive music — music that changes in tempo, style, and complexity in response to gamers' actions — is definitely more effective. Film scores are intricately timed and tailored to accentuate every frame in a movie; games need a way to mold music around game events.

Interactive music is promising, and Microsoft's inclusion of DirectMusic for generating interactive music in games is good news for composers and developers. With DirectMusic Producer, the composition and editing tool for DirectMusic tracks, the composer can create a certain mood and atmosphere in response to changes in the game by abstracting and varying certain parameters and characteristics such as the tempo, volume, chord progressions, a drum pattern, or short snippets of melodies. DirectMusic receives cues from the game about the state of the game, and this causes the music to change as the gamer explores the gaming environment. The use of DLS and DLS2 in DirectMusic ensures that the same instruments are heard on all playback devices.

DirectMusic can use the CPU to generate music, which allows every sound card to reproduce a DirectMusic track exactly. This has a drawback, though, because CPU processing time that is used for the music takes away important processing time that a game may need to handle the AI or render graphics. If hardware manufacturers support DirectMusic and DLS, this situation may be alleviated, but most manufacturers, including Creative, do not provide DLS2 compatibility.

This has led to the current state of music today, where recorded tracks are the most common means for creating game music, probably because musicians are familiar with the straight-ahead recording techniques used to produce linear pieces of music, and would rather not learn a new and complex tool like DirectMusic. Also, because music is a subtle medium that often hides under the surface, it often receives less attention during the development process of a game. Moreover, gaming technology and advancements are largely focused on "wow" factors, like 3D graphics, game engines, multiplayer features, and 3D sound. These factors, and others, have hindered widespread use of DirectMusic in games.

> A few games, notably those from Monolith Productions (http://www.lith.com), have used DirectMusic.

Will we see interactive music in the future? It all depends on whether gamers let developers and hardware manufacturers know that this is what they want.

Sound Effects in Games

Sound effects are important in any game, especially for arcade and action games, like first-person shooters. Watching a rocket launcher go off on the screen isn't as exciting if it isn't accompanied by a deep, satisfying explosion when the rocket explodes in the enemy's face. A well-engineered sound engine and sound effects can put you in the heat of the battle. In many first-person shooter games, like Half-Life, you can listen to the realistic rattle of a machine gun being fired while some of the rounds ricochet off the walls around you and empty cartridges fall to the ground. If sound effects weren't important, people would still be content with silent movies, even today!

Sound effects are used for many reasons, and among them are these:

- To give the player a sense of place by playing environmental sound effects, such as the crash of waves when the player is near the sea.
- To provide ample feedback in response to gamers' actions: for example, when a spell is cast, an appropriate sound played back lets users know the effectiveness of the spell.
- To steer the gamer in a certain direction by playing a sound of, say, a waterfall at 120 degrees behind the gamer using 3D-positional audio.
- To tell the player of impending danger through consistent use of audio cues, such as the increasing loudness of footsteps.
- To scare the gamer by playing random animal growls, deep laughing voices, and rumbling sounds.

Before the Sound Blaster

Before the Sound Blaster came into the picture in 1989, games did not have an easy way to play back recorded sound effects. Most developers forced the music synthesizer in the AdLib to produce sound effects by creating instruments and algorithms that mimicked sound effects, but the results never came close to real, prerecorded sounds. More complex waveforms, like the voice of a singer, are nearly impossible to synthesize without the use of advanced synthesis techniques and significant computing power, which most PCs did not have at that time.

The Sound Blaster–Compatible Era

The Sound Blaster had 8-bit, mono DACs that allowed prerecorded Wave files to be stored on disk and played back when needed. This feature gave game developers the power to trigger realistic recorded sound effects and voices in their games and ushering in the terms *audio card* and *sound card*. The best thing about the Sound Blaster was that it was affordable, not costing much more than the popular AdLib card, while offering more bells and whistles like an integrated gaming port, and Wave audio recording and playback. This helped Creative quickly gain market share.

Two of the landmark games that placed the Sound Blaster on many shopping lists were Wing Commander and its sequel, Wing Commander II: Revenge of the Kilrathi. The music, composed by George Sanger (also known as The Fat Man), dynamically rose and fell in mood and intensity as the player engaged in dogfights, finally ending with a relieving and majestic fanfare, which signaled the end of a successful mission. The games were groundbreaking in the use of cinematic cut scenes that told the story in a movielike, wide-screen frame on the monitor. The characters and storyline unfolded gradually as the characters conversed, just as in a movie, while the on-screen text illuminated the dialogue and story line.

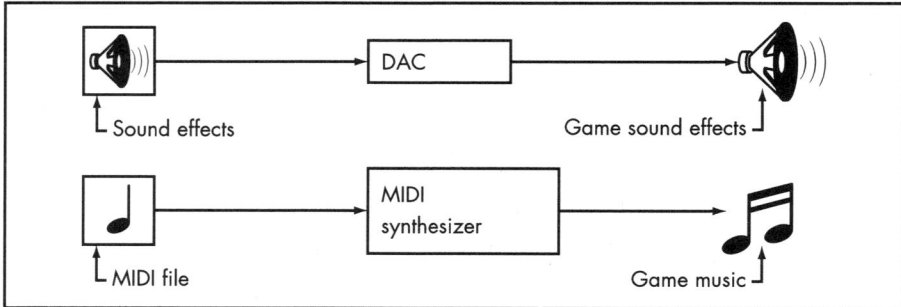

Figure 10.4: Early games used the MIDI synthesizer for music and the DAC of the sound card for sound effects

Wing Commander II upped the ante by retailing optional speech packs that used the Wave playback capability on a Sound Blaster or compatible sound card to enable game characters to speak in their real voices. This enhanced players' attachment to the characters, and their involvement with the story line grew. Games that usually depend on graphics, fast-moving enemies, and increasing the odds to excite gamers could now use sound and music and the subtle variation and intonation of the human voice to engage the emotions of players and tell a compelling story.

With the advent of games like Wing Commander, many developers started using Wave playback of sound effects and voices to enhance their games, and the Sound Blaster was christened the de-facto standard in PC sound. Just as AdLib compatibility allowed the Sound Blaster to support the hundreds of existing game titles and quickly gain acceptance in the market, the widespread use of Wave playback on the Sound Blaster made the "Sound Blaster-compatible" tag the thing to look for when shopping for non-Creative sound cards.

Newer generations of the Sound Blaster gradually increased the Wave playback quality. The Sound Blaster Pro added 8-bit stereo support, and the Sound Blaster 16 finally upped the sound card to the much-desired 16-bit, 44.1-kHz, CD-quality mark. This standard remained in the subsequent Sound Blaster 32 and Sound Blaster AWE cards, until the Live! increased support to 16-bit, 48-kHz sound. At or above CD quality, sound cards can adequately reproduce most of the frequency range that humans can hear, enabling game developers to employ crisp and dynamic sound effects.

DirectSound and Sound Mixing

Most sound cards in that time have only one DAC to decode a stereo audio stream to analog format, but games normally have many sounds playing at the same time, so some form of mixing has to be implemented. In the early days, when DOS games were still predominant, most game developers had their own algorithms and software code to perform mixing. After the game engine did the mixing, it would send the results directly to the sound card's DAC.

However, when Windows (especially Windows 95) became widespread on desktops, games could no longer access the sound card directly and had to go through the operating system. The PC now can multitask and run several applications simultaneously, so there is a need to regulate the use of the hardware among all the applications that are running. As you can imagine, requiring the software to go through a few layers of the operating system API and drivers to send data to a graphic card or sound card slowed down game performance considerably, compared to performance when instructions are sent to the hardware directly. To alleviate this problem, Microsoft introduced an efficient and low-latency set of technologies under the name DirectX, allowing game developers better and more efficient access to key hardware components on the PC that games often use. This includes DirectDraw for graphics, DirectInput for game controllers, and DirectPlay for network gaming.

Get more information and download the latest DirectX from http://microsoft.com/directx.

DirectX includes a component called the DirectSound API that allows games to access the sound card using a standard set of instructions. This is a huge improvement over the technology of the DOS environment, because developers need not write special code in their games to support all the different sound cards on the market. They can now write their games to play sound through DirectSound, and hardware manufacturers simply have to produce DirectSound-compliant drivers so that their sound cards can translate the DirectSound instructions that games send through the DirectSound API into instructions that their sound card can understand.

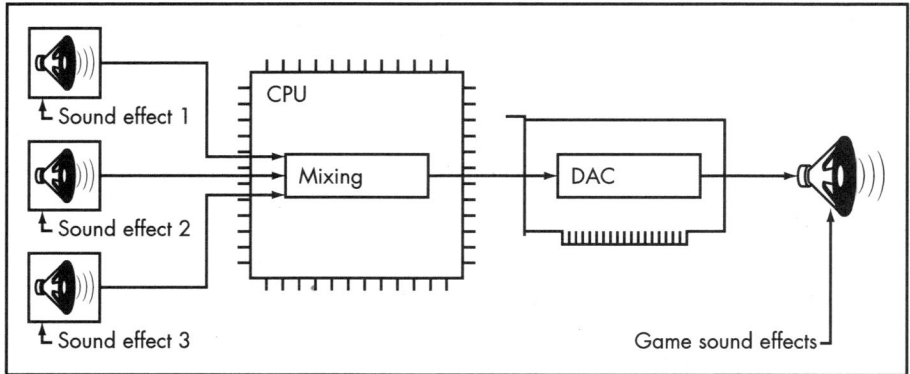

Figure 10.5: Early games and sound cards without hardware mixing will use the CPU to mix several sounds together before sending a single output to the DAC for playback

DirectSound includes built-in support for Wave mixing, alleviating developers of the job of writing Wave-mixing routines in their games. Like DOS games, which had to implement their own mixing algorithms, Windows games that use DirectSound may find fewer CPU resources for their games if the sound card does not have a feature known as *DirectSound acceleration*. As with music playback, it is better to let the sound hardware perform common audio tasks like mixing, leaving the CPU power available for other parts of the game.

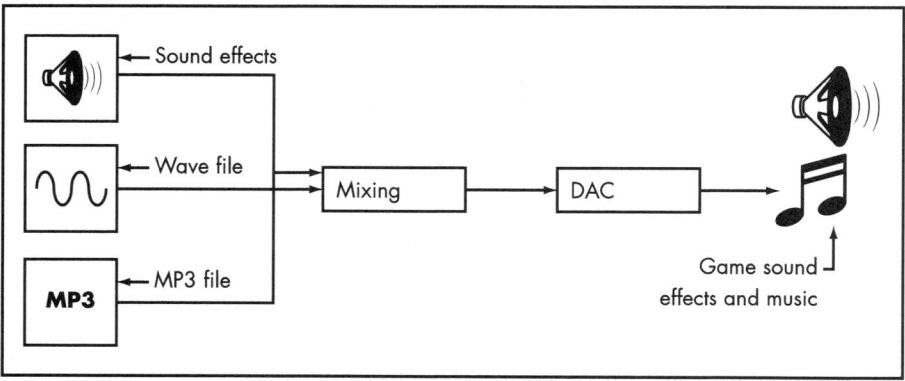

Figure 10.6: Current games use the mixing capability of sounds cards to play back sound effects, as well as music (read from the CD typically in Wave or MP3 format)

Today, with most PC games released on the Windows platform exclusively, DirectSound support in the drivers is a must. DirectSound acceleration is found on most PCI sound cards as well. The Live! and other cards, like the Sound Blaster AWE series, support DirectSound acceleration by taking the information from DirectSound and mixing multiple sounds using hardware on the sound card. (Older sound cards, like the Sound Blaster, Sound Blaster Pro, and Sound Blaster 16, do not have DirectSound acceleration.) The Live! supports acceleration of 64 DirectSound streams simultaneously, while other sound cards support 128 or more.

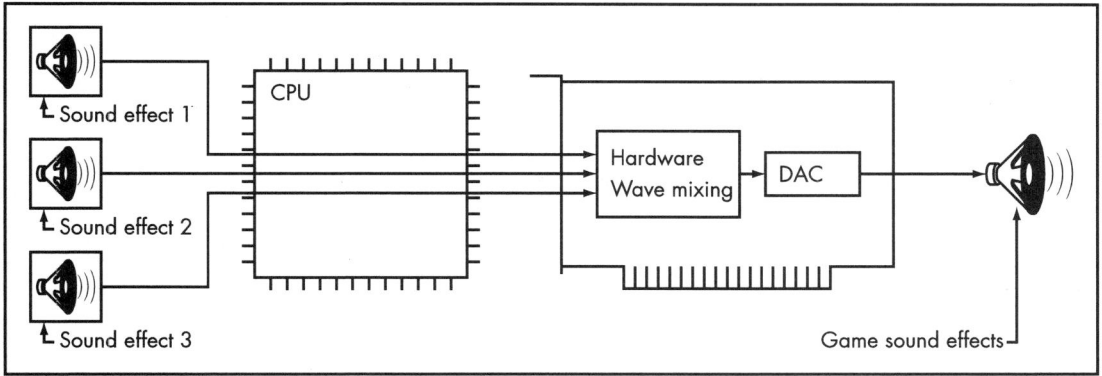

Figure 10.7: Sound cards with DirectSound acceleration allow the sounds to bypass the CPU and go directly to the sound card's hardware mixing

> DirectSound attempts to fall back to its software-mixing algorithm if no more hardware streams are available for accelerated mixing.

3D Positioning

Positional audio has been touted for many years as a technology that will revolutionize the sound card industry. Sound can be placed anywhere in a 360-degree circle around the listener, enabling games to envelop the player with sound effects. This can also provide important audio cues to the gamer, such as the direction and distance of an approaching adversary.

Actually, 3D sound has existed for quite some time, but mainly as stereo expansion, which takes a conventional stereo sound source and modifies it so that it sounds like it is coming from a much wider area than the two front speakers. This form of 3D does not place sound in a particular location around the listener and is less desirable for use in games.

Read more about virtual surround in Chapter 6, "Speakers."

In 3D positioning, the "3D" represents the ability to locate sounds at any point on a 360-degree circle around, and above or below, the player. Most 3D positioning APIs have a number of features to enable realistic 3D audio, such as volume controls to simulate distance from the listener, panning controls to allow sounds to move dynamically from one angle to another, and controls to alter the speed of sound in relation to the listener. The Doppler shift—the change in pitch of a sound source moving toward and away from the listener—can also be set.

Figure 10.8: 3D positioning allows sounds to be placed above, below, behind, and in front of the listener. Sounds can also be located far away from the listener, like the helicopter in the diagram, or near to the listener with a louder volume, like the barking dog.

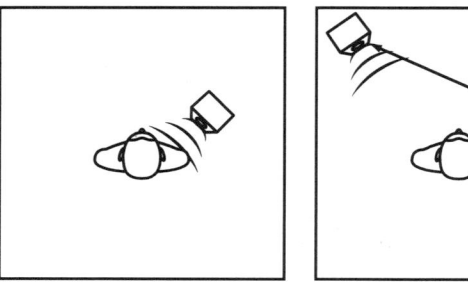

Figure 10.9: Movement of a sound source affects the angle and the distance from the listener

> **Doppler Shift**
> When you are inside a car, the sound of the engine and the movement of the car will be at a consistent pitch. However, if you are on the sidewalk and a car whizzes past you, you will hear a quick rise in pitch as the car nears your position, and the sound will slowly decrease in pitch and volume as the car moves away. The Doppler shift is caused by the rapid compression and decompression of air in the environment due to quick-moving sound sources.

In addition, 3D positioning has to keep track of several parameters to provide a consistent sound field. It needs to keep track of the position of the player, as well as the location and velocity of a sound source, to calculate where the sound source can be placed in relation to the listener. Most of the sounds are *point sources*: sounds that emanate at a particular point in 3D space and can be heard in all directions.

Sound cones are used to simulate the narrow dispersion of sound spanning a particular angle, such as speech coming out of a person's mouth. In these cases, it is louder when the listener is directly in front of the person than when he is behind the person. Such complex effects can be modeled with sound cones. When the player changes his position from the sound cone, the 3D positioning API automatically modifies the volume and other parameters.

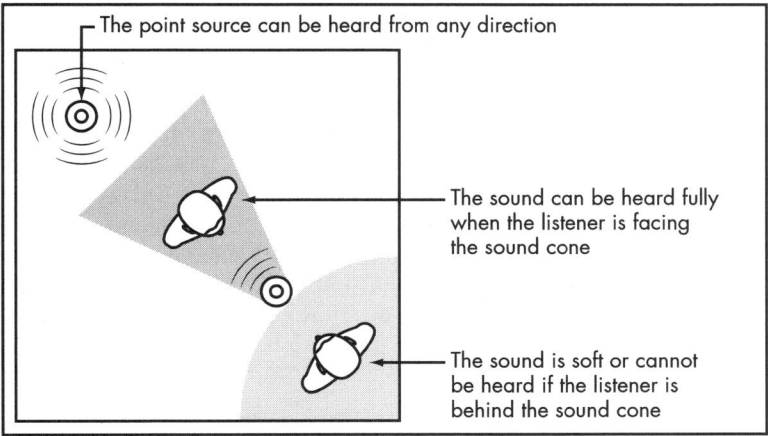

Figure 10.10: Point sources and sound cones

It was not easy to achieve 3D positioning in earlier systems, because most sound cards and speaker systems were designed to support the common two-speaker stereo configuration. Sound card manufacturers who wanted to implement 3D positioning had to first deal with the problem of generating audio that would seem to the listener to come from any direction—but using only two speakers. The Live! solves this problem by using two rear speakers to reproduce sounds that are positioned behind the listener. It requires more equipment and effort in setting up, but the results are much better than virtual 3D positioning with two speakers.

DirectSound3D and A3D

Microsoft's DirectX 3 API introduced a new component called DirectSound3D that allowed game developers to define and place sounds in a 360-degree space. However, the version of DirectSound3D that came with DirectX 3 used a proprietary virtual 3D positioning algorithm that did not sound realistic and relied entirely on the CPU to perform the processing. Sound card makers were also disappointed that the DirectSound3D API did not allow 3D positioning instructions generated by the game to be passed on to the drivers. This prevented sound cards from implementing acceleration and 3D positioning in hardware for DirectSound3D.

Aureal, an experienced sound technology firm with a history of 3D and virtual audio research, took this opportunity to bring its groundbreaking positional audio technology to the PC market in the form of A3D. The A3D API implemented a variation of the DirectSound3D features that works only with Aureal's own Vortex DSPs. The A3D sound cards, together with the A3D API, allowed game developers an easy and effective way to add 3D sound to their games. The API bypassed the DirectSound3D API altogether because it had its own 3D positioning specifications. Aureal also had very effective virtual surround technology that made it possible to obtain affordable 3D positioning on the PC with only two speakers. Even before the Sound Blaster Live! was announced, A3D and Vortex sound cards already had a respectable gaming audience.

Microsoft realized that to make DirectSound3D the standard API, it had to allow sound card drivers to receive the positioning parameters that games set in the DirectSound3D API. When the gates to this very important component opened in DirectX 5, manufacturers quickly took advantage of this new ability to support hardware acceleration. The Live! relies exclusively on the DirectSound3D API for 3D positioning. By then, the A3D API was also quite popular, so Creative quietly installed an A3D wrapper with the drivers. This wrapper pretends to be an A3D API, making the Live! appear like an A3D-compatible sound card. It takes the game's A3D instructions and translates them into equivalent DirectSound3D instructions that the Live! drivers understand. Some A3D-specific parameters for 3D audio are lost in the process, but the results are quite good in general.

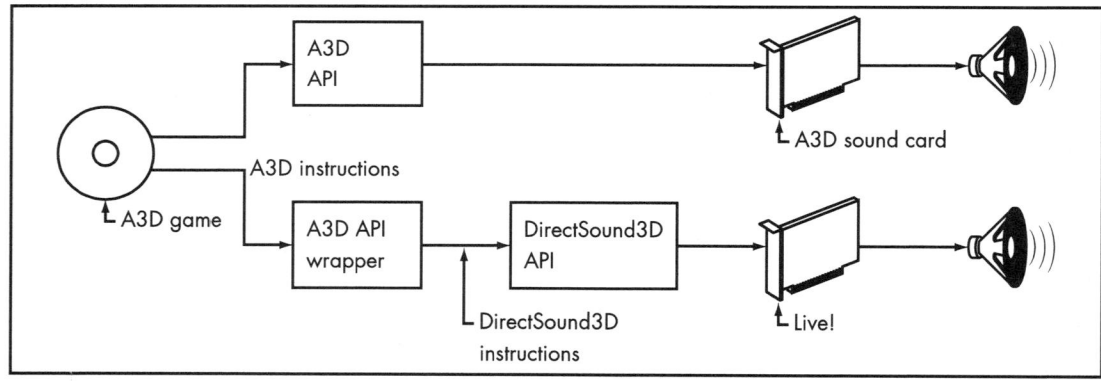

Figure 10.11: The way A3D is supported on the Live! and a real A3D sound card is slightly different

> You can find the A3D wrapper in most driver installations. The wrapper is in the form of an a3d.dll file that can be found in Windows' system or system32 folder.

After the Live! came on the market, there was a period of intense competition with Aureal, and legal bouts ensued. At the consumer front, there were numerous debates among supporters of the EAX and A3D 2.0 camps as to which technology was superior and provided more realistic results. Unquestionably, Aureal had one of the best two-speaker 3D positioning technologies, and each API had its merits. Unfortunately, the legal wrangling caused cash flow problems for Aureal, and the company was forced to cease operation.

Creative bought Aureal's intellectual property, including A3D technology. Creative has stated that it would not be using the A3D brand name, but after paying so much money to purchase Aureal's technology, most people concluded that Creative would probably incorporate some of that technology into future EAX versions without announcing it as such.

OpenAL

Open Audio Library (OpenAL) is an audio and 3D positioning API similar to DirectSound and DirectSound3D. It has several advantages, one of which is open-source licensing that allows developers to freely use and participate in development of the API without being subjected to any licensing fee. It is also cross-platform and includes support for different operating systems, such as BeOS, Linux, Mac OS, and of course, Windows.

Visit the OpenAL Web site at http://www.openal.org.

OpenAL was spearheaded by Creative and Loki Entertainment. Loki Entertainment specialized in licensing and porting games from other platforms to the Linux operating system. The company ported games such as Soldier of Fortune, Tribes 2, and Unreal Tournament.

Most developers of Windows games continue to use DirectX for sound, but a few games like LucasArts' Jedi Knight II: Jedi Outcast use OpenAL. Developers of games on operating systems like Linux are also looking at OpenAL as an easy means of supporting 3D sound in their games. Like the A3D wrapper, OpenAL support is implemented in Windows by translating OpenAL instructions used by games into equivalent DirectSound3D instructions.

> OpenAL support is contained in an OpenAL32.dll file, and is installed in Windows' system or system32 folder along with the drivers. Games that use OpenAL may also install the file in the game's installation folder.

3D Streams

The performance of a CPU depends on the power of the chip, which can be measured in many ways. The most popular is the MHz (clock speed) rating. Similarly, sound chips and DSPs used in sound cards also have an upper limit to their processing ability. This limits the number of stereo (DirectSound) and 3D (DirectSound3D) streams that can be mixed simultaneously.

The processing needed to alter a sound and place it in 3D space and allow it to adapt as parameters change in real time is not trivial compared to the simple processing needed to mix normal stereo streams together for playback. Therefore, most sound cards support fewer 3D streams than 2D streams. The very first Live! drivers supported only eight 3D streams, because Creative claims acoustic research has shown that most people cannot discern more than eight 3D-positioned sound sources at once. However, some considerations arose:

- Many games frequently use more than eight sounds simultaneously.
- Ideally, every positioned sound should be consistent in 3D space; the ninth or tenth sound, for instance, should not be downgraded to 2D and emanate from all speakers.
- It is not desirable to fall back to DirectSound3D's software rendering mode because of the high CPU requirements and the difference in quality between the sound card's 3D positioning algorithms and DirectSound3D's simple software-based 3D audio renderer.
- Gamers and developers requested for more 3D streams.
- The competition supported more 3D streams.

Creative increased the number of streams to 32 by releasing a driver upgrade, and now all Live! cards support 32 streams by default. Creative has not increased this number in the three years since it changed it from 8 to 32, and many have speculated that it is not possible to increase the number of 3D streams further because 32 comes close to the limit of the EMU10K1.

EAX

EAX is a set of technologies that enables sound enhancement by processing and altering sound. Much of EAX for gaming is focused on the API and the ability to alter sound effects and make them more relevant to the audio characteristics of the location and environment of the player. EAX works together with DirectSound3D by obtaining the 3D-positioned sound sources and applying EAX processing to them.

To learn more about EAX and how to make it work with 3D and non-3D sound sources, read Chapter 8, "EAX." You can also visit Creative's EAX site at http://eax.creative.com.

EAX 1.0

EAX 1.0 introduces the core of the EAX technology: reverberation. Reverb simulates the reflection of sound and produces an echo effect that gives game players information about their gaming environment. Such audio cues help the gamer determine the shape and size of a room, for instance, and the material that makes up the walls or surroundings. When materials absorb sound, there is less reflection of sound, and therefore less reverberation.

Without EAX, gamers can tell the direction of a sound when DirectSound3D is used, but they cannot determine the environment that the sound is in. Voices from behind you while you are in a sewer sound entirely different from those when you are in a huge hall, even though the sound remains behind you.

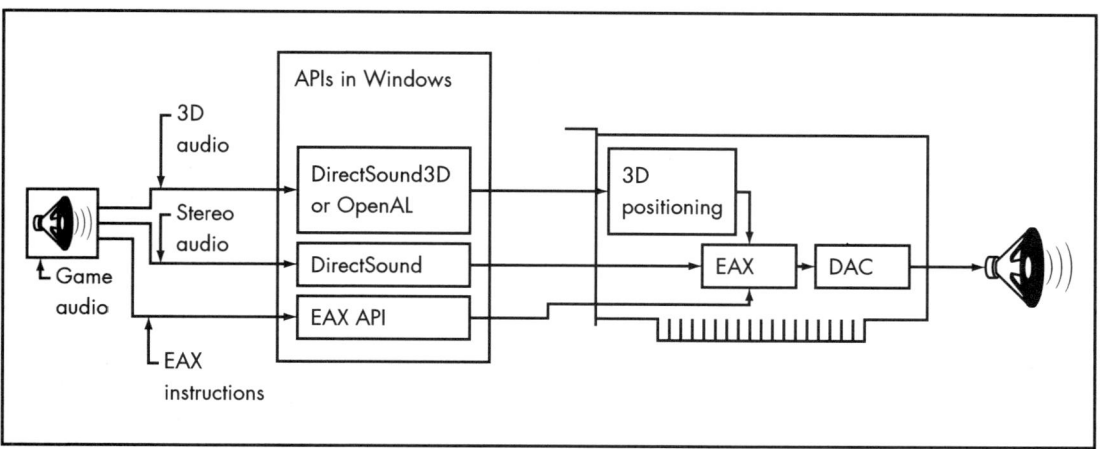

Figure 10.12: Stereo and 3D sound streams go through EAX processing before being output. The game uses the EAX API to send instructions to the EMU10K1 to set the correct effects.

EAX features a collection of around 30 presets, such as Auditorium, Cave, Hallway, Forest, Sewer Pipe, and Underwater, to allow developers to quickly add EAX effects to simulate environments that are common in many games. Developers also can modify some more detailed aspects of each preset like the reverb level, decay, and time damping to tweak them to the particular gaming environment.

EAX is applied to games similarly to the way you would apply EAX to normal audio sources, using the Surround Mixer or EAX Control Panel. When the player is in a tiny room, you can apply the Room preset, and this preset will stay in effect until the player moves into another environment, such as a tunnel. When the player crosses the boundary of two rooms with different presets, the game will trigger the EAX API to switch presets on the Live!

It takes considerable skill and a good ear to implement effective EAX in games. Unfortunately, many games tend to go overboard with EAX by setting the reverberation levels so high that they diminish the effect of 3D audio. This makes it difficult for listeners to pinpoint the exact location of a 3D sound source, because the reflections of a sound will come from other angles (and speakers) as it bounces off the walls that enclose the area. Too much EAX, especially with highly reverberant presets like Concert Hall and Sewer Pipe, will drown out 3D positioning, and the reverberation itself will sound unrealistic.

EAX 2.0

The next version of EAX was quickly introduced in 1999 in response to Aureal's new A3D 2.0 API. It included new tools to enable developers to separate a game level into different rooms with different EAX settings. Developers could make use of their game's 3D geometry to make this compartmentalization. Also, more controller parameters were added: for example, to allow room sizes to be changed.

EAX 2.0 also added key support for the simulation of obstacles that block sound from directly traveling to the listener in a gaming environment. Let's take a look at the two elements of EAX 2.0 that Creative has often used to market this feature in EAX: occlusions and obstructions.

Occlusions

Occlusion come from the word *occlude*, which means to prevent the passage of or cause something to become closed. This terms applies well to sound in rooms and enclosed areas. Imagine standing outside a room when a loud commotion is going on inside. All the sounds occurring in the room will be contained within the room's walls, but the full impact of the sound will not be heard outside the room because the walls that enclose the room absorb much of the sound.

If you want to hear what is going on, you could open the door slightly, and this small gap will allow some of the sound to leak out of the room. However, if you stand to the side and far away from the door, the sound will still be muffled:

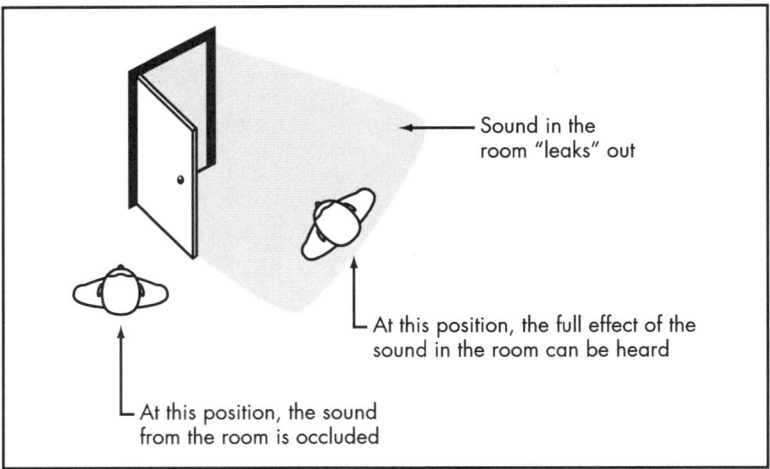

Figure 10.13: The slightly ajar door causes some of the sound from the room to be heard by listeners near the doorway

an occluded effect. Similarly, if you are inside the room and an explosion occurs outside, the blast will be muffled by the time the sound waves reach you.

Also if you replace concrete walls with a less dense material, like wood, more sound will be able to pass through the walls, and therefore the muffling effect will be less pronounced.

Obstructions

Sound can also be muffled when an object prevents the sound waves from reaching the listener's ears directly. For instance, if you are playing a first-person shooter game and there is a barrier in between the cracking sound of burning coal ahead of you, the higher frequencies of the sound will be muffled because the walls absorb and reflect most of the sound.

However, you will probably still be able to hear a faint sound of burning coal because some of the reflected sound will still reach you after it bounces off other objects in the room and moves around the object (a process known as *diffraction*).

More muffling occurs when objects are denser or when the angle of diffraction is large. The effect is less pronounced when most frequencies of the sound can pass through the object, as with a thin sheet of cloth. All these parameters can be set in the EAX 2.0 API.

> Higher-treble frequencies are especially susceptible to the muffling effect because they tend to travel in a straight line and will be absorbed or reflected away. This is also the reason why Chapter 6, "Speakers," mentions that it is best to place speakers so that the tweeters are directly at ear level and the high frequencies have a direct line of sight to your ears.

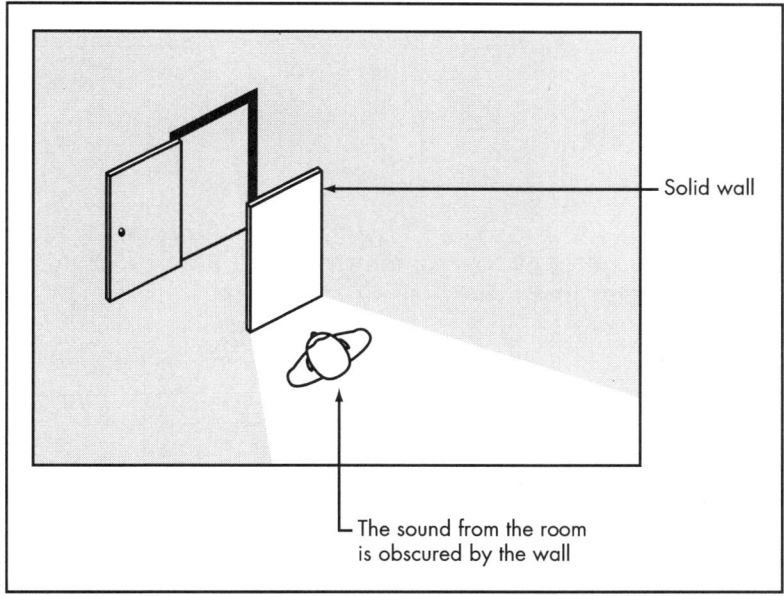

Figure 10.14: A solid wall absorbs sound from the room

EAX 3.0

To stave off competition from Aureal, Creative announced EAX 3.0. The new features in this version were to give developers new tools to provide the "ability to use and tune localized reflection clusters or isolated individual reflections, to continuously 'morph' between environments, and to further improve distance rendering and naturalness with Creative's proprietary statistical reverberation model" (quoted from the press release).

This press release was issued in March 1999, but Creative never delivered. Instead, the company decided to hold back these features for more than two years. In September 2001, these features finally saw the light of day in the EAX

Advanced HD technology available, unfortunately, only on the Sound Blaster Audigy cards. It is unlikely that the Live! will get these new features because they would diminish the value of the Audigy cards, even if it is technically possible for the EMU10K1 to support these features.

> Live!Ware 3 was released by Creative, and many assume that it includes EAX 3.0. However, Live!Ware 3 came with EAX 2.0.

The chief complaint about current EAX 1.0 and 2.0 implementations is the lack of realistic transitions between environments as the player moves between different types of rooms with different reverb characteristics. When the player crosses the boundary between two rooms, the EAX effect is abruptly switched, and any sound that is currently reverberating is immediately affected. The ability to gradually change the parameters from one environment to another over some time is one key improvement to EAX that should have been provided with the Live! cards.

I3DL2

Interactive 3D Audio Level 2 (I3DL2) is an initiative by the Interactive Audio Special Interest Group (IA-SIG) to standardize guidelines for a minimum set of features for 3D audio to be used in various applications, such as games, browsers, and multimedia software. The first, level-1 guidelines largely focused on 3D positioning and are based on Microsoft's DirectSound3D API.

> Many companies, including Creative and Microsoft, are members of the IA-SIG.

I3DL2 is a subset of EAX 2.0 and includes similar features, such as obstruction, occlusion, and reverberation effects. Games and sound cards that support I3DL2 need to implement support for the API in their software and drivers, just like EAX. Microsoft has added full support for I3DL2 in DirectX 8. The Live! drivers do not directly support I3DL2. Developers should use DirectX 8 instead.

EAGLE

EAGLE—short for Environmental Audio Graphical Librarian Editor—is the tool used by game developers to add EAX by graphically marking out the boundaries of different rooms and setting EAX parameters. EAGLE imports the 3D geometry of a game level and allows developers to walk through the level and define EAX parameters for every object and room to have EAX occlusion, obstruction, or reverberation effects applied.

The parameters are saved in an EAL file and shipped with the game. When the game is running, it sends the coordinates of the player in the level to the EAX

Manager, which is part of the drivers. The EAX Manager reads the coordinates from the game and relates them to the EAL file to retrieve the EAX parameters that are applicable to the player's current location. The game receives the EAX parameters and sets them in the EAX API. (The EAX Manager acts as a translator and does not automatically change the EAX parameters on the game's behalf.)

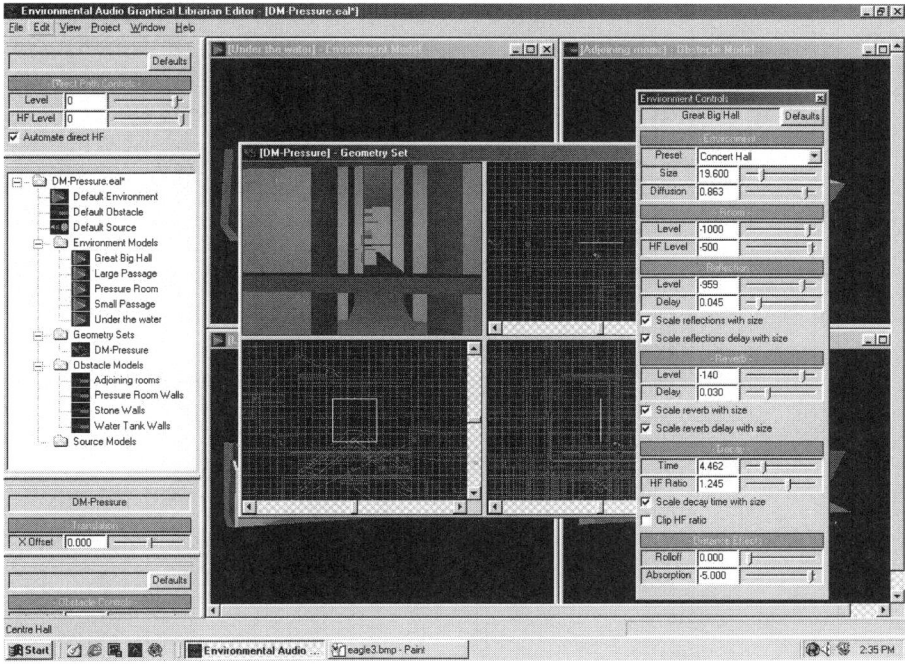

Figure 10.15: EAGLE in action

If a game does not have 3D locations and maps, the developer need not use EAGLE. Using the EAX API will suffice. After all, EAGLE does not replace the EAX API. It just gives developers a visual tool for setting EAX parameters in accordance with 3D maps of their games. Other games, like strategy games, which use an overhead view of the game world, could manually use the EAX API to switch environments without the need for EAGLE.

Dolby Digital API

Dolby Digital is the most prevalent surround sound format in DVDs. It provides six digital channels of audio for a 5.1 speaker configuration, commonly adopted by home theater systems. Until recently, no common method existed for games to include or play back Dolby Digital audio.

> The Dolby Digital API is implemented in ac3api.dll, which can be found in Windows' system or system32 folder.

During the Game Developer's Conference in March 2001, Creative introduced the Dolby Digital API, which gives developers a standardized library of tools to access the Dolby Digital decoding feature on the Live! 5.1 cards. This will allow developers to send Dolby Digital/AC-3–encoded 5.1 audio to the Live! for playback on the connected speakers. We wait with bated breath for this new wave of games!

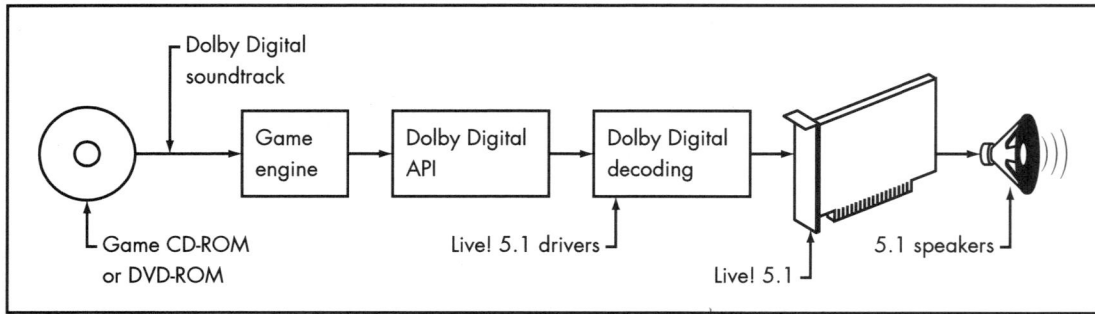

Figure 10.16: The Dolby Digital API allows games with surround soundtracks to be decoded by the Live! 5.1 for playback on 5.1 speakers

Read more about the Dolby Digital decoding capability of the Live! 5.1 in Chapter 11, "Watching Movies." You can find out more about 5.1 speaker support in Chapter 6, "Speakers."

3D Sound on the Live!

Certain processes need to occur for the sound card to perform 3D positioning and use EAX. Games come with a library of sound effects that are triggered and placed in 3D space using a 3D positioning API such as DirectSound3D or OpenAL. If 3D is not supported, it would probably use DirectSound (the 2D/stereo audio component of DirectX). Here is a rough picture on what goes on behind the scenes:

- Games provide the sound file and 3D positioning parameters to DirectSound3D or OpenAL.
- Games also set the EAX or I3DL2 environmental effects and obstruction simulation parameters.
- The Live! drivers have components that understand the DirectSound3D or OpenAL and EAX or I3DL2 instructions. The drivers translate these high-level instructions into equivalent low-level instructions that work on the EMU10K1.

- The EMU10K1 is programmed to perform the specific types of positioning and environmental effects set by the developer. The algorithms are sent to the DSP so that it can apply the effects to incoming sounds without any significant CPU power or frequent need for the driver running on the PC to check and control the rendering process.
- The sound files received by the drivers from the high-level APIs are sent to the EMU10K1 for processing and playback.
- The 3D sounds are positioned, and EAX effects are applied. (The algorithms used by the sound card's DSP to achieve this will also vary, depending on the number of speakers it is set to utilize.)

Speaker Configuration

When the Live! renders 3D audio and EAX, it is aware of the current speaker configuration and places sounds to the best of its ability using the available speakers. Therefore, it is important that you make sure that you have the correct speaker settings in the Surround Mixer. Also use the Test feature to ensure that each speaker is connected correctly and not accidentally swapped.

> If you have Creative or Cambridge SoundWorks speakers such as the DTT2500, DTT3500, or Inspire 5700, which come with a decoder box, the CMSS mode should be set to Fourpoint/5.1 so that all the front and rear channels from the Live! card can be heard. The speakers will not use the rear channels when set to CMSS Music or Movie mode.

Chapter 6, "Speakers," mentioned the use of height positioning on the Live! APIs like DirectSound3D allow developers to locate sounds above and below the listener. The 3D engine on the Live! implements these instructions through HRTF and virtual audio in any speaker mode.

Let's run through each speaker mode and find out how 3D positioning is affected by the different speaker modes.

2 Speakers Mode

The Live! uses HRTF and virtual surround algorithms to simulate sounds coming from the rear speakers. You will need to sit centrally, with both front speakers at the same distance from your ears, to obtain a realistic sonic image. Sound in this mode will not be as realistic as in the 4 Speakers and 5.1 Speakers modes.

4 Speakers Mode

The Live! uses four speakers to place audio in 3D space. In a typical four-speaker 3D positioning configuration for games, one speaker is placed in each of the four corners of the room. This setup provides realistic 3D positioning in most cases. Many developers also use a four-speaker configuration when programming their games for DirectSound3D and EAX.

TIP *If the game does not use 3D positioning, the rear speakers will duplicate the sound played back in the front speakers. This duplication results in a surround effect, but does not sound like 3D audio.*

> A process called *crosstalk cancellation* is performed so that sounds localized in one direction do not go to your other ear (which is normally the case because the sounds get reflected off other objects in the room). A simple example would be to make sure that a sound from the left speaker only comes from that side. Basically, the Live! will invert the sound from the left speaker and play the inverted signal on the right speaker so that it cancels out any remaining sound that goes to the right ear. Crosstalk cancellation is also performed in the 2 Speakers and 5.1 Speakers modes.

5.1 Speakers Mode

The 5.1 configuration adds a center channel to a four-speaker setup. The Live! 5.1 drivers will take into account the center speaker when positioning sounds in 3D space. This will produce a more accurate front soundstage and 3D positioning, especially if you place the left, right, and center speakers farther apart. This mode will be less useful if your room forces you to place the left and right speakers close together. In this case, just two front speakers will give a good front image for 3D positioning.

TIP *The Live! 5.1 will not produce any audio on the center speaker if the game does not use 3D positioning APIs like DirectSound3D or OpenAL.*

Headphones Mode

Headphones have an advantage over other types of speakers, because the sound travels directly to each of your ears without any chance of it being affected by the environment or traveling to your other ear. Thus, processing like crosstalk cancellation, like those used for speakers, is usually not necessary. The Live! uses a form of virtual surround similar to that for the 2 Speakers mode to simulate a 360-degree sound field. The sound that is played back is also slightly different from that in the speaker modes and is tweaked to perform well with most headphones.

Live!Surround Mode

Live!Surround encodes 3D positioning into a Dolby Surround–compatible format that works with AV receivers and decoders that have the Dolby Surround or Dolby Pro Logic logo. As in the 5.1 Speakers mode, Dolby Surround has a center speaker, and this provides a better front soundstage, especially if there is sufficient room to spread out the three front speakers. However, the surround speakers are mono, and all output the same sound, so sounds that the game developer places to come from behind will not be as accurate as when two discrete surround speakers are available, as in the 4- and 5.1 Speakers modes.

Playing Games with the Live!

Regrettably, many game publishers do not state the form of audio support provided by their games, like they do for the graphics and CPU. This makes it hard for buyers to tell whether a game supports 3D audio or EAX. The following are some ways to find out, as well as some information on how they would behave, and tips to correctly configure the games.

Games with 3D Positioning

Some games are able to detect the presence of the Live! and enable 3D sound, while most default to stereo mode, requiring you to go into the game's audio/sound configuration screen to turn on 3D positioning. The menu item may use many different terms, such as "3D sound," "DirectSound3D," "DS3D" or "OpenAL." Some game developers may also have a single "EAX" on/off option that enables both EAX and 3D positioning together, since nearly all EAX sound cards also support 3D positioning.

> Games with 3D positioning do not necessarily use EAX. 3D positioning and EAX can work exclusively, but together, they would definitely produce a better game audio experience.

Some games may also show a list of typical speaker configuration modes for selection. There may be options like "stereo speakers," "surround," or "quad speakers." This scheme is very vague, and you will have to guess and choose the one that is closest to your setup, or contact the publisher's tech support for further assistance.

> Other than the speaker configuration, there are no 3D positioning parameters that can be changed on the Live!

Is It in 3D?

If you are using a four- or 5.1-speaker setup, it may be difficult to tell if a game is using a 3D positioning API because the front channels are duplicated in the rear speakers. One way to tell is to listen closely for any panning sounds. If you are playing a first-person shooter game, you can also find a particular object that is making a constant sound and spin your character around. If the sound moves between the left and right speakers, but never seems to come only from the rear speakers behind you, the game probably does not support 3D audio.

Check the Front/Rear Balance

As explained above, 3D positioning works in all speaker modes of the Live! However, if you use four or 5.1 speakers, the FAD slider in the mixer should be set correctly, and not at the maximum or minimum position. This ensures that both the front and rear speakers are playing correctly for an accurate 3D sound field. Also, if your speakers have a front/rear balance knob, make sure that they are set correctly, since it works together with the FAD slider in the mixer to affect the relative volume of the front and rear speakers.

Not Everything Is in 3D

A game with 3D positioning does not mean that it uses 3D exclusively for all the sound that is playing. The game would also use standard stereo streams for audio tracks like voice-overs and music — sound that does not need to be positioned in 3D. If you are using four or 5.1 speakers, the stereo streams would be duplicated in the rear speakers, as well. This behavior is similar for other stereo nongame audio played with other applications like media players. The only exception is when CMSS is turned on.

3D Positioning and CMSS

You may have read in Chapter 6, "Speakers," that the Live! has a CMSS (Movie mode) that can upmix a stereo sound source to surround in any of the speaker modes. On two speakers or headphones, this creates a virtual surround effect, and with four or 5.1 speakers, the rear channels output the processed surround sound.

CMSS could possibly garble 3D positioning if it was also applied to sounds that are already positioned in 3D. Fortunately, this is not the case, as CMSS is applied only to stereo audio streams. Most games use a mixture of stereo and 3D streams, so with CMSS turned on, the stereo streams, like the musical score, will be processed with a surround effect.

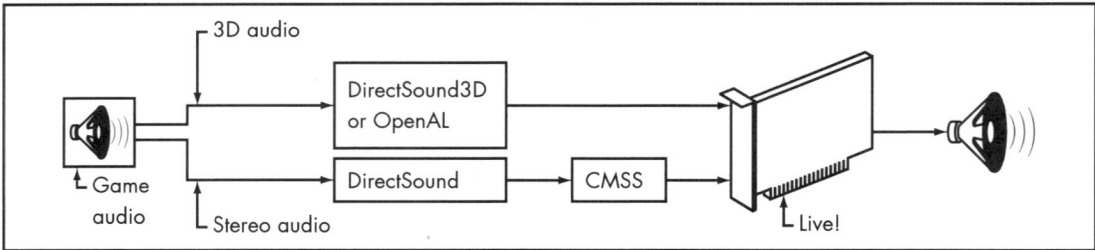

Figure 10.17: CMSS affects only the sounds in the game that use stereo audio (DirectSound)

With a four- or 5.1-speaker setup and CMSS enabled, the rear speakers will not carry a duplicate of the front speakers, but instead carry the CMSS-processed surround channels. You can choose to enable or disable CMSS, depending on whether you like its surround effect or a simple front-to-rear duplication of the stereo streams would sound better to your ears. The Live! handles 3D-positioned sounds similarly, regardless of the CMSS setting.

Games with EAX Support

Many games that support EAX will have an EAX logo on the box, along with other common logos like the Windows and Intel Pentium logos. (Earlier games may carry the older Environmental Audio logo.) Some game publishers may not display the logo on the box or within the game, but may indicate EAX support in the game's specifications. You can also check the publisher's Web site for the system requirements.

Games that support EAX may turn it off by default and wait for you to go to the configuration screen to enable it, or they may automatically detect the presence of an EAX sound card and enable support. Once enabled, the game will be able to switch the EAX parameters of the Live! to correspond to the gaming environment that you are in.

> EAX support is likely to be available in a game if it installed an eax.dll, EaxMan.dll, msseax.m3d, or msseax2.m3d file somewhere in its installation folder.

EAX Without 3D Positioning

It is possible for games to feature EAX support (and sometimes even have the EAX logo printed on the box) without using 3D positioning APIs like DirectSound3D or OpenAL. In such games, standard stereo game audio will have effects added to them.

Detecting EAX

If you are having a hard time telling if a game has EAX, you can turn off EAX in the Surround Mixer and play an audio CD or MP3 file before loading the game. Notice the unreverberated quality of the music that is playing. Once the game is loaded, move to a level or map that has lots of reverberation, like a cave or tunnel. Listen closely to the music for any form of reverberation. If there is reverb, the game probably has EAX support, because it had automatically turned on effects when there were no effects before the game was started.

EAX Outside of Games

Unlike many other sound cards, EAX on the Live! is not a game-exclusive technology. You can apply EAX to any sound source that is playing back on the Live!, such as an MP3 player or even your own voice through a microphone. Any effect that is set in the Surround Mixer or EAX Control Panel will be disabled during a game with EAX support. The correct preset will be restored once the EAX game exits to the desktop.

Tweaking EAX Levels

Sometimes, games may use reverbs that are too heavy for your tastes. Fortunately, this can be dialed down with the EAX presets available in the Surround Mixer and EAX Control Panel. Choose the No Effects or EAX—Normal Effects presets to get the full impact of EAX. If you find that a game's EAX effects are too pronounced, set EAX — Light Effects. You can also disable EAX in any game by choosing Disable EAX.

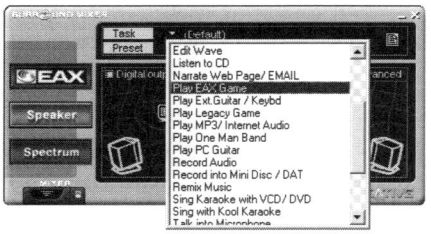 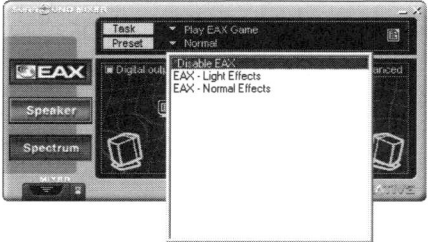

Figure 10.18: In the Surround Mixer, select Play EAX Game in the task list, and in the preset list that pops up, choose the amount of EAX to be applied

If these presets are not satisfactory, you can also refer to Chapter 8, "EAX," for instructions on how you can use the EAX Control Panel to manually set the maximum reverb level that can be applied on the Wave output of the Live!.

Games Without EAX Support

Games that do not have EAX support are termed *legacy games*. For such games, you can use the Surround Mixer or EAX Control Panel to specify an EAX preset that is applied to all sounds in the game (similar to applying EAX to nongame audio).

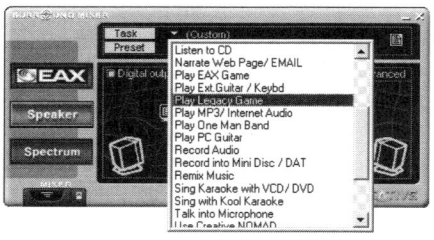 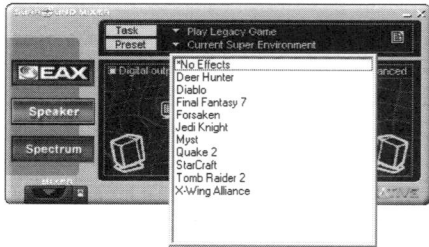

Figure 10.19: In the Surround Mixer, select Play Legacy Game in the task list, and in the preset list that pops up, choose a preset for the game

The Live! comes with a few presets for some older games. If you use the EAX Control Panel and set the effects, you'll notice that the game presets make use of one of the common reverb presets available. For example, the Starcraft preset uses the Quarry 1 EAX preset with a setting of 20 percent. Because the presets are actually quite generic, you can use them on other similar games, as well. You can also use the EAX Control Panel to manually increase or decrease the reverb amount to make the effect stronger or weaker.

TIP *You can duplicate the Starcraft preset by setting the EAX preset to Quarry and changing the reverb amount to 20 percent. (You can duplicate any other preset using the same technique.)*

11

WATCHING MOVIES

Advancements such as accelerated video cards, multimedia-capable CPUs, and storage media such as DVDs have enabled PCs to be full-blown home entertainment systems. And what better way to be entertained than to watch a great movie? The Live! brings movie watching on the PC to a new level with its multispeaker support and ability to play back surround formats such as Dolby Digital. First, let's take a look a quick look at the evolution of surround sound throughout the years.

From the Cinema to the Living Room

Hollywood is undoubtedly the hotbed for innovations in audio and surround sound. Introduced in the 1970s, Dolby Stereo gradually became the sound standard for movies, especially when films like *Star Wars* showed the world how multiple channels of sound can be exploited for dramatic impact. Dolby Stereo (known as Dolby Surround in the consumer market) became the ubiquitous surround sound format for theaters and home video before the arrival of Dolby Digital in the late 1990s.

Matrix Surround

Engineers of early surround sound technology found themselves facing an interesting challenge: how to deliver four channels of audio in the two channels found in the common stereo configuration. Dolby Surround processing was specifically engineered around this limitation by using a matrix encoding system that allows two extra channels (the center and surround) to be transparently mixed into the left and right speakers. When played back on a normal stereo system, it sounds like any other stereo program, but when a Dolby Surround or Dolby Surround Pro Logic decoder is used, the encoded Dolby Surround channels can be recovered.

Encoding

Like many other audio formats, creating a Dolby Surround soundtrack requires an encoding process. Sound engineers and designers create the sound, and place them among the speakers in a surround configuration. The surround sound is encoded and decoded while the soundtrack is created, allowing the designers to monitor the results in real time. The resulting encoded soundtrack is ready to be distributed over widely available stereo delivery media. When the stereo sound is passed through a Dolby Pro Logic decoder in the home, the same signals are reproduced as heard in the mixing studio.

> Dolby Surround is also known as Dolby Stereo when applied to film projected in cinemas and theaters.

Dolby Surround is the dominant surround sound format because of its ability to be stored in the ubiquitous stereo format found on almost all media, from CDs, MiniDiscs, and LDs to stereo VHS tapes and television broadcasts. Many television shows today are delivered in Dolby Surround, and virtually all home theater receivers and amplifiers are capable of decoding this format. Even though newer digital surround formats like Dolby Digital and DTS are available for DVDs and satellite TV, Dolby Surround has remained in use.

Decoding

After the filmmakers encode the soundtracks, the cinema operators and consumers will have to purchase the equipment to recreate the soundtrack. Such equipment includes a Dolby Surround decoder. In the home, three decoding technologies are available, and most of them are built in to home theater receivers, surround decoders, and some 5.1 multimedia speaker systems.

Dolby Surround

Dolby Surround was the first matrix decoding process made available to home theaters. It uses a passive decoder to extract the surround channel from the left and right speakers and provides a total of three channels of audio: left, right, and surround. It is passive because the decoder does not analyze and adapt to changes in the soundtrack, nor can it remove what is sent to the surround speakers from the original left and right channels. This design was used because electronics were not as advanced at that time, and it provided a good balance between electronic complexity and cost—an especially sensitive issue in the cost-conscious consumer market.

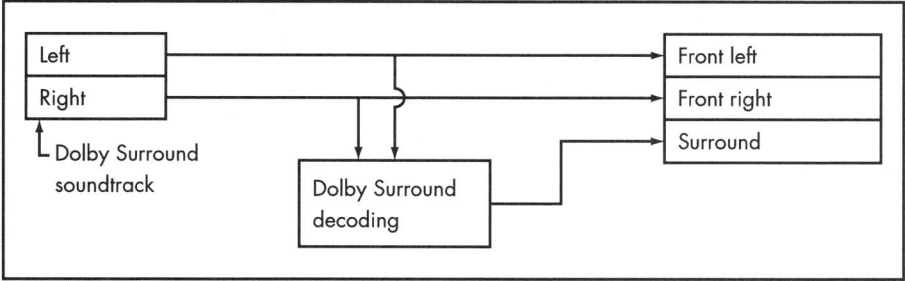

Figure 11.1: The Dolby Surround decoding process

Dolby Surround Pro Logic

In 1987, Dolby introduced an improved decoder dubbed Dolby Surround Pro Logic that performs active instead of passive decoding. The decoder actively monitors the encoded Dolby Surround stereo signal to determine where to place sounds. This provides more directionality, because sounds can be steered among the speakers. The decoded center and surround channels are removed from the original left and right channels, improving channel separation. In addition to the surround channel, this decoder can pick out sound that appears on both the left and right channels and redirect it to a center channel. These new features have gained widespread acceptance and made three-channel Dolby Surround decoders obsolete.

> The logic steering system used by Pro Logic is the same as those available on professional Dolby Stereo cinema processors.

Limitations of Matrix Surround

However, matrix surround has its limitations. There are essentially only two channels to carry all the sound. As a result, only one surround channel is played back on both surround speakers in a typical home theater setup, so it is not possible to play different sounds on each speaker. This makes it difficult for filmmakers to do neat things like make sound effects spin around the audience. Also, the surround channel is limited to midrange frequencies.

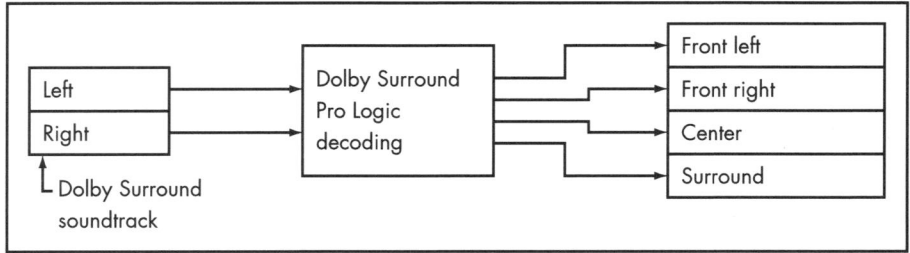

Figure 11.2: The Dolby Surround Pro Logic decoding process

A common artifact, easily identifiable when sounds meant for one channel leak into another channel, is that dialogue can commonly be heard, at a lower volume, in the surround channel as well. A workaround was implemented by adding a few milliseconds of delay to the sound playing back on the surround speakers so that the human ear hears the sound from the front speakers first and identifies it as coming from the front. (This is known as the *Haas effect*.) Also, music that would be best heard only from the left and right speakers is often collapsed to the center speaker.

Nearly all of these problems are now overcome with more advanced signal processing techniques for matrix decoding, like those employed in Dolby Pro Logic II and DTS Neo 6, among the many other solutions that have been developed.

Dolby Surround Pro Logic II

In 2000, Dolby finally updated its matrix decoding technology with the new Dolby Pro Logic II decoder, eliminating many of the shortcomings of standard Pro Logic decoding, while taking advantage of the improved quality in stereo movie delivery formats like VHS Hi-Fi and digital television systems. The decoder now can reproduce full-range stereo surround channels, has a music mode that works with non–Dolby Surround material, and produces a more 5.1-like surround effect from existing stereo material. Pro Logic II is rapidly appearing as a standard feature in home theater equipment and overtaking Pro Logic as the standard matrix decoding system.

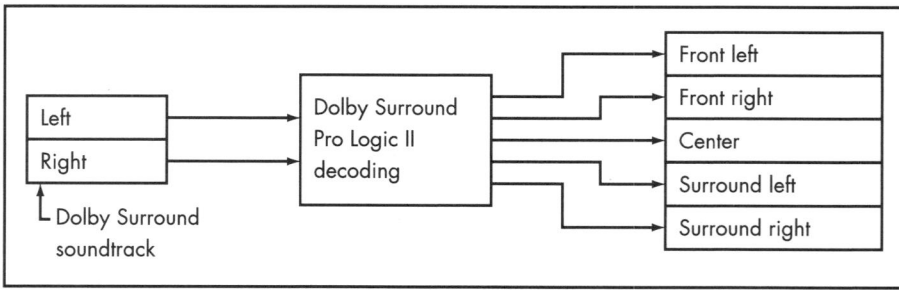

Figure 11.3: The Dolby Surround Pro Logic II decoding process

Discrete Multichannel Surround

In the late 1990s, improvements in electronics and DSPs enabled new sound processing possibilities at a cost acceptable to the consumer market. Why try to hide channels in one another when new technology allows each channel to be stored and delivered separately?

Dolby Digital

So two decades after matrix encoding was introduced and refined, Dolby introduced the new Dolby Digital format, which allows up to six channels of audio to be encoded and stored digitally. The format provides five full-range channels that cover the entire audible frequencies of 20 Hz to 20 kHz and also adds a low-frequency effects (LFE) channel dedicated to reproducing powerful low bass effects twice as loud as the other channels can. This configuration is known as 5.1, with the .1 representing the LFE channel because it requires only about one-tenth the bandwidth and storage space of the other full-range channels.

Each of the six channels in a Dolby Digital setup—left, right, center, surround left, surround right, and LFE—has a corresponding audio channel in the soundtrack. Filmmakers are free to place sound on any of the five main speakers without fear that sound will interfere or bleed into other channels as in a matrixed system. The full-range channels, especially the surrounds, play back sharp, clear sound, for a more precise and involving soundstage compared to the single midrange surround channel provided by Dolby Surround.

> In 1992, *Batman Returns* became the first film to use Dolby Digital.

The two surround speakers are used to create ambience and play directional sound effects, while the dialogue and many sound effects come from the center speaker and correspond with the on-screen action. The left and right speakers are used mainly for music and for occasions when the sound is off-screen or when more impact is needed in the front soundstage.

In cinemas, the LFE channel is used to store extra bass information to drive separate subwoofers. In the home, the LFE channel may be mixed into the front speakers, or mixed with bass from other channels and played on a subwoofer, depending on the available speaker configuration.

Today, Dolby Digital is the common surround sound technology for DVDs and digital satellite broadcasts. Some console platforms can output Dolby Digital soundtracks, while on the PC side, Creative has introduced a Dolby Digital API to allow PC games to reproduce Dolby Digital soundtracks through the Sound Blaster Live! 5.1's Dolby Digital decoding capability.

DTS

DTS is another multichannel sound format developed by Digital Theater Systems. It is quickly gaining acceptance in DVDs as an arguably higher-quality alternative to Dolby Digital. DTS allocates higher bit rates for the surround soundtracks and uses different encoding techniques from Dolby Digital. It was originally developed as a multichannel surround format for music. Director Steven Spielberg played an instrumental role in bringing the cinema version of DTS to Hollywood for his groundbreaking 1993 box office hit, *Jurassic Park*. As with Dolby Digital, most DTS soundtracks on DVDs provide five channels of full-range audio and a .1 LFE channel.

> Sony Dynamic Digital Sound (SDDS) is another multichannel sound format that is commonly used in films and cinemas. However, Sony has no plans to introduce it in the consumer market.

More Technology, More Channels

5.1 channels was not enough. The filmmakers for the highly anticipated 1999 film *Star Wars Episode I: The Phantom Menace* wanted more directional control of the surrounds, and the solution was to add a new center surround channel. This enhancement is known as Surround EX. In movie theaters, surround speakers are mounted on the left side, right side, and behind the audience. For a traditional 5.1 configuration, the left half of the back speakers play the sounds from the left surround channel, while the right half plays the sounds from the right surround channel.

Theaters upgraded with Surround EX had all their back speakers routed to reproduce sound from the new center surround channel. This allowed sounds to be positioned directly behind the audience instead of having them play on both the left surround and right surround channels to simulate a sound from the rear-center position. In home theaters, one or two center surround speakers are added to the back of the listening position for a six- or seven-speaker configuration. This requires manufacturers of AV receivers to add extra amplification circuitry for the extra speakers.

Find out more about Dolby technologies for home theater and multimedia at http://www.dolby.com.

Dolby's implementation of Surround EX is dubbed Dolby Digital Surround EX. The consumer equivalent, Dolby Digital EX, is gradually becoming affordable enough for midrange and budget home theater systems. DVDs with Dolby Digital EX soundtracks are still carried over conventional 5.1 Dolby Digital soundtracks, with the center surround channel matrix-encoded into the left and right surround channels. Home theater receivers that do not support Dolby Digital EX soundtracks will reproduce the left and right surrounds as they are found in the soundtrack, but equipment that recognizes Dolby Digital EX will be able to matrix-decode the rear surround channel (using a technique similar to the way Pro Logic decodes the center channel from a stereo source) and send it to the center surround speakers.

 DTS also has a similar implementation called DTS-ES Matrix 6.1 that uses the company's matrix encoding and decoding systems to add and extract a center surround channel from 5.1 DTS soundtracks. To circumvent inherent problems with matrix encoding, DTS also introduced the DTS-ES Discrete 6.1 format, which can also be found in some DVD titles. Unlike the other formats, DTS-ES Discrete 6.1 stores the center surround channel separately, bypassing the need for matrix decoding to extract the center surround channel. Currently, DTS-ES Discrete 6.1 is the only consumer format to support 6.1 channels in the digital soundtrack. (Dolby Digital EX and DTS-ES Matrix 6.1 are still delivered over 5.1 digital soundtracks.)

> There are some AV receivers that support DTS-ES Matrix 6.1, but not DTS-ES Discrete 6.1 decoding. However, DTS-ES Discrete 6.1 soundtracks can still be played on equipment only capable of decoding DTS-ES Matrix 6.1 soundtracks; the center surround channel can still be retrieved. To find out more about how this is achieved, visit http://www.dtsonline.com.

These new technologies are just beginning to appear in home theater systems and for some DVD titles. They will arrive on the PC when the technology and cost of sound cards and multimedia speakers are right for the PC audio market.

> Dolby's *Surround EX* and the *ES* in DTS-ES both mean extended surround and indicate the presence of a center surround channel, which can be decoded by compatible surround decoders.

Encoding in Digital Formats

Dolby Digital used to be called Dolby AC-3, after the encoding technology that Dolby developed to reduce digital audio signals to more manageable sizes. This reduction is necessary to make the soundtrack coexist with existing film and projection equipment, and to allow many channels of sound to be stored on DVDs or delivered over digital television broadcasts.

> Dolby Digital supports sample rates of 48, 44.1, and 32 kHz, and because it can contain one (mono) to six (5.1) channels of audio, the bit rate of the compressed AC-3 audio can range from 32 to 640 kbps.

Why is encoding necessary? Consider audio CDs. They typically store 16-bit, 44.1-kHz audio that is adequate to cover the range of sounds that we can hear, and each CD can store only 74 minutes of stereo audio. Most movies run at least 90 minutes. Add to that the requirement of storing five full-range CD-quality channels, and you can see that this all adds up to a need for a substantial amount of storage space. Moreover, DVDs have to store both video (which itself has to be squeezed down to a manageable size with MPEG-2 video compression so that it can fit on a single disc) and audio. Although DVDs can store significantly more data than audio CDs, many DVD titles now come on double-disc sets because the content easily exceeds the capacity of a single disc, especially when many supplements are included.

Dolby Digital and DTS perform processing known as *perceptual audio coding* (explained further in Chapter 12, "Creating a Music Library"), which is akin to audio compression technologies like MP3 and Sony's ATRAC and ATRAC3, used in the company's MiniDisc and flash memory audio players. These compression technologies use digital audio and signal processing algorithms to determine which parts of the sound cannot be perceived by the ear and so can be removed, while at the same time preserving the most significant portions of the sound so that it is able to represent the original sound as accurately as possible.

> The main feature that sets Dolby Digital and DTS apart from MP3 and ATRAC is the surround format support for more than two channels. Differences aside, all of these technologies discard imperceptible audio information to reduce storage space.

What About THX?

THX is not a surround sound format but a set of quality standards and technical criteria for movie reproduction. Therefore, there are no such things as a "THX soundtrack" or a "THX surround format." THX certifications are wide ranging, from certifications for cinemas and media like LaserDiscs and DVDs, to audio certification for surround soundtracks and home theater equipment. To earn a "THX Certified" label, products have to meet stringent criteria.

For surround sound, THX builds on existing surround sound standards like Dolby Surround and Dolby Digital, adding specifications and technology for THX home theater receivers, decoders, and speakers so they can closely reproduce what is heard when the movie soundtrack is created on the film dubbing stage. These standards ensure great compatibility and performance benchmarks for THX-certified products.

In the PC world, THX certification is not an important criterion for most buyers, as the company is largely focused on film audio. Nevertheless, THX certifies multimedia PCs and their most important component: multimedia speakers. High-end speaker models from Altec Lansing, Klipsch, and Logitech have earned this certification. However, this does not mean that these speakers incorporate the same THX surround sound enhancements found in high-end (and very costly) home theater equipment.

Summary of Common Surround Formats

The following table summarizes the common surround formats and the channels that can be obtained from their soundtracks.

Table 11.1: Audio Channels Output by Common Surround Decoding Technologies

Format/ Channels	Front Left	Front Right	Front Center	Surround Left	Surround Right	Surround Center	LFE (.1 Channel)
Stereo	✓	✓					
Dolby Surround	✓	✓		ONE SURROUND CHANNEL			
Dolby Pro Logic	✓	✓	✓	ONE SURROUND CHANNEL			
Dolby Pro Logic II	✓	✓	✓	✓	✓		
Dolby Digital	✓	✓	✓	✓	✓		✓
Dolby Digital EX/ Surround EX	✓	✓	✓	✓	✓	✓ (Matrix decoded from surround left and surround right channels)	✓
DTS	✓	✓	✓	✓	✓		✓
DTS-ES Matrix 6.1	✓	✓	✓	✓	✓	✓ (Matrix decoded from surround left and surround right channels)	✓
DTS-ES Discrete 6.1	✓	✓	✓	✓	✓	✓ (Discrete)	✓

Surround Setups

A typical Dolby Surround Pro Logic or Dolby Digital home theater uses five speakers spread around the listening area. The center channel is usually placed close to the screen, while the left and right speakers are located on the sides to allow the front soundstage to be sufficiently spread out. The surround speakers are placed to the left and right or behind the listening area to provide an enveloping sound field. A subwoofer is usually added to reproduce low bass effects common on film soundtracks, especially in action movies.

Find out more about speaker positioning in Chapter 6, "Speakers."

There are many ways to configure a surround setup to accommodate the number of speakers in the system. You should have at least five main speakers to accurately reproduce the multichannel soundtrack. The subwoofer can be omitted if the front-left and front-right speakers are full range and have woofers large enough for adequate bass reproduction. Even then, subwoofers are a good addition because the woofer drivers in subwoofers are much larger and can produce much more bass than typical woofer drivers in full-range speakers. They can also go much lower than smaller woofers, and the better ones, with huge drivers of 10 inches in diameter or more, can pump out bass at a deep, rumbling 10 to 40 Hz.

If all of the main channels are satellite speakers, a subwoofer definitely is necessary. Most 5.1 multimedia speaker systems use satellite speakers, so a woofer unit will almost always be provided to supply the bass for all the five main speakers.

> If a source has an LFE track but you do not have a subwoofer, most receivers and the Live! 5.1 can be set to redirect audio in the LFE channel to the left and right speakers.

We do not recommend forgoing the center channel on a home theater setup, but if it is absolutely necessary to do so, receivers can redirect center channel audio to the left and right speakers. The Live! 5.1 also does this automatically when you change speaker modes in the Surround Mixer. Leaving out the center speaker on a PC is fine if the left and right speakers are close together and provide a sufficiently realistic front soundstage without giving a feeling that there is a gap in the center.

Configuring AV Receivers and Decoders

AV receivers, amplifiers, and decoders normally allow you to configure settings for each speaker, but many also divide the speakers into three main groups: front, center, and surround. A wide (wide range) or large setting will send the entire frequency range from the channel to the speaker, and a normal or small setting will redirect low bass to the front speakers (for the center channel) or the subwoofer output (for the front or surround speakers). The center speaker will probably have a phantom setting that allows you to send the center channel equally to the left and right speakers when you do not have a physical center speaker connected.

Note: Many lower-end and multimedia 5.1 speaker systems with decoders do not have such settings.

Another issue, mentioned in Chapter 6, "Speakers," is the matching of speakers. Just as you would not use different types of left and right speakers in a stereo system, you should avoid unmatched speakers in a home theater. If you do vary speaker types, sounds may change in timbre and quality when they move among the different types of speakers. Ideally, all five speakers should be of the same brand and product range so that their tonal characteristics match. However, the surround speakers can be slightly different from the front speakers because the surround channel is used and positioned differently for movies, and the main soundstage is typically concentrated in the front three speakers.

> Dolby Surround and Pro Logic decoding restricts the surround channels to 100 Hz to 7 kHz, which is generally midrange sound. However, newer technologies like Dolby Digital, DTS, and even the new Pro Logic II do not have this limitation, so if you are upgrading your home theater, older surround speakers designed for midrange reproduction may need to be upgraded, as well.

In 3D positional audio in games, however, using the same speakers for the front and surround channels is important for accurate movement of sound among the speakers. Buying home theater or multimedia speakers in a package determined by the manufacturer or speakers of the same product range lessens the chances of mismatched speakers, as they will probably be matched sonically even if they are not physically identical.

> The built-in speakers of some television sets can be hooked up as the center channel; however, because of the huge disparity in quality between television speakers and loudspeakers, the television speaker may actually impair the front soundstage.

Not Everything Is 5.1!

Although modern DVD titles with surround sound technologies like Dolby Digital normally have 5.1 audio, they can also store fewer channels. For instance, a classic movie with a mono soundtrack can be stored in a Dolby Digital–encoded 1.0 soundtrack. Dolby Digital soundtracks can range from mono (one channel) to 5.1 (six channels), while DTS allows up to 7.1 (eight channels).

Some Dolby Digital soundtracks are only 2.0 (stereo), and some DVDs, like Disney's *Tarzan*, have a 5.0 soundtrack that omits the .1 LFE channel. The lack of a .1 LFE channel does not mean that there is an absolute absence of bass. Most soundtracks are mixed with sufficient bass information in the front channels. The LFE is an option for filmmakers to mix in extra bass for cinemas and home theater setups with powerful subwoofers (and a larger budget).

Dolby Surround Soundtracks Encoded in Dolby Digital

Many DVDs also come with stereo Dolby Surround soundtracks to ensure backward compatibility with stereo sound systems and Pro Logic decoders, and to contain alternate language or commentary tracks. These Dolby Surround tracks are matrix encoded and then compressed with the same Dolby AC-3 audio coding algorithm, but they use only two channels (stereo) and are sometimes stored on DVDs with an indicator to tell the decoder to automatically switch to Pro Logic decoding. This automatic switching cannot be done with non–Dolby Digital soundtracks, like those delivered over the air or stored in audio CDs.

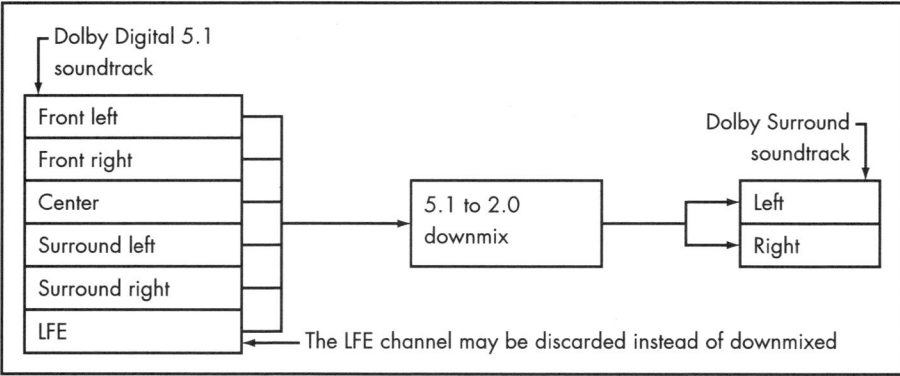

Figure 11.4: Downmixing is performed by converting a 5.1 soundtrack to a Pro Logic–compatible 2.0 soundtrack

Playing 5.1 Soundtracks on Fewer Speakers

Some DVDs include only a 5.1 soundtrack and not a stereo soundtrack. This makes them difficult to reproduce on stereo or the popular four-speaker configuration of multimedia PCs. Discarding channels would not make sense because removing channels, for example, the center channel that contains most dialogue, would result in a loss of significant parts of the soundtrack. Therefore, the Dolby Digital specifications require the DVD player to support *downmixing* of 5.1 to stereo Dolby Surround–compatible tracks. This allows any stereo system or Pro Logic decoder to play back the sound contained in all channels of a 5.1 soundtrack, although less accurately. Downmixing is also performed by software DVD players, allowing 5.1 soundtracks to be played back on the two or four speakers commonly used with PC sound cards like the Live!

Home Theater on the PC

In 2000, the popularity of DVDs boomed, and the PC became a DVD playback alternative to the typical TV and DVD player combination, especially for homes and dormitories with limited space. Sound card manufacturers responded with 5.1 decoding and six-channel outputs on their sound cards. A PC with a 450-MHz or faster CPU, a video card with DVD decoding acceleration, a DVD-ROM drive, and a software DVD player will provide good-quality DVD playback.

Most video cards released after 1999 support some form of DVD and MPEG-2 acceleration that takes over some of the steps necessary to decode and display the video on a DVD.

Figure 11.5: PowerDVD and WinDVD are two of the most popular software DVD players in Windows

In fact, the high-resolution and non-interlaced video from the monitor (VGA) output of graphic cards can provide a very affordable big-screen home theater solution when connected to a front projector or other displays. A sound card like the Live! can also be used to pass an unaltered Dolby Digital or DTS signal from a DVD disc to an external home theater receiver. Add a DVD-ROM drive, a TV tuner and capture card with time-shifting software, a wireless keyboard, and a wireless mouse into a sleek PC case, and you'll have a machine that some people term a *home theater PC* (HTPC). (The more expensive solution would be to use high-end home theater equipment such as line doublers, progressive scan DVD players, screens and video projectors, and other costly options.)

On the other end, most users use their PCs not as a dedicated playback machine for a home theater system, but as a budget DVD playback system, using the computer monitor and a stereo or a multichannel multimedia speaker system. The speakers and decoding quality are very important components to get a satisfying surround experience, because of the huge dynamic range of movie soundtracks—from the whisper quiet to deafening loudness when the action heats up. Most multimedia speakers have satellite speakers with similar audio characteristics, and this should provide a smooth soundstage as sounds shift among the speakers.

> Most DVDs are *region coded* so that movie studios can control the distribution of their movies in different parts of the world. The flash ROM firmware of DVD-ROM drives manufactured after 2000 (known as RPC-2 drives) makes them lock to a particular region after playing DVDs of a particular region a few times. The earlier RPC-1 drives did not have this locking feature implemented in the firmware; the software DVD player performed the region locking, which was easy to bypass.

> DVDs are copy protected, and a software DVD player is required to unlock them. Copying the VOB files from the DVD-ROM drive directly to the hard drive will not make them playable.

Surround Sound on the Live!

There are many ways to get surround sound into the Live! Depending on the speaker configuration and the model of the Live! card, the Live! can be used for surround sound decoding or as an intermediary to pass surround soundtracks to an external decoder such as a home theater receiver, decoder, amplifier, or affordable set of multimedia speakers with a built-in hardware decoder.

Playing Matrix Surround Soundtracks

Because matrix surround soundtracks are delivered as standard stereo signals, and sound cards like the Live! work primarily with stereo sound sources, you can send the outputs of the Live! to a matrix surround decoder to extract the additional channels. But first, let's find out the ways you can get stereo and matrix surround-encoded sound into the Live!:

- Connect audio output from external AV equipment, such as an LD player or stereo VCR, to the Live! You can do this with the analog inputs on the Live!'s backplate or a digital I/O device like the Live!Drive. (Digital inputs on digital I/O devices can also be used, because they also accept stereo digital signals.)
- Play stereo sound with the PC. For example, you could play a video or audio clip using your favorite media player.

When non-matrix-encoded (stereo) sources are passed through matrix surround decoders, the results may vary. With Pro Logic decoders, the sound field may be collapsed to the center speaker, with very little sound heard on the left and right speakers. Newer decoding technologies, such as Pro Logic II, DTS Neo 6, and the lesser-known Circle Surround by SRS Labs, are designed to work with non-matrix-encoded (stereo) sources as well.

> If a Dolby Surround soundtrack is delivered in mono format, as with a mono television broadcast, the stereo and surround information cannot be properly decoded.

Unfortunately, these newer matrix surround decoding technologies have not yet been available on sound cards. Many sound card manufacturers believe users want only Dolby Digital and DTS playback on their sound cards, but due to the pervasiveness of matrix-encoded stereo sound sources, users also want their equipment to convert stereo sound sources to multichannel (a process known as *upmixing*) so that a 4- or 5.1-channel speaker setup is not wasted. As you will read later, the Live! has a CMSS mode that does this.

> **Auto-detection of Matrix-Encoded Soundtracks**
> A stereo sound source may or may not be encoded with Dolby Surround or other forms of matrix surround encoding. This makes it difficult for audio equipment to detect encoded soundtracks and turn on the appropriate decoder automatically. Most audio and video recordings that are encoded this way will carry a logo, like the Dolby Stereo or Dolby Surround logo.
>
> The only exception is for Dolby Surround soundtracks encoded digitally with Dolby AC-3, as explained above in the section "Dolby Surround Soundtracks Encoded in Dolby Digital." A tag embedded in the digital data tells the decoder to turn on Pro Logic decoding automatically. Of course, the decoder must be Dolby Digital compatible and the audio must be from a digital source like DVD, because older Dolby Surround and Pro Logic decoders do not support digital inputs or the AC-3 format that carries the tag.

External Decoding

The Live! does not support Pro Logic or Pro Logic II decoding, but if you own a home theater receiver, surround decoder, or a multimedia speaker that supports Pro Logic decoding, you can connect the Live!'s front stereo outputs (either analog or digital) to the receiver and perform decoding externally. If you connect to a receiver in this way, make sure the Live!Surround speaker setting is turned off because the matrix-encoded stereo soundtrack should be unaltered as it goes out to the external decoding equipment. Because Live!Surround processes and modifies all sound that is played through the Live! to make it compatible with a Pro Logic decoder, soundtracks that already have matrix-encoded channels will be encoded a second time by Live!Surround, producing undesirable results.

To correct this, set the speaker mode to 2 Speakers, 4 Speakers, or 5.1 Speakers so that the external matrix surround decoder receives an unmodified stereo signal. You can connect to the speakers using the analog front line output or the coaxial and optical outputs available on digital I/O devices like the Live!Drive.

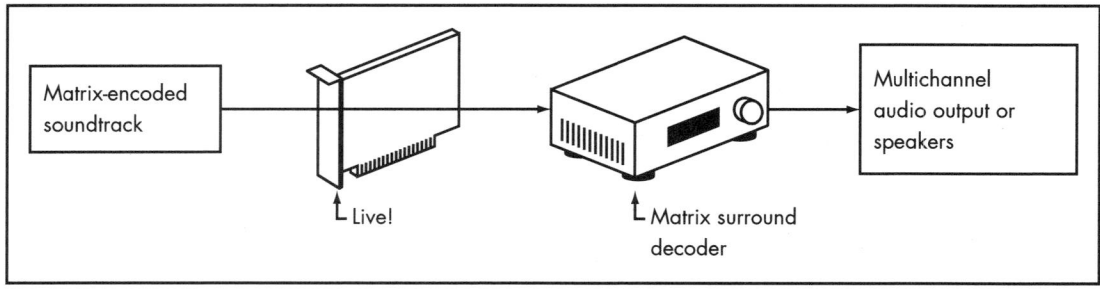

Figure 11.6: A matrix-encoded surround soundtrack is input into or played on the Live!, and the stereo output is sent to an external decoder to obtain the surround channels

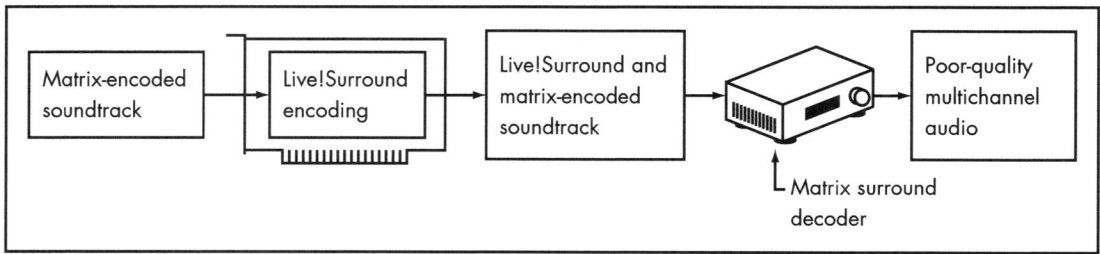

Figure 11.7: If Live!Surround is turned on while using an external matrix surround decoder, any matrix-encoded audio will be decoded a second time by the Live!Surround process, before it is decoded. This may result in poor surround sound.

Change back to Live!Surround when you are playing games with 3D positioning; you need the Live! to convert the 3D sound to a Pro Logic–compatible signal for the receiver.

Here's a summary on how you can connect the Live! to an external decoder to listen to matrix-encoded soundtracks:

Table 11.2: External Decoding for Matrix Surround Soundtracks

Sound Sources	Any matrix surround–encoded stereo sound played and controllable by the mixer.
Speaker Modes	2 Speakers, 4 Speakers, or 5.1 Speakers. Do not use Headphones and Live!Surround modes, because these alter the stereo (matrix-encoded) sound that is being played back.
Speaker Types	**Home theater:** Four-channel (without the center channel) or five-channel setup. A subwoofer is optional. **Multimedia speakers:** Most 5.1 multimedia speakers with Dolby Digital decoders will also support Pro Logic decoding with analog inputs. (5.1 multimedia speakers without decoders are not compatible with this external decoding method.)
Other Requirements	The speaker or sound system that receives the sound from the Live! must have a decoder or AV receiver with Dolby Surround, Dolby Surround Pro Logic, or Dolby Surround Pro Logic II, or some other matrix decoder, such as Circle Surround or DTS Neo 6.
Software Settings	None.

Table 11.2: External Decoding for Matrix Surround Soundtracks (continued)

Connections	Connect the Live!'s front outputs to the decoder or AV receiver. You can use either the analog line outputs on the backplate or the optical or coaxial digital outputs (if your decoder supports digital input).

Sound Card Decoding with CMSS

The Live! has a Creative Multi-Speaker Surround (CMSS) setting that can be activated in the Surround Mixer and PlayCenter. Also called Movie Mode in the Surround Mixer, CMSS works in a way similar to Dolby Surround decoding: it processes the left and right channels and derives the extra channels. Non-matrix-encoded soundtracks such as music can also be used with CMSS, but as with other matrix decoding technologies, the results will vary depending on the characteristics of the audio track itself.

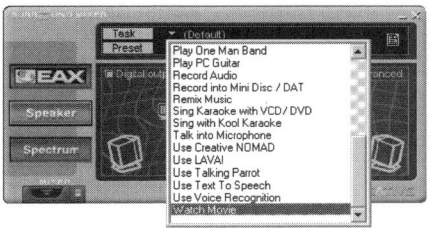 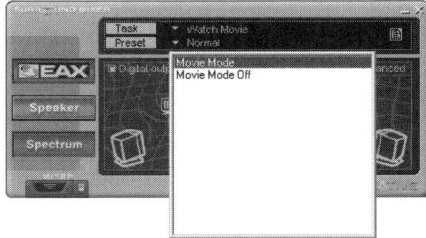

Figure 11.8: In the Surround Mixer, select Watch Movie in the task list, and in the preset list that pops up, select Movie Mode to turn on CMSS

Figure 11.9: To turn on CMSS in PlayCenter, change it to Player view and click the arrow to the left of the EAX logo to open the number pad. Click the small CMSS word below and select Stereo Enhancement Mode.

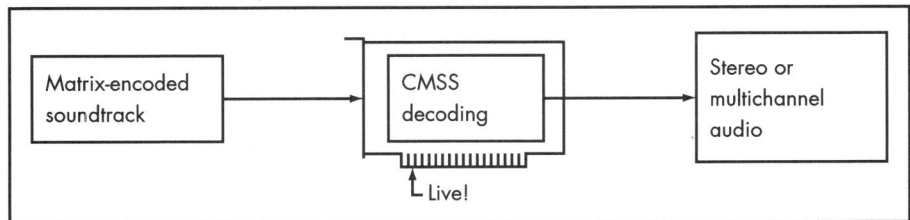

Figure 11.10: CMSS decoding is performed within the Live! and output to the connected speakers

Watching Movies **319**

> On early versions of the Live! drivers, CMSS may cause the rear speakers to be excessively loud and the surround sound to crackle. You can try using the front-rear balance slider in the mixer to correct this, but the best solution is to install the latest drivers.

CMSS automatically applies the decoding algorithm to any stereo sound that is playing through the Live! In 2 Speakers mode, it expands the stereo sound field to produce a surround effect with two channels. However, to obtain the most realistic surround playback with CMSS, you will need at least four-channel speakers. The rear-left and rear-right speakers will play the surround information that CMSS derives from the mixer's output. CMSS will include the center channel if a Live! 5.1 is set to 5.1 Speakers mode.

Table 11.3: CMSS Decoding for Matrix Surround Soundtracks

Sound Sources	Any stereo sound played through the mixer.
Speaker Modes	Any mode.
Speaker Types	Any speaker configuration.
	However, at least a four-channel configuration is recommended so that the surround speakers can provide the best effect. CMSS will accommodate a five-channel configuration and take into account the center speaker during decoding. Virtual surround will be used with the 2 Speakers and Headphones modes.
Other Requirements	None.
Software Settings	Use the Speaker window in the Surround Mixer or PlayCenter to turn on CMSS (also known as Movie mode in the Surround Mixer).
Connections	Speakers connected to the sound card.

Playing Digital Surround Soundtracks

DVDs are the most popular source of digital surround soundtracks, with all discs using the Dolby Digital format, and some titles featuring an alternate DTS soundtrack. A DVD is physically similar to a CD, but you can differentiate it by looking for the DVD logo printed on the label. The PC must have a DVD-ROM drive to be able to read a DVD. A software DVD player is also required, and it does the same things as a consumer DVD player: it reads the data on the DVD in the DVD-ROM drive, decodes the AC-3 or DTS audio and the MPEG-2 video, and sends the results to the video and sound cards.

> **TIP** *Make sure that you have DMA enabled for your DVD-ROM drive. (The Help file for the software DVD player will have instructions.) This will enable large chunks of data to be quickly transferred from the DVD-ROM drive to the DVD playback software without using too much CPU power, which can be put to better use to decode the video and audio. It will also prevent the audio from skipping, especially on PCs with slower CPUs.*

> DVDs can also include a standard uncompressed stereo PCM soundtrack like that of a CD. This soundtrack is uncompressed, unlike AC-3– or DTS-encoded material. Such soundtracks are more common for music DVDs, where sound quality and detail are of utmost importance.

Another less common source of Dolby Digital sound is AC-3 files. The Live! 5.1 driver CD comes with a few AC-3 files (with .ac3 file extensions) to showcase the Dolby Digital decoding abilities built into the driver. You can play them using PlayCenter or a DVD playback software. AC-3 files are not common and are seldom available on the Internet for download.

Here are three ways that digital surround soundtracks can be played on the Live!

External Decoding: S/PDIF Passthrough

S/PDIF passthrough sends compressed Dolby Digital or DTS signals directly to the digital outputs of the Live!, and therefore requires an external Dolby Digital or DTS decoder, which can be commonly found in home theater receivers and 5.1 multimedia speakers that has a decoder built in.

> Some 5.1 multimedia speakers do not have decoders built in and rely solely on the DVD playback software or sound cards like the Live! 5.1 to decode Dolby Digital. For such setups, use the other two decoding methods covered next.

For S/PDIF passthrough, the software DVD player puts the sound card into S/PDIF passthrough mode. As data is read from the DVD, the AC-3 or DTS soundtrack is transferred directly to the sound card's digital outputs without any processing or decoding. When S/PDIF passthrough is in effect, the digital outputs will no longer contain any of the other sound that is played through the mixer, because the software DVD player takes control of the digital output. (The analog outputs still play the sound from the mixer, but not the sound from the DVD.)

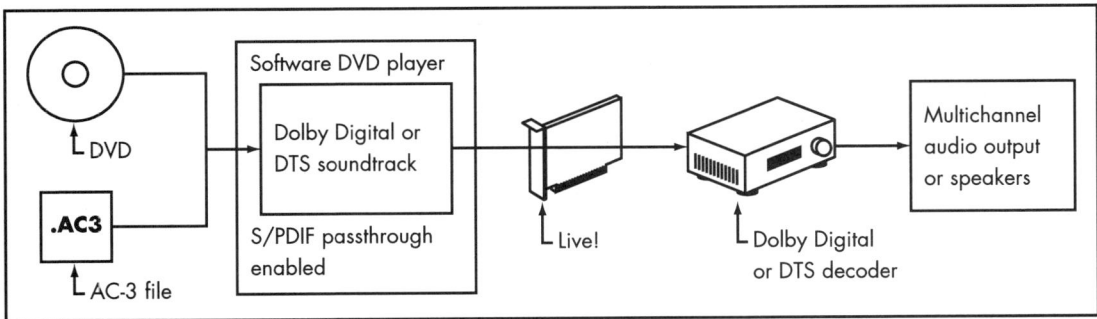

Figure 11.11: The Dolby Digital or DTS soundtrack passes through the sound card unaltered, to an external decoder

S/PDIF Passthrough with Digital DIN Speaker Systems

If you connect the Live! to a speaker system that has Digital DIN connectors, the front channels carried over the Digital DIN cable will be used to transport the digital surround soundtrack when S/PDIF passthrough is activated. As a result, the sound from the mixer will not play through the front speakers when passthrough is in effect.

Older Digital DIN speakers like the DTT2500 allow Dolby Digital signals only on their coaxial input and not on the Digital DIN input. The DTT2500 will ignore the digital soundtrack over its Digital DIN input. For such speakers, you will need to use a coaxial or optical cable to connect the speaker's Dolby Digital input to the digital output of a digital I/O device such as the Live!Drive.

On the other hand, newer Digital DIN speakers like the DTT3500 and the Inspire 5700 will detect a Dolby Digital or DTS signal over the Digital DIN cable and switch to the correct decoding mode. In this case, you do not need to connect another digital cable from the Live! to the decoder. Similarly, properly configured home theater receivers and decoders connected digitally to the Live! should be able to differentiate between a standard stereo signal and a surround-encoded signal and automatically switch to the correct decoding mode.

Driver Issues

S/PDIF passthrough is not a well-established standard and has a long history of problems arising from the combination of operating systems, software DVD players, and Creative's drivers. In fact, S/PDIF passthrough was not working correctly with the Windows 2000 Live! drivers until a year after the release of the Windows 2000 OS in February 2000. If you are running Windows 2000, be sure to install Service Pack 2 (SP2) or later because versions prior to SP2 do not support S/PDIF passthrough (even if the Live! drivers are the latest version).

Many older PCs with outdated drivers will experience problems such as lack of sound and unsynchronized or skipping sound and video. You can download Service Packs for Windows using the Windows Update service at http://windowsupdate.microsoft.com. Also download the latest drivers from Creative to ensure trouble-free operation.

Player Support

Not all software DVD players support S/PDIF passthrough, but many are beginning to regard this as an important feature. The two most popular players are PowerDVD (http://www.cyberlink.com.tw) and WinDVD (http://www.intervideo.com). In addition to S/PDIF passthrough support, they offer software decoding when an external decoder is not available. (See the next section, "Software Decoding.")

> A demo of PowerDVD is included in the CD-ROM. S/PDIF passthrough is functional in the demo version.

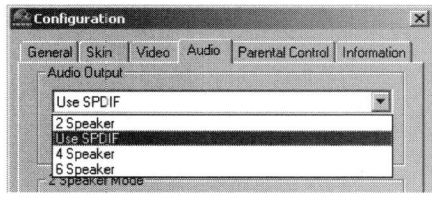 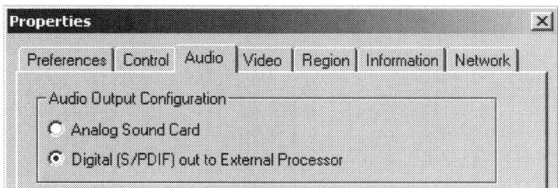

Figure 11.12: S/PDIF passthrough is enabled in PowerDVD by selecting the Use SPDIF option. In WinDVD, select the Digital (S/PDIF) out to External Processor option.

Table 11.4: S/PDIF Passthrough for Digital Surround Soundtracks

Sound Sources	DVDs with Dolby Digital or DTS soundtracks, or AC-3 (Dolby Digital) files.
Speaker Modes	Any mode. The setting does not matter because the mixer and speaker outputs are bypassed completely when S/PDIF passthrough is activated.
Speaker Types	**Home theater:** Typically, five speakers connected to a home theater receiver or amplifier. A subwoofer can be added for enhanced bass. **Multimedia speakers:** A 5.1 multimedia speaker system with a built-in Dolby Digital and/or DTS decoder.
Other Requirements	**Software:** A software DVD player that supports S/PDIF passthrough on the Live! **Digital outputs:** A digital I/O device such as the Live!Drive for digital output. The receiver must support the same digital input (either coaxial or optical). Alternatively, for newer Live! cards, you can use the mini-jack digital output to get a digital audio signal from the Live! (Before you proceed with this method, read the section titled "Obtaining a Digital Output" in Chapter 3, "The Sound Blaster Live! Hardware.") **Decoding support:** The sound system receiving the digital signal from the Live! must support Dolby Digital and/or DTS decoding.
Software Settings	**Software DVD player:** Set it to use S/PDIF passthrough. This setting is usually found in the Audio or Speakers section of the Configuration/Setup screen and is often marked S/PDIF Output. **Speaker settings:** For Live! 5.1 cards, do not enable the AC-3 Decode feature in the Advanced mixer settings window, or the drivers will intercept the passthrough signal and decode it instead of passing it unaltered to the digital output. **Mixer:** The Wave and master volume controls cannot be used to set the volume because the mixer is bypassed. Use the volume control on the decoder/receiver/amplifier.
Connections	**Coaxial Out:** Connect a coaxial cable from the digital I/O device to the decoder/receiver/amplifier. **Optical Out:** Connect an optical cable from the digital I/O device to the decoder/receiver/amplifier. **Newer Live! cards:** Use a mini-jack–to–RCA cable. Connect the mini-jack to the mini-jack digital output on the Live!'s backplate, and the white RCA plug to the coaxial input of the decoder/receiver/amplifier.

Software Decoding

Software decoding relies on the abilities of the DVD player software, which in turn uses the CPU to perform the actual decoding of sound that is obtained from the DVD. Software decoding works in a few ways, depending on the number of speakers the Live! is configured to use:

- The ability to convert from a 5.1 soundtrack to stereo is a basic and necessary requirement since sound cards primarily work with stereo sound sources.
- Because four-channel multimedia speakers are common in the PC world, software DVD players also need to decode and downmix a 5.1 soundtrack to four speakers. The center channel is mixed into the front-left and front-right speakers, and the .1 LFE channel is either discarded or mixed into the front speakers (depending on the particular software's implementation). The two front and two rear channels is then sent to the speakers.
- When coupled with a 5.1 sound card like the Live!, software decoding negates the need for a more costly external decoder or multimedia speaker with a decoding unit. The sound that goes out to the six-channel outputs of the sound card are already in 5.1.

TIP *With software decoding, the volume can be controlled in the mixer, unlike with S/PDIF passthrough.*

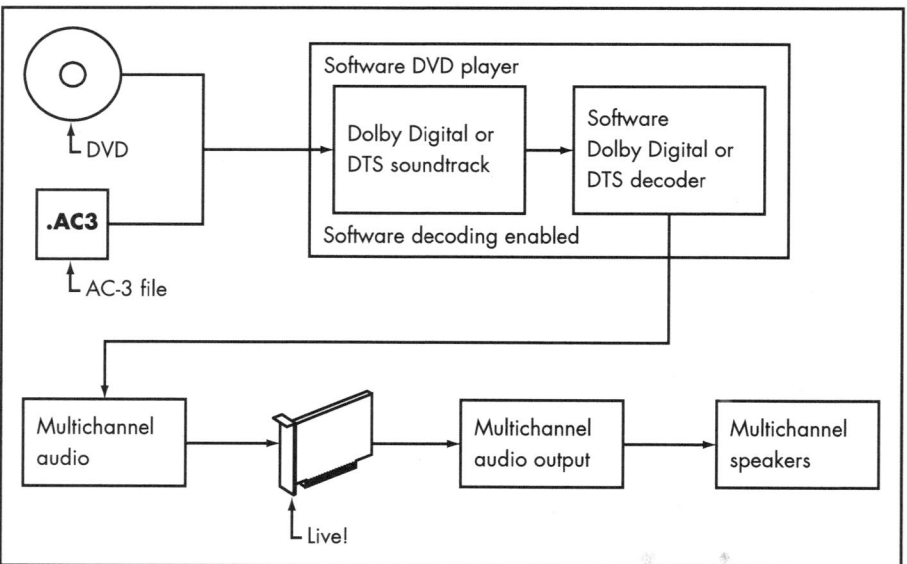

Figure 11.13: Software decoding relies on the CPU to decode Dolby Digital or DTS soundtracks and send the multichannel soundtrack to the Live!'s audio outputs

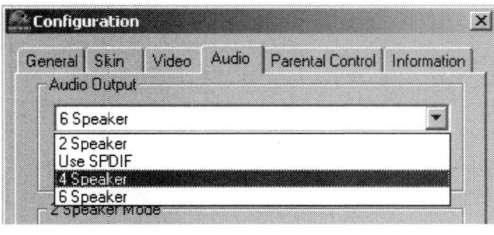 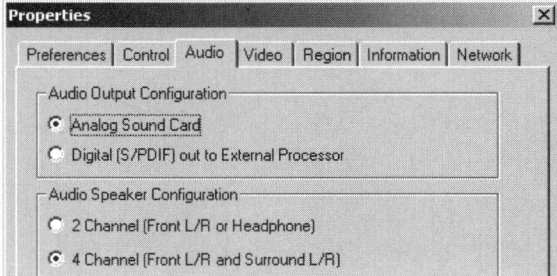

Figure 11.14: Software decoding can be enabled in PowerDVD by choosing the 2 Speaker, 4 Speaker, or 6 Speaker modes. In WinDVD, select the Analog Sound Card option and choose the number of speakers used.

Table 11.5: Software Decoding for Digital Surround Soundtracks

Sound Sources	DVDs with Dolby Digital or DTS soundtracks, or AC-3 (Dolby Digital) audio files.
Speaker Modes	2 Speaker, 4 Speaker, or 5.1 Speaker. (For Headphones, read the section "Headphones" later in this chapter.)
Speaker Types	**Home theater:** Connect the Live!'s 4 or 5.1 outputs to the discrete RCA inputs on the receiver. (Not all receivers have discrete 5.1 inputs.)
	Multimedia speakers: A multimedia speaker system with any number of speakers.
Other Requirements	**Software:** All software DVD players can downmix to stereo, but if you want to downmix to four speakers, check that the software supports four-channel downmixing with the Live!'s 4 Speaker mode. If you are using a Live! 5.1 with 5.1 speakers, check that the software has a 5.1 or six-channel setting.
Software Settings	**Software DVD player:** Set the player to the appropriate speaker mode, according to the Live!'s speaker setting (in the Speaker window of the Surround Mixer).
	Speaker settings: Set the speaker mode to correspond to the number of speakers that you are using. Use the 2 Speaker, 4 Speaker, or 5.1 Speaker mode. Do not use Live!Surround.
	Mixer: The Wave and master volume controls are functional, unlike with S/PDIF passthrough.
Connections	**Home theater:** Connect the Live!'s 4 or 5.1 outputs to the discrete inputs on the receiver. (Not all receivers have discrete 5.1 inputs.)
	Other speaker systems: Connect them to the outputs on the Live!

Each software DVD player may perform decoding and downmixing differently, and this affects the sound quality and positioning of audio among the speakers. In particular, the LFE channel could either be mixed into the main left and right channels (which is preferred), or be discarded entirely. If you use less than 5.1 speakers, poorly designed players may also discard the channels of the unavailable speakers, instead of playing them back in other available speakers.

An effective way to ensure that all channels are reproduced or downmixed correctly is to use a DVD test disc or the THX Optimode feature found on many

THX-certified DVD titles. They usually have a surround speaker test that plays noise or test sound pattern on each individual speaker in turn. By listening to such test sequences, you can check that all speaker channels are reproduced correctly and not discarded.

Many times, when the .1 LFE channel is tested, there is no rumbling bass sound at all, indicating that the LFE channel is discarded during downmixing. Look for a setting in the software DVD player to redirect the LFE channel to the front-left and front-right channels.

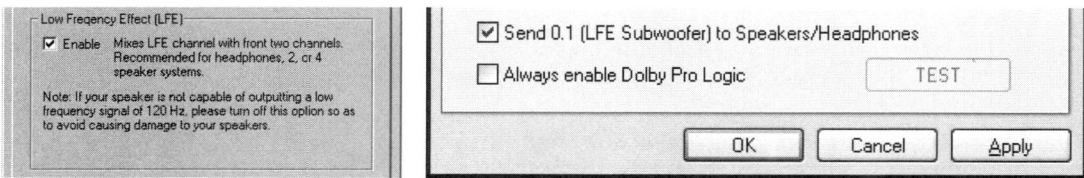

Figure 11.15: Redirecting the LFE channel to the main speakers in PowerDVD and WinDVD

Sound Card Decoding: Dolby Digital Decoding

Dolby Digital decoding is available only on the Live! 5.1 and not the first- and second-generation Live! cards. Contrary to popular belief, the decoding is actually performed by the CPU, and not by the EMU10K1 or a separate DSP on the Live! card. This makes it similar in concept to the decoding done by a software DVD player. The difference is that to use the built-in decoder on the Live! 5.1, the software DVD player has to be set to S/PDIF passthrough mode, as if it were supposed to send the surround soundtrack to an external decoder (as described earlier in the section "External Decoding: S/PDIF Passthrough").

> Most 5.1 sound cards that claim to support Dolby Digital decoding actually rely on software decoding in DVD playback software such as PowerDVD and WinDVD. Unlike the Live! 5.1, these sound cards do not have Dolby Digital decoders in the drivers.

The drivers will detect that the software DVD player is trying to open the digital output in S/PDIF passthrough mode and will jump into action and capture the sound and decode it. The CPU will perform the decoding, and the drivers will send the sound to the speakers. Any speaker mode can be used—the drivers will handle the downmixing.

> The Live! 5.1 cards do not support DTS decoding; therefore, you will need to rely on an external DTS decoder or a software DVD player with DTS decoding capability to carry out the decoding.

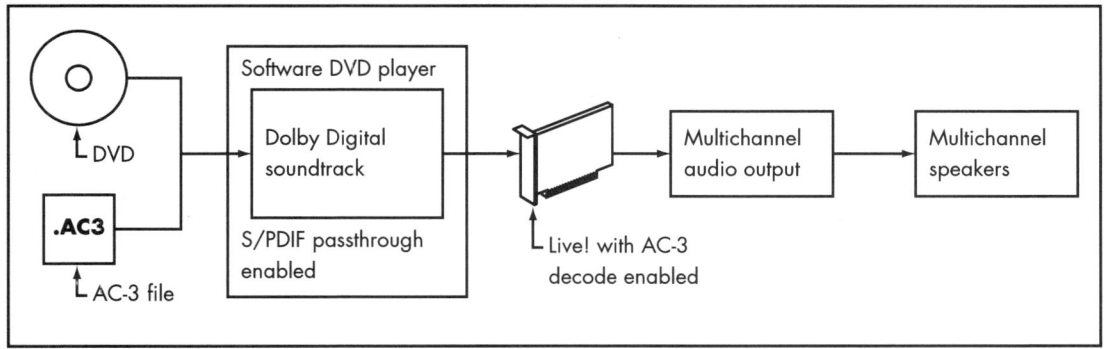

Figure 11.16: The Dolby Digital soundtrack from the DVD or AC-3 file is sent to the Live! for decoding

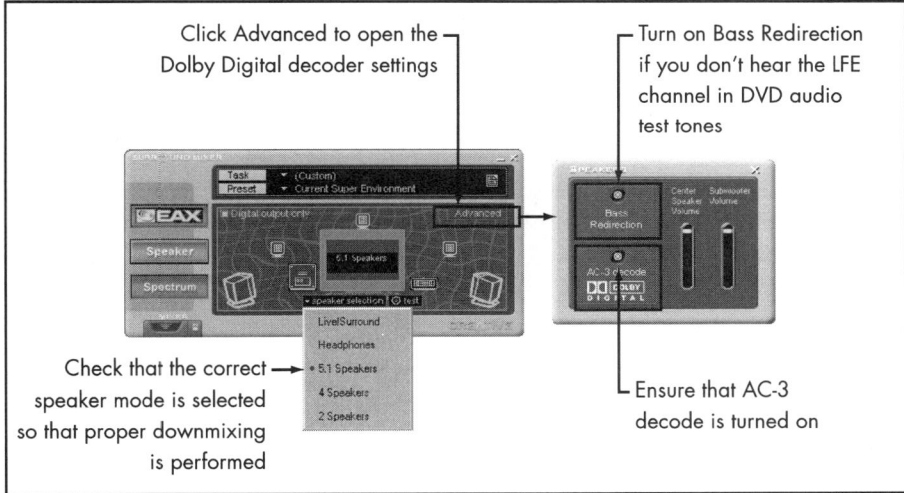

Figure 11.17: How to set AC-3 decoding in the Surround Mixer

> When you enable or disable AC-3 decoding on the Live! 5.1 while playing a DVD using S/PDIF passthrough, the changes will be effective only when the playback is stopped and started again or when the playback software is closed and restarted.

Some issues with the drivers and hardware prevent the Live! from obtaining compressed soundtracks (such as Dolby Digital) from the digital (coaxial or optical) inputs provided by digital I/O devices; therefore, you cannot use the Live! 5.1 as a Dolby Digital decoder. For instance, you cannot connect a consumer DVD player to the digital input on a Live!Drive and play Dolby Digital and DTS soundtracks because the digital inputs on the Live! recognize only the PCM stereo audio format (16 bits, up to a maximum of 48 kHz). The soundtracks must be from a source that is read by the PC, like a DVD in a DVD-ROM drive, or AC-3 files stored on the hard drive or CD-ROM, and played by media player software.

Table 11. 6: Sound Card Decoding for Digital Surround Soundtracks

Sound Sources	DVDs with Dolby Digital or DTS soundtracks, or AC-3 (Dolby Digital) files.
Speaker Modes	Any mode.
	If the 5.1 Speakers mode is not used, the Live! will downmix the soundtrack accordingly.
Speaker Types	**Home theater:** Connect the Live! 5.1's analog outputs to the six discrete inputs on the receiver. (Note that not all receivers have discrete 5.1 inputs.) When Dolby Digital decoding of the Live! 5.1 drivers is not used with the 5.1 Speakers mode, the drivers will discard the LFE channel.
	Multimedia speakers: A multimedia speaker system with any number of speakers.
Other Requirements	A software DVD player with S/PDIF passthrough support.
Software Settings	**Software DVD player:** Set the player to S/PDIF Output mode.
	Speaker settings: Set the mode to correspond to the number of speakers that you are using.
	When connecting to a home theater system's discrete 5.1 inputs, do not set the speaker mode to Live!Surround. Instead, use the 5.1 Speakers mode.
	Mixer: The Wave volume control does not work, but the master volume control can be used to regulate the volume.
Connections	**Home theater:** Connect the Live! 5.1's six analog outputs to the discrete inputs on the receiver. (Not all receivers have discrete 5.1 inputs. Sound card decoding cannot be used if the receiver does not have discrete 5.1 inputs.)
	Other speaker systems: Connect them to the outputs on the Live!

Choices, Choices!

There are obvious differences in the way matrix-encoded and digital soundtracks are played on the Live! Furthermore, there are different ways to play these two forms of surround, and it can be daunting task choosing a setup that's suitable. Let's work through the choices.

Matrix Surround Soundtracks

Matrix decoding of stereo sound sources requires either the use of an external decoding unit, like a Pro Logic AV receiver, or the CMSS (Movie Mode) available in the Live! drivers. For matrix surround-encoded sources like Dolby Surround soundtracks, the ideal choice is an external Dolby Surround Pro Logic decoder, or even better, a Pro Logic II decoder. These decoders require extra hardware, and if they are not available to you, the CMSS mode is a good compromise.

> If you are using a 5.1 speaker setup with a Live! 5.1, the CMSS mode is the only way to upmix stereo soundtracks to 5.1 in order for the center speaker to be used.

Digital Surround Soundtracks

Digital soundtracks have to be decoded, either by an external decoder or with the CPU (which is definitely more cost-effective). If you are one of the lucky people who have a home theater right beside your PC, you should definitely hook up the Live! to your AV receiver for some serious sound. Otherwise, a Live! paired with a four- or 5.1-channel multimedia speaker system and software decoding would be great for watching DVDs.

Live! 5.1 owners have another task: choosing between sound card decoding and software decoding. Both sound very close in quality so you will need to do some listening tests to find out what your ears prefer. A good way to decide is to play DVDs that you are familiar with, because you know how they should sound. Also, some software DVD players even come with DTS software decoding (usually the more costly versions), which is an added bonus because the Live! 5.1 cannot decode DTS soundtracks.

> If you set a software DVD player to S/PDIF passthrough mode and turn on AC-3 decode in the Live! 5.1 while playing back a DTS soundtrack, no sound will be heard. DTS DVDs also come with a Dolby Digital soundtrack for compatibility, so be sure to use the menus to choose the correct soundtrack.

Generally, hardware or external decoders have a slight edge over software implementations because of the higher-quality external DACs and dedicated DSPs. On the other hand, going the hardware route costs much more, even with multimedia speakers that have decoders; fortunately, the software route remains a good-quality solution.

Two or Four Speakers

Of course, 5.1 is the best configuration for movie surround, but your room layout and space may dictate a different sound system. Just two speakers are a little inadequate for the high-octane surround soundtracks in today's movies. Even when virtual surround is used to simulate the surround speakers with two speakers, most people do not find the results realistic.

Four speakers work much better. In a four-channel setup, the center speaker (used for dialogue localization) is missing, so the front-left and front-right speakers should be placed fairly close to one another to prevent a "hole in the middle" effect in the front soundstage. Try placing the speakers around four feet apart; do not place them too close together or the front soundstage will be compressed, making the sound seem more like mono.

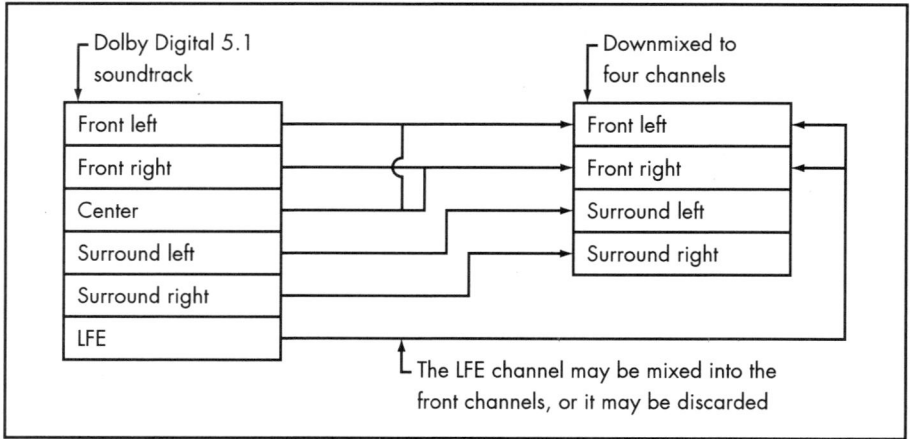

Figure 11.18: A 5.1-channel soundtrack is downmixed to a four-channel output by mixing the sound from the center and LFE channels to the front-left and front-right channels

Decoding matrix surround-encoded soundtracks with CMSS works with any speaker mode, as it is designed to adapt to the speaker configurations available with the Live! If you are using stereo speakers, virtual surround is used to give the illusion of more speakers. A four-channel setup has the benefit of the surround speakers, which can properly reproduce ambient and surround cues embedded in movie soundtracks.

For digital surround sources, automatic downmixing built in to software DVD players will be able to convert 5.1 soundtracks to stereo or four-speaker setups, as long as you have set the speaker mode correctly in the player's configuration (not forgetting the speaker configuration of the Live!, as well). Some software even comes with Dolby Headphone decoding, so that you can get a realistic surround experience from a standard two-driver headphones (described later). If you have a Live! 5.1 with a two or four speakers, you can also use the Dolby Digital decoder in the drivers, which will downmix the 5.1 soundtrack to your particular speaker configuration.

5.1 Multimedia Speaker Systems and Home Theater Receivers with Discrete 5.1 Inputs

A configuration using a 5.1 multimedia speaker system and home theater receiver with discrete 5.1 inputs works best with the Live! 5.1 cards, because you can individually send each of the six channels in a 5.1 configuration to the sound system. With such a setup, you can take maximum advantage of the built-in Dolby Digital decoding in the Live! 5.1 drivers. In addition, DTS decoding is now supported by some software DVD players, making decoding of high-quality DVD soundtracks possible at a low cost.

5.0 or 5.1 Home Theater or Multimedia Speakers with Dolby Digital or DTS Decoding

A sound system consisting of 5.0 or 5.1 home theater or multimedia speakers with Dolby Digital or DTS decoding will have a built-in decoder that will decode Dolby Digital or DTS signals from software players that have S/PDIF passthrough enabled. Home theater system speakers are typically more powerful than multimedia speakers and will give you a great movie experience, especially when the PC is connected to a screen or projector that takes advantage of the high-resolution (800 by 600 or higher) upscaling of DVDs by video cards.

Headphones

Headphones used to be a poor proposition for a satisfying surround sound experience, because the sound produced goes directly to your ears and gives you an

"in the head" experience, as if the sound is originating at the center your head. With advancements in digital signal processing, however, this now does not have to be the case. A particularly cost-effective and realistic solution is the Dolby Headphone technology supported by some software DVD players. This is a virtual audio algorithm that takes the individual channels decoded by Dolby Digital and places each of them "farther" from your head, as if the speakers were in a typical home theater arrangement. The "rooms" (that is, the presets) in Dolby Headphone can be changed. One of them is based on a typical film audio mixing soundstage used to create surround soundtracks, and works great for movies, while the other is optimized for music playback.

Dolby Headphone is one of the most realistic virtual surround implementations for movie viewing with headphones. However, if this is not available to you, the CMSS movie mode in the Live! is a compromise. It does not place the speakers farther away like Dolby Headphone, but it virtualizes the surround channel so that you actually hear audio cues that seem to come from behind.

TIP *Take care of your ears when watching movies with headphones, because the large dynamic range of movie soundtracks may cause you turn up the volume on softer scenes, but when loud sound effects are suddenly played, your ears may get hurt.*

To use Dolby Headphone, make sure you use 2 Speakers, 4 Speakers, or 5.1 Speakers mode. Do not use the Headphones and Live!Surround modes in the Speaker settings of the Surround Mixer, because these modify the Dolby Headphone signal produced by the software DVD player. (In fact, any sound that is played through the Live! in the Live!Surround or Headphones modes will be altered.)

On the other hand, if you want to use the drivers' CMSS to get virtual surround, you can also use the Headphones speaker mode. One of the speaker modes may sound better than the Headphones mode to you, so experiment with the modes while playing a surround soundtrack. In this case, the software DVD player should be set to downmix the soundtrack to a Dolby Surround–compatible stereo signal so that CMSS can decode it with greater accuracy.

PART FOUR
CREATING AUDIO

12

CREATING A MUSIC LIBRARY

Digital audio takes up a hefty amount of storage space. An eight-gigabyte hard drive can hold only about 12 to 15 audio CDs before it is full. Research into how we hear sound has led to the development of audio compression technologies like MP3 that can reduce digital audio to one-tenth its original size. Along with easy-to-use jukebox programs, you can compile digital music libraries and store them right on your PC! There are numerous advantages. You can:

- Have every album and song at your fingertips.
- Never again be confined to the track order of a CD.
- Easily mix and play music from different albums, artists, and musical styles.
- Get rid of the songs you dislike.
- Store different sequences of tracks in playlist files and retrieve them at any time.
- Spin your music like a pro, with crossfading, EQ, and other special audio effects.

You can regard a music library as a virtual CD jukebox with the capacity for hundreds and possibly thousands of CDs! Two important advances make this possible. The first is the decreasing price of mass storage media, like hard drives and writeable CDs. Just ten years ago, a one-gigabyte hard drive was unheard of in consumer PCs, but today, tens of gigabytes are the norm. With storage space so affordable, many music files can be stored and quickly retrieved with just a few mouse clicks.

The second advancement is audio compression.

Audio Compression

The most important technological advancement that contributed to the digital music boom is audio compression. Many compression formats and techniques are available, but the MP3 format is the most popular. Why is audio compression necessary? A minute of CD-quality stereo audio (at 16 bits, 44.1 kHz) consumes about 10 megabytes of storage space. Now consider downloading an entire album, which may be as large as 650 megabytes for 74 minutes of CD-quality audio!

Formats like ATRAC3, MP3, WMA, the open-source Ogg Vorbis, and even surround sound formats like AC-3 (used in Dolby Digital) and DTS, all rely on audio compression to keep file sizes down so that audio can be distributed and recorded on media with less space. *Psychoacoustics* (the scientific study of how sound is perceived) are used to make this compression effective. This spawned efficient compression technologies that rely on *perceptual coding*. When we know how we hear sound, we can take advantage of its properties to find out what we cannot hear and reduce the amount of data that is needed to represent an audio recording.

The amount of data is reduced by discarding some of the original audio information that is deemed to be insignificant to the human ear. The information that is removed cannot be retrieved again; therefore, this form of compression is generally known as *lossy compression*.

A few other uncommon audio compression formats exist that use *lossless compression*. Lossless compression is used for common file compression on computers: for instance, it is used in the popular Zip file format, where every single bit of data can be reconstructed from the compressed file. This form of compression, where no data is lost during the process, results in larger file sizes than lossy compression. Therefore, most audio compression formats use lossy compression to obtain the smallest possible file sizes.

Consider that uncompressed Wave audio (PCM) tries to capture and represent sound as accurately as possible, but audio compression tries to determine how it sounds to humans and then store only audio information that is absolutely necessary for it to sound good to the human ear. The following few sections discuss some commonly employed psychoacoustic properties.

Frequency Masking

As acute as our ears are, there are sounds that we simply cannot hear. A common hearing phenomenon that is used to compress audio is *frequency masking*. This phenomenon causes louder sounds of a particular frequency to mask softer sounds that are of the same frequency. Imagine that very noisy construction work is going on nearby while you are talking. The person next to you will barely hear you because the construction noise is much louder and masks your voice, because the noise also occurs in a frequency range similar to that of your voice. To make yourself heard, you can raise your voice until the vibrations in the air produced by your vocal cords are stronger than the sound waves from the construction site, and your friend can hear you once again.

Temporal Masking

Another property of human hearing is that the ears need a moment to recover after hearing a loud sound before they can hear a soft sound. For instance, when a very loud sound stops, it will be a few moments before the ears recover enough for you to hear a softer sound that has been there all the while. Audio compression removes the softer sounds that immediately follow a loud sound, thereby making the compressed file smaller.

Hearing Range

We all know that the human ear can typically pick up sound in the range 20 Hz to 20 kHz, so many audio compression formats discard audio data that is outside this range.

Sensitivity

The ear requires that sound be of certain loudness before it can be perceived. The loudness required differs over the human hearing range. Mid-frequency sounds, like voices, are easier to pick up when soft than a high-pitched sound at the same volume, which cannot be heard unless it is louder than the sensitivity limit of humans. Sensitivity level is the most common characteristic of human hearing used to compress audio because much of the audio data outside this sensitivity range can be discarded.

Stereo Encoding

For most music, the left and right channels play sound with few differences. This gives audio compression another way to remove unnecessary information: by representing sounds that occur on both the left and right speakers only once. The other alternative is to use simple stereo encoding, where the left and right channels are compressed and stored individually.

Codecs

Compression and decompression algorithms are commonly based on psycho-acoustic models and can be converted to software code and implemented in a *codec* (which stands for coder/decoder). The software code runs on the CPU and allows creation and playback of compressed audio files. The codec can also be embedded in hardware, like a dedicated DSP chip in a portable MP3 recorder and player. For every compression format that you want to play with your software or hardware player, the particular codec should be supported. Most software and media players can be upgraded with new codecs downloaded from the Internet, but hardware players are generally limited to the formats they are advertised to work with.

> The coding/compression process requires significantly more CPU processing power than the decoding process.

The coder is used only once — by the person who compresses the file for distribution — while the decoder is used by everybody who receives the file and wants to play it back. When the compressed sound file is played, the decoder will process the compressed data to re-create the audio. The resulting output from the decoder is a digital audio format that the sound card can recognize, which is typically standard PCM Wave audio supported by all sound cards.

> Some audio players, like Winamp, use their own codecs, while many others rely on the codecs installed in Windows to play compressed audio (and video, as well). You can determine the codecs installed in your PC by checking the Sounds/Multimedia settings in Windows Control Panel.

> Codecs for a particular compression standard — for example, MP3 — can be produced by many developers. The method used to encode and decode the audio may vary, but the resulting compressed file will adhere to the compression standard. This provides room for developers to improve the sound quality of their encoding and decoding techniques while retaining the format of the file so that it can work on existing players.

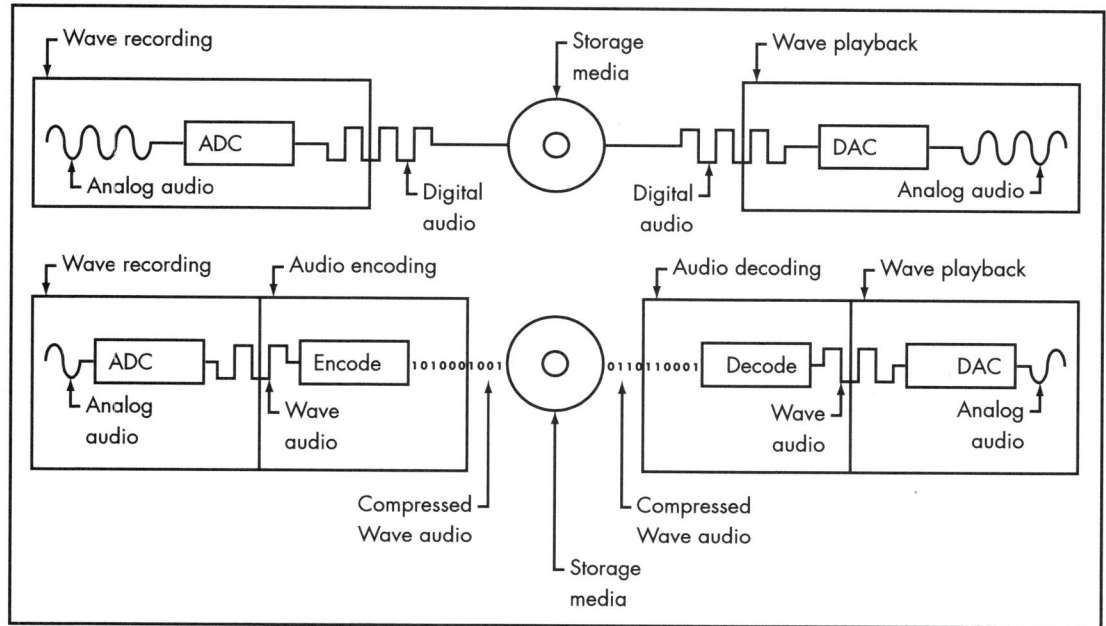

Figure 12.1: Compared to recording and playback of uncompressed PCM Wave audio, compressed audio requires an extra encode stage when creating the media file, and the decode stage is performed each time the compressed file is played back

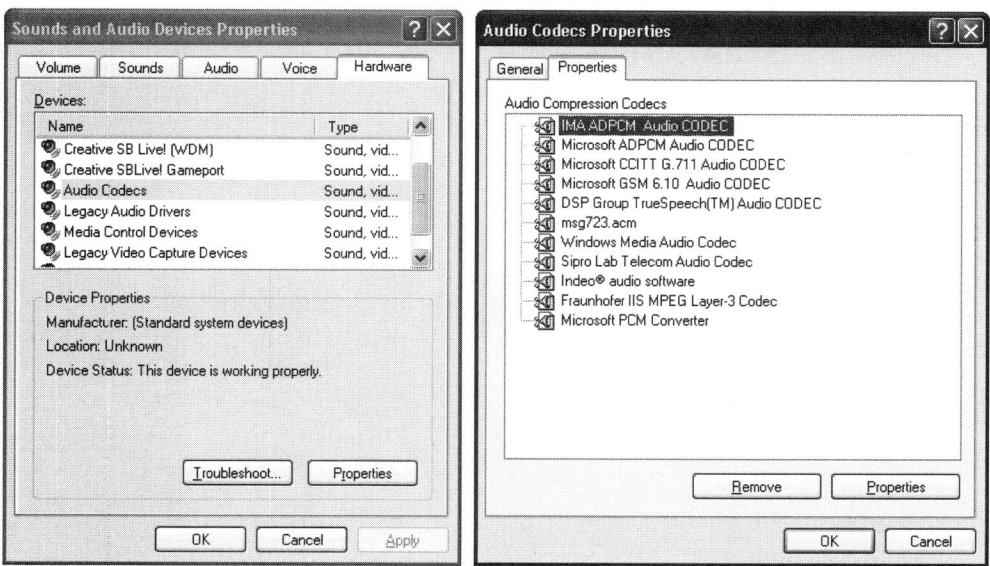

Figure 12.2: Highlight "Audio Codecs" and click the Properties button to see the list of audio codecs installed in Windows

The MP3 Phenomenon

Although there were many compression standards before, MP3 was the audio format to gain wide acceptance and popularity because it allows audio files to be squeezed down to very manageable sizes, and at the same time keeps the audio quality close to the original. In 1998, the small file sizes produced by MP3 caught the attention of many users who wanted to exchange music through their bandwidth-limited Internet service providers (ISPs) and modems. This led to the explosion of MP3-trading and file-sharing networks that are common today.

Consumer electronic manufacturers also jumped on the bandwagon and introduced many devices with MP3 playback capability, especially for portable audio devices. Tiny portable MP3 players using flash memory are now favorites on many shopping lists. Portable CD players are enhanced to play MP3 files written on CD-R and CD-RW discs, while those looking to carry an entire music library in their pockets can buy portable players that use multi-gigabyte hard drives originally meant for notebook computers. Home deck-sized audio players with hard drives and CD-ROM drives can also be found, and some car CD players and changers also have MP3 playback capability.

> **What's Legal?**
> MP3s aren't illegal, although there are some companies with certain commercial interests that would rather have you believe that the very existence of MP3 is illegal. Under most copyright laws around the world, you have every right to make copies of purchased CDs, albums, and other recordings for personal use. Even then, the recording industry is now exploring ways to stop consumers from obtaining music directly from audio CDs and preventing them from working on CD-ROM drives in computers. You should be aware that distributing or selling copyrighted works to others is not legal in most parts of the world.

The MP3 Standard

The popular MP3 codec is an abbreviation of MPEG Audio Layer 3 (and not MPEG-3, as it is often mistakenly called) and is designed to be used as soundtracks for video compressed with MPEG-1 and MPEG-2. The Motion Picture Experts Group (MPEG) defines audio and video compression standards that are widely adopted by the industry. The processes are divided into phases, with different target applications. The MPEG-1 phase, completed in 1992, has been widely adopted in digital video and Video CD formats, among many others. The more complex MPEG-2 is used in DVDs and other digital video formats, including satellite TV broadcasts, and MPEG-4 is quickly gaining acceptance as a low-bandwidth compression format for smaller devices such as PDAs and mobile phones, and for streaming video over the Internet.

> A new MP3 Pro format was introduced in 2001. It has backward compatibility with MP3 and higher compression ratios. However, it has yet to gain wide acceptance.

MPEG audio is also separated into three layers, known simply as Layer 1, Layer 2, and Layer 3. As the layer number increases, the complexity of the encoder and decoder increases, and the resulting sound quality will also be improved. A higher layer will also provide more compression, resulting in a smaller sound file. Hence, a Layer 1 audio file will be larger than a Layer 3 file of the same playback duration, since the encoder is less complex, making it compress faster but also perform less processing, resulting in less data being discarded, or compressed, and consequently, a larger sound file. Layer 3 is the best audio coding scheme and is used to create MP3 files. It makes use of the psychoacoustic properties described earlier and adds a few other tricks to keep the audio size down while retaining a large measure of the audio quality of the original file.

> For backward compatibility, higher-layer decoders have to support playback of audio encoded using lower layers. Thus, an MP3 player should also be able to decode Layer 1 and Layer 2 audio.

When creating MP3s, several factors and settings can be modified to obtain the desired trade-off between file size and sound quality. Among these are sample rate, bit rate, and joint stereo.

Sample Rate

MP3s can be created at sample rates of 48 kHz, 44.1 kHz, and 32 kHz. You should normally compress MP3s at 44.1 kHz, as this will retain most of the quality of CD audio. 48 kHz can be used for sound sources that are at 48 kHz, like DAT recordings. The 32-kHz rate can be used when file size has to be kept to a minimum, for example, to be transferred to a portable MP3 player with limited memory capacity or streamed over the Internet, or when the sound source does not require CD quality, as with voice recordings.

Bit Rate

The bit rate determines how much data is used to represent every second of audio. If fewer bits are allocated, less data is used to represent the sound, and the resulting MP3 will be lower in quality, especially the high-frequency components like cymbals and hi-hats. Typical MP3 bit rates range from 32 kilobits per second (kbps) to 320 kbps. Because the bit rate allocated to represent every second of audio is the same throughout the MP3 file, this type of bit rate allocation is commonly known as constant bit rate (CBR) allocation.

> A byte of data equals 8 bits.

> The general consensus is that a higher compression rate, resulting in a lower bit rate, will sound worse than audio with a higher bit rate.

To keep file sizes small but still get good CD-quality MP3 audio, compress at 128 kbps. Some of the nuances of the original sound may be lost, especially at the higher frequencies, but the file will remain close to the original. The quality can be improved by moving up to 160 kbps or 192 kbps. Many users regard 192 kbps as the "sweet spot" between file size and sound quality. If you want minimal loss of quality from the original, consider using 256 kbps or 320 kbps. Properly encoded MP3 files with compressions rates higher than 256 kbps are very close to CD quality, making them suitable for good CDs that you would like to keep at the highest quality.

TIP *If you are encoding audio for streaming over the Internet, do consider your potential audience. Many users may be on 56-kbps modems, so sound quality has to be sacrificed to reduce the bit rate to, for example, 30 kbps. And most 56-kbps modems don't run at the maximum of 56 kbps because of overhead, noise, and attenuation in the phone lines and potential slowdown from traffic on the Internet.*

Many encoders also support an extension to the MP3 standard known as variable bit rate (VBR). Instead of fixing each second of audio at a certain bit rate, the rate fluctuates, with different bit rates used depending on the complexity of the sound at each short interval. How does this work? When compressing Wave audio to MP3, the encoder has the opportunity to evaluate the audio. It uses certain pre-programmed techniques to determine the complexity of an audio passage at a point in time and allocates the bit rate necessary to adequately represent that sound.

TIP *Be sure to check the documentation of your hardware or software MP3 player before building your music library, because some players do not support VBR correctly. Some poorly implemented players that do play VBR files may have erratic time displays that jump about instead of steadily incrementing the time every second.*

A relatively simple passage, such as a prolonged bass sound with a consistent waveform, can be represented with less data, so the encoder may use only 32 kbps for the few seconds when the bass sound is playing alone. However, when the track gets busy, and more complex audio and high-frequency information is present all at once — for example, cymbal crashes and complex orchestral passages — more information is necessary to represent that portion accurately, so the encoder may switch to 192 kbps or higher.

> In addition to MP3, many other compression standards use VBR, although CBR is still dominant.

In most cases, VBR (as compared to CBR) will be able to further reduce the file size of an MP3 soundtrack, while preserving audio quality. Most encoders use a percentage slider to determine how generous to be when allocating the bit rate. Set the slider to the maximum, and you may find that the encoder will often use 256 kbps and 320 kbps for complex audio passages. Set it lower, and the encoder may use only 128 kbps for complex audio passages, while trying its best to allocate a lower bit rate for less complex audio to minimize the file size. Unlike with CBR, the encoder has no way to determine the bit rate it will use for the entire soundtrack until it has evaluated it during encoding, so the resulting file size cannot be known beforehand.

Joint Stereo

The size of audio files typically doubles when going from mono to stereo when other parameters (particularly the bit rate and sample rate) remain the same, because two channels of audio (instead of one) have to be individually recorded. But MP3's Joint Stereo encoding alleviates this burden somewhat. At bit rates at and below 160 kbps, turning on Joint Stereo in the settings of your encoder will result in the best sound quality. Sound that occurs on both the left and right speakers will be encoded only once, and the extra bits saved can be used to represent other, more significant information that helps increase the sound quality of the compressed audio. At 192 kbps and higher, Joint Stereo has less of an impact on the sound quality, because the allocated bits are sufficient for normal stereo encoding. Nevertheless, some listening tests have also shown that Joint Stereo can still benefit higher bit rate recordings, depending on the characteristics of the tracks and the capability of the encoding software.

Audio Sample

CD Folder: Chapter 12 - Creating a Music Library
Files: 128 kbps Joint Stereo.mp3 and **128 kbps without Joint Stereo.mp3**
Compare the two audio files both encoded at 128 kbps, but one with Joint Stereo and one without.

> **Recompression**
> Although a well-compressed audio file can be barely discernible from the original, some data is always discarded in the process because MP3 compression is lossy. If you decode and recompress an audio file many times, some audio artifacts may become evident. To illustrate this, we have compressed a piece of music. Most people doing digital audio work use uncompressed Wave files to edit and archive digital audio. They convert these files to MP3 only after the final version is produced.

Audio Sample

CD Folder: Chapter 12 - Creating a Music Library
File: Re-encode.mp3
This track was re-encoded 18 times from the original, using 128 kbps and Joint Stereo. You can clearly hear the audio artifacts once too much data is discarded by a lossy encoding process. If you're interested, you can look in the **Re-encode - Intermediate Tracks** subdirectory for the intermediate tracks that were created during the re-encoding process.

Audio Software: PlayCenter and Winamp

PlayCenter is Creative's do-it-all audio playback and jukebox application that was created and introduced with the Live! cards. It has many features:

- Playback of various audio formats such as MP3, Wave, and WMA files and audio CDs.
- Time scaling to speed up or slow down the audio without affecting the pitch.
- Quick access to EAX presets.
- Features to quickly copy and compress CDs to MP3 and WMA formats.
- Support for MP3 encoding up to bit rates of 320 kbps, including VBR encoding.
- Playback of video files, VCDs, and DVDs (this feature can be used with the time-scaling feature).
- Easy playback of MIDI files with SoundFonts. If a SoundFont has the same file name as a MIDI file, PlayCenter will automatically load the SoundFont before playing the MIDI file.
- Integration with Nomad portable MP3 players. When the Nomad product line was launched, PlayCenter was upgraded to provide capabilities to rip and transfer audio to and from these devices.
- With the Live! 5.1, the ability to use the built-in Dolby Digital decoding feature to play back AC-3–encoded 5.1 surround audio files.

> PlayCenter for the Live! cards is currently at version 2.50 (at the time of writing). If you have an older version, request the latest version from Creative. If you have Windows XP, remember to patch PlayCenter to the latest version, there are some reported compatibility issues.

Nullsoft's Winamp is the Internet's most popular MP3 player and is consistently being updated and tweaked. It has been a favorite for many users because of its simple and effective user interface and snappy load times, especially compared to the more cumbersome and feature-loaded jukebox programs.

Figure 12.3: The full-featured Jukebox view and smaller Player view available in PlayCenter

Winamp is a player and does not support MP3 ripping and recording features found in full-featured jukebox programs. However, it does have many other features:

- A plug-in architecture to allow new playback, sound effects, and equalization features to be added to the player.
- Support for additional audio formats such as MIDI, MODule, WMA, and Wave. Support for new audio formats can be easily added by downloading a codec.
- Support for visualization plug-ins to allow graphics to dance with the music.
- Downloadable skins to change the look of the player.

Figure 12.4: Winamp is made up of a main window, the playlist window, the equalizer window, and the browser window

Creating a Music Library **345**

> We have included Quintessential Player (QCD), another popular media player. It has an excellent audio CD playback with CDDB integration, plays many popular audio formats, and even supports the same plug-ins that Winamp uses. Download the latest version from http://www.quinnware.com.

Ripping CDs

You probably have many audio CDs in your collection. Good news! CDs are the easiest and most convenient way of getting music into your PC in all its pristine digital quality. All you need is software capable of digitally transferring audio CDs to computer files and a CD-ROM, DVD-ROM, or CD-RW drive. This procedure is commonly known as *ripping*. The technical term for this procedure is *DAE*, which stands for *digital audio extraction*.

The software will put the drive into DAE mode, read the audio track digitally, and write it to an equivalent PCM Wave format on the hard drive. Because CDs are 16-bit, 44.1-kHz media, the resulting Wave files from a DAE operation will also have the same bit rate and sample rate. Once you obtain the Wave files, you can encode them to MP3 or any other format, or even edit them using Wave editors such as SoundForge before encoding them. (Chapter 13, "Recording Audio," covers recording and editing Wave audio in more detail.)

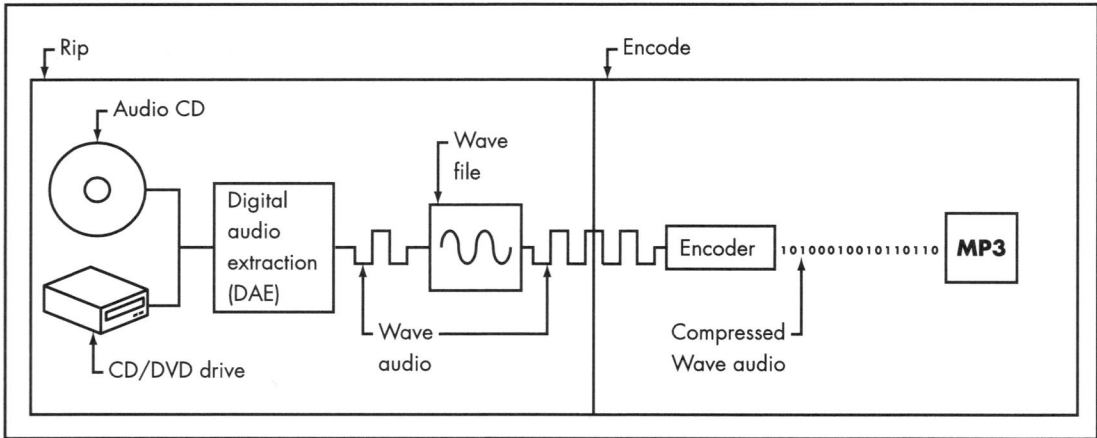

Figure 12.5: The steps needed to rip and encode an audio CD to a compressed audio file like MP3

> **TIP** *Register with CDDB and configure PlayCenter so that it automatically logs on to the CDDB database on the Internet to retrieve the correct album title, artist, and track names for the CD. If the CD is not commercially available and is custom made, the track names will not be found.*

Many CD ripping and jukebox applications, such as PlayCenter, can perform the rip-and-encode process all in one step. All you have to do is to select the audio CD tracks that you want to convert to MP3 or WMA, and PlayCenter will do the job automatically and add the tracks to your music library. You can rip from a CD in the background while other media files are playing.

The speed of the ripping stage depends largely on the DAE capability of your optical drive. Most drives can rip an entire 74-minute audio CD in less than 10 minutes. But if the drive is faulty or has poor DAE support, clicks and other audio artifacts may appear in the output Wave files. If this occurs, try lowering the DAE speed or turn on error correction in the configuration of the ripping software.

> **TIP** *Exact Audio Copy (http://www.exactaudiocopy.de) is widely regarded as one of the best CD audio extraction tools. Its features and advanced error correction capabilities ensure that the resulting audio is free of noise.*

> The music industry has started to introduce protected discs that exploit the differences between optical drives used in PCs and consumer audio CD players. Audio extracted from these protected CDs will produce static and noise that may damage speakers if played too loud. However, when these discs are played back on standard CD players, they work fine. You will not be able to rip or transfer the music from such discs to a portable MP3 player.

The speed of the encoder depends on how the encoder is configured. Some encoders can be configured to encode in high-quality mode, and the process will take more time. The speed of the CPU is the most important factor in determining encoding speed. A faster CPU will encode MP3s faster.

Other Ways to Get Audio

Besides ripping music from CDs, you can get audio from any other source and add it to your music library. Here are some ways:

- Use file-sharing applications like those that use the Gnutella or Direct Connect networks. These applications let you connect, search, and share files with all other users who are on the same network.
- Visit Web sites such as MP3.com that host music from independent artists.
- Some online stores, music sites, and record labels occasionally offer downloadable previews of current or upcoming releases, although many only sell formats that prevent you from using it on another PC or writing it to a CD.
- Use PlayCenter to record MIDI files as MP3s.
- Use a sequencer or DJ application to create your own music mixes and save them as MP3s.
- Record from cassette tapes or LPs to Wave files and use an encoder to compress the audio files for digital archiving.

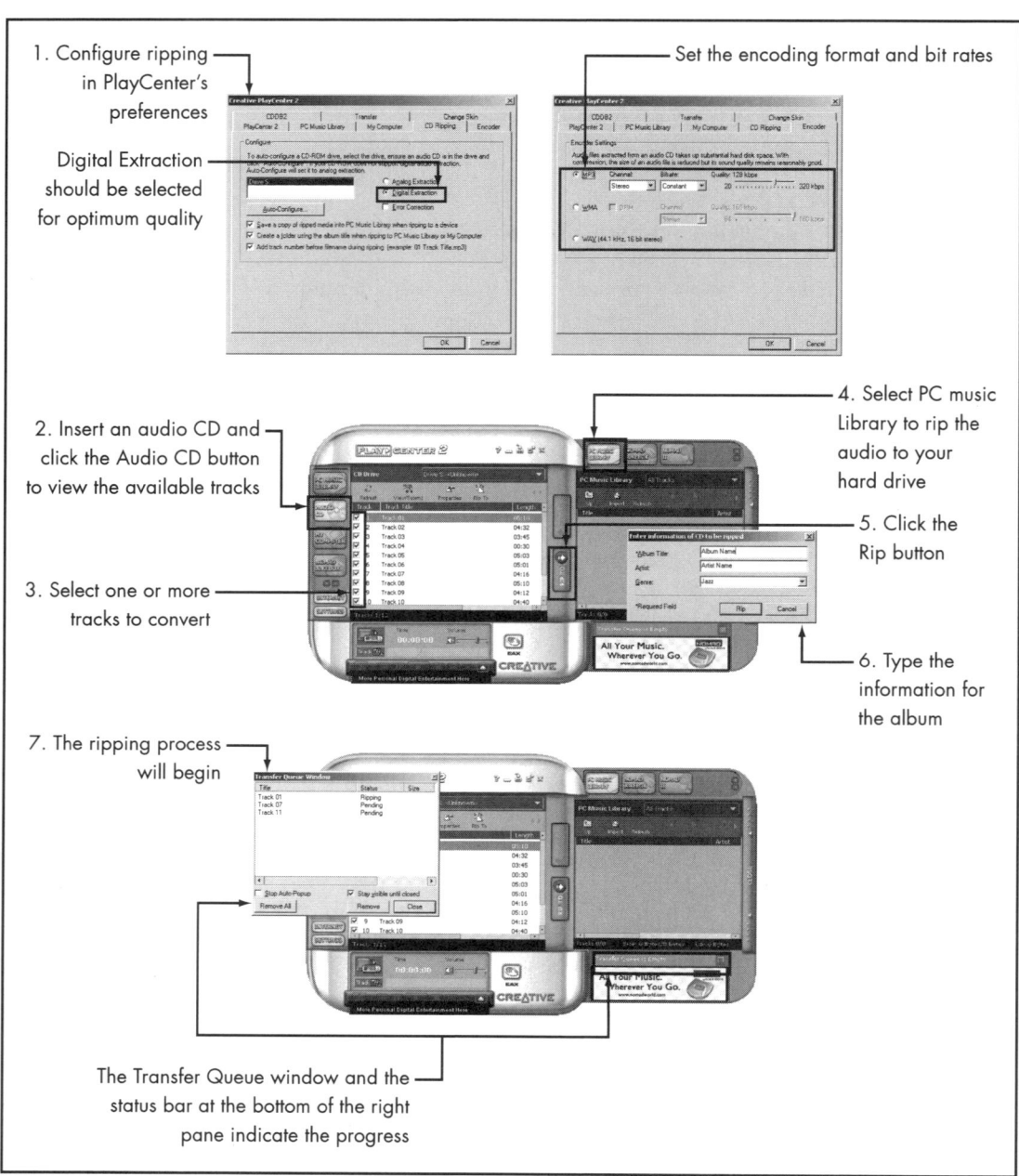

Figure 12.6: Using PlayCenter to rip an audio CD

Chapter 13, "Recording Audio," covers digital audio recording in greater detail.

Recording with PlayCenter

With PlayCenter, you can also record MP3 and WMA files from audio files and CDs. To do this, navigate to the desired playlist, album, artist, genre, or folder that has the track you want to record. You can also switch among PC Music Library, Audio CD, and My Computer to find the track that you want to record. Once this is done, there are a few ways to begin recording:

- To record the entire track from start to finish, click the Record button, and the recording will start automatically. (The playback of the file will be triggered automatically.)
- To record part of a track, play the track and quickly click the Record button when playback reaches the portion that you want to record.

When the track ends, the recording will stop, and PlayCenter will prompt you for a name to store the audio file. It will be found in the Recordings subfolder of the configured Media Folder that PlayCenter uses to store all audio files (usually C:\Media\Music). You can stop the recording before the track ends by clicking the Stop button.

> When the record feature is used on an audio CD track, PlayCenter will not perform direct ripping of CD audio to MP3 files. Instead, PlayCenter will play the track in real time and record it again, which may result in loss of audio quality. Use this method for CD audio tracks only when you want to add EAX to MP3 files; otherwise, use the rip option for the most accurate conversion.

> PlayCenter switches the Live!'s record source (in the mixer) to What-U-Hear mode when it starts to record and changes back to the previous setting when recording is complete. Make sure that the volume of your What-U-Hear slider is loud enough, or the resulting audio file may be too soft. If any other sound plays during the recording, it will be included, so ensure that no background applications or instant messengers are running.

If an EAX preset is enabled or changed before or during recording, it will also be present in the final recording. Remember to turn off EAX when recording a file that already has EAX added to it, or two effects will be layered, resulting in excessive reverberation.

Tweaking the Audio

Audio players provide many options for tweaking and modifying the audio to suit your listening equipment and audio source. Some of the more common types of effects are discussed here.

Equalization

Equalization is commonly used for earphones. Because earphones are usually very poor in bass, nearly every portable player has an enhanced bass option to boost the lower frequencies to adequate levels discernible with an earphone. Most portable players also have fixed equalization presets that boost different frequency ranges, and these presets are commonly named Jazz, Rock, and Pop.

Unlike the fixed equalization features found in many portable consumer audio players, software equalizers go one step further by dividing the frequency range into different bands and allowing increasing or decreasing of volume within each band. With this finer control, you can slowly tweak the equalization to compensate for limitations in the playback equipment, resulting in a more pleasing and fuller sound that is closer to your liking. Most media players also include several presets and allow you to save the current settings to new presets so that they can be easily recalled later.

> PlayCenter does not have an equalizer.

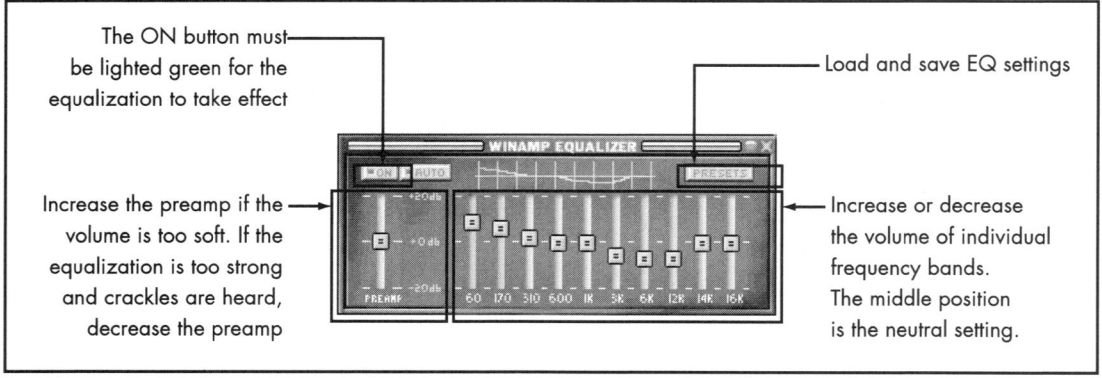

Figure 12.7: Winamp's graphic equalizer allows you to increase or decrease the volume of various frequency bands

TIP *If a media player has an equalizer, the settings will most likely affect only the audio that is produced by the media player itself, and not any other sound that happens to be playing through the sound card at the same time. The only equalization settings that affect all sound output are those that are set in the sound card's mixer, including bass and treble controls (and also the EAX presets).*

Plug-ins

Winamp is designed with a plug-in architecture so that the audio that is being played back can be piped through an input, output, or DSP/Effect plug-in for further processing and modification. Visualization plug-ins add new graphical effects to the player, and some even use 3D acceleration in video cards. Every imaginable plug-in that alters the behavior and sound in Winamp can be found on Winamp.com. You can find tools to add virtual surround to playback, equalize and clean up the sound, crossfade tracks like what radio stations and DJs do, and even run several plug-ins at the same time.

Time Scaling

PlayCenter has a very useful feature that can speed up or slow down audio (and even video) files from two to six times the normal playback speed. Normally when a file is speeded up or slowed down, the pitch of the sound also increases or decreases, making it difficult to listen to. Using the EMU10K1, the Live! can adjust the pitch up or down in tandem with the change in playback speed so that the original pitch is preserved.

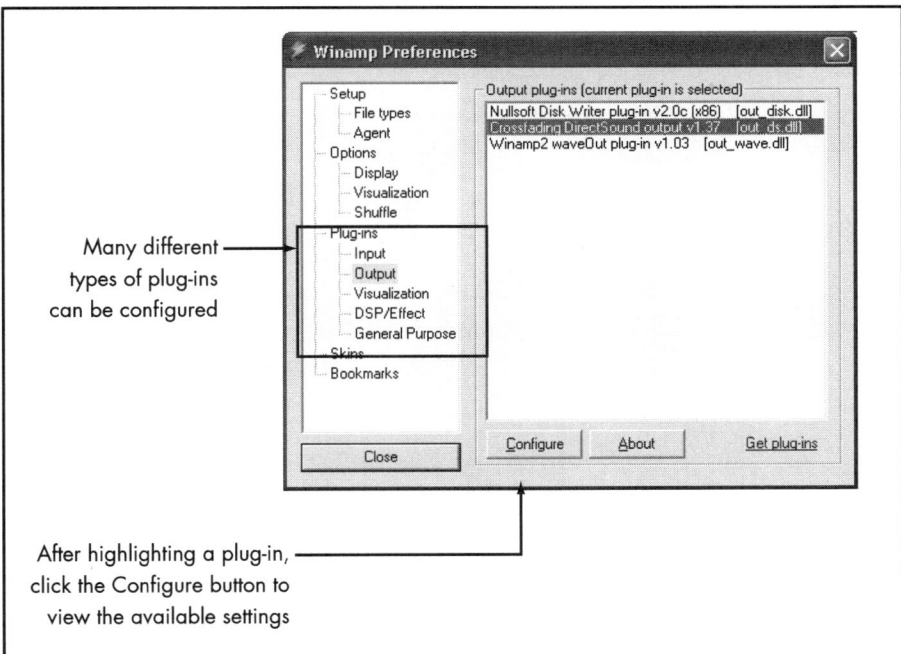

Figure 12.8: Changing plug-ins in Winamp Preferences

Creating a Music Library **351**

> Time scaling was not in the very early versions of PlayCenter, so if you have a very early first-generation Live! card with very old Live!Ware drivers, do remember to update to the latest version.

Organizing Your Music

The possibility of storing thousands of small audio files in large storage devices has introduced an interesting problem: how can we organize and quickly access the music we want, with minimal mouse clicks and agony?

The easiest way is to mirror the real world by storing individual albums and CDs in folders. With all music in one central location, jukebox applications like PlayCenter, (and even some hardware MP3 players) exploit this organization by allowing categorization and searching of audio tracks by criteria such as artist name and musical genre. You can:

- Rearrange and shuffle tracks from various artists and albums.
- Play and shuffle all the songs of a particular artist from one or all of that artist's albums.
- Select and play tracks that belong to a particular musical style to flow with your mood.

Other possibilities abound; you are limited only by the capability of the playback software!

Organizing with PlayCenter

PlayCenter lets you build a music library within the Media folder that you specified in the configuration. All files that are in the music library can be found within the subfolders of the Media folder. You can also add audio files located elsewhere as part of the audio library.

When songs are recorded or ripped from CDs, they will be automatically stored in the Media folder. You can also configure PlayCenter to automatically create a folder with the name of the album being copied. By using the information obtained from the MP3 tracks in the library, PlayCenter will automatically categorize the files by artist and genre. The drop-down menu at the top offers three ways of viewing the music library: by album, artist, or genre or as a list of all the tracks in the library.

PlayCenter also provides a simple playlist feature that lets you add, remove, and rearrange files. You can also drag individual tracks or use the Shift-Up Arrow and Shift-Down Arrow keys to rearrange the order of the tracks. Files in a playlist can be from different albums, but the file must already be in an album before it can be added to a playlist. Use the Import button to add files to the music library.

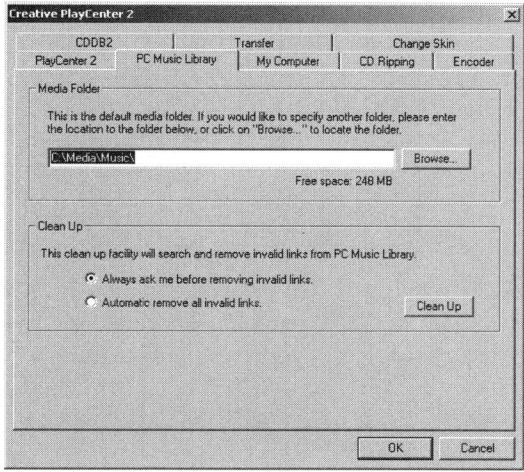

Figure 12.9: The PC Music Library tab of PlayCenter's Preferences allows you to set the location of the Media folder

Winamp's Playlist

Winamp is a simpler application than PlayCenter and does not keep track of your libraries automatically or bind you to a particular music library and folder. In its place is a simple playlist management feature that allows you to add and rearrange music files in any arbitrary order. After this is done, you can save the playlists to any location on the hard drive and recall them later. You can also quickly load Winamp and begin playing the songs on the playlist by double-clicking the playlist in Windows Explorer.

TIP *Playlists store links or references to the music files, so if you move some of the files around, you will have to remove the file from the playlist and add it again. Unlike Winamp, Play-Center stores its playlists internally. Changes are automatically saved without any intervention.*

More Tips

As you get familiar with your favorite media player and jukebox applications, you will be able to navigate your ever-growing digital music library with ease, and drag and drop will help you move and play files quickly. You may also want to copy or back up your music to other forms of storage media.

Drag and Drop!

Dragging and dropping is a very efficient way to get things done quickly. To play an audio track, simply drag the file from a Windows Explorer window or the desktop and release the mouse button when the cursor is within the window of a media

Creating a Music Library **353**

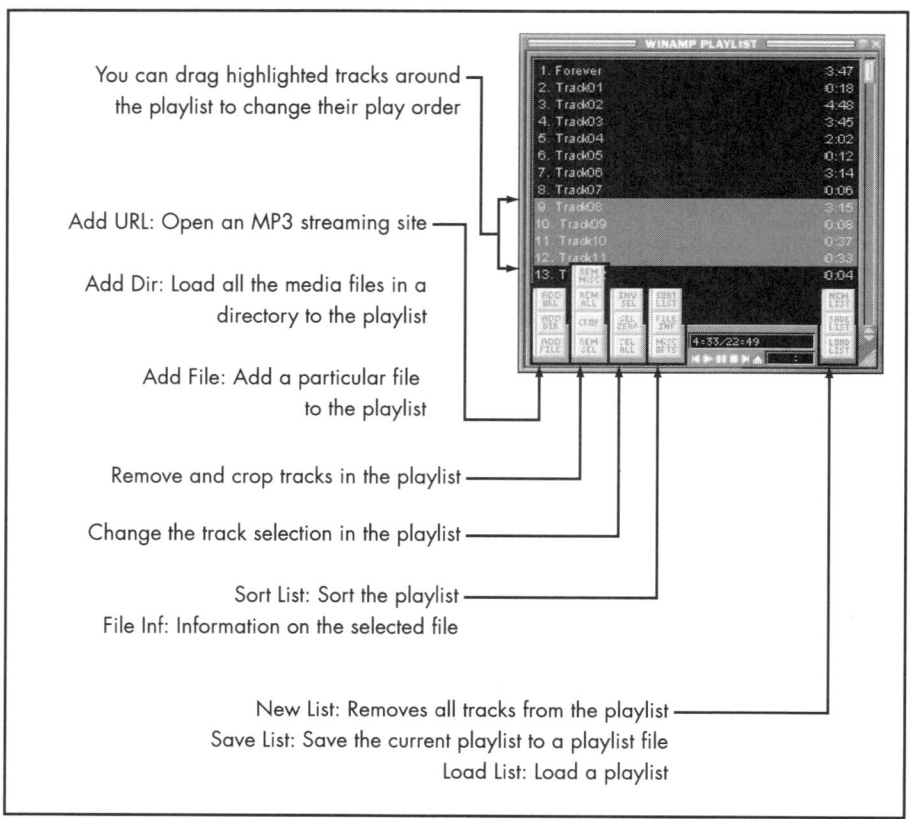

Figure 12.10: Organizing a playlist in Winamp

player application. Winamp also allows you to select and drop multiple files onto the playlist. Just open one or more Windows Explorer windows and find the folders where the audio files are stored, and you can quickly drag them from Explorer into the current playlist. This saves you the trouble of having to go the File, Open, or Add dialog boxes and slowly navigate through the hard drive and subfolders to find a particular album or track.

Archiving Your Music

The hard drive provides a quick and efficient way to keep all your music files in one place, but no computer component lasts forever, especially because hard drives are mechanical components on which high rotational speeds and heat can cause gradual wear and tear. Many people know that hard drives will fail sooner or later and back up all their important files to removable storage or mirror their files to a second hard drive. You should do that with your music files, too!

One easy way to store music files is to use a CD writer to burn your music collection to blank CD-R discs. CD-R discs are very affordable considering the

650-MB to 700-MB file sizes they provide for data storage. Always use a reputable brand if you want to store music files permanently. Most CD writing software supports burning of MP3 files to standard audio CDs that works with consumer CD players.

Some consumer and car CD players also support playback of MP3 files stored as data files on a CD-R or CD-RW disc. This eliminates the need to write the files to standard audio CDs (uncompressed PCM audio takes up more space). By storing the MP3 files as they are without converting them to CD audio, you can also quickly transfer the files to a portable MP3 player or share them with others over the Internet.

Other alternatives are Zip disks and other removable storage media. You can also use packet-writing software to turn CD-RW discs into large floppy disks and allow arbitrary copying and erasing of files from the disc. These forms of storage media are very useful when you have a PC at work and want to shuttle your music from your home to your office. Some CD-MP3 players will also recognize such packet-written discs.

13

RECORDING AUDIO

Playing back digital audio (converting digital data to an analog signal) is only half of the functionality of a sound card today. Any modern sound card can also record audio (converting an analog signal to digital data). The Live! is capable of recording not only from analog sources, but also from digital sources and from a mix of the two. Recording from a digital source, however, is really nothing but converting the input signal to the correct format and performing some level conversion and adding effects when necessary.

The audio source used for recording, as well as the recording level, is determined by the mixer settings. For good results, it is important to select the recording sources and set the recording levels correctly. This is described in the section "Mixer Settings for Recording" later in this chapter.

Recording Sources and Equipment

As described in previous chapters (Chapters 3, 4, 5, and 7 in particular), the Live! has a multitude of audio inputs. All of these can be used as recording sources, but you should be aware of the following two limitations when recording audio:

- **You can record from only one audio source at a time.** This problem often can be solved by using the virtual recording source called What-U-Hear, in which case all the sound sources that are played back by the sound card will also be recorded. In this mode, you cannot listen to some inputs and record from others; for example, you cannot record from the microphone if it is muted.
- **You can record from only one *analog* audio source at a time, even using What-U-Hear.** The fact that you cannot record from more than one analog source at a time is a limitation of the Live! hardware, and there is no easy way to overcome it. Either you'll have to record the sound sources separately, or you'll have to use an external mixer.

Analog Inputs on the Live! Card

All Live! models come with enough analog inputs for most types of recordings. The backplate of the Live! card has an analog mini-jack line input and a mini-jack microphone input. These require different signal levels, so make sure that you use the right one.

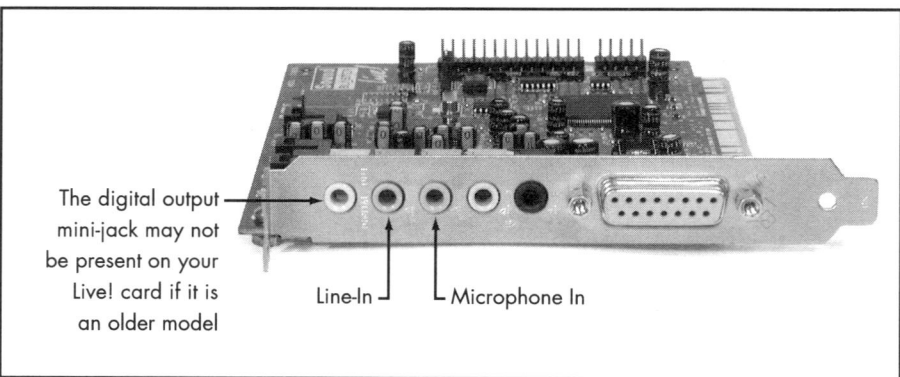

Figure 13.1: Analog audio inputs on the backplate of a Live! card

All of the audio inputs on the circuit board of the card (for internal connections in the computer), such as the CD Audio, TAD, and AUX inputs, can also be recording sources. In addition to the connectors on the card itself, you can add a Live!Drive or another digital I/O card or front panel, for a greater selection of analog recording sources.

Line In

The line-in connector, found on all Live! cards (colored blue on many models), can be used to record from any stereo analog line-level source. *Line level* refers to the signal strength of the electrical signal and is the type of signal that you can expect from the outputs of most electronic devices. See Chapter 5, "Connecting Devices," for a more detailed description of signal levels and the types of devices that you'll commonly connect to this input.

> The output of most record players is not line level and should therefore not be connected directly to the line input of the Live! One way to connect such a device is to connect it to the Phono input of an amplifier and, if available, connect a line-level output on the amplifier (such as the tape output normally used for recording to a cassette recorder) to the line input of the Live!

Microphone

The microphone input (colored pink on most cards) is used to connect and record from—you guessed it—a microphone. Microphones give a very weak signal that needs to be amplified many times to be comparable to a line-level signal. If you connect a line-level source to the Mic input, the signal will be amplified way beyond clipping, and you may even risk damaging the microphone amplifier on the sound card.

On-Board Inputs

Although you may have few occasions to do so, you can record from any of the on-board inputs, as well. For example, you can select CD Audio as the recording source and record while playing back a CD with your CD-ROM or DVD drive. However, most optical drives can read audio tracks digitally with digital audio extraction (DAE), making this way of recording tracks less desirable.

Live!Drive Inputs

If you are lucky enough to have a Live!Drive, you have some additional choices of recording sources. If the software is correctly installed, you should have the option of selecting the Live!Drive's inputs (such as Line In 2) as recording sources in the mixer, following a process similar to that for recording from the main analog inputs.

Digital Inputs

The Live! is designed to have the audio signal stay in the digital domain as long as possible. Therefore, it would be natural to do the actual recordings digitally, whenever possible. However, most Live! cards offer few digital inputs, and none on the backplate for connecting external digital audio equipment.

The I^{2}S and CD Digital inputs (which, unfortunately, are missing on a few Live! models) can be used to record digitally from, for example, MPEG decoder cards and CD and DVD drives inside your computer. As explained in Chapter 4, "Accessories Galore," however, you need an add-on such as the Live!Drive or one of the many available digital I/O boards to get external digital inputs.

Recording from a Digital Source

Recording from a digital source is similar to recording from an analog source. You select the digital input as the recording source in the mixer, run your favorite audio editor, and start recording.

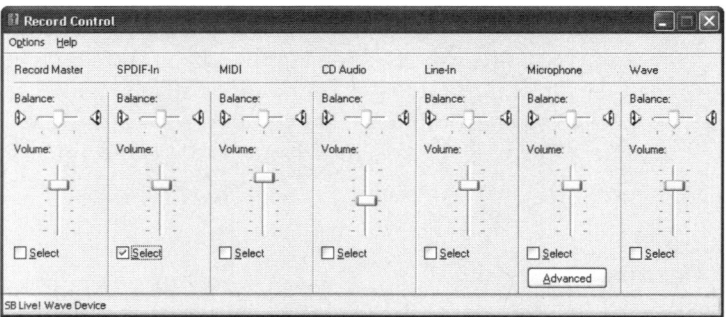

Figure 13.2: The Windows mixer with the digital S/PDIF-In selected as the recording source

Note that the recording level affects digital sources, as well. Unfortunately, the Live! drivers and other software do not offer any feature to bypass the mixer such that no level conversion is performed, which is important for users who want to make perfect digital copies with every single bit replicated exactly. The Live! will perform any necessary sample rate conversion when recording from sources with different sampling rates.

Mixer Settings for Recording

The mixer is where you control what should be recorded and what should not be. Some audio editors let you control the mixer settings from within the program (such as in a recording dialog, along with a volume meter, to easily set the recording level). Otherwise, simply open the Live! mixer to adjust the recording settings (as described in detail in Chapter 7, "The Mixer").

Recall from Chapter 7 that both the Live! mixer and Windows' built-in mixer let you select the recording source and set the recording level. Because the Live! mixer is the application of choice for most Live! users, we will focus on this application, although you can go back to Chapter 7 for a description of how the Windows mixer is used, as well.

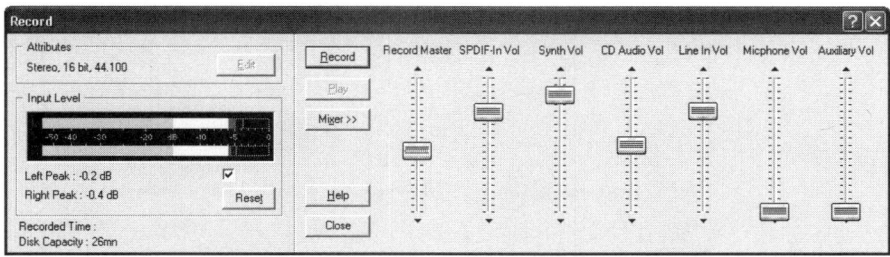

Figure 13.3: Some Wave editors, like WaveLab, let you adjust the recording levels from within the program

Selecting the Right Source for Recording

The recording source and level are set in the leftmost part of the Live! mixer. You can record from only one source at a time, unless you use the What-U-Hear source; in that case, the unmuted play sound sources (in the middle section of the mixer) are recorded. Before you record, simply select the input that you intend to record as the recording source in the mixer.

> Even if you use What-U-Hear, note that you can still use only one analog audio source for recording. This is because of a limitation of the Live! hardware, and there is no way around it other than using an external mixer to mix several analog sources.

Adjusting the Recording Level

With the slider below the recording source selector, you can set the recording level for that particular source. For good results, it is important that the recording level is set carefully. These guidelines should help you set an appropriate level:

- Set the recording level as high as possible.
- While setting the recording level as high as possible, make sure that the entire dynamic range of the Live! and the recorded audio format is used. While it is possible to increase the level of the recorded material after it is recorded, audio artifacts like hiss that are present in low quantities will also be increased in tandem, and this may lead to excessive noise and loss of quality.
- Avoid clipping at any price! Clipping occurs when high-volume sections and peaks in the input are louder than what can be captured when recording. This problem is fixed simply by lowering the recording level. Clipping causes very nasty clicks and distortion when played back and will very likely ruin what you've recorded.

Recording Audio **361**

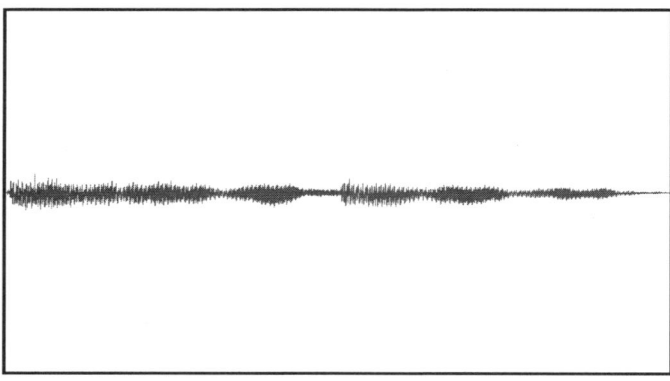

Figure 13.4: This piece of audio is recorded at levels that are too low

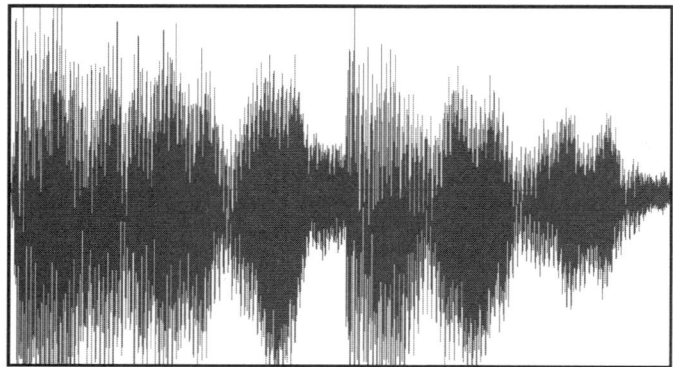

Figure 13.5: The same piece of audio recorded using a recording level that is too high. Notice how the loudest parts get clipped off at the top and bottom.

- To prevent clipping, it is essential that the audio editor has some sort of volume meter that shows the peak levels of the recorded signal. Set the recording level so that the peaks are about 3 to 6 dB (about 30 to 50 percent) below the maximum level. This way, you will get a good level while still leaving some room for unexpected peaks in the audio signal that otherwise would lead to clipping.

TIP *Another less accurate way is to play back the audio and watch the level meter. Set the record levels such that the maximum (usually marked red) is reached only occasionally at the loudest parts of the audio.*

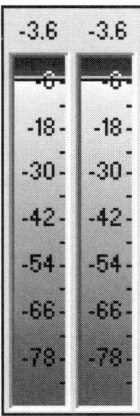

Figure 13.6: VU (volume) meters to monitor the recording level in SoundForge

Recording with EAX Effects

Normally, an audio source is recorded without effects (dry), though you may hear effects while you record it if an EAX preset is selected. The only way to record with effects is to use What-U-Hear as the recording source. In other words, the following procedure can be used to record from an audio source with the effects included:

1. Use the EAX Control Panel to make sure that the desired effect is applied to the audio source(s) from which you will record.
2. Open the Live! mixer. Mute all audio sources except those from which you will record.
3. Select What-U-Hear as the recording source.
4. Open the audio editor to check the recording level using the audio editor's volume meters or by creating test recordings. Adjust the recording level in the mixer, if necessary.
5. Start recording.

Note that this process assumes a few limitations, as highlighted in Chapters 7 and 17. For example, you cannot easily record from a single source with effects while playing something else (as is sometimes necessary, for example, for recording vocals or external instruments with reverb in an audio sequencer).

Audio Editing Basics

There is a wealth of programs for recording and editing audio files, from very simple programs such as the Sound Recorder, which ships with Windows, to professional applications with many advanced features.

Figure 13.7: Windows Sound Recorder. It will let you record audio, but has very limited editing capabilities.

Most audio editors provide a similar set of basic features. The audio being edited is usually presented as one waveform diagram (or two, for stereo), with the vertical position representing the sound intensity at any time, and the horizontal axis representing the time.

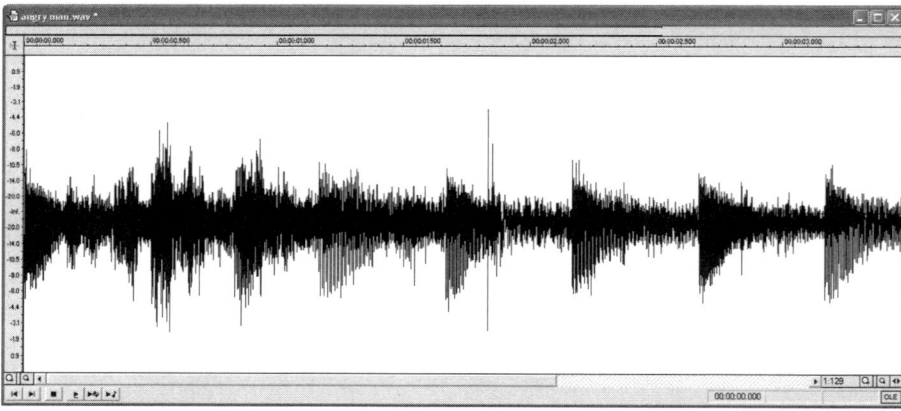

Figure 13.8: Example of a sound file presented as a waveform in a sound editor window (SoundForge)

All Wave editors give you basic functionality such as the ability to copy, cut, paste, and delete selected parts of the audio. Most will also let you record audio directly to disk (as opposed to recording into memory), in which case only the free space of your hard disk limits the length of the audio you can record. Some Wave editors will let you process the audio file in various ways, such as by adjusting and/or normalizing the level, adding echoes and other effects, and so on.

Various audio editors have been bundled with various Live! packages, including Creative WaveStudio, SoundForge XP, and WaveLab Lite. These are all quite similar, and all provide an adequate set of features for most audio editing tasks.

Recording Audio

Before you start recording audio, some programs present a dialog box where you can set the format of the new recording (resolution and bits, sample rate, mono or stereo) and preview the recorded audio level with a volume meter. Others require you to create a new sound file and specify its type and parameters before recording, while displaying volume meters elsewhere.

Try to record at the highest possible sample size and sample rate supported by the sound card; it is always a good idea to work with and store a high-quality version of the recording. In the case of the Live!, record at 16-bit, 48 kHz. Subsequently, you can convert the recording to a lower sample size and rate.

> Lower sample rates (like 22 kHz sampling rates representing frequencies at up to 11 kHz) cannot represent audio up to the 20 kHz limit of our hearing, like 44.1 kHz or 48 kHz can. 32 kHz is used by many television broadcasts, providing acceptable-quality audio with an upper frequency of 16 kHz.

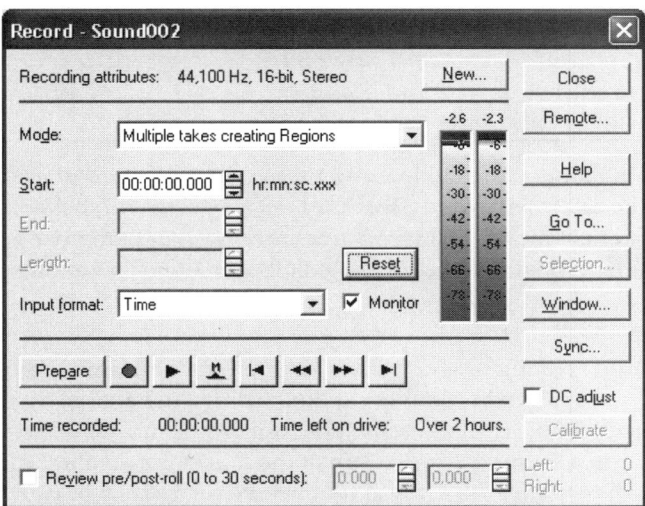

Figure 13.9: The recording dialog in SoundForge

As explained earlier, it is important that you carefully set the recording level. A too-low recording level may result in a noisy recording. If you set the recording level too high, clipping and distortion may occur.

Memory Requirements

Uncompressed PCM wave audio data (which is what you'll get when you record audio) takes plenty of space on your hard drive. One minute of CD-quality audio (16-bit, 44-kHz stereo) takes up about 10 megabytes on your disk, and thus one song can easily consume 50 to 100 megabytes.

TIP *Defragment your hard drive occasionally, as a fragmented hard drive places different parts of the recorded audio in different areas on the disk, creating a greater chance of audio skipping when the audio recording software writes audio data to disk. Skipping occurs especially on old hard drives that have difficulty sustaining the required 180 kbps transfer rate required for CD-quality audio.*

The following table shows how much space one second and one minute of audio will consume, depending on the audio format used.

Table 13.1: Amount of Data Required for One Second and One Minute of Uncompressed Audio at Common Sampling Rates

Format	1 Second	1 Minute
8-bit, 22-kHz mono	21.5 KB	1.26 MB
8-bit, 22-kHz stereo	43.1 KB	2.52 MB
8-bit, 44-kHz mono	43.1 KB	2.52 MB
8-bit, 44-kHz stereo	86.1 KB	5.04 MB
16-bit, 22-kHz mono	43.1 KB	2.52 MB
16-bit, 22-kHz stereo	86.1 KB	5.04 MB
16-bit, 44-kHz mono	86.1 KB	5.04 MB
16-bit, 44-kHz stereo	172.3 KB	10.07 MB
16-bit, 48-kHz mono	93.8 KB	5.49 MB
16-bit, 48-kHz stereo	187.5 KB	10.99 MB

In addition, when editing a sound file, the audio editor may require several times the amount of storage space for working copies of the file, undo buffers, and so on, so a couple of gigabytes of free space on your hard drive is a good thing to have when you want to record and edit longer audio files at high quality.

Normalizing

Many audio editing programs have a normalization feature. *Normalizing* means scaling the amplitude (volume) of the recorded material so that the loudest part of the sound will reach a certain level, usually the maximum level. For example, if the peak in a sound file is –6 dB (half the maximum amplitude), normalizing it to the maximum level (–0 dB) will simply scale the volume by two.

In many cases, it is desirable to normalize the sound files that you've recorded, especially when you want to write them to CD. This way, you know that all your sounds will be played back at about the same volume. If you keep the level as high as possible, background noise is reduced, and you also won't have to turn the volume up as high on your amplifier or speakers.

Cutting, Trimming, and Other Editing

Audio editing software lets you highlight parts of the recorded material and cut, copy, paste, and delete parts, just as you can with text in a word processor. In most cases, you can also process or add effects (such as normalize) to only a part of the audio file.

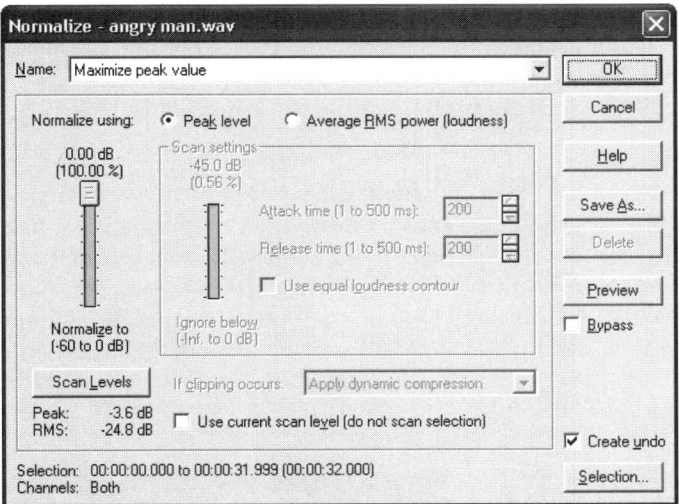

Figure 13.10: Normalization options in SoundForge

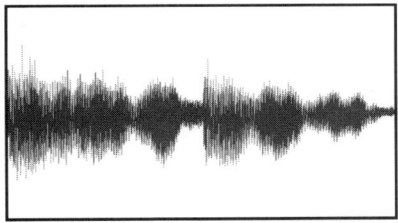 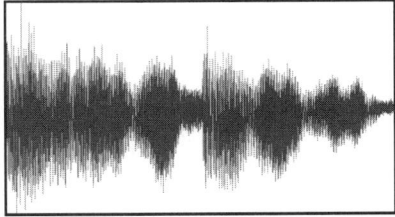

Figure 13.11: Waveform before (left) and after normalization (right). Notice how the peaks barely touch the bounds of the waveform window after normalization.

After you've recorded a piece of audio, you may have some unwanted silence at the beginning and/or end because you didn't click Record at exactly the right moment. Nothing is easier to fix. Simply select the silent part and use Cut or Delete in the audio editor to remove the part. It is always a good idea to trim your recorded material this way. Some audio editors even have automatic trimming features.

Adding Effects

It is not uncommon among audio editors to have a selection of non–real-time effects that you can apply to the whole or part of the audio file. These effects are not real time because they take time to process and modify the audio file before you can hear the changes. Conversely, EAX effects are real-time effects because they are applied immediately to any audio source. Here are some of the common effects that are routinely used on recorded audio.

Fade In and Fade Out

Fade in and fade out are non–real-time effects. For example, many audio editors offer a fade-out feature, where you select a part (usually the end) of the audio file, and the program gradually decreases the volume over the highlighted section.

Compression

Another useful effect, although somewhat difficult to master, is compression. Compression (in this context) means lowering the loudest parts of an audio signal to even out the dynamics of the signal. Most compressors have at least four parameters for controlling compression: the *threshold* level, above which the compressor will be triggered to lower the output; the *ratio*, which specifies how much the level above the threshold will be compressed; and the *attack* and *release* times, which control how quickly the compressor reacts to peaks and returns to no compression, respectively.

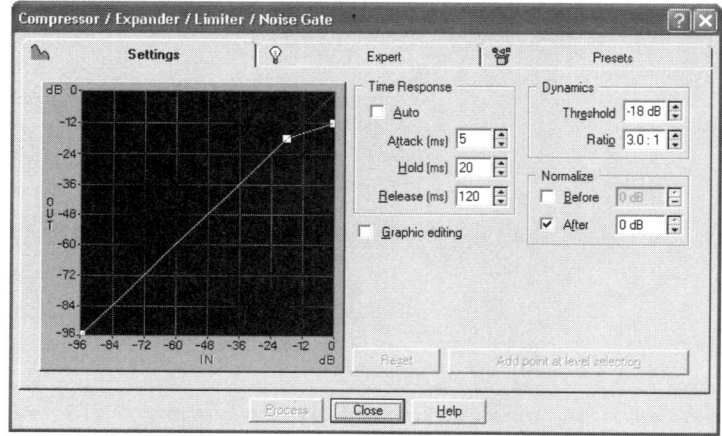

Figure 13.12: The compression dialog in WaveLab Lite gives you the attack and release times, an additional hold time, and the compression threshold and ratio. In addition, WaveLab can automatically normalize the material before and/or after compression.

Compression can be used in many situations, such as to make the level of recorded vocals more even and to increase the average volume of a song (by lowering the peaks to be able to increase the overall volume without causing clipping). Fast compression (short attack and release) with very high ratios is known as *limiting*, because it effectively limits the output signal to below the threshold.

Figure 13.13: The original version of a vocal track with varying levels as picked up by a microphone (left), and the compressed (and somewhat amplified) version on the right. Notice how the overall level of the recording is evened out with the compression.

Equalization

Equalization is another effect that is sometimes essential. The equalizer lets you boost or reduce the levels of the different frequencies of a sound. In fact, the bass and treble controls in the Live! mixer make up a very simple (two-band) equalizer. The more advanced graphical equalizers found in audio editors have a larger number of fixed frequency bands, whose individual levels can be controlled.

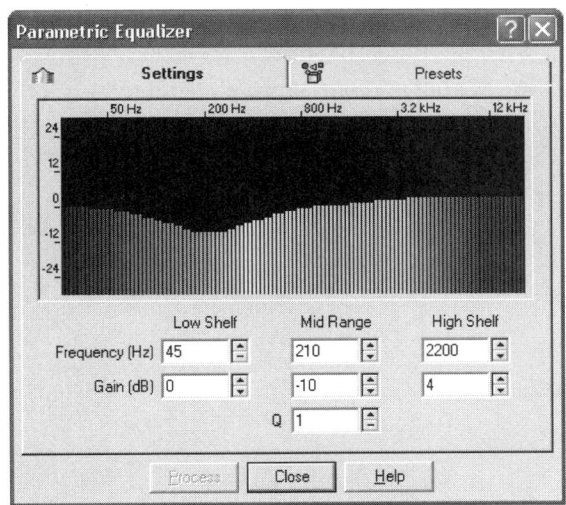

Figure 13.14: The parametric equalizer in WaveLab gives you a graphical display of the resulting frequency curve

A more advanced variation of an equalizer is the *parametric equalizer*, which allows more parameters to be controlled, such as the modification of the range of controllable frequencies. This function is very useful if you need to eliminate or emphasize a particular, known frequency component of a sound.

Other Effects

Some audio editors let you add effects similar to the Live!'s EAX effects (such as echoes, reverb, and chorus). In many cases, however, you can use the Live!'s internal effects, which are very customizable and let you hear the result of a change to a parameter in real time. Try them out and experiment to get the best results. The Undo feature is one keystroke away!

After Recording

You can do many things to recorded audio files:

- Write them to audio CDs with a CD-RW drive and an inexpensive, blank CD-R disc. Do make sure the files are 16-bit 44.1-kHz Wave files. Some CD writing software will also perform conversion so that you need not manually use an audio editor to convert them.
- Convert them to MP3 format. Grab one of the available MP3 encoders, like the popular open-source Lame encoder, and you can compress Wave files to more manageable sizes and share them over the Internet.
- Mix them into your home videos if you are editing them on the PC.
- Play them back and record them to an external audio recorder with the analog or digital outputs of the Live!
- Deliver them in Web pages by using lower sample rates and sizes, and saving them to file formats supported by the browser like AIFF, Wave, or Flash.

PART FIVE
COMPOSING MUSIC

14

MIDI EXPLAINED

You may take for granted the fact that a synthesizer today can be controlled by another synthesizer, computer, or other electronic device, but keep in mind that before MIDI, which was introduced only some 20 years ago, no such communication standard for musical instruments existed.

> 1950s – In the first large synthesizers, all parts (modules) of the system were connected by patch cables. At this time, synthesizers were more objects of research at universities than musical instruments. In most cases, any custom-made device could be used to control the synthesizer (such as a keyboard module), as long as it sent the right type of electrical signals for this particular system.
>
> 1960s – The first commercial synthesizers, such as the Minimoog, were designed to be played live and offered no way of remote control.
>
> 1970s – The first common way of controlling synthesizers was by using control voltages, or CVs. In this case, the voltage on a cable represented the frequency of the note to be played. This, together with a signal called Gate,

which turned the note on and off, is found in many old synthesizers, drum machines, and other electronic music instruments.

1980s – MIDI, standardizing both the electrical interface and the digital communication between musical instruments, is introduced and quickly adopted by manufacturers of digital musical instruments.

Overview of MIDI

MIDI, introduced in the early 1980s, provides a standardized way for musical instruments (and sometimes other equipment) to talk to each other. It is standardized in the sense that there are a number of basic *messages* that most MIDI devices understand, such as "play the note C in octave 4" or "add some vibrato on MIDI channel 3."

It is important to keep in mind that *MIDI itself does not contain any sound*. Instead, MIDI carries notes and other messages to tell an instrument what to play. Just as you can't expect two piano players to sound exactly the same even if you give them the same sheet of notes to play, you will not necessarily get exactly the same result if you send the same sequence of messages to two different synthesizers.

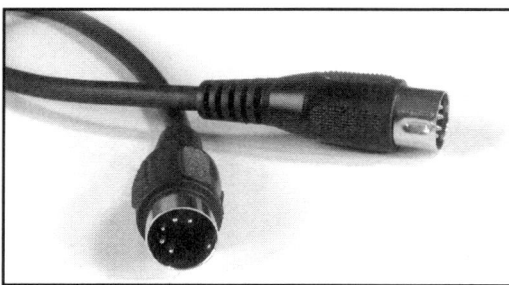

Figure 14.1: Standard MIDI cables

The five-pin DIN connector was chosen as the standard connector on MIDI cables. Standard MIDI cables can be found in any well-stocked music store. For reliable operation, you shouldn't use cables longer than 50 feet (15 meters).

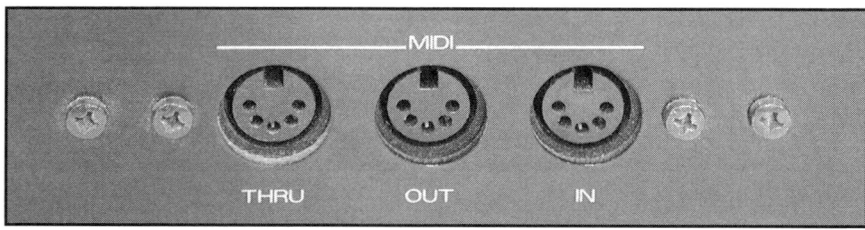

Figure 14.2: Look for these connectors on your synthesizer or other electronic music instrument. If they're there, you can connect it to any other MIDI instrument or a Sound Blaster Live – equipped computer.

In addition to the "language," the MIDI standard also contains electrical specifications to make sure that any two MIDI devices can easily be connected using standard MIDI cables. Because MIDI messages are short, the amount of data that needs to be transferred in every unit of time is usually small. Therefore, data is transmitted at a low speed (for details, see "MIDI Hardware" below). In rare cases, where large amounts of data need to be sent at one time, the slow speed of MIDI can cause slight (but annoying) delays. A couple of milliseconds delay is hardly noticeable, but delays of 20 milliseconds or more can be a problem, particularly in very tight electronic music.

On the other hand, there are several other sources of delays in a MIDI system besides the actual data transfer. Some MIDI instruments react slowly to MIDI data, especially when large amounts arrive in a short time period. The timing of a sequencer is not always perfect either—in fact, the faster and more advanced computers and operating systems become, the more timing problems seem to occur. Windows in particular has traditionally not been very well suited for programs that rely on precise timing, although with today's powerful computers, the timing of pure MIDI data is rarely a problem unless too many applications are running in the background.

Today, some aspects of the MIDI protocol may seem strange or limiting, and indeed they are. Keep in mind that this standard was created at a time when synthesizers were very limited compared to those of today, and although it may be far from perfect, we should be glad that there is a standard like MIDI at all. Imagine how much worse life would be for electronic musicians if each manufacturer had its own "standard" for communication!

MIDI Hardware

Physically, MIDI is an asynchronous serial interface (there's no separate synchronization signal) that transmits at a data rate of approximately 31,250 bits per second, a very slow speed measured by today's standards, and slower than many 56 kbps modem dial-up connections, too. MIDI data is transmitted in bytes. Every byte consists of 8 data bits (that make up the actual value of the byte) and one *start bit* and one *stop bit* (to synchronize the data flow). This makes every transmitted byte 10 bits in size.

One byte of information, 10 bits including start and stop bits, will therefore take 10 / 31,250 = 0.000320 seconds = 320 microseconds per byte. For example, a chord of 6 notes, where each "note on" message is 3 bytes will take 3 * 6 * 320 microseconds = 5.76 milliseconds to transmit. This delay is probably not noticeable, but add a few drums, a bass, and some other instruments that play notes at the very same moment, and you can see why timing problems can occur when many notes that are supposed to sound at the same time are delayed by slow data transmission.

Note that the type of electrical interface described in the MIDI specification is used only for devices with physical MIDI connectors (such as when you connect external synthesizers and drum machines). In the case of a sound card, like the Live!, the MIDI data never leaves the computer and is transferred via the PCI bus (or ISA bus, for old sound cards), which is faster than standard MIDI communication by an order of several magnitudes.

A Little About Sequencers

The subject of MIDI messages brings us to another common term used when speaking about computer-generated music and MIDI: *sequencer*. A sequencer basically is a device that can record and play back sequences of MIDI data.

> Some purists may disagree on this definition because the term *sequencer* was applied to many analog devices that could play back only programmed (not recorded) sequences of notes. However, this kind of sequencer was only common before the MIDI era.

In many ways, a sequencer is a lot like a tape recorder. But while a tape recorder records actual sound, the sequencer records only the notes (the MIDI messages). Therefore, the sequencer depends on the synthesizer to play back the music. Unlike a tape recorder, a sequencer will let you record one instrument at a time and then play back all these recordings simultaneously. Most sequencers will also let you save and load your work and edit the data in various ways.

Most early sequencers were separate boxes. However, MIDI was introduced at a time of rapid development in computer technology, and soon computers were equipped with MIDI interfaces (the necessary electronics to connect the computer to other MIDI devices). Some computers (like many models of the Atari) even had this feature built in, which made them very popular for music. With the computer being able to receive and transmit MIDI messages, sequencers could be implemented in software. With a large screen, a keyboard, and a mouse, computer sequencers became very powerful and provided increased possibilities for editing the recorded sequence. In addition, they could use the computer's relatively large memory and disks to store work.

Nowadays, the term *sequencer* almost exclusively refers to sequencer software, although you can find synthesizer workstations with built-in sequencers and even stand-alone sequencers if you look for them.

> ### Hexadecimal Numbers
> When referring to the actual data of MIDI messages, numbers are often written in *hexadecimal* (hex) format. Whereas the decimal system that we normally use has 10 elements (0 to 9), the hexadecimal system has 16 elements (0 to 9 and A to F). Thus, the hexadecimal value E is equivalent to 14 in decimal format, and the decimal value 10 is equivalent to A in hexadecimal format. To distinguish the two numbering systems in this book, hexadecimal numbers will be preceded by the *0x* prefix, like this: *0x7*.
>
> In a two-digit decimal number, the leftmost digit is the tens value, and the second digit is the ones value. In hexadecimal format, the principle is the same, but instead the first digit is the sixteens value. This may seem a bit confusing at first. A few examples may be useful:
>
> The hexadecimal number 0x7 is 7 in decimal format.

The hexadecimal number 0xB is 11 in decimal format (B = 11).
The hexadecimal number 0x24 is 36 in decimal format (2*16 + 4 = 36).
The hexadecimal number 0xBE is 190 in decimal format (B = 11 and E = 14; therefore, 11*16 + 14 = 190).

In a three-digit number, the leftmost digit is the hundreds value (10*10 = 100) in decimal format, and 256s value (16*16 = 256) in hexadecimal format. However, the data in the MIDI protocol is sent as 8-bit bytes, in which the possible numbers range from 0 to 255—and 255 (0xFF) is the highest number that can be written with two hexadecimal digits; therefore, we won't have to worry about hex numbers with three or more digits. This is, by the way, exactly the purpose of writing numbers in hexadecimal. An 8-bit value (such as a byte in a MIDI message) can always be written with two hexadecimal digits, where the first digit represents the first 4 bits, also known as the *high nibble*, and the second digit represents the last 4 bits, the *low nibble*.

If you need to calculate or convert numbers between hexadecimal and decimal formats, the Windows calculator can be switched to scientific mode, where both decimal (Dec) and hexadecimal (Hex) formats are available, as well as the A through F keys for hexadecimal input. If you switch to binary (Bin) mode, you will see the values of the actual bits in a number (although any initial zeroes will not be displayed).

A Simple Example

To get a better understanding of the MIDI protocol, let's start with an example. Imagine that you've connected a MIDI keyboard to a computer that's running a sequencer. When you press a key on the keyboard, a MIDI message is sent to the computer. The MIDI message contains, in this case, the information that a key was pressed. It also contains a number between 1 and 16 called the *MIDI channel*—something we'll talk more about later. Further, the message contains information about *what* key was pressed and finally *how hard* it was pressed (assuming that the MIDI keyboard was able to sense this).

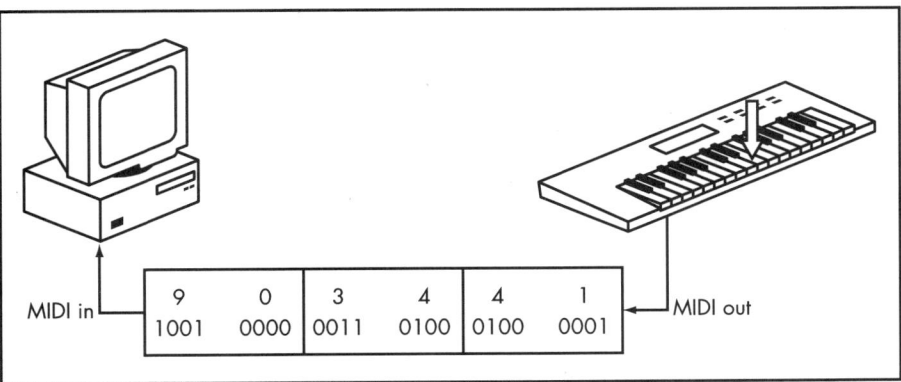

Figure 14.3: A simple MIDI message. As you will see later, this is a note on message.

A similar message is sent when you release the key. In this case, it will contain the information that a key was released, the MIDI channel, and information about what key was released.

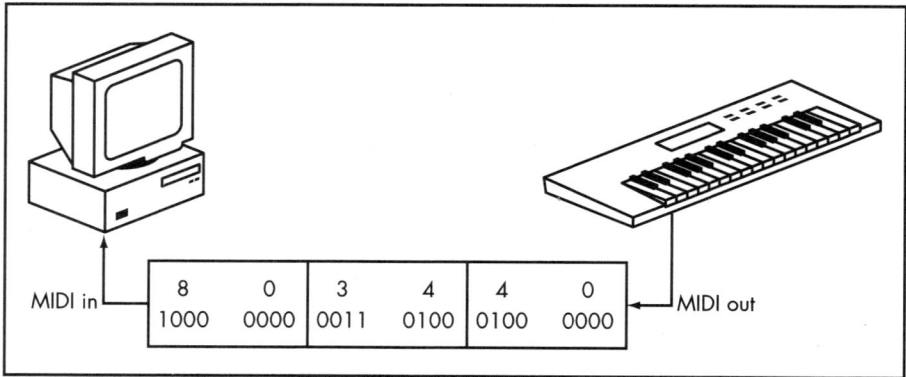

Figure 14.4: *The* note off *MIDI message sent when the key is released*

If the sequencer is recording, it will store these messages, together with information about when they were received, in the computer's memory. On playback, the same sequence is sent back to the MIDI keyboard (or to any other MIDI instrument that you've selected).

The Structure of a MIDI Message

With no or very little understanding of MIDI, you are likely to find a sequencer quite confusing. This section presents an overview of MIDI messages, including the types of messages and when they are used.

A MIDI message consists of one or a few binary numbers sent in a row. Each such number is 1 byte (8 bits) in size, meaning it can have a value between 0 and 255, for a total of 256 possible values (because each binary bit has one of two possible values—usually referred to as 0 and 1—8 bits give $2*2*2*2*2*2*2*2 = 2^8 = 256$ possible values).

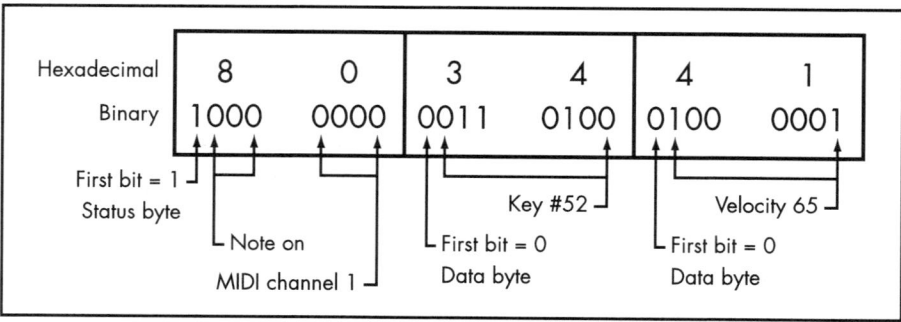

Figure 14.5: *A complete MIDI message in detail*

The first byte of a MIDI message is called a *status byte,* and it contains information about the data that will follow it. The first bit of a status byte is always set to 1. The next three bits determine the *type* of MIDI message (the different types of MIDI messages are explained later in this chapter). The remaining four bits identify the *MIDI channel,* a value between 1 and 16.

If the status byte is omitted (which a receiving MIDI device is able to determine by looking at the first bit of the first byte, which is always set to 1 in status bytes), the status is assumed to be the same as the last status byte received. This is known as the *running status* and is also part of the MIDI specification (see Appendix A, "The MIDI Specification").

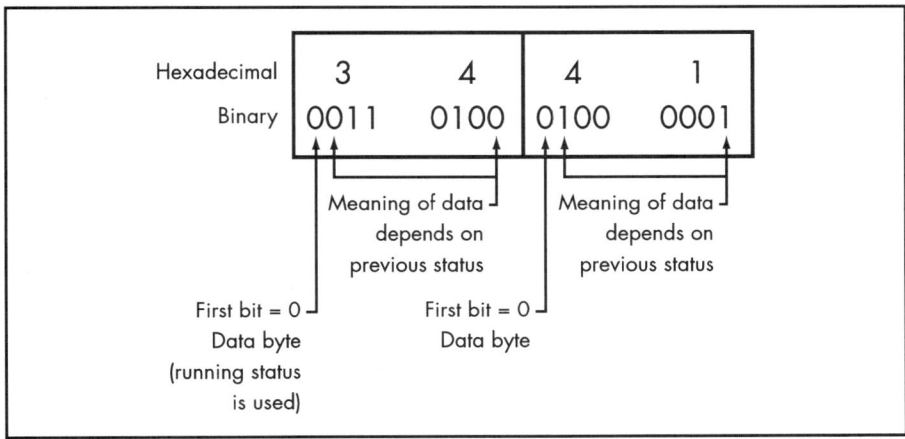

Figure 14.6: A MIDI message using running status

After the status byte comes a number of data bytes, depending on the type of message. In the example in the preceding section, the status byte contains the information that a key had been pressed and identifies the MIDI channel to be used. The data bytes that follow such a message contain the number of the key that has been pressed and the velocity value (how hard it was pressed). Because the first bit of every status byte is set to 1, the first bit of every data byte must be set to 0. As a consequence, only seven bits of each byte are left for the data, resulting in 128 possible values (usually numbered 0 to 127 rather than 1 to 128). This is why many values in a sequencer range from 0 to 127.

If we had only one synthesizer that could play only one instrument at a time, the MIDI channel information would not be needed. However, virtually every modern synthesizer can play several different instruments at a time. Therefore, for each note (or other MIDI message) we send, we need to include information about what instrument it refers to.

Normally, one instrument is associated with one MIDI channel. For example, a synthesizer may be programmed so that every time a "play note" MIDI message is received on MIDI channel 1, a piano sound is used, and every time a similar message is received on MIDI channel 2, a flute sound is used. As mentioned earlier, MIDI channel numbers range from 1 to 16, and therefore one synthesizer cannot (normally) play more than 16 different instruments at one time. In fact, this is one of the serious limitations of the MIDI protocol. There are ways to get around this, though, as you'll discover later in this chapter in the section, "The Live! Synthesizers."

MIDI Message Types

Not surprisingly, the MIDI specification defines many types of messages in addition to those that turn notes on and off. The following list summarizes the eight main types of MIDI messages:

Note on/off. This type of MIDI message is sent whenever a key is pressed (note on) or released (note off) on a MIDI keyboard, or when a MIDI sequence is played back with a sequencer. Every note-on and note-off status byte is followed by two data bytes containing the note number and the velocity (which is usually not used with note off). The MIDI specification states that a note number of 60 is a middle C.

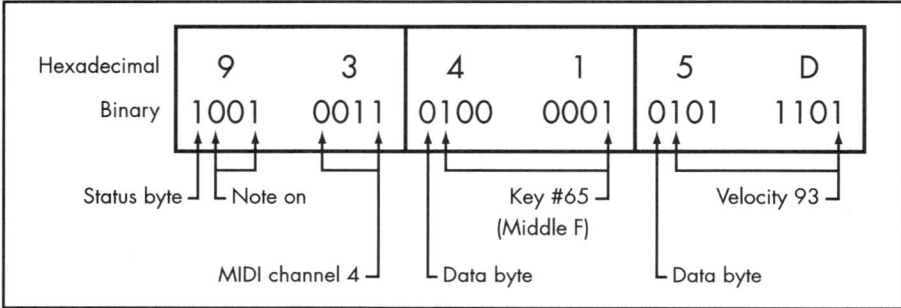

Figure 14.7: A note on MIDI message

Pitch wheel. This type of message contains information about the position of the pitch wheel or joystick found on many synthesizers and keyboards. Pitch wheel messages are sent only when the wheel or joystick is moved. Changes in pitch should affect only one instrument, so this type of message also contains information about the MIDI channel. Because 128 possible values (which is the maximum for one data byte) are too few to accurately represent the position of the pitch wheel, two data bytes follow every pitch wheel status byte, for a total of 128*128 = 16,384 possible positions.

Key aftertouch. Some keyboards are aftertouch sensitive: that is, they sense the amount of pressure applied to a key that is being held down. This information is transmitted via MIDI, which as a key aftertouch message. An aftertouch status byte is followed by two data bytes, containing the note number and the pressure value.

Channel aftertouch (channel pressure). MIDI keyboards that support this type of aftertouch (see the following chapter on MIDI keyboards) will send this type of MIDI message instead of key aftertouch. Because the pressure value in this case is not specific to any note but common to all notes playing on a MIDI channel,

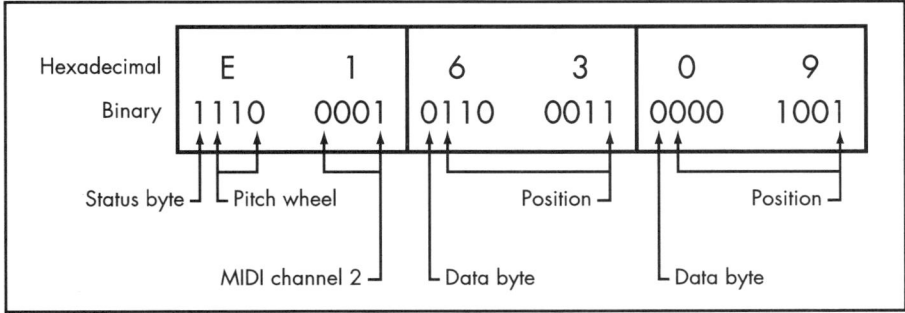

Figure 14.8: A pitch wheel MIDI message

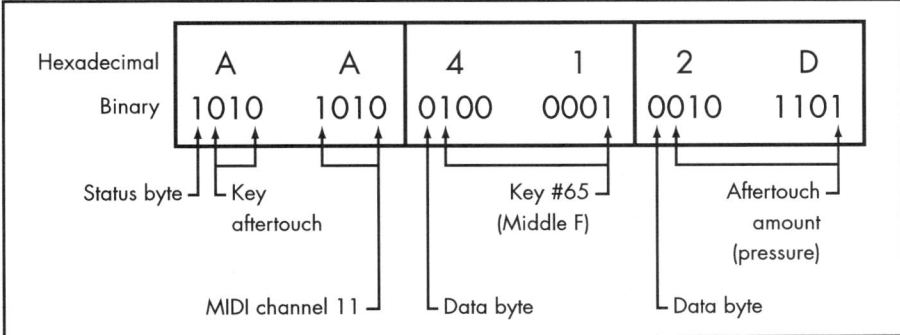

Figure 14.9: A key aftertouch MIDI message

only one data byte, containing the pressure value, follows a channel aftertouch status byte.

Control change. One large group of messages is called control changes (CC), or controllers. This type of message is used to control certain parameters of a MIDI channel. For example, at the end of a long saxophone note you may want to add some vibrato (using the modulation wheel on a MIDI keyboard) to make the sound more natural. For this, and many other purposes, you use control change messages.

Basically, all types of MIDI messages that don't have a type of their own are found in this category. A large number of control changes and their purposes are described in the MIDI specification. A more in-depth description of the control change messages that you can use with the synthesizer on the Sound Blaster Live! is found in Chapter 17, "Sequencer Basics," and in Appendix E, "The Sound Blaster Live! MIDI Implementation."

A control change status byte is always followed by two data bytes. The first byte indicates the type of control change. For example, a value of 1 means modulation, which usually adds vibrato as in the preceding example. The second data byte

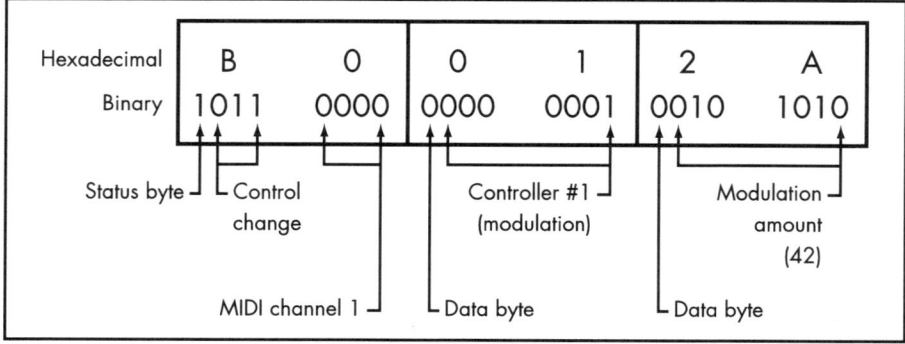

Figure 14.10: A control change MIDI message; in this case, control change 1 (modulation)

contains the controller's new value—for example, the modulation amount. What the second byte means in other cases depends on the type of control change.

Patch change (program change). A patch change message tells a synthesizer what instrument to use on a certain MIDI channel. It is also sometimes known as a program change message, where *patch* and *program* are both synthesizer-speak for *instrument*.

A typical patch change message may contain the following information: "use instrument number 12 on channel 2." Unfortunately, the MIDI specification itself doesn't say anything about how instrument (patch) number 12 sounds, and that is where additional standards, such as General MIDI (discussed later in this chapter), become important. Because only one data byte follows a patch change status byte, a maximum of 128 different patches can be selected with this method. This was certainly enough when the MIDI specification was created, but today many synthesizers (including the Live!) can have far more than 128 instruments. In this case, sets of 128 patches have to be arranged in banks that are selected with a special type of control change message. This is explained in more detail in the Chapter 16, "SoundFonts."

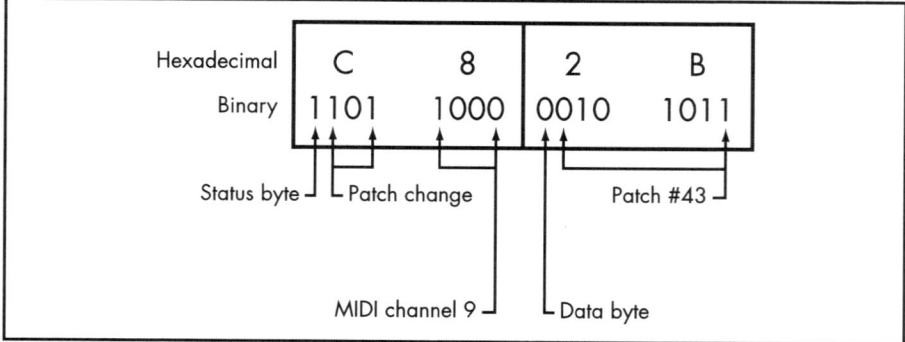

Figure 14.11: A patch change MIDI message

System messages. One completely different type of MIDI message is the system message. System messages are not specific to any particular MIDI channel, but instead to the entire MIDI system. System messages include MIDI start, stop, and continue, as well as MIDI clock and song position messages, used to synchronize sequencers. These messages are not among the most commonly used, but they are useful in certain cases. Many system messages are only one byte long.

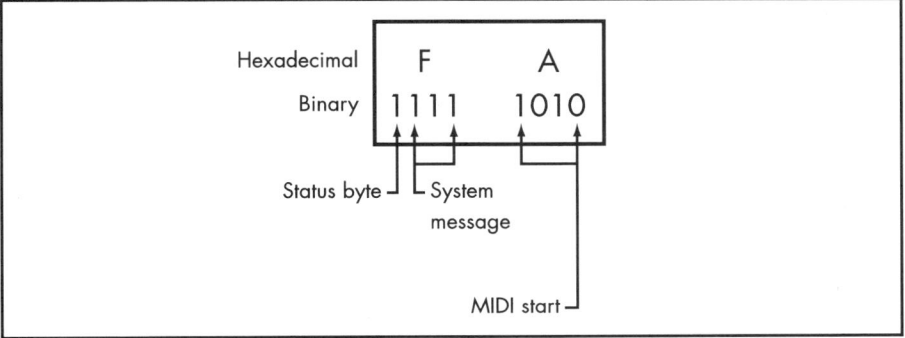

Figure 14.12: Example of a system message: MIDI start

System exclusive. The last type of MIDI message, which is actually a type of system message, is the system exclusive (SysEx) message. System exclusive messages are used when larger amounts of data are to be transferred over MIDI to a specific device. A system exclusive message can have any number of data bytes. For example, all the parameters necessary to describe a sound in a programmable synthesizer can be transferred with a SysEx message to a computer for permanent storage.

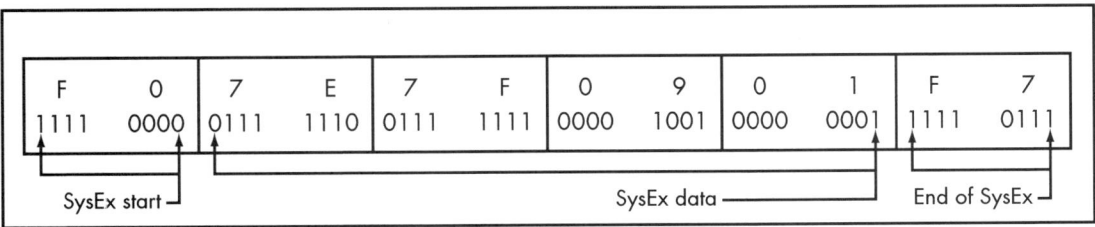

Figure 14.13: Example of a short system exclusive message. A system exclusive message always starts with 0xF0 and ends with 0xF7.

General MIDI and Other Standards

At the time when the MIDI specification was created, synthesizers were neither capable of sounding nor meant to sound like real instruments. As they evolved and new synthesis techniques became widespread (especially wavetable synthesis), realistic sound became a possibility. As mentioned earlier, the MIDI protocol specifies no way to tell a synthesizer to use a particular type of instrument sound—

only an instrument number. General MIDI (GM), introduced in 1991, offers a solution to this and a few other limitations of the MIDI specification.

General MIDI includes a table that associates each of the 128 patch change numbers with a certain type of instrument. On a General MIDI–compatible synthesizer, patch number 19 is always a rock organ, and patch number 57 is a trumpet. The first entries in this table are shown here; the rest can be found in Appendix B, "The General MIDI Sound Set."

Group	Prog #	Instrument name
Piano	1	Acoustic grand piano
	2	Bright acoustic piano
	3	Electric grand piano
	4	Honky-tonk piano
	5	Rhodes piano
	6	Chorused piano
	7	Harpsichord
	8	Clavinet
Chromatic percussion	9	Celesta
	10	Glockenspiel
	11	Music box
	12	Vibraphone

General MIDI also specifies that MIDI channel 10 is used for drums. All other channels (1 to 9 and 11 to 16) can be used for other instruments. On the drum channel, different keys trigger different drum sounds. General MIDI specifies what drum sound corresponds to what key.

The last part of the General MIDI standard sets some basic requirements for a General MIDI–compatible instrument. These include a minimum number of notes that can be played simultaneously and a basic set of control change messages that the instrument should respond to.

Standard MIDI Files

The most important reason for a standard like General MIDI is that it makes playback of MIDI sequences recorded using one General MIDI–compatible instrument possible using any other GM-compatible instrument (at least in theory). A standard MIDI file (SMF; usually ending with the extension .mid) contains the MIDI data (the MIDI messages and the relative time for each message) necessary to play back a song on a General MIDI–compatible instrument. Because MIDI files contain only the MIDI messages and no sound, they tend to be small in size and can be easily edited.

There are two common types of standard MIDI files: type 0 and type 1. The main difference between them is that in the former, the MIDI data is saved in the order it should be played back, whereas in the latter, the tracks are saved separately. Most sequencers can read and save both types of standard MIDI files.

> A third type of MIDI file, type 2, is defined as well. A type-2 MIDI file contains one or more independent single-track patterns. Type-2 MIDI files are not commonly used, though.

A standard MIDI file usually begins with MIDI messages that assign the correct instruments (patch changes) and relative volumes of each MIDI channel (control changes) and other similar initialization commands. Consequently, at the beginning of a song, many MIDI messages have to be sent in a short time over a rather slow MIDI connection. Because of this, and the fact that many synthesizers and other MIDI devices respond slowly to certain MIDI messages such as patch changes, it is a good idea to leave the first bar empty of notes. If you do this, you can be sure that all MIDI channels will be properly initialized when the actual playback starts.

Using a General MIDI SoundFont as synth bank (see Chapter 16, "Sound-Fonts"), which is the default after installation, the Live! is fully GM compatible. Quite high-quality GM SoundFonts are included in the software bundle, making the Live! very well suited for MIDI file playback. This, of course, assumes that the MIDI file is actually created for playback on a General MIDI–compatible instrument (which is almost always, but not necessarily, the case). Some MIDI files may require GM or XG compatibility for correct playback.

The Problems with General MIDI

That a MIDI file can be correctly played back with any GM instrument is a truth — but not the whole truth. Although General MIDI specifies that patch number 0 is a grand piano, for instance, it does not tell in more detail *how* a grand piano sounds. This leads to problems when sound programmers have different opinions about how certain instruments should sound. Even with instruments that have sounds that most people easily recognize, there's another problem: namely, that it is often difficult to reproduce a particular sound on a synthesizer. For instance, it is almost impossible to achieve a natural piano sound from an electronic music instrument, unless the synthesizer uses wavetable synthesis.

For these reasons, a standard MIDI file will hardly ever sound exactly the same on two different GM-compatible instruments. In many cases, a MIDI file will sound just fine on the synthesizer it was created with, but very unpleasant on another. You can see for yourself by downloading some of the many free General MIDI SoundFonts available on the Internet and playing back the same MIDI file using different SoundFonts.

GS and XG

General MIDI was created many years ago, and synthesizers have become more advanced since then. Some synthesizer manufacturers have attempted to extend GM with better synthesizer specifications, more sounds, more drum kits, and so on.

First out was Roland with the *GS* (which is believed to stand for General Standard or General Sound) format. The standard is based on General MIDI and adds variations on many of the original GM instruments. GS also has some new drum kits, such as jazz, electronic, and orchestral kits, in addition to the standard GM kit. A full list of GS sounds and drum kits can be found in Appendix B. GS also requires that a MIDI device respond to certain control change MIDI messages in addition to those already defined in GM. A GS-compliant instrument should also have a built-in effects unit, with reverb and chorus effects. Using the appropriate SoundFonts, the Sound Blaster Live! is almost compatible with GS and fully compatible with GM. Otherwise, most GS-compatible instruments are made by Roland.

> A few features are still missing in the MIDI specification of the Live! MIDI Synth, making it not quite fully GS compatible. For example, effects types must be selected via SysEx messages, which are not supported on the Live!

XG (which stands for Extended GM) is a standard introduced by Yamaha, and is similar to GS. XG was created a few years after GS and, not surprisingly, defines more instruments and drum kits than GM and sets additional requirements for the effects unit. The XG standard also specifies some requirements other than the instrument sound set. For example, certain MIDI messages are defined for sound editing (which can't be used on the Sound Blaster Live!). Thus, with the right SoundFont, the Sound Blaster Live! can be compatible with the XG sound set, but not fully XG compatible. XG sound set compatibility may be enough for some MIDI files created for the XG format, however.

General MIDI 2 (GM2)

In late 1999, the MIDI Manufacturer's Organization proposed a successor to the General MIDI standard, General MIDI 2. This standard is similar to GS and XG, but is not specific to any manufacturer. The most notable improvements over General MIDI are:

- Larger minimum polyphony (32 voices)
- More control changes now mandatory, including filter and envelope parameters
- Two simultaneous drum channels
- A number of SysEx messages defined for precise control of among other things the effects units
- 87 new instrument variations and a total of 9 drum kits

At the time of writing, only a few hardware instruments support the General MIDI 2 standard, so it still remains to see whether this new standard will become as huge a success as its predecessor.

With the appropriate SoundFont, the Live! can be made compatible with the General MIDI 2 sound set. Other parts of the standard (most notably the control change implementation and SysEx support) would require a revised set of Sound

Blaster Live! drivers for full GM2 compatibility. At the time of writing, Creative has not revealed any plans to support GM2.

Synthesizer Basics

It may seem strange to dedicate half a chapter of a book about the Sound Blaster Live! to synthesizer basics. The reason for doing so, though, is that the Live! has very powerful synthesis capabilities, and some general knowledge of the subject will prove useful in many situations.

A Brief History of Synthesizers

The history of electronic musical instruments starts about a century ago. The first pieces of electronics that could (even with the best will) be called synthesizers, however, were not built until several decades later, and even then they didn't look much like the compact, small, and easy-to-use (okay, *relatively* easy to use) electronic instruments of today. Among the first synthesizers were giant modular synthesizers, where the various components of the synthesizer were separate boxes. These synthesizers were programmed by connecting the inputs and outputs of the modules with cables and turning switches and knobs on the modules themselves. These monsters where initially found only at universities and other institutions.

The next step in synthesizer evolution occurred when these large systems were shrunk to, together with a keyboard, fit into a small (again, relatively speaking) box that could actually be carried to gigs and fit into studios. Suddenly, a product that people were willing to buy existed. At this time, synthesizers were based on analog electronics (discrete electronic components, rather than integrated circuits and microprocessors). This made creation of any kind of memory for storing settings difficult. Consequently, when a musician had turned the knobs and buttons and created a cool sound, he or she had to remember or write down all the settings for it. Analog electronics also tend to be somewhat unreliable, and the instruments had to be tuned often because the sound-generating circuits inside were quite temperature sensitive. Despite all this, some people still find the sound of classic analog synthesizers warmer and richer than the sound of today's synthesizers.

In the late 1970s, digital electronics found its way into not only computers but many other electronic devices, including synthesizers. First, the control electronics of many synthesizers turned digital so that instruments could be equipped with memories for saving and recalling the synthesizer's settings. Later, with more powerful digital electronics, the sound generators of the synthesizer turned digital as well, resulting in more reliable and powerful instruments. With the introduction of fully digital instruments, new synthesis techniques (such as frequency modulation) could be used.

Other Electronic Instruments and Studio Equipment

In a music studio, you will find many other types of gear. Because both hardware and software often try to look and feel like another piece of studio equipment, it is good to have a basic understanding of the most common devices found in a music studio.

Drum Machines

A *drum machine* is basically a synthesizer specialized to create drumlike sounds. Drum machines often also have the ability to play and edit drum patterns so that they can be used without a sequencer. Just as there are different types of synthesizers, there are different types of drum machines using different techniques to produce the sound.

Synthesizer Modules

A *synthesizer module* is nothing but a synthesizer without a keyboard. In a music studio, it is common to have several synthesizers. Because one keyboard can be used to play many synthesizer modules via MIDI, this approach saves both space and money. Synthesizer modules and effects units are often mounted on standard-sized (19-inch-wide) racks.

Effects Units

In a studio, you will most likely find several types of effects units and other sound processing gear. Common effects include reverb, delay, chorus, flanger, and phaser. Other common sound processing devices (that you normally wouldn't call effects units) are *compressors, limiters, enhancers,* and *equalizers.* Because the Live! has an integrated effects unit on board, most of these effects are described elsewhere in this book. In fact, it is very common for synthesizers and other electronic musical instruments to have their own built-in effects units.

The Mixer

Figure 14.14: A 16-channel mixer

The mixer can be said to be the heart of many music studios. The audio outputs of all synthesizers, drum machines, effect units, and often a few microphones are connected to the mixer board. The most basic purpose of a mixer is to mix the sound from many sources and to provide the ability to control the relative level of each sound in the mix. Every audio input to a mixer board is called a channel, and the number of channels on a mixer board ranges from a few to hundreds. More reasonable numbers of channels, such as 4, 8, 12, or 16, are commonly found in home studios. An external mixer may be necessary if you plan to use the Live! together with several other sound sources.

Sound Cards

Early computers were not designed to create sound. Usually, at the best, they could produce short beeps. With the quick evolution of the computer, not least for games and entertainment, the need for the computer to be able to play sound became obvious. Early home computers and video game machines (which technically are pretty much the same thing), like the Commodore 64 and Nintendo Entertainment System, were all able to produce music. With the advent of more advanced computers like the Commodore Amiga and Atari, playback of digitally recorded (sampled) sound became possible. In all of these computers, sound and music were handled by custom chips that were standard parts of the computers.

The IBM PC, which at the time of computers like the Amiga and Atari wasn't particularly useful for games, was mainly a business machine and had virtually no sound support (other than the small built-in speaker still found in PCs today). As the PC found its way into homes, things slowly started to change. The early Sound Blaster models were among the first sound cards to arrive for the PC. Finally, the PC could make some noises! Of course, there are many generations of sound cards between these early models and the Sound Blaster Live! of today.

More details about the evolution of sound cards can be found in Chapter 1, "The Evolution of Sound on the PC."

Most sound cards contain some type of synthesizer to be used for music (even though its importance for the typical user is not quite as obvious as before because most of today's games use prerecorded audio tracks). In this case, the synthesizer is simply a chip on the card, and the output from the synthesizer chip and the normal Wave channel are normally mixed.

Most of the first synthesizer chips on sound cards used a simple type of synthesis, known as FM, resulting in rather plastic and toylike sounds—not at all close to any real instruments. You could certainly not expect high-quality MIDI file playback from such a card.

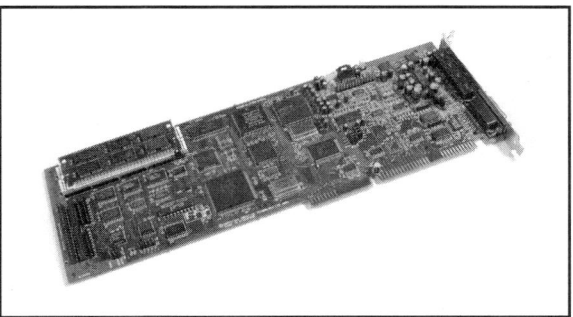

Figure 14.15: The Sound Blaster AWE32

MIDI Explained

Things changed with the Sound Blaster AWE series of cards. They were the first consumer cards to offer a high-quality on-board wavetable synthesizer and effects unit, just like the Live! does. The most distinctive feature of a wavetable synthesizer is that the sounds are based on prerecorded sounds. This gave the AWE card a much more natural sound when playing MIDI. This fact also made the AWE series of cards popular for hobby musicians as an alternative to expensive synthesizer modules or professional sound cards.

The AWE cards introduced one more feature that was important for hobby musicians: the ability to go beyond the standard GM sound set, using a technology called SoundFonts.

Synthesizer Jargon

To help you further explore the area of electronic musical instruments, what follows are some terms commonly used when comparing synthesizers. You'll find them particularly useful when comparing the capabilities of different instruments.

Polyphony

The *polyphony* of a synthesizer refers to the number of sounds, or *voices*, it can play simultaneously. The first synthesizers were *monophonic*: they could play only one note at a time. Modern synthesizers can often play 32 or more notes at a time.

To make things a little bit more complicated, though, one instrument sound may use more than one voice. For example, a combined piano and string instrument may consist of a piano sound and a string sound played simultaneously, thus requiring two voices for every note you play. If a synthesizer has 32-voice polyphony and every note takes two voices, the effective polyphony is only 16 voices.

A polyphony of 32 voices or so is enough for most types of music. In rare cases, though—for example, when playing very large chords with heavily layered sounds or playing long parts with the sustain pedal down—you may run out of unused voices. To reduce this possibility, the synthesizer built in to the Live! hardware has 64 voices, which is comparable to, and in many cases more than, the polyphony of modern stand-alone synthesizers.

Multitimbrality

Multitimbrality refers to the number of different types of instruments (different timbres) that can be played by the synthesizer at one time. Early synthesizers could play only one instrument sound at a time, even though they sometimes were able to play several notes with the same instrument.

When a synthesizer can play two different instruments at one time, it is said to have two *parts*. Therefore, we may today say that a synthesizer is 8- or 16-part multitimbral. One part on a synthesizer normally corresponds to one MIDI channel. Because of the 16-channel limit of the MIDI protocol, synthesizers are normally not more than 16-part multitimbral. This can be a limitation if you want more than 16 different instruments to play at one time. One way to get around this is to equip the synthesizer with two or more MIDI-in connectors. Because different MIDI data can be sent to each MIDI-in port, this effectively results in 16

MIDI channels per port, for a total of 32. In recent years, synthesizers with dual MIDI-in connectors have become common.

In the case of a sound card, adding another MIDI-in port for another 16 MIDI channels is simply done by modifying the drivers. In the case of the Live!, the hardware synthesizer has two MIDI-in ports, named A and B.

MIDI Capabilities of the Live!

The Live! is a great tool for beginning with MIDI, or if you are already an experienced MIDI musician, freely composing virtually anything you can imagine. Let us take a look at some of the basic features of the card.

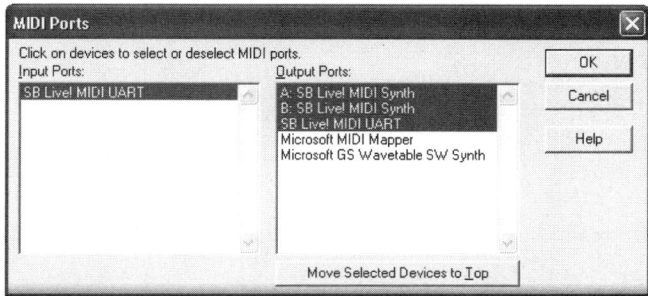

Figure 14.16: The Live! synthesizers, as listed in the Cakewalk sequencer's MIDI port selection window

The Live! Synthesizers

You might not know it, but a Sound Blaster Live! has not one but several quite different synthesizers. Because these are physically located on the Live! card inside your computer, no MIDI connectors or cables are needed to use them. Instead, the MIDI-in and out ports of the sound card are known as *MIDI ports*. MIDI software displays a list of available in and out ports. Figure 14.16 is from the Cakewalk Sequencer.

In this case, not one but five MIDI-out ports are available, all of which are explained in the following paragraphs. Note that because these are not physical ports, the actual number of ports installed and their names are determined by the drivers and operating system installed. The Microsoft GS Wavetable SW Synth in the screenshot is a software synthesizer that comes with Windows 2000 and XP, and not with the Sound Blaster Live!

The MIDI Mapper is not really a MIDI port at all. Instead, the MIDI Mapper always points to the default MIDI playback synthesizer in the system. The port that the MIDI Mapper uses can be set on the Control Panel, in the Multimedia section. For MIDI sequencing, you will normally specify the real ports and avoid the MIDI Mapper.

The following table summarizes the features of the synthesizers on the Live!.

Table 14.1: Summary of Features of the Synthesizers on the Sound Blaster Live!

	SB Live! MIDI Synth	Creative S/W Synth	FM Synthesizer Emulation
Software/hardware	Hardware	Software	Software
Polyphony (voices)	64	Max. 1,024 (See description)	20 (as on the OPL3 FM synthesizer chip)
MIDI channels (parts)	32	16	16
SoundFont support	Yes	No	No
Effect settings per channel	Yes	No	No
Operating systems	Windows 95/98/ME/2000/XP	Windows 95/98/ME	Windows 95/98/ME

The SB Live! MIDI Synth

Of all synthesizers found on the Live!, the SB Live! MIDI Synth is the most powerful. The fact that this synthesizer is implemented in hardware (in the EMU10K1 chip, which is thoroughly described in Chapter 18, "The EMU10K1 Digital Audio Processor") makes it reliable and low on processor use, leaving more computer resources for other tasks, such as audio mixing in an audio sequencer. This synthesizer also has the largest number of supported features. For example, SoundFonts can be used to expand its set of available instruments. You can also set the EAX effects levels independently on each MIDI channel. Furthermore, it supports a large set of MIDI controllers to make your MIDI music more expressive.

When using the Sound Blaster Live! with a sequencer, this synthesizer should be your synthesizer of choice—simply because it sounds best. It has a 64-voice polyphony, so running out of voices with this synthesizer is rarely a concern.

Why A and B?

The maximum number of MIDI channels is 16 (because of a limitation in the MIDI protocol), but the Sound Blaster Live! engineers used a trick to get around this. By adding another MIDI port to the SB Live! MIDI Synth, they increased the number of MIDI channels, and thereby the synthesizer's multitimbrality, to 32 (16 channels per port).

The SB Live! MIDI synthesizer A and B, therefore, point to the same synthesizer, and the 64 available voices are arbitrarily divided between these two ports. Normally, you would start using the 16 MIDI channels of port A. If this is not enough, then additional MIDI channels from port B can be used. An exception would be if you need more than one drum part (MIDI channel 10), in which case you are forced to use both MIDI ports.

The Software Synthesizer

The Creative S/W Synthesizer (available only on Windows 95/95/ME) is a software wavetable synthesizer. This means that all of the calculations needed to produce the sounds are performed in the computer's main processor (CPU) rather than in the SB Live! hardware. Therefore, the synthesizer will consume some additional system resources when used.

Because this is a software synthesizer, the actual implementation lies in the Sound Blaster Live! drivers. In the first driver release, this synthesizer had a polyphony of 64 voices, but because all processing occurs in software, this figure could be easily increased by minor changes to the code. Creative found a use for this number in its marketing approach, and the software synthesizer's polyphony is, with the latest drivers, an almost insane 1,024 voices. Anyone who has worked with electronic music, however, realizes that this is just a fantasy number. First of all, playing 1,024 voices simultaneously with a software synthesizer will require a large amount of CPU power. What makes this value even more ridiculous is that no piece of music will ever require anywhere this number of voices to be played at one time.

> Marketing is why the figure 1,024 appears in the product name of some Live! models. In fact, the numbers included in Creative product names are largely a mess. The 16 in Sound Blaster *16* referred to its ability to play back and record 16-bit audio. The *32* in AWE32 is the number of voices in the EMU8000 synthesizer on the chip. The *64* in AWE64 is the sum of the number of voices in the EMU8000 synthesizer and the software waveguide synthesizer. The *64* in PCI64 refers to the number of voices in the software wavetable synthesizer; as does the *128* in PCI128. And who knows what the *512* in PCI512 stands for.

The final, and perhaps most important, reason that very few people use this synthesizer is that it lacks SoundFont support; instead, it uses a special type of wavetable sound set (with a file extension of .cfm). One General MIDI–compatible sound set is included with the drivers. As far as the author knows, except for a few additional GM sets of larger size, no other sound sets of this format have ever been released—and there is no tool for creating your own! The sounds played by this synthesizer are generally of lower quality than those of the SB Live! MIDI Synth. Thus, unless you have some particular reason not to, use the SB Live! MIDI Synth for sequencing.

FM Synthesizer Emulation

Because previous generations of Sound Blaster cards included a Yamaha OPL FM synthesizer, the DOS drivers include a software emulation of this chip. Unfortunately (though some people absolutely hated the sound of this synthesizer), there's no such emulation in the Windows drivers, so even though some people miss this synthesizer, it is dead and buried and not likely to come back.

MIDI Ports for External MIDI Instruments

In the list of available MIDI ports, you will also find ports named SB Live! MIDI UART or SB Live! MIDI out and SB Live! MIDI in, depending on the driver version and operating system you're using. These ports do not point to any of the synthesizers described previously. MIDI data instead is sent to or received from the external MIDI connectors of the card.

> UART is short for *Universal Asynchronous Receiver and Transmitter*, the electronics needed for receiving and transmitting MIDI signals to and from external devices.

You should select these ports if you use external MIDI instruments. For example, if you use a MIDI keyboard for input to the sequencer, select the SB Live! MIDI UART or SB Live! MIDI in as the input port, as in Figure 14.16. You'll find more about how to connect external MIDI gear in the next chapter.

When this MIDI device is used, the MIDI out on both the Joystick/MIDI connector and the digital I/O device will receive the same MIDI signals.

Summary of the MIDI Devices of the SB Live!

Each MIDI device will provide 16 MIDI channels, so that in sequencing software, you can layer different tracks of musical instruments together in separate channels to create a piece of music. With the above 4 MIDI devices, the Live! has a total of 64 MIDI channels available when you are using a MIDI sequencing software that lets you use all four ports at once for MIDI composition. For software that relies on the Windows preferred MIDI device setting, only one can be used at any time. This includes the Windows Media Player.

> The specifications of the Live! list 48 MIDI channels; they do not take into account the SB Live! MIDI UART device, which also provides another 16 MIDI channels if you have an external MIDI hardware capable of generating MIDI music.

Each of these MIDI synthesizer devices uses different ways to generate MIDI audio and supports a different number of polyphony, which determines the number of sounds that can be played back by the synthesizer simultaneously. 64-voice polyphony is the norm for most uses.

Table 14.2: MIDI Devices on the Sound Blaster Live!

MIDI Device	Synthesizer	Polyphony	Description
A: SB Live! MIDI Synth B: SB Live! MIDI Synth	Hardware synthesizer in the EMU10K1	64 voices (automatically distributed between both A and B SB Live! MIDI Synth devices)	Makes use of the hardware synthesizer in the EMU10K1 to play MIDI files. This will offload the playback of MIDI files to the Live!, freeing the CPU for other tasks. To use SoundFonts and the built-in MIDI effects of the Live!, like reverb and chorus, either of these devices has to be used. This is the preferred setting.
SB Live! MIDI UART	MIDI out on the backplate's Joystick/MIDI connector and digital I/O devices like the Live!Drive	Depends on the MIDI hardware connected to the MIDI out	Use this when you wish to play MIDI files with external MIDI hardware connected to the MIDI output of the Live!
SB Live! S/W (Software) Synth	Uses the CPU to generate MIDI music	1,024 voices	This device provides a rudimentary General MIDI sound and does not support SoundFonts. It should be used only as a last resort as it takes up CPU processing time to generate music. You should normally use the A: SB Live! MIDI Synth device for the best sound quality and performance. Only available in Windows 95/98/ME.

TIP *You can also use the second B hardware synthesizer in sequencers for extra MIDI channels to work with.*

TIP *If you are sequencing music and the polyphony of the other MIDI devices is used up, you can use the SB Live! Software Synth (if available) to fill up some of the instrument parts.*

In general, hardware synthesizers have the best MIDI quality, support more realistic effects, and use little CPU time compared to software synthesizers. You would normally use the hardware synthesizer built in to the EMU10K1 by choosing the SB Live! MIDI Synth.

15

CONNECTING MIDI INSTRUMENTS

As mentioned in the previous chapter, MIDI refers not just to the "language," but also the connectors, cables, and electrical properties of the communication between instruments. Therefore, most instruments that "speak" MIDI will have one or more MIDI connectors, which are five-pole DIN connectors.

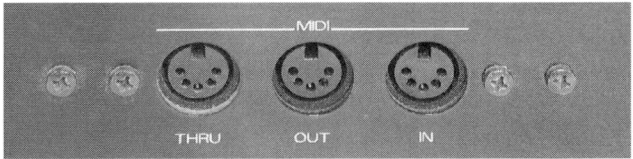

Figure 15.1: Typical set of MIDI connectors on a synthesizer

To create MIDI music, you need three things. First, you need a sound source: the synthesizer. This can be the synthesizer of the Sound Blaster Live!, a separate hardware synthesizer, a synthesizer module (a synthesizer without a keyboard), or a software synthesizer in your computer.

Second, you need a sequencer to record and play back the music. Chapter 17 will teach you how to pick a sequencer, as well as the basics of using one.

Finally, to be able to use the sequencer, you need a way of entering the notes. While using the mouse or the computer keyboard directly within the sequencer program may work for some types of music, it certainly doesn't for others. A good MIDI keyboard is therefore highly recommended, and this chapter will help you choose the right one.

The MIDI Interface on the Live!

The Sound Blaster Live!, like many other sound cards, has a MIDI interface so that you will be able to connect any external MIDI devices such as synthesizers, keyboards, drum machines, and effect units to the computer.

The Original Live! with a Digital I/O Card

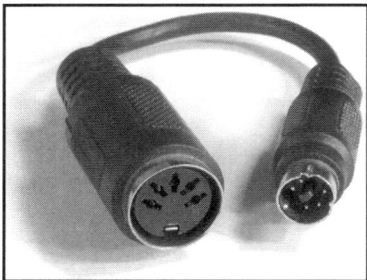

Figure 15.2: MIDI-DIN to standard size MIDI connector cable

The original Live! with a digital I/O card has separate MIDI in and out connectors. Unfortunately (due to size constraints), they are not standard-sized MIDI connectors. You will need special converter cables to turn these connectors into normal MIDI connectors. Because only one such converter cable was included in some versions of the original Live! package, you may have to order another converter cable. If so, they are available from the Creative online store, as well as some well-stocked music and computer stores.

Live!Drive and Live!Drive II

Both the Live!Drive (also known as Live!Drive I) and Live!Drive II have standard MIDI in and MIDI out connectors on the front, so if you are lucky enough to have one of these, just plug in your MIDI cables and start playing!

Live!Drive IR

Unfortunately, there wasn't enough room on the front panel of the Live!Drive IR to fit standard-sized MIDI connectors, so the same type of Mini-DIN connectors as are found on the digital I/O card of the original Live! were used. Consequently, converter cables are necessary to connect normal MIDI cables to this connector.

At least one should be included with the card. If you need another one, it can be purchased from the Creative online store, as well as some well-stocked music and computer stores.

Other Live! Models

Figure 15.3: Splitter cable for the joystick port

The rest of the Live! models do not have dedicated MIDI connectors. Instead, they use a method commonly found on sound cards, where some of the pins on the joystick connector (the oblong, flat, 15-pole connector on the back of the card) are used for MIDI. In this case, you need a splitter cable that will give you both a joystick connector and MIDI in and out. (Actually, this feature can be used on all Live! models. However, this is the same MIDI in and out as on the digital I/O card or Live!drive—not a second one—so if you have real MIDI connectors, there's hardly any point in using a splitter cable in the joystick port.) As this is the same on many sound cards, this type of cable can usually be found in well-stocked music and computer stores (or if you have the skills to build it yourself, finding the instructions on the Internet isn't hard).

Sample Setups

To make it easy to see how MIDI is used in practice, what follows are a few examples of how MIDI gear can be connected in typical studio setups.

Example 1: MIDI Keyboard to Synthesizer Module

Suppose you have one MIDI keyboard and one synthesizer. To be able to play the sounds on the synthesizer module, you must connect the MIDI keyboard to the module using MIDI. You would therefore connect the MIDI out on the keyboard to the MIDI in on the module. When this is done, every time you play something on the keyboard, messages are sent via the keyboard's MIDI out to the module with information about what notes were played and, if the keyboard is velocity sensitive, velocity information.

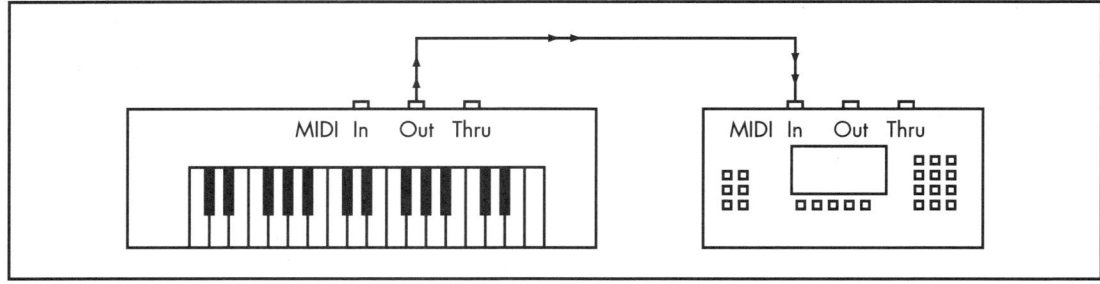

Figure 15.4: Example1: MIDI keyboard connected to synthesizer module

Example 2: MIDI Keyboard and Sequencer

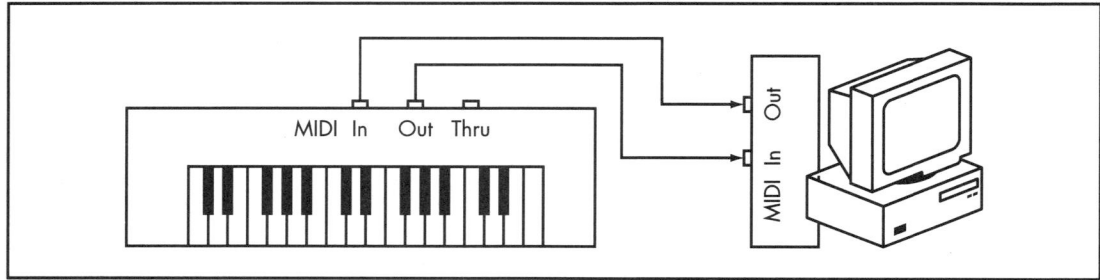

Figure 15.5: Example 2: MIDI keyboard connected to computer-based sequencer

If you need to connect a computer running a sequencer and a keyboard-equipped synthesizer (which is a common home studio setup), the sequencer must be able to receive all MIDI messages that the synthesizer transmits when you play the keyboard. Therefore, the synthesizer's MIDI out is connected to the computer's MIDI in. But this is not enough, particularly if you plan to use the sounds of the synthesizer. The main purpose of the sequencer is to be able to play back what was previously recorded. Therefore, the computer's MIDI out should be connected to the synthesizer's MIDI in. In this case, MIDI messages can go in both directions, and you'll get the ability to both record and play back sequences of MIDI messages.

MIDI Thru

Many MIDI devices have three MIDI connectors. The last one (where MIDI in and out are the first two) is called MIDI thru. Everything that goes into the MIDI in, and only that, will be echoed on the MIDI thru connector. This feature is commonly used to chain several MIDI instruments together, and unless you have a large studio setup (in which case you probably know most of this anyway), you won't need this feature.

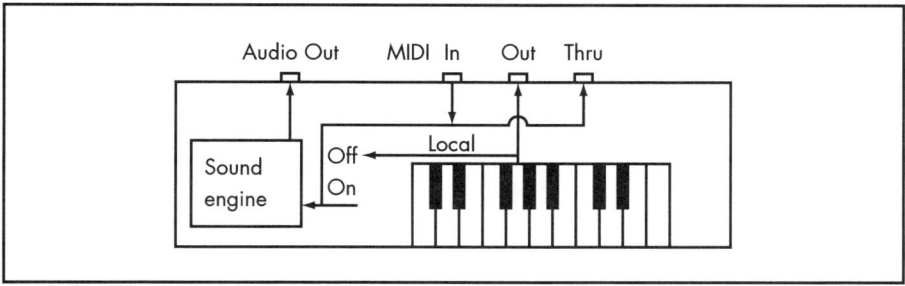

Figure 15.6: Signal routing in a synthesizer

Using a MIDI Keyboard for Input

To efficiently create music with a MIDI setup, you need a way to enter notes in real time. While many options exist, the far most popular is using a MIDI-equipped piano-like keyboard. Let's look at some of the details concerning this.

Choosing the Right MIDI Keyboard

Basically, there are two ways you can go when you purchase a MIDI keyboard. You can use the sounds of *another* synthesizer or sound module, and buy a dedicated MIDI keyboard that doesn't contain any sounds at all. Such a keyboard simply transmits MIDI data when you press the keys. Sometimes, particularly when they are used to control other MIDI instruments in a studio, such keyboards are known as *keyboard controllers, master keyboards,* or *mother keyboards.* If you are planning to use the Live! synthesizer as the sound source, purchasing this type of keyboard may save you money. MIDI keyboards like this can be found in all price ranges, starting at around $100, and they come in all sizes and with different features. Most of the common features are outlined here. For certain types of electronic music, a very simple keyboard is often enough.

You can also buy a new or used synthesizer, home keyboard, or anything that sends MIDI when you play it—but simply to use its keyboard. A 10- or 15-year-old synthesizer is often quite limited when it comes to sounds, but it may have a high-quality keyboard and many useful MIDI features. Of course, if it does contain some nice sounds, it's very possible to use it together with the Live! for creating music.

When looking for a good MIDI keyboard, here are a few things to consider:

Number of keys. How many keys you need on the keyboard usually depends on what type of music you are going to create. If you are used to the piano, chances are that you will prefer a keyboard with more keys. On a synthesizer keyboard, 61 keys (five octaves) and above is common. Dedicated MIDI keyboards may be found with fewer keys. If you don't need the extra keys, there is usually no point in getting them—they will only fill your desk and empty your wallet. When in doubt, however, go to your nearest music store and try a few different sizes and keyboard types. Many keyboards, especially those with fewer keys, can easily be transposed, or shifted, one or more octaves up or down.

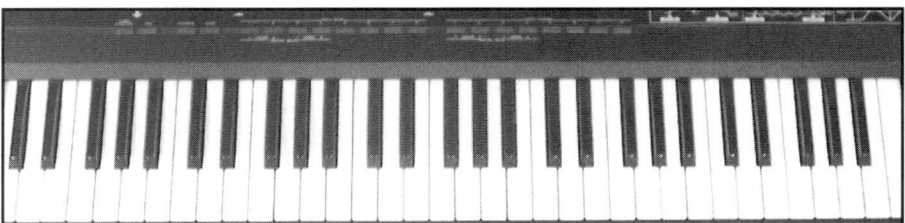

Figure 15.7: A 61-key keyboard—a common size, and good enough for most purposes

Type of keys. There are different types of keys on MIDI keyboards, too. Most keyboards can be said to be either *weighted* or *unweighted*. Unweighed keyboards are keyboards with the normal type of synth keys; they are usually quite light and made of plastic. A weighted keyboard has the feel of a piano keyboard, with some weight added to each key. The latter type of keyboard is more expensive and is often found in digital pianos. The type of keyboard you choose is, of course, a matter of taste. For many types of music, unweighted keys are fine. If you're looking for the perfect piano feeling, however, weighted is the way to go.

Velocity sensitivity. If the keyboard is velocity sensitive, it will sense how hard (or more correctly, at what speed) you press the key and transmit this information via MIDI. Velocity sensitivity is a common feature today, and it is certainly recommended if you're trying to create any kind of music that is not totally electronic. Usually, when you hit a key harder, the note will be played louder. If this feature is missing on a keyboard, a default velocity value will be transmitted when you press a key. In a computer-based sequencer, you can easily edit these values manually after you've recorded a part, but velocity sensitivity can save you a lot of time and, if you're a decent keyboard player, help you create more natural sounding music.

Pitch-bend wheel or joystick. On many MIDI keyboards, you will find a wheel or a joystick (or sometimes even buttons, although they don't give you as good control as the alternatives) located at the left side of the keyboard. This is used to alter, or bend, the pitch of a playing note, as you can do on many real instruments. While it takes a while to master, once you do, it can be hard to live without.

Modulation wheel/joystick. On many real instruments, you can add a slight vibrato at the end of long sustained notes to make them sound more alive. On a MIDI keyboard, this is often accomplished with a *modulation wheel* (or with the combined pitch-bend/modulation joystick found, for example, on many Roland synthesizers). Depending on the synthesizer and the type of sound you're playing, this wheel may add effects in addition to vibrato, which is why it's called a modulation wheel rather than a vibrato wheel. Like the pitch-bend wheel, it takes a while to master, but it can be very useful once you do. Some keyboard controllers have separate pitch and modulation wheels.

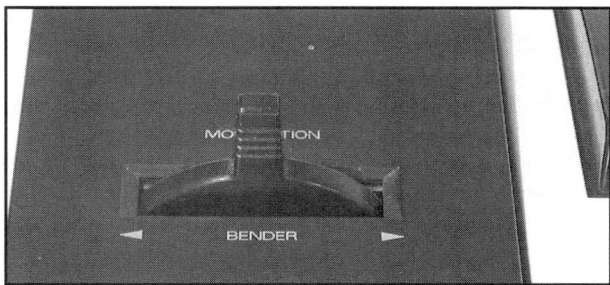

Figure 15.8: Pitch-bend and modulation joystick on a Roland synthesizer

Sustain pedal.   Many MIDI keyboards let you connect a *sustain pedal*. A sustain pedal works just like the right pedal on a piano. When it's pressed down, notes will not stop playing until you lift your foot from the pedal. If you play the piano, you will most likely appreciate this feature.

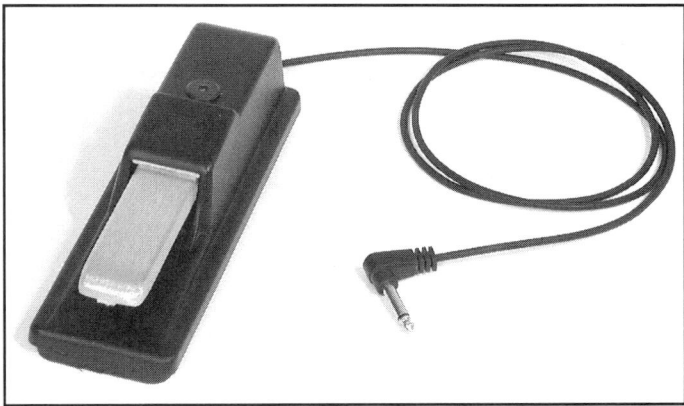

Figure 15.9: Sustain pedal

Aftertouch (pressure) sensitivity.   On some keyboards, you can press down a key a little harder to add certain effects to the sound in much the same way as with the modulation wheel. The type of effect depends on the synthesizer and the instrument you're playing. You may be able to, for example, add vibrato or growl to a saxophone or brightness to a synth pad. There are two types of aftertouch. The aftertouch can be specific to each key, so that you can add aftertouch to only certain notes; this is known as *key aftertouch*. The other, more common type of aftertouch sends a value to the current MIDI channel. In this case, it makes no difference what key is pressed down—the aftertouch value affects all notes playing on that MIDI channel. This is known as *channel aftertouch*, or *channel pressure*.

Expression pedal.   Some MIDI keyboards let you connect another pedal, called an *expression pedal*. This type of pedal, however, is not either simply up or down, like a sustain pedal, but it can have any value in between. Its use depends on the synthesizer and the sound you are playing, but it's commonly used to control the volume of the current instrument. This feature is probably more useful for live performances than for studio work.

Local on/off. If you are using a synthesizer as a MIDI keyboard and plan to use its sounds together with the sounds of the synthesizer on the Live!, make sure that a feature called local control can be turned off. When local control is off, any keys that you press on the synthesizer's keyboard will not trigger any notes on the keyboard's internal synthesizer. Only the MIDI data will be transmitted. If this MIDI data is sent to a sequencer, it can be instantly sent back to the synthesizer to be played. This is the preferred mode when the synthesizer is connected to a sequencer.

Figure 15.10: Menu on a synthesizer to set local control

Example: The Author's Choice

Everyone has his or her own personal taste, and I do not want to recommend any specific brand or models. What follows is just an example to give you a concrete setup that works well with the Sound Blaster Live!. If you want a keyboard for MIDI input, try different options to find one that suits *you*—not me!

I purchased a used Roland D-50 synthesizer a couple of years ago. Most of the time, I do not use its built-in sounds at all. Instead, I have connected the MIDI out of the D-50 to the MIDI in of the Sound Blaster Live! and play the sounds of the Live! with the keyboard of the D-50. I chose it because I like the feel of the keyboard and because it has all the features mentioned in the preceding list. This is certainly true for many other types of synthesizers, as well, so it may be a good idea to visit your local music store to see if it has any used equipment to offer.

Figure 15.11: Roland D-50

For the times when I'm away from home but bring my computer, I use a BlasterKey MP3, which is a simple MIDI keyboard controller from Creative. It is relatively small and, while not extremely light, is only a fraction of the weight of the rather heavy D-50. It's connected directly to the MIDI/joystick port of the Live! and does not need anything else, not even a power cord. Although it lacks many of the features (like a pitch-bend wheel) and the nice feeling of the D-50, it has 49 relatively good velocity-sensitive keys, and using it sure beats using the mouse or keyboard for note input.

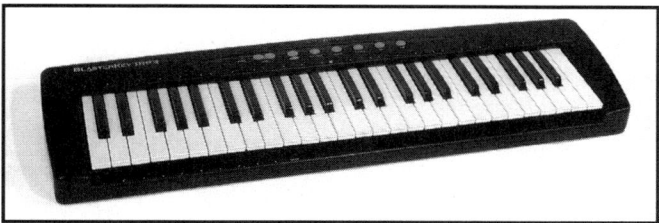

Figure 15.12: BlasterKey MP3

Software Synthesizers

With the increasing speed of computers, a large number of programs designed to replace sound-generation hardware such as synthesizers, samplers, and drum machines has appeared. Many of these programs receive MIDI and can therefore be controlled from any sequencer.

Types of Software Synthesizers

Just as there are different types of hardware synthesizers (including analog synthesizers, virtual analog synthesizers, various types of digital synthesizers and samplers, and drum machines), there are many types of software synthesizers available. Because the PC is very flexible, almost any type of software can be written for it. However, because of the rather limited processing power of a PC (compared to the dedicated custom chips found in most synthesizers), some types of synthesis are more suitable for software synthesizers than others. Many software synthesizers take advantage of the PC's better user interface compared to that of most regular synthesizers, as well as the ease of upgrading software to incorporate new and exciting features.

Among the many available types of software synthesizers, you'll find General MIDI playback modules, drum machines (often with built-in pattern sequencers), virtual analog synthesizers, modular synthesizers (where you construct your own synthesizer from basic building blocks), and even entire virtual studio racks!

In fact, many cheaper sound cards don't even have a hardware synthesizer, but use a software synthesizer supported by the particular hardware (for, among other things, low latency) to play back MIDI music. This is also the case when the Creative S/W synthesizer, which is available with most Live! drivers for Windows 95/98/ME, is used.

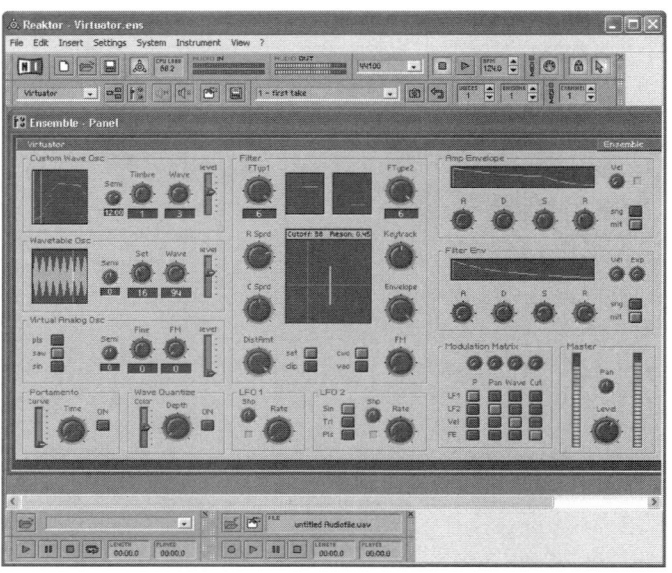

Figure 15.13: Two software synthesizers: Native Instruments' Reaktor (top) and Propellerhead Software's Reason (bottom)

Many manufacturers let you download free trial versions of their software. Because the choice of synthesizer is much a matter of taste, as well as price, you should compare a few and judge for yourself. Of course, because the Live! already has a great hardware synthesizer with plenty of power, high sound quality, and SoundFont support, a software synthesizer is far from necessary. It some cases, however, it might inspire you with its new sounds, new user interface, and new possibilities.

Some software synthesizers are mainly designed for playback of GM MIDI files. One example of this is the Microsoft software synthesizer that comes with some of the later versions of Windows, enabling playback on hardware without wavetable synthesis support. Another example is the Virtual Sound Canvas (which is a software equivalent of Roland's popular line of Sound Canvas GM Synthesizer modules), of which you'll find a demo on the CD.

The Pros and Cons of Software Synthesizers

Recently, software synthesizers have significantly increased in both popularity and quality. A few years ago, computers did not have anywhere near the audio processing power of the custom chips found in hardware synthesizers. While modern hardware synthesizers are still more powerful than software synthesizers running on today's computers, the latter have a couple of advantages that make them worth considering in many situations.

A software synthesizer is normally designed to run on your computer without any extra hardware. This, of course, makes it cheaper to buy a software synthesizer than a hardware synthesizer, assuming that you already have a decent computer to run it on. Second, while most hardware synthesizers often offer no more than a small display and a few knobs or sliders, a software synthesizer can use the entire PC monitor, mouse, and keyboard as its user interface. Furthermore, it can use the hard drive to load and store data, and in some cases it can automatically synchronize with MIDI and audio sequencers in various ways to make life easier for musicians.

Processing Power

All this comes at a price, of course. First, software synthesizers rely on your computer's processing power (where the main processor is usually the limiting factor). Sound synthesis is a computationally intensive task, so your computer may not be able to live up to your expectations. And there's not really any point in buying the latest, fastest, and most expensive computer only to be able to run a software synthesizer smoothly, unless you're desperately in need of the particular advantages it might offer.

The limited power of your computer often becomes more obvious when you're running both a sequencer and a software synthesizer, and perhaps also recording all audio data to disk at the same time. While the software synthesizer itself might run fine, a sequencer requires quite a lot of free system resources to ensure proper timing.

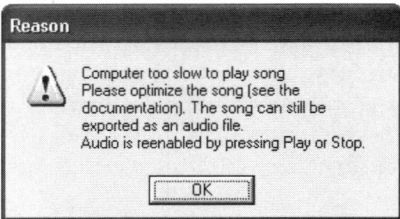

Figure 15.14: Make sure that you have a fast computer before running a software synthesizer

Latency

Another problem with software synthesizers is *latency*. Latency is the time from when a note is triggered until the result is played. A hardware synthesizer has dedicated processors that do nothing but synthesize sound. A computer, on the other hand, has only one processor that has to perform all the tasks of a modern operating system, including responding to user input, performing disk access, and running other programs in the background. Because of this, something may temporarily interrupt the sound generation, which will immediately cause audio dropouts if the sound is played immediately after it is generated.

To solve this problem, software synthesizers normally calculate the sound to be played a little bit in advance and use *buffers* that store short bits of precalculated sound before it's actually played back. If these buffers are too large (such as 100 milliseconds or even seconds), there will be a noticeable delay between the time a key is pressed on your MIDI keyboard and the time the sound is played. Because this delay, or *latency*, is a fixed time, this is generally not a problem when playing back prerecorded MIDI files, because all tracks will be equally delayed. However,

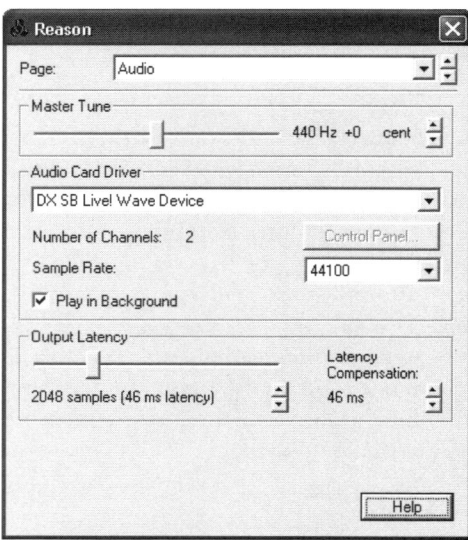

Figure 15.15: Audio settings in the Reason software synthesizer

the problem with latency becomes apparent when you are playing live, and when you try to synchronize the software synthesis with other audio or MIDI playback.

A faster computer will usually handle those interrupts in sound generation more quickly, reducing the need for large buffers. A slow computer, on the other hand, may require a large buffer (high latency) to produce smooth playback. The specific synthesizer used, as well as the drivers, both have a large impact on the required buffer size. High-performance audio drivers, such as ASIO, can sometimes reduce the latency to almost the same response time as you can expect from hardware synthesizers. Unfortunately, Creative does not provide ASIO drivers for the Live!

Note that improved drivers, better-performing software synthesizers, and faster computers have together made latency less of a problem today than it was not long ago.

> ASIO is a type of sound card driver optimized for low-latency audio playback on hardware that supports it. It was created to give Steinberg's audio sequencers (Cubase VST) better performance, but it has since been adopted by some other software developers, as well.

A MIDI Loopback Device

A PC-based sequencer will send MIDI data to any MIDI out ports on the computer. Software synthesizers are usually able to listen only to MIDI in ports. Clearly, some sort of device that connects a MIDI out port to a MIDI in port is necessary to connect a sequencer to a software synthesizer. Such a device is usually referred to as a *MIDI loopback device* and is a small piece of software that gives the system one or more virtual MIDI in and MIDI out ports. Any MIDI data sent to such a MIDI out port is simply sent back to the corresponding MIDI in port.

> A software synthesizer also may install its own driver and thus get its own MIDI out port, just like the software synthesizer on the Live! or Microsoft's software synthesizer included in Windows 2000. There's also a technology called ReWire (originally developed for Propellerhead Software's ReBirth software synthesizer) that lets you connect software with ReWire support to the Cubase VST audio sequencer.

Hubi's MIDI LoopBack Device

Probably the most famous MIDI loopback device program for Windows is *Hubi's MIDI LoopBack Device*, which is included on the CD. This program installs a number of loopback MIDI in and out ports on your system (four by default). Installation is simple and described in the included documentation. Hubi's MIDI loopback device has proved itself to work very well under Windows 95, 98, and ME. Because of the differences in the operating systems, however, it will not work with Windows NT, 2000, or XP.

Figure 15.16: The installation of Hubi's LoopBack Device driver is similar to the installation of a hardware driver, using the Add New Hardware Wizard. Detailed installation instructions are provided with the driver itself.

Figure 15.17: After the installation of the driver, you can configure the number of ports to use and other settings

MIDI Yoke

MIDI Yoke is similar to Hubi's MIDI LoopBack Device and works with all present versions of Windows, including 2000 and XP (although the NT/2000/XP version should not be considered as stable as its 95/98/ME counterpart). Installation and configuration is just as simple (see the included documentation). The program can be downloaded for free from http://www.midiox.com.

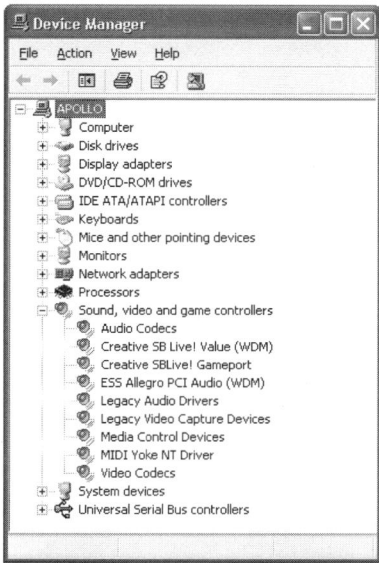

Figure 15.18: MIDI Yoke successfully installed under Windows XP

Using the Loopback Device

Using the loopback device is simple once you understand what the program actually does: In your sequencer, select one of the loopback device's MIDI out ports as the MIDI out port to use. Then select the corresponding MIDI in port as the port that the software synthesizer will listen to. When this is done, all MIDI data sent by the sequencer to the loopback device's MIDI out port will be sent to the software synthesizer's MIDI in port. This is like connecting the MIDI out to the MIDI in port of your Live!, only without the need for any cables or other hardware.

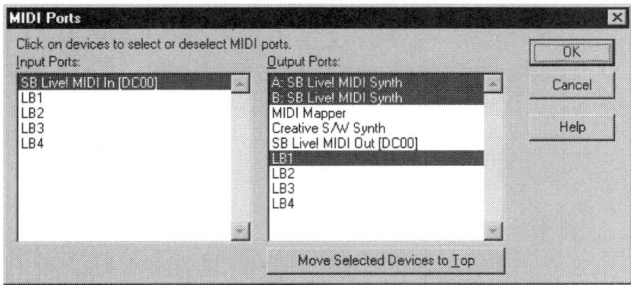

Figure 15.19: To use the loopback device, we choose one of its out ports as the MIDI out port in my sequencer (in this case Cakewalk Pro Audio)

Connecting MIDI Instruments **411**

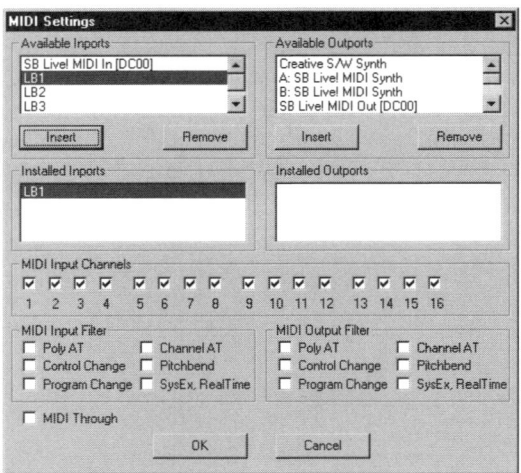

Figure 15.20: In the software synthesizer (Reaktor was used for this example), we choose to receive MIDI data from the corresponding in port of the loopback device

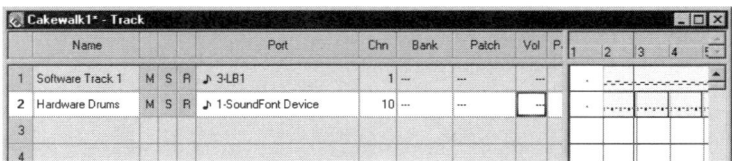

Figure 15.21: For sequencer tracks using the loopback port, any MIDI data is now sent to the software synthesizer

16

INTRODUCTION TO SOUNDFONTS

This chapter is devoted entirely to Sound-Fonts, a technology introduced with the AWE cards by Creative and E-MU, a manufacturer of synthesizers and electronic musical instruments that is now a subsidiary of Creative. Among other things, E-MU designed the synthesizers and effects units of the AWE series of sound cards, as well as those of the Sound Blaster Live!

The chapter will give you to the basic concepts of how to get, load, and use SoundFonts, as well as how to edit and create your own SoundFonts using the most popular SoundFont editor available: Vienna SoundFont Studio.

What Is a SoundFont?

On a wavetable synthesizer, like the hardware synthesizer of the Live!, two sets of information are required to describe an instrument. The first is the waveform data, the *samples*, that contain the basic sound. The second is the settings for the amplifiers, filters, low-frequency oscillators, and other components of the synthesizer, plus some information about the correspondence between keys and samples. SoundFont is a standard format for synthesizer instruments invented by

E-MU. A SoundFont file contains both the samples and the synthesizer information. One SoundFont may contain many samples and instruments, and therefore we often speak of a SoundFont as a bank of instruments.

SoundFont®

Figure 16.1: The SoundFont logo

Currently, the number of musical instruments that support SoundFonts is limited. The Sound Blaster 32, AWE32, AWE64, Audigy, and Live! cards support them, as well as the Audio Production Studio (APS) and a few other cards from E-MU. Some software synthesizers on the PC and Mac can also use SoundFonts (without any SoundFont support in hardware).

SoundFont files usually end with the extension .sbk or .sf2, where the former (short for *sound bank*) is the earlier type of SoundFont used almost exclusively with the AWE cards, and the latter is the current format (SoundFont 2), which is the most common today.

Where to Find SoundFonts

Because the SBLive! MIDI Synthesizer is based on SoundFonts only, it is totally useless without them. A good first step in exploring the possibilities of Sound-Fonts is to try some different ones and see the difference they can make. Let us therefore see what options there are for finding these files.

> To get you started, we've included some demo versions of commercial SoundFonts on the CD.

The Standard SoundFonts

Included with the Sound Blaster Live! drivers is a basic SoundFont that contains all the presets in the General MIDI and GS specifications, the GM and GS drum kits, and the MT-32 presets on variation bank 127. This SoundFont contains about 2 MB of samples. Most installation packages also contain 4- and 8-MB versions of the GM and GS sound sets for higher-quality MIDI playback. If installed, these can usually be found in the same place as the 2-MB SoundFont, namely in C:\Program Files\Creative\SBLive\Program or C:\Program Files\Creative\SBLive\SFBank (where C:\Program Files\Creative\SBLive\ is the default SBLive! installation path, and maybe different on your system). The files are called 8mbgmsfx.sf2 and 4gmgsmt.sf2. They are included on most installation CDs, so if they are not installed, insert your installation CD and search for *.sf2 files, and you should find them. Then you can simply copy the files to the location mentioned here. The 4- and 8-MB versions are usually not included in the Web downloadable versions of Live!Ware.

The following table summarizes the sound sets included with the standard GM SoundFonts.

> The MT-32 is a sound module made by Roland that has 128 preset sounds, although these are arranged differently from those in the General MIDI specification. Few MIDI files are created for this sound set, so you will most likely not find any use for this sound set. A chart of the MT-32 sound set is found in Appendix D, "The MT-32 Instrument List."

Figure 16.2: The standard GM/GS SoundFont banks

Table 16.1: Summary of the Standard GM SoundFonts Included with Most Sound Blaster Live! Installations

	Sample Size	Presets	GM	GS	MT-32	Included with All Web Packages
2gmgsmt.sf2	1,790 KB	328	✓	✓	✓	✓
4gmgsmt.sf2	3,897 KB	329	✓	✓	✓	
8mbgmsfx.sf2	7,205 KB	138	✓			

SoundFont Archives on the Web

Many musicians sooner or later find the 128 GM sounds rather boring and uninspiring. One of the more common questions about the Live! is where to find new SoundFonts. Good places to start are SoundFont archives on the Web. Because tools for creating SoundFonts are freely available, there are plenty of SoundFonts you can download for free from various Web sites. Of course, the quality of free SoundFonts may not always be what you hope for, so to find the perfect guitar sound, you may have to try a couple of banks. Because SoundFonts often include large amounts of sound data, the file sizes tend to be large, which is not a good thing for people with slow connections to the Internet.

SoundFonts that you download from archives on the Net are often compressed to reduce the file size and download time. If you get a file that does not end in .sbk or .sf2 but, for example, .zip, .rar, .arj, .sfArk, .sfpack, or something else, you can assume it's a compressed file and needs to be decompressed before it can be used.

A file ending in .zip or .rar can be decompressed with the WinZip (see http://www.winzip.com) and WinRar (see http://www.rarsoft.com) utilities, respectively. The .sfArk and .sfpack file extensions indicate that the file has been compressed with special SoundFont compression programs such as sfArk from Melody Machine (see http://www.melodymachine.com) and SFPack from Megota Software (see http://www.megota.com) to reduce their file sizes for a quicker download.

Commercial SoundFonts

More and more instruments support SoundFonts, and you can now buy commercial SoundFonts in all sizes, genres, and price ranges on CDs or on the Web, for direct downloading. This is certainly a more expensive option than using free SoundFonts, but commercial SoundFonts are generally of very high quality. Commercial SoundFonts can normally be found where sample CDs for other hardware samplers are sold.

There are also examples of very high quality SoundFonts that were custom made for the SoundBlaster Live!, such as Grand Piano One from StudioAX (see http://www.studioax.com) or the Utopia Live! General MIDI SoundFont (see http://www.utopialive.com). In many cases, MP3 songs demonstrating the SoundFonts are available for downloading—a great help when in doubt. You can also listen to the demos of these two SoundFonts in the CD-ROM.

The SoundFont Control Panel

The SoundFont Control Panel is part of the Live!Ware drivers and is included on the installation CD shipped with your sound card. If you don't have the installation CD, you will need to obtain the drivers-only package that can be downloaded from the Sound Blaster Web site.

If Live!Ware is installed, you can open the SoundFont Control Panel by selecting the SoundFont option in AudioHQ.

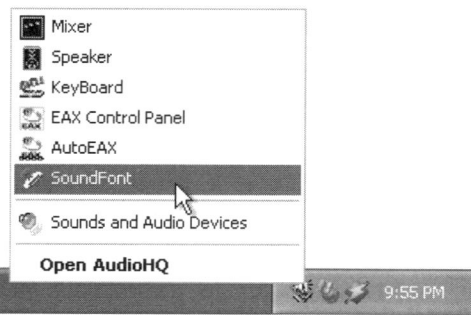

Figure 16.3: Open the SoundFont applet from the AudioHQ menu...

Figure 16.4: ...or from the Creative Launcher. If neither of these are installed, AudioHQ can be accessed from the Start menu as well.

Replacing the Synth Bank

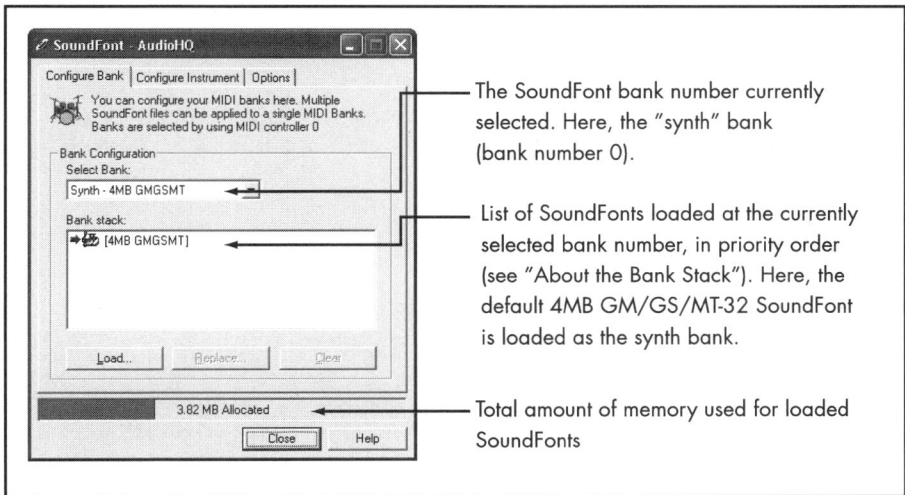

Figure 16.5: The first tab (Configure Bank) of the SoundFont applet

The *synth bank* is the first SoundFont bank (number 0). Whatever SoundFont is loaded at this bank number is used by default for MIDI playback. Because General MIDI files should be played back using a set of GM instruments, a GM SoundFont is usually loaded at this location, although you can load any SoundFont here, or even leave this bank empty (in which case you will not be able to play back MIDI files).

Changing the synth bank is easily done using the SoundFont Control Panel. On the first tab of the panel, Configure Bank, you can specify what SoundFonts are loaded at what bank numbers. To replace the synth bank, select Synth from the drop-down list (if it is not already selected). In the "Bank stack" list in the same tab, the synth SoundFont is then displayed. Select it and click Replace. You can now select a new SoundFont to be used for MIDI playback.

If you get an error message saying that there's not enough SoundFont cache memory available, you need to increase the SoundFont cache (see the section "SoundFont Cache and Other Options" later in this chapter for information on how to do this).

When you've replaced the synth bank, try playing back a MIDI file to hear the difference. Because any SoundFont can be loaded as the synth bank, playback of

MIDI files may not be correct unless you have chosen a SoundFont containing the General MIDI instrument set.

Loading Additional SoundFonts

Just as you can replace the synth bank (number 0) with another one, new Sound-Fonts can be loaded to other bank numbers. To load a SoundFontas, say, bank number 1, just select this bank from the drop-down list and click the Load button. Once a bank has been chosen, it is displayed in the "Bank stack" list.

Clicking Clear will remove the selected SoundFont from the "Bank stack" list and remove it from memory.

Clicking Replace will replace the selected SoundFont with a new one of your choice. Note, though, that this feature requires SoundFont cache memory to hold both the old and new SoundFont simultaneously. Therefore, when handling large SoundFonts, it may be a better idea to select the SoundFont, clear it, and then load the new one rather than using the Replace feature.

About the Bank Stack

You may have wondered why the list is called the bank stack, or why there's even a list. Wouldn't it be enough to simply show the name of the SoundFont loaded at the selected bank number? The answer is that the Live! drivers and software let you do more than simply load one SoundFont at one bank number. At every bank number, you can stack any number of SoundFonts "on top of" each other. The topmost bank in the stack in which the selected instrument exists will be used.

To clarify things a little, Figure 16.6 shows an example of when SoundFont stacking is useful: Imagine that you have a General MIDI SoundFont that you really like, except for the guitar sounds. However, you have another SoundFont containing better-sounding versions of the same guitar sounds on the original General MIDI locations, and nothing more. Loading the General MIDI Sound-Font at the bottom of the stack and the guitars SoundFont on top of that makes the Live! select the General MIDI sounds for all presets but the guitars, where instead the guitar SoundFont is used.

When you load multiple SoundFonts to one bank number, the top of the stack is indicated by an arrow in the "Bank stack" list (see Figure 16.7).

Variation Banks

Some SoundFonts contain presets not only in the bank you've loaded it to, but also in later banks. These additional banks are usually referred to as *variation banks*. The GS standard, for example, defines a couple of variation banks containing more presets in addition to the 128 General MIDI presets (see Appendix C, "The GS Instrument List" for a complete list).

If you load any of the included GM/GS SoundFonts as the synth bank, you'll notice that several of the banks say "Used by bank 000," meaning that the Sound-Font loaded as bank 0 has presets in this bank, too. You can still load additional SoundFonts on top of variation banks (see Figure 16.8).

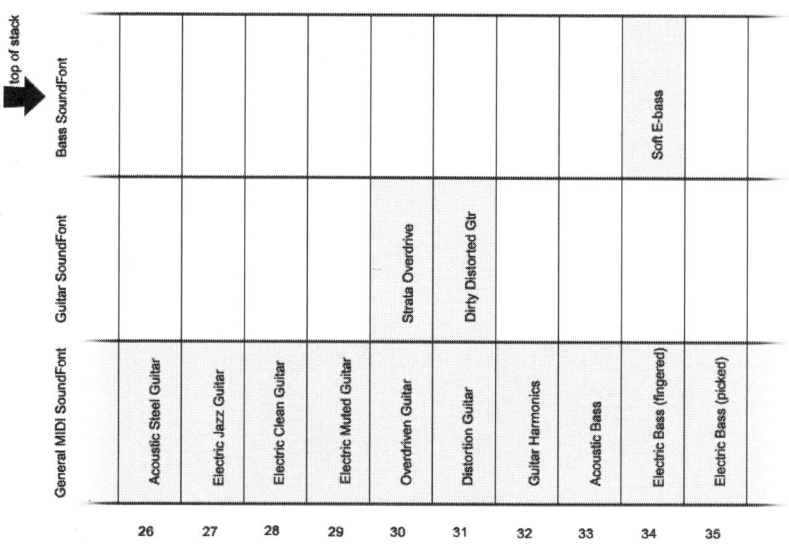

Figure 16.6: In this picture, three SoundFonts are stacked: A GM SoundFont at the bottom, a guitar SoundFont, and a bass SoundFont at the top. If instrument 27 is selected, the instrument from the GM SoundFont is used because this instrument doesn't exist higher up in the stack. If instrument 34 is chosen, however, the Soft E-bass instrument from the bass SoundFont is used because it exists in the topmost bank. Instrument 30 would similarly select the Strata Overdrive instrument.

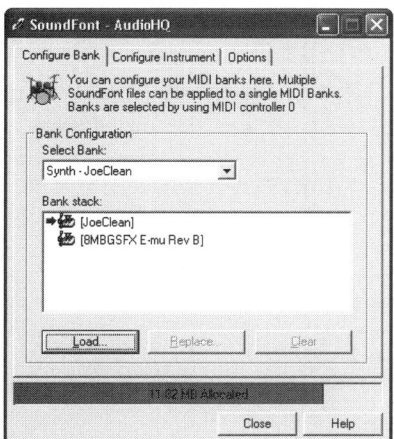

Figure 16.7: The JoeClean guitar SoundFont stacked on top of the 8 MB default SoundFont bank. Whenever the selected instrument exists in the JoeClean bank, this version will be used. If the instrument is missing, the version from the 8 MB GM bank is used.

The SoundFont containing the variation banks is sometimes called the *parent bank*. Because the parent bank and its variation banks belong together, you need

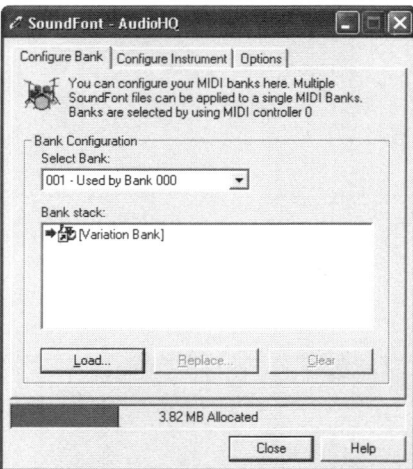

Figure 16.8: The synth bank uses bank 1 for variations

to select the parent bank when you want to remove any variation. Trying to remove a variation bank directly will generate an error message.

Replacing One or More Presets

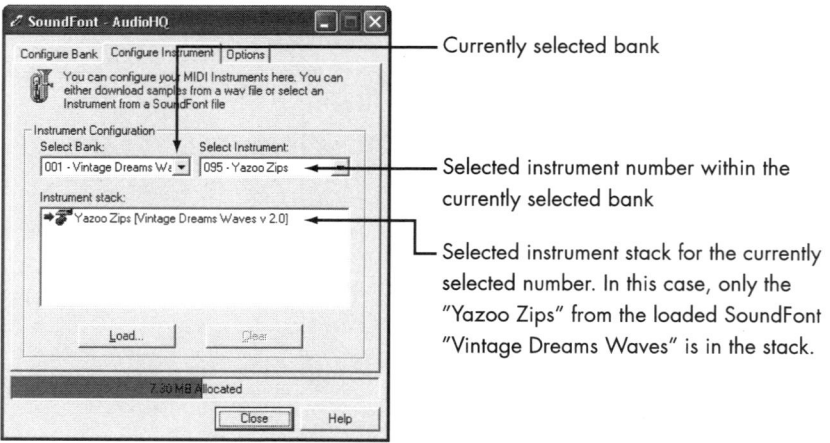

Figure 16.9: The second tab (Configure Instrument) of the SoundFont applet

Switching to the second tab of the SoundFont Control Panel, Configure Instrument, lets you view and replace individual instruments in a loaded SoundFont bank.

You can replace an instrument with either a .wav file or an instrument from another SoundFont bank. In the latter case, you cannot select the instrument in the new SoundFont bank that should be used, so this feature is best used with SoundFonts that contain a single instrument. On the other hand, when using a

.wav file, you cannot control the root key (the pitch at which the sample should be played), so if you load a tuned instrument as a .wav file, you may need to transpose the track in your sequencer.

Replacing a single instrument is very straightforward. In the AudioHQ, switch to the Configure Instrument tab and select the bank number and the instrument within that bank to replace. Click the Load button, and you can select a SoundFont or a .wav file to replace the selected instrument. Instruments that are part of a multi-instrument SoundFont get a different icon than individually loaded instruments. An instrument that was loaded in this way can be cleared by selecting it and clicking the Clear button. You cannot, however, clear individual instruments from SoundFonts loaded on the first tab of the SoundFont Control Panel.

Actually, just as you can load several SoundFonts on top of each other in the bank stack, you can load several instruments on top of each other in an *instrument stack*. This stack works exactly the same way as a bank stack: when one instrument is selected, the topmost available instrument is used. Just as in the bank stack, the top of the instrument stack is indicated by an arrow.

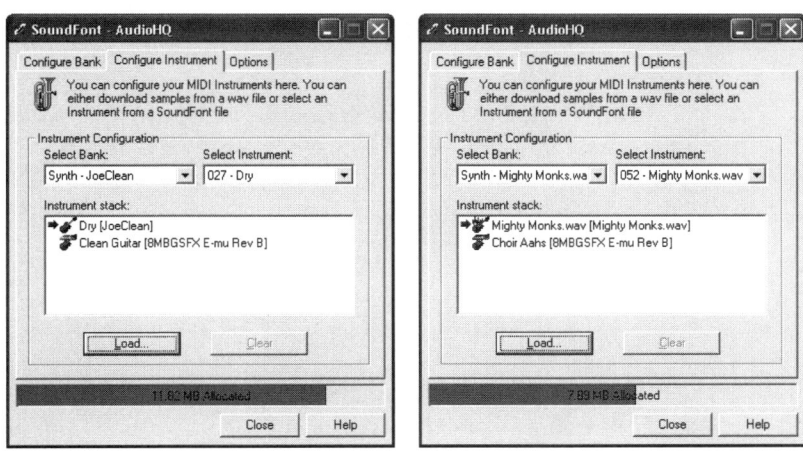

Figure 16.10: Individual instruments in the loaded SoundFont replaced by another SoundFont and a .wav file

SoundFont Cache and Other Options

Because there is no memory on a Sound Blaster Live! card itself, SoundFonts are loaded into the memory (RAM) of your computer. On the Options tab of the SoundFont Control Panel, you can set the maximum amount of memory that can be used for SoundFonts. This memory is called the *SoundFont cache* and is set by moving the slider in the SoundFont Cache box. The maximum SoundFont cache size that can be set depends on your computer's memory size. Normally, the maximum is about half the amount of memory available in your computer.

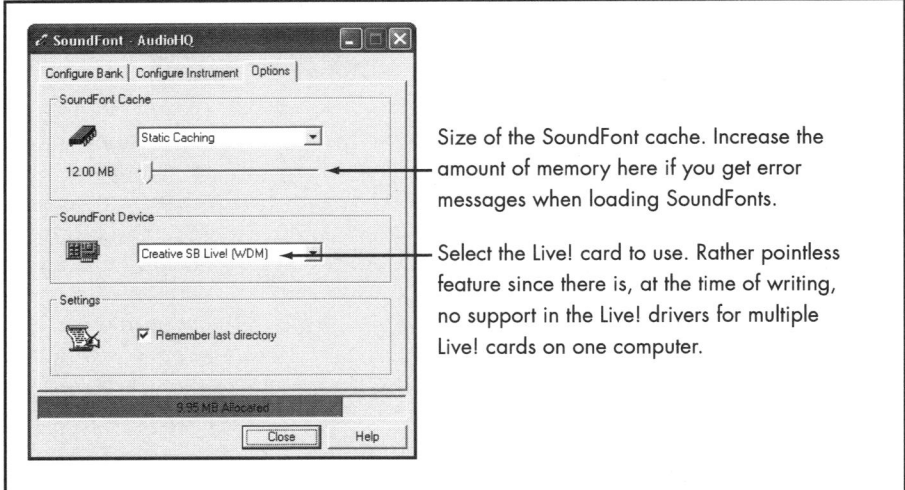

Figure 16.11: The third tab (Options) of the SoundFont applet

> Although half the amount of RAM in your computer can be used to load SoundFonts, you should keep in mind that the EMU10K1 chip can see a maximum of only 32 MB at a time. When more than 32 MB of Sound-Fonts are loaded, the Live! drivers use a clever system of controlling *which* 32 MB are visible to the EMU10K1 at any time. However, it is not possible to load and play one single sample that is more than 32 MB, no matter how much RAM you have in your computer.

The amount of SoundFont cache used is always shown at the bottom of the SoundFont Control Panel (where the red part of the bar represents the used part). If at any time when loading or replacing SoundFont banks or instruments you run out of SoundFont cache (which results in an error message), increase the SoundFont cache size here (if possible) and try again. Don't worry about setting a value that is too high here. If the SoundFont cache is not used, it is still available for other programs. You can also specify how this memory is managed (the caching algorithm), although all Live! drivers so far offer only one setting: static caching.

Although no Live! drivers (yet) support multiple Live! cards in one computer, on this tab you can also select which of the sound cards with SoundFont support to control.

Creating Your Own SoundFonts: Introduction to Vienna SoundFont Studio

Although using preprogrammed SoundFonts for your compositions is a huge improvement over relying solely on the standard GM sound set, being able to create and edit your own SoundFonts is the key to getting the full power from your Sound Blaster Live! A few programs for this purpose exist, but the most common and popular one is Vienna SoundFont Studio, developed by E-MU and Creative Labs.

Getting and Installing the Software

Unfortunately, Vienna SoundFont Studio program was not included in the software bundle of many versions of the Sound Blaster Live! (partly because a version of Vienna with full Sound Blaster Live! support was not ready at the time of the initial release of the SBLive!). However, the program can be downloaded free of charge from the Sound Blaster Web site (http://www.soundblaster.com). At the time of this writing, version 2.3 is the most recent version.

The installation procedure is simple. If you got the program from the Net, the downloaded file is most likely in Zip format, which can be decompressed with a utility like WinZip. When the file is decompressed, you are left with an installation program named setup.exe. Run this program, and it will, after asking you for an installation directory (the default installation path is usually fine), automatically install the program and create the program icons on the Start menu. If you have any audio editing applications installed on your computer, the installer may also ask you to select one to use for sample editing.

After installation, the program can be found on the Start menu under Programs • Creative • Vienna SoundFont Studio. Note that a Sound Blaster Live! (or other sound card with SoundFont support) is required to run the program.

The Program Parts

When you start Vienna, the window will be split into several sections.

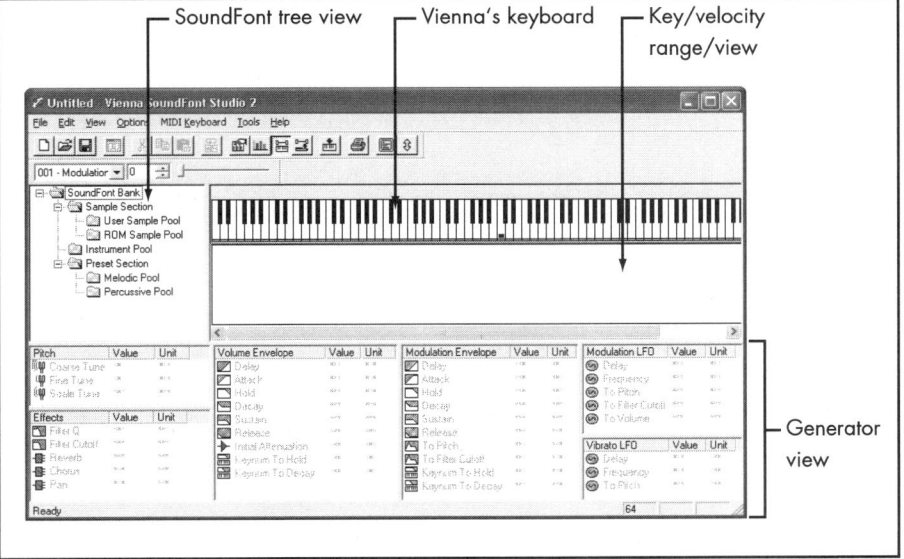

Figure 16.12: Vienna's main window

Introduction to SoundFonts **423**

At the bottom of the program window is the *generator view*, from which all synthesizer parameters (pitch, effects, envelopes, and low-frequency oscillators) are controlled. On the left side, a *tree view* shows the structure of the current SoundFont, much like the Windows Explorer. On the right side, you will find the *key/velocity range view*, with Vienna's keyboard at the top and any active samples and their ranges shown below. As in most Windows programs, there is also a menu bar and a toolbar, in this case including the MIDI controller bar where you can set the value of any supported MIDI controller.

Playing Sounds

Editing a SoundFont without being able to listen to the result every time you make a change is a nearly impossible task. Fortunately, there are a few ways to play a sound while you are editing it. Which method you use depends on your personal preference and available equipment.

Note that the sound that is played is always the selected sample, instrument, or preset in the SoundFont tree view (or part of it, if it is selected in the key/velocity range view). Therefore, to try the methods described here, you may first want to load a SoundFont into Vienna and select a preset to play.

The status bar at the bottom of the window always displays the last note number (or key/octave, if you have set this in the preferences) that was played.

Using a MIDI Keyboard

If you have a MIDI keyboard connected to your Sound Blaster Live!, it can be used to play the currently selected sound. First make sure that the MIDI keyboard is properly connected to the MIDI interface of the Sound Blaster Live! Then select MIDI In Devices from the MIDI Keyboard menu. Select the MIDI in port that corresponds to your external MIDI interface (which would be SB Live! MIDI UART or SB Live! MIDI In on a Live!) and click OK. Now you should be able to use your keyboard for instrument playback.

Using the Mouse

The mouse can be used to play the Vienna keyboard. A key is pressed as long as you hold down the left mouse button on a key. You can use the right mouse button to play sustained notes (which don't stop playing when you release the mouse button). Click the key again to release the note.

Using the Computer Keyboard

If you don't have an external MIDI keyboard connected to your Live!, the computer keyboard can be used for the same purpose. When the Vienna keyboard is active (click anywhere on it to make it active), the keys A thru K on your computer's keyboard can be used to play one octave of notes. The octave is selected with the 1 to 9 and 0 keys.

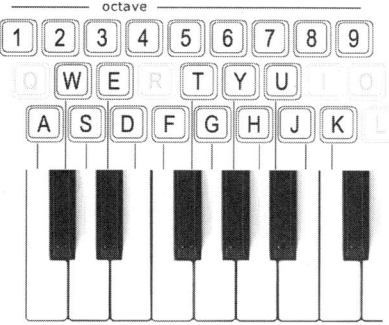

Figure 16.13: The computer keyboard keys and their corresponding keys on a piano keyboard

Using the Controller Toolbars

If your MIDI controller keyboard can't generate all control change messages recognized by the SB Live! MIDI Synth, or you're using the keyboard or mouse to play SoundFonts, you can use up to four *MIDI controller bars*. MIDI controller bars are shown and hidden using the View menu. These bars let you set the value of any supported MIDI controller. You can use this feature to check how the current instrument or preset responds to a control change value that you can't generate otherwise. Only the control changes that are recognized by the SB Live! MIDI Synth, plus pitch bend and aftertouch (pressure), are supported.

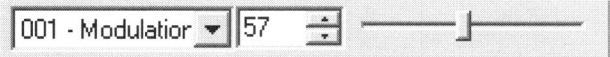

Figure 16.14: A controller toolbar is used to test the sound with various levels of modulation

If you want to reset all the controller values, or if some note becomes stuck (which may happen if a note-off message is lost in a transmission), there are two options on the MIDI Keyboard menu—Reset All Controllers, and All Notes Off—that will come in handy. These restore all controller values to their default settings and turn off all notes, respectively.

The SoundFont Structure

To successfully build your own SoundFonts from scratch, it is important to understand the structure of a SoundFont. While this structure may seem unnecessarily complex for creating a single preset (which is the SoundFont term for a finished instrument sound), this type of structure is very useful when creating larger projects.

To stay on a concrete level, let's imagine that we are to create a grand piano SoundFont. This is certainly not the first thing you would try, since creating a good-sounding piano SoundFont requires great skill in sampling and SoundFont

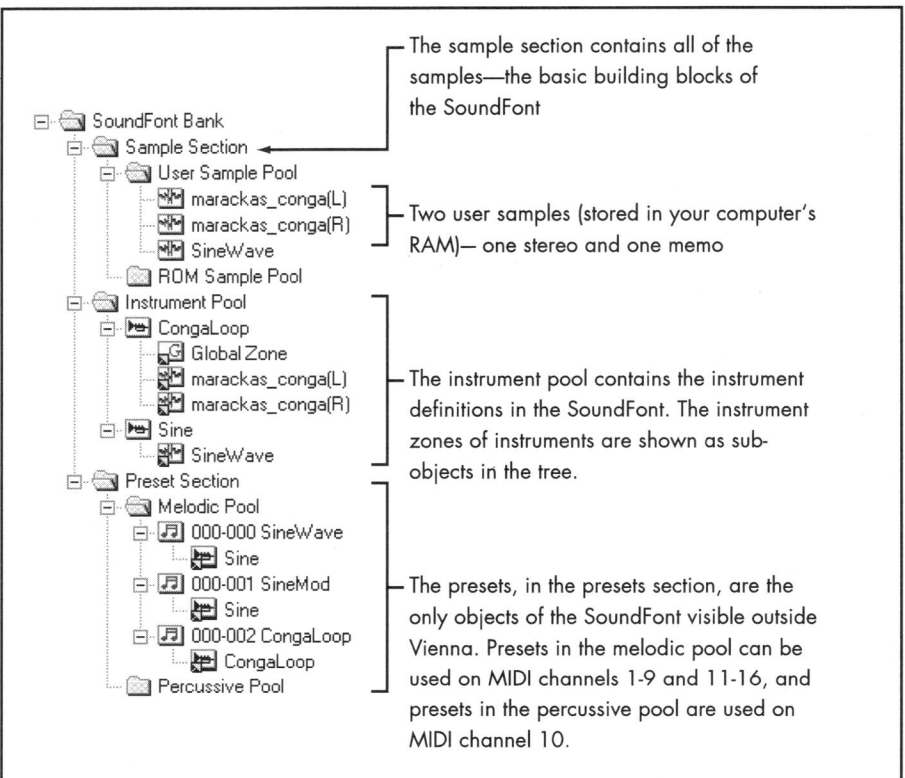

Figure 16.15: The stucture of a SoundFont shown as a tree

programming techniques, but it serves as a good example of how SoundFonts are structured.

Samples

The samples are the basic building blocks of a SoundFont. Any number of these pieces of audio can be included in a SoundFont. The samples in a SoundFont are displayed in the Sample Section folder of the SoundFont tree view. In our grand piano example, several samples would be necessary, because not only the pitch but the whole timbre of the sound changes across the keyboard range.

A sample may also include looping points. When the playback reaches the end looping point, it starts over at the start looping point. This way, short sound samples can be played as long as necessary.

Finding good looping points is often a difficult task, but it is almost necessary in this case because a piano will sound for about half a minute if the key is held down, and such amounts of sample data won't fit in your computer's memory.

Instruments

In an instrument, samples are combined with synthesizer settings to create the desired basic sound. In the piano SoundFont example, the piano samples from the sample section are laid out to cover different parts of the keyboard range. The amplifier envelope parameters are set to simulate the dynamics of a grand piano, and the individual samples may be panned a little differently, and so on.

If all this is done in the instruments section, why do we need presets at all? Read on to find out.

Presets

The preset section is the part of the SoundFont that is visible to the outside world. If a user loads a SoundFont for use in a sequencer, the user can choose among only the available presets.

Presets are simply a means of combining and customizing the available instruments. In many cases, there is a one-to-one correspondence between instruments and presets. In our example, we may be satisfied with the piano instrument we created and just create a piano preset based on the piano instrument. However, to make the SoundFont more useful, we could create a few variations on the piano, all using the piano instrument, with some minor changes in the synthesizer parameters for each preset. For example, to create a softer piano, we can lower the cutoff frequency of the filter somewhat. Or imagine that we've created a nice string orchestra instrument as well; not only can we create the piano and string presets, but these can be combined into a piano/string pad preset.

At this point, you may think it would have been a simpler solution to copy instruments rather than introducing an extra preset layer. Well, let's say that we later decide to improve our piano by using new and better samples. If we had copied it to every instrument, we would have to make the necessary changes to each one. Now we can instead change the single piano instrument, and the improvement will automatically affect all presets based on it.

Getting Your Own Sample Material

If you choose to create your own SoundFonts from scratch, you need some sample material to start with. This is, in many cases, the hardest and most crucial part of creating a good SoundFont. Sampling a grand piano with good results, for example, takes a lot of practice. If you happen to own another synthesizer, it may be a good instrument to practice on, especially because synthesizers are very easy to sample (just plug its output into the line-in port of the Live!).

Of course, you don't have to sample the material yourself. There are plenty of instrument samples, drum loops, and other useful material available from various sources on the Net. It is also possible to use the samples from other SoundFonts. When using such material, just make sure that you have the author's permission to use the sound in your SoundFonts.

The Sample Section

The samples in the current SoundFont are listed in the Sample Section folder of the SoundFont tree view. If you can't see it, click the plus next to the SoundFont Bank folder to expand it and view its subsections. The Sample Section folder contains two subsections when expanded: User Sample Pool and ROM Sample Pool.

When using Vienna with a SoundFont-compatible sound card that has read-only memory (ROM) containing samples, these samples will automatically show up in the ROM Sample Pool. The AWE cards are examples of such cards. The Live!, however, does not have any such feature and relies entirely on the computer's main memory to store samples.

To listen to any sample, select it from the User Sample Pool list by clicking it; you will then be able to play it.

Importing .wav Files

Any sample that you import into Vienna will be placed in the User Sample Pool. Vienna can import .wav audio files of virtually any frequency and 8- or 16-bit resolution. To load a sample, right-click the User Sample Pool folder and select Import User Sample(s) from the menu that appears. A file selector will ask for the name of the samples you want to load. Pick one or more files and click Import. The sample will now show up in the User Sample Pool. If the file is in stereo, two samples, the left and right, will be imported.

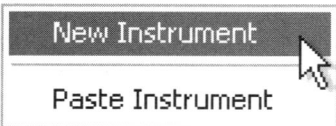

Figure 16.16: The shortcut menu that appears when you right-click in the sample pool

In the file selector, you can select several samples by holding down Ctrl while clicking each sample. You can also hold down Shift and click the first and last samples in a list, and all the samples in between will also be selected.

Creating New Samples

Vienna does not have any built-in functions for creating new samples. However, when properly configured, it can create a new empty sample, start your favorite Wave editor to let you fill it with something useful, and import the sample back when you quit the Wave editor. To try it, right-click User Sample Pool and select New User Samples from the menu. This feature is most useful when you plan to record your own samples.

Looping

An instrument that should be able to play long sustained notes, such as a piano, flute, or string ensemble, will usually require the samples to be looped. A looped sound has two looping points. When the playback reaches the end of the loop, it is continued at the beginning of the loop. Carefully set looping points can have a huge impact on the quality and realism of a SoundFont.

Looping is controlled from the looping dialog box that opens when you double-click a sample (or select Loop from the right-click menu). To get full control over the loop settings, make sure that the entire dialog window is visible. If you see a button named Loop Settings, click it to view the settings used to fine-tune the loop.

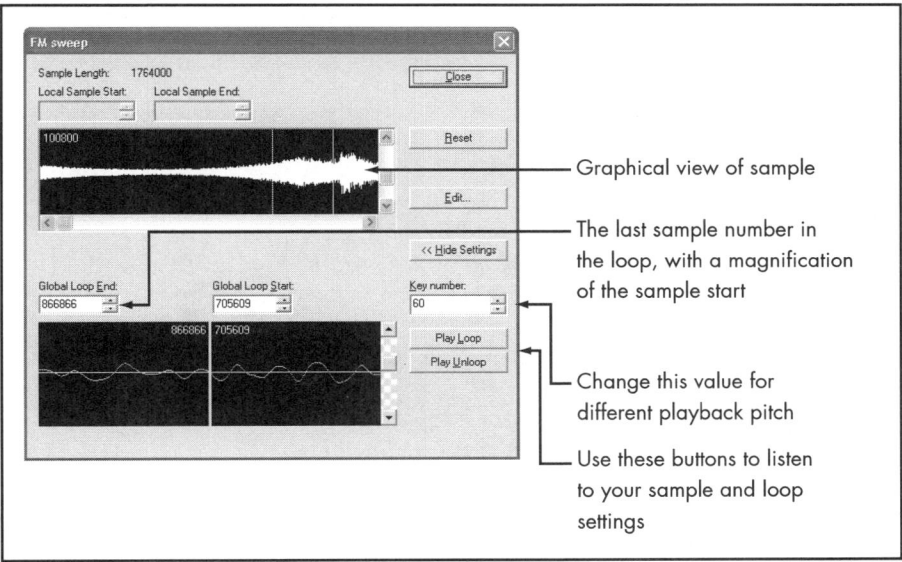

Figure 16.17: Vienna's sample loop dialog

The top of the Loop dialog box shows a graphical representation of the sample. Two vertical lines (green and blue) show the start and end looping points. At the bottom of the dialog box, two views show the last part of the sample before the end of the loop and the very beginning of the loop.

The general rule is to set the looping points at positions that make the transition from the end of the loop to the start of the loop as seamless as possible. Try to set the start and end looping points on points at the same level on the waveform (such as when the waveform crosses the center line on a rising edge). Audible clicks and other noises occur when the start and end looping points don't match. The small waveform views at the bottom of the dialog box, as shown here, will help you with this process.

If you're creating a synthetic sound, sometimes one single waveform cycle is enough to make up the entire loop. If you're trying to replicate a classical musical

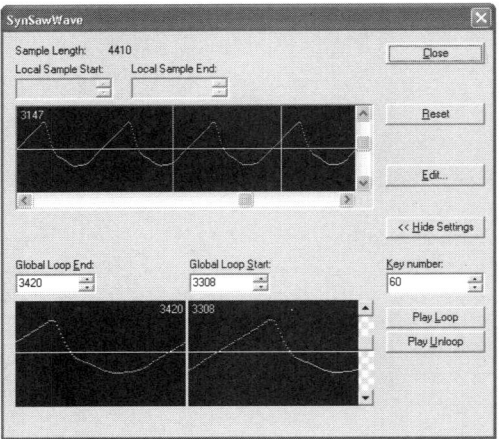 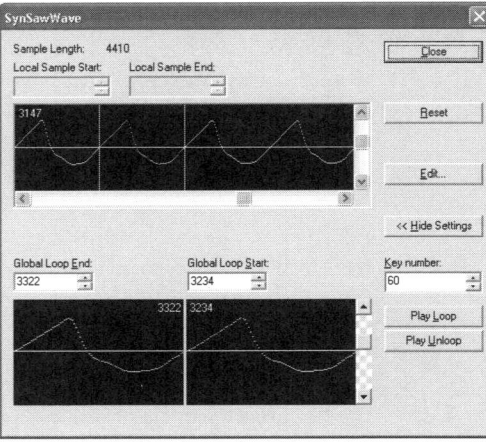

Figure 16.18: An example of bad loop settings (left). Notice the difference in amptitude of the sample at the very end and beginning of the loop (you can see it clearly at the border between the bottom two windows). This will most likely produce noise when played back. A corrected version of the loop (right). The end and start of the loop fit perfectly together, as you can clearly see in the bottom windows.

instrument, say a piano or a guitar, the longer the loop, the less the risk that the sample will sound repetitive and artificial. Instruments like the latter are among the hardest to faithfully reproduce on a synthesizer, so don't give up if you find it hard to create good loops at first. Also note that some samples are more suitable for loops than others.

You can play your loop at any time to check how it sounds by clicking the Play Loop button. You can also set the playback pitch (in semitones) by changing the Key Number value above the Play button.

To make things a little more complicated, there are two types of looping points: *global* and *local*. The global looping points are set at the sample level, and the local looping points are relative to the global looping points (and are controlled at the instrument level; see the next section). Most of the time, you will set good global looping points for each sample and not use the local looping points (that is, you will set the offset to 0).

Creating Instruments

Okay, folks. This is where the fun starts—or, at least, this is where we put the synthesizer to work and whatever you're working on starts to sound good.

To create a new instrument, right-click the instrument pool and select New Instrument from the menu that appears. Name the new instrument and click OK. Another dialog box will now ask you to select a number of samples from the sample

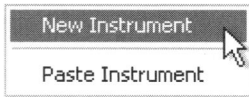

Figure 16.19: The instrument pool shortcut menu

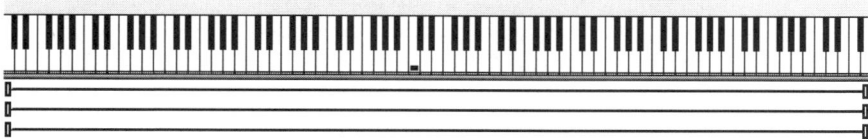

Figure 16.20: The key range view with three zones. The zone ranges are shown as the black lines with handles at both ends below Vienna's keyboard. In this case, all three zones span the entire keyboard.

pool. The selected samples will automatically be added to the new instrument. You can, of course, add and remove samples manually later if you need.

After you click the Add button, the instrument and its samples will appear in the SoundFont tree view as *instrument zones*. The instrument zones will also show up as bars in the key/velocity range view, below Vienna's keyboard.

By default, an instrument zone will span the entire key range of your MIDI controller, although this behavior can be changed in the preferences. As you'll see later, there are many times you need to restrict the range of keys where a sample is played. To do this, simply select the sample you want to change and drag either end of the bar that represents its range (you may have to scroll the window horizontally to find the ends). Another way to do this is to right-click the key range of a zone and select MIDI Set Range. You'll be asked to press the lower and the upper key of the current zone, and the range will then be automatically adjusted. The note numbers (or key/octave) of the selected range are displayed in the status bar.

The *root key* of a sample zone is an important parameter that must set to tell Vienna what pitch the sample was originally recorded at. For example, if you record a middle E on a piano, you should set the root key to a middle E (which is MIDI key number 64), or the sample will not be played back at the correct pitch. The root key of the selected instrument zone is indicated by a red arrow above Vienna's keyboard when the sample is selected. To change it, either right-click the sample in the SoundFont tree on the left and select Properties, or right-click the key/velocity range below Vienna's keyboard and select MIDI Set Root Key. If you choose the latter option, all you have to do is press the key on your MIDI keyboard that corresponds to the note that was originally sampled. Otherwise, simply enter the key number in the dialog box.

Getting Creative with Zones: Multisamples, Splits, and Layers

You've probably realized by now that you can use more than one sample in one instrument. This is very useful in many cases. One sample is seldom enough to re-create the full range of an acoustic instrument. Even though the synthesizer can play the sound at different pitches, on a real instrument, the actual timbre of the sound of low notes is usually pretty different from that of higher ones. To make this less of problem, an instrument is often sampled playing different notes, and each such sample is assigned to a narrow range of keys. This technique is called *multisampling* and is achieved in Vienna by loading several samples to one instrument and assigning them to different key ranges without overlap.

Splits are similar to multisamples, but whereas a multisampled instrument contains several samples of the same sound, in a split one part of the keyboard plays one instrument and another part plays a totally different instrument. For example, you might create an instrument with two samples where the lower keys use one zone playing a bass guitar and the higher keys play an electric piano. Also, you can add more instrument zones than two; just add more samples and adjust the instrument zone ranges below Vienna's keyboard.

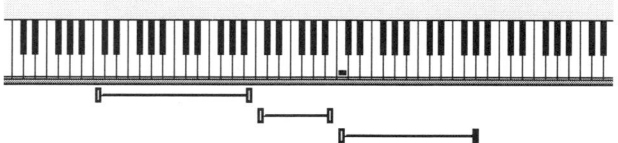

Figure 16.21: Key ranges of the zones in a multisampled instrument

Consider this extreme example: When you create a drum kit, you normally assign one unique instrument to each key. To simplify the process of creating such an instrument, there's a checkbox labeled "Assign each sample to individual key" in the Add Samples dialog box. If you check it, Vienna will ask what key number to assign to each sample. These are the normal MIDI key numbers, where middle C is 60.

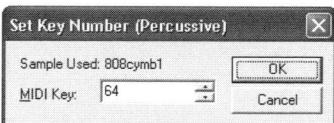

Figure 16.22: Dialog for assigning samples to individual keys when the Assign each sample to individual key *is selected*

In some cases, you might want to play several samples simultaneously when you hit a key. This is called *layering*. For example, you could create a full brass orchestra by layering different brass samples. To do this, just make several zones overlap, and they will all be played when you play a note in their common key range.

You also may want to use a special type of layering for stereo samples. A stereo sample is, in Vienna, two separate samples: one for each speaker. These should usually be played at the same time and use the same key range (panned to the left and right extremes; see the next section).

Velocity Range and Velocity Splits

Not only can you change the samples played according to the key that you press, but you can also play different samples according to how hard you press the key (on a velocity-sensitive MIDI keyboard). It may sound strange at first, but imagine a snare drum hit by a drumstick. When hit hard, not only will it sound louder, but the sound will be quite different from the sound when the drum is hit softly. Many synthesizers, samplers, and drum machines will simply play the sound at a lower volume when you press the key with a lower velocity on a MIDI keyboard. Vienna, however, will let you select the velocity range where an instrument zone should be played.

Try loading two different samples and assign them both to the same key range in one instrument. Then select Velocity Range from the View menu, or click the corresponding button on the toolbar. Note that the keyboard view changes to a gradient where (for some reason) blue represents soft and black represents hard. By default, key zones are played at any velocity (unless otherwise specified in the preferences), but just as you can change the key range in the key range view, you can drag the edges of the instrument zones to adjust the velocity range. If you want to play one sample when the key is hit softly and another when it's hit hard, just make sure that one zone covers one half of the velocity range and the other zone covers the other half. And if you want even more accuracy, you can create even more complex *velocity splits*, as this technique is called.

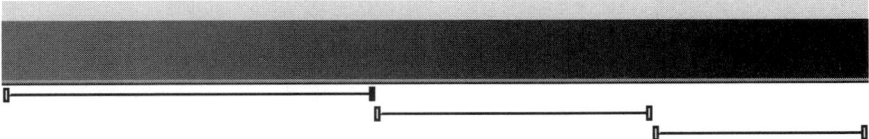

Figure 16.23: The velocity range view showing the zones of an instrument with a velocity split

Exclusive Classes

Yet another feature supported by SoundFonts is *exclusive classes*. If you assign two or more instruments to an exclusive class, only one of them can play at any given time. The classic (and by far the most common) example of when this is useful is in a drum kit where you have samples of a hi-hat played both open and closed. Obviously, a hi-hat can't be both open and closed at the same time, so in this case, both the open and the closed hi-hat sample would belong to the same exclusive class. Thus, if an open hi-hat sound is being played, playing the closed hi-hat sound will shut it off immediately.

You can have several exclusive classes in one SoundFont, and even within one instrument. To assign an exclusive class to two or more zones, right-click the zone in the key range view and select Properties. In the Exclusive Class field, enter any number except 0 to make the instrument belong to that exclusive class.

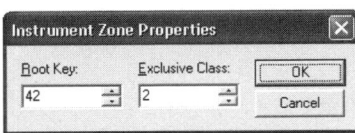

Figure 16.24: In this example, the instrument zone belongs to exclusive class 2

Looping—On the Instrument Level

For each instrument zone, you can decide whether the corresponding sample should be looped. If you right-click an instrument zone in the SoundFont tree view and select Loop, you will open a Loop dialog box, similar to the one used on the sample level. Here, however, you have a checkbox to choose whether you want to enable looping for this sample in the particular instrument zone. You can also adjust the looping points using something called local looping points (which are really offsets from the global looping points that are defined on the sample level). Usually, you will set good global looping points for a sample on the sample level and won't need to adjust the local looping points. If you do want to use different looping points for the same sample in different instruments, however, this is where to do it.

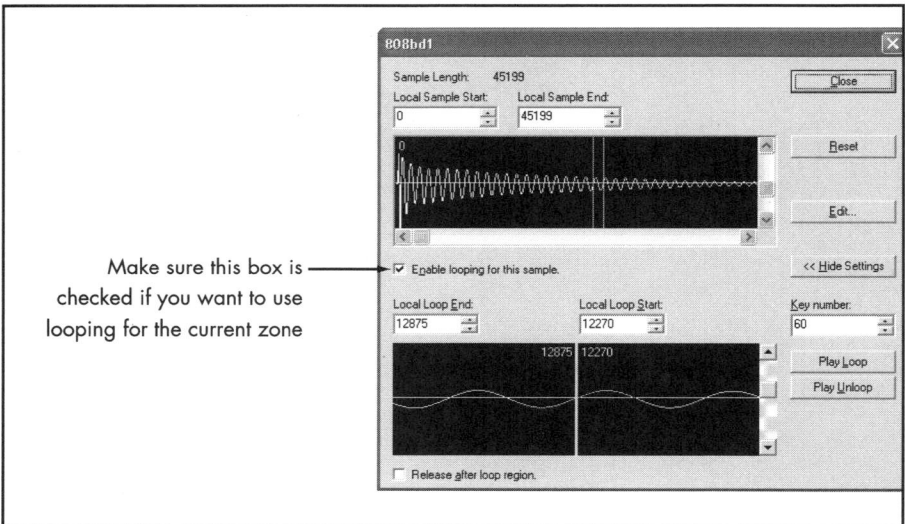

Make sure this box is checked if you want to use looping for the current zone

Figure 16.25: The loop properties dialog box of an instrument zone. Notice the checkbox that allows you to turn looping of a certain sample on and off.

Generators

Until now, we've used only the upper part of the Vienna window. When an instrument zone is selected, you'll note that all of the fields in the window panes at the bottom of the screen are filled with values (if you don't see one or more of these panes, drag the edges of the panes to move or resize them). These are synthesizer parameters, or *generators*, as they are known in Vienna, and you can use different settings for each of the instrument zones in your SoundFonts. Each parameter, such as the Filter Q value, affects the way that the instrument sounds. While the large number of parameters may seem confusing if you have little or no experience programming synthesizers, this is certainly one of the strengths of the SB Live! MIDI Synthesizer. For an introduction to the common building blocks of a synthesizer and to get a better understanding of some of the concepts that will follow, be sure to read Chapter 14, "MIDI Explained" (if you haven't done so already), before continuing.

When you click a synthesizer parameter in the generator view, a dialog box will open where you can change the generator's value. A generator will use a default value unless assigned a new value to it. All edited values are shown in red.

Pitch	Value	Unit
Coarse Tune	0	semitones
Fine Tune	0	cents
Scale Tune	100	cents

Effects	Value	Unit
Filter Q	0	dB
Filter Cutoff	20000	Hz
Reverb	0	%
Chorus	0	%
Pan	0	%

Volume Envelope	Value	Unit
Delay	0.001	sec
Attack	0.001	sec
Hold	0.001	sec
Decay	0.001	sec
Sustain	100	dB
Release	0.001	sec
Initial Attenuation	0	dB
Keynum To Hold	1	X
Keynum To Decay	1	X

Modulation Envelope	Value	Unit
Delay	0.001	sec
Attack	0.001	sec
Hold	0.001	sec
Decay	0.001	sec
Sustain	100	%
Release	0.001	sec
To Pitch	0	cents
To Filter Cutoff	0	cents
Keynum To Hold	1	X
Keynum To Decay	1	X

Modulation LFO	Value	Unit
Delay	0.001	sec
Frequency	8.176	Hz
To Pitch	0	cents
To Filter Cutoff	0	cents
To Volume	0	dB

Vibrato LFO	Value	Unit
Delay	0.001	sec
Frequency	8.176	Hz
To Pitch	0	cents

Figure 16.26: Vienna's generator view. From left to right: Pitch, filter, effect and pan settings, volume envelope settings, modulation envelope settings, and LFO settings

Pitch

The Pitch category of the generator view has three parameters. *Coarse tune* changes the pitch of the current instrument zone any number of semitones up or down. In most cases, however, you'll change the zone's root key to get the desired pitch.

Fine tune lets you tune the instrument zone ± 99 cents (where 100 cents make one semitone). This is useful if the original sample is slightly out of tune. There's no automatic tuning feature in Vienna, so you'll have to trust your ears. Of course, in most cases the sample will be correctly tuned when recorded.

Scale tune is a feature that you'll probably use less often than the other two. By default, the difference in pitch between two adjacent keys is 100 cents (one semitone). Using this generator, this value can be changed to anywhere between 0 (all keys play the same pitch) and 1,200 cents (every key plays one octave higher than the previous one). Although there are exceptions, this feature is most useful with sound effects and nontuned instruments.

Audio Sample

CD Folder: Chapter 16 - Introduction to SoundFonts
File: Vienna Tune.wav
The tuning audio example illustrates the three types of tuning you can adjust. The first example is a series of five notes and the same five notes transposed up using the coarse tuning. In the second part, the five notes are detuned using the fine-tune option. Listen carefully. The third example illustrates (with the same five notes) what can be achieved using a non-semitone scale.

Effects, Filter, and Pan

Effects is a slightly misleading name for this section of Vienna. Under Effects, you'll find not only what we normally refer to as effects, reverb, and chorus, but also pan and the filter parameters.

Most people who have programmed synthesizers are familiar with the concepts of filters. Basically, a filter removes certain frequencies of the sound. In the case of the SB Live! MIDI Synthesizer, the filter is a *low-pass filter*, meaning that frequencies below a certain *cutoff frequency* pass through the filter, and higher frequencies are removed. You can set the cutoff frequency for the filter (in hertz) by clicking the corresponding generator. From the beginning, the filter frequency is set to the highest frequency, letting virtually all the frequencies in the original sample through. Lowering the filter cutoff frequency produces a darker, less brilliant sound.

Filter Q, or *resonance*, as it is often called, is another filter parameter commonly found on synthesizers. If you increase the filter Q, the frequencies around the cutoff frequency will be emphasized. The result is often a thinner sound. In modifying the cutoff frequency, a filter Q value higher than 0 is often used to produce sounds that are very typical for synthesizers. Try adding some Q to an instrument zone (for best effect, use a tuned sample with a wide frequency range) and play it with different filter cutoff values to hear the difference.

Reverb and *chorus* control the level of effects added to the sounds on playback. Note that it is much easier to add reverb and chorus to an instrument from the sequencer than it is to remove it, so it's better not to overuse these effects. Sometimes, however, you may want to add an effect such as reverb to one zone within an instrument and play another zone dry (with no effects). In such cases, increasing these effect levels is the way to go.

Pan is the placement of the instrument zone between the two speakers in a stereo setup. A value of –50 makes all sound come from the left speaker, a value of 0 makes it come equally from both speakers, and a value of 50 makes it come from the right speaker only. When you add stereo sample pairs to an instrument, these are automatically panned to the left and right extremes.

Audio Sample

CD Folder: Chapter 16 - Introduction to SoundFonts
File: Vienna Effects.wav
The first two examples play the same notes with different filter settings, first with no resonance (Q=0), later with resonance. The next two examples demonstrate the reverb and chorus effects, and finally the set of notes is played with different pan settings.

Volume Envelope

The purpose of an *envelope* is to control the value of another synthesizer parameter over time. The envelopes for the SB Live! MIDI Synth consist of six values: delay, attack, hold, decay, sustain, and release. Many samples are supposed to be played the way they are, without a volume envelope. In many cases, however, especially with looped samples, you will need to control the volume at different times from the moment a key is pressed. Real instruments have different volume envelopes. For example, a xylophone has a very short attack and decay, producing a short and distinct sound. Most synth pads and many string sounds, on the other extreme, use very long attacks and decays for a very smooth transition between notes and chords. For an illustration of what a volume envelope does, study the sketch shown here:

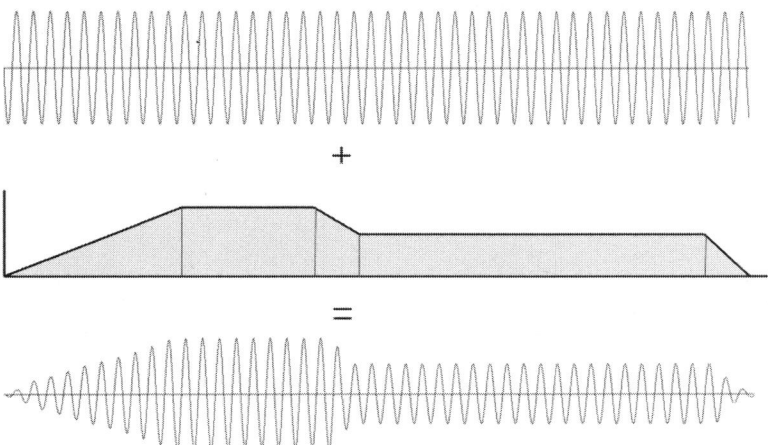

Delay is the time (in seconds) before the sample starts sounding after a note on. Usually, the sample is supposed to play as soon as you hit the key—that is, with a delay of 0. A delay is useful, for example, to create interesting effects when layering sounds.

Attack is the time (also in seconds) from when a sample starts playing until it reaches its maximum level. A large attack value makes a soft, slow start. Note that if you are using a sampled sound that has a long attack itself, this parameter can only make it longer, not decrease the attack time.

Hold is the time that the sound will play at its maximum level before the level starts decreasing.

Sustain is the level that should be sustained as long as the key is still pressed. A string orchestra may have a maximum sustain level (playing at maximum level until the key is released), whereas a xylophone will have a sustain level of 0, because no matter how long you hold down the key, the produced sound will always be very short.

Decay is the time it takes for the level to fall from the maximum (hold) level to the sustain level. This parameter is measured in seconds, as well.

Release is the time it takes from the moment a key is released until the sound stops. Some sounds, like that of an electric organ, will stop sounding almost immediately when the key is released, thus using a short release time. Other sounds, such as slow synth pads, may use a very long release.

TIP *Use a simple waveform, such as a saw or a square wave, and play with these parameters to get a feeling for what they do. An envelope contains many parameters, so some practice is required until you master this feature.*

The *initial attenuation* parameter lets you reduce the overall volume of the instrument zone if it is too loud compared to the other instrument zones, or if the current instrument is too loud compared to the other instruments. An attenuation of 0 dB means that the zone is played at full volume.

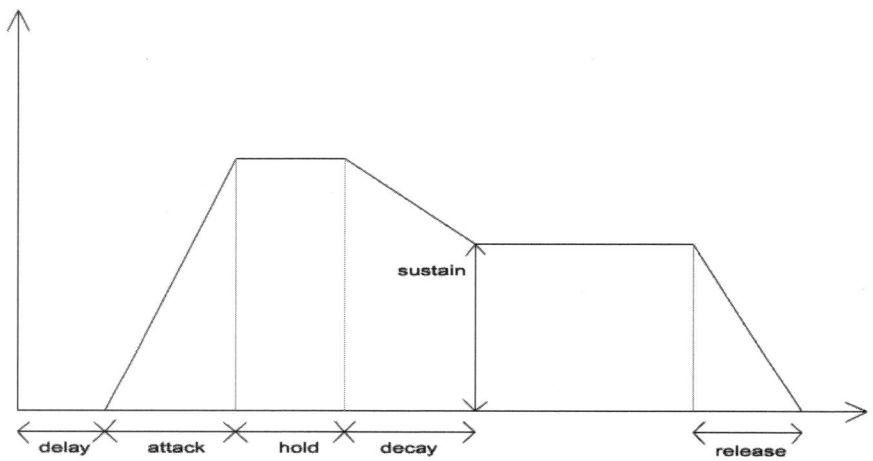

Figure 16.27: ASDR envelope

When keynum to hold and keynum to decay are set to 1, the key number pressed does not affect the hold and decay parameters of the volume envelope. When set to a lower value, a higher note will cause shorter hold or decay, and when set to a higher value, a higher note will cause longer hold or decay. A higher note, in this case, is a note over 60 (middle C).

Audio Sample

CD Folder: Chapter 16 - Introduction to SoundFonts
File: Vienna Volume Envelope.wav
In this example, the same (simple) waveform is played back using three different volume envelopes: Flat (very short attack, full sustain, very short release), very short attack and a short decay (like a marimba), and lastly with a long attack and a long release.

Modulation Envelope

The SB Live! MIDI Synthesizer can use two envelopes for each note played. The first one, as described previously, controls the volume over time. The second one, the *modulation envelope*, can be used to control, or *modulate*, the filter frequency or the playback pitch, or both, over time.

The delay, attack, hold, decay, sustain, and release parameters are exactly the same as for the volume envelope, so once you master one envelope, you know how to use them both. You can control keynum to hold and keynum to decay for this envelope, as well. New in the modulation envelope are the to pitch and to filter cutoff parameters.

To pitch is a measure of how much this envelope modulates the pitch. This is most useful for sound effects and enables you to change an instrument zone's pitch over time. If you set this parameter to a positive value, the pitch will rise as the envelope rises. If you set it to a negative value, the pitch will instead fall when the envelope rises.

To filter cutoff lets you control the filtering by an envelope—a very useful feature for many types of sounds. For example, a synth bass may be created from a simple saw wave by setting a volume envelope with a fast attack, and by setting a modulation envelope to let more high frequencies pass through the filter at the very beginning of the sound, giving it a sharper attack. Or you may want to create a filter sweep by adding some Q (resonance) to a sound and use a relatively slow filter envelope to let the filter slowly open or close.

When you set this parameter to a positive value, the modulation envelope is added to the filter frequency. By default the filter frequency is already set at maximum (to let all frequencies pass through the low-pass filter), so you need to first set the filter cutoff parameter to a lower value, or this parameter has no effect. Likewise, if you specify a negative value, the envelope is subtracted from the cutoff frequency, which therefore must be greater than the lowest possible value.

Audio Sample

CD Folder: Chapter 16 - Introduction to SoundFonts
File: Vienna Modulation Envelope.wav
This audio example demonstrates some of the effects that can be achieved using modulation envelopes (to control filter and pitch settings).

Low-Frequency Oscillators (LFOs)

Each low-frequency oscillator basically generates a sine wave at a frequency lower than human hearing. The output of the LFO is not played as sound, but is used to modulate other synthesizer parameters, just like the envelopes. The SB Live! MIDI Synthesizer has two low-frequency oscillators, or LFOs, per voice. One can be used to modulate pitch (for vibrato effects), and the other can be used to modulate pitch, filter cutoff frequency, or volume, or any combination of the three. Both LFOs have two parameters to control their respective behaviors: delay and frequency:

Delay, measured in seconds, is the time between the moment a key is pressed and the moment the oscillator starts taking effect. This can be anywhere from 0 (the oscillator starts immediately) to 10 seconds.

Frequency is the speed at which the LFO oscillates, measured in hertz (that is, cycles per second). If you use it to create vibratos, use your ears to find a suitable frequency. Somewhere around 3 Hz might be a good starting point to simulate natural vibratos, but the value depends on the instrument you're creating.

To use either of the LFOs to control the pitch (vibrato), set the to pitch parameter to a value other than 0. Because a sine wave is negative half of the cycle and positive the other half, in most cases you won't notice any difference between the positive and negative values of this parameter. For natural vibratos, use a relatively low value here; a higher to pitch value combined with a lower frequency value will produce a sirenlike sound.

To filter cutoff, which is available only for the modulation LFO, does just what the name implies: it modulates the filter cutoff frequency. This is great for wah-wah effects and can also produce effects similar to those of big fans or helicopter rotor blades. Just as when you use modulation envelopes, do not set the filter cutoff parameter to the extreme values or you may not hear the full effect of the modulation LFO.

To volume is also available only on the modulation LFO. This parameter makes the LFO modulate the volume, creating tremolo-like effects. A little bit of LFO-to-volume can also be useful for creating more natural sounding vibrato effects.

The modulation control change, by the way, adds to the to pitch parameter of the modulation LFO.

Audio Sample
CD Folder: Chapter 16 - Introduction to SoundFonts
File: Vienna LFO.wav
This example shows different effects that can be achieved with the LFO.

The Global Zone

Any instrument can have at most one *global zone*. A global zone is a special type of zone that is not associated with any sample or key range (so you may actually wonder why it's called a zone). The generators associated with the global zone, however, affect all other zones of the instrument. Using a global zone might come in handy, for instance, when you are creating a multisampled instrument. All normal instrument zones use samples from the same real instrument and should probably be treated similarly. Thus, instead of setting exactly the same generator values for each zone, you can create all of the zones without touching the generators and add a global zone that sets the generator values for all zones. Even with a global zone, you can still tune the parameters of the other zones individually.

You create a global zone by right-clicking the instrument in the SoundFont tree view and selecting Global Zone from the menu that pops up (see Figure 16.28). Once the global zone is created, you can edit its generators as with any other zone.

Creating Presets

Presets are the only objects in a SoundFont that can be seen and used outside Vienna. Samples and instruments are only building blocks to create presets. The fact that they are called *presets* is a little unfortunate, because these are actually

Figure 16.28: A global zone as part of an instrument

what most other programs (including the SoundFont Control Panel) refer to as *instruments*.

There are two types of presets: *melodic* and *percussive*. The difference between a melodic and a percussive preset is that percussive presets are used on MIDI channel 10, and melodic presets can be used on any of the other 15 MIDI channels.

Creating a preset, whether it is melodic or percussive, is similar to creating an instrument. The major difference is that where an instrument is built from one or more samples (through instrument zones), a preset is built from one or more instruments. Each preset consists of one or more preset zones, each referencing an instrument, and an optional global zone.

Creating a New Melodic Preset

In the SoundFont tree, right-click Melodic Pool, under Preset Section (click the small plus sign if the Preset Section subsections aren't visible). From the menu, select New Melodic Preset. A dialog box now lets you specify the bank number, preset number, and name of the new preset.

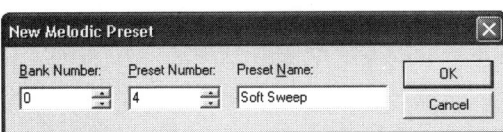

Figure 16.29: Creating a new melodic preset

The bank number controls the bank number at which the preset should be available, relative to the bank number to which the SoundFont was loaded. When the number is set to 0, the preset appears at the bank number where the SoundFont was loaded. If you set it to a higher value, such as 2, and load the SoundFont as bank number 5, the preset will be available at bank number 7. This type of setting is used, for example, to create variation presets of the GS banks. In most cases, however, you'll leave this number at 0.

The preset number specifies the value of a patch change MIDI message that should be sent to use this preset. If you're creating a bank of custom sounds, the first instrument would (normally) be preset number 0, the second preset number 1, and so on. If you, however, are creating a SoundFont to replace a certain GM preset (by loading it on top of the GM bank in the bank stack), you should instead use the number of the preset you want to replace.

Choose a descriptive preset name. Not only will it be easier to edit and update the bank in the future, but the preset name will also be displayed by sequencers and other applications that have built-in SoundFont support. In many simple banks, or banks with few presets, the extra step of first creating one or more instruments and then the presets may seem unnecessary. In these cases, there will often be a one-to-one correspondence between instruments and presets, and they will usually use the same names.

When you click OK, you'll be able to select one or more instruments to use as preset zones. This procedure is the same as when you initially selected samples for an instrument, and the selected instruments will appear as preset zones under the new preset.

Editing Preset Zones

Preset zones are very similar to instrument zones. You can edit the key range and velocity range by selecting the desired view for Vienna's keyboard and drag the ends of the bar representing the zone. Multisampling, splits, velocity splits, and layering can be created at this level or at the instrument level, depending on what you find suitable for the project. In general, it's a good idea to create splits and layering at the instrument level and, if necessary, collect several multisamples or velocity splits at the preset level, so it is easier to reuse individual instruments in more than one preset.

There's no root key associated with a preset zone because is a property of a sample. If you want to transpose an instrument zone, you should use the coarse tune generator.

Editing Generators at the Preset Level

Generators for presets are, just like at the instrument level, specific to one zone and can be edited in the same way. The main difference is in some units and ranges. Many parameters, such as filter cutoff and the time parameters of the envelopes, are not expressed as absolute values, but are relative to the values specified in the corresponding instrument (marked with an X in the Unit column). For example, 2.0 X means twice the instrument's value. Also, the scale tune parameter is not available at the preset level.

Many times, you will use the settings from the instruments in the preset right away, without touching the generators on the preset level. In other cases, you can customize the instruments that make up a preset. This makes it easy to use customized versions of one instrument in many presets, and if you make any changes or improvements to the instrument, they will immediately affect all presets that use it.

Adding a Global Preset Zone

One, and only one, global zone can be added to a preset. The preset global zone serves the same purpose as at the instrument level: namely, to provide an easy way to change the generator values of all other zones. No instrument will be associated with a preset global zone.

The Percussive Section

Presets in the percussive section are created exactly the same way as in the melodic section. There is one minor exception, however: You cannot create percussive drum presets in banks other than the current one. In other words, when you create a percussive preset by right-clicking Percussive Pool and selecting New Percussive Preset from the menu, you are asked for only the preset number and the name.

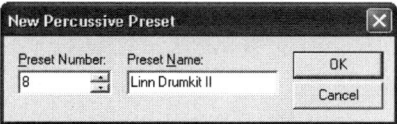

Figure 16.30: Creating a new percussive preset

How to Overcome the Channel 10 Limitation

As the name suggests, the percussive section should be used for drums and other percussive instruments, as MIDI channel 10 will always use presets from this section. Because there is only one MIDI channel 10, you can only use one percussive preset for each MIDI port. (On the SB Live!, you can therefore use a maximum of two percussive presets at a time, because the SB Live! MIDI synthesizer has two MIDI out ports: A and B.) To overcome this limitation, you can create drum kits and other percussion sounds as melodic presets, which will then be available on all MIDI channels except 10.

The Advantage of the Sample-Instrument-Preset Structure

When you start designing a SoundFont, think about what you want the instruments and presets of your SoundFont to be. If you are creating a multisampled piano SoundFont with six samples across the keyboard, you might start by creating the basic piano instrument by assigning the individual samples to instrument zones. Then you can use this instrument for all of the presets in your SoundFont, either to create small variations of the original piano instrument or to create splits and layers with other instruments. An advantage of this approach is that if you later improve the piano, for example, if you improve the multisampling by adding a few more samples to the piano instrument, all the presets using the piano instantly take advantage of this.

A Full Example

Enough theory? In the following example, you'll see how to create a SoundFont from scratch and transform a rather short and simple piece of sound data into something useful and expressive.

Before We Start

Regardless of the SoundFont you're going to create, you'll need some basic sound data to start with. This tutorial will not cover the process of obtaining the samples, which may involve anything from sampling an orchestra with microphones to using sounds directly off a CD. If you're creating, say, a piano SoundFont, you might have sampled different keys and velocities of a real piano. Whatever the source of your samples, make sure that you are actually allowed to use them for this purpose. This is particularly important if you plan to release your SoundFont commercially or as a free download.

The example here aims to create a synth bass instrument. The samples can be found on the CD, and I recommend you to listen to them before you try the example. These samples were not obtained by sampling a real instrument, but created with a sound-generating piece of software named Stomper. To be able to play high pitches while still getting a good sample rate for the sound played back at low pitches, the samples were obtained using three waveforms playing an A note and playing them back at their original pitches at three octaves (where A0 is the note at the lowest octave and A2 is the note at the highest octave).

At every step, the SoundFont created so far can be found on the CD, as well.

> The program Stomper was originally written to create drum sounds similar to those found in analog drum machines. The program has, however, now been extended to contain different synthesizer waveforms, as well as filters and can thus very well be used to create the basic waveform data for instruments. For more information about the program, see the author's Web site, at http://www.master-zap.com.

Step 1: Loading the Samples into Vienna

If you haven't done so already, start Vienna. The first thing you need to do is to bring these three samples into Vienna so you can start playing with them. As described earlier, this is done by right-clicking in the sample pool in the SoundFont tree on the left side of the window and selecting Import User Sample(s). In the dialog box, select the three samples to be used and click Import, and they will appear in the SoundFont tree view.

Step 2: Looping the Samples

Since these samples are quite short, you need to add looping points to get a sustained sound. Double-clicking a sample opens the Loop dialog box (see Figure 16.31). A graphical representation of the waveform is shown in the upper half of the window. Below this, the two smaller windows should display a short piece of the waveform around the start and end of the loop (if they do not, make sure the full dialog box is shown by clicking the Loop Settings button).

By default, the looping range is set as the entire waveform. Click Play Loop to listen to the current loop setting and note that the sample simply plays over and over again. Because this is a synthetic instrument, looping one single cycle of the waveform is fine (see the following figure). When sampling real instruments, however, longer loops are required for a good result.

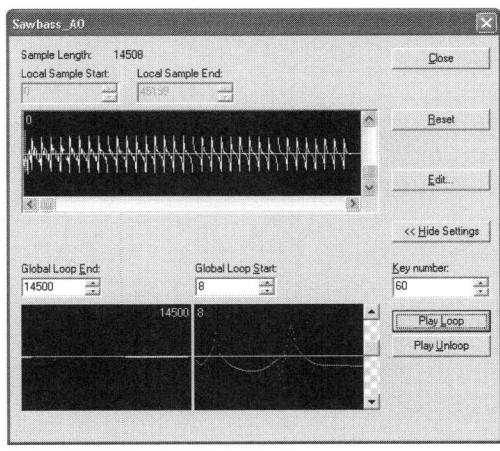

Figure 16.31: Opening the loop settings dialog for our imported sample

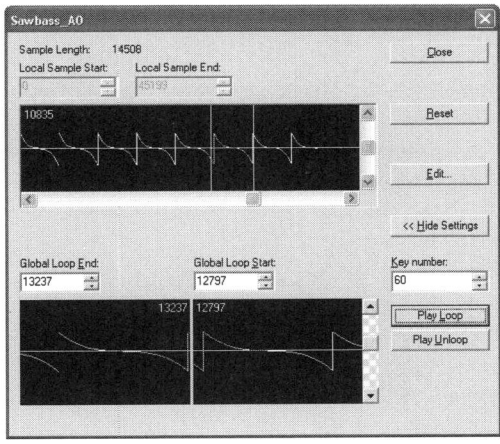

Figure 16.32: Define a coarse looped section of the sample, one cycle long

Placing the looping points is the tricky thing here—and it is even trickier when working with samples of real instruments. In the sample window, drag the looping point markers so that they enclose exactly one cycle near the end of the waveform, as shown in Figure 16.32. The view can be zoomed in and out with the left and right mouse buttons or the vertical scroll bars. Extreme fine-tuning can be done by altering the values (in samples) of the Local Loop Start and Local Loop End fields.

Use the Play Loop button to check how your loop sounds. The Key Number field controls the pitch of the playback. If you make the loop section too short or too long, the sound will change pitch when it enters the loop. When you're satisfied with the first sample, repeat the procedure for the next two samples (or, to save time, load the Step2.sf2 file from the CD).

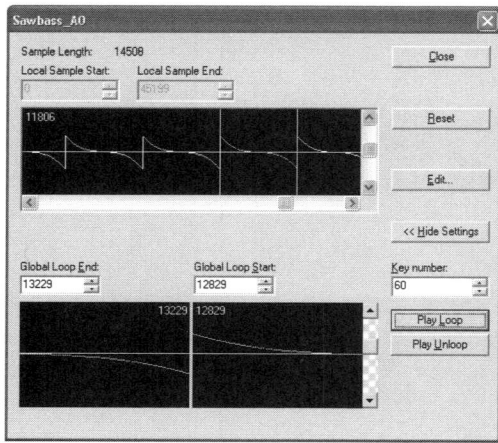

Figure 16.33: The fine-tuned loop

Step 3: Creating the Instrument

When the basic samples have been created and loop points have been defined, it's time to create the instruments we need. One instrument may consist of several samples layered or split across the keyboard range, or in some cases a combination of these. In this example, you will create one synth bass instrument using three samples at different octaves split across the keyboard.

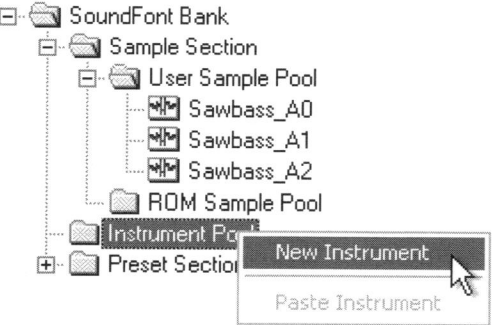

Figure 16.34: Right-clicking in the instrument pool gives you these choices

To create the instrument, right-click the Instrument Pool section of the SoundFont tree view and select New Instrument from the menu. A dialog box will ask for the name of the new instrument. For the example, you can name the instrument Sawbass, after the sawtooth-like waveforms used. Another dialog box will appear, as shown in Figure 16.35.

For each sample used in the new instrument, a new instrument zone needs to be created. When you select the samples to be used in the instrument from this dialog box, these zones will automatically be created.

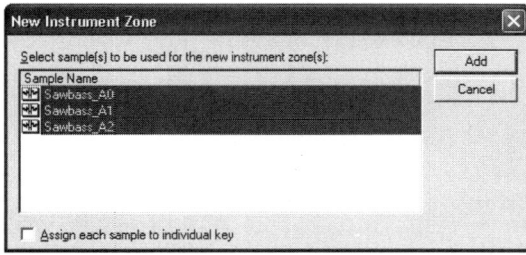

Figure 16.35: Creating a new instrument using all the imported samples

The new Sawbass instrument will now appear in the Instrument Pool section of the SoundFont tree view, and the instrument zones (named after the samples they use) will appear, too. The key range of each instrument zone is shown as a bar below Vienna's keyboard.

Make sure that looping is enabled for each sample used by opening the Loop dialog box and checking the "Enable looping for this sample" box. The looping points have been set already, so there's no reason to change the local looping points of the samples.

Step 4: Adjusting Key Ranges

By default, each instrument's key range will span the entire keyboard. In this example, however, the A0 sample is meant to be used for the lower keys, A1 for one octave in the middle, and A2 for the keys above that.

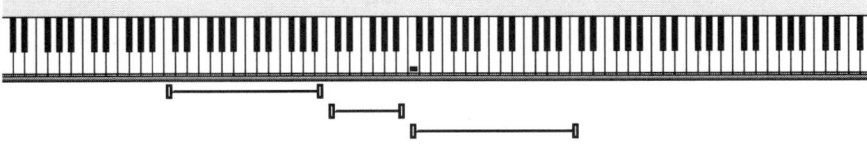

Figure 16.36: Adjusting the key ranges of our newly created zones to create a multisampled instrument

Drag the ends of each instrument zone until each key corresponds to exactly one instrument zone as pictured here. Although not applicable in this example, it is certainly possible for instrument zones to overlap (that is, for samples to be layered). You should keep in mind that every layer requires one voice when played back by the SB Live! MIDI Synth. Even with a polyphony of 64 voices, massively layered sounds may eventually lead to the lack of free voices.

Try playing some notes with the Vienna keyboard or your MIDI keyboard. Notice that there's a slight change in timbre when you cross a split point. This happens because lower sample rates contain fewer of the high-frequency components. The sudden change of sample rate therefore results in a noticeable change in sound. This, combined with the difficulty of recording similar samples over an instrument's entire musical range, is why the multisamples of many acoustic instruments such as pianos, flutes, and so are often very noticeable. Try listening carefully to a sample piano instrument, such as the one in the standard GM

Introduction to SoundFonts **447**

banks, and you'll see. The best way to avoid this phenomenon is to create dense multisample zones. This, however, requires far more work at the sampling stage, as well as more sample memory.

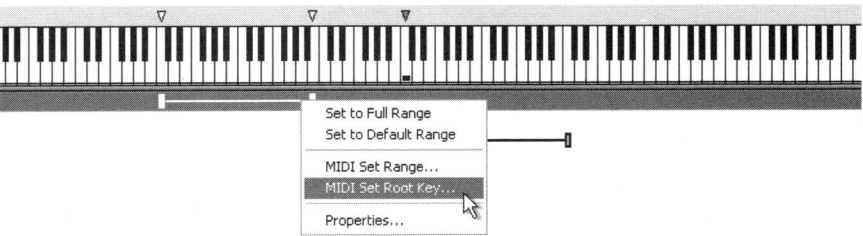

Figure 16.37: Here, we set the root key by pressing a key on our MIDI keyboard. If you are not using a MIDI keyboard, select Properties instead and adjust it manually.

You also want to make sure that the samples are played back at the correct pitch. This is done by right-clicking an instrument zone and selecting MIDI Set Root Key (if you have a MIDI keyboard connected to your computer) and pressing a key or by editing the zone properties. Because these samples are A notes at three different octaves, the root key are correspondingly set to A in different octaves (where A0 is the low octave, A1 is one octave higher, and A2 is two octaves higher). Load the Step4.sf2 file to see how it's done. Note that when an instrument zone is selected, its root key is shown in Vienna's keyboard.

Step 5: Adding a Global Zone

Despite all our looping and instrument zone creation efforts, we still don't have something that sounds like a synth bass. To get this, we need to adjust the generators for the instrument. This could be done for each instrument zone individually, but because all zones will use the same settings, we will add a global zone that will affect all samples of the instrument.

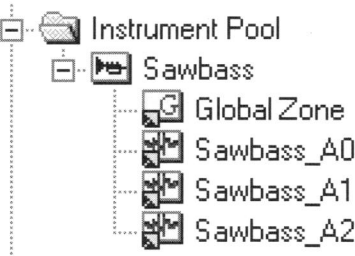

Figure 16.38: Our sawbass instrument with a global zone

In the instrument pool, add a new global zone by selecting this option from the right-click menu of the Sawbass instrument. Now you're ready to tweak those synthesizer parameters, also known as *generators*.

The waveform contains far too much high frequencies, resulting in a sound that is too bright and harsh. Simply lowering the filter cutoff frequency will solve this problem. To give some additional character to the sound, however, we will allow more high frequencies at the very beginning of the sound, giving it a sharper attack. Do this by adjusting the filter envelope. You can also adjust the volume envelope. Basically, however, a synth bass is supposed to sound as long as a key is pressed, which is the default setting of the volume envelope. Consequently, only minor changes need to be made to the volume envelope.

Although the generator section of Vienna may seem a bit confusing at first, mastering it is one of the keys to creating good instruments and presets. Experiment a lot and listen to the results while adjusting parameters.

Step 6: Creating a Preset

All of the previous steps are worth nothing unless we create one or more presets in the SoundFont. As mentioned earlier, presets are the only components of a SoundFont that are visible outside Vienna. In many cases, there is a one-to-one correspondence between instruments and presets, but a preset can consist of more than one instrument and even change the generator values.

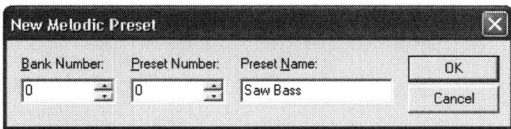

Figure 16.39: At this step, we're adding a preset as number 0 in the first bank

Create a new melodic preset in the SoundFont tree view. You'll be asked for a preset name, as well as bank and preset numbers. Saw Bass will do as the instrument name. The bank number is not an absolute value, but relative to the position where the SoundFont is loaded. Unless you're creating a GS bank or something similar, you can safely leave this value at 0. The preset number is the number within the SoundFont. Because this is our first preset, set it to 0, as well.

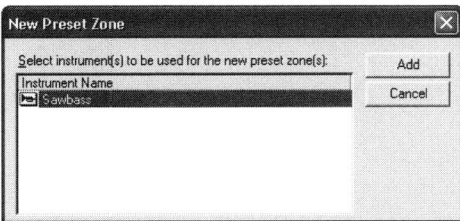

Figure 16.40: A new zone is added to the SawBass preset

Another dialog box appears, where you can select the instruments that will make up the new preset. Because you've created only one instrument so far, select the one and only Saw Bass and click Add. Preset zones are similar in concept to the instrument zones you encountered earlier, but preset zones are made up of entire instruments rather than single samples.

In this case, the instrument will use the entire keyboard range, so no adjustments need to be made here. If you save the SoundFont now, you have a working SoundFont that can be used with any MIDI sequencer or other MIDI software. However, now that you've done all this, why not create another preset based on the Saw Bass instrument?

Step 7: Creating Another Preset

You can create another preset, this time called Resonant Synth Bass, in the same way as in the previous step. This time, select the preset and start fiddling with the generator parameters. To get that real synth sound, turn up the resonance (also known as the Q) of the filter.

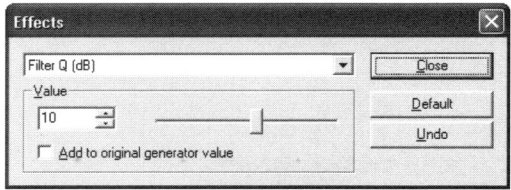

Figure 16.41: In the second preset using the same instrument, we add some resonance (Q) to the filter

In the example, the volume envelope decay is increased and the filter envelope decay value decreased. Try adjusting these (and other) parameters and listen to the result to see how they affect the sound.

Listening to the Result

The file Step7.sf2 is the finished SoundFont. A short sample MIDI file that uses only these two instruments is included. Load Step7.sf2 as bank 1 and play the included Sawbass Example.mid file (or, if you like, the Sawbass Example.mp3 file) to see what you've just created. For comparison, play the original waveforms once again. If you didn't know what a wavetable synthesizer could do before, you should have an idea by now....

SoundFont Management

You can open and edit any SoundFont 2 files (files ending with .sf2) directly with Vienna, including the General MIDI SoundFonts that were included in the SB Live! installation package. When a SoundFont is opened, all of its samples, instruments, and presets can be viewed in the SoundFont tree and edited as described previously. Saving is just as easy. Just select Save or Save As from the File menu, and the current SoundFont will be saved in the SoundFont 2 format.

TIP *Although Vienna is very stable on most systems, you should save your work often during editing. If you save your work under different file names every time, you will also be able to go back to an older version in case you realize that you've made a mistake somewhere during editing.*

Copying Samples, Presets, and Instruments from Other SoundFonts

Since only one SoundFont can be edited at a time, you cannot copy or drag objects between open files as you can in many other programs. Instead, you use the *Bank Manager* for this purpose. You open the Bank Manager by selecting this menu item from the File menu.

In the Bank Manager, you can import another SoundFont by clicking the Import Bank button. When you have selected a SoundFont, its samples, instruments, and presets will be displayed in the SoundFont tree of the Bank Manager. You can now select an object, copy it (by clicking the Copy button), and without closing the Bank Manager, go back to the SoundFont being edited and paste it.

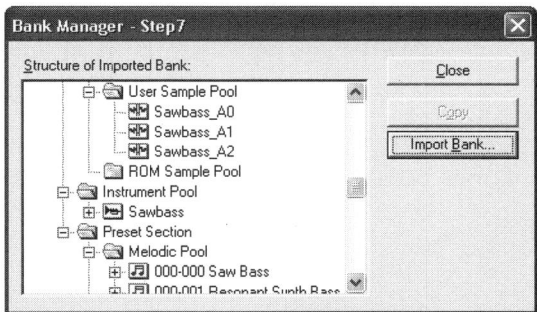

Figure 16.42: The Bank Manager after importing the SoundFont from step 7 of the tutorial

To copy a sample, select the sample from the user sample pool in the Bank Manager. Then go back to Vienna and highlight the user sample pool. Select Paste from the File menu; you will be asked for a name (where the original name is used by default), and the sample will be copied to the SoundFont being edited.

Instruments and presets are copied in a similar way. Highlight the instrument or preset to be copied in the Bank Manager, and click Copy; then highlight the instrument pool or one of the preset sections and paste it. Note that if you copy an instrument, all samples that the instrument uses are copied, as well. Copying a preset copies both the instruments and samples required.

Converting Other Formats into SoundFonts

Old SoundFonts (ending with .sbk, short for sound bank) can be imported into Vienna after they have been converted to SoundFont 2 files. This conversion occurs automatically when you try to open such a file. In the File dialog box that appears when you select Open from the File menu, choose SoundFont 1.0 Banks as the file type and select a file to open. Vienna will now ask you whether you want

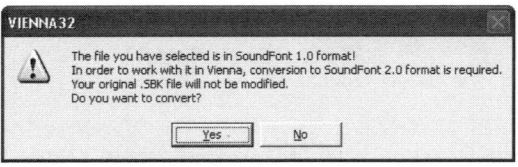

Figure 16.43: When you open a SoundFont 1 file (.sbk), you'll be asked to let Vienna convert it to the SoundFont 2 format

to convert the selected bank to a SoundFont 2 file. If you click Yes, Vienna creates a new .sf2 file with the same name and contents as the original bank and opens it for editing.

Other Features of Vienna

This chapter is meant to be a guide to Vienna and to describe the basic use of the program. For more information, you can always turn to Vienna's help system (select Help Topics from the Help menu). This provides a good and detailed reference covering all the details of the program. If you are unsure of a specific function of Vienna not covered here, chances are that you will find it in Help.

Information and Statistics

Select Information from the File menu to enter information about a SoundFont. Some information, like the date of creation and file version, can't be changed. You should, however, enter the full bank name and author name and, optionally, copyright information and comments. The bank name entered here is the name that will be displayed in the SoundFont Control Panel (or any other software) when the SoundFont is loaded.

Statistics, also found on the File menu and as a button on the toolbar, is useful to quickly see the number of samples, presets, and instruments in the current bank, as well as the total size of the user sample data.

Print

You can print a detailed description of a SoundFont by selecting Print from the File menu. The printout will include tables of the presets (including the instruments used for each preset), the instruments (including samples used), and the samples in the current SoundFont, with plenty of information in each category.

Full-Screen Editing

If you have a low-resolution display, at resolutions like 640 * 480 or 800 * 600, you may find the Full-Screen Editing toggle, located on the right side of the toolbar, useful. When you click it, Vienna's window will occupy the entire screen area. Click it again to go back to the previous window size.

Next to this button on the toolbar is the Full Tree toggle. Clicking this button will hide the generator view. Clicking it again will restore it. This toggle is particularly useful when creating instruments or presets with many zones.

Tools

As you might have noticed, the menu bar includes the Tools menu. The first option, Wave Editor, lets you choose what program to use for Wave editing. Because Vienna doesn't have the capabilities to edit samples, every time you choose to create a new sample or edit an existing one, the program you've chosen here will be run.

In the window that opens, a list of Wave editors is displayed. Choose the one you want (such as WaveStudio) by selecting it. If you have another program installed on your computer that doesn't show up in the list, simply click the No Editor Assigned line and click Assign to select the program file to be used.

The Mixer menu item, when selected, launches the Sound Blaster Live! mixer (assuming that it's installed on your system). Vienna 2.3 also includes a Control Panel menu item (though it has always been disabled (dimmed) on the author's system, and there's no documentation about it in the help files).

Preferences

At the bottom of the Options menu, select Preferences to bring up the Preferences window. This window provides tabs with various options, most of which you will never need to touch.

On the first tab, Ranges, you can select the default key and velocity ranges that should be used for new zones.

On the Options tab, you will find some miscellaneous options. It may seem more natural to use the key and octave instead of a MIDI number to represent a key. If you prefer this notation when keys are displayed (such as in the status bar), make sure that the first option, "Display MIDI-Key number instead of Octave-Key," is unchecked. Leaving it checked, however, may give you a good sense of what notes MIDI key numbers correspond to. Be careful if you deselect "Always save unused samples and instruments," or Vienna will automatically remove unused material that you might want to use later. However, if this is what you want, it's a very useful feature to make sure that you don't waste any precious memory. Most of the options here are rather self-explanatory, and they are also described in Vienna's help system.

On the Color Scheme tab, you can choose the colors for changed generator parameters, as well as the loop start and end.

Finally, the settings on the fourth tab, Devices, let you select which MIDI out port to use for SoundFont playback while editing. If you have, for example, both an AWE32 and a Sound Blaster Live! in your computer, you can switch between the two here. Some information, such as the amount of RAM that is available for SoundFonts, is also displayed. Almost any SoundFont-capable hardware on your computer can be selected here (such as the two MIDI ports of the Live!, the AWE32, AWE64, E-MU, APS, and so on).

17

SEQUENCER BASICS

As explained previously, a sequencer (nowadays) is something that can record sequences of MIDI data and play them back. Many sequencers also have sophisticated features for editing and arranging the recorded data in various ways.

Most software sequencers speak MIDI rather than being specific to a particular synthesizer or other device. This makes it possible to use all of the special features of the Live! with virtually any sequencer. Some sequencers also have handy features such as built-in SoundFont support.

Rather than trying to explain all of the features of most sequencers (which could fill an entire book on its own), this chapter will focus on how to set up sequencers to work optimally with the Sound Blaster Live! and to use all of the latter's special features, such as SoundFonts and Live!-specific MIDI messages. A very basic description and example of how to use a sequencer is provided at the end of this chapter for beginners.

Finding the Right Sequencer

If you start looking for a sequencer, you will soon notice that there are many of them available. Because MIDI is the universal language for electronic musical instruments, which most sequencers are based on, virtually any sequencer can be used together with the Sound Blaster Live!

Bundled Software

Sequencer software, such as Cubase or Cakewalk, is bundled with the Live! models targeted at musicians. If you are unsure as to whether your model contains sequencer software, check the installation and/or application CDs that came with the card. The bundled versions are often "lite" versions; that is, versions with a limited set of features compared to the top-of-the-line programs in the respective sequencer family. However, do not think that this is necessarily a bad thing. In fact, for a beginner, the large number of features found in the more expensive sequencer packages will most likely seem overwhelming, and most of the time you will likely end up using just a small set of all the features offered.

Choosing Your Own

If you don't have a sequencer already, there are plenty available to buy, and even some for free. A good place to check is at a local music store that sells electronic music equipment. Usually, such a store will have both a good selection of programs and staff with the experience to help you choose the right one. Once again, if you are a beginner, it may be a good idea to start off with one of the less advanced (and thus cheaper) versions of the programs. Some manufacturers offer demo versions of their software on their Web sites that you can download and try before you decide.

Table 17.1: Some of the Most Popular Sequencers for the PC

Sequencer	Manufacturer	Web Site
Cakewalk, SONAR	Twelve Tone Systems	http://www.cakewalk.com
Cubase, Cubasis	Steinberg	http://www.steinberg.net
Digital Orchestrator	Voyetra	http://www.voyetra.com

Most MIDI sequencers have a similar structure, and once you know one, you will quickly feel familiar with most other sequencers. One major feature that you should consider when you buy a sequencer is whether you need it to play audio tracks as well as MIDI. This ability to play both has become a common feature among the well-established sequencers available today, and it may not add very much to the price. Audio tracks and audio effects, however, put more stress on your computer, so if you have a low-end computer, don't expect very good performance when running several tracks and effects at once. You'll find more on audio sequencers later in this chapter.

Installing and Configuring Your Sequencer

Installation of a sequencer is usually pretty straightforward. On the installation CD, you'll find an installation program that takes you through the process of setting up the sequencer on your system. Usually, you'll be asked which directory to install the files and what components to install. If the sequencer has support for audio tracks, it may run an additional program to examine and test your sound card for best performance.

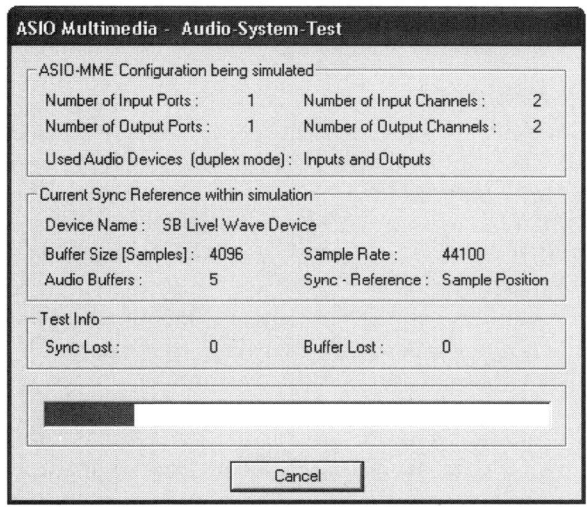

Figure 17.1: Cubase's automatic audio configuration tool is run at installation

If the program needs details about your audio setup, you will most likely find these explained in the manual. When you install the program or the first time you run it, most sequencers will ask you to specify which MIDI in and MIDI out ports to use. This is an important step, but your responses can be changed later; this step is explained later in this chapter in the "Selecting the MIDI Ports" section.

Here are a few things to consider before you install a sequencer:

- A sequencer relies on high-precision timing to deliver smooth playback of your songs. If you have many programs running in the background (check the taskbar and system tray at the bottom of your screen), there's a risk that performance will be affected, leading to lag and delay of notes.
- If you have installed many programs and have run your system for a long time since the current version of Windows was installed, it may be worth considering a fresh installation, even though it's a lot of work and requires access to the Windows installation discs and all of your software. If you have the option of running the sequencer on a separate machine or on a separate Windows installation on the computer, choosing this option reduces the risk of problems significantly. Music software and other programs unfortunately don't always work very well together.

- If the sequencer supports audio tracks and you plan to use them heavily, you will need both a fast processor and a fast hard drive. The faster, the better. Otherwise, check the manual to see what the requirements for running the program are, and make sure that you have a little bit of a margin. Also make sure that the sequencer runs on the operating system you are using.

In many cases, however, simply installing and running a sequencer on an existing system works fine. You can always try installing the software on your computer and, if it doesn't run as well as expected, use the preceding tips to find a better solution. Some sequencer manuals also provide useful tips for optimizing system performance for that particular sequencer.

Selecting the MIDI Ports

Before you can use the sequencer, it must know what MIDI in and MIDI out ports to receive data from and send data to. If you have a SB Live! installed, at least the SB Live! MIDI in or SB Live! MIDI UART (depending on the operating system and drivers) MIDI in port, and the SB Live! MIDI out or SB Live! MIDI UART, and SB Live! MIDI Synth A and B MIDI out ports should be available. You might also find the software synthesizer, Creative S/W Synth, among the out ports.

In most sequencers, you can choose any combination of the preceding, and any other ports you might have on your system, to use for MIDI communication. Some sequencers (like Cubase) skip this step and let you choose among all available MIDI out ports for each track.

Cakewalk will require you to select which MIDI ports to use for MIDI input and output. Open the MIDI Devices dialog box and highlight the ports you may use. Cakewalk will then let you choose among the selected MIDI out ports for each track in the sequencer. It will also record MIDI input from any port selected for MIDI in.

In most versions of Cubase, you will select among all available MIDI out ports for each track, eliminating the need for a MIDI Devices selection.

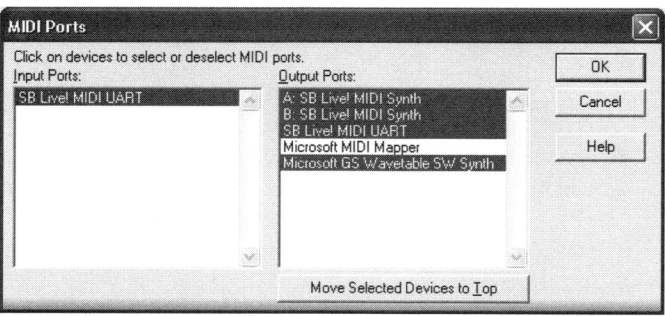

Figure 17.2: Select MIDI Devices from the Options menu in Cakewalk Pro Audio 9, and this dialog box will appear, letting you select the MIDI in and out ports to use. The ports depend on the drivers and operating system that you are using. In the screenshot, Live!Ware 3 for Windows XP is used.

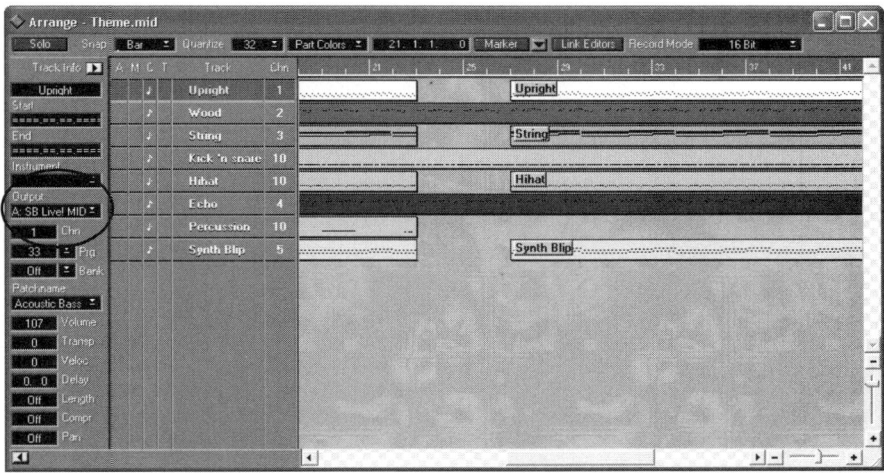

Figure 17.3: In Cubase, you select the MIDI port for each track

The Building Blocks of a Modern Sequencer

Most modern MIDI sequencers have a very similar structure, although the details differ from program to program. If you are already familiar with how to use a sequencer, you can skip this part. If you are not, this section will give you a basic idea of what a sequencer is and how to use it.

The Track or Arrange View

Almost all MIDI sequencers are built on a concept known as *tracks*. Each track can be thought of as one member of your orchestra, where each member plays one instrument. Tracks in a sequencer are a little more flexible, though. While a track is always associated with one MIDI channel (and therefore one instrument), most sequencers will let several tracks play using the same MIDI channel. For example, you might use one track for a bass guitar (MIDI channel 1), one for an electric organ (MIDI channel 2), and three for playing the drums and percussion on MIDI channel 10.

The *track* view (or *arrange* view, as it is known to Cubase users) can be said to be the main view of a MIDI sequencer. Commonly, the track view will show all tracks of a song as horizontal bars. Each bar displays the track name, track properties (such as MIDI channel and MIDI port used), and some coarse representation of the song data itself. Most modern sequencers allow a virtually unlimited number of simultaneous tracks.

In addition to the most important settings such as which MIDI port and MIDI channel to use for a track, virtually all sequencers provide fields where you can specify properties such as instrument, bank, volume, and pan. Some sequencers also let you transpose and delay tracks individually.

The former category of properties (instrument, bank, volume, and so on) is nothing but a shortcut for sending certain MIDI messages on playback. For example,

Sequencer Basics **459**

if you specify a volume of 80 on a track belonging to MIDI channel 4, the sequencer will send a control change 7 (channel volume) on MIDI channel 4 every time playback starts. If this field is missing, you can instead insert this control change message at the very beginning of your song. These fields provide a convenient way of changing the most common properties of a MIDI channel.

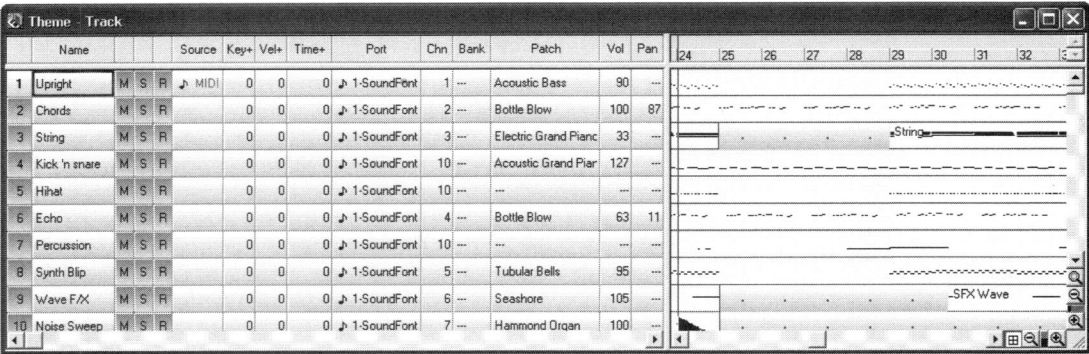

Figure 17.4: Cakewalk's track view

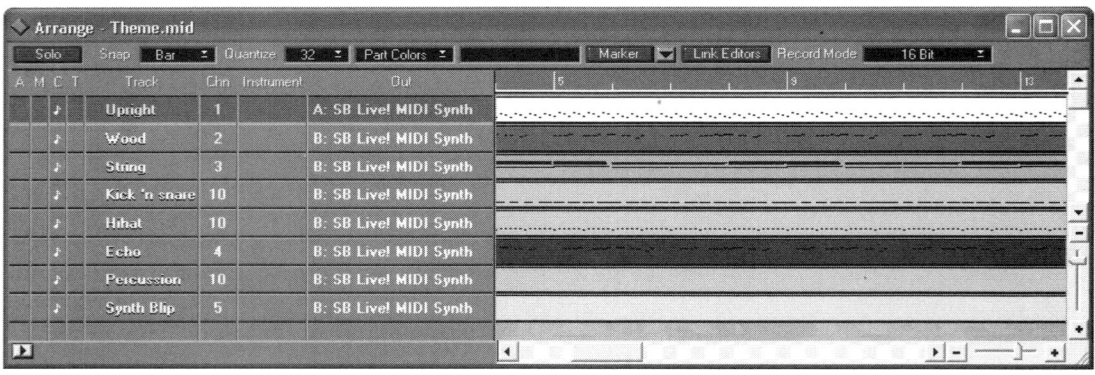

Figure 17.5: Cubase's arrange view

TIP *Most of the track properties are specific to MIDI channels rather than sequencer tracks. Therefore, although the sequencer may allow it, you may get undesirable effects if you use different settings on tracks that are assigned to the same MIDI channel.*

Piano Roll and Other Edit Views

When it comes to editing MIDI data, most sequencers give you a choice of several representations of the parts you've recorded.

The *piano roll* view (simply known as *edit* in Cubase) is a common view for note editing. It displays the recorded notes (and often some additional information such as control change messages and note velocities) in a grid, with time on

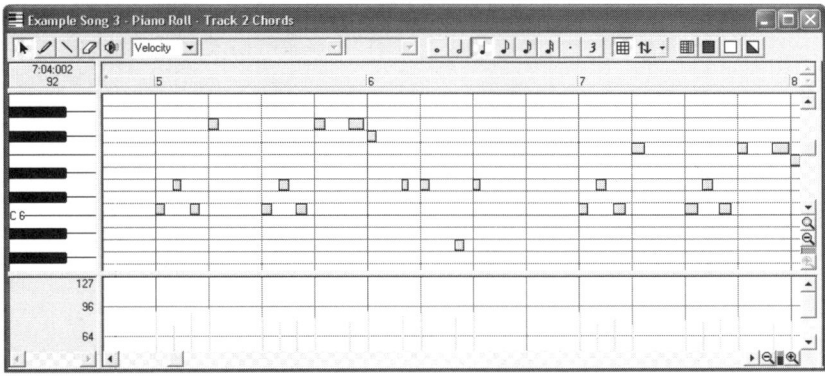

Figure 17.6: The piano roll in Cakewalk. Notes are represented as bars in the grid in the upper part of the window. Each note's velocity value is shown as a line below.

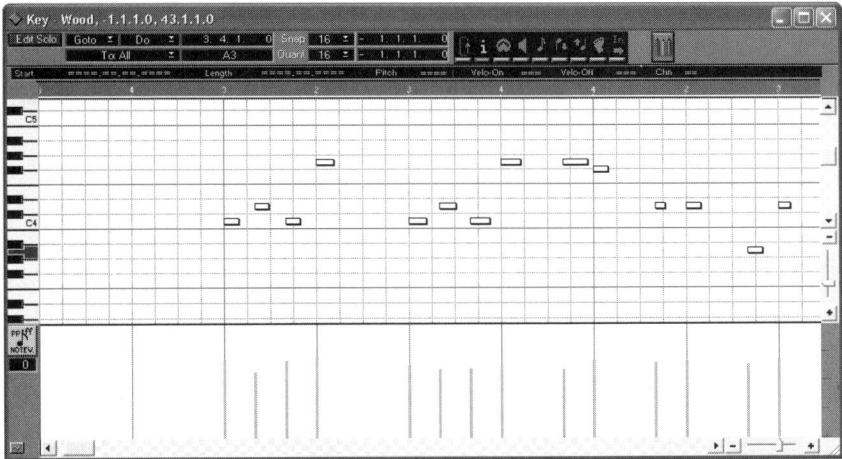

Figure 17.7: An edit window in Cubase

the horizontal axis and the note keys on the vertical axis. From this view, individual notes can easily be modified, added, or deleted.

Some sequencers offer a *staff* or *score* view, where the events on a track are displayed just like notes on paper. This view may be great if you are used to reading music on notation sheets rather than as they appear when you use the piano roll view. The staff view generally doesn't offer the same precision as the piano roll view, though, and may lack some of the more advanced editing possibilities of the latter.

In the *event list*, all MIDI events are displayed as rows in a list. While this view doesn't give you a very good overview of the track, it may be useful for performing certain specific tasks, such as inserting a certain type of event at a specific time or viewing a compact summary of all MIDI events that a track contains.

Sequencer Basics **461**

Figure 17.8: The staff view in Cakewalk provides a musician-friendly means of editing note events

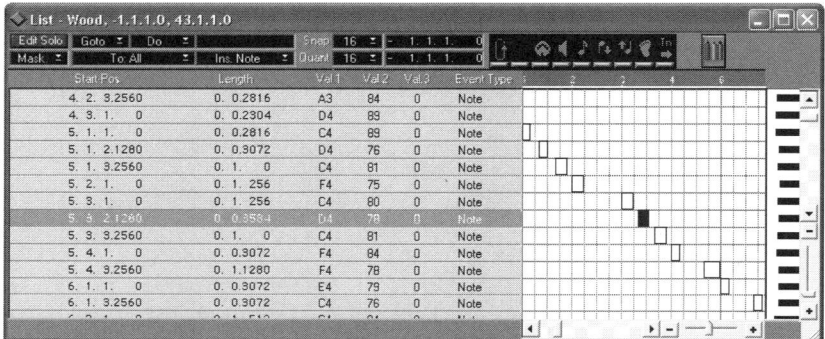

Figure 17.9: The event list in Cubase. One row corresponds to one MIDI event, such as a note or a control change.

> **TIP** *Most sequencers include many more features than the simple building blocks just described. Even if you think you understand the general concepts, it is usually a good idea to read the manual or the online help for your sequencer to discover everything the program has to offer.*

Basic Sequencer Use: Recording Tracks

A complete guide to using sequencers could fill a book on its own, so every single feature in a modern sequencer cannot be described here. Instead, the following steps in the process of creating a simple song are meant to provide an example for those who are not familiar with basic sequencer use. More advanced features, such as Live!-specific control changes and NRPNs, are explained later in this chapter.

Tracks (that is, the different instruments) are normally recorded one by one. Just as in real life (but perhaps even more so when all instruments are played on a keyboard), it is difficult (and not always necessary) to get every note exactly on the right beat. A few tricks can (and should) be used to overcome this problem.

Tempo

All sequencers have a tempo setting that controls the speed of playback. Some will let you change the tempo within a song, and some will let you set just one tempo for the entire song. In any case, when recording tracks, it is very important that you stay close to the tempo played by the sequencer.

> Tempo is usually measured in *beats per minute* (BPM). A tempo of 120 BPM means that the sequencer will play 2 beats (quarter notes) per second. (120 beats per minute / 60 seconds per minute = 2 beats per second).

Figure 17.10: The tempo setting in Cakewalk

The Metronome

Most sequencers have a *metronome* feature that will, when enabled, play a sound (through the PC speaker, the computer's audio channel, or a MIDI note) on every quarter, usually with the first quarter of each beat emphasized. Make sure that you turn on this feature for the first tracks you record, or you will not be able to follow the sequencer's tempo. Once you have one or a few tracks with a distinctive rhythm, you can turn off this feature, because these tracks themselves will give you the tempo during recording of additional tracks. It could, therefore, be a good idea to start by recording a basic drum track, although that depends very much on the type of song, as well as your personal preferences.

Quantization

The metronome will help you to keep the tempo only during recording. The next problem you will most certainly face, particularly when recording percussive instruments such as drums, is that the notes don't fall exactly on the beat. A common feature of sequencers, *quantization*, is useful to correct this. When you quantize a set of notes, each note will be moved to the nearest of a fixed number of positions per beat. For example, if you have recorded a hi-hat on every eighth note, you can apply quantization to the nearest eighth note to make sure that all notes are in their intended positions.

Figure 17.11: Cubase's metronome settings

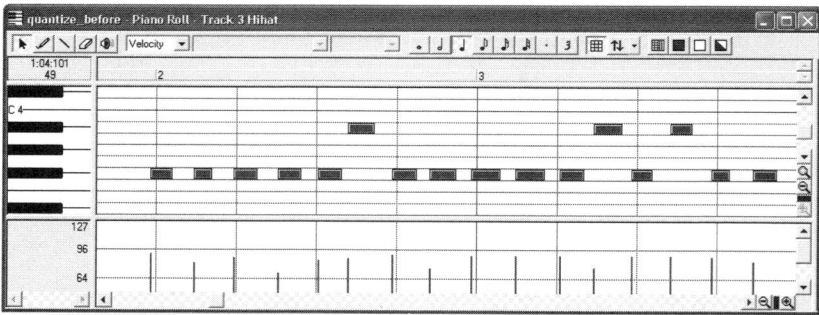

Figure 17.12: The hi-hat track before quantization. The notes are not very well aligned to the beat.

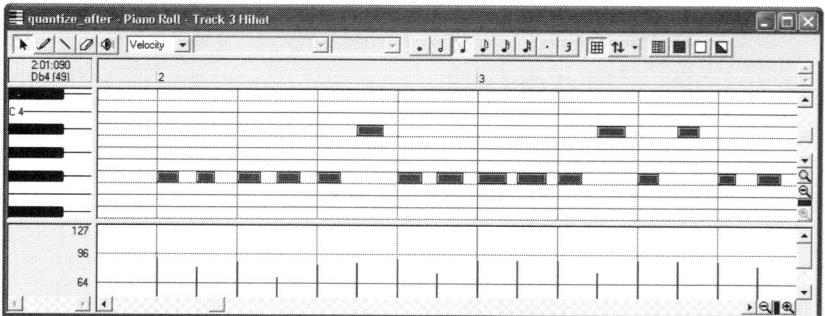

Figure 17.13: After quantization, every note is played back at exactly the right moment. Note that no quantization of the note length has been done—quantization was applied only to the start times.

Audio Sample

CD Folder: Chapter 17 - Sequencer Basics
Files: Quantize Before.mid and **Quantize After.mid**
Listen to the examples yourself! The bass drum, snare, and hi-hat tracks were recorded separately. The Quantize Before.mid file contains the originally recorded tracks, and Quantize After.mid contains the same tracks with the notes quantized to the nearest sixteenth.

You should note a few things about quantization. First, quantization only moves notes to the nearest note value specified. Thus, if the recorded notes do not follow the tempo very well or are too far away from their intended positions, quantization may not work very well. Consequently, it is still important to do a good job on the original recording (which takes practice). Second, the most basic quantization moves all notes to the exact note positions specified. Although most professional musicians are very exact when playing, this type of "perfect" quantization may produce quite unnatural sounding music. Although it is great for many types of electronic music, you should use quantization with caution if you want to produce natural sounding music.

Some sequencers provide more advanced types of quantization. For example, it is not uncommon to let the user specify the amount of quantization. A setting of 50 percent may move all notes halfway toward the "perfect" quantized values, leaving some natural feel in the recording.

Some sequencers let you quantize the notes when recording. Others may let you quantize selected notes while editing a song, and in some cases you can keep the unquantized material on the track and let the sequencer quantize it in real time on playback, which makes it easier to undo and change quantization settings.

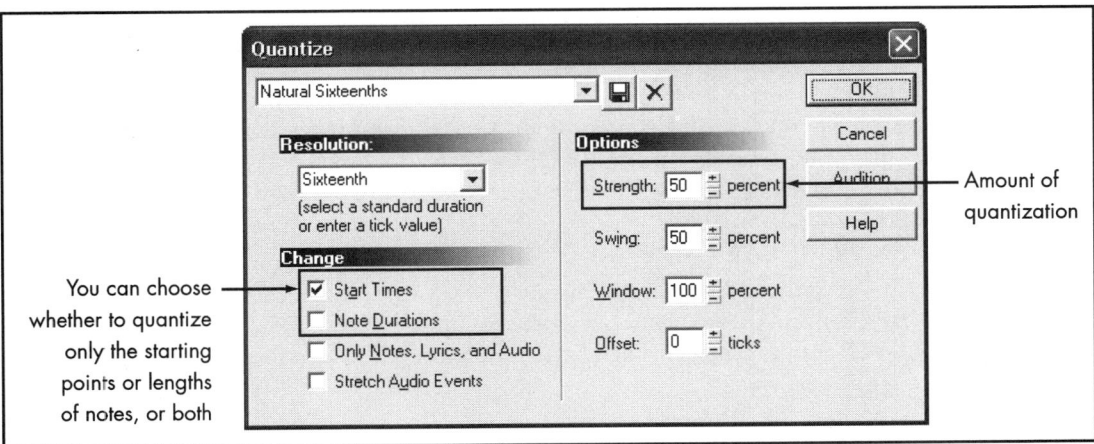

Figure 17.14: Cakewalk Pro Audio 9's quantize options

Recording in Real Time

The normal way to record notes is to play the part in real time using a MIDI device as input. The sequencer will act much like a multitrack tape recorder, although it will record MIDI messages rather than the audio itself.

Most beginners discover that recording in real time is usually a bit trickier than just playing, because you have to follow the tempo of the sequencer (as played by the metronome and/or the already recorded tracks). Most sequencers will let you set the number of "count in" beats: that is, the number of beats played by the metronome before the actual recording starts. If you are recording a complicated part, there are a number of things you can do to improve your chances of success:

- The first (and most important) thing is, of course, to practice. You won't master MIDI sequencing in one day. If you use some sort of MIDI keyboard for input, you will naturally find real-time recording a bit easier if you already play the keyboard, particularly if you've played in an orchestra or a band.
- Because a MIDI sequencer does not record the audio itself, but rather the notes you play, you can decrease the tempo while recording. Once you are satisfied with the part, you can go back to the previous tempo setting. Sometimes, drastic tempo changes, such as halving the tempo, are necessary, depending on the complexity and speed of the part you are recording and your playing skills.
- If all else fails, you should consider a non–real-time recording method, as described in the next section. Even if you have very limited piano skills, a basic MIDI keyboard used for non–real-time input can take you very far, especially if you are creating electronic music that does not require the "human touch" that you get from real-time recording.

Non–Real-Time Recording

When it comes to non–real-time recording, most sequencers give you at least two choices: you can either enter the notes directly into an editor (such as the piano roll) using your mouse and computer keyboard, or you can use a feature known as *step recording* to record note by note using your MIDI keyboard.

Using the Editor Views

Entering the notes directly into one of the sequencer's editors is a time-consuming process, and there is generally no point in doing so unless the piece that you are about to record is too complex to play in real time and too irregular for step recording.

Step Recording

Step recording is a great (and quick, when you master it) way to record even, regular sequences of notes without having to worry about timing, and with the ability to immediately erase the last notes if you play the wrong ones. When you step record, you play the notes (or chords) one by one, and they are all entered as evenly spaced notes of the same length. The length and duration of the notes are set prior to recording.

Creating a track with a hi-hat on every sixteenth note is a piece of cake with step recording, as is the creation of many types of short, melodic sequences commonly found in electronic music. Different sequencers use different approaches to step recording. Cakewalk has a special dialog box for step recording, whereas Cubase lets you step record notes directly into the piano roll editor.

To make step recording even more useful, many sequencers let you skip note positions when you step record, as well as enter chords. This makes it possible (and even easy after some practice) to create quite irregular sequences without having to record the material in real time.

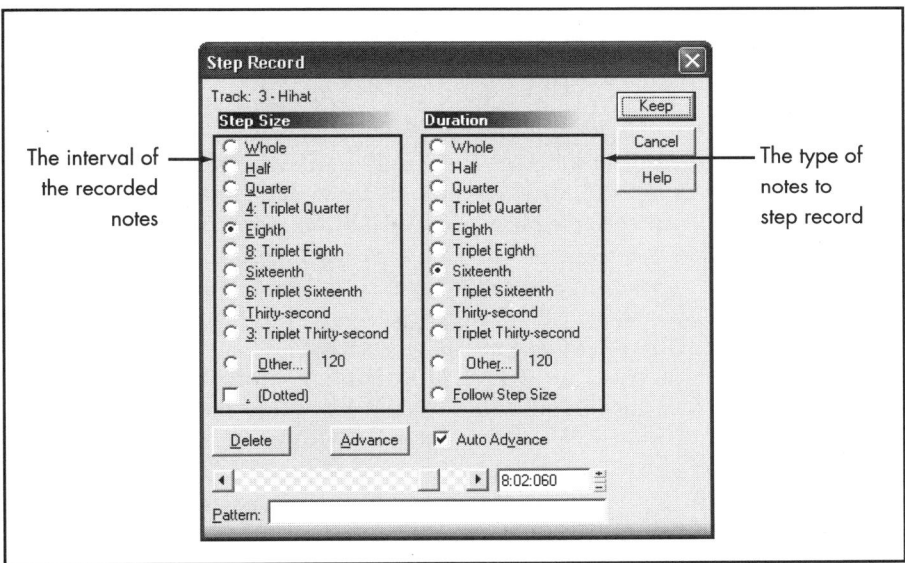

Figure 17.15: Step recording dialog box in Cakewalk Pro Audio 9

To successfully step record irregular sequences, try to find a rhythm when recording and use a keyboard shortcut or MIDI key to skip notes—having to use your mouse within a sequence of notes can be very distracting.

Using SoundFonts

When you are sick and tired of the 128 General MIDI instruments that come with the card (okay, there are also a few variations in the GS sound set), it is time to start looking at SoundFonts. With SoundFonts, you will never run out of new, exciting instruments. And SoundFonts can be used in just about any MIDI sequencer, although some sequencers offer some nifty features that make life even easier.

SoundFont Support in Cakewalk

Recent versions of Cakewalk and SONAR have built-in SoundFont support. As an example, we will look at how Cakewalk Pro Audio 9 handles SoundFonts.

Cakewalk's approach to SoundFonts lets you specify locations on your computer where you store SoundFonts, and for each song you can select which SoundFonts to use. These settings are saved together with the rest of the song so you don't need to worry about loading all the SoundFonts every time you open the song again.

Configuring Instruments

For each MIDI out port, Cakewalk keeps track of what type of instrument is connected to it. This makes it possible to display the correct instrument names and show the supported controllers and so on for each port. Cakewalk has built-in SoundFont support, so we need to tell it only that the SB Live! MIDI Synth A and B are SoundFont devices, and Cakewalk will automatically find the correct instrument names and other settings.

To know how to handle different synthesizers and other musical instruments, Cakewalk uses something called *instrument definitions*. An instrument definition defines what features are available and how various things should be done on a specific instrument.

Versions of Cakewalk that have SoundFont support will detect that a MIDI out port has SoundFont support as soon as you create a track using it and will create a SoundFont Device instrument definition for the port. So, first of all, for the first track, select the SB Live! MIDI Synth A or B as the MIDI out port. Select Instruments from the Options menu. A dialog box appears that lets you select the type of instrument definition used for each channel of all selected MIDI out ports. Make sure that the SB Live! MIDI Synth A and B ports use the SoundFont Device definition, by selecting all channels from these ports (hold down the Ctrl key and click

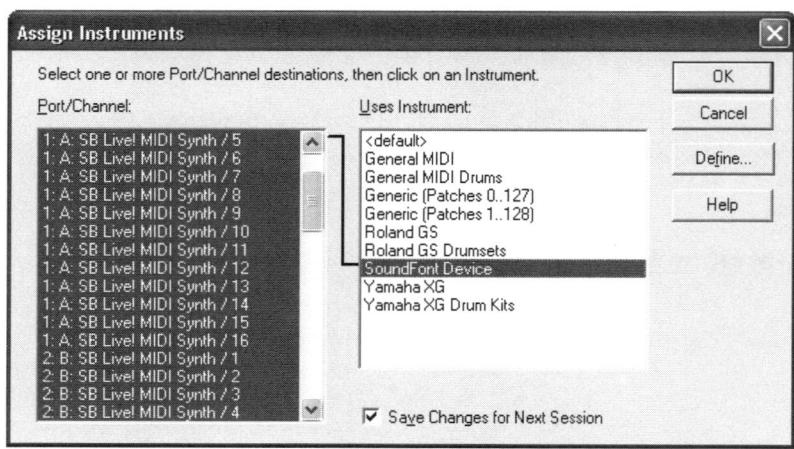

Figure 17.16: Assign Instruments dialog box in Cakewalk Pro Audio 9. Make sure that all channels of the SB Live! MIDI Synth use the SoundFont Device instrument definition.

to select multiple items, or click the first item and Shift-click the last item in a row to select all items in between), and select the SoundFont Device instrument definition on the right.

Normally, this selection is handled automatically for ports that are determined to have SoundFont support. When you are using the SoundFont Device instrument definition, the name of the out port in the tracks view will change to SoundFont Device.

Creating Your Own Instrument Definition

If you already have the SoundFont Device instrument definition, you can simply use it and skip this section. However, there is nothing magic about the SoundFont device instrument (except how Cakewalk finds the patch names), and you can easily edit this instrument definition or even create your own. To do so, follow these steps:

1. With the SoundFont Device selected, click Define in the Assign Instruments dialog box. Another dialog box will pop up, showing all available instrument definitions and their properties in a treelike view on the left side of the screen. On the right side, you will see all available properties for the various settings, and you can drag the correct setting from here to any instrument definition on the left.

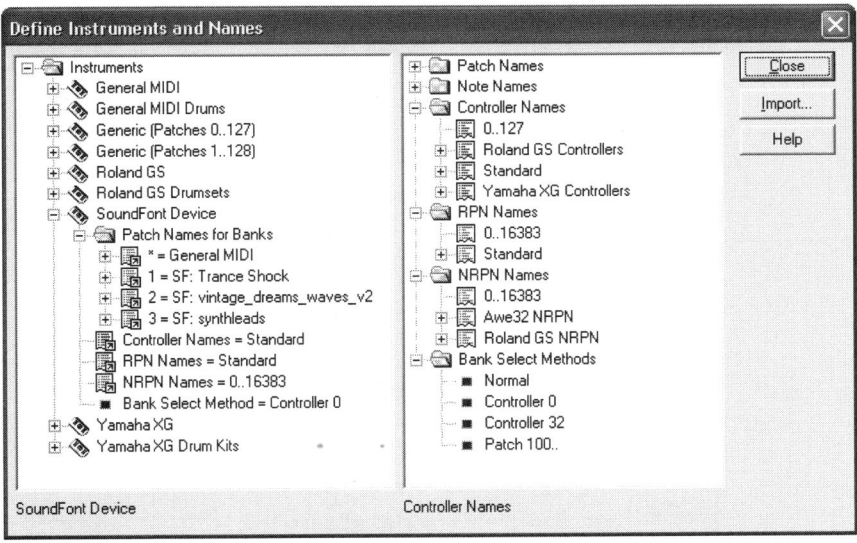

Figure 17.17: Cakewalk's dialog box for creating your own instrument definitions

When you're creating an instrument definition for a SoundFont device, note these important items in this dialog box: the bank selection method, the patch names, and the controller names.

2. Set the bank selection method, defining which MIDI messages to send to change SoundFont, to Controller 0 Only, because the Live! supports "only" 128 banks at a time and thus ignores controller 32, which is used in rare cases when more banks are supported.

3. Patch names are, in the case of the SoundFont Device, not generated from a pre-defined list as in most cases, but from the SoundFonts loaded in memory. Therefore, you should not assign anything to this setting but instead let Cakewalk take care of it.

4. Set controller names to Standard (which includes most of the controllers on the SB Live! MIDI Synth), or use a custom setting based on the SB Live! MIDI implementation (described in Appendix E, "The Sound Blaster Live! MIDI Implementation"). You can also set the controller names to, for example, "Roland GS Controllers" which will include all the supported controllers, plus a few extra that have no function on a Live!

5. Additionally, you can create a definition of all the RPNs and NRPNs supported by the Live! (or use the AWE32 NRPNs, which are supplied with many Cakewalk versions) and assign the RPN/NRPN definition to the SoundFont Device. In theory, doing this would make the use of NRPNs on the Live! very easy. In practice, certain aspects of Cakewalk limit the usefulness of this approach, as you will see later. Nevertheless, assigning the supported set of NRPNs here is better than just selecting Standard. For more information about NRPNs, see "Introduction to RPN and NRPN" later in this chapter.

Loading SoundFonts Within Cakewalk

When you use a version of Cakewalk that has SoundFont support, you do not load SoundFonts with the SoundFont applet as you normally would, because Cakewalk has its own SoundFont management system. This way, Cakewalk can save information about what SoundFonts were loaded at what bank numbers along with your song (if you save it in Cakewalk's own .wrk format). Thereafter, every time you load the song, the SoundFonts will be loaded, as well.

Figure 17.18: The finished instrument definition for the SB Live! MIDI Synth

NOTE *Only the names of the loaded SoundFont files are saved with a song, not the SoundFonts themselves. Therefore, make sure that you don't delete or move SoundFonts that you use in songs, or Cakewalk will not be able to find them when you load the song.*

To bring up the window where you load SoundFonts within Cakewalk, select SoundFonts from the Options menu. The main part of the window consists of a list with the loaded SoundFonts and their corresponding bank numbers. Even though you may have loaded SoundFonts using the SoundFont applet, as described before, they will not be available within Cakewalk (except for the Synth bank).

It is a good idea to first specify the folders on the computer where you store SoundFont files.

1. Open the SoundFonts dialog box by selecting SoundFonts from the Options menu.
2. Click the Locations button.

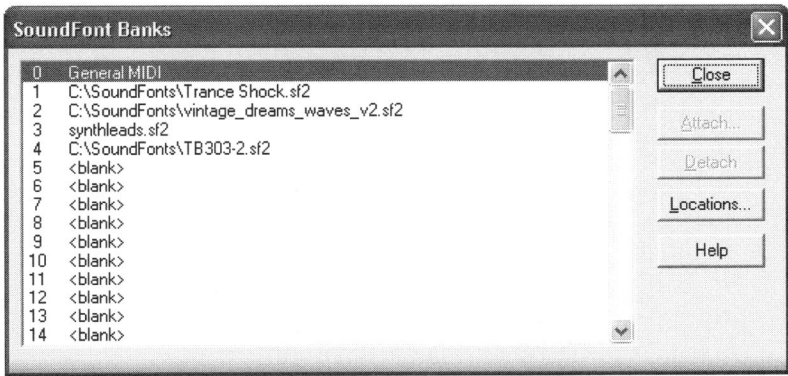

Figure 17.19: Cakewalk's dialog box for SoundFont management

3. In the window that opens, you will be asked to enter a list. This list is simply the paths of the folders where you keep SoundFonts. For example, if you store SoundFonts in a folder called SFonts under Music on your D: hard drive, you would enter *d:\music\sfonts* as the list.

Figure 17.20: If this is the folder containing your SoundFonts . . .

Sequencer Basics **471**

4. If you have several folders containing SoundFonts, you enter them all, separated by semicolons, like this: *d:\music\sfonts;d:\work\music\SoundFont;e:\sf2.*

Figure 17.21: . . . this is what you would type in the Locations dialog box

To assign a SoundFont to bank number, select it from the list, click Attach, and pick a SoundFont file. To remove a SoundFont, select it in the list and click Detach. Note that the first bank, number 0, is assumed to be a General MIDI bank by Cakewalk and cannot be changed.

Using SoundFont Banks on MIDI Tracks

For any MIDI track in the track view, you can select which bank to use in the Bank field. If the track corresponds to a SoundFont device, the bank number and name of the loaded SoundFont will be shown here. For example, if you loaded the Vintage Dreams Waves SoundFont as bank number 5, first select the MIDI out port and a MIDI channel; then type *4* (or click the plus button four times) in the Bank field to use this SoundFont for the selected track. When you select instruments (patches), the correct names from the SoundFont will appear in this field.

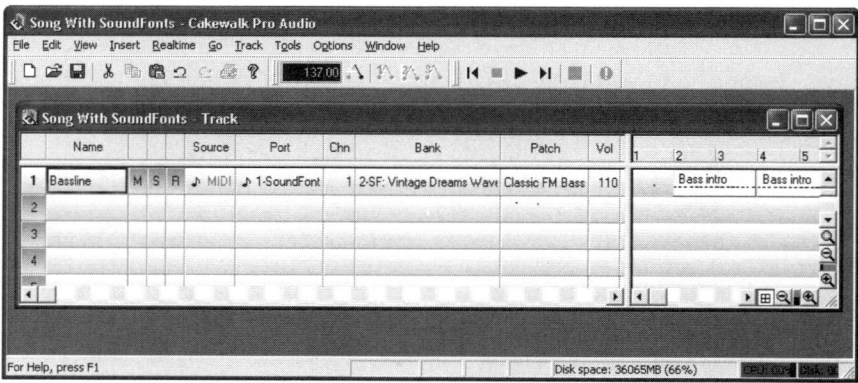

Figure 17.22: Track using a custom SoundFont in Cakewalk

SoundFont Support in Cubase

Cubase takes a somewhat different approach to SoundFont support than Cakewalk. Instead of requiring loading and maintaining SoundFont information explicitly, Cubase relies on the SoundFonts that you've loaded with the SoundFont applet and provides a simple but quick and powerful method of choosing among the available instruments. In addition, recent versions offer the functionality of managing Sound-Fonts within the sequencer, and store this information in your song.

Configuring Cubase for SoundFont Support

Assuming that you're using a version of Cubase with SoundFont support, making Cubase use your loaded SoundFonts is very easy. To use a SoundFont on a particular track, follow these steps:

1. Use the SoundFont Control Panel to load the banks you want to use in your song, as described in the previous chapter. You can also remove or load additional SoundFonts while Cubase is running.

2. To use SoundFonts within the sequencer, first select a MIDI track and make sure it points to either of the SB Live! MIDI Synth ports.

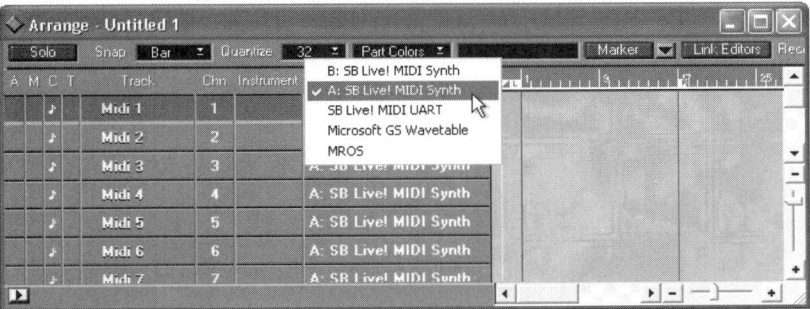

3. Right-click the instrument field, select Setup Instruments, and check whether SoundFont is selected for Patchname Source. If this option is missing, it is probably either because the drivers aren't correctly installed or the version of Cubase you're using doesn't support SoundFonts.

Sequencer Basics **473**

4. Open the track information panel on the left side of the screen. In the Banks field, select which SoundFont bank to use and what type of MIDI message to use to select it. If this is not already done, set the type of MIDI message to Send MSB First (and nothing else).

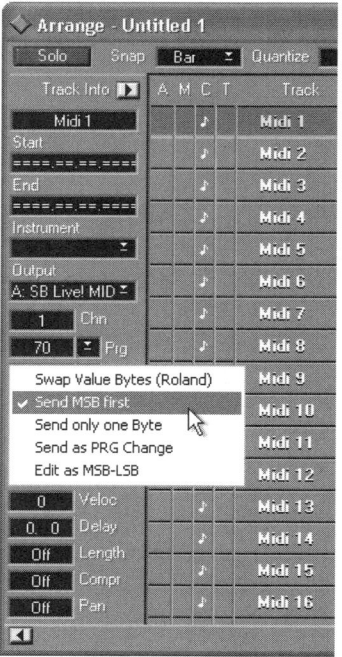

5. You can now select among the loaded SoundFonts by clicking the large field next to Bank. Choose one and notice how the instrument names change those of the selected SoundFont when you click the Patchname field.

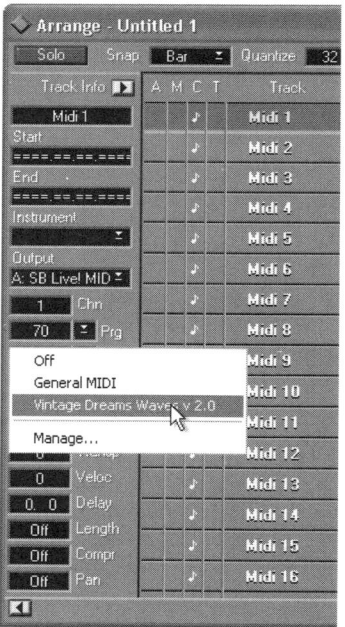

If the instrument (patch) names are displayed correctly but bank switching doesn't seem to work, make sure that the right method for selecting banks is selected.

TIP *Although Cubase will recognize and use SoundFonts loaded with the SoundFont Control Panel, you can manage SoundFonts from within Cubase, as well. To open the SoundFont manager, select Manage from the Bank Menu of the Track Info pane.*

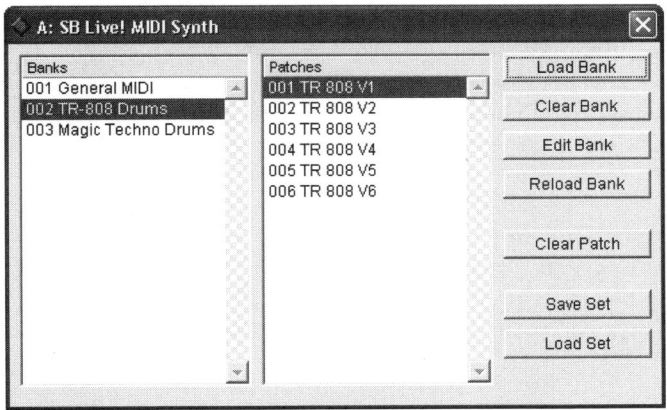

Figure 17.24: The SoundFont manager in Cubase

Using SoundFonts in Any MIDI Sequencer

Even though many sequencers have built-in SoundFont support nowadays, you can use SoundFonts with just about any MIDI sequencer. In fact, changing banks in Cubase or Cakewalk is just a convenient way to send a bank select MIDI message to a MIDI out port and save these settings along with the songs. The real benefit of built-in SoundFont support is that the sequencer will be able to display the correct patch names for any SoundFonts that may be loaded in memory.

Using the Bank Field

If your sequencer has a Bank field for each track, it can most likely be used to automatically switch between banks. Just make sure that only control change number 0 is sent when you change the value of this field. Using only control change 0 is the most common case and can usually be set in your sequencer's preferences, or as in Cakewalk, for instance, in the instrument definition used.

Without native SoundFont support, the patch names will not be shown correctly for loaded SoundFont banks. Instead, you'll see either the instrument number or the corresponding General MIDI instrument name. In this case, there's not much you can do. To select an instrument, change the bank and patch number and play a few notes on your MIDI controller keyboard to verify that the right instrument is selected.

TIP *While the lack of native SoundFont support makes it somewhat harder to find the right instrument, you can always open the SoundFont applet and switch to the second tab to quickly get a list of the instruments available in a loaded SoundFont bank.*

Changing Banks Manually

You should know by now that each MIDI channel has exactly one instrument assigned to it. By default, instruments from the first SoundFont in memory, the Synth bank, will be used. To use an instrument from another bank in memory on a MIDI channel, all you need to do is to send a bank select message on that channel containing the number of the new bank.

Because a bank select message is nothing other than control change number 0, this is easily done either by opening a view of the track where you can "draw" controller values or by using the event list to insert the controller.

> For MIDI instruments that have a large number of banks, the MIDI specification suggests the use of a combination of control changes 0 and 32 to select banks. The SB Live! MIDI Synth, like most other synthesizers, uses only control change 0, making it possible to choose among up to 128 banks.

You will usually want to select the instruments before a song starts playing, so the best place to insert a bank select message is at the very beginning of the song. A good practice is to leave one blank bar at the beginning of your song to make sure that any MIDI messages used to initialize the channels (such as bank select) are sent before any notes.

The first method, using the controller view (which is often embedded in the piano roll view), is as follows:

1. Open the window where you can draw controller values (normally the piano roll) and switch to control change 0 (bank select).
2. At the beginning of the song, simply insert a control change with the value equal to the number of the loaded SoundFont to be used, as shown here.

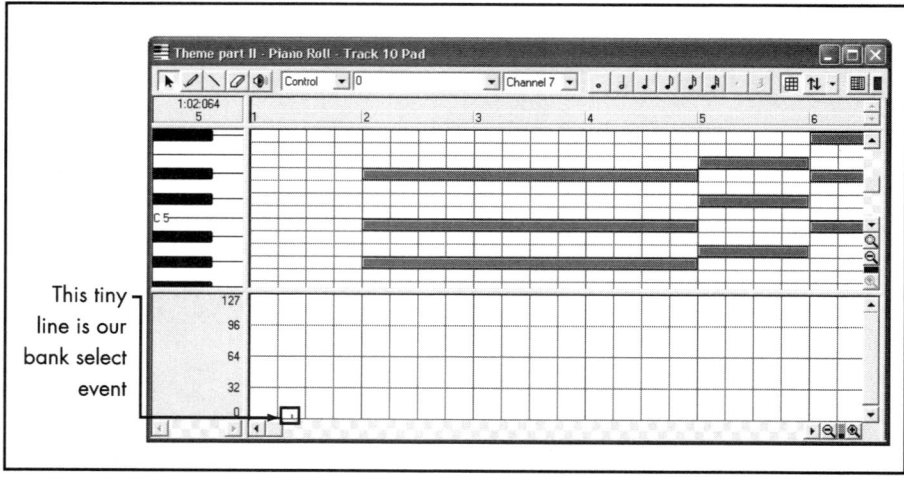

Figure 17.25: A bank change inserted using Cakewalk's piano roll editor

Because this procedure may require some fine precision with the mouse, using the event list may be a better idea:

1. Open the event list view (assuming that your sequencer offers this view).
2. Insert a new MIDI event. Set the type of the new event to Control Change, the control change number to 0, and the value to the number of the bank you want to use.
3. Set the time value of the event to the very beginning of the song to make sure that this message is sent before any other MIDI messages on that track.

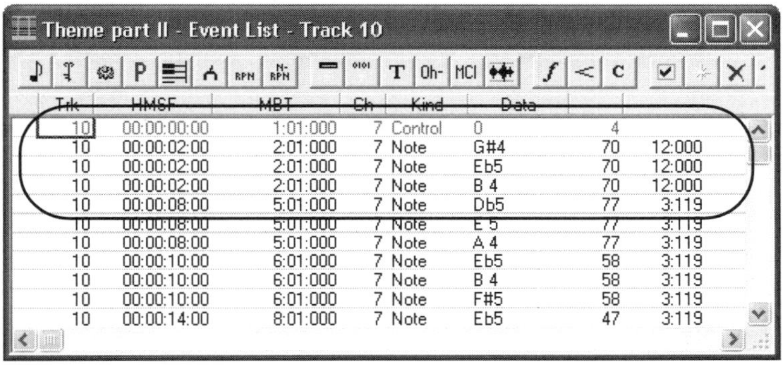

Figure 17.26: The event list gives you better control when inserting bank select messages

Keep in mind that MIDI messages are not automatically sent the moment you insert them. After you've manually inserted a bank select message at the beginning of a track, set the playing position to the beginning of the song and play the first bar or so. This way, the bank select message is sent to the MIDI port. You can verify that the channel uses an instrument from the new bank by playing a few notes on your MIDI keyboard.

Using MIDI Controllers

MIDI controllers, or control changes if we refer to the corresponding MIDI messages, were mentioned back in Chapter 14, and several times since then. Indeed, control changes are important to spicing up your sequencer work a little.

Control changes are used to control anything that doesn't have a specific type of MIDI message of its own. This includes the modulation amount (commonly used for vibrato effects), sustain pedal state (up or down), bank select messages (to use your custom SoundFont banks, as you've seen examples of), and many other items. The complete list of defined control change numbers can be found in Appendix A, "The MIDI Specification."

> Note that a control change message is always sent to a specific MIDI channel, so if you add some vibrato to one instrument (or, in other words, to one MIDI channel), all other instruments are unaffected.

Entering MIDI Controllers

If your MIDI keyboard has a modulation wheel or joystick, ribbon controller, sustain pedal, expression pedal, breath controller, or virtually any other device to give you extra real-time control, chances are that it will send control change messages when this device is used. Control changes are recorded, like any other MIDI events, by the sequencer.

Once recorded, the sequencer will let you edit the recorded controller values. Often, this can be done in the same view as the one where the note events are shown. Like other events, controller values can be added, deleted, and modified.

Note that, although they are technically different, pitch bend and aftertouch are usually edited the same way as MIDI controllers in a sequencer.

Controllers on the SB Live! MIDI Synth

Like all synthesizers, the Sound Blaster Live! MIDI Synth supports only a subset of the control changes defined in the MIDI specification. This section describes when, why, and how to use each and every one of the supported controllers.

The following table shows the control changes that are supported by the SB Live! MIDI Synth. A more detailed description of each one of them can be found in the paragraphs that follow.

Table 17.2: Supported Control Changes on the SB Live! MIDI Synth

CC#	Name	Parameter Meaning	Description and Use*
0	Bank Select	Bank number	Selects the SoundFont bank number to select instruments from on a particular MIDI channel.
1	Modulation	Modulation amount	Increases the LFO-to-pitch parameter of the instrument, producing a vibrato.
6	Data Entry	Data value (MSB)	Most significant byte of an RPN or NRPN data value.
7	Main Volume	Channel volume	Sets the main volume of a MIDI channel.
10	Pan	Position (where 0 = left, 64 = center, 127 = right)	Positions an instrument in the stereo field.
11	Expression	Relative channel volume	Sets the relative main volume of a MIDI channel.

Table 17.2: Supported Control Changes on the SB Live! MIDI Synth (continued)

CC#	Name	Parameter Meaning	Description and Use*
38	Data Entry	Data value (LSB)	Least significant byte of an RPN or NRPN data value.
64	Sustain Pedal	0–63 = off, 64–127 = on	Controls whether the notes on a MIDI channel are sustained.
91	Reverb Depth	Reverb amount	Sets the amount of reverb on a MIDI channel.
93	Chorus Depth	Chorus amount	Sets the amount of chorus on a MIDI channel.
98	NRPN LSB	NRPN (LSB)	Least significant byte used to select an NRPN.
99	NRPN MSB	NRPN (MSB)	Most significant byte used to select an NRPN.
100	RPN LSB	RPN (LSB)	Least significant byte used to select an RPN.
101	RPN MSB	RPN (MSB)	Most significant byte used to select an RPN.
120	All sounds off		Immediately turns off all sounds on the target MIDI channel.
121	Reset all controllers		Sets all controllers of the target MIDI channel to their default values.
123	All notes off		Turns off all notes on the target MIDI channel.

* Specific to the SB Live! MIDI Synth

Note that the effects controllers (except for the reverb, if you are using recent drivers) can be remapped to other numbers and can be replaced by other effects.

The best way to understand the effect of a controller is to listen to it. The CD contains many short MIDI files, named Control Example <controller>.mid (and corresponding .wav files, if you prefer those), where <controller> is the exemplified controller. Control Example.mid is the original MIDI file, and the Control Example All.mid is the same MIDI file with all the controllers from the other examples added to it.

CC0: Bank Select

You use control change 0 to select a SoundFont bank number from which to select the instrument for a particular MIDI channel. You must use this controller to use any loaded SoundFont bank other than the Synth bank. To use CC0, simply send control change 0 with a value of the bank number where the SoundFont that contains your instrument is loaded.

The use of SoundFonts and the bank select controller is discussed in more detail in the section "Using SoundFonts" in this chapter.

CC1: Modulation

As you may recall from the synthesis basics, modulation simply means that something is used to change the behavior of something else. For example, a low-frequency oscillator can be used to modulate the pitch of an oscillator, resulting in a vibrato effect. Usually, this type of control change message is sent when the position of a modulation wheel or joystick on a MIDI keyboard has changed.

The value of a control change 0 message controls the amount of modulation of an instrument. Modulation is not necessarily the same as vibrato. Different synthesizers, and even different instruments on the same synthesizer, may produce different results when applying modulation to an instrument.

On the Sound Blaster Live! MIDI Synth, modulation values higher than zero increase the LFO-to-pitch value of the SoundFont instrument, effectively resulting in a vibrato effect (depending on the initial amount and the LFO frequency). This can be used to add some vibrato to long notes to simulate the playing style of a brass, wind, or string player.

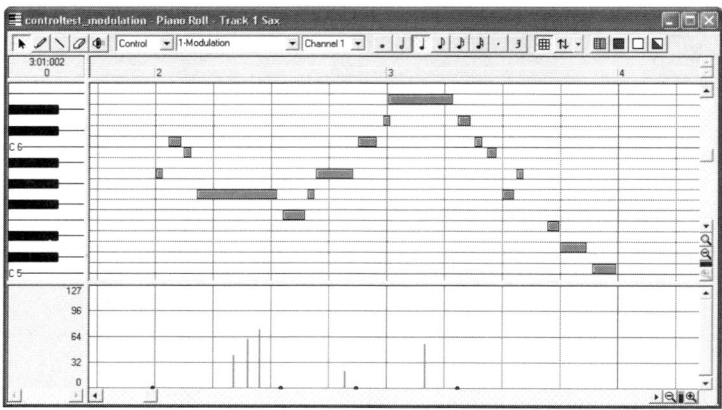

Figure 17.27: Some vibrato at the end of long notes. This effect was added by hand; a modulation wheel or joystick would have produced more dense control changes.

Audio Sample

CD Folder: Chapter 17 – Sequencer Basics
Files: Control Example Modulation.mid, Control Example Modulation.wav
This example can be found on the CD. (For comparison, the same file without the controllers added is available as Control Example.mid and Control Example.wav.) Listen carefully and compare the two.

CC6 and CC38: Data Entry

Control changes 6 and 38 are used together to control the value of a registered parameter number (RPN) or a nonregistered parameter number (NRPN). RPNs and NRPNs and examples of how they can be used are presented in the section "Introduction to RPN and NRPN" later in this chapter.

CC7: Volume

Control change 7 is used to control the volume of a MIDI channel. In your sequencer, you most likely already have a field or a slider to control the volume of each track. What happens when you change this value is that a control change 7 with the new value is sent to the corresponding MIDI channel. Because virtually all sequencers have this feature, you normally don't need to enter volume control changes manually.

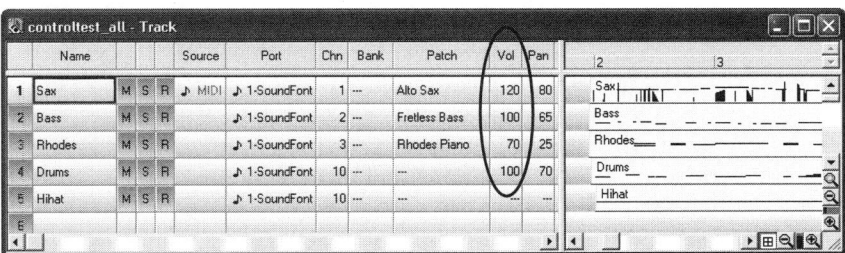

Figure 17.28: The track or arrange view in Cakewalk and Cubase with the volume fields highlighted

To apply other volume effects such as rapid, pulsating volume changes or tremolo effects and fade in and fade out, control change 11 can be used. This way, you can still easily use CC7 to control the relative volumes of all MIDI channels.

CC10: Pan

The pan value controls the placement of an instrument between the two speakers in a stereo setup. A value of 64 centers the instrument in the stereo field (the instrument is played equally loud in both speakers), and the closer to the extreme values you get, the closer to the left or right speaker the instrument will seem to come from.

Many sequencers offer control over the pan of a channel on the track level, just as for the volume. Use this parameter! Panning the channels (wisely—don't overdo it) can greatly improve the overall feeling of a song. If you are creating a piece of classical music, you can study the positions of the individual instruments in an orchestra and choose the pan values according to this. If you are creating popular music, you may have to just trust your instincts. Note that you can get interesting effects by changing the pan values of instruments within a song rather than using a value for the whole track.

Don't be afraid to experiment.

Also note that some instruments already have pan values other than center stored in the SoundFonts. You'll find a good example of this if you try the toms in the GM drum set. These are panned slightly from left to right to simulate their positions in a drum kit. Also, some effects (like chorus) widen the stereo panorama of an instrument, which at the same time reduces the effect of the pan.

Audio Sample
CD Folder: Chapter 17 – Sequencer Basics
Files: Control Example Pan.mid and Control Example Pan.wav
In this example, the instruments have been panned slightly compared to the original version. Make sure to play back the example using at least two well-separated speakers.

CC11: Expression

What is known in the MIDI specification as expression simply controls the volume of an instrument on the Live! If you've followed this discussion so far, you should be thinking: Isn't that exactly what CC7 did? Yes it is; however, these controls are both very useful and should be used slightly differently.

Imagine that you are recording a piece of music with some very soft and some very loud parts. To control the volume of the instrument, you could draw the volume with control change 7. However, if you need to change the overall volume of this instrument later, you would have to draw all these volume changes again (and you probably wouldn't get it quite right anyway). A better approach is to use CC11. The value of this controller is normally set to 127. If you set it to a lower value, however, you'll lower the volume of the channel, just as with CC7. Consequently, CC7 and CC11 together determine the volume of the channel. If the volume of CC7 is set to 75 percent of the maximum volume, and CC11 is set to 50 percent of the maximum volume, then you'll get a volume of 0.75 * 0.5 = 0.375, or about 38 percent of the maximum value.

To use this controller for a fade out, you simply draw a straight line of controller values from 127 to 0 over the bars where the fade out should be. Just make sure that you put a controller with a value of 127 at the beginning of the track, too, or the channel volume will still be 0 when you play the song again.

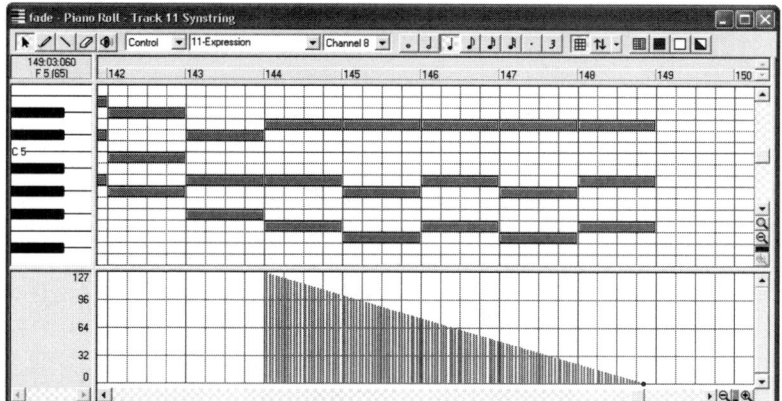

Figure 17.29: Controller 11 used to fade out a track of synth strings

When used in real time, the expression control change is often generated by an *expression pedal* connected to your MIDI keyboard. Unlike a sustain pedal, this type of pedal senses how far it is depressed and sends a data value between 0 and 127 accordingly.

TIP *For an example of a more creative use of this controller, see "Volume Effects Using CC11" later in this chapter.*

CC64: Sustain Pedal

If you have a sustain pedal connected to your MIDI keyboard, a CC64 message will be sent every time you press or lift your foot from the pedal. Because the state of a sustain pedal is either down or up (on or off), any value between 0 and 63 is interpreted as off, and any value of 64 or above is interpreted as on.

When the sustain pedal is down (on), note-off messages on this MIDI channel will not have any effect until the state changes to off. In other words, the sustain pedal has (virtually) the same effect as on a piano.

CC91: Reverb Depth

The reverb depth control change sets the amount of reverb used for an instrument, where 0 is completely dry and 127 is the maximum effect level, where the maximum effect level is the setting of the master reverb level in the EAX Control Panel.

Audio Sample
CD Folder: Chapter 17 – Sequencer Basics
Files: Control Example Reverb.mid and Control Example Reverb.wav
Some reverb is added to the saxophone and drum channels. For correct playback of the MIDI file, make sure that the master reverb level in the EA applet is at least halfway up.

CC93: Chorus Level

The chorus level controller sets the amount of chorus for an instrument. The absolute chorus level is determined by the same factors as for the reverb level.

Audio Sample

CD Folder: Chapter 17 – Sequencer Basics
Files: Control Example Chorus.mid and Control Example Chorus.wav
Chorus is added to the bass and Rhodes tracks. Again, if you play the MIDI file, make sure that the master chorus level is set higher than 0 percent.

The preceding descriptions of how to control effects are far from complete. Fortunately, the next section focuses on the effects of the Live! and how to use them with MIDI.

CC98 and CC99: NRPN

The CC98 and CC99 controller pair is used to select the nonregistered parameter number (NRPN) parameter to be controlled with the corresponding CC6 and CC38 data entry controller pair. How this is done and the use of NRPN on the Live! are discussed in more detail in the section "Introduction to RPN and NRPN" later in this chapter.

CC100 and CC101: RPN

A combination of CC100 and CC101 is used to select a registered parameter number (RPN) parameter to be controlled with the CC6 and CC38 data entry controller pair. See the section "Introduction to RPN and NRPN" later in this chapter for examples of how to use RPN.

CC120: All Sounds Off

Sending a CC120 message turns off all sound on the MIDI channel it's targeted to. This includes any sound that would normally be produced after the notes are released. The data value of this control change is ignored. This control change could, for example, be sent by a sequencer to quickly mute a MIDI channel.

CC121: Reset All Controllers

Control change 121, when sent to a MIDI channel, sets the values of all supported controllers to their default values. The data value is ignored. You (or, more often, a media player) can send this control change, for example, between MIDI files to make sure that the controller settings of the previous file played do not affect the playback of the current one.

CC123: All Notes Off

A CC123 message has the same effect as sending a note-off message to every note being played on the target MIDI channel. Normally, the MIDI controller or sequencer keeps track of the notes being played and eventually sends the corresponding note-off message. If a note-off message is lost in transmission, however, this controller can be sent to recover from the situation. It can also be used to reduce the number of note-off messages that must be sent when playback of a song suddenly stops (as when the user clicks the Stop button on a sequencer).

Note that there's a difference between CC120 and CC123. While CC120 guarantees to immediately turn off all sound on the target channel, CC123 merely turns off the notes. Some instruments will still sound for a moment after the note is released.

Common Controller Problems

The value of a controller stays the same until it is changed (or a CC121 message is received). This can sometimes create problems when you are jumping back and forth in a song, which is common during sequencing.

One of the most common examples of this problem occurs when a sustain pedal is used. When a track is recorded in real time, the control changes of the sustain pedal are recorded, as well. Imagine that you play back the track later and stop the playback at a moment when the sustain pedal is down. If you go back and start playback from where the sustain pedal should be up, the state of the sustain pedal will still be down (unless the sequencer has a method of handling this type of situation), and the track will not be correctly played back.

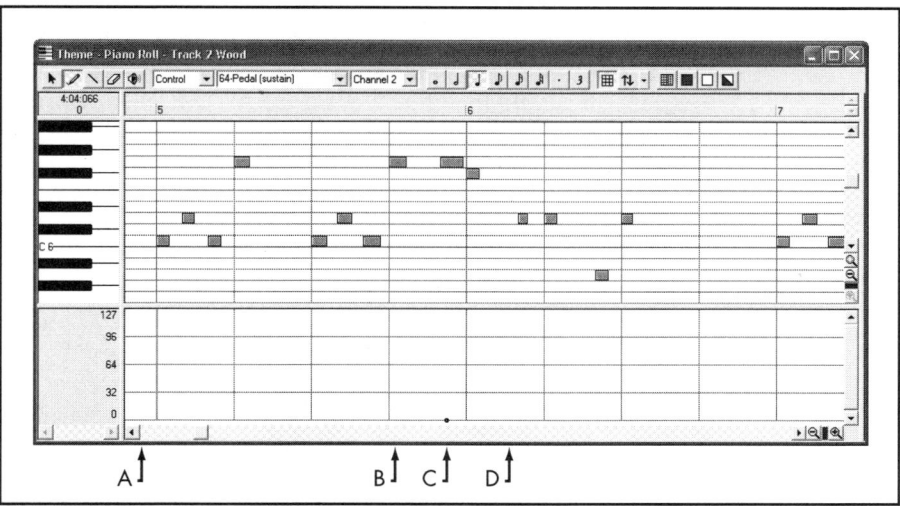

Figure 17.30: The sustain pedal is turned on at (a) and turned off at (c). If the playback is stopped at point (b) and restarted at point (d), the sustain pedal will still be on beyond (d), even though it shouldn't be. Advanced sequencers have features that fix this problem.

Some sequencers have a feature that, at the beginning of playback, searches the previous bars for any previous controller messages and automatically sets any found controllers to their intended values. This feature is called Searchback in Cakewalk and Chase in Cubase.

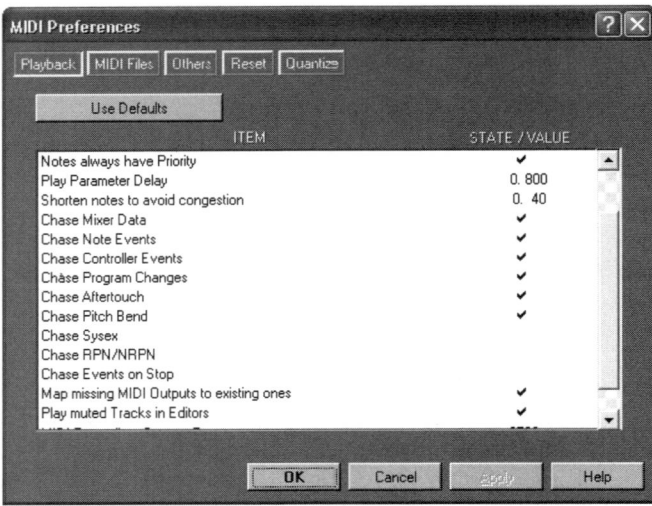

Figure 17.31: Chase options in Cubase's MIDI preferences

Controlling Effects

The EAX effects system on the Live! is very flexible, and fortunately you can use (almost) the full power of the effects unit of your Live! for MIDI music. Many synthesizers (including the EMU8000 on the AWE32 and AWE64 cards) have two effects units: one for reverb and one for chorus. Often, there are a few different types of each, such as reverbs that simulate a few different sizes of rooms or halls. For each MIDI channel (effectively, for each instrument in your song), you can control how much of the sound is sent to each of the effects units. A sound without any effects is usually referred to as *dry*, whereas a sound with effects in it is called *wet*.

Built in to the Live! is a programmable effects unit. The fact that it is programmable means, in this case, that effects algorithms can be downloaded to the chip and used on a sound source. This is done by the Live! drivers, and with a simple driver update, it's therefore possible to improve the effects or even add new types. The same effects that are used for Environmental Audio (EAX) are also used for MIDI music. To simulate different sound environments, reverb (a very dense echo) plays an important role in EA. Fortunately, reverb is an equally important effect in music, and MIDI musicians can take advantage of the good-sounding and very customizable reverb effects offered on the Sound Blaster Live! Other effects that are more useful for musicians (and sometimes just to create weird effects) are chorus, distortion, and ring modulation, to mention a few—all of which can be produced by the Live!'s effects unit.

Effects require a lot of computations, so you cannot use an infinite number of different effects at the same time. More specifically, with the current Live! drivers, four effects can be used simultaneously. Two of these effects can be used on MIDI tracks, so you have to carefully pick the effects to use in a project. What's

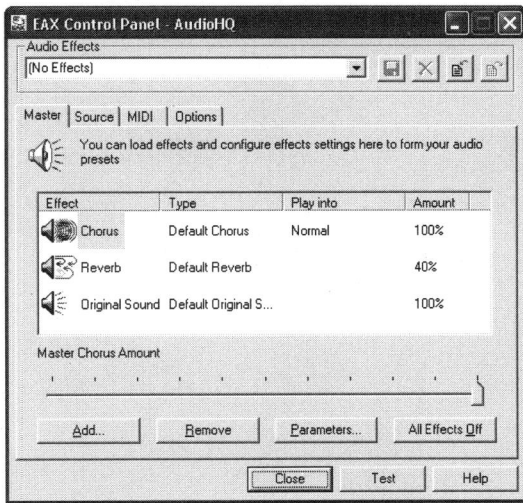

Figure 17.32: The master effects settings in the Environmental Audio applet

even worse is that with recent drivers, the reverb is always one of these two effects, which brings the number of effects you can freely choose down to one. In other words, available for your compositions, you will have reverb plus one more effect. By default, chorus will be the second effect (because GS, XG, and GM2 all assume that a chorus effect is available), but you can replace this with more a exotic effect such as pitch shift, vocal morpher, or any other available EAX effect.

Selecting and Configuring Effects

The effects settings of the Live!, whether it's used for games, MIDI music, or any other application, are always controlled from the Environmental Audio applet.

Using the Default Effects with MIDI

By default, reverb and chorus are the two loaded effects. To use them on the instruments in your sequencer, follow these easy steps:

1. On the first tab of the Environmental Audio applet (Master) shown above in Figure 17.32, make sure that the effects are loaded. To hear the effects, you need to set their values to more than 0. To do this, select each of the effects respectively and drag the slider to the desired value. For chorus, you'll most likely want to use a full 100 percent; for reverb, a smaller percentage may be enough, but it's a matter of the type of music you want to create.

2. By default, these effects will be applied to all sound sources. Because pre-recorded music already contains the proper number of effects, you will most likely turn off the effects for all sources but MIDI. To do this, switch to the second tab (Source). Select each of the sources in the drop-down box and set the chorus and reverb levels to 0 percent.

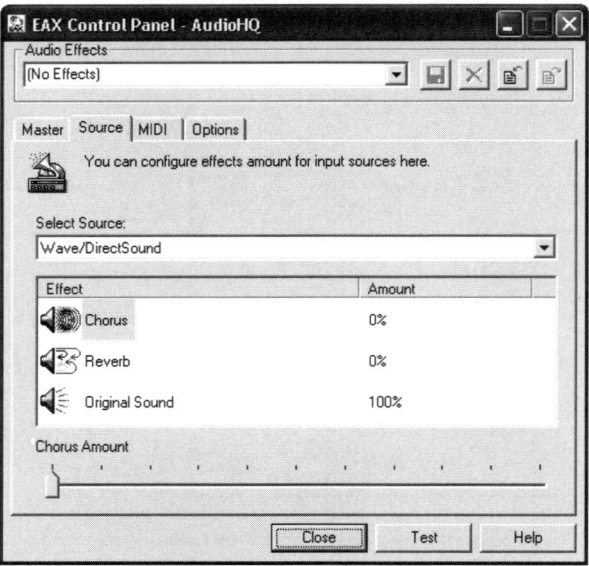

Figure 17.33: On the second tab of the EA applet, you can control the effects levels on individual sound sources

Each MIDI channel has its own effects levels, so these levels are not set on this tab but rather by using control change MIDI messages.

3. Switch to the third tab of the EA applet (MIDI). This is where you specify which control change numbers control which effects. On almost any

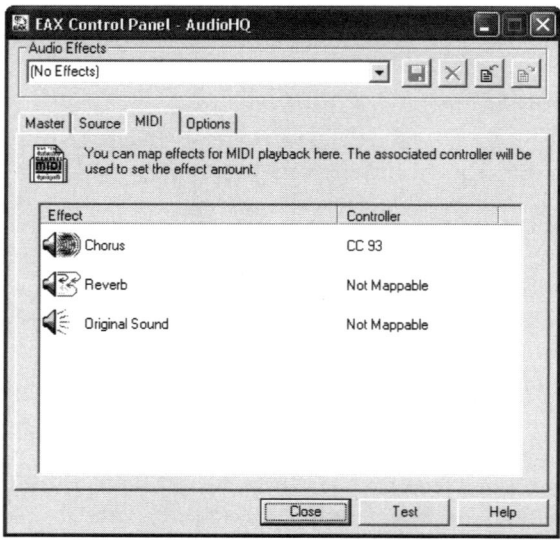

Figure 17.34: On the third tab of the EA applet, you associate the loaded effects with control change numbers in MIDI tracks

synthesizer, CC91 controls the amount of reverb, and CC93 controls the amount of chorus. Although these can be changed, these are the default settings of the Live!, too, so you only need to verify the settings. If you are using Live!Ware 3, you will notice that reverb is listed as not mappable. This simply means that CC91 is used for reverb, and that this cannot be changed.

4. If the sequencer is not already running, start it and add control change messages to the tracks that you want to apply effects to. If your sequencer has a fancier way to apply effects (like a reverb and chorus setting for each track, or a MIDI mixer window from which effects levels can be controlled), feel free to use it instead.

The effects level is controlled by the value of the controller that you insert on a track. Keep in mind, though, that the effects level on an instrument is not necessarily proportional to the value of the corresponding controller. There are three factors that control the amount of effects on an instrument:

- The master effect level, as set in step 1. Changing this value affects the effects levels on all MIDI channels (and other sources on which effects are used).
- The controller value. Generally, the higher the controller value, the more of the corresponding effect is added to the sound.
- The SoundFont. Remember from the previous chapter that information about effects levels can be stored in the actual SoundFont. As a consequence, zeroing the controller does not always mean that you get a completely dry sound. This can sometimes be a problem and is a good reason not to unnecessarily add effects to the SoundFonts themselves — in most cases, the same thing can be done with controllers. To fix this problem, you'll have to either manually edit the SoundFont in Vienna or a similar program, or use some tricky combinations of NRPNs—a topic that will be covered later in this chapter.

Customizing Effects

Fortunately, you do not have to use the same type of reverb, chorus, or whatever effect you may be using for every occasion. When you install Live!Ware, many different types of reverb and other effects are available to choose from. If none of the preset effect variations suits you, you can even create your own.

The reverb is, without competition, the most customizable effect available on the Live!, and you will find a large number of reverb types available. The following steps describe how to change the type of reverb used, although the same procedure can be used to select a preset type of any of the other effects, as well.

1. Open the Environmental Audio applet and select the first tab (Master).
2. In the list of loaded effects, there is a Type column. To change the reverb type, click the Reverb row of this column, and a drop-down list will appear.

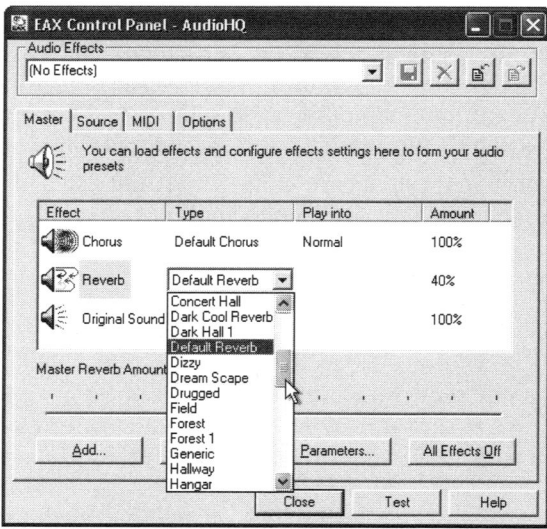

Figure 17.35: The EA applet lets you select from the many preset effect types

3. From the drop-down list, select one of the (many) available presets. If you, for example, want a fairly long and bright reverb, you can try the Stone Corridor preset. You can test the effects settings by clicking the Test button at the bottom of the window. The test sound (which is a drum loop by default) is played by the Wave channel of the Live!, so the effect must be enabled for this source (on the Source tab), or you won't hear any effect at all.

Most of the presets are created for games and sound effects, so you may need to customize the effects settings to find that perfect sound for your MIDI tracks. Creating your own effect presets is a relatively easy procedure (although the number of parameters and their meanings can sometimes be a bit overwhelming):

1. Make sure that you can actually test the effect before you start tweaking it. It's very difficult to create good effects without being able to hear the result while editing its parameters.

2. Select the effect from the list of loaded effects on the first tab of the EA applet and click Parameters. Another window appears, containing a list of parameters for that effect (as shown in Figure 17.36). Reverb is the most customizable type of effect, with over 25 individual parameters (with Live!Ware 3), all affecting the resulting sound.

3. Tweak the values of the various parameters until you're satisfied with the sound. Don't be afraid to experiment. Actually, you'll probably need some experimenting, because the number of parameters can be large, and there is no reference manual that lists all of them. The most important parameters for each effect are listed at the end of this section, however.

4. Type a name for the new effects preset in the combo box above the parameter list and click the Save button (the floppy-disk icon). Now you can use this

effect preset just like any other by selecting it in the Type column on the EAX Control Panel (see Figure 17.37).

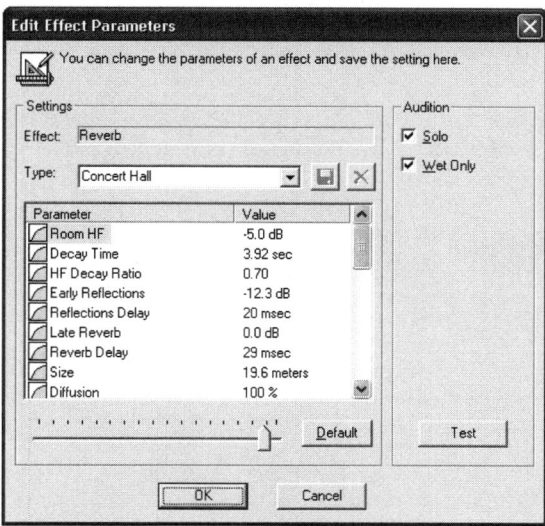

Figure 17.36: The parameter-editing dialog box for the reverb effect. This is the ultimate tool for customizing your effects settings.

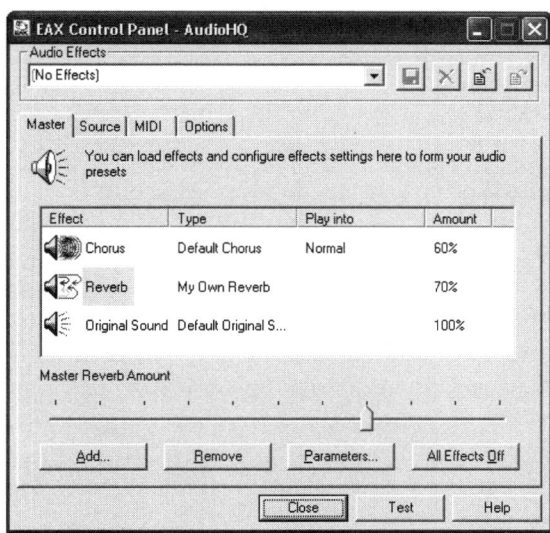

Figure 17.37: Using your own reverb type in the EA applet

Using Other Effect Types

Even though you can do a lot with what you learned so far, you are not limited to variations of reverb and chorus. You can load completely different types of effects, customize them, and map them to controllers to use them in your sequencer. Here's how:

1. On the Master tab of the EA applet, click the Add button to load a new effect. You'll be presented with a list of available effects programs (in addition to those that are already loaded).

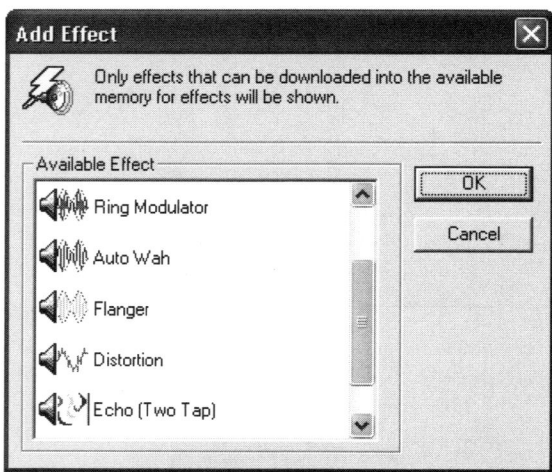

Figure 17.38: This dialog box lets you select from the available effects. Effects that are already loaded are not listed in the dialog box.

2. Once loaded, the effect will appear, together with the reverb and chorus, in the list of loaded effects (see Figure 17.39). Note that a maximum of four different effects can be used at one time (of which reverb and chorus are two), so you may need to select one of the loaded effects and click Remove to be able to load another one.

3. Set the amount to the desired level and, if you want, remove the new effect from sources other than MIDI by setting its level to zero for the sources on the second tab of the applet.

4. To use the effect with MIDI, you need to assign a controller to the new effect to control the amount used on each instrument. To do so, switch to the MIDI tab. Remember that you can use only two effects on MIDI at the same time. Reverb is one of them, and if chorus was the other one before, you need to unmap it from its controller. This is done by selecting chorus in the Effect list and setting the value in the Controller column to Not Mapped.

5. Select your new effect and map it to a control change number in the Controller column (see Figure 17.40). The MIDI specification isn't very specific about control changes and effects, so you can select any of the free

controllers in the list. This controller can now be used in your sequencer to control the amount of the new effect.

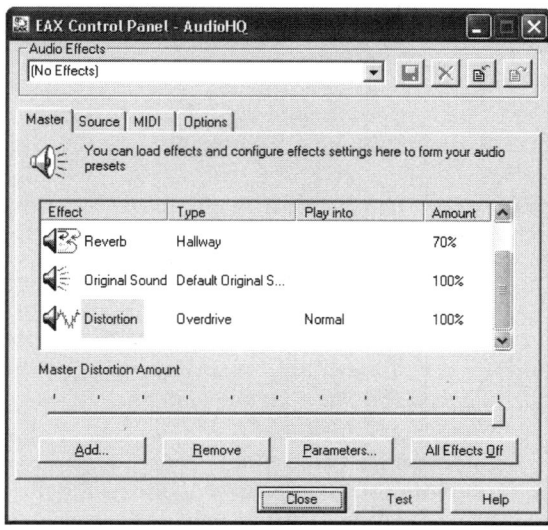

Figure 17.39: A new effect, distortion, has been loaded

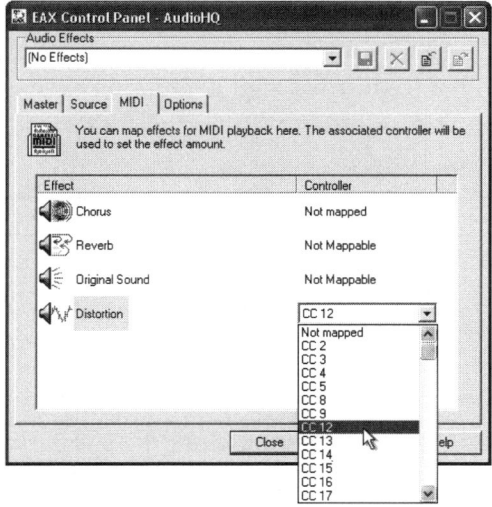

Figure 17.40: After unmapping the chorus effect, the newly added distortion effect is here associated with controller 12

A Note on Recording Effects

Although covered in more detail in another part of this book, how to include the effects is one of the most common sources of confusion when recording MIDI music. If MIDI is selected as the recording source in the mixer, the effects will *not* be recorded along with the music. To record the effects, you must select What-U-Hear as the recording source (and, preferably, mute all sources but MIDI).

The Available Effects

Since the first Live!Ware version, the number of effects and, perhaps more important, the quality and customization capabilities of the effects have increased significantly. Live!Ware 3 offers ten effects with varying levels of customizability. The effects, their uses, and their most important parameters (for customization) are summarized, from a musician's perspective, here.

Reverb

A good reverb is hard to live without when creating music. Reverb simulates the dense type of echo you find, for example, in a large, empty hall, although many types of reverb can be created to simulate the ambience of just about any type of room. Among the presets, you'll find concert halls, different types of rooms, drain pipes, and caves, just to mention a few.

Using reverb on certain instruments can enhance the richness of a song significantly. Once you discover it, be careful not to overuse it—it's easy to add too much of it in a mix. It tends to be most useful for bright, soft, lead-type instruments, as well as some percussion instruments. Basses and bass drums generally do not sound good with longer reverb effects, although reverb is used to some extent on the snare drum. Bright and frequently played instruments, like a hi-hat, may add some noise to the mix when too much reverb is used, so be careful!

The following table describes the most important parameters of the reverb effect.

Table 17.3: Important Parameters of the Reverb Effect

Parameter	Meaning and Use
Room HF	The level of high frequencies in the reverb. An empty room with hard walls will create much high-frequency content, and objects in a room (fabrics in particular) tend to damp the high frequencies.
Decay Time	The length of the reverb. Larger rooms will generally have longer decay times, while a fraction of a second may be enough to simulate a small, damped room.
Early Reflections	The level of the first reflections that come shortly after the original sound.
Reflections Delay	The delay between the original sound and the early reflections.
Late Reverb	The level of the dense, thick reflections that come after the early reflections.
Reverb Delay	The delay between the original sound and the late reverb. Short values make a very smooth reverb; longer delay times can create very interesting effects.
Size	This parameter affects a number of other parameters, simulating rooms of different sizes.
HF	The highest frequency that the reverb will contain.

Chorus

Chorus is a commonly used effect that creates a fatter sound by adding one or more slightly delayed copies of the sound. Further, the delay is modulated by an LFO, and optionally, some feedback can be introduced. Controlled by the phase parameter, each copy of the sound can be made out of phase and panned differently, creating a wider stereo effect.

Chorus is great for certain types of instruments, like some guitars and basses. A string section can be made incredibly thick and rich with a bit of chorus added to it. Use chorus selectively, however. Don't add a lot of chorus to each and every instrument in a song.

The most important parameters of the chorus are described in the following table.

Table 17.4: The Most Important Parameters of the Chorus

Parameter	Meaning and Use
Delay	The delay between the original and the copy of the sound. Depending on the delay size, certain frequencies may be canceled out, and others may be emphasized.
LFO Rate	The speed at which the LFO modifies the delay parameter.
LFO Depth	The amount of modulation on the delay time that the LFO will add. More modulation creates a somewhat wavy sound.
Feedback	Adding some feedback will introduce new harmonics to the sound. This can produce special effects.
Phase	The phase difference between the copies of the sound. A phase difference of 180 degrees means that one copy is an inversion of the other.

Flanger

Flanger is a very distinguishable effect, similar to chorus. Compared to chorus, flanger uses shorter delay times, resulting in more cancellation and addition of frequencies. As in the case of chorus, the copies of the sound can be phased differently and panned to the left and right speaker. The effect can be used on many types of instruments and sounds, including guitars, leads, and vocals. The parameters are similar to those of chorus.

Echo (Two Tap)

The two-tap echo is a simple echo effect with different delay, feedback, and panning settings for the two taps. These are the main parameters to control the two-tap echo:

Table 17.5: Some of the Most Important Parameters of the Two-Tap Echo

Parameter	Meaning and Use
Tap1 Delay Time	The time between the original sound and the first tap. Increase this value to get a longer echo (larger room), and decrease it to get a shorter echo.
Tap1 -> Tap2 Delay Time	The time between the first and second taps.
High-Frequency Damping	Causes some of the higher frequencies to be absorbed every time the sound bounces off an object. The less damping, the brighter the echo will sound.
Regeneration	This parameter controls the amount of feedback in the echo process. If the value is set to 0 percent, only the first two taps can be heard; large values produce repeated taps.
Tap Spread	Controls how wide the echo is—in other words, how far the echo taps should be panned to the left and right speakers.

Distortion

Most people know what an overdriven or distorted guitar sounds like. The distortion effect lets you create this sort of sound, as well as distort any other imaginable sound. With a bit of practice, the distortion effect can be used to produce realistic-sounding guitar solos, as well as many other type of interesting effects. Don't be afraid to experiment with distortion! The effect can produce everything from a slight overdrive effect to real heavy-metal sound.

Table 17.6: Important Parameters of the Distortion Effect

Parameter	Meaning and Use
Edge	The distortion amount. The higher the edge value, the more distorted the sound will be. Smaller values simulate soft overdrive, and higher values simulate heavy distortion.
Gain	Distortion amplifies the sound, producing a very loud result, but you can use this parameter to lower the output level. Generally, the more distortion you use, the more you need to lower the output level to produce a similar volume.
Pre-Dist Lowpass Cutoff	By changing this value, you can ensure that only the lower frequencies of a sound will be distorted.
Post-Dist EQ	These parameters control the frequency content of the distorted result. The lower the bandwidth, the narrower the frequency band of the effect around the center frequency.

Auto Wah

The auto wah effect is similar to the wah-wah effect commonly used with guitars and some other types of instrument. A wah-wah effect essentially is a (resonant) filter. Instead of the filter being controlled with a low-frequency oscillator (as in a regular wah-wah effect), however, the cutoff frequency is controlled by a simple attack-release envelope, triggered every time a peak is detected. The following table describes its most important parameters.

Table 17.7: The Most Important Parameters of the Auto Wah Effect

Parameter	Meaning and Use
Attack Time	The time from the moment a peak is detected until the cutoff frequency reaches its highest value.
Release Time	The time it takes for the cutoff frequency to fall back to its original level.
Resonance	Filter resonance. Higher values will produce a more wah-like effect, but often a thinner sound.
Peak Level	The sound level above which peaks are detected. The lower the value, the smaller the peaks in the sound that will trigger the envelope.

Ring Modulator

Ring modulation is a conceptually simple effect that multiplies two sounds. If, at one moment, the two sound levels are 60 percent and 40 percent of maximum, the output sound level is 0.6 * 0.4 = 0.24, or 24 percent of maximum. In this case, one of the sounds is the input sound, and the other is the output of a simple waveform oscillator with adjustable frequency. In other words, the result will be a (fast) modulation of the input signal's amplitude. See the following table for its settings.

Table 17.8: Important Parameters of the Ring Modulator Effect

Parameter	Meaning and Use
Frequency	The modulation frequency. Different values produce a different type of sound.
Highpass Cutoff	Low frequencies can be removed from the result by increasing the highpass cutoff frequency.
Waveform	The shape of the second waveform used in the ring modulation process. A sine wave produces the smoothest and least distorted result.

Pitch Shifter

A pitch shifter changes the pitch of a signal in real time—in other words, without changing its playback speed. Without going into too much detail, to produce a good result, this process requires quite sophisticated effects algorithms and plenty of computational power. For a consumer product, the Live! does a pretty good job with this effect, although it's not something you'll want to use to transpose a finished mix a couple of semitones up or down.

One problem is that unless you set the original sound's master level to 0 percent (which would affect all other MIDI channels, as well), you can't use this effect solo on an instrument. This makes the effect less useful for MIDI work, although I encourage you to still try it. Layering a sound one octave above the original, for example, can produce a rich effect.

The tuning parameters simply control how much up or down the original sound should be tuned. A coarse tune of 12 semitones will shift the sound one octave up or down.

Vocal Morpher

The vocal morpher is essentially a filter, controlled by an LFO, that amplifies certain controllable frequencies that are strong in different sounds produced by the human voice. This effect will likely not be especially useful in your MIDI tracks.

Frequency Shifter

Most likely, you'll find this effect more useful to play with than to use for MIDI music. The frequency shifter lets you shift the audio a specified number of hertz up or down (or both, since you can set the direction independently for each speaker). To get the full effect, you should not mix the result with the original audio, and you should therefore set the original sound to 0 percent. Unfortunately, you can't control the original sound level for individual MIDI channels, and setting the original sound master level to 0 percent would cancel all original sound. Also, unlike the pitch shifter, the frequency shifter shifts all frequencies in the original sound a fixed amount up or down rather than scaling by a fixed ratio. This makes the effect less useful for tuned instruments.

Saving Environment Presets

When you have created the perfect effects settings for a song, it is important to save the settings, or they will be lost the next time you start your computer. Optionally, you can check the "Always save changes automatically" setting on the Options tab, to make sure that changes are saved.

To save an environment preset, type a name for it in the combo box at the top of the window and click the Save button (the floppy-disk icon), as shown in Figure 17.41. You can also export the effects settings to a file, for example, to store the preset together with your song, by clicking the Export Environment button.

TIP *Note that only the effects and their preset types are saved in the environment preset. If you have made any customizations to an effect, you must first save it as a new preset.*

Introduction to RPN and NRPN

You can think of the registered parameter number (RPN) and nonregistered parameter number (NRPN) within the MIDI specification as a number of extra controllers.

RPN

The same RPNs have the same meaning on different MIDI instruments. The pitch bend range (number of semitones that the pitch wheel can bend a note) on a synthesizer, for example, does not have any control change number defined. Still, many MIDI devices support changes to the pitch bend range of an instrument via

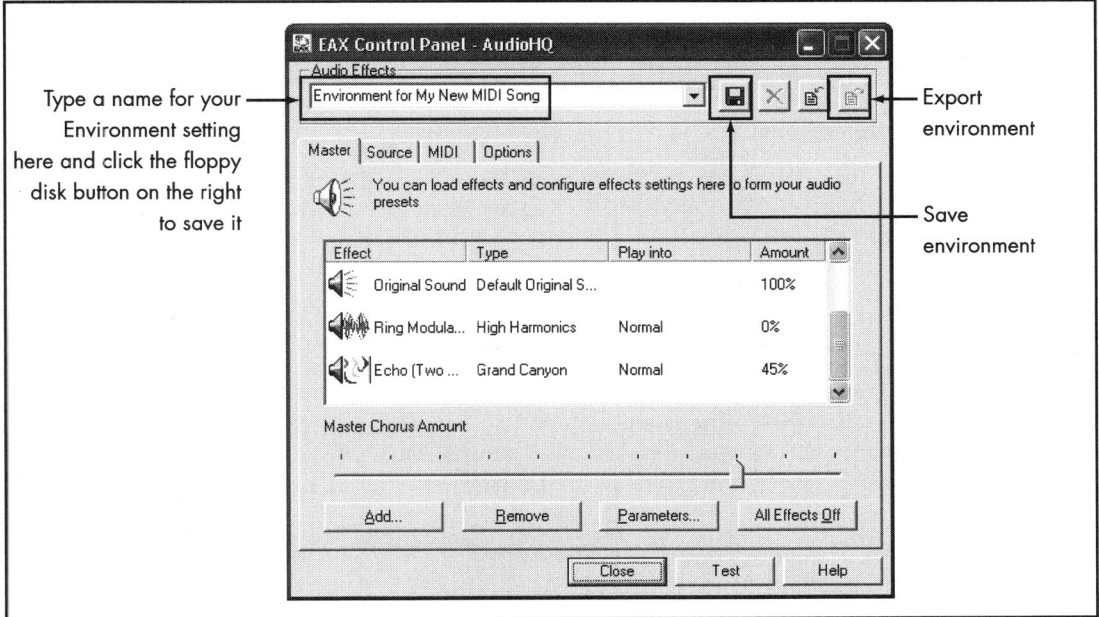

Figure 17.41: Once you are satisfied with your effects configuration, you can save it as an environment preset

MIDI. RPN 0 was defined for this purpose and can be used to change the pitch bend range of a MIDI channel on any instrument that supports it.

NRPN

NRPNs, on the other hand, have different meanings on different MIDI instruments. Parameters that are specific to a particular instrument and don't have control change numbers associated with them can, if the instrument supports it, instead be controlled by NRPNs.

On the Live!, most SoundFont parameters (such as filter, envelope values, and LFOs) can be controlled by NRPNs. Using the same NRPNs on a synthesizer without SoundFont support may give no or totally different results.

How RPN and NRPN Messages Are Sent

Technically, RPN and NRPN are a series of control change messages and are thus specific to the MIDI channel they are sent to. Both the RPN or NRPN and its corresponding value are made up of two MIDI bytes (one most significant and one least significant byte; see "About MSB and LSB" in Appendix A, "The MIDI Specification"); both the RPNs or NRPNs and their data values range from 0 to 16,383.

An RPN message is sent as follows:

1. The most significant byte (MSB) of the RPN is sent via control change 101.
2. The least significant byte (LSB) of the RPN is sent via control change 100.
3. The MSB of the RPN data (the new value) is sent via control change 6.
4. The LSB of the RPN data (the new value) is sent via control change 38.

An NRPN message is sent similarly, although the first control changes would be 99 and 98 rather than 101 and 100. Consequently, to change the value of an RPN or NRPN, up to four control changes are required.

Sequencers with RPN and NRPN Support

Because an RPN or NRPN message is simply a series of control changes, these messages can be used with virtually any sequencer. However, some sequencers have specific support for RPN and NRPN messages, in which case you don't have to manually calculate the values for the MSB and LSB.

This is a great feature, because calculating MSB and LSB values of RPN and NRPN data is not something that a musician should have to do—that's what we use computers for! The only problem arises when the Sound Blaster Live! expects values in the range 0 to 127, and the sequencer displays values in the full 0 to 16,383 range. Needless to say, unless your sequencer has a special way of dealing with this situation (such as keeping track of the valid range for each NRPN), using this features will not work. Keep in mind, though, that you can instead use control change 38 only.

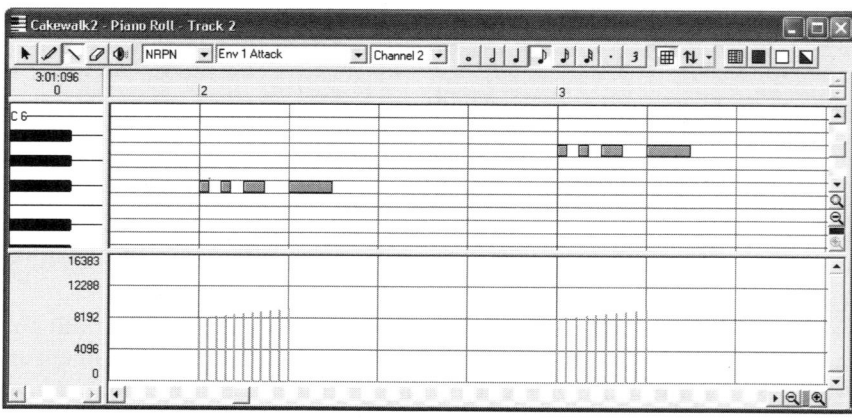

Figure 17.42: Cakewalk's built-in NRPN support, here with the AWE NRPN set used in the instrument definition. Note the range of the controller values.

RPNs on the SB Live! MIDI Synth

Only four RPNs were defined in the original MIDI specification. The Live! currently supports three of them: pitch bend range, global coarse tuning, and global fine-tuning.

RPNs on the Sound Blaster Live!, despite their sometimes misleading names, affect only the instrument on the MIDI channel they are sent to. If, for example, you move the global fine-tuning value of MIDI channel three 45 cents up, all the other MIDI channels will remain at default tuning.

Changing the Pitch Bend Range

The pitch bend range of an instrument, or the maximum number of semitones the pitch of the instrument can be altered by a pitch wheel or joystick, is normally set to two semitones. Although in many cases this range gives good control during playback, you may sometimes need a higher value.

Changing the pitch bend is easily done with the following sequence of control change messages, which together form an RPN message:

CC#	Value	Description
101	0	These two control changes together select RPN 0.
100	0	
6	NN	Where NN is the desired pitch bend range (in semitones).

Be sure to place these MIDI messages on the track using the instrument whose pitch bend range you intend to change. All other instruments will keep their previous pitch bend range setting; only the instrument on this MIDI channel is affected. Also remember that you need to send these MIDI messages to the synthesizer before the pitch bend range is changed. Therefore, a good place to put these messages is at the beginning of the track so that they are sent before playback starts.

For example, if you've chosen a synthlead instrument on MIDI channel 1 and need one full octave (12 semitones) of pitch bend range, you would insert the control change messages shown here at the start of the track (here viewed using Cakewalk's event list).

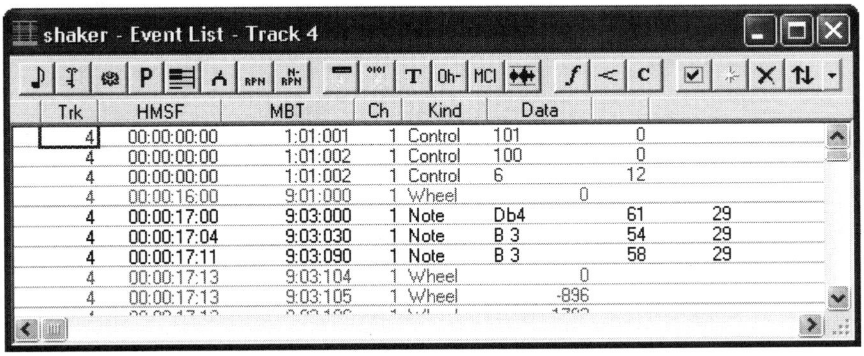

Figure 17.43: The top three lines set the pitch bend range of this MIDI channel to 12 semitones instead of the default 2

Alternatively, with a sequencer that has special support for RPN and NRPN, you can use the RPN directly. Because CC6 is the MSB of an RPN message, the number of semitones must be multiplied by 128 to get the data value.

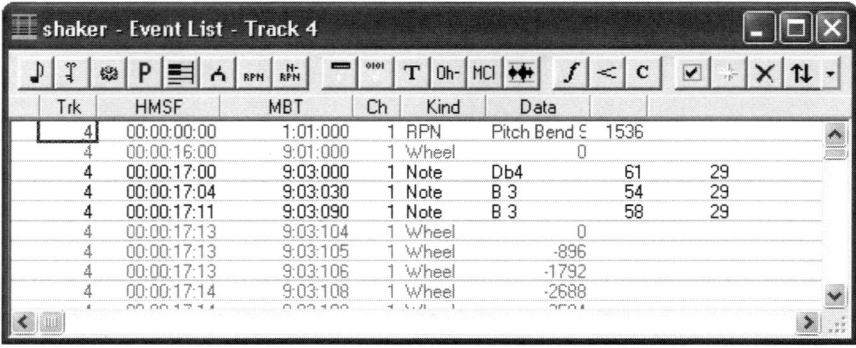

Figure 17.44: An alternative (and easier) way to set the pitch bend range, provided that the sequencer has support for RPNs

> When using extreme pitch bend ranges (usually a few octaves, depending on the instrument used), the maximum pitch that can be played by the SB Live! MIDI Synth may be a limiting factor. In this case, you'll notice that the pitch bend stops before you've reached the expected note. Should this happen, there isn't much to do but change your song and accept that the SB Live! MIDI Synth isn't perfect.

Changing the Global Coarse Tuning

Global coarse tuning is a somewhat misleading name because, on the SB Live! MIDI Synth, it affects only the current MIDI channel. Changing the global tuning of the SB Live! MIDI Synth transposes all notes played on this particular MIDI channel one or more semitones up or down. To change the global tuning of a MIDI channel, insert the following MIDI messages on a track:

CC#	Value	Description
101	0	These two control changes together select RPN 2 (global coarse tuning).
100	2	
6	XX	Where XX is the desired global coarse tuning (in semitones). The default (no transpose) is 64.

If you send a global coarse tuning value of 64, notes are not transposed. A value of 65 means that all notes are transposed one semitone up, a value of 62 means that notes are transposed two semitones down, and so on.

Because the same effect can be achieved with virtually any sequencer, there are few cases when this feature is useful. Global coarse tuning was most likely implemented for completeness of the MIDI implementation of the SB Live! MIDI Synth.

Changing the Global Fine-Tuning

Just like global coarse tuning, global fine-tuning is used to change the pitch of all played notes on a MIDI channel. Global fine-tuning lets you control the pitch within ±100 cents (±1 semitone) in very fine steps. If you need this full resolution, however, you will find the global fine-tuning somewhat tricky to change manually.

Unless your sequencer has explicit support for RPNs, to change the global tuning you need to calculate and use both the MSB (CC6) and LSB (CC38) values, as described in "About MSB and LSB" in Appendix A, "The MIDI Specification." The data value is therefore as follows:

```
Value = CC6*128 + CC38
```

This is a value between 0 and 16,383. Note that 8,192 is the default tuning, 0 is 100 cents down, and 16,383 is 100 cents up. Therefore, to change the fine-tuning, insert the following MIDI messages on a track:

CC#	Value	Description
101	0	These two control changes together select RPN 1 (global fine-tuning).
100	1	
6	XX	The desired tuning, in XX*128 + YY steps. One step corresponds to a change in pitch of 100/8,192 cents.
38	YY	

The difficulty here might be calculating the XX and YY values for the desired pitch. Let's say we want to change the pitch of the current MIDI channel 15 cents up. A full 100 cents up would be 8,192 steps from the default pitch, so 15 cents must be (15/100)*8,192 steps from the default value, which is 8,192, so the new number of steps would be as follows:

```
(15/100)*8,192 + 8,192 = 9,423.8 ≈ 9,424
```

To get the XX value, we divide this value by 128. The YY value is the remainder of this division:

```
9,424 / 128 = 73 (remainder 80)
```

So, to get the desired pitch, we send the above sequence of MIDI messages with XX = 73 and YY = 80.

> The remainder is calculated using the mod operator in the Windows calculator. See "About MSB and LSB" in Appendix A for more information.

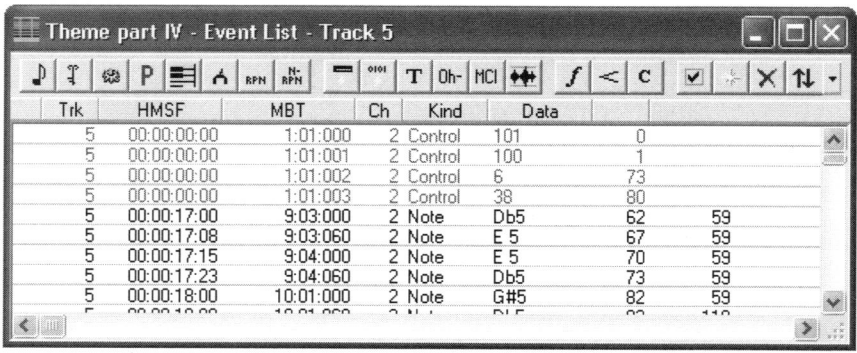

Figure 17.45: Adjusting the global tuning of the instrument on the current MIDI channel

Note that the YY value affects only the pitch 1/128 of the XX value. In many cases, you don't need this very fine precision. In such cases, the fine-tuning can be adjusted using control change 6 only, just as with coarse tuning. Then a CC6 value of 64 is the normal pitch, and one step corresponds to a change in pitch of 100/64 (about 1.56) cents.

If, on the other hand, the sequencer explicitly supports RPN messages, changing the global tuning with full precision is a piece of cake. Simply use RPN 1 with the desired tuning (9,424. as calculated in the previous example).

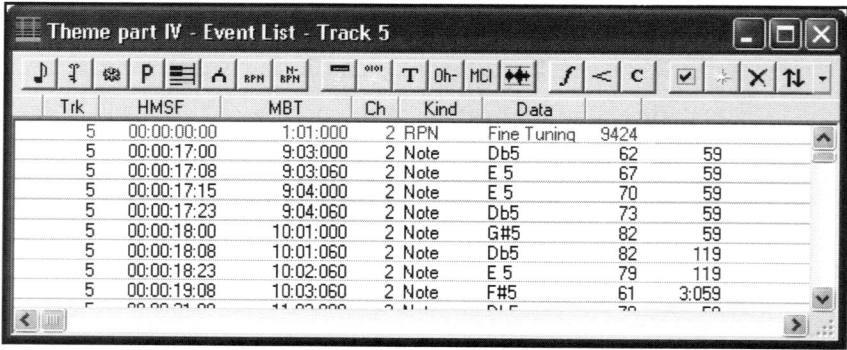

Figure 17.46: The alternative way of adjusting the global tuning in a sequencer with RPN support

NRPN: The Key to Real-Time SoundFont Control

NRPNs, nonregistered parameter numbers, are another type of control change message that are of great importance if you want to dig into the most advanced features of the SB Live! MIDI Synth's MIDI implementation. Just like RPNs, NRPNs control parameters of the synthesizer, usually specific to one MIDI channel. While each RPN has a well-defined meaning, the meaning of an NRPN MIDI message is totally up to the manufacturer of the synthesizer—in our case, Creative.

So what did the Creative engineers give us for the NRPNs of the SB Live! MIDI Synth? Since the advent of the AWE32 (Creative's first card with SoundFont support), we have been able to control almost all parameters (or, more correctly, generator values) of each instrument in the SoundFont using NRPNs. This opens great possibilities. Imagine (or better still, try—read on to find out how!) controlling filter resonance and cutoff parameters, volume envelope parameters, LFOs, and so on in real time on any of your tracks. You will particularly find this to be a cool feature if you are creating electronic music, but even in acoustic types of music it can occasionally be useful for tweaking the SoundFonts.

How to Use NRPN Messages

Just like the RPN messages described in the previous section, NRPN messages are sent using a couple of control changes. Control changes 98 and 99 select the SoundFont parameter to be controlled, and control changes 6 and 38 are used (as MSB and LSB) to set the parameter's value. The reason that the controllers are used in pairs is to get a wider range of values than the 128 possible values that one single MIDI data byte gives. We use two bytes, so we can enter data in the range 0 to 16,383. How this works is described in more detail in "About MSB and LSB" in Appendix A.

To further complicate things, many of the SoundFont parameters can have negative values. Therefore, to set a SoundFont parameter to 0, you will need to send a value of 8,192 (halfway between 0 and 16,384). Anything below this is considered a negative value.

A value of 8,192 is represented by CC6 = 64, CC38 = 0. By default, the drivers seem to assume the value of CC6 to be 64, so if you are controlling a parameter with valid values in the range 0 to 127 (such as filter cutoff), you can use only CC38 and never have to worry about CC6.

The parameter to be controlled is selected using control changes 98 and 99. Because there are fewer than 128 parameters that you can edit, CC99 is not used and must be set to 127. The value of CC98 will then select any of the available SoundFont parameters. For example, filter cutoff frequency is controlled by number 21, so after you set CC99 to 127 and CC98 to 21, CC38 can be used to control the filter cutoff value. Because the valid range for filter cutoff is 0 to 127, CC6 does not have to be used.

TIP *A full table of available SoundFont parameters, their NRPNs, and allowed ranges appears in Appendix E, "The Sound Blaster Live! MIDI Implementation."*

The following table shows the control change numbers used to control SoundFont parameters on the SB Live! MIDI Synth.

Table 17.9: Control Changes Used to Enter NRPN MIDI Messages

CC#	Name	Description
6	Data Entry Coarse	Most significant byte of the NRPN value. Set to (Actual Value + 8,192) / 128.
38	Data Entry Fine	Least significant byte of the NRPN value. Set to (Actual Value + 8,192) mod 128 (mod is the modulo operator—that is, the remainder of integer division).
98	NRPN Coarse	The SoundFont parameter to be changed. See the table in Appendix E.
99	NRPN Fine	Should always be set to 127.

> The SoundFont 2 Technical Specification describes another NRPN implementation that is not compatible with the implementation described in this chapter (which is the most commonly used).

Example: Filter Cutoff

One of the simplest (and probably most useful, because it is essential in modern electronic music) examples of real-time SoundFont control is the process for changing the filter parameters in real time. If you want to try the following example yourself, you can use the original MIDI sequence on the CD as realtime_filter_step1.mid. Note that the example requires synthleads.sf2 (also included) to be loaded as bank 1.

1. First, I assigned a track to MIDI channel 1 of the SB Live! MIDI Synth and step recorded a short sequence of sixteenths onto it. Then I copied that take to fill the track and did some basic editing using the piano roll. Because we're going to control filter cutoff in real time, I chose the Resonant Lead instrument from the synthleads.sf2 SoundFont.

   In addition to the synthlead track, I added a smooth choir/string background on MIDI channels 4 and 5.

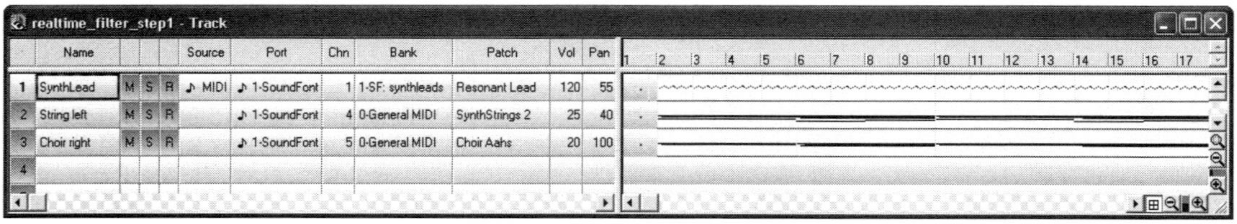

Figure 17.47: Assigning a synthlead track and adding a smooth choir/string background

For your own experiments, or simply to try this example, the sequence is available on the CD as Realtime Filter Step 1.mid. If you prefer to simply listen to the sequence, the corresponding audio clip is Realtime Filter Step 1.wav.

2. Once we have the basic sequence, we need to insert the correct NRPN messages on the synthlead track. Using the event list editor, I inserted two control changes at the very beginning of the track. CC99 is always set to 127, and according to the NRPN controller table in Appendix E, CC98 should be set to 21 to control filter cutoff.

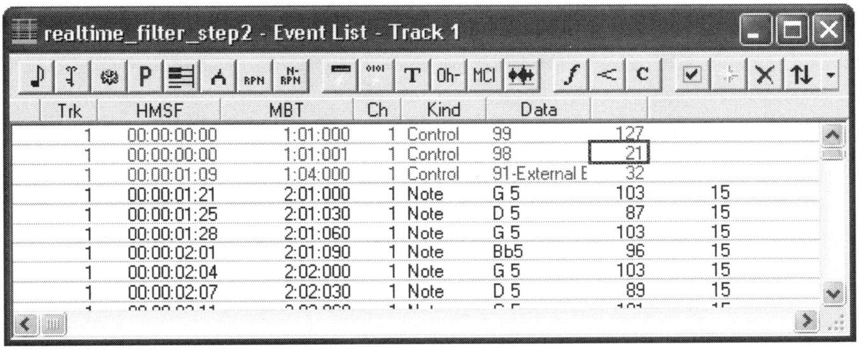

Figure 17.48: Track configured for real-time control of filter cutoff

3. We can now use controller 38 to directly control the filter cutoff frequency. I opened the synthlead track in the piano roll/controller editor and selected controller 38. Using Cakewalk's line tool, I painted a smooth set of control changes.

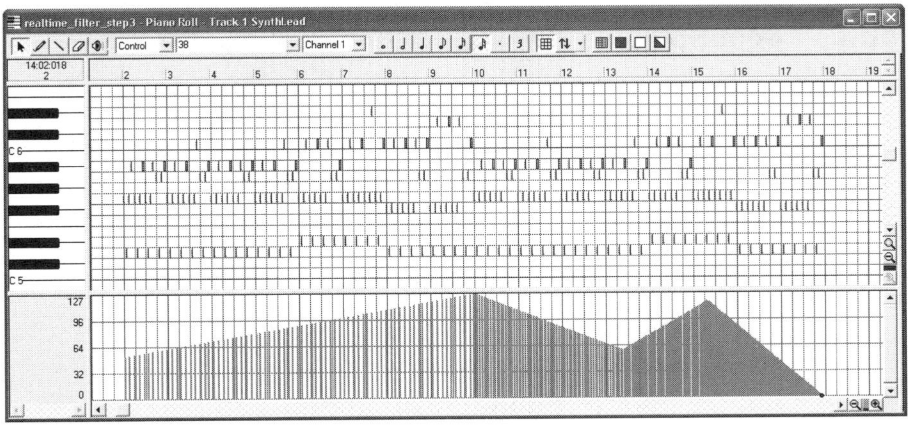

Figure 17.49: The filter cutoff values inserted as controller 38 events on the track

Audio Sample

CD Folder: Chapter 17 – Sequencer Basics
File: Realtime Filter Step 3.wav
The result of this step is included as an audio clip on the CD.

4. Just to add a little extra something to the sequence, I created two more tracks on MIDI channels 2 and 3. After copying the contents of the synthlead track to both of these channels, I panned them slightly differently and delayed them two and three 1/32 notes (which is, respectively, 60 and 90 ticks in Cakewalk).

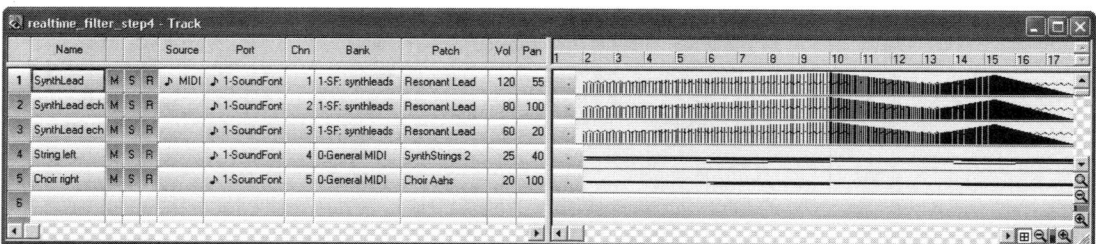

Figure 17.50: The finished sequence

Audio Sample

Folder on the CD: Chapter 17 – Sequencer Basics
File: Realtime Filter Step 4.wav
You can listen to the final result in **Realtime Filter Step 4.wav**.

After trying this feature, or simply listening to the result, you will realize just how useful the real-time SoundFont control is.

Audio Sequencers

More often than not, modern sequencers can handle audio tracks in addition to MIDI. The difference between a MIDI and an audio track is that whereas a MIDI track consists of notes and other MIDI events, the audio track contains the actual sound. Consequently, an audio track is not dependent on a synthesizer to be played back and can contain any type of sound. A common use for audio tracks is to add vocals and effects to a piece of MIDI music. Because audio tracks consist of pre-recorded sound rather than notes, they cannot be edited as freely as MIDI tracks.

TIP *Audio tracks are mixed together and played back using the Live!'s Wave channel—not using MIDI. If you need to adjust the balance between MIDI and audio tracks, adjust the levels of the MIDI and Wave channels in the mixer.*

Configuring Audio Settings

Although most installation programs run diagnostic software to fine-tune the performance of the sequencer on your system, you should at least look at the settings yours has made to ensure that you get optimal results. Most audio sequencers have an audio settings dialog box or something similar where you can choose among the various available audio drivers and set buffer sizes for playback.

Just like a software synthesizer, the audio sequencer must prepare a little bit of audio at a time to ensure smooth playback and store it in a buffer. This effectively means that the audio may be slightly delayed compared to the MIDI sound. This delay is known as *latency*. Most audio sequencers can compensate for this by delaying the MIDI notes by the same amount, but nevertheless latency may be annoying at times, and it complicates real-time work such as recording.

Optimizing Software

While the performance of an audio sequencer is heavily dependent on your computer, there are a few things you should keep in mind to make sure you get the best possible results with your current equipment.

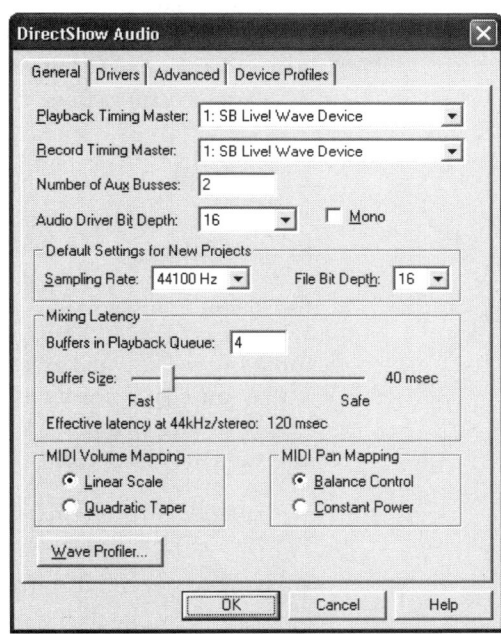

Figure 17.51: Cakewalk's audio settings. From this dialog box, you can control the buffer size (and thereby the latency) and several other settings.

- To minimize the latency, you can often adjust the **buffer size**. The smaller the buffer size, the less latency you will get. This benefit comes at a price, however. Smaller buffer sizes require more power from your computer and are more likely to produce clicks, dropouts, and all sorts of undesired noises. Similarly, the more tracks you play back at the same time, the greater the likelihood that such unwanted effects will occur.

- Different **audio drivers** may perform differently. The normal Windows multimedia drivers are generally not very well optimized for real-time applications such as audio sequencing. DirectX drivers, if available, are made to give improved performance and use fewer of your computer resources, which normally translates into the ability to handle more simultaneous tracks and reduced latency. ASIO drivers, where available, are optimized for low-latency playback of audio tracks and usually give superior performance compared to both the Windows and DirectX drivers. If your sequencer lets you choose which type to use, try all available types and see which provides the best performance on your system.

Optimizing Hardware

If you are upgrading your computer, note that three factors (in addition to the sound card you are using) are important for the performance of an audio sequencer:

- A **fast processor**. Because audio mixing and effects are largely handled by the system processor, a fast processor will let you do more things at the same time.
- **Plenty of memory**. The more audio data that can be stored in memory, the better. Plenty of memory is always a good thing when working with large pieces of sound data, and with today's memory prices, you get a lot for your money.
- A **fast hard drive**. In many cases, the audio tracks will not fit in memory but have to be loaded from the hard drive in real time during playback. This puts a lot of stress on your computer's hard drive, and a slow one can easily become a bottleneck. If you are buying a new hard drive, keep in mind that audio data takes lots of space and tends to fill up drives quickly, so get as large a drive as possible.

Using Audio Tracks

Generally, audio sequencers are designed to make audio tracks look and feel as similar to MIDI tracks as possible. There are a couple of important differences, though.

Recording Audio Tracks

When recording audio tracks, keep in mind that what is recorded is not the MIDI input but the sound card's audio input. Assuming that you are using a Live!, the actual source is determined by the recording source setting in the Live! mixer. The following example shows how to add vocals to a song using a microphone and Cakewalk Pro Audio.

1. Connect the microphone to the mic input of your Sound Blaster Live! or Live!Drive (see Chapter 5, "Connecting Devices").

2. Open the Live! mixer and select the microphone as the recording source (see Figure 17.52). Set a level low enough that there's no risk of clipping, but still as high as possible to reduce . Set a level low enough that there's no risk of clipping, but still as high as possible to reduce noise from the microphone amplifier. Finding an optimal level may require a few tries.

> **TIP** *Many microphones require additional amplification of the signal. You can click the small plus sign above the microphone icon in the mixer to apply an additional 20 dB of amplification to the signal.*

3. To hear what you are singing, leave the microphone source unmuted. You should use headphones for listening, both to reduce the risk of feedback and to make sure that none of the background music is recorded with the microphone.

4. Set the Live!'s Wave input as the source for the newly created track in Cakewalk. A mono track is fine since you are recording from a microphone.

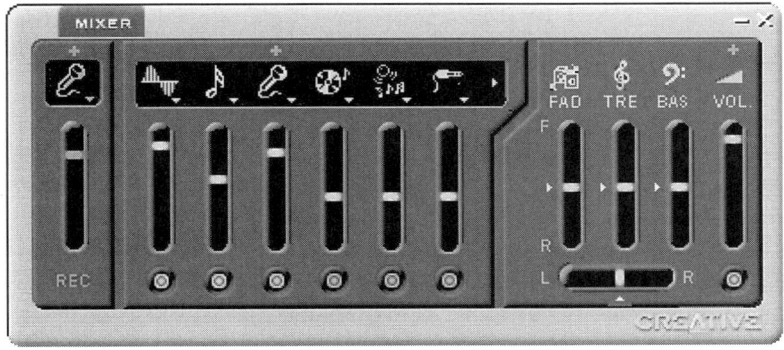

Figure 17.52: These settings will let you record from a microphone while playing back MIDI and Wave channels

5. Make sure that you have enough disk space and start recording!

This procedure will record the vocals without any Environmental Audio effects. Although you can easily add effects (such as reverb, which is very useful for vocals) to the mic input in the EA applet, there's no simple way to record it. Normally, you would set the recording source to What-U-Hear, but in this case, that would record all of the music that is played back, as well. There are four possible solutions to the problem:

- Record the voice without listening to the background tracks. This is not a very good option, because it is hard to follow the pitch and tempo of the music when you can't hear it. Some sequencers can provide you some visual aids here, but you will most likely still prefer one of the other options.
- Use the effects on playback. If the vocal is the only audio track, you can simply add reverb to the Wave channel using the EA applet. If you are using more audio tracks, however, all tracks will be affected using this method.
- Rerecord the track with effects. In other words, mute all other tracks (or use the sequencer's solo feature, if available), set the recording source to What-U-Hear, and mute all but the Wave source (in the mixer) and then add the

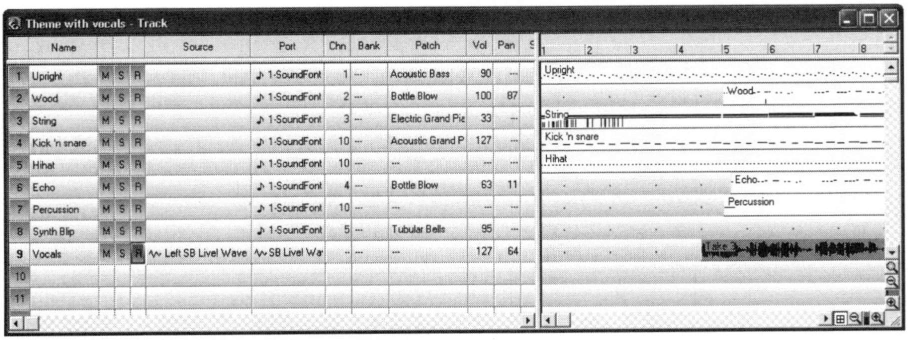

Figure 17.53: Cakewalk's track view with the newly recorded audio track at the bottom

Sequencer Basics **511**

reverb to the Wave channel (in the EA applet) and play back the vocal track while recording it to a new track. This may sound a bit complicated, but it also may be the best option in this case. Just make sure that you remember to remove the reverb effect from the Wave channel after you've finished recording and to restore the mixer settings! The old vocal track can now be discarded, although you may want to simply mute it or save the original track to have the option of going back to it.

There may also be a fourth option: to use the software effects that many audio sequencers provide. This may, in many cases, be the easiest solution, and some software effects are of high quality, so you should definitely see if these effects are available to you. Software effects, such as reverb, will require a substantial amount of precious processing power, however, and few are as flexible and good sounding as the Live!'s built-in effects.

Mixdown

If the number of simultaneous audio channels and software effects begins to become too large for your computer to handle, the sequencer may offer the option of mixing any number of tracks (with software effects) into one single audio track. Note that once the tracks are merged, you cannot edit the individual parts and effects that compose the track, so be sure to save your work, including the individual sound files, before you do a mixdown.

So you have your MIDI and audio tracks and want to turn them all into one single audio file? Normally, this is a piece of cake:

1. Create a new (stereo) audio track that will contain the final mix.
2. In the mixer, set the recording source to What-U-Hear and mute all playback sources except the MIDI and Wave channels (see Figure 17.54). If either Wave or MIDI is too loud or too weak, you should adjust it now.
3. Start recording in the audio sequencer. Once recording is finished, the new track should contain an audio copy of both your audio and MIDI tracks. You can now save this track as an audio file and do whatever you want with it (burn it as a CD track, convert it to an MP3 file, and so on) (see Figure 17.55).

Automation

Some sequencers offer ways to automate and simplify some of the more complicated MIDI tasks. The learning curve of these features may be steep, but can in some cases save you a tremendous amount of work. What follows are a few examples of automation features in the Cubase and Cakewalk sequencers.

Mixermaps and StudioWare Panels

Cubase lets you add functionality to its MIDI mixer by using a type of plug-in known as *mixermaps*. There are several mixermaps available that are custom made for the Sound Blaster Live! These let you control parameters specific to Creative cards, such as the NRPN controllers, in real time.

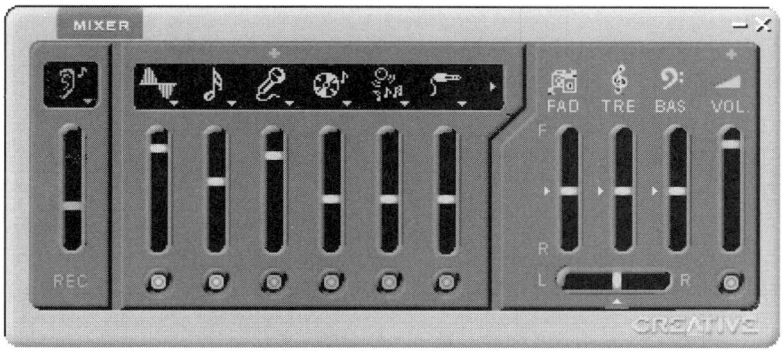

Figure 17.54: The Live! mixer prepared for the final mixdown

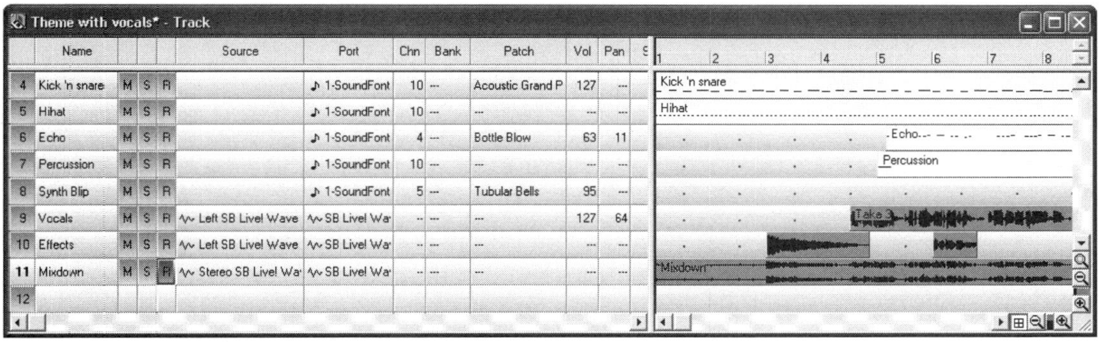

Figure 17.55: The final mix is now recorded to the audio track at the bottom

Cakewalk has a concept that is similar to Cubase's mixermaps, called *StudioWare panels*. A StudioWare panel is a window that contains a set of controls that can be programmed to control various parameters, such as the NRPN controllers (see Figure 17.56). Just like Cubase mixermaps, StudioWare panels are available that are customized for the Live! You should check for such options in your sequencer, because this type of feature may save you lots of work and give you an additional level of control over your songs.

CAL

If you are looking for the ultimate level of control, the advanced versions of Cakewalk has its own built-in programming language: Cakewalk Application Language (CAL). A full CAL tutorial is far beyond the scope of this book, but for an example of how it can be used, consider the following CAL program:

```
(do
        (word pan 64)
        (forEachEvent
                (do
                (= pan (random 0 127))
```

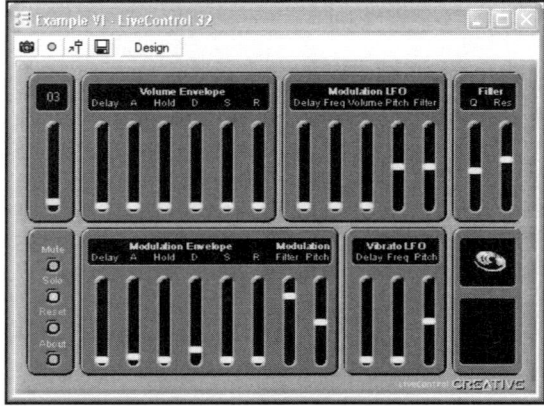

Figure 17.56: The excellent LiveControl StudioWare panel by Xplain

```
                    (if (== Event.Kind NOTE)
                        (insert Event.Time Event.Chan CONTROL 10 pan)
                    )
                )
            )
)
```

This program assigns a random pan value to each of a number of notes. When it is run, a variable named pan is declared on line 2. The next line tells Cakewalk to perform a certain action for every event that is currently selected, namely to assign a new random value (between 0 and 127) to the variable pan. If the current event is a note, then the program will insert a control change 10 with the value of the pan variable at the same time and channel as the note event.

TIP *More information about how to create and run CAL programs is available from the Cakewalk manual, help files, and Web site (http://www.cakewalk.com).*

Sequencing Tips and Tricks

Don't Give Up!

After reading this chapter, you may feel like you need to be an Einstein to even comprehend the basics of MIDI sequencing. Sure, there's a lot to the subject, and this chapter gives you only a very brief overview (from a Live! user's perspective). If you have never run a sequencer before, the process may seem confusing and overwhelming. Don't fear, however. Play around with the settings and try the different features and see what they do. Soon you will get the basics, and then things will start falling into place.

Experiment!

This can't be stressed enough: use your imagination to create music. Avoid getting stuck following a lot of rules about how to create "good" music. If you run out of inspiration, try using new instruments and SoundFonts, play with some new features or settings in your sequencer, or sample something weird and create a SoundFont from it (but watch out for copyright issues!).

Get to Know Your Sequencer!

The sequencer is the most important tool you will use here to create MIDI music: learn it! This chapter may give you the very basics, but to get the most out of your software, spend some time reading the manuals or online help. Spending 20 minutes reading the manual may save you several hours of frustration later.

Try Some Cool MIDI Effects!

With a bit of imagination, MIDI can be used to simulate common audio effects. Look at the following two examples to see how it can be done.

MIDI Echo

Assuming that you can spare a few MIDI channels (use the SB Live! MIDI Synth B port if you run out of them otherwise), you can easily create a useful echo effect by adding a few extra tracks to your song:

1. For a two-tap echo, create two new tracks in your sequencer and assign them to different (unused) MIDI channels.
2. Copy the contents of the original track to both of the new tracks. If the sequencer allows linking (in which case any updates to the original contents update the copies as well), you may want to use it.
3. Set the volume of the echo tracks lower than that of the original tracks. The tracks should use the same instruments.
4. Delay each of the echo tracks differently. Usually you will want to delay the tracks a number of note values, such as by one quarter note or three eighth notes, although you should feel free to experiment here. Some sequencers have a delay setting for each track that you can use. Otherwise, you will have to move the actual note events.
5. For a more intense effect, try panning the echo tracks differently.

You can hear the effect of a MIDI echo on the synthlead channel in the realtime_filter_step4.wav file. To see the difference it makes, compare it to realtime_filter_step3.wav, in which the effect is missing.

Volume Effects Using CC11

You can do some more creative things than add fade in and out with controller 11 (expression). For example, you can CC11 with alternating high and low values synchronized to the tempo of a song to produce a tremolo-like effect on the long sustained notes—a great effect for electronic music!

Audio Sample

CD Folder: Chapter 17 – Sequencer Basics
Files: CC11 Tremolo.mid and CC11 Tremolo.wav

You'll find the example as a MIDI file on the CD, and the corresponding audio file. Note that the MIDI file requires synthleads.sf2 as user bank 1 for correct playback.

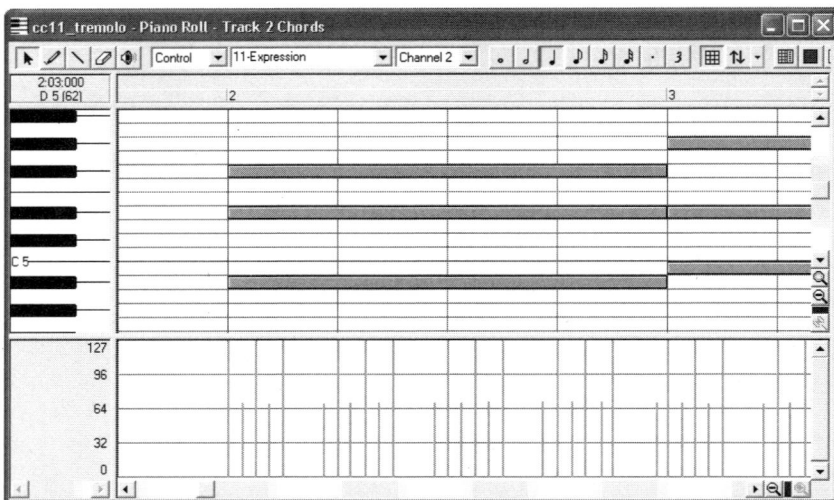

Figure 17.57: Produce fast, rhythmic volume changes with controller 11. For the best effect, be sure to put the controller events on even note values.

18

THE EMU10K1 DIGITAL AUDIO PROCESSOR

It has been mentioned earlier in this book, but in case you didn't know it already, the EMU10K1 is the chip responsible for virtually all audio processing on the Live!—the brain of the card. This chip handles everything from sample rate conversion to EAX effects.

A Backgrounder

Earlier sound cards from Creative, such as the Sound Blaster 16, AWE32, and AWE64, were fundamentally different in the way they were built. While these cards were (at the time) rich in features, every feature required its own circuitry and special chips. The audio signal interconnections between the different parts of the cards were usually analog, making the cards large and noisy.

A very good example is the AWE32. It was the card with the largest number of features at the time it was introduced, but because each feature required its own set of chips, the card was physically huge. It was lengthy, reaching all the way from the back to the front of your computer, and its noisy output annoyed many of its users.

Figure 18.1: Compare the size of an AWE32 card and a Live!

With the introduction of the Live!, the design philosophy changed. The basic new idea was, instead of putting a lot of chips for different purposes onto a board and laying out the required interconnections, to combine as many features of the sound card as possible in one single integrated circuit. Within the chip, audio signals were kept within the digital domain so that no unnecessary noise or other artifacts would be introduced. This one integrated circuit eventually became the EMU10K1, and the reduced costs of producing a single chip, compared to many chips, as well as a smaller circuit board, enabled sound card manufacturers like Creative to make these sound cards more affordable.

The EMU10K1 Chip

The EMU10K1 Digital Audio Processor, or EMU10K1, was designed by Creative and E-MU (a respected manufacturer of electronic music instruments and now a subsidiary of Creative). Creative uses the chip to power all cards in the Live! series, while E-MU used it in the (now discontinued) more professional Audio Production Studio (APS) card, targeted at music studios.

Looking at a Live! card, the EMU10K1 processor is easy to spot. The chip is mounted in a square, black plastic package with metal pins on all four sides. Inside the plastic package, connected to the metal pins, is the microchip itself, measuring 6.7 by 6.5 millimeters. The chip contains about 2.5 million transistors, just slightly less than the (first) Pentium processor.

Figure 18.2: The EMU10K1 chip on a Live! board – you can't miss it

Many Functions on One Chip

The primary goal of the EMU10K1 was to provide powerful hardware support for DirectSound, DirectSound3D, and Creative's proprietary DirectSound 3D extension, EAX. In addition, the chip features a powerful wavetable synthesizer with all the components necessary to support SoundFonts, flexible playback and recording modes, analog and digital mixing, and sample rate conversion.

Sample Rate Conversion

All audio processing within the chip is kept within the digital domain. While the A/D and D/A converters of the Live! support a maximum resolution of 16 bits per sample, internal processing is performed with greater precision (32 bits) to make sure that the sound quality is not affected by rounding errors in the audio processing and mixing algorithms.

All audio processing is also performed at a fixed sampling frequency, namely 48 kHz. This frequency was chosen with the DVD standard in mind. This means that at any point where an audio signal enters the EMU10K1, whether it comes from an analog input, such as the Line In connector, or a digital S/PDIF input or is generated within the chip itself (such as when an audio or MIDI file is played back), the signal is immediately converted to 48 kHz. This way, without any additional circuitry, the Live! can support a large number of recording sample rates, from 8 kHz to 48 kHz.

The 48-kHz Sample Rate Conundrum

We should also highlight the often-debated "limitation" of the EMU10K1. Most consumer PCI sound cards, as well as motherboards with built-in sound chips, are all designed around Intel's AC'97 (Audio Codec '97) specification, which standardizes the way in which sound cards are designed and interfaced with other components used to build them, as well as to other hardware components and operating systems running on the PC. This specification allows manufacturers of sound chips (also referred to by Intel as DCs, short for digital controllers), such as the EMU10K1 DSP used in the Live!, to easily interface with the wide range of

AC'97 chips available to perform the most common sound card functions, such as D/A and A/D conversion, providing analog inputs and outputs, mixing of multiple audio signals. Thus, a manufacturer can design a sound chip with proprietary technology and features, but have the inputs and outputs comply with the interface standards outlined in the AC'97 specifications. Generic AC'97-compatible programs such as AC'97 mixers will also work with any sound card that uses an AC'97 chip.

> The Live! uses the AC'97 chip to convert digital audio from the EMU10K1 to analog for the Line Out 1 (Front) connector. Additional DACs are used for the Line Out 2 (Rear) connector and the Line Out 3 (center/subwoofer) output (available on 5.1 Live! cards). Therefore, the audio quality from speakers connected to these outputs depends on the quality of the AC'97, as well as the DACs that are used by the sound card manufacturer.

The EMU10K1 is coupled with an AC'97 codec chip. If you look closely at the chips on the Live! card, you'll see a small one that has "97" as part of its part number, like the Sigmatel STAC97 series and Creative's CT1297 used on most Live! cards. Creative uses different AC'97 chips on different production runs of the Live!, and there are slight sound quality differences between them, especially with signal-to-noise ratio (SNR).

Figure 18.3: AC'97 chips on the first-, second-, and third-generation Live! cards

> Some adventurous engineers have even removed the Live!'s AC'97 chip and soldered higher-quality ones for improved sound quality.

Because the AC'97 codec includes DACs to convert digital audio data to analog sound that we can hear, all the audio processing performed by the EMU10K1, such as the playback and mixing of 3D audio in games or the adding of EAX to a music CD, must be sent to the AC'97 codec to be decoded and played back. The

AC'97 codec also provides a S/PDIF output capability that is used to provide digital output from the Live!

However, the AC'97 standard is defined such that the codec accepts digital audio only at 48 kHz, not the slightly lower 44.1-kHz rate that standard audio CDs and many desktop musicians work with. The engineers who designed the EMU10K1 decided to use the 48-kHz rate in all the operations of the DSP, so any audio that is sent and processed by the EMU10K1 will ultimately be converted to a 48-kHz sampling rate. An analog input device such as a microphone or even an 8-bit, 8-kHz digital output of a digital audio player connected digital to a digital I/O device of the Live!, will be converted to 16-bit 48-kHz by the ADCs on the EMU10K1 before further processing, for instance, before mixing and adding of EAX effects are performed on the sound.

A consumer sound chip will be much more complex, and definitely more expensive to make, if it has to maintain all of the audio input to the sound card at their original sample rates. E-MU, the company that developed the EMU10K1 DSP for the Live! cards, also mentions some benefits in promotional material: that the EMU10K1 running at 48 kHz, compared to 44.1 kHz, provides superior fidelity, and that many consumer digital audio devices, such as DAT tapes, surround sound in DVDs, and satellite broadcasts, are increasingly using 48 kHz, making it the ideal choice for audio production.

> An external digital audio device feeding digital audio to the Live! at 48 kHz may not be running in synchronization with the clock timing of the EMU10K1; therefore, each sample (or "pulse") of data (of the 48,000 sent out each second) has to be delayed so that it can synchronize with the clock rate of the EMU10K1. This delay occurs for 48 kHz as well as non-48 kHz digital audio input to the Live!

To avoid resampling the 48-kHz processed audio back to another sample rate—for example, the common 44.1-kHz—E-MU decided to fix all digital outputs from the Live! at 48 kHz. This includes digital outputs on any digital I/O devices attached to the Live! Over the years, many users have asked if there is a way to bypass this, but it is not possible because this is how the hardware was designed. This has caused some disappointment among users who are doing digital audio work and want bit-perfect copies of digital audio data, instead of having it converted from 44.1 kHz to 48 kHz and back. Many other most costly professional sound cards can do this, but not the Live!, as it was Creative's intention to produce a cost-effective sound card for the general consumer.

The good news is that most digital audio equipment comes with sample rate converters that can convert from the Live!'s 48-kHz output to the device's supported sampling rate. For example, the MiniDisc format stores audio at 44.1 kHz, which limits it to work with digital audio at 44.1 kHz. Fortunately, many MD recorders have built-in sample rate converters to convert from the most common

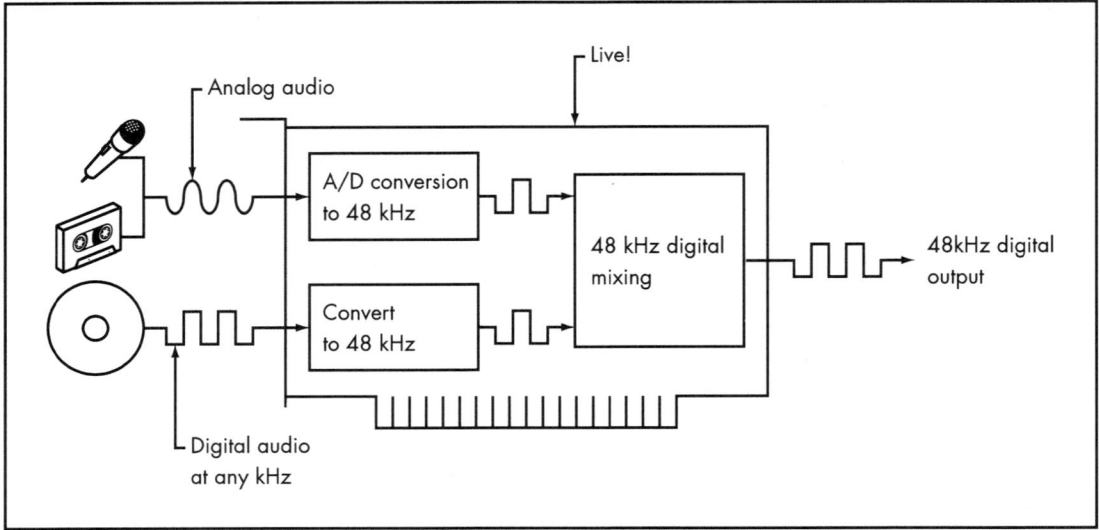

Figure 18.4: 48-kHz sample rate

sampling rates passed to the digital inputs to 44.1 kHz. When purchasing such equipment, especially older-generation digital audio recorders, do check for a sample rate converter, especially if you intend to record digitally from the Live!

On the other hand, do not be alarmed! Most users will not notice any signal degradation because of the fixed 48-kHz sample rate of the EMU10K1. It hardly affects the audio quality or features of the Live!, except the above issues when recording from the Live!'s digital output. Recording MP3s to MiniDiscs and other digital audio recorders work without a hitch because a huge majority of them support recording of audio at 48 kHz.

The FX8010 Effects Processor

Without a doubt, the EMU10K1 and the Live! card were designed with the serious gamer in mind, to deliver hardware-accelerated 3D-positional audio (using four or more speakers) and environmental audio effects such as echoes, damping, and reverb.

The way Creative and E-MU chose to realize this was by integrating a digital signal processor (DSP)—the FX8010—into the EMU10K1 chip. A digital signal processor is a processor with a special set of instructions to quickly process streams of audio data. The FX8010 is fully programmable and can therefore be customized to perform different types of audio processing depending on the application. Its use in the Live! ranges from 3D positioning and EAX effects in games to effects (such as reverb and chorus) for MIDI music and effects on digital audio streams: for example, pitch shifting for karaoke. The FX8010 is also responsible for the mixing of digital audio sources.

In fact, the FX8010 can be found not only as part of the EMU10K1 in the Live! series of cards, but also as a stand-alone chip. For example, the FX8010 is responsible for the effects processing in the E-MU Mantis digital mixer.

Because the FX8010 is a general digital signal processor, its functionality depends on the effects program that it is loaded with. In the case of the Live!, every time you (or a game) select a new EAX effect, a new program is loaded into the processor by the drivers. Therefore, the features of the Live! are very much dependent on its drivers. As Creative likes to point out, the fact that the effects processor is fully programmable also means that the drivers can be updated to include new and/or improved effects programs (or other features) to enhance the Live! without requiring any changes in hardware.

The Wavetable Synthesizer

The other main feature of the EMU10K1 is its wavetable synthesizer. More details about how the wavetable synthesizer on the Live! works can be found in Chapter 16, "Introduction to SoundFonts." For here, though, let's just say that wavetable synthesis is a technique based on prerecorded sound, and is commonly used in synthesizers today. The wavetable synthesizer of the EMU10K1 is hard-wired into the chip and cannot be upgraded or modified. (Don't confuse the hardware synthesizer of the EMU10K1 with the software synthesizer included with most Live! drivers. While the latter may offer up to an almost insane 1,024 voices, it takes its power from your computer's main processor and does not support SoundFonts.)

The synthesizer has a polyphony of 64 voices—a polyphony comparable to that of other synthesizers. Naturally, it has all the necessary features required for full hardware SoundFont support: one oscillator (the basic sound source), one resonant low-pass filter, an amplifier, two envelopes, and two low-frequency oscillators, per voice. If you have used Vienna (or another SoundFont editor) to create your own SoundFonts, you are already familiar with these basic synthesizer structures. You may also have noticed that many instruments consist of several samples played simultaneously, increasing the complexity and richness of instrument sounds, but effectively reduces the polyphony of the synthesizer. Therefore, the synthesizer can play back 64 notes at a time only when each instrument uses exactly one voice.

The oscillator contains a sample rate converter that resamples the current voice's playback rate to the internal audio processing sample rate of 48 kHz. To minimize quantization noise at low sample playback rates, the chip uses an 8-point interpolation algorithm for the sample rate conversion, resulting in a softer and less noisy sound.

SoundFont Support

In addition to the preceding, the only other requirement for SoundFont playback is driver support. The SoundFont files, which are loaded into the computer's main memory, contain the audio data required for the wavetable oscillator, as well as the settings for the other synthesizer elements. When a MIDI note is triggered, it is the driver's responsibility to look in the currently loaded SoundFonts, determine what sounds should be played, and send the appropriate commands to the EMU10K1 to play back the note. Thus, SoundFont support is as much a matter of drivers and software as hardware.

PCI Bus Communication

Unlike some earlier sound cards, (like the AWE cards), the Live! does not have its own memory for storing sample data, nor does it have the large audio buffers commonly found on older sound cards. Instead, whenever the Live! needs data (whether it is sample data for the wavetable synthesizer or waveform data for plain sample playback), it relies on being constantly fed small portions of data, stored in the computer's main memory, via the PCI bus.

If you have a background in computer engineering (or simply know a lot about how computers work internally), you may recall that virtually all modern computers (including PCs) use a technique called virtual memory to map blocks (or pages) of physical memory (which may be spread out over the memory, or in some cases even written to disk) to logically continuous memory areas. As a consequence, the EMU10K1 needs to have its own translation tables for conversion between logical memory addresses and physical pages. The size of this table limits the amount of memory that the EMU10K1 can see to 32 MB. Later versions of the Live! drivers supported SoundFonts larger than 32 MB, loading them by changing this conversion table on the fly during playback. The E-MU APS drivers, on the other hand, never got around this limitation.

If a playing audio stream runs out of data, you'll likely hear audible clicks or noises. To prevent this, every time an audio buffer is running low on data, a PCI bus request is sent to fill the buffer. The request is given priority according to how much data is left in the buffer. While this is a flexible and quite efficient approach, it is known to work less than perfectly with some motherboard chipsets and other hardware, particularly when the load is already high on the system bus (such as during the transfer of large blocks of graphics).

THE MIDI SPECIFICATION

The MIDI specification (version 1.0) was written in 1984 by the MIDI Manufacturers Association (MMA). Note that the information presented here is an abbreviated and simplified version of the original MIDI specification. Parts of the specification have been left out. If you need the full document, it can be purchased from MMA or found online. Many useful tables and links can be found at harmony-central.

> The MMA Web site can be found at http://www.midi.org. A copy of the MIDI specification can be found at http://www.borg.com/~jglatt/tech/midispec.htm. The address for Harmony Central is http://www.harmony-central.com.

MIDI Messages

As mentioned in Chapter 14, the MIDI protocol describes how information should be transferred between instruments as what are known as *messages*. A MIDI message consists of one *status byte* (unless running status is used; see the discussion later) optionally followed by a number of *data bytes*.

The highest bit of a status byte is always 1, which means that the values of a status byte range from 0x80 to 0xFF. The high nibble specifies the type of message (where bytes starting with F are somewhat special since they don't belong to any particular MIDI channel). In a data byte, the highest bit is always 0, and therefore values range from 0x0 to 0x7F (0 to 127).

> **TIP** *For a description of the hexadecimal numbering system, see Chapter 14.*

Voice Messages

Status bytes with high nibbles ranging from 8 to E indicate the beginning of *voice messages*. In a voice message, the lower nibble specifies the MIDI channel that the message belongs to (0 to F, or as humans usually prefer to count them, 1 to 16). One or two data bytes (with a value between 0 and 127) always follow a voice message. The following table describes the different types of voice messages and the data bytes that follow each type of message. Any following data bytes are sent in the order they are described in the table.

Table A.1: MIDI Voice Message Types

Message Type	Status Byte	Data Bytes	Description
Note Off	0x80 to 0x8F	Note number Velocity	Indicates that a particular note should be released. This does not necessarily mean that the note will immediately stop sounding. The first data byte represents the note number (where 60 is a middle C). The second data byte, the release velocity, is seldom used.
Note On	0x90 to 0x9F	Note number Velocity	Indicates that a particular note should be played. The first data byte is the note number. The second data byte is the velocity (the amount force used to press the key). This value often controls the volume of the played note, but can control other parameters well, depending on the instrument. A sending device that does not sense velocity should use a default value of 64.
Aftertouch (key aftertouch)	0xA0 to 0xAF	Note number Pressure amount	This is the amount of pressure applied to a particular note on an instrument that supports key aftertouch (as described in Chapter 15). The first data byte is the note number, and the second data byte is the amount of pressure.
Controller (control change)	0xB0 to 0xBF	Controller number Controller value	Sets the value of a controller used to control any parameters on the instrument other than those that have a specific type of MIDI message. The first data byte specifies what controller number to change. A list of common controller numbers appears later in this appendix. The second data byte is the new value of the controller.

Program change (patch change)	0xC0 to 0xCF	Program number	A program change message tells the device to change the instrument (known on some devices as the program, preset, or patch, as well as the instrument) on a particular MIDI channel (part). The single following data byte is the new patch number to be used. For devices with more than 128 patches, bank change messages (a type of control change) are used.
Channel pressure (channel aftertouch)	0xD0 to 0xDF	Pressure amount	This is the non-note-specific equivalent of the key aftertouch. The value of the data byte is the current pressure amount.
Pitch wheel	0xE0 to 0xEF	Pitch wheel value (2 bytes)	A pitch message specifies that the pitch bend wheel (or joystick on some MIDI controllers) has been moved to a new position. To get sufficient precision, 2 data bytes are used to specify the value (see "About MSB and LSB" later in this appendix). A value of 8192 means that the wheel is centered. The actual number of semitones that the pitch wheel can transpose the pitch is usually adjustable on the instrument and/or via MIDI.

> Some devices use a Note On message with a velocity value of 0 instead of a Note Off message. This has the advantage that it allows running status (explained later) to be used more efficiently.

About MSB and LSB

Some MIDI messages require data with more than 128 possible values. Since every byte has a 128 possible values, 2 bytes will yield 128 * 128 = 16,384 possible values. To get this precision, one *most significant byte* (MSB) and one *least significant byte* (LSB) are used. The MSB is worth 128 times the LSB.

This extra precision may be used by some controllers (such as controller that has a coarse and a fine controller associated with it, although both are not always used), the pitch bend wheel, and the RPN and NRPNs.

The following formula can be used to convert an MSB-LSB pair to its corresponding value:

```
Value = MSB * 128 + LSB
```

For example, a message with MSB = 42 and LSB = 109 together forms the value 42 * 128 + 109 = 5,485.

Converting the other way is a little trickier. The MSB is the integer part of the value divided by 128, and the LSB is the rest of the division. In other words:

```
MSB = Value/128
LSB = Value mod 128
```

Mod, in the preceding formula, is the modulo operator, which simply gives the remainder of integer division. It can be found in the Windows calculator by switching to the scientific view.

For example, the value 5,485 would be converted as follows: The calculation 5,485/128 yields about 42.85. The integer part of this quotient, and therefore the MSB, is 42. We then use the Windows calculator to calculate 5,485 mod 128 and get the result 109, which is our LSB.

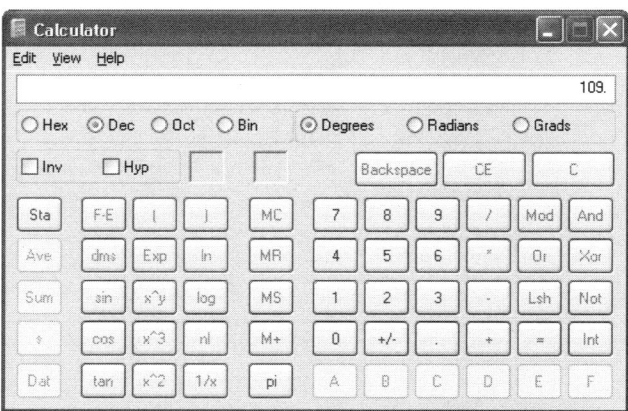

Of course, in most cases, the sequencer will perform these calculations for you.

Running Status

The communication between MIDI instruments is slow, but you can use *running status* to reduce the amount of MIDI data transmitted. When running status is used, status bytes are sent only when the status changes; otherwise, the previous status is assumed.

For example, if a chord with six notes is sent using running status, a Note On status byte is sent with the first Note On message. Only the data bytes of the remaining five Note On messages are sent. Using running status, 13 bytes of MIDI data are necessary to play this cord as opposed to 18 bytes without running status. This reduces the delay caused by transmission of the data from 5.76 to 4.16 milliseconds.

Control Change Numbers

Control changes (CC) can be used to change virtually any simple parameter on a MIDI device (for more complicated tasks, SysEx messages, discussed later in the section "System Exclusive (SysEx) Messages," are used). Many control change numbers are specified by the MIDI specification, although synthesizers normally respond to only a minority of these. The important control change numbers for Live! users are described in detail in Chapter 17. Therefore, the following table lists the names of the defined controllers. A thorough description of each one is found in the original MIDI specification. Controllers received by the Live! are marked with an asterisk.

Control Change Number	Controller Name
0*	Bank select
1*	Modulation wheel (coarse)
2	Breath controller (coarse)
4	Foot pedal (coarse)
5	Portamento time (coarse)
6*	Data entry (coarse)
7*	Volume (coarse)
8	Balance (coarse)
10*	Pan position (coarse)
11*	Expression (coarse)
12	Effect control 1 (coarse)
13	Effect control 2 (coarse)
16	General-purpose slider 1
17	General-purpose slider 2
18	General-purpose slider 3
19	General-purpose slider 4
32	Bank select (fine)
33	Modulation wheel (fine)
34	Breath controller (fine)
36	Foot pedal (fine)
37	Portamento time (fine)
38*	Data entry (fine)
39	Volume (fine)
40	Balance (fine)
42	Pan position (fine)
43	Expression (fine)
44	Effect control 1 (fine)
45	Effect control 2 (fine)
64*	Hold pedal (on/off)
65	Portamento (on/off)
66*	Sostenuto pedal (on/off)
67	Soft pedal (on/off)
68	Legato pedal (on/off)
69	Hold 2 pedal (on/off)
70	Sound variation
71	Sound timbre
72*	Sound release time
73*	Sound attack time
74	Sound brightness
75	Sound control 6
76	Sound control 7
77	Sound control 8
78	Sound control 9
79	Sound control 10
80	General-purpose button 1 (on/off)
81	General-purpose button 2 (on/off)

Control Change Number	Controller Name
82	General-purpose button 3 (on/off)
83	General-purpose button 4 (on/off)
91*	Effects level
92	Tremolo level
93*	Chorus level
94	Celeste level
95	Phaser level
96	Data button increment
97	Data button decrement
98*	Non-registered parameter (NRPN) (LSB)
99*	Non-registered parameter (NRPN) (MSB)
100*	Registered parameter (RPN) (LSB)
101*	Registered parameter (RPN) (MSB)
120*	All sound off
121*	All controllers off
122	Local keyboard (on/off)
123*	All notes off
124	Omni mode off
125	Omni mode on
126	Mono operation
127	Poly operation

For many controller types, there is one controller number for fine values and one for coarse values. This is because the 128 possible steps of one control change were believed to not be enough in all situations. In most cases, however, only the coarse controllers are used.

> In most cases, reverb is mapped to CC 91 and chorus to CC 93. EAX effects can be remapped, however, so that the SB Live! MIDI Synth responds to other control changes than those marked.

Examples of Voice Messages

A few examples of simple voice MIDI messages and their meanings are provided here.

0x93 0x4D 0x55   Since the high nibble of the status byte is 9, this is a Note On message. The low nibble is 3, which is the MIDI channel (although, since MIDI channels are numbered 1 to 16 rather than 0 to 15, the message is actually for MIDI channel 4). The note number is 0x4D = 77 (which is an F on the keyboard). The note should be played with a velocity value of 0x55 = 85. Consequently, the message means "Play an F on MIDI channel 4 with a velocity of 85."

0xC0 0x16   This is, according to Table A.1 on page 526, a program (patch) change message, for MIDI channel 1 (since the low nibble of the status byte is 0). The following data byte is the patch number, in this case 0x10 = 16, although patches are also normally numbered starting with 1, making this a 17. The patch number 17 is a Hammond Organ on General MIDI instruments.

0x33 0x40   Observing that 0x33 is less than 0x80, the first byte is a data byte. Thus, this is a valid MIDI message only if running status is used. In this case, however, we need to know the previous status to know the meaning of these data bytes. For example, if the last status was Note On, this message would mean that note number 51 should be played with a velocity value of 64.

System Messages

MIDI messages whose status bytes have a value between 0xF0 and 0xFF are called *system messages*. The reason for this name is that they are not specific to any particular MIDI channel. Unlike with voice messages, the low nibble of the status byte specifies the type of voice message.

Two subtypes of system messages have been defined: System Common messages (0xF0 to 0xF7) and System Real-time messages (0xF8 to 0xFF). The MIDI standard specifies the system messages listed in the following table.

Table A.2: System Common and System Real-time MIDI Messages

Message Type	Status Byte	Data Bytes	Description
SYSTEM COMMON MESSAGES			
System Exclusive (SysEx)	0xF0 0xF7	See description.	A status byte of 0xF0 indicates the beginning of a SysEx data transfer. SysEx messages are used to transfer large amounts of data between two specified MIDI devices (see below). A SysEx data transfer always ends with a status byte of 0xF7. Any number of bytes can be sent in between.
MTC Quarter Frame	0xF1	Time code value	Used for synchronization of some MIDI playback devices.
Song Position	0xF2	Song position (2 bytes)	Used to set the location where the playback of a slave sequencer or similar device will start.
Song Select	0xF3	Song number	Used to select the song number (or something similar, such as the pattern on a drum machine) to be played.
Tune Request	0xF6		Intended for the tuning of analog synthesizers; rarely used.

Table A.2: System Common and System Real-time MIDI Messages (continued)

Message Type	Status Byte	Data Bytes	Description
SYSTEM REAL-TIME MESSAGES			
MIDI clock	0xF8		A MIDI clock message is optionally sent 24 times per quarter note to synchronize playback. This can, for instance, be used to synchronize delays or LFO rates on a synthesizer to the sequencer's playback tempo.
Tick	0xF9		Send by some devices in 10-millisecond intervals to keep slave devices synchronized.
MIDI Start	0xFA		Used to tell a slave device, such as a sequencer or a drum machine, to start playback.
MIDI Continue	0xFB		Used to tell a slave device to continue playback at the current song position.
MIDI Stop	0xFC		Used to tell a slave device to stop playback.
Active sense	0xFE		Some devices send an active sense message every 300 milliseconds (unless any other MIDI messages are sent). A receiving device can then assume that the connection is broken if it stops receiving active sense messages.
Reset	0xFF		Any MIDI device that receives this message should reset itself to its default state.

> MTC is an abbreviation for MIDI time code, which is a type of messages used to control and keep different types of playback and recording devices (not necessarily musical instruments) synchronized.

For a more detailed description of the various system messages, see the full MIDI specification. Status bytes other than those listed in the preceding table are not defined by the MIDI specification and are ignored by MIDI devices.

System Exclusive (SysEx) Messages

System Exclusive messages are used when device-specific data needs to be transferred between two devices. For example, all parameters that make up one instrument, or even an entire set of instruments on a programmable synthesizer, can be transferred from a computer to replace the existing ones.

A system exclusive message starts with 0xF0. The next byte is an ID number specific to the instrument's manufacturer. Any number of data bytes follows next, ending with 0xF7. The purpose of these data bytes is determined by the manufacturer of the device. Commonly, a byte representing the model follows the manufacturer ID, to make sure that the SysEx message is received only by the type of instrument it was meant for.

There is a lot more to SysEx messages than is described here, but they normally are not used with the Sound Blaster Live!; read the full MIDI specification if you want to find out more.

B

THE GENERAL MIDI SOUND SET

General MIDI Programs

Group	Prog #	Instrument name	Group	Prog #	Instrument name
Piano	1	Acoustic grand piano	Reed	65	Soprano sax
	2	Bright acoustic piano		66	Alto sax
	3	Electric grand piano		67	Tenor sax
	4	Honky-tonk piano		68	Baritone sax
	5	Rhodes piano		69	Oboe
	6	Chorused piano		70	English horn
	7	Harpsichord		71	Basoon
	8	Clavinet		72	Clarinet
Chromatic percussion	9	Celesta	Pipe	73	Piccolo
	10	Glockenspiel		74	Flute
	11	Music box		75	Recorder
	12	Vibraphone		76	Pan flute
	13	Marimba		77	Bottle blow
	14	Xylophone		78	Shakuhachi
	15	Tubular bells		79	Whistle
	16	Dulcimer		80	Ocarina

Group	Prog #	Instrument name	Group	Prog #	Instrument name
Organ	17	Hammond organ	Synth lead	81	Square lead
	18	Percussive organ		82	Saw lead
	19	Rock organ		83	Calliope
	20	Church organ		84	Chiff
	21	Reed organ		85	Charang
	22	Accordion		86	Voice
	23	Harmonica		87	Fifths
	24	Tango accordion		88	Bass + lead
Guitar	25	Acoustic nylon guitar	Synth pad	89	New age
	26	Acoustic steel guitar		90	Warm
	27	Electric jazz guitar		91	Polysynth
	28	Electric clean guitar		92	Choir
	29	Electric muted guitar		93	Bowed
	30	Overdriven guitar		94	Metallic
	31	Distortion guitar		95	Halo
	32	Guitar harmonics		96	Sweep
Bass	33	Acoustic bass	Synth F/X	97	Rain
	34	Electric bass (fingered)		98	Soundtrack
	35	Electric bass (picked)		99	Crystal
	36	Fretless bass		100	Atmosphere
	37	Slap bass 1		101	Brightness
	38	Slap bass 2		102	Goblins
	39	Synth bass 1		103	Echoes
	40	Synth bass 2		104	Sci-fi
Strings/ Orchestra	41	Violin Ethnic		105	Sitar
	42	Viola		106	Banjo
	43	Cello		107	Shamisen
	44	Contrabass		108	Koto
	45	Tremolo strings		109	Kalimba
	46	Pizzicato strings		110	Bag pipe
	47	Orchestral harp		111	Fiddle
	48	Timpani		112	Shanai
Ensemble	49	String ensemble Percussive		113	Tinkle bell
	50	Slow string ensemble		114	Agogo
	51	Synth strings 1		115	Steel drums
	52	Synth strings 2		116	Woodblock
	53	Choir aahs		117	Taiko drum
	54	Voice oohs		118	Melodic tom
	55	Synth voice		119	Synth drum
	56	Orchestral hit		120	Reverse cymbal

Brass	57	Trumpet F/X	121	Guitar fret noise
	58	Trombone	122	Breath noise
	59	Tuba	123	Seashore
	60	Muted trumpet	124	Bird tweet
	61	French horn	125	Telephone ring
	62	Brass section	126	Helicopter
	63	Synth brass 1	127	Applause
	64	Synth brass2	128	Gun shot

General MIDI Drum Preset Map

	Note #	Drum preset		Note #	Drum preset
	27	High Q		58	Vibra-slap
	28	Slap		59	Ride cymbal 2
	29	Scratch push C4	C4	60	High bongo
	30	Scratch pull		61	Low bongo
	31	Sticks		62	Mute high conga
	32	Square click		63	Open high conga
	33	Metronome click		64	Low conga
	34	Metronome bell		65	High timbale
	35	Kick drum 2		66	Low timbale
C2	36	Kick drum 1		67	High agogo
	37	Side stick		68	Low agogo
	38	Snare drum 1		69	Cabasa
	39	Hand clap		70	Marackas
	40	Snare drum 2		71	High whistle
	41	Low tom 2	C5	72	Low whistle
	42	Closed hi-hat		73	Short guiro
	43	Low tom 1		74	Long guiro
	44	Pedal hi-hat		75	Claves
	45	Mid tom 2		76	High wood block
	46	Open hi-hat		77	Low wood block
	47	Mid tom 1		78	Muted cuica
C3	48	High tom 2		79	Open cuica
	49	Crash cymbal 1		80	Mute triangle
	50	High tom 1		81	Open triangle
	51	Ride cymbal 1		82	Shaker
	52	Chinese cymbal		83	Jingle bell
	53	Ride bell	C6	84	Belltree
	54	Tambourine		85	Castanets
	55	Splash cymbal		86	Mute surdo
	56	Cowbell		87	Open surdo
	57	Crash cymbal 2		88	

THE GS SOUND SET

The GS sound set includes all the GM programs and the GM drum kit plus the following extensions:

GS Program Variations

Prog #	Bank #	Instrument name	Prog #	Bank #	Instrument name
5	8	Detuned electric piano 1	32	8	Guitar feedback
6	8	Detuned electric piano 2	39	8	Synth bass 3
7	8	Coupled harpsichord	40	8	Synth bass 4
15	8	Church bell	49	8	Orchestra
17	8	Detuned organ 1	51	8	Synth strings 3
18	8	Detuned organ 2	62	8	Brass 2
20	8	Church organ 2	63	8	Synth brass 3
22	8	Italian accordion	64	8	Synth brass 4
25	8	Ukulele	81	8	Sine wave
26	8	12-string guitar	108	8	Taisho koto
26	16	Mandolin	116	8	Castanets
27	8	Hawaiian guitar	117	8	Concert bass drum
28	8	Chorus guitar	118	8	Melodic tom 2
29	8	Funk guitar	119	8	808 tom
31	8	Feedback guitar			

GS Drum Kits

Prog #	Name	Description
1	Standard	The standard General MIDI drum kit.
9	Room	Similar to the standard kit. Some ambience is added to some of the drum sounds.
17	Power	Similar to a standard kit, but with more "punch" in the bass and snare drums.
25	Electronic	Synthetic drum sounds similar to those found in analog and digital drum machines.
26	TR-808	The drum kit from the Roland TR-808 drum machine.
33	Jazz	Similar to the standard drum kit.
41	Brush	A standard kit where some of the drums are played with brushes.
49	Orchestra	Concert bass drums, snares and timpani.
57	F/X	Collection of sound effects.
128	MT-32	The drum/effects kit from the MT-32 sound module.

THE MT-32 SOUND SET

The MT-32 Programs

These programs are found in bank number 127 of the 2gmgsmt.sf2 and 4gmgsmt.sf2 files. Note that the SBLive! is not fully compatible with the controller and SysEx set of the MT32. Therefore, MIDI files created for the MT-32 that uses e.g. modulation and aftertouch may differ in playback from an actual MT-32 while played back with the SBLive!.

Prog #	Instrument name	Prog #	Instrument name
1	Acou Piano 1	65	Acou Bass 1
2	Acou Piano 2	66	Acou Bass 2
3	Acou Piano 3	67	Elec Bass 1
4	Elec Piano 1	68	Elec Bass 2
5	Elec Piano 2	69	Slap Bass 1
6	Elec Piano 3	70	Slap Bass 2
7	Elec Piano 4	71	Fretless 1
8	Honkytonk	72	Fretless 2
9	Elec Org 1	73	Flute 1
10	Elec Org 2	74	Flute 2
11	Elec Org 3	75	Piccolo 1
12	Elec Org 4	76	Piccolo 2
13	Pipe Org 1	77	Recorder
14	Pipe Org 2	78	Pan Pipes

Prog #	Instrument name	Prog #	Instrument name
15	Pipe Org 3	79	Sax 1
16	Accordion	80	Sax 2
17	Harpsi 1	81	Sax 3
18	Harpsi 2	82	Sax 4
19	Harpsi 3	83	Clarinet 1
20	Clavi 1	84	Clarinet 2
21	Clavi 2	85	Oboe
22	Clavi 3	86	Engl Horn
23	Celesta 1	87	Bassoon
24	Celesta 2	88	Harmonica
25	Syn Brass 1	89	Trumpet 1
26	Syn Brass 2	90	Trumpet 2
27	Syn Brass 3	91	Trombone 1
28	Syn Brass 3	92	Trombone 2
29	Syn Bass 1	93	Fr Horn 1
30	Syn Bass 2	94	Fr Horn 2
31	Syn Bass 3	95	Tuba
32	Syn Bass 4	96	Brs Sect 1
33	Fantasy	97	Brs Sect 2
34	Harmo Pan	98	Vibe 1
35	Chorale	99	Vibe 2
36	Glasses	100	Syn Mallet
37	Soundtrack	101	Windbell
38	Atmosphere	102	Glock
39	Warm Bell	103	Tube Bell
40	Funny Vox	104	Xylophone
41	Echo Bell	105	Marimba
42	Ice Rain	106	Koto
43	Oboe 2001	107	Sho
44	Echo Pan	108	Shakuhachi
45	Doctor Solo	109	Whistle 1
46	School Daze	110	Whistle 2
47	Bellsinger	111	Bottleblow
48	Square Wave	112	Breathpipe
49	Str Sect 1	113	Timpani
50	Str Sect 2	114	Melodic Tom
51	Str Sect 3	115	Deep Snare
52	Pizzicato	116	Elec Perc 1
53	Violin 1	117	Elec Perc 2
54	Violin 2	118	Taiko
55	Cello 1	119	Taiko Rim
56	Cello 2	120	Cymbal
57	Contrabass	121	Castanets
58	Harp 1	122	Triangle
59	Harp 2	123	Orche Hit

Prog #	Instrument name	Prog #	Instrument name
60	Guitar 1	124	Telephone
61	Guitar 2	125	Bird Tweet
62	Elec Gtr 1	126	One Note Jam
63	Elec Gtr 2	127	Water Bell
64	Sitar	128	Jungle Tune

THE SOUND BLASTER LIVE! MIDI IMPLEMENTATION

This appendix lists the MIDI capabilities of the Live! for the two main synthesizers of the Live!: the SBLive! MIDI Synth and the Creative Software Synthesizer. The MIDI implementation of the Sound Blaster Live! is dependent on the drivers used. The charts that follow refer to the Live!Ware 3 drivers.

The MIDI Implementation Chart

For every MIDI device, a document known as a MIDI implementation chart should exist (it is usually found in the manual or in a separate document). The MIDI implementation chart describes the MIDI capabilities of the device in a standardized way. In this chart, you can easily see what types of MIDI messages a device will receive and transmit. Such charts can be useful in determining whether two MIDI devices will work well together.

MIDI Implementation Chart: – SBLive! MIDI Synthesizer

WAVETABLE SYNTHESIZER WITH SOUNDFONT SUPPORT
Sound Blaster Live! MIDI Synth (Live!Ware 3 Drivers)

Function	Transmitted	Recognized	Remarks
MIDI Channel	X	1–16	
Mode	X	3	

Function		Transmitted	Recognized	Remarks
Note Number		X	0–127	
Note On		X	9n	Velocity = 0–127
Note Off		X	8n	Velocity = 0–127
Key Aftertouch		X	X	
Channel Aftertouch		X	O	
Pitch Bend[*1]		X	O	+/– 2-octaves pitch bend sensitivity recognized
Control Change[*1, *2]	0	X	O	Bank select
	1	X	O	Modulation
	6	X	O	Data entry
	7	X	O	Main volume
	10	X	O	Pan
	11	X	O	Expression
	38	X	O	Data Entry
	64	X	O	Sustain pedal
	91	X	O	Reverb Depth
	93	X	O	Chorus Depth
	98	X	O	NRPN LSB
	99	X	O	NRPN MSB
	100	X	O	RPN LSB
	101	X	O	RPN MSB
	120	X	O	All sounds off
	121	X	O	Reset all controllers
	123	X	O	All notes off
Program Change		X	O	0–127

Notes [*1] All channels (including that for drums) respond to MIDI volume.
Default power up: Bend = 2 semitones, Master volume = 100, Controllers normal.

[*2] Additional control change numbers can be mapped to EAX effects.

Mode 1: Omni on, poly   O: Yes
Mode 2: Omni on, mono   X: No
Mode 3: Omni off, poly
Mode 4: Omni off, mono

MIDI Implementation Chart: Creative Software Synthesizer

SOFTWARE WAVETABLE SYNTHESIZER
Creative S/W Synthesizer (Live!Ware 3 Drivers)

Function		Transmitted	Recognized	Remarks
MIDI Channel		X	1–16	
Mode		X	3	
Note Number		X	0–127	
Note On		X	9n	Velocity = 0–127
Note Off		X	8n	Velocity = 0–127
Key Aftertouch		X	X	
Channel Aftertouch		X	O	
Pitch Bend[*1] recognized		X	O	+/– 2- octaves pitch bend sensitivity
Control Change[*1]	0	X	O	Bank select
	1	X	O	Modulation
	6	X	O	Data entry
	7	X	O	Main volume
	10	X	O	Pan
	11	X	O	Expression
	32	X	O	Bank select
	64	X	O	Sustain pedal
	66	X	O	Sostenuto
	72	X	O	Attack time control
	73	X	O	Release time control
	98	X	O	NRPN LSB
	99	X	O	NRPN MSB
	100	X	O	RPN LSB
	101	X	O	RPN MSB
	120	X	O	All sounds off
	121	X	O	Reset all controllers
	123	X	O	All notes off
Program Change		X	O	0–127

Notes [*1] All channels (including that for drums) respond to MIDI volume.
Default power up: Bend = 2 semitones, Master volume = 100, Controllers normal.

Mode 1: Omni on, poly   O: Yes
Mode 2: Omni on, mono   X: No
Mode 3: Omni off, poly
Mode 4: Omni off, mono

RPNs on the SBLive! MIDI Synth

The Sound Blaster Live! MIDI Synth supports some of the most common Registered Parameter Numbers (RPNs): Pitch Bend Range, Master Fine Tuning, and Master Coarse Tuning.

Table E.1: Registered Parameter Numbers on the SB Live! MIDI Synth

LSB	Name	Range	Default	Unit	Description
0	Pitch Bend Range	1–127 semitones	2	1 semitone	The coarse adjustment (CC6) specifies the pitch bend range in semitones. Fine adjustment (CC38) is ignored.
1	Master Fine Tuning	0–16383 (±100 cents)	8192	(200/16384) cents	The value specified by CC6 * 128 + CC38 specifies the fine- tuning.
2	Master Coarse Tuning	0–127	64	1 semitone	The value specified by CC6 is the coarse tune. Default (normal tune) is 64. A value of 63 transposes all instruments one semitone down.

Apparently, the SB Live! RPN implementation does not fully comply with the MIDI standard. The fine adjustment of the pitch bend range is ignored, making it possible to specify the pitch bend range only in whole semitones. The master tuning, both coarse and fine, are implemented according to the MIDI specification.

NRPNs on the SB Live! MIDI Synth

The NRPN specification of the SB Live! MIDI Synth is not included in the Sound Blaster Live! documentation, and according to Creative it is not part of the official SB Live! MIDI implementation. However, the NRPN implementation of the Live! seems to be almost exactly the same as that of the AWE cards. The following table is based mainly on the NRPN implementation of the AWE cards; because of the differences between the synthesizers, the actual implementation (especially the units and ranges) may therefore differ slightly from what appears in the table.

Table E.2: Non-Registered Parameter Numbers on the SB Live! MIDI Synth

NRPN	LSB	Name	RT	Range	Unit	Description
16256	0	LFO 1 Delay	No	0, 5900	4 ms	Delay from 0 to 22 seconds.
16257	1	LFO 1 Frequency	Yes	0, 127	0.084 Hz	Frequency from 0 to 10.72 Hz.
16258	2	LFO 2 Delay	No	0, 5900	4 ms	Delay from 0 to 22 seconds.
16259	3	LFO 2 Frequency	Yes	0, 127	0.084 Hz	Frequency from 0 to 10.72 Hz.
16260	4	Envelope 1 Delay	No	0, 5900	4 ms	Delay time from 0 to 22 seconds.
16261	5	Envelope 1 Attack	No	0, 5940	1 ms	Attack time from 0 to 5.9 seconds.
16262	6	Envelope 1 Hold	No	0, 8191	1 ms	Hold time from 0 to 8.2 seconds.

NRPN	LSB	Name	RT	Range	Unit	Description
16263	7	Envelope 1 Decay	No	0, 5940	4 ms	Decay time from 0.023 to 23.7 seconds.
16264	8	Envelope 1 Sustain	No	0, 127	0.75 dB	Sustain level from full level to off.
16265	9	Envelope 1 Release	No	0, 5940	4 ms	Release time from 0.023 to 23.7 seconds.
16266	10	Envelope 2 Delay	No	0, 5900	4 ms	Delay time from 0 to 22 seconds.
16267	11	Envelope 2 Attack	No	0, 5940	1 ms	Attack time from 0 to 5.9 seconds.
26268	12	Envelope 2 Hold	No	0, 8191	1 ms	Hold time from 0 to 8.2 seconds.
26269	13	Envelope 2 Decay	No	0, 5940	4 ms	Decay time from 0.023 to 23.7 seconds.
26270	14	Envelope 2 Sustain	No	0, 127	0.75 dB	Sustain level from full level to off.
16271	15	Envelope 2 Release	No	0, 5940	4 ms	Release time from 0.023 to 23.7 seconds.
16272	16	Initial Pitch	Yes	–8192, 8191	1 cent	Tuning between –8192 and 8181 cents.
16273	17	LFO 1 to Pitch	Yes	–127, 127	9.375 cents	The affect of LFO 1 on pitch. From –1 to +1 octave at peaks.
16274	18	LFO 2 to Pitch	Yes	–127, 127	9.375 cents	The affect of LFO 2 on pitch. From –1 to +1 octave at peaks.
16275	19	Envelope 1 to Pitch	No	–127, 127	9.375 cents	The affect of Envelope 1 on pitch. From –1 to +1 octave at peaks.
16276	20	LFO 1 to Volume	Yes	0, 127	0.1875 dB	The affect of LFO 1 on volume. Values smaller than 64 cause a positive phase modulation, maximum 12 dB at peaks. Values greater than 64 cause negative phase modulation.
16277	21	Initial Filter Cutoff	Yes	0, 127	62 Hz	Controls the filter cutoff frequency from 100 to 8000 Hz. (note that this is not an absolute value but the initial filter cutoff).
16278	22	Initial Filter Resonance	No	0, 127		Selects one of 16 resonance coefficients, where values 0– to 7 select the first entry in the table that follows, 8 to 15 select the second entry, and so on. Simply put, higher value means more resonance.
16279	23	LFO1 to Filter Cutoff	Yes	–64, 63	56.25 cents	The affect of LFO 1 on filter cutoff. Negative values cause negative phase modulation.

Table E.2: Non-Registered Parameter Numbers on the SB Live! MIDI Synth (continued)

NRPN	LSB	Name	RT	Range	Unit	Description
16280	24	Envelope 1 to Filter Cutoff	No	−127, 127	56.25 cents	The affect of Envelope 1 on Filter Cutoff. Negative values cause negative modulation.
16281	25	Chorus Effects Send	No	0, 255		Chorus Effects Send, where 0 is dry and 255 is maximum effect.
16282	26	Reverb Effects Send	No	0, 255		Reverb Effects Send, where 0 is dry and 255 is maximum effect.

A Yes in the RT column indicates that this parameter can be used in real time: that is, that this sound parameter can be changed while a note is being played.

Resonance Coefficients Table

The following table lists the resonant filter's audio properties for different resonance coefficients (see the "Non-Registered Parameter Numbers" table in the previous section).

Table E.3: Resonance Coefficient Table for the SB Live! MIDI Synth

Coefficient	Low Fc Cutoff Frequency (Hz)	Low Q (dB)	High Fc Cutoff Frequency (kHz)	High Q (dB)	DC Attenuation (dB)
0	92	5	Flat	Flat	−0.0
1	93	6	8.5	0.5	−0.5
2	94	8	8.3	1	−1.2
3	95	10	8.2	2	−1.8
4	96	11	8.1	3	−2.5
5	97	13	8.0	4	−3.3
6	98	14	7.9	5	−4.1
7	99	16	7.8	6	−5.5
8	100	17	7.7	7	−6.0
9	100	19	7.5	9	−6.6
10	100	20	7.4	10	−7.2
11	100	22	7.3	11	−7.9
12	100	23	7.2	13	−8.5
13	100	25	7.1	15	−9.3
14	100	26	7.1	16	−10.1
15	100	28	7.0	18	−11.0

INDEX

Note: Italicized page numbers refer to illustrations.

Numbers

2 Speakers mode, 170–72, 182, 183, 225, 297
3D positioning, 285–90, 299–300, 301
3D sound, 296–97
4 Speakers mode, 172–76, 297
4.1 channel FPS2000 (speaker), 174
4.1 speakers, 139, 142–44
44.1 kHz sample rate, 519–22
48 kHz sample rate, 522, 523
5.1 Digital DIN speakers, 179
5.1 home theater system, *147*
5.1 Live! cards, 520
5.1 multimedia speaker systems, 139–40, 146
5.1 speakers, 144–46
5.1 Speakers mode, 176–80, 298

A

absolute measurements, 27–28
AC-3 decoding, 204, 205
AC'97 codec chip, 520–21
AC'97 mixer program, 205, 520
AC'97 standard, 521
accessories, 69–101
    See also Live!Drive
    digital I/O cards, 70–72
        digital output module, 77–78
        vs. Live!Drive, 101
        optical, 73–77
        S/PDIF Bypass, 96–101
acoustics, 185
active subwoofers, 153

A/D conversion, 36–37, 519
AdLib card, 4, 12, 276, 282
AdLib synthesizer, 4
AdLib-compatible cards, 277
Advanced Linux Sound Architecture (ALSA), 259
Advanced Signal Processor, 12
aftertouch sensitivity, 403
ALSA EMU10K1 (Live!) driver, 259
alsa-project.org, 259
Altec Lansing ATP3 2.1 multimedia speaker system, *142*
amplification ratings, 161–63
amplified signals, 105
amplitudes, 27
analog, 104–15
    See also connectors
    connecting analog equipment, 109–14
    vs. digital, 31–33
    signals, 104–5
analog caveat, 214
analog connectors, 79–82, 113, 163–64
analog inputs, 358–60
analog outputs, 115
analog-to-digital conversion, 6, 35
application program interface (API), 235
APS (Audio Production Studio) card, 78, 256, 414, 518
APS software, 256
APSLive! card, 255
archiving music, 354–55
arrange view, 459
ASDR envelope, *438*
ASIO sound card drivers, 409
ATRAC3 format, 336
attack times, 367, 437
AUD_EXT extension connector, 52, 71, 75, 92
    diagram of, 96

AUD_EXT extension connector
    (continued)
    EMU10K1 chip support of signals in, 56
    interfaces with, 87
    pins on, 53–55
    signals from, 86
    on sound cards, 93
AUD_EXT_2 connector, 89
Audigy cards, 256, 294, 414
audio, 23–38, 508–12
    See also recording audio
    compressing, 336–37
    editing, 363–70
        adding effects, 367–70
        cutting/trimming, 366–67
        memory requirements, 365–66
        normalizing, 366
        before starting, 365
    hardware acceleration, 270–71
    how we hear, 24–30
        positioning sound, 28–28
        sound waves, 25–28
        vibrations, 24–25
    MIDI music playback option, 268–70
    mixing, 200
    samples
        CC11 Tremolo.mid, 516
        CC11 Tremolo.wav, 516
        Control Example Chorus.mid, 483
        Control Example Chorus.wav, 483
        Control Example Modulation.mid, 480
        Control Example Modulation.wav, 480
        Control Example Pan.mid, 482
        Control Example Pan.wav, 482
        Control Example Reverb.mid, 483
        Control Example Reverb.wav, 483
        creating music library, 343, 344
        FM synthesis.wav, 9
        piano.wav, 26
        Quantize Before.mid and Quantize After.mid, 465
        Realtime Filter Step 3.wav, 508
        Realtime Filter Step 4.wav, 508
        Sample Rate Comparison.wav, 35
        Sample Size Comparison.wav, 8

screech.wav, 26
Vienna Effects.wav, 436
Vienna LFO.wav, 440
Vienna Modulation Envelope.wav, 439
Vienna Tune.wav, 435
Vienna Volume Envelope.wav, 438
Wavetable synthesis.wav, 9
    settings for, 508
    settings that don't work, 271
    software for, 344–46
    sound in digital domain, 31–38
        A/D and D/A conversion, 36–37
        analog vs. digital, 31–33
        digital audio, 33
        sampling, 33–36
        working with digital audio, 38
    sound playback and recording, 266–68
    sources available on Live! cards, 200–204
    tweaking, 350–51
    ways to obtain, 347–49
audio analyzers, 214
audio card, 282
Audio Codec '97 specification, 519
audio drivers, 509
audio hub, 10–11
audio levels, 114
Audio Production Studio (APS) card, 78, 256, 414, 518
Audio tab, 266
audio tracks, 510–12
AudioHQ's Device Controls applet, 84, 100
AudioHQ's SoundFont Control Panel, 269, 416–17, 421
auto wah effect, 496
automatic speaker muting, 79
automation, 512–14
Aux In 2 input, 82, 126
AUX_IN connector, 42, 51
AV equipment, 141
AV receivers, 160–61, 165, 178, 182, 188, 190
AWE cards, 390, 413, 428, 524
AWE32 cards, 14, 414, 486, 504, 518
AWE64 cards, 414, 486

B

backplate audio jacks, 56–58
Backplate Joystick, 62–63
Bank field, 475
Bank Manager, 451
bank select controllers, 479–80
bank stack, 418
BAS (bass), 25, 211
beats per minute (BPM), 463
binary system, 35
BIOS settings, 262
BlasterKey MP3 keyboard controller, 405
BNC coaxial cables, 107
BNC-to-RCA adapters, 116
BPM (beats per minute), 463
budget. *See* buying decisions
buffers, 408, 509
bundled software, 456
buying decisions, 153–63
    budget, 161
    features, 159–61
    magnetic shielding, 158
    number of speakers, 153–54
    power and amplification ratings, 156–58
    research and listening, 161–63
    sound quality, 154–56
    space constraints, 158–59

C

cable receivers, 128–29
Cakewalk Application Language (CAL), 513–14
Cakewalk Pro Audio 9, *465, 467, 468, 469*
Cakewalk sequencer software, 514
    bundled with Live! models, 456
    loading SoundFonts within, 470–72
    selecting MIDI ports, 458
    staff view, *462*
    tempo setting, *463*
    track view, *481*
CAL (Cakewalk Application Language), 513–14
Cambridge SoundWorks, 17, 19, 143
    4.1-channel FPS2000 speaker, 174, 175
    5.1 speaker system, 177
    DTT2500 speaker, 175, 179
    DTT3500 speaker, 59, *146*, 180
    FourPointSurround FPS1000, 143
    FPS2000 Digital, 58
    MegaWorks 210D speaker, 175
    MegaWorks 510D speaker, 175, 180
    speakers, 297
cards, sound. *See names of specific cards*
CBR (constant bit rate), 341, 343
CC11 Tremolo.mid, 516
CC11 Tremolo.wav, 516
CD Audio recording source, 218
CD Digital inputs, 200, 359–60
CD players, 124–25, 340
CD_IN analog connection, 44–45, 218
CD_IN connectors, 46–47
    drivers connected to, 48
    hiss in, 50–51
    pin assignments of, 42
CD_SPDIF connectors, 46–47, 120
CD_SPDIF digital connection, 45
    clarity of, 50–51
    recording source used in, 218
CD_SPDIF internal connector, 200
CD-ROM drives, 43–45, 340
CD-RW discs, 340
CDs, ripping, 346–47
center speakers, 144–46, 188–89
changing speaker modes, 167
channel aftertouch, 380–81, 403
channel pressure, 403
chorus control, 436
chorus effect, 495
chorus level controllers, 484
clipping, 215
C/MS (Creative Music System), 12
CMSS (Creative Multi-Speaker Surround), 182–83
CMSS mode, 297
CMSS Movie modes, 177, 300
coaxial cables, 116–17
coaxial connections, 77, 99–100, 171
codecs, 337–39
coder/decoder, 338
coding/compression process, 338

Color Scheme tab, 453
COM port, 175
compressing audio, 336–37
computer keyboard, 424
computer's main processor (CPU), 392
condenser microphones, 81, 134
Configure Instrument tab, 420, 421
configuring
    instruments, 468
    sequencer, 480
connecting devices, 103–36
    analog, 104–15, 109–14
        See also connectors
    signals, 104–5
    digital signals, 115–36
        CD players, 124–25
        Coaxial cables, 116–17
        digital connectors on Live!, 122–23
        Digital Outputs, 119–20
        DVD players, 131–32
        headphones, 133
        making connection, 121–22
        microphones, 134–35
        MiniDisc, DAT, and digital recorders, 129–31
        MP3 players, 132–33
        optical connectors, 117–19
        satellite and cable receivers, 128–29
        tape players, 125–26
        TV sets and VCRs, 126–28
    speakers, 167–84
        2 Speakers mode, 170–72
        4 Speakers mode, 172–76
        5.1 Speakers mode, 176–80
        Headphones mode, 180
        Live!Surround mode, 180–82
        speaker technologies on Live!, 182–84
connectors
    analog
        1/4-inch jacks, 107–8
        1/8-inch jacks, 108–9
        Aux In 2 input, 82
        headphone Out jack, 79–80
        on Live!, 113–15
        Mic In 2/Line In 2 connector, 80–81
        RCA jacks, 106–7

digital, 82–83
extension, 52–56, 86–89
    See also AUD_EXT extension connector
    SPDIF_EXT, 52, 55–56, 75, 92
internal, 41–51
    AUX_IN, 42
    choosing connection method, 50–51
    Inter-IC sound (I^2S), 42–43
    obtaining audio from optical drives, 44–49
    pin connectors, 51–52
    playing audio CDs, 43–44
    TAD, 41–42
MIDI, 62–63, 70
optical, 91, 117–19
constant bit rate (CBR), 341, 343
control change messages, 499
control changes (CCs), 381
    CC0, 479–80
    CC1, 480
    CC6, 480
    CC7, 481
    CC10, 481–82
    CC11, 482–83
    CC38, 480
    CC64, 483
    CC91, 483
    CC93, 484
    CC98, 484
    CC99, 484
    CC100, 484
    CC101, 484
    CC120, 484
    CC121, 484
    CC123, 484–85
Control Example files
    Chorus.mid, 483
    Chorus.wav, 483
    Control Example.mid, 480
    Modulation.mid, 480
    Modulation.wav, 480
    Pan.mid, 482
    Pan.wav, 482
    Reverb.mid, 483
    Reverb.wav, 483
Control Panel, 228–30, 416–18

controller problems, 485–86
controllers, SB Live! MIDI Synth, 478–85
   bank select controllers, 479–80
   chorus level, 484
   data entry, 480
   expression, 482–83
   modulation controllers, 480
   nonregistered parameter number (NRPN), 484
   notes off, 484–85
   pan, 481–82
   registered parameter number (RPN), 484
   reset controllers, 484
   reverb depth, 483
   sound off, 484
   sustain pedal, 483
   volume, 481
copying, 451
CPU (computer's main processor), 392
creating music library. *See* music library, creating
Creative Gameport Joystick, 252
Creative Inspire 5700 speaker systems, 59, 180
Creative Inspire speakers, *159*
Creative Keyboard, 84
Creative Miscellaneous Devices, 252, 260
Creative MultiMedia Interface device, 252
Creative Multi-Speaker Surround (CMSS), 182–83
Creative Music System (C/MS), 12
Creative SB16 Emulation device, 252
Creative SB Live! Gameport device, 252
Creative Signal Processor (CSP), 12
Creative speaker system, 177, 297
Creative S/W synthesizer, 392, 406, 458
Creative's Digital DIN connector, 179
Creative's digital I/O cards, 119
Creative's Live!Drive. *See* Live!Drive
CreativeWaveStudio (sound editor), 26
crosstalk cancellation, 298
CSP (Creative Signal Processor), 12
CT4620 Live! card, 71, 72, 75, 92
CT4660 Digital I/O card, 70, 71, 72, 96, 175
CT4670 Live! card, 70
CT4760 Live! card, 77
CT4770 Optical Digital I/O card, 73, 74, 75
CT4800 DIO module, 74
Cubase sequencer software
   arrange view in, *481*
   bundled with Live! models, 456
   configuring for SoundFont Support, 473–74
   event list in, *462*
   metronome settings, *464*
   selecting MIDI out ports, 458, *459*
   SoundFont manager, *475*
   SoundFont Support in, 472–73
custom instrument sounds, 278–79
cutoff frequency, 436
cutting, 366–67

D

D/A conversion, 36–37, 519, 520
DAC (sound card), 147
DAC units, 37
DACs (digital-to-analog converters), 6
DAE (digital audio extraction), 46, 218, 346, 359
DAE mode, 346
DAT (digital audio tape), 73, 117, 128, 129–31
data connection, 46
data entry controllers, 480
dB (decibel), 27
DB-25 joystick connector, 62
DCC (digital compact cassette), 117
DCC recorders, 117
DCs (digital controllers), 519
decay time, 437
decibel (dB), 27
decimal (Dec), 377
default device, 267
default effects, 487
delay time, 437, 439
Desktop Theater DTT2500 Digital, 58
Device Manager, 47, *253*
devices, connecting. *See* connecting devices
diffraction, 292–93
digital audio, 6, 33, 38

Index **555**

digital audio extraction (DAE), 46, 218, 346, 359
digital audio tape (DAT), 73, 117, 128, 129–31
digital compact cassette (DCC), 117
digital connectors, 82–83, 122–23, 164
digital controllers (DCs), 519
Digital DIN backplates, 86, 88, 175, 176
Digital DIN cable, 165, 166, 180
Digital DIN connectors, 165–68
    to connect Digital DIN backplate, 88
    number of pins, 71
    support of S/PDIF signals, 123
Digital DIN input, 58–59, 120, 122, 123, 180
Digital DIN output, 100, 119–20, 167, 175, 176
Digital DIN signals, 166
Digital DIN speakers, 77, 119
Digital DIN-to-Digital DIN cable, 120, 174, 175
digital domain, sound in, 31–38
    A/D and D/A conversion, 36–37
    analog vs. digital, 31–33
    digital audio, 33
    sampling, 33–36
    working with digital audio, 38
Digital In/Out jack, 73
Digital Input/Output (DIO), 73
digital inputs, 70, 359
digital I/O cards, 119–20
    bundled with first Live! card, 58, 398
    connector for, 87, 94
    digital output module, 77–78
    enhancing capabilities with, 52
    vs. Live!Drive, 101
    optical, 73–77
    passing signals to, 86
    solution of cramped backplates, 70–72
    use to get optical or coaxial digital outputs from Live!, 164
    used with Live!Drive, 87
digital I/O devices
    affect from sampling rate, 70
    connectors on for speakers, 163
    digital input on, 97, 115
    digital outputs on, 170
    Live!Drive, 216

matching audio connectors with, 160
    pairing with Live! card, 122
    recording sound from, 266
    support sample rates, 120
digital I/O solutions, 52
digital mini-jack-to-mini-jack cable, 175
digital output module, 77–78
digital outputs, 70, 119–20
digital recorders, 129–31
digital signal processor (DSP), 40, 522
digital signals, 115–16, 115–36
    CD players, 124–25
    Coaxial cables, 116–17
    connecting devices, 136
    digital connectors on Live!, 122–23
    digital outputs, 119–20
    DVD players, 131–32
    headphones, 133
    making connection, 121–22
    microphones, 134–35
    MiniDisc, DAT, and digital recorders, 129–31
    MP3 players, 132–33
    Optical connectors, 117–19
    satellite and cable receivers, 128–29
    tape players, 125–26
    TV sets and VCRs, 126–28
digital S/PDIF input, *360*, 519
digital vs. analog, 31–33
digital-to-analog converters (DACs), 6
DIN connectors, 76–77, 85, 91, 374
DIN MIDI cables, 91
DIO (Digital Input/Output), 73
DIO module, 77
DirectMusic, 280
DirectSound acceleration, 284
DirectSound APIs, 241, 268, 283–85, 294
DirectSound3D sound card, 16, 201, 270, 287–88
DirectX, 283, 288
DirectX 3 API, 288
DirectX 8 API, 279
disk operating system (DOS), 238
distortion effect, 496
DLS (Downloadable samples), 279
DLS2 specifications, 279
Dolby Digital, 30, 60, 274

AV receiver, 144
decoding, 128, 177
DVD playback, 148
multichannel audio format, 116, 121
outputs, 201
receiver, 148–50
signals, 117, 128, 131
Dolby Digital 5.1 decoding, 144
Dolby Digital/AC-3-encoded 5.1, 296
Dolby Digital API, 274, 295–96
Dolby Digital/DTS audio formats, 165
Dolby Headphone, 180
Dolby Pro Logic, 30, 148–50, 182
Dolby Surround, 30
Doppler shift, 286
DOS (disk operating system), 238
DOS drivers, 259–62
Downloadable samples (DLS), 279
dragging, 353–54
Drive Properties, *48*
driver-only releases, 244
drivers, 235–71
    determining version, 250–51
    DOS drivers and Sound Blaster 16 Emulation, 259–62
    how works, 235–37
    kX project, 256–57
    Linux, 257–59
    patches for, 245
    stability of, 254–56
    type available, 253–54
    verifying installation, 251–53
    in Windows, 238–55
        evolution of, 238–41
        for Live!, 244–50
        VXD and WDM Drivers, 241–44
dropping, 353–54
drum machine synthesizer, 388, 405
dry signal, 233
dry sound, 486
DSP chip. *See* EMU10K1 Digital Audio Processor (DSP) chip
DSP (digital signal processor), 40, 522
DSP/Effect plug-in, 351
DTS multichannel audio format, 116, 121
DTS signals, 117, 204
DTS surround decoders, 165

DTS surround sound signals, 60
DTT2500 speaker, 175, 177, 297
DTT3500 speaker, 177, 297
DVD decoder card, 43
DVD playback software, 165
DVD players, 131–32, 144
DVD standard, 519
DVD/MPEG-2 decoder card, 146
DVD-ROM drive, 144
dynamic microphones, 81

E

EA applet, 488, *491*, 511
EAGLE (Environmental Audio Graphical Librarian Editor), 17, 294–95
EAL file, 295
EAX API functions, 222
EAX (Environmental Audio eXtensions), 16, 18, 222–34, 290–95
    compatible sound cards, 223
    Control Panel, 228–30, 301, 302
    EAX 1.0, 290–91
    EAX 2.0, 291–93
    EAX 3.0, 293–94
    effects
        adding, 367
        controlling, 486
        recording with, 363
        uses for, 224–25
    environment controls in Surround Mixer, 225–28
    Environmental Audio Graphical Librarian Editor (EAGLE) used to add, 294–95
    how works, 223
    Interactive 3D Audio Level 2 (I3DL2), 294
    levels, 301–2
    presets, 230, 349
    processing, 154
    standard, 223
    support, 224, 301, 302
    using, 224–25
EAX Manager, 295
eax.dll file, 301

EaxMan.dll file, 301
echo effect, 495–96
edit view, 460, 466
editing audio, 363–70
    adding effects, 367–70
    cutting, trimming, and other editing, 366–67
    memory requirements, 365–66
    normalizing, 366
    before starting, 365
effects, 436
    adding, 367–70
    configuring, 487–94
        customizing, 489–91
        using other types, 492–94
    controlling, 486–87
    customizing, 231–32, 489–91
    default, 487
    editing parameters, 232–33
    recording, 363, 487–89, 493–94
    selecting, 487–94, 494–98
        customizing, 489–91
        using default, 487–89
        using other types, 492–94
    uses for, 224–25
    volume, using CC11, 515
electronic instruments, 387–88
E-MU APS drivers, 524
E-MU (electronic musical equipment manufacturers), 13, 78, 222, 521
E-MU Mantis digital mixer, 522
EMU10K1 Digital Audio Processor (DSP) chip, 517–24, 518–22
    adjusting pitch with, 351
    background of, 517–18
    capabilities of, 222–23, 243, 255
    connection to and from, 53
    containing programmable effects-processing unit, 223
    effects processing done within, 200
    enables Creative to add new capabilities to, 244
    features, 519
    function of, 40–41
    FX8010 effects processor, 522–23
    inability to encode and compress multiple audio channels, 150
    interface with AC'97 chips, 519–20
    internal 48-kHz sample rate used by, 120
    PCI bus communication, 524
    responding and generating sound, 236
    signals from, 52, 75, 92
    wavetable synthesizer, 523–24
EMU10K1F.sys file, 251
EMU10K1.vxd, 251
EMU8000 synthesizer chip, 10, 14, 393, 486
EMU8008 synthesizer chip, 10, 15
EMU8710 synthesizer chip, 10
enhancers, 388
Ensoniq AudioPCI design, 16
envelope control, 436–37
environment controls, 225–28
environment presets, 498
Environmental Audio, 222. *See also* EAX (Environmental Audio eXtensions)
Environmental Audio applet, *486*, 486
Environmental Audio effects, 511
Environmental Audio eXtensions. *See* EAX
Environmental Audio Graphical Librarian Editor (EAGLE), 17, 294–95
environments, 230
equalizers, 388
equipment, recording, 358
event list, 461, *462*
Exact Audio Copy, 347
exclusive classes, 433
excursion, 139
expression controllers, 482–83
expression pedal, 403–4, 483
extension connectors, 52–56, 86–89
    See also AUD_EXT extension connector SPDIF_EXT, 55–56
external MIDI instruments, 393
external sound sources, 203
External Volume Control, 262–65

F

FAD (Front/Rear Balance), 211, 300
Fat Man, The (George Sanger), 232
FAT32 support, 239
FCC label, 64
filter, 436

filter cutoff, 439, 440, 506–7
Filter Q filter parameter, 436
fine tune, 435
FireWire connection, 46
flanger effect, 495
FM (frequency modulation) synthesis, 275
FM synthesis.wav, 9
FM Synthesizer Emulation, 393
FM synthesizers, 4, 12, 277
frequency, 25
    masking, 337
    speed, 439–40
frequency modulation (FM) synthesis, 275
frequency shifter effect, 498
front panel, 358
front speakers, 186–88
Front/Rear Balance (FAD), 211, 300
full-duplex support, 15
Full-Screen Editing toggle, 452
FX8010 effects processor, 223, 522–23

G

gain, 81
Game Blaster card, 12
games, 274–302
    3D positioning, 285–90
    3D Sound on Live!, 296–97
    Dolby Digital API, 295–96
    EAX (Environmental Audio eXtensions), 290–95
        EAX 1.0, 290–91
        EAX 2.0, 291–93
        EAX 3.0, 293–94
        Environmental Audio Graphical Librarian Editor (EAGLE), 294–95
        Interactive 3D Audio Level 2 (I3DL2), 294
    EAX Support, 224
    with Live!, 299–302
    movie soundtracks setting benchmark for, 274
    music in, 275–81
        custom instrument sounds, 278–79
        General MIDI devices, 277
        General MIDI (GM) standard, 277–78
        interactive music future, 280–81
        recorded audio, 279
    sound effects in, 281–85
    speaker configuration, 297–99
General MIDI 2 (GM2), 386–87
General MIDI-compatible instrument, 384
General MIDI-compatible synthesizer, 384
General MIDI devices, 277
General MIDI files, 417
General MIDI (GM) standard, 277–78, 383–84
General MIDI instrument, 475
General MIDI playback modules, 405
General MIDI SoundFonts, 269, 385, 450
General Standard or General Sound (GS) format, 385–86
generators, 434–40, 448
    effects, filter, and pan, 436
    global zone, 440
    low-frequency oscillators (LFOs), 439–40
    modulation envelope, 438–39
    pitch, 435
    volume envelope, 436–38
Generic AC'97-compatible programs, 520
global coarse tuning, 502–3
global looping, 430
global zone, 440, 448–49
GM instruments, 386
GM2 (General MIDI 2), 386–87
Gravis Ultrasound, 13–14
grounding, 108
GS (General Standard or General Sound) format, 385–86
GS Wavetable SW Synth, 269, 391

H

hardware synthesizer, 397
headphones, 79, 133, 153, 171
Headphones modes, 180, 183, 225, 298
head-related transfer function (HRTF), 183–84, 193
hearing range, 337
height positioning, 184

hexadecimal (Hex) formats, 376–77
hibernation, 247–48
hi-fi systems, 140–41
hiss, keeping Live! card free of, 215–16
hold time, 437
home theater systems, 139, 147–51
HRTF (head-related transfer function), 183–84
Hubi's MIDI LoopBack Device driver, 409–10

I

I^2S (Inter-IC sound), 42–43
I2S_IN connector, 75
I3DL2 (Interactive 3D Audio Level 2), 294
IA-SIG (Interactive Audio Special Interest Group), 279
IDE cables, 93
Import User Sample, 444
infrared (IR) receiver, 86
initial attenuation, 438
Inspire 5700 (speaker), 297
installing
    drivers, 251–53
    Live!Drive, 92–95
    sequencer, 457–59
instrument definitions, 468, 469
Instrument Pool section, 446, 447
instrument stack, 421
instrument zones, 431
instruments, 382
    copying, 451
    creating, 430–34, 446–47
Instruments dialog box, *468*
Integrated Drive Electronics. *See* Intelligent Drive Electronics (IDE)
Intelligent Drive Electronics (IDE), 44
Intel's AC'97 specification, 205, 519, 520
intensities, comparing ratio of, 27
Interactive 3D Audio Level 2 (I3DL2), 294
Interactive Audio Special Interest Group (IA-SIG), 279
interactive music, 280–81
Inter-IC sound (I^2S), 42–43
internal connectors, 41–51
    AUX_IN, 42
    choosing connection method, 50–51
    Inter-IC sound (I^2S), 42–43
    obtaining audio from optical drives, 44–49
    pin connectors, 51–52
    playing audio CDs, 43–44
    TAD, 41–42
Internet archives, 415
Internet service providers (ISPs), 340
IR (infrared) receiver, 86
ISPs (Internet service providers), 340

J

Joint Stereo, 343
joystick, 402
JP3 pins, 52

K

kbps (kilobits per second), 341
kernel, 243
kernel mixer (KMixer), 242
key aftertouch, 380, 403
Key Number field, 445
key ranges, 447–48
keyboard controllers, 401
keys, 401–2
key/velocity range view, 424
kilobits per second (kbps), 341
Klipsch (company), 143
Klipsch ProMedia 4.1 (speaker), *144*
KMixer (kernel mixer), 242
kX project, 256–57

L

late reverb, 233
latency, 408–9, 509
layering, 432
LED (light-emitting diode), 117
LFO frequency, 480

LFOs (low-frequency oscillators), 439–40
LFO-to-pitch value, 480
light-emitting diode (LED), 117
limiting, 368, 388
Line In, 114
Line In 2 input, 75, 115
line level signals, 104, 359
Line Out, 114
Line Out 1 (front) connector, 56, 133, 171, 520
Line Out 2 (rear) connector, 56–57
Line Out 3 (center/subwoofer) output, 520
line-in connector, 359
line-in jack, 58
Line-In2/Microphone2, 80
Linux (operating system), 256–59
Live! sound card, 163–68, *178*
    3D Sound on, 296–97
    analog inputs on, 358–60
    EAX processing, 154
    games with, 299–302
    how routes, mixes, and resamples audio, 200–205
        audio sources, 200–204
        S/PDIF passthrough, 204–5
    keeping hiss free, 215–16
    Line Out 1 connector, 171
    MIDI capabilities of, 391–95
    support for
        analog connectors, 163–64
        changing speaker modes, 167
        connecting for S/PDIF passthrough, 164–65
        digital connectors, 164
        Digital DIN connectors, 165–67
Live!Drive, 78–96, 164
    adding for greater selection, 358
    analog connectors, 79–82
    compatibility, 92
    connecting to AUD_EXT connector, 92
    digital connectors, 82–83
    vs. digital I/O cards, 101
    DIN connectors on, 85
    extension connectors, 86–89
    Headphone Out connector, 171
    how works, 96
    inputs, 359

    installing, 92–95
    models, 89–90, 89–91
    obtaining optical connectors, 91
    origin of, 78–79
    other connectors, 83–86
    standard MIDI connectors on, 398
Live!Drive I. *See* Live!Drive
Live!Drive II
    connecting, 85, 90, 124, 126, 398
    history of, 78
    S/PDIF bypass feature, 122
Live!Drive IR, 17, 126
    connecting, 126, 398–99
    IR receiver, 85, 86, 90–91
    S/PDIF bypass feature on, 122
Live!Surround speaker mode
    3D positioning encoding, 298–99
    on Live! card, 148
    matrix encoding on, 180–82
Live!Ware (program), 244
loading SoundFonts, 418
local looping, 430, 445
local on/off, 404
Logitech Xtrusio DSR-100 (digital speakers), 165
Loki Entertainment, 289
Loop dialog box, 434
Loop Settings button, 444
looping samples, 444–46
lossless compression, 336
lossy compression, 336
low nibble, 376
low-frequency oscillators (LFOs), 439–40
low-level analog signals, 104–5
low-pass filter, 436

M

magnetic shielding, 158
master keyboards, 401
matrix encoding, 180
MB_PRO connector, 52
Media folder, 352
Megota Software, 416
melodic presets, 441
Melody Machine, 416

memory requirements, 365–66
messages, 374
    structure, 378–80
    types, 380–82
metronome feature, 463, *464*
Mic In 2/Line In 2 (switchable microphone), 80
microphones, 134–35, 359
Microsoft. *See names of specific products*
MIDI, 373–95
    capabilities of Live!, 391–95
    general MIDI and other standards, 383–87
    overview of, 374–83
        example, 378
        hardware, 375
        message types, 380–82
        sequencer, 376
        structure of message, 378–80
        synthesizer
            basics, 387–90
            jargon, 390–91
MIDI cables, *374*, 374, 398–99
MIDI channels, 377–80
    changing banks manually, 476
    changing properties of, 460
    controlling volume of, 481
    effects levels on, 488
    setting EAX effects on, 392
MIDI connector cable, *398*
MIDI connectors, 62–63, 71
MIDI controller bars, 424, 425
MIDI controller keyboard, 475
MIDI controllers, 477–78, 484
MIDI data, 85, 375, 401
MIDI devices, 76–77, 398
    summary of, 394–95
    three MIDI connectors on, 400–401
    understanding of messages, 376
MIDI Devices dialog box, 458
MIDI echo, 515
MIDI events, 461
MIDI files, 484, 519
MIDI inputs, 76–77
    connectors, 398, 400, 401
    ports, 390–91, 457, 458

MIDI instruments, 476
    connecting
        MIDI interface Live!, 398–99
        MIDI loopback device, 409–12
        sample setups, 399–401
    software synthesizers, 405–9
    using MIDI keyboard for input, 401–5
MIDI interfaces, 376, 398–99
MIDI keyboard, 424, 477, 480
    choosing, 401
    for input, 401–5
    to Synthesizer Module, 399–400
MIDI loopback device, 409–12
MIDI Manufacturers Association, 279
MIDI Mapper, 391
MIDI messages, 400, 459–60, 476–77
MIDI music playback option, 268, 268–70
MIDI outputs, 76–77, 85, 88
    connectors, 398, 400, 401
    ports, 411, 457, 458
MIDI ports, 393, 477
    inputs, 390–91, 457, 458
    outputs, 411, 457, 458
MIDI sequencing, 216, 394, 456
MIDI Set Range, 431
MIDI Set Root Key, 431
MIDI specification, 476, 477, 482
MIDI standard, 375
MIDI Synth. *See* SB Live! MIDI Synth
MIDI synthesizer, 229, 259
MIDI thru connector, 400–401
MIDI tracks, 472, 510–12
MIDI UART device, 394
MIDI Yoke, 410–11
minicomponent systems, 140
Mini-DIN connectors, 85, 86, 398–99
Mini-DIN plug, 166
Mini-DIN-to-DIN adapter cable, 91
MiniDisc devices, 73, 117, 129–31
MiniDisc format, 117
MiniDisc products, 119
Mini-jack Digital Out connector, 174
mini-jack digital output, 58–62, 100, 123
    obtaining, 60–61
    on Second-Generation Live!, 59
    summary of, 61–62
    on Third-Generation Live!, 59–60
mini-jack optical output, 124

mini-jacks, 170
    for Digital DIN adapter cable, 120, 166, 167
    for female Digital DIN adapter cable, 174, 175
    plugs, 108–9
    for RCA cables, 114, 124, 125, 163, 170, 173, 181
mixdown, 512
mixer strip, 205
Mixer window, 205
mixermaps, 512–13
mixers, 11, 199–220, 388–89
    audio, 200
    how Live! routes, mixes, and resamples audio, 200–205
        audio sources, 200–204
        S/PDIF passthrough, 204–5
    keeping Live! hiss free, 215–16
    recording audio, 216–19
    settings, recording, 360–63
    using, 205–14
        Surround Mixer, 207–14
        Volume Control, 205–7
    volume controls in software, 219–20
models, 89–91
modifying, audio, 350
modular synthesizers, 405
modulation controllers, 480
modulation envelope, 438–39
modulation wheel, 402
Molex 70553 connectors, 41
Molex connector, 65
monophonic, 390
mother keyboards, 401
motherboard, threat of, 20–21
Motion Picture Experts Group (MPEG), 340
mouse, 424
movies, 303–31
    common surround formats, 311
    discrete multichannel surround, 307–9
    encoding in digital formats, 309–10
    home theater on PC, 314–16
    matrix surround, 304–6
    soundtracks of, 274
    surround setups, 311–14
    surround sound on Live!, 316–31
    THX standards, 310

MP3 codec, 340
MP3 files, 341, 349
MP3 format, 336, 340–44
MP3 playback capability, 340
MP3 players, 132–33, 340
MP3 Pro format, 341
MP3 recorder, 338
MPEG audio, 341
MPEG Audio Layer 3. *See* MP3 codec
MPEG (Motion Picture Experts Group), 340
MPEG-1 format, 340
MPEG-2 format, 340
MPEG-4 format, 340
MPEG/DVD decoders, 42
msseax2.m3d file, 301
msseax.m3d file, 301
MT-32 sound module, 415
multichannel audio, 29–30
multimedia, 10, 13
multimedia speakers, 141–47
    2.0 speakers, 141–42
    2.1 speakers, 142
    4.1 speakers, 142–44
    5.1 speakers, 144–46
    USB speakers, 146–47
multisampling, 431
multitimbrality, 390–91
music, 275–76
    archiving, 354–55
    custom instrument sounds, 278–79
    in games, 275–81
    General MIDI devices, 277
    General MIDI (GM) standard, 277–78
    interactive future, 280–81
    recorded audio, 279
music cards, 4–5
music composition, affordable, 9–10
music library, creating, 335–55
    audio compression, 336–37
    audio software, 344–46
    codecs, 337–39
    MP3s, 340, 340–44
    organizing music, 352–55
    ripping CDs, 346–47
    tweaking audio, 350–51
    ways to obtain audio, 347–49
music synthesis, 8
muting, 208–9

N

Native Instruments' Reaktor software synthesizers, *406*
New Melodic Preset, 441
New User Samples, 428
non-Creative sound chips, 20
non-real-time recording, 466
nonregistered parameter number (NRPN), 480, 484
    controllers for, 484
    key to Real-Time SoundFont Control, 504–8
    messages, 505–6
    and registered parameter number (RPN), 498–500
normalizing, 366
notes off controllers, 484–85
NRPN. *See* nonregistered parameter number (NRPN)
Nyquist's Theorem, 33–34

O

occlusion, 292
OEM models, 65–66, 200
OEM (original equipment manufacturer), 65–66
On-Board inputs, 359
Open Audio Library (OpenAL), 289
Open Sound System (OSS), 258
OpenAL32.dll file, 289
opensource.creative.com (Web site), 258
operating system (OS), 235, 237
OPL3 FM synthesizer chips, 8
optical connections, 91, 99–100, 117–19
Optical Digital I/O Card, 73–77, 98, 115, 128
    enabling S/PDIF bypass for, 124
    Line In 2 input found on, 88
    support of S/PDIF bypass feature, 78, 96
Optical Digital I/O Card II, 73
optical fiber cable, 118
Optical In, 82
Optical In connector, 83

optical I/O card. *See* Optical Digital I/O Card II
optical I/O devices, 117, 119, 124
Optical Out, 83
Optical TOSLink cable, 118
Optical TOSLink outputs, 171
optical/TOSLink outputs, 77
optimizing
    hardware, 510
    software, 509
organizing music, 352–55
original equipment manufacturer (OEM), 65–66
OS (operating system), 235, 237
oscillators, 41
OSS (Open Sound System), 258
Other Advanced Controls, 209
outputs, 88

P

pan, 436, 481–82
parameter-editing dialog box, *491*
parametric equalizer, 369
parent bank, 419–20
passive subwoofer, 153
patch change, 382
PCB (printed circuit board), 40
PCI bus communication, 518
PCI (peripheral component interconnect), 10
PCI sound cards, 519
PCM audio, 116, 120, 165
PCM format, 165
PCM Wave audio decoder, 338
PCM Wave format, 346
peak music power output (PMPO) rating, 157
peaking, 215
perceptual coding, 336
Percussive Pool, 443
percussive presets, 441, 443
peripheral component interconnect (PCI), 10
Philips, 117
phono cables, 106

piano roll view, 460
piano.wav, 26
pickup, 30
pitch, 435, 439
pitch shifter effect, 497–98
pitch wheel, 380
pitch-bend, 402, 500–501
placement, of speakers, 185–95
    center speaker, 188–89
    front speakers, 186–88
    subwoofers, 194–95
    surround speakers, 190–94
Play Control, 205
Play Loop, 444, 445
PlayCenter (software), 344–49, 352
playing sounds, 424–25
PlayStation 2 (gaming hardware), 274
plug-ins, 351
Plug-n-Play standard, 13
PMPO (peak music power output) rating, 157
point sources, 286
Polk Audio AMR-150 (digital speakers), 165
polyphony, 10, 390
portable CD players, 340
positioning
    See also placement, of speakers
    games with 3D audio, 192
    surround sound, 190
POST (power-on self-test) procedure, 51
power ratings, 156–58
powered subwoofers. *See* active subwoofers
power-on self-test (POST) procedure, 51
Preferences window, 453
presets
    copying, 451
    creating, 440–43, 449–50
    EAX (Environmental Audio eXtensions), 230–34
    environment, 498
    preset zones, 442
pressure sensitivity, 403
Primary Sound Driver device, 268
printed circuit board (PCB), 40
processing power, 407
program change, 382

Propellerhead Software's Reason software synthesizers, *406*
PS/2 keyboard, 86
psychoacoustics, 336
purchasing. *See* buying decisions

Q

QCD (Quintessential Player), 346
quantization feature, 463, *464*, 465
Quantize After.mid file, 465
Quantize Before.mid file, 465
Quintessential Player (QCD), 346

R

Radio Corporation of America, 106
rate conundrum, 519–20
rate conversion, 519
ratio, 367
RCA adapters, 111
RCA cables, 106–7, 115, 116, 126, 141, 159, 170
RCA coaxial connectors, 117, 128
RCA connectors, 124
RCA inputs, 110, 173, *178*, 210
RCA jacks, 114, 117, 125, 126, 130, 131, 170, 173, 178
RCA line input, 115
RCA line-level outputs, 124
RCA output, 160
RCA output jacks, 114, 125, 126
RCA plugs, 60, 110, 116, 126
RCA-to-mini-jack cable, 124
RCA-to-RCA cable, 124
read-only memory (ROM), 428
real time, recording, 466
realistic instruments, 9
Realtime Filter Step 3.wav file, 508
Realtime Filter Step 4.wav file, 508
Reason software synthesizers, *406*
recording audio, 216–19, 266–68, 357–70
    analog inputs on Live! card, 358–60
    controlling, 206, 213

recording audio *(continued)*
    dialog, 365
    editing, 363–70
        adding effects, 367–70
        cutting/trimming, 366–67
        memory requirements, 365–66
        normalizing, 366
        before starting, 365
    equipment for, 358
    levels, 361–63
    mixer settings for, 360–63
    non-real-time, 466
    real time, 466
    sources, 358
    sources and equipment, 358
    starting, 365
    step, 466–67
    tracks, 462–67
reference sound, 27
registered parameter number (RPN), 480, 484
    controllers, 484
    and nonregistered parameter number (NRPN), 498–500
    on the SB Live! MIDI Synth, 500–504
release times, 367, 437
RemoteCenter software, 86
reset controllers, 484
resonance filter parameter, 436
Resonant Synth Bass, 450
reverb, 229, 436, 483, 494
ring modulator effect, 497
ripping CDs, 346–47
RMS (root mean square) rating, 157
Roland D-50 synthesizer, 404
Roland MT-32 synthesis, 275–76, 415
Roland Sound Canvas, 278
Roland synthesizer, *403*
ROM (read-only memory), 428
ROM Sample Pool, 428
root key, 431
root mean square (RMS) rating, 157
RPN. *See* registered parameter number

S

sample rate, 33
Sample Size Comparison, 8, 35
samplers, 10
samples
    copying, 451
    loading, 444
    looping, 444–46
Sanger, George (composer), 282
satellite, 128–29
Sawbass instrument, 447
SB Live! MIDI Synth, 259, 269, 447, 476
    bank select controllers, 479–80
    chorus level controllers, 484
    data entry controller, 480
    expression controllers, 482–83
    MIDI implementation, 504
    modulation controller, 480
    nonregistered parameter number (NRPN) controllers, 484
    notes off controllers, 484–85
    pan controllers, 481–82
    registered parameter number (RPN) controllers, 484
    reset controllers, 484
    reverb depth controllers, 483
    sound off controllers, 484
    sustain pedal controllers, 483
    volume controllers, 481
SB Live! MIDI Synth A, 458
SB Live! MIDI Synth B, 458
SB Live! MIDI UART, 458
SB16 emulation, 260, 262
scale tune, 435
score view, 461
screech.wav, 26
SCSI (Small Computer System Interface), 46
Searchback feature, 485
sensitivity level, 337
sequencer, 376, 455–516
    audio, 508–12
    automation, 512–14
    available effects, 494–98
    building blocks of, 459–62
    choosing, 456

controller problems, 485–86
controllers on SB Live! MIDI Synth,
    478–85
    bank select, 479–80
    chorus level, 484
    data entry, 480
    expression, 482–83
    modulation, 480
    nonregistered parameter number
        (NRPN), 484
    notes off, 484–85
    pan, 481–82
    registered parameter number
        (RPN), 484
    reset, 484
    reverb depth, 483
    sound off, 484
    sustain pedal, 483
    volume, 481
controlling effects, 486–87
finding, 456
installing and configuring, 457–59
nonregistered parameter number
    (NRPN), 504–8
recording tracks, 462–67
registered parameter number (RPN),
    498–504
saving environment presets, 498
selecting and configuring effects,
    487–94
    customizing, 489–91
    using default, 487–89
    using other types, 492–94
SoundFont support
    in Cakewalk, 468–72
    in Cubase, 472–75
tips and tricks, 514–16
using MIDI Controllers, 477–78
using SoundFonts in, 467, 475–77
settings, 271
setups, sample, 399–401
sf2 files, 414
Shift-Down Arrow keys, 352
Sierra On-Line (game company), 276
Sigmatel STAC97, 520
signals, analog, 104–5
signal-to-noise ratio (SNR), 520

SIMM memory modules, 14
Small Computer System Interface
    (SCSI), 46
SMF (standard MIDI file), 384
SMP (Symmetric Multiprocessing)
    systems, 247, 250
SNR (signal-to-noise ratio), 520
software
    See also names of specific software
    audio, 344–46
    bundled, 456
    optimizing, 509
    synthesizers, 405–9
    volume controls in, 219–20
SONAR sequencer software, 468
Sondius WaveGuide software synthesizer, 14
Sony, 117
Sony/Philips Digital Interface Format. *See*
    S/PDIF (Sony/Philips Digital
    Interface Format)
sound bank, 414
Sound Blaster 1.0, 6–11, 9–10
    audio sample, 8, 9
    music synthesis, 8
    realistic instruments with wavetable
        synthesis, 9
    sound card as an audio hub, 10–11
    Wave audio, 7
    wave audio for music, 8
Sound Blaster 16 ASP card, 7, 9, 12–13
Sound Blaster 16 card, 12–13, 283
Sound Blaster 16 emulation card, 259–62
Sound Blaster 16 MultiCD card, 13
Sound Blaster 16 PnP card, 13
Sound Blaster 16 SCSI-2 card, 13
Sound Blaster 16 Value card, 13
Sound Blaster 32 cards, 10, 283, 414
Sound Blaster Advanced WavEffects
    (AWE) card, 13–14
Sound Blaster AWE32 card, 9, 13–14, *389*
Sound Blaster AWE64 card, 14–15
Sound Blaster AWE64D (OEM) card, 15
Sound Blaster AWE64 Gold, 73
Sound Blaster AWE64 Gold card, 14–15
Sound Blaster AWE64 Value card, 15
Sound Blaster AWE cards, 8, 9, 10, 17,
    278, 283

Sound Blaster AWE series, 284
Sound Blaster compatibility, 19–20
Sound Blaster Live!, 7, 11, 15–16
Sound Blaster Live! 5.1 series, 17
Sound Blaster Live! MP3+ card, 16–17
Sound Blaster Live! Platinum card, 16–17
Sound Blaster Live! Player card, 16–17
Sound Blaster Live! Value card, 15–16
Sound Blaster Live! X-Gamer card, 16–17
Sound Blaster PCI 64 card, 19
Sound Blaster PCI cards, 19
Sound Blaster PCI platform card, 15
Sound Blaster Pro, 12, 283
sound cards, 10–11, 41, 282, 389, 524
sound cones, 287
sound effects, 281–85
sound, evolution of, 3–21
    advancements in, 17–19
    first Sound Blaster, 6–11, 9–10
        audio sample, 8, 9
        music synthesis, 8
        realistic instruments with wavetable synthesis, 9
        sound card as an audio hub, 10–11
        Wave audio, 7
        wave audio for music, 8
    future of, 20, 21
    history of Sound Blaster, 11–21
    motherboard threat, 20–21
    music cards, 4–5
    past and present, 19
    Sound Blaster compatibility, 19–20
    sound in real world, 5–6
    timeline of Sound Blaster, 11–17
        1989 Sound Blaster, 12
        1991 Sound Blaster Pro, 12
        1992 Sound Blaster 16, Sound Blaster 16 ASP, and Wave Blaster, 12–13
        1994 Sound Blaster AWE32, Vibra Pro, and Vibra 16, 13–14
        1995 Wave Blaster II, 14
        1996 Sound Blaster AWE64 and Sound Blaster AWE64 Gold, 14–15
        1997 Sound Blaster AWE64 Value, Sound Blaster AWE64D (OEM), EMU8008, and Vibra 16x, 15
        1998 Sound Blasters based on Ensoniq AudioPCI, Sound Blaster Live!, and Sound Blaster Live! Value, 15–16
        1999 Sound Blaster AudioPCI 128, Sound Blaster Live! Platinum, Sound Blaster Live! Player, Sound Blaster Live! MP3+, and Sound Blaster Live! X-Gamer, 16–17
        2000 Sound Blaster Live! 5.1 series, 17
sound, how we hear, 24–30
    positioning sound, 28–28
    sound waves, 25–28
    vibrations, 24–25
sound intensity, 27
Sound Mapper, 268
sound off controllers, 484
sound playback, 266–68
sound, positioning, 28–30
sound quality, 154–56
Sound Settings, 265–71
sound sources, 208
sound waves, 24–25, 25–28
SoundFonts, 9–10, 413–53, 475–77
    applets, *417*, 470, 472–73
    banks, 472, 475
    Control Panel, 416–18, 452
    creating, 422–24
    creating instruments, 430–34
    creating presets, 440–43
    Device instrument, 469
    features of, 452–53
    files, 523
    full example of, 443–50
        adding global zone, 448–49
        adjusting key ranges, 447–48
        creating instruments, 446–47
        creating preset, 449–50
        loading samples into Vienna, 444
        looping samples, 444–46
        before starting, 443–44
    generators, 434–40

effects, filter, and pan, 436
global zone, 440
low-frequency oscillators (LFOs), 439–40
modulation envelope, 438–39
pitch, 435
volume envelope, 436–38
getting sample material, 427–30
loading, 470–72
management, 450–52, 470–72
playing sounds, 424–25
structure of, 425–27
support, 472, 473–74, 475
   in Cakewalk, 468–72
   in Cubase, 472–75
variation banks, 418–22
what it is, 413–14
where to find, 414–16
SoundForge (sound editor), 26, *363*, *365*
Sounds/Multimedia settings, 338
sources, recording, 358
space constraints, 158–59
S/PDIF (Sony/Philips Digital Interface Format), 43, 83, 115–16, 120, 521
bypass, 96–101, 122, 128
connections, 82
data, 82, 124
inputs, 60, 82, 83, 96, 120
output bracket, 14
outputs, 73, 83, 121, *172*, 248
passthrough mode, 204–5, 247, 248–49
   connecting for, 164–65
   switching to, 172
signals, 59, 82, 117, 119, 120, 123, 124
SPDIF_EXT extension connector, 52, 55–56, 75, 92
SPDIF-In/Auxiliary2 input, 82
speakers, 137–95
   See also headphones; *names of specific speakers*
   buying, 153–63
      budget, 161
      features, 159–61
      magnetic shielding, 158
      number of speakers, 153–54
      power and amplification ratings, 156–58

research and listening, 161–63
sound quality, 154–56
space constraints, 158–59
configuring, 297–99
connecting, 167–84
   2 Speakers mode, 170–72
   4 Speakers mode, 172–76
   5.1 Speakers mode, 176–80
   Headphones mode, 180
   Live!Surround mode, 180–82
   speaker technologies on Live!, 182–84
home theater systems, 147–51
multimedia, 141–47
   2.0 speakers, 141–42
   2.1 speakers, 142
   4.1 speakers, 142–44
   5.1 speakers, 144–46
   USB speakers, 146–47
placement of, 185–95
   center speaker, 188–89
   front speakers, 186–88
   subwoofers, 194–95
   surround speakers, 190–94
sound from, 138–40
stereo audio systems, 140–41
subwoofers, 152–53
support on Live! sound card, 163–68
   analog connectors, 163–64
   changing speaker modes, 167
   connecting for S/PDIF passthrough, 164–65
   digital connectors, 164
   Digital DIN connectors, 165–67
splitter adapters, 111
splitter cable, *399*
stability, drivers, 254–56
staff view, 461, *462*
standard for EAX, 223
standard MIDI file (SMF), 384
standard SoundFonts, 414–15
start bit, 375
step recording, 466
stereo audio systems, 29, 140–41
stereo encoding, 337
stereo expansion, 183
stereo mini-jack-to-RCA cables, 126

Index **569**

stereophonic sound, 29
Stomper (software), 444
stop bit, 375
streaming, 279
studio equipment, 387–88
StudioAX, 416
StudioWare panels, 513
subwoofers, 142–44
   active, 153
   multimedia speakers, 144–46
   placement, of speakers, 194–95
   speakers, 152–53
Surround Mixer, 207–14, 291, 296, 301, 302
   advanced controls, 210
   analog caveat, 214
   audio analyzers, 214
   environment controls in, 225–28
   muting, 208–9
   record control, 213
   sound sources, 208
   tone and volume controls, 210–13
surround speakers, 190–94
sustain level, 437
sustain pedal, 403, 483, 485
switchable microphone, 80
Symmetric Multiprocessing (SMP) systems, 247, 250
synth bank, 417, 476
Synthesizer Module, 399–400
synthesizer module synthesizer, 388
synthesizers, 387
   basics of, 387–90
   hardware, 397
   software, 405–9, 407–9
   vocabulary of, 390–91
system exclusive (SysEx) message, 383, 386

T

TAD connector, 41–42
tape players, 125–26
tempo setting, *463*
temporal masking, 337
threshold level, 367
Timbre sound, 155
time scaling, 351

timeline of Sound Blaster, 11–17
   1989 Sound Blaster, 12
   1991 Sound Blaster Pro, 12
   1992 Sound Blaster 16, Sound Blaster 16 ASP, and Wave Blaster, 12–13
   1994 Sound Blaster AWE32, Vibra Pro, and Vibra 16, 13–14
   1995 Wave Blaster II, 14
   1996 Sound Blaster AWE64 and Sound Blaster AWE64 Gold, 14–15
   1997 Sound Blaster AWE64 Value, Sound Blaster AWE64D (OEM), EMU8008, and Vibra 16x, 15
   1998 Sound Blasters based on Ensoniq AudioPCI, Sound Blaster Live!, and Sound Blaster Live! Value, 15–16
   1999 Sound Blaster AudioPCI 128, Sound Blaster Live! Platinum, Sound Blaster Live! Player, Sound Blaster Live! MP3+, and Sound Blaster Live! X-Gamer, 16–17
   2000 Sound Blaster Live! 5.1 series, 17
toe in method, 186
tone controls, 210–13
Tools menu, 453
Toshiba Link (TOSLink), 83
   cables, 83
   connectors, 83, 117, 118, 119
   inputs, 119, 124
   jacks, 118
   outputs, 119
   plugs, 83
   TOSLink-to-TOSLink optical cable, 171
track view, 459, 472
transducers, 134
transistor-transistor logic (TTL), 61
TRE (treble), 25, 211
tree view, 424, 426, 431, 434, 446, 447, 449
trimming, 366–67
TRS plugs, 108
TRS signals, 117
TTL (transistor-transistor logic), 61
TV sets, 126–28
TV/FM tuner cards, 42
type-2 MIDI file, 385

U

Universal Asynchronous Receiver and Transmitter (UART), 394
universal serial bus (USB), 46
unofficial drivers, 245
unweighed keyboards, 402
USB connection, 132
USB speakers, 146–47
USB support, 239
USB (universal serial bus), 46
User Sample Pool, 428
Utopia Live! General MIDI SoundFont, 416

V

variable bit rate (VBR), 342–43
variation banks, 418–22
VCRs, 126–28
velocity
    range, 432–33
    sensitivity, 402
    splits, 432–33
Vibra 16 chip, 13–14, 15
Vibra Pro chip, 13–14
vibrations, 24–25
VideoLogic (company), 143
VideoLogic ZXR-500 (speaker), *145*
Vienna Effects.wav, 436
Vienna LFO.wav, 440
Vienna Modulation Envelope.wav, 439
Vienna SoundFont Studio, 422–24
Vienna Tune.wav, 435
Vienna Volume Envelope.wav, 438
Vintage Dreams Waves SoundFont, 472
virtual analog synthesizers, 405
virtual device drivers (VXDs), 241, 242
Virtual Sound Canvas software synthesizers, 407
virtual surround, 183
vocal morpher effect, 498
voices, 390
VOL (Play Control Volume), 211
VOL_CTRL connector, 51
VOL_CTRL Pins, 263–64
volume, *363*, 440
    controls, 205–7, 210–13, 219–20, 262–65, 481
    effects, 515
    envelope, 436–38
VXDs (virtual device drivers), 241, 242

W

.wav audio files, 7, 8, 420–21, 428
Wave Blaster card, 12–13
Wave Blaster II card, 14
Wave/DirectSound sound source, 230
WaveLab Lite, *368*
waveOut API, 268
Wave/PCM format, 116
wavetable synthesis, 9, 277
wavetable synthesizer, 523–24
weighted keyboards, 402
wet sound, 486
What-U-Hear record source, 213, 361
    icon behavior because of, 226
    selecting in mixer, 214
    settings, 218
    volume of, 349
    when to use, 217
Winamp (software), 344–46, 353–54
Windows 2000 (operating system), 240, 247, 248
Windows 98 (operating system), 239
Windows 9x (operating system), 241, 245–46
Windows ME (operating system), 239
Windows NT (operating system), 239–40, 247
Windows (operating system)
    audio
        hardware acceleration, 270–71
        MIDI music playback option, 268–70
        settings that don't work, 271
        sound playback and recording, 266–68
    Control Panel, 338
    Device Manager, 251–53
    Driver Model (WDM), 240–41, 242, 243–44, 256

Windows (operating system) *(continued)*
    drivers in, 238–55
        evolution of, 238–41
        for Live!, 244–50
        VXD and WDM Drivers, 241–44
    Hardware Quality Labs (WHQL), 237
    multimedia, 265–71
    SB16 emulation driver, 262
    Sound Recorder, *364*
    WaveOut API, 248–49
Windows XP (operating system), 240–41, 250
WinRar, 416
WinZip (compression software), 416
WMA format, 336
woofer. *See* subwoofers

X

XG (Extended GM), 386
Xtrusio DSR-100 (digital speakers), 165

Y

Yamaha OPL2 synthesizer chips, 8
Yamaha's DB50XG cards, 13
Y-cable, 126

Z

ZXR-500 speaker, *145*

More No-Nonsense Books from **NO STARCH PRESS**

THE BOOK OF OVERCLOCKING
Tweak Your PC to Unleash Its Power

by SCOTT WAINNER *and* ROBERT RICHMOND

If you don't mind voiding the manufacturer's warranty on your CPU, overclocking is for you. Learn how not to fry your system while souping up everything from the Pentium II to the latest Athlon XP and Pentium 4. Sections on cooling, troubleshooting, and benchmarking make sure you get the most out of your machine.

2002, 304 PP., $29.95 ($44.95 CDN)
ISBN 1-886411-76-X

JIN SATO'S LEGO® MINDSTORMS™
The Master's Technique

by JIN SATO

LEGO legend Jin Sato shares his way of thinking about designing MINDSTORMS robots like his famous robotic dog, MIBO, in this landmark book.

"Every LEGO Mindstorms enthusiast should have this book next to their LEGO storage bin." — Slashdot

2002, 364 PP., $24.95 ($37.95 CDN)
ISBN 1-886411-56-5

STEAL THIS COMPUTER BOOK 2
What They Won't Tell You About the Internet

by WALLACE WANG

This bestseller will open your eyes to the Internet underground, with coverage of everything from viruses and password theft to Trojan Horse programs and encryption. The CD-ROM includes over 200 anti-hacker and security tools.

"An engaging look at the darker side of the information superhighway."
— *Amazon.com*

2000, 462 PP. W/CD-ROM, $24.95 ($38.95 CDN)
ISBN 1-886411-42-5

LINUX MUSIC & SOUND
How to Install, Configure, and Use Linux Audio Software
by DAVE PHILLIPS

This is an in-depth introduction to recording, storing, playing, and editing music and sound on Linux, with over 100 MIDI applications on the CD-ROM.

"This is an excellent reference both for basic sound procedures and for programs currently available for the Linux musician." — Sys Admin

2000, 408 PP. W/CD-ROM, $39.95 ($61.95 CDN)
ISBN 1-886411-34-4

PROGRAMMING LINUX GAMES
Building Multimedia Applications with SDL, OpenAL™, and Other APIs
by LOKI SOFTWARE, INC. *with* JOHN R. HALL

This complete guide to developing Linux games discusses important multimedia toolkits (including Simple DirectMedia Layer) and teaches the basics of Linux game programming.

2001, 426 PP., $39.95 ($59.95 CDN)
ISBN 1-886411-49-2

Phone:

1 (800) 420-7240 OR
(415) 863-9900
MONDAY THROUGH FRIDAY,
9 A.M. TO 5 P.M. (PST)

Fax:

(415) 863-9950
24 HOURS A DAY,
7 DAYS A WEEK

Email:

SALES@NOSTARCH.COM

Web:

HTTP://WWW.NOSTARCH.COM

Mail:

NO STARCH PRESS
555 DE HARO STREET, SUITE 250
SAN FRANCISCO, CA 94107
USA

UPDATES

Visit **http://www.nostarch.com/sblive_updates.htm** for updates, errata, and other information.

ABOUT THE AUTHORS

Lars Ahlzen is the founder of the "Live! Center" website (http://listen.to/sblive) and a Computer Science and Engineering student at Chalmers University of Technology in Gothenburg, Sweden.

Clarence Song is a software engineer living in Singapore, and an avid technology, multimedia, and AV enthusiast. He runs the popular "ALive!—Sound Blaster Live! Resource" website.